Food & Material Culture
Proceedings of the Oxford Symposium on Food and Cookery 2013

Food & Material Culture

Proceedings of the Oxford Symposium on Food and Cookery 2013

Edited by Mark McWilliams

Prospect Books
2014

First published in Great Britain in 2014 by Prospect Books, Allaleigh House, Blackawton, Totnes, Devon, TQ9 7DL.

© 2014 as a collection Prospect Books.
© 2014 in individual articles rests with the authors.

The authors assert their moral right to be identified as authors in accordance with the Copyright, Designs & Patents Act 1988. No part of this publication may be reproduced, stored in a retrieval system or transmitted in any form or by any means, electronic, mechanical, photocopying, recording or otherwise, without the prior permission of the copyright holders.

ISBN 978-1-909248-40-3

The photograph on the front cover is by Toby Coulson.
The photograph on the back cover is of the Chesterfield tureen and cover by Paul de Lamerie, 1736–7. Courtesy of the Metropolitan Museum of Art, New York. See the paper by Carolin C. Young for more details.

Design and typesetting in Gill Sans and Adobe Garamond by Tom Jaine.

Printed and bound in Great Britain by Jellyfish Solutions.

Contents

Foreword   9
    Mark McWilliams

Plenary Papers

Autarchic by Design: Aesthetics and Politics of Kitchenware   11
    Diana Garvin

Sporks, Pestles and Peelers: Why Kitchen Technology Matters   20
    Bee Wilson

The Soup that Went into the Tureen: Connecting the Dots between Food and Material Culture   33
    Carolin C. Young

Symposium Papers

The Future of Tableware and Cooking Vessels   48
    Ken Albala

Salt-pot / *Tuz Testisi*: A Salt and Terracotta Water Cooler from Turkey   56
    Nilhan Aras

Towards an Anthropology of Bimby Food-processors in Italy   62
    Elisa Ascione

Digital Gastronomy   70
    Adrian Bregazzi

Bottles, Glasses and Contrasting Beer Cultures in Belgium and the United States   80
    Anthony F. Buccini

The Bamboo Tea Whisk in Japanese Tea Tradition   90
    Voltaire Cang

Trench Fare: Cooking under Fire, France 1914–1918   100
    Kyri W. Claflin

The Significance and Symbolism of Sugar Sculpture at Italian Court Banquets   111
    June di Schino

Refrigeration and the Americanization of Immigrants in the First Half of the Twentieth Century   123
    Betsey Dexter Dyer and Jonathan Brumberg-Kraus

Shaken, not Stirred: the Story of Mixers and Mixing   135
    Len Fisher, Janet Clarkson and Alan Parker

Food and Material Culture

Napkins and Handkerchiefs in Early Modern Drama — 141
Joan Fitzpatrick

Kitchen Knives: the New Bling — 151
Peter Hertzmann

Tsatsal: the Symbolism and Significance of Mongolian Milk Spoons — 161
Sharon Hudgins

Katai: Coconut Scrapers — 175
Phil Iddison

Moulds for Shaping and Decorating Food in Turkey — 184
Priscilla Mary Işın

An Examination of Elite Consumption Trends in Ceramic Tableware in Georgian Ireland — 197
Tara Kellaghan

The Cow Creamer and the 'Cudster' — 208
Llio Teleri Lloyd-Jones

How to Make Solar Cooking Global: a Beginner's Guide — 214
Jeremy MacClancy

The Rise of the Picnic Hamper — 224
Diana Noyce

Vessels and Equipment Used by Street Food-vendors in Istanbul — 234
Banu Özden

Ushnān and Perfuming the Banquet — 241
Charles Perry

A Federal-era Kitchen: Hampton's Stew Stove, Iron Oven and Hearth — 248
Patricia Bixler Reber

Table Manners and what they Looked Like — 256
Gillian Riley

Endless Eating: the Indian *Thali* — 264
Caroline Rowe

'Let's all go eat at the Automat': Machines and Miracles in New York City — 272
Laura Shapiro and Rebecca Federman

The First Thousand Years of Pottery in Prehistoric Oxfordshire — 281
Emilie Sibbesson

Making Muscular Machines with Nitrogenous Nutrition — 289
Lesley Steinitz

Nefs: Ships of the Table and the Origins of Etiquette — 304
David C. Sutton

Turkish Coffee: *arte & factum*, Paraphernalia of a Ritual from Ember to Cup — 314
Aylin Öney Tan and Nihal Bursa

The Material Culture of the Classical Greek Banquet — 325
Stephanos Tanis

Food and Material Culture

A 'Knack' for Cooking: what are the Required Tools? *Amy B. Trubek*	336
The *Quederah*: the Everyday Cooking Pot of Talmudic Times *Susan Weingarten*	344
The Role of Extra-domiciliary Kitchens in Great Household Victualling Strategies, *c.* 1400–1600 *Ryan Whibbs*	354
Kee Wah Bakery's Mooncake Packaging Makeover in the 1990s *Jennifer Wong*	365
The Waurás in Brazil Have a Pan that Speaks to the Fire *Marcia Zoladz*	374
Our Kitchen in 1940s Baghdad *Sami Zubaida*	385

Foreword

Over the last decade or two, the study of material culture has become a major trend in the humanities, shifting the foci of whole fields from texts to objects. That some kinds of scholarship so long ignored the stuff, ordinary and extraordinary alike, of human life seems difficult to imagine.

For those who think about food, though, none of this is new. Food itself is a kind of material culture, albeit ephemeral, and it has always been intimately related to the objects used to gather, store, prepare, serve and eat it. After all, 'dish' refers both to the plate itself and to the food served upon it. One gives name to the other.

And at least etymologically, material culture comes first. 'Dish', for example, has been used in English to refer to a plate or other serving object since as early as 700 CE, according to the *OED*, preceding its use to name the food on the plate by over eight centuries. That makes sense: the pot comes before the soup.

The pot itself was the subject of an early Oxford Symposium in 1988, and this year the Symposium expanded its focus to consider all the material culture of food. The range of symposiasts' papers – almost all included in this volume – suggests the extraordinary scope of discussions during three lovely summer days in Oxford: from coffee grinders to coconut scrapers, picnic baskets to Turkish salt-pots, eighteenth-century stew stoves to twenty-first century 3D printers, plastic sporks to bling knives.

Some of those objects showed up in the amazing collection of 'tube food' – foods of all sorts in squeezable tubes – that accompanied welcoming drinks on Friday evening; others begged to be identified on the bring-and-buy tables. As usual, meals were the centre of conversation and celebration, and this year several were designed around the Symposium's theme. At the opening dinner prepared by Stevie Parle, symposiasts were asked to grind their own spice mixes with mortar and pestle; as a result, each group of diners enjoyed a slightly different meal. By the final meal, an Ethiopian lunch, utensils were left untouched as everyone ate with their hands. In between, feasts of Middle Eastern and Brazilian fare were prepared with the usual skill and aplomb by Tim Kelsey and his staff at St Catherine's.

The papers collected here capture the remarkable variety of topics covered this year. They reflect as well the committed scholarship, relentless curiosity, and joyous play that characterizes the Symposium itself. For their help in preparing this volume, I would particularly like to thank Elisabeth Luard, Ursula Heinzelmann, Helen Saberi, Peter Hertzmann, and Tom Jaine.

Mark McWilliams
Editor, Oxford Symposium on Food and Cookery

Autarchic by Design: Aesthetics and Politics of Kitchenware

Diana Garvin

In October 1935, Italian Fascist dictator Benito Mussolini heralded the invasion of Ethiopia, and with it, the establishment of Italian East Africa. One month later, the League of Nations countered with a raft of economic sanctions. By choking off Italy's foreign supply of wheat and other basic materials, the League of Nations hoped to crush the regime's imperialist ambitions. With this bout of international fist-shaking, domestic policy crashed headlong into the domestic sphere. Autarchy emerged.

Broadly speaking, autarchy meant producing and consuming Italian products, privileging domestic goods over foreign ones. On the national level, the regime promoted this policy by introducing a raft of plans to rationalize and modernize Italian industry. Popular magazines and books translated these policies into recommended practices for everyday life. Italian economic self-sufficiency meant that domestic labour such as shopping, gardening and cooking took on a heightened political charge. When autarchy entered the home, it headed straight for the hearth. In the private sphere, politics spoke through the idiom of design.

A new approach to the material culture of Fascist Italy
Cultural historians of the Italian Fascism have tended to focus on regime-sponsored initiatives rendered on a grand, public scale. Art historians have emphasized the diffusion of style via commercial and graphic design. Taking these conversations into the domestic realm demonstrates how political and commercial aims mutually reinforce and ultimately coalesce in the aesthetics of cooking utensils, dishware and appliances. In short, culinary paraphernalia promoted autarchy to Italian women through design.

If economic policy takes material form in kitchenware, then this incarnation demonstrates that the regime infiltrates the domestic sphere and modifies its aesthetics for national ends. So it stands to reason that Italian citizens experienced Fascist policies of autarchy not only at political rallies in the public piazza, but also in the home through the objects they handled every day. This line of logic further suggests that the kitchen stands as a synecdoche for the national larder. Ultimately, these objects exemplify the collusion of design and politics in the hearth of the home.

Of course, designers may or may not have explicitly allied themselves with the regime and its promotion of autarchy. But living and working in Fascist Italy meant that designers were subject to the political and artistic trends of the day. These tendencies inevitably influenced the conditions of manufacturing and sale. All these objects are

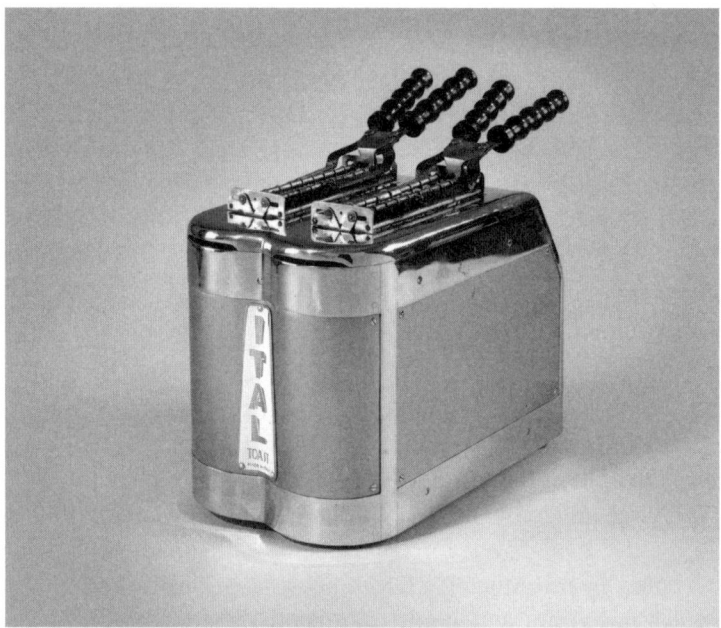

Figure 1. Toaster, Milan, manufactured by ItalToast, chrome (Wolfsonian Institute, Miami, xx1990.393; photo. Lynton Gardiner).

imbued with concerns for autarchy because they were produced in a time marked by such concerns. Ultimately, the significance of these objects in the context of the private home tells us more about the history of daily life than does the intentionality of the designer and his professed political stance. This essay focuses on the observable, physical properties of the plates, toasters, sugar bowls, and what these aesthetics meant in the context of Italy's Fascist period. These objects represent the material connection between the regime, industry and consumers – the physical point at which politics touch the individual through design.

From autarchy to aesthetics: the modern and the traditional

Autarchy, an abstract economic policy, takes concrete form in the aesthetics of the kitchen objects that Italian women used every day. Two broad categories emerge: modern and traditional. Each style evokes a specific set of culinary practices to encourage autarchical eating. Innovative designs, bright colours and shine characterize the modern objects. This group dazzles the viewer with its futuristic aesthetic of streamlined curves and knife-sharp angles. Forms evoke speed and efficiency. Functional objects associated with energy (electric appliances) and stimulants (tea and coffee sets) predominate.

In contrast to the modern objects, the traditional pieces comfort rather than thrill. Simple forms and muted colour palettes of sepia and sage prevail. Larger and heavier than the modern objects, these pieces provided decoration for bare walls and cupboards.

Bucolic motifs like wheat heads and home-made loaves of bread repeat in the same dish, suggesting the abundance and the fertility of the countryside.

Modern, functional objects

These objects construct and promote a set of culinary practices that bring politics into the kitchen by translating autarchy into two aesthetic categories. Turning to the first group, what design elements make these objects feel modern, and how does that modernity work to encourage autarchic cooking and eating? Approaching the question of modernity iteratively rather than attempting to define it from the start demonstrates the meaning of modernity in the specific context of culinary implements and cooking methods. First, metalwork, particularly in silver hues, gives this impression. Domestically produced aluminium and chrome evoke the idea that using autarchic materials imbue the cook with a modern sensibility. Along similar lines, writers and artists of the day such as F.T. Marinetti and Mario Sironi conflated the physical properties of metal with idea of modernity. Metalwork signals a shift from old cooking methods, such as heating food over an open hearth, to new ones, such as toasting bread with electricity in a chrome-plated appliance. The material composition of these objects casts the daily practice of autarchy as chic. This aura of style is a particularly important move for autarchy, because foreign products previously reigned as the height of fashion. A visually dazzling Italian teacup represented a cultural shift – it signalled the beginning of the end of France and England's monopoly over style in Italian homes.

In addition to being composed of autarchic materials, metal-based electric appliances such as the ItalToast Toaster decrease cooking time and effort. Designed in Milan, this electric chrome toaster features two sets of adjustable heat level controls. The construction allows the cook to minutely control multiple facets of the cooking process by turning dials and pushing buttons. A flashing red alert light the need for attention previously required of the cook. By automating these elements, the toaster abstracts the cooking process from the original combination of fire, pan and bread into a Taylorist succession of manual, rather than full-body, operations. So this object sends a message of modernity in its physical aesthetics, in that it is metal with streamlined curves and shine, but also in its function. Cooking faster and with less effort means cooking in a modern way. Speed marks the object in its design and in its use. This toaster suggests that increasing the speed of cooking while diminishing the effort involved was a positive practice that marked the cook as fashionably modern. By accelerating production in the kitchen, this object translates the abstract concept of autarchy into a daily practice for the domestic sphere.

Aesthetics of smooth flow also emerge in Friuli-Venezia-based designer Galvani's ceramic tea set, produced in Pordenone *circa* 1935. This piece exemplifies how design provides a concrete means for creative negotiation of the politicized questions of autarchy. This tea set evokes modernity two of the same elements as the ItalToast toaster: gleam and novel form. Although ceramic, the tea set's black glaze and smooth

Figure 2. Galvani, Tea Set, Pordenone, c. mid-1930s, ceramic (Wolfsonian Institute, Miami, 84.7.27.9; photo. Lynton Gardiner).

Figure 3. Arrigo Finzi, Tea and Coffee Set, c. 1935, manufactured by Le Argenterie d'Italia, metal and wood (Wolfsonian Institute, Miami, 83.9.11.2; photo. Silvia Ros).

texture throw off light. Sharp colour contrast of matte orange on the oval-shaped handles and knob finials energizes the visual composition. Brightness draws attention to the rendering of the cup handles: while traditional in that the oval form allows for a modified handgrip of the cup, the ovoid form departs from the formerly diffuse English teacup handle style, a dainty ear-shaped curve. Form (novel), material (clay) and aesthetics (modern) mark this tea set as conceived and manufactured in Italy, making it an autarchic product.

What would this object have meant in physical context? The teapot, creamer and sugar bowl would have been filled in the kitchen then moved to a salon or living room for service. The kitchen constitutes a private space, whereas the salon provides a semi-public area for receiving guests. Traditions of tea drinking in Italy tended to be bourgeois and gendered female, and further invoked an association with Great Britain that could be highly problematic for sanction-bound Italy. It is the class-based and foreign tradition of tea service, rather than the product itself, that becomes problematic under the sanctions. For this reason, design provides a powerful intermediary to redefine this meal pattern as Italian.

Not only is afternoon tea a foreign ritual, but tea itself is also a foreign product. How then to rebrand tea, as well as coffee, sugar and chocolate, as Italian, and thus autarchic? Advertisements often conflated colonial people with dark-coloured products, suggesting that both manpower and food were raw materials to be seized in order to fuel Italian bodies and industry. Similarly, these foods provide energy as stimulants but have little nutritional value. This last fact provides for an interesting connection to the aesthetics of modernity, in that stimulants provide a means to meet the call for ever-increasing speed. Aesthetics of streamlining further support this acceleration.

Being both decorative and functional, this tea set beautifies the table and contains products prior to consumption. In contrast to the ItalToast toaster, these objects do not change cooking method. Rather, these objects serve a translational need by rebranding a foreign ritual and product as autarchic. By serving tea to guests in with this explicitly Italian service, the lady of the house could mark herself as patriotic, even chic, with her up-to-the-moment awareness of the Fascist political climate.

Similar tropes emerge in a tea and coffee set designed by Arrigo Finzi, produced by Le Argenterie d'Italia in Milan. Also dating from *circa* 1935, this set evokes modernist aesthetics in its materials, design, use and associated foods. We see this in the novel octagonal base and fluted concentric bands encircling the central container, and the sharply sculpted rectangular spouts, all topped by the star-shaped knobs.

Autarchic materials and streamlined form both evoke modernity. The decision to depart from previous coffee and tea set forms, rather than to update them, can be read as a bid to mark these objects as the material bearers of new ideas in Italian design. Ultimately, we see that modern kitchen objects offer chicness and worldliness to promote autarchic practices. But in doing so, they also evoke the problematic associations of modernity with hyper-acceleration, colonialism and imperialism.

Figure 4. Lino Berzoini, 'Non Sciupate il Pane' [Don't Waste Bread], Albisola (Savona), c. 1933, bread plate, manufactured by Casa Giuseppe Mazzotti, ceramic, 8 inches diameter (Wolfsonian Institute, Miami, 84.7.1.4; photo. Silvia Ros).

Figure 5: Virgilio Retrosi, 'Amate il Pane' [Love Bread], Rome, 1927, bread plate, manufactured for Fabbrica Ceramiche d'Arte [Ceramic Arts Factory], ceramic, 14 inches diameter (Wolfsonian Institute, Miami, 84.7.30; photo. Bruce White).

Decorative traditional objects

Some kitchen objects overtly trumpet political messages with text and graphics rather reflect or incarnate the political climate with elements of design. This brings us to the second category of objects. How do the aesthetics of these objects evoke simplicity and a sense of the rural? And how do these traditions promote autarchy? Decorative bread plates offered the ample, flat surface area necessary for detailed pictorial odes to autarchy. Bread consumption (how much, how often, by whom) sent charged political messages whether or not the consumer wished to do so because of widespread grain scarcity and a national push for conservation. Being placed in the kitchen or dining room and thus highly visible around mealtimes, these objects were meant to display and communicate the importance of bread conservation when such messages could have the greatest effect on rationing behaviours.

Designer Lino Berzoini heralded bread conservation in a rustic plate produced by Casa Giuseppe Mazzotti and Motta *circa* 1933 bearing the message, '*Non sciupate il pane*', 'Don't waste bread', in pale yellow letters. This plate's raised design suggests display rather than service. The messages of this plate would be read in the same context as other wall hangings of the mid-1930s, such as the ubiquitous images of the Duce. The plate, like the Duce, watches over the dining process. In this way, this ceramic plate attempts to diminish bread consumption in the individual's home as one part of a larger push for autarchic eating on a national scale.

But how do the plate's aesthetics promote autarchic eating? Rusticity and domesticity converge in the plate's kitchen scene, simply composed of an open hearth and a woman working at a long farmhouse table. A countrified aesthetic marks Berzoini's colour choices. The plate's muted earth tones range from sienna to sage, sparked by the buttery shade of the wording, the bread, and the blonde-haired baker. Yellow unites the composition by highlighting the connection between the baker and her family's bread. The tranquil kitchen space depicted here provides an effective advertisement for autarchic practices by evoking the peace and plenty of a socially conservative imaginary national past.

Production, rather than consumption, of bread inspires the decoration. With fourteen rolls completed on the bench, and another in her hands, she happily engages in this time-consuming labour. Daily practices of autarchy, such as managing bread consumption, belong to the realm of women's labour. The high number of rolls, along with ample sacks of flour and a large container of flour at the woman's feet, suggest plenty even as the words below her feet warn against waste. With no speaker apparent, these words assume the quality of a Biblical commandment. This plate would have been mounted on the wall and commands from on high, 'Thou shalt not waste bread'. Whether the plate's owner took this edict so seriously we cannot say. But the plate's celebration of baking is clear. Because the imagery focuses on food production even as the use of a serving plate implies its consumption, this image imbues the simple choice of whether or not to reach for another piece of bread as a matter of national importance.

In the next example, the voice of the State calls out to the diner in poetic rather than religious terms. This ostentatiously rustic bread plate bears the opening phrases of Mussolini's propagandistic poem, '*Amate il pane*' [Love bread]. Sienna wheat chaffs and midnight-blue cornflowers at the wide lip of the plate wreathe the injunction, 'Amate il pane, cuore della casa, profumo della mensa, gioia del focolare' [Love bread, heart of the home, perfume of the table, joy of the hearth]. The authoritative capitalized words evoke the dictatorial language of the '*Non sciupate il pane*' plate.

The centre of the plate shows the open fireplace of a country kitchen, flanked by stylized wheat chaffs drawn in a relatively larger scale than the kitchen. By using the open hearth as a backdrop for Mussolini's verse, Retrosi casts the country kitchen as the symbolic space for daily autarchic practices such as conserving bread. Both plate and poem define the kitchen through the slippery fusions and elisions of consumer and consumed. While the phrasing and title ('*Amate il pane*') suggests that bread is the '*cuore della casa*', the heart of the home more typically refers to the kitchen or fireside. Positive emotive terms such as '*amate*', '*cuore*' and '*gioia*' elevate bread eating from a rote act of filling the belly to pious ritual of quasi-religious significance, as with the consumption of the host. Bread, the product, rather than the kitchen, the space, defines the emotional centre of the home. Being so precious, only the State has the authority to oversee the daily rite of bread consumption. In sum, we see that rural aesthetics and tradition promote autarchy by evoking a sense of peace to be gained through productivity and obeisance to regime calls for autarchy.

The political power of common things

Industrial design colludes with politics not only because it possesses the capacity to travel from the public sphere to the private, but because it is a form of intervention in daily life that passes largely undetected by the object's user. Message reception need not depend on text: meaning can be read in extent and type of decoration, intended and actual use, materials, size and heft of objects. Put more broadly, objects need not be created with the goal of controlling population in order to possess a controlling function; they may act as political interventions by dint of their creation in a time and place infused with such reins.

To broaden the frame from object to kitchen, and from kitchen to the national larder, one might ask: Was the ideal kitchen aesthetic of the 1930s modern or traditional? These two categories have been useful in helping us to identify the specific culinary practices that these objects promoted. But ultimately, this categorization presents a false dichotomy. Elements of an old-fashioned kitchen do not capture the difficult working conditions of actual kitchens so much as they provide a re-writing of productive, Italian, socially-conservative past to promote contemporary calls for autarchy. Indeed, nothing could be more modern. Further, every kitchen would have featured a mix of these objects – both modern toasters and traditional bread plates.

Autarchic by Design: Aesthetics and Politics of Kitchenware

Modernity and tradition come together under the aegis of autarchy and point to what is at stake in the aesthetics of kitchen objects. With the onset of the League of Nations' economic sanctions against Italy and the regime's responding call for autarchy to neutralize this threat, questions of domestic production and consumption assumed a heightened importance. Promotion of autarchy crossed spheres, encompassing the public via linguistic translations and pushes for increased productivity in factories, farms and mines, and the private via calls to the home cook to get more out of less. She was to Taylorize her movements, as if in a factory to get more work out of less physical energy, and to make judicious decisions with food products, providing the family with more nutritional energy out of less food.

The regime generally did not concern itself with making these dictates explicit. Rather, major kitchenware firms and designers translated the regime's broad calls for autarchy into specific practices for their core consumers. Economic prudence and trendiness also played significant roles in shaping popular aesthetics. Within the general frame of obeisance to the regime via promotion of autarchy, designers took variant approaches with regards to how such consent manifests in prescribed actions.

When speaking of food and the kitchen in this political context, the significance of the connection between the body and the national body assumes heightened importance. In a time and place that held repetitive, daily practices to be productive of particular types of bodies and minds, the kitchen offered a potent material governmental dimension. National economics enter the private sphere through mass-produced texts and objects, that is, through narrative and also through design. This shift contributed to the development of a definition of autarchy that is specific to women and defined as a set of daily, primarily culinary, practices. But more broadly, it also supported governmental efforts to institutionalize the kitchen, to control this productive space through the form and function of the most mundane of objects. These familiar kitchen tools show that regulatory controls are not always as big as prison or hospital. Sometimes they are as small as a sugar bowl.

Sporks, Pestles and Peelers: Why Kitchen Technology Matters

Bee Wilson

A spork, drawn by Annabel Lee, inspired by cutlery in an early twentieth-century catalogue from J. Jacquotot.

The spork is a hybrid eating implement, a cross between a spoon and a fork. In disposable plastic form, it is used by fast-food restaurants as a kind of lowest common denominator of cutlery. But sporks are also made in sturdier forms – from thicker plastic, stainless steel or wood – for people who have some reason to minimize the amount of cutlery they hold. Campers use them; as do soldiers packing a kit, though the military spork is often more like a Swiss army knife. So do people who have lost the use of one arm; and, more prosaically, parents packing children's lunchboxes (I myself scoffed at the spork until my daughter switched from packed lunches to school dinners). Some sporks have a spoon at one end and a fork at the other, while some have a single curved end that serves as both fork and spoon. The spork is what theorists of technology call a joined tool – two inventions combined. Other examples would be a camera-'phone or a pencil with a rubber on the end.

Two things that seem obvious about the spork are that it is a) very modern and b) deeply comical, but both these impressions require further scrutiny. Despite its contemporary appearance, there are plenty of antecedents for the spork. One example is the sucket fork of early modern times, which had a fork on one end for spearing a sweetmeat and a spoon on the other for spooning up the delicious sweet syrup. A still older forerunner would be the Roman multitool on display in the Fitzwilliam Museum, Cambridge, an ingenious eating device from the third century AD that combines a pear-shaped spoon, a three-pronged fork, a spatula, a pick, a spike and a knife. Most modern sporks look feeble by comparison.

Yet if the thing itself is old, the word is relatively new. It was first recorded in a dictionary in 1909 but didn't enter popular usage until the 1970s.[1] The word 'spork' is somehow hard to say with a straight face and has given rise to a whole genre of spork jokes on the internet. For instance:

> Dear Fork,
> I understand that we haven't spoken since you ran away with dish, but I thought you should know that we have a son. His name is Spork. He has your hair.
>   Sincerely, Spoon.

What makes the spork funny is its hybrid nature and name, which sounds undignified. In addition to sporks, there are spifes, sporfs, knoons and the knork, all of which sound absurd, though in his paper on the possible future of tableware, Ken Albala argues that the knork is in fact rather useful: a fork with the cutting edge of a knife but not one so threatening that you daren't put it in your mouth.

Part of why sporks and knorks are funny – both funny ha ha and funny peculiar – is that unlike almost every other form of tableware or food technology in general, they are hard to categorize or place – whether in terms of cuisine or manners or culture. One of the major recurring themes in this year's symposium papers is the connection between culinary objects and culture in its widest sense. The importance of any kitchen technology goes beyond function and enters the realm of symbol. Sharon Hudgins in her paper on Mongolian milk spoons tells us that these spoons have an importance in nomad culture that is highly symbolic. Voltair Cang says the same of the Japanese bamboo tea whisk or *chasen*, which wasn't just about whisking powdered tea and hot water in the most efficient manner – it was and is a symbol of Japan.

Even now, the material culture of cooking is more symbolic and even quasi-magical than we often notice. Many cooks gravitate towards particular pots when they cook, not because they make the food taste better, but because we like the feel of them in our hands or some feeling of security that they bestow, like household gods. Peter Hertzmann draws our attention to kitchen knives as the new bling, pointing out that consumers – professional chefs as well as amateurs – often choose expensive knives as much for their status as on grounds of function.

The material culture of food carries symbolic freight. It needs to *mean* something and we feel unsettled by something like the spork that is so indeterminate and apparently meaningless.

Perhaps, however, the spork's comical lack of dignity also reflects a wider notion that kitchenware as a subject is somehow trivial flimflam – uninteresting or shallow or merely antiquarian. This year's Symposium is welcome for redressing an imbalance that has existed for too long in food history – and indeed in the wider food culture – which is an obsession with ingredients at the expense of techniques or equipment. Cooking technology has been a strangely neglected subject. On the one hand, it has been neglected by historians of technology, who have traditionally given priority to gunpowder and airships over refrigeration and gas ovens, but it has also been neglected by historians of food, which is odder. In 2000, Cambridge University Press published a two volume, 4000 page *World History of Food* which included nutrition, vegetarianism, culture and countless ingredients from buckwheat to coconut to sea turtles but managed to have nothing on kitchens and their equipment or on changing culinary techniques and tools.[2] This matters. I mean, how do you cook the sea turtle? I'm guessing in the shell, but I'd like to be told. When we focus on ingredients and forget what is done to them, half the story is missing. We change the texture, the taste, the nutritional content and cultural associations of ingredients simply by using different tools and techniques to prepare them.

To some extent, the obsession with ingredients at the expense of material culture is understandable. What makes food interesting is the fact that we want to eat it, whereas the appetite we feel on viewing a cake tin is only by proxy. Food itself is surely the most important of all material cultures. The great psychologist of food Paul Rozin has said that 'the mouth is the principle and most salient route of entry of material things into the body.'[3] To eat is to take matter from outside ourselves and to place it inside, a deeply intimate process. Conversely, you can't eat a kitchen. You can't digest a wooden spoon. You can't taste the metal of the pan in the grains of the risotto; or, if you can, something has gone wrong.

Nevertheless, in the remainder of this paper I want to explore some of the ways in which the utensils of eating and cooking are just as intimate and important a part of who we are as the food they interact with.

Unlike the spork, the material culture of food is not a laughing matter. The tools we choose to cook and eat with from decade to decade or from century to century both reflect and shape our society, arguably as much as other markers such as government, economic structure, religion and marriage arrangements. Access to kitchen equipment also affects our health. A 2014 study by Bradley M. Appelhans et al. demonstrated that among a sample of 103 low-income American families, ownership of kitchen tools predicted how many home-cooked meals children would eat. While 100% of the households owned at least one refrigerator, fewer than 80% had a cutting board, a ladle, a whisk, a grater or a kitchen table. Families who lacked these supplies understandably ate fewer 'home-prepared dinners'.[4]

Entire culinary cultures hinge on cooking food one way and not another: on using this vessel and not another; on grilling this and frying that. In his paper about the Baghdad kitchen of his youth in the 1940s, Sami Zubaida recalls the strong conviction among cooks that chicken must be boiled before it is roasted, a conviction which persisted even after the chickens had changed, rendering it an empty ritual. Archaeologists gathering sherds of broken pottery have always seen that cooking vessels are central to the identity of a community, and they like to name people after the pots they left behind, such as the Beaker folk of the third millennium BC, who travelled across Europe from the Spanish Peninsula eventually reaching Britain around 2000 BC. Wherever they went, they left traces of reddish brown, bell-shaped clay drinking vessels. Our own culture has so much stuff that pottery has lost some of its former importance, but it is still one of the few universal possessions. Perhaps many hundred years from now when our culture is buried by some apocalypse or other, archaeologists will dig up our remains and name us the mug community, a people who liked our ceramics to be brightly coloured, large enough to accommodate high volumes of comforting caffeinated drinks, and above all, dishwasher proof.

Because cooking technologies have always been a feature of human society, they offer a fascinating test case for the problem of continuity and change which runs through all of history. In some ways, what we are doing when we walk into our kitchens and apply heat to raw ingredients is not so different from the first moments of cooking as imagined by Richard Wrangham in *Catching Fire*, where he sees cooking as the decisive moment at which we ceased to be upright apes and became fully human.[5] Much has changed since the first cooking fires, however. The fact that we have kitchens to walk into at all is noteworthy. The history of the material culture of food is often phrased as 'how has the kitchen changed over time', which is really to ask the wrong question. It implies that we moved incrementally from cave-age kitchens, with rocky work surfaces, through to the kitchen islands and glass splashbacks of today. To phrase the question like this is to forget that the room itself – a purpose-built space in which to cook, never mind the labour-saving devices and electric switches – is itself a very recent invention, at least in a home setting (professional kitchens have a different history). For the vast majority of history, most people have had no separate room in which to cook. All cooking would have taken place, probably in a single cauldron, over a single fire, whose purpose was to heat the house and boil water as well as cook, and whose smoke was inescapable. In such dwellings the kitchen was everywhere and nowhere.

Today in the developing world, people still cook in a similar way, with disastrous consequences. The World Health Organization estimates that smoke from cooking fires causes 1.5 million deaths a year, which is worth remembering anytime someone suggests that the history of cooking is a trivial subject.[6] One of the great things about the modern separate kitchen – which as a mass phenomenon only arrives in the twentieth century – is that not only is it a far better workspace for cooking – creating the possibility of cooking as a leisure pursuit – but it also offers an escape from cooking when you shut the door.

So the kitchen is one of the ways our material culture is new. And the organization of our kitchens is also new; and indeed would be baffling in many ways to our ancestors. I'm not talking especially about high-tech gadgetry such as sous-vide machines – apart from the electrical precision of it, to heat food in a water bath strikes me as a very old way to cook, reminiscent of the geyser cookery of Iceland or even the steaming methods of ancient pit ovens. A more noteworthy fact about the modern kitchen would be the absence of fire and the presence of ice.

Whereas in the past, cooking was always organized around fire – the word focus comes from the Latin for fireplace because the fire was the thing on which the whole

A nineteenth-century kitchen range, after Webster, drawn by Annabel Lee.

household was focused – the focal point now (except in kitchens with Aga-style cast iron ranges) is the fridge whose arrival has changed so much about how we shop and cook and eat. Paul Levy once wrote about what a disaster it is when a freezer malfunctions and all of the carefully husbanded provisions become unusable: 'pounds and pounds of tomatoes, frozen whole as they ripened in the greenhouse, now collapsed like pricked balloons'.[7] When we can't think what else to do, we open the fridge door and stare into it long and hard as if it will provide the answers to life's great questions. It used to be flames that people stared into. Now it is ice we look to first, to provide us with dinner.

This question of continuity and change is also seen in some of the smaller technologies of food whose presence in our lives we take for granted. Consider two objects that you would find in any kitchen shop today: a granite pestle and mortar and a double-bladed ergonomic vegetable peeler. Neither of them is particularly remarkable. They are certainly not decorative or beautiful. They are probably not the sort of gadgetry that most people associate with 'kitchen technology', such as futuristic Pacojets and anti-griddles. But they do represent technology nevertheless. These quite unassuming objects illustrate some rather surprising things about the tools with which we fill our kitchens, especially about how much has changed in the material culture of cooking and how much has stayed the same. The first thing is that we should be much more startled than we are by the fact that these two objects are coexisting, sitting side by side. They look perfectly natural together. Yet they belong to completely different stages in the history of our technological development.

One of them, the pestle and mortar, is somewhere between ten and twenty thousand years old. The earliest stone mortars have been found in the Levant, in the Middle East, going back around twenty thousand years.

Sporks, Pestles and Peelers

By the time of the Romans the pestle and mortar was already an object that had undergone various refinements in its design, whether beautiful limestone mortars with handles at the edges, goblet shaped ones or basalt ones with three little tripod feet. We have nothing over the Romans when it comes to mortars. They also had wonderful sieves, frying pans, double-boilers, casserole dishes, ladles, colanders and more. What the Romans didn't have was anything like the ergonomic vegetable peeler. Then again, nor did the Elizabethans or the Victorians or the Edwardians or indeed the generation of the Second World War. Such peelers are a mere twenty years old, having arrived in the final decade of the twentieth century. It is a more recent invention than the electric oven or the microwave and far more recent than the pressure cooker or the waffle iron. It's a small thing, but good vegetable peelers – which I would define as ones that do an efficient job of removing a fine layer of peel without hurting your hand – have only been in our lives since 1990 (or 1989 if you come from the States).

Peeling vegetables used to be one of the most annoying jobs in the kitchen. For centuries, the default method was with a paring knife. In the right hands – skilled hands – the paring knife is an excellent tool, but it requires immense concentration to remove every scrap of peel without also gouging your own thumb. By the mid-twentieth century, peelers were available, but they were bothersome in various ways. The Lancashire with its crude fixed blade and handle tied with string, which removed wasteful chunks of potato along with the string; or the swivel-action metal peelers of France, which had a highly effective blade but whose waffled chrome handle would stab into your hand as you peeled. Preparing mashed potatoes for a large family gathering could leave you with peeler-related blisters.

The breakthrough only happened when Sam Farber, a retired housewares designer, attempted to come up with something that would help his wife Betsey, who had arthritis in her hands. The result was the OXO Good Grips peeler, whose brilliant idea was that to make a peeler that was both comfortable and efficient, so that you had to pay as much attention to the handle as to the blade. It was included as a design classic in the Museum of Modern Art exhibition Counter Space in New York in 2010.[8] It spawned a brand-new market in peelers: today's kitchenware shops are flooded with peelers in every pretty colour, C-shaped and U-shaped and Y-shaped. The owner of one UK kitchenware store told me that whereas twenty years ago he would have stocked just two peelers, now he stocked 60 different ones, allowing for all the colour variations.

But just because a technology exists doesn't mean we have to use it. As I've said, I think this object is the most wonderful step forward. My mother disagrees. Breakfast for her is ritualistic. Every morning, after her toast, she eats either an apple or a pear, which she laboriously peels using a table knife. It used to upset me that she was losing so much of the fruit along with the peel and so I started buying her peelers as presents. But whenever I went to stay with her and breakfast came around, I noticed that the peelers remained stubbornly in the kitchen drawer and she got out her trusty old table knife as she always had done. Eventually, I asked her why she wasn't using one of the peelers and she replied that she just couldn't get on with it. You could say that this a morality tale about how grownup daughters shouldn't be so bossy with their mothers, nor should they give them lectures disguised as presents, and I'd have to agree. But I'd also suggest that my mother's – to me, somewhat illogical – attachment to her table knife illustrates another theme that recurs in the history of culinary objects which is that new technologies in the kitchen, even beneficial ones, are often greeted with suspicion and outright rejection when they first appear.

Cooks are conservative beings, masters of quiet repetitive actions which change little from day to day or year to year. Given that communities define themselves by cooking food one way and not another, it's hardly surprising that once our hands have become used to a certain way of doing things, we don't want to give it up, even if there is another potentially more efficient way available. We are back to the question of symbolism. This emotional conservatism in the kitchen can be seen even when the stakes are much higher than peeling fruit.

The gas oven, for example, represented a huge improvement in the saving of labour and the speed with which meals could be prepared, over the hearths and cast-iron kitcheners that came before. When they became widespread in domestic kitchens from the 1880s onwards, they liberated people – especially women – from all the pollution and labour of a fire. Yet many people hated the idea of gas, fearing they would either be poisoned or die in an explosion if they cooked with it.[9]

The same cooks who toiled in the tropical heat, pollution and filth of a coal-fired range feared that gas was a dangerous form of cooking. Besides, they preferred to do things just as their mothers and grandmothers did – which I'm sure is also how my own mother feels about her table knife for peeling fruit. And, as I'm sure she would say, people have been peeling fruit with knives for hundreds of years before Mr Farber and his OXO Good Grips brand came along.

The story of the ergonomic peeler may be very short, but if we forget the handle and focus on the blade, it becomes part of the history of the knife, which is actually the most ancient of all cooking techniques. The knife is the oldest tool in the cook's armoury, older than the management of fire by somewhere between one and two million years, depending on which anthropologist you believe. The primary job of knives was to do some of the work that feeble human teeth cannot. Unlike lions, we lack the ability to tear meat from a carcass with our bare teeth, so we invented ever-sharper cutting tools to do the job for us. The story of knives and food is not only about cutting tools getting ever sharper and stronger, however. It is also about how we tame the alarming violence of these utensils. The Chinese did it by confining their knife-work to the kitchen, reducing food to bite-sized pieces with a massive cleaver-like instrument, out of sight. Europeans did it first by creating elaborate rules about the use of the knife at table – the subtext of all table manners is the fear that the man next to you may pull his knife on you – and, second, by inventing 'table knives' so blunt and feeble that you would struggle to use them to cut people instead of food. In medieval times, the ergonomic peeler would have been completely superfluous, because everyone had their own personal knife that they carried with them wherever they went and brought out at mealtimes whenever they needed to peel, slice or cut anything, whether it was a chewy crust of bread, some meat or a piece of fruit. And because they were cutting things all the time, people must have had fluent knife skills. The habit of carrying your own sharp knife with you was as much a bedrock of Western culture as Christianity, the Latin alphabet and the rule of law. Until – suddenly – it wasn't. So much of what we believe about utensils is determined by culture, but cultural values are not fixed and eternal. From the seventeenth century onwards there was a great upheaval in European attitudes to knives.

The first change was that knives started to be pre-laid on the table, joined by that new-fangled implement, the fork. This divested knives of their former magic. Rather than being specially tailored to an individual owner, cases of identical knives were now bought and sold by the dozen and laid out impersonally for whoever happened to sit down. The second change was that table knives ceased being sharp. They were thus divested of their power too. The *raison d'être* of knives is to cut. It takes a civilization in an advanced state of politesse – or passive aggression – to devise on purpose a knife that does a worse job of cutting. In more ways than one we are still living with the consequences of this change today.

The familiar part of the story has to do with manners: the 'civilizing process' described by the sociologist Norbert Elias whereby Western patterns of behaviour at the table changed and people became revolted by ways of eating that had once seemed acceptable, whether it was picking up meat with fingers or producing sharp knives at meals.[10]

But there's another less familiar story, about how the table knife and fork actually had an impact on our bodies. From the 1960s onwards, an anthropologist called C. Loring Brace started looking into the problem of the human overbite. This overbite refers to the way that the top layer of our teeth fits over the bottom layer, like a lid on a box. The opposite of an overbite is the edge-to-edge bite seen in apes where the top incisors clash against the bottom ones like a guillotine blade. Initially, Brace assumed that the overbite must have emerged in humans around the time of the adoption of agriculture roughly 10,000 years ago, until he found that the edge-to-edge bite actually persists much longer. After studying numerous skulls, he found that the overbite only emerges around 200-250 years ago in the Western World. It is not therefore a product of evolution – the time-frame is far too short. Rather, it seems to be a response to the way we cut our food during our formative years. In the days before the table knife and fork, the main method of eating was something that Brace has christened 'stuff and cut'. First, grasp the food – perhaps a piece of hard cheese, a chewy sausage or a crusty chunk of bread. Then clamp it between your teeth. Finally, rip or cut off the main hunk of food being careful not to slice your lips in the process.[11]

With the adoption of the knife and fork, for the first time people – from childhood onwards – were cutting their food into small pieces before eating it, rather than clamping larger pieces in their mouths as they had done in the days of sharp knives and no forks. Brace's thesis was that whereas previously the clamping action of eating had limited the eruption of the teeth in the jaw to an edge-to-edge bite, once we ate small morsels, our teeth continued to erupt into an overbite.

How can we be sure, as Brace is, that it was cutlery that brought about this change in our teeth? The short answer is that we can't. Modes of eating were far more various than just 'Stuff-and-cut', and not all food required the incisor's clamp. People also supped soups and potages, nibbled on soft crumbly pies, spooned up porridge and polenta. And yet Brace's theory does seem the best available fit with the data. There is a clincher in the form of China. In China, the overbite emerged 900 years earlier, coinciding with the adoption of chopsticks which went along with food being cut into tiny morsels before it arrived at table. The differing attitude to knives in East and West had a graphic impact on the alignment of our jaws.

The arrival of table knives had many other consequences. It went along with a long slow decline in knife skills. Except for chefs, knowledge of how to handle a knife, never mind keep one sharp, has become a minority pursuit in modern societies. The way we are taught to hold our table knives is with your forefinger over the spine, to avoid any gesture reminiscent of violence. The trouble is that many of us then apply this same hold to kitchen knives, where it is ineffectual and actually dangerous, because if your finger slips you will cut yourself.

The surprising thing about our lack of knife skills is that it matters so little. Being able to wield a sharp kitchen knife accurately is a huge pleasure but no longer necessary for survival. Our food system enables us to feed ourselves even when we lack the most rudimentary cutting abilities. Bread comes ready-sliced and vegetables can be bought ready-diced. When something needs to be really finely chopped or shredded, a food processor will pick up the slack. One of the few things that can't be done mechanically – outside of professional kitchens where they have giant potato rumblers – is peeling, another factor explaining the emergence of the ergonomic peeler.

This object belongs to a very particular moment in history: to a kitchen that has no servants – because people didn't generally worry too much about whether peeling vegetables was painful when servants were doing the job. It is suggestive of a worldview of cooking as a pleasurable leisure activity rather than drudgery. And it is a tool aimed at people who want to get good culinary results with the minimum of skill. A paring knife puts the onus on the user to follow the curve of the carrot or apple. An ergonomic peeler does all the tricky angling for you. It is virtually foolproof and it needs to be.

The question, however, is how an object like this co-exists with this other one – the pestle and mortar, which is so many thousands of years older? Part of the answer is that old and new do sit side by side in the material culture of kitchen. While many tools have become obsolete – the weight-powered spitjack, the sugar nipper – many others have endured for centuries, such as the mezzaluna, these lovely two-handled curved knives in the shape of a half moon, which are just as useful now for chopping herbs as they were in the aristocratic Italian kitchens of the sixteenth century. No design has yet improved on the mezzaluna and it has an advantage over the knife, which is, to quote Nigella Lawson, that with the mezzaluna 'both my hands are engaged and thus it is impossible for me to cut myself'.[12]

The persistence of the pestle and mortar in our kitchens is arguably rather different from the mezzaluna. While it looks very similar in form to those with which our Neolithic ancestors pounded grains and tubers, its function has been radically transformed. Many cooks now regard their personal pestle and mortar with fondness. We often select them as much on aesthetic grounds as based on their function. This is because in our cooking lives it is a pretty much superfluous and therefore ornamental piece of technology. It may be a nice way to make curry pastes when we don't feel like washing up the food processor, but we don't need it to grind flour or pulverize sugar, which comes ready-pounded in bags. Nor do we need it for pepper, which can be ground far quicker and more easily in a pepper grinder. The pestle and mortar is a fun thing that we use on a whim when we are feeling like being leisurely in the kitchen – for example, when we decide one sunny morning that we'd like to make some pesto from scratch, relishing the sensation of crushing the waxy pine nuts against the hard surfaces and inhaling the marvellous scent of basil.

The pestles and mortars of the past were both more necessary and far more painful tools to use, being vital if bone-aching aids in the task of generating enough belly-filling calories for survival. By the end of the Stone Age, mortars were sometimes incorporated into a house; there are giant basalt mortars set in the ground, as part of a courtyard where women and servants would have sat for hours grinding. This way of life continued one way or another for centuries – and still does in the developing world. A visitor to the Highlands of Scotland in 1800, T. Garnett, watched as two women ground grain in a rotary quern, another grinding device, 'singing some Celtic songs all the time'.[13] It's easy to romanticize this way of life – the slower pace of existence, the comradeship forged around the grindstone. But Middle Eastern burial sites indicate that using these grinding tools put a heavy strain on women's bodies: female skeletons show signs of acute arthritis, with the knees, hips and ankles all severely worn by kneeling down and rocking back and forth to crush grain against stone.[14]

At least these grindstones were necessary. As time went on, the pestle and mortar became associated with elaborate forms of cuisine for the wealthy which seemed to make a fetish out of the amount of labour they required. The Romans had a whole class of dishes called mortaria, made in the mortar, and medieval cooks made mortrews, mortar-pounded concoctions of white boiled meats and almonds ideal for those with bad teeth. There were many reasons why highly refined foods were so highly prized. The mingling together of many pounded ingredients corresponded to medieval Galenic ideas about temperament and balance. Later, in Renaissance times, processing became a kind of alchemy: a desire to distil things down until all you were left with was the very essence or inner kernel of a foodstuff.

But when considering the technologies of grinding, pounding and so on, we cannot get past the labour question and pre-industrial patterns of work. Highly processed foods were favoured by the rich not despite the labour they caused – the number of people they wore out – but because of it. Take this recipe for pancakes from the fourteenth-century advice book *Le Menagier de Paris*, dating from *c.* 1393: 'First, get a copper pan and melt a large quantity of salted butter. Then take eggs, some warm white wine' – which goes in place of our milk – and the 'fairest wheaten flour'. Then beat it all together, 'long enough to weary one person or two'. Only then is the batter done. There is startling nonchalance in this 'one person or two', conjuring up a kitchen in which there is a standing army of servants, arrayed like so many utensils.[15]

A recipe like this gives some clue as to why it was so late in the day that labour-saving implements arrived in the kitchen. The harsh fact is that there was very little interest in saving labour when the labour in question was not your own. The phrase 'labour-saving' first enters the language in 1791, but it would be another half century before it finally came to the kitchen. In the second half of the nineteenth century in both the United States and Great Britain, the market was suddenly flooded with labour-saving culinary devices, many cheaply made from tin: there were raisin seeders, potato mashers, coffee mills, cherry pitters, apple corers. Many were heavy apparatus clamped to the table like a mincing machine. What explains their sudden emergence? A supply-side argument would talk about the industrial revolution and the existence of a glut of cheap metal. But industrialization – particularly in the States – also went along with a reduction in the number of servants that middle-class women could call upon to help them in the kitchen. Many of these labour-saving devices were a disappointment. There were no fewer than 692 separate patents issued for egg beaters issued in America between 1856 and 1902. But not one of the designs, so far as I can tell, was an improvement on the trusty old French balloon whisk invented in the sixteenth century.[16]

The real labour saving only came with the electric kitchen of the twentieth century and tools such as the Cuisinart – introduced to the U.S. from France by Carl Sontheimer in the 1970s, which Craig Claiborne, the *New York Times* food critic, compared as an invention to 'the printing press, cotton gin, steamboat, paper clips, Kleenex'.[17] The Cuisinart's impact was actually far from universal – as of 2014, fewer than 20% of low-income American families studied owned one – but for those who did acquire one, the food processor made the kitchen a different place. Cooks could whizz things so easily that, as so often with a new technology, there was a zealous over-use for a while. In the 1970s Elizabeth David dined out with Julia Child at a celebrated London restaurant. Child commented that what they were eating could be called Cuisinart cooking. David noted that 'about seven dishes out of ten on that restaurant menu could not have been created without the food processor'.[18]

David herself was part of a backlash towards more robust French and Italian provincial cooking in which the individual ingredients were discernible. Soups and stews became chunky, a way of parading that no processor had been used. Fine-textured food lost its cachet. Now it was the rustic and the irregular that were prized. The pestle and mortar was revived as a symbol of all that was low-tech, hand-made and artisanal. In its first incarnation, the pestle was used because there was no other way to grind the ingredients that needed to be ground. Now, pestles are used stubbornly and through choice as a way of slowing down the cooking process. Its persistence in our kitchens is arguably a very good sign – an indication that, at least among the demographic of households lucky enough to possess cutting boards and ladles and whisks, we are among the first generations in history who can choose how to cook at home based on whim and desire rather than necessity.

To return to the question of how a pestle and mortar can coexist with an ergonomic peeler, the answer is partly that appearances can be deceptive. Our pestles are not as ancient as they seem, because they perform a diametrically different function in our cooking lives from ancient grindstones. Conversely, the ergonomic vegetable peeler – if we see it as a cutting tool – is part of a history stretching back two million years and thus far more familiar to our ancestors than it first seems. They are both examples of the constant, restless reinvention that goes on in cooking, which is what makes the material culture of food such an important window into the wider history of human culture and which is why, unlike the spork, the subject is far from laughable.

Kitchen and eating tools will doubtless continue to evolve in the future, although my own feeling is that the kitchen of the future will look more like the kitchen of the past than most futurologists allow. I can't foresee the wooden spoon becoming obsolete just yet. During the Second World War, an American kitchen company toured the country showing off a kitchen of the future.[19] One of its futuristic elements was that instead of pots and pans, it had recessed heating units hidden under the work surfaces, which looked a bit like washing machines. The idea of a kitchen beyond pots and pans sounds like something from the futuristic cartoon *The Jetsons*. The war ended, however, and people continued to cook with pots and pans, and to cut vegetables with knives, and to heat things with fire and to drain them in sieves. In an energy-scarce future, cooks may turn to green pans, or layer vegetables up in multiple steamers set over a single burner, but in the end, this is not so unlike the Victorian *batterie de cuisine* or the medieval cauldron. Even in a dystopian future where – as is sometimes predicted – all meals were reduced to a pill, we would still need the material objects of the kitchen for their symbolic qualities. As with my mother and her table knife, they make us feel safe. Things like pestles and peelers seem to anchor us in the concrete world of things, which perhaps is more valuable than ever in an era when so much of life is virtual.

The history of the kitchen may be short, but the history of culinary equipment is as long as humanity. We still surround ourselves with our household gods, whether it's Mongolian milk spoons or bling knives, shoring ourselves up against the unknown. We will never get beyond the technology of cooking itself. Sporks may come and go, microwaves rise and fall, but the human race will always have kitchen tools. Fire, hands, knives; we will always have these.

Notes

1. *OED*, 'spork'; see also Bee Wilson, *Consider the Fork: A History of How We Cook and Eat* (New York: Basic Books, 2012), pp. 204-08.
2. *The Cambridge World History of Food*, eds. Kenneth F. Kiple and Kriemhild Coneè Ornelas (Cambridge: Cambridge UP, 2000).
3. Paul Rozin, 'The socio-cultural context of eating and food choice', *Food Choice, Acceptance and Consumption*, ed. Halliday MacFie and Herbert L. Meiselman (London: Chapman & Hall, 1996), p. 83.
4. Bradley M. Appelhans, Molly E. Waring, Kristin L. Schneider, and Sherry L. Pagoto, 'Food preparation supplies predict children's family meal and home-prepared dinner consumption in low-income households', *Appetite* 76 (2014), pp. 1-8.
5. Richard Wrangam, *Catching Fire: How Cooking Made us Human* (New York: Basic Books, 2009).
6. Wilson, p. 91.
7. Paul Levy, *Out to Lunch* (London: Chatto & Windus, 1986).
8. Juliet Kinchin and Aidan O'Connor, *Counter Space: Design and the Modern Kitchen* (New York: MoMa publications, 2010).
9. See Christina Hardyment, *From Mangle to Microwave: the Mechanization of Household Work* (Cambridge: Polity, 1990).
10. Norbert Elias, *The Civilising Process*, trans. Edmund Jephcott (Oxford: Blackwell, 1994),
11. For Brace's work on the overbite, see, for example, C. Loring Brace 'Occlusion to the Anthropological Eye', *The Biology of Occlusal Development*, ed. James McNamara (Ann Arbor, MI: U Michigan P, 1977), pp. 179-209; 'Egg on the Face, *f* in the Mouth and the Overbite', *American Anthropologist*, New Series, 88:3 (1986), pp. 695-97; 'What Big Teeth you Had, Grandma!', *Evolution in an Anthropological View* (Lanham, MD: AltaMira, 2000), pp. 165-99. See also Helke Ferrie, 'An Interview with C. Loring Brace', *Current Anthropology*, 38:5 (December 1997), pp. 851-917.
12. Nigella Lawson, *Kitchen: Recipes from the Heart of the Home* (London: Chatto & Windus, 2010), p. 5.
13. Wilson, p. 152.
14. Neil MacGregor, *A History of the World in 100 Objects*, (New York: Viking, 2010), p. 35.
15. *The Goodman of Paris* (*Le Menagier de Paris*, c. 1393), ed. and trans. Eileen Power, (London: Folio Society, 1992).
16. On the great American egg beater bubble, see Marion Harland, *Common Sense in the Household* (New York: Scribner, Armstrong, & Co., 1873); also Don Thornton, *Beat This: The Eggbeater Chronicles* (Sunnyvale: Offbeat Books, 1994).
17. Craig Claiborne, 'She Demonstrates How to Cook Best with the New Cuisinart', *New York Times*, 7 January 1976, p. 64.
18. Elizabeth David, *French Provincial Cooking* (London: Penguin, 1998), p. 9.
19. See Kinchin and O'Connor.

The Soup that Went into the Tureen: Connecting the Dots between Food and Material Culture

Carolin C. Young

Food and material culture marry symbiotically together. One can consume fruit picked directly from the tree (a gesture our current generation rates highly because of its emblematic purity and rarity), but food usually gets presented in some kind of serving dish, whose characteristics derive from its utilitarian as well as symbolic functions. An especially beautiful vessel lends respect to that put into it and may be perceived as enhancing the experience of eating it, an aesthetic captured in Proverbs 25:11: 'A word fitly spoken is like an apple of gold in a setting of silver.'

That verse inspired the title of my first book and encapsulates my belief that food and the objects surrounding it should always be studied in tandem, even by those whose primary interest lie with one or the other. This paper outlines a few examples of the ways in which combining the two fields together has yielded important discoveries and concludes with some cautionary tales of mistakes resulting from their unnatural separation. Although these examples have been drawn from European history, primarily of the eighteenth and early nineteenth centuries, they elucidate principles that extend to any place or period.

Vincent La Chapelle and the Chesterfield tureen

The soup tureen that arrived on élite European tables from the late seventeenth century was that era's most dazzling dining accessory. At their most magnificent, tureens are veritable works of art on a par with the finest sculptures. Among the most famous of these, the so-called Kingston tureens, designed by Juste-Aurèle Meissonier (1695–1750) in France in 1734–1735 for the English Duke of Kingston, feature swirling shell-inspired forms that exemplify the rococo style at its most exuberant.[1] During this same period, French silversmith Thomas Germain (1673–1748) executed equally impressive tureens in an entirely different, monumental style that included highly articulated still-life sculptures of fish, freshly hunted birds and boars' heads.

These glamorous objects reflect the attenuated elegance of the French court of the ancien régime (and for some represent just why a revolution needed to take place in 1789). However, as this fashion spread across the Continent, Great Britain and its colonies, tureens took on more modest but no less playful forms. Tin-glazed earthenware and soft-paste porcelain served as especially popular materials from which to make them in workshops from Denmark to Portugal. Chinese export porcelain versions appealed to the colonial market.

Figure 1. One of the pair of 'Kingston' tureens and platters designed by Juste-Aurèle Meissonier, made by Pierre-François Bonnestrenne and Henri Adnet, Paris, c. 1735–40, silver. Courtesy of the Cleveland Museum of Art.

Figure 2. Boar's head tureen, lid, and stand by Thomas Germain, Paris, 1733–1734, silver. Courtesy of the Detroit Institute of Arts Museum.

The Soup that Went into the Tureen

Fashionable shapes included vegetable and animal forms such as cabbages, asparagus, turkeys and eels. Nevertheless, in spite of the rather obvious fact that all of the above are edible, at no point when I was a student of the decorative arts with Christie's Education in the 1990s did any of my eminent silver and ceramics professors mention anything about how these objects were used or what went into them. It was this omission that inspired me to study food history. With gourmand leanings, I was naturally curious to know about the soup that went into the tureen.

Happily, a generation of forerunners was already hard at work paving the way. About a dozen years earlier, Barbara Ketcham Wheaton had published her seminal book, *Savoring the Past*. She devotes a chapter to the refinement of French cuisine in the Age of Enlightenment at Louis XIV's court at Versailles and then explains its evolution through the eighteenth-century.[2] The new cooking found its match in the innovative *service à la française* method of presenting symmetrically laid out dishes on the table in a small series of courses, each including myriad dishes. To illustrate how this was done, Wheaton reproduced period diagrams, including one from the 1742 edition of Vincent La Chapelle's *Cuisinier moderne*, which originally appeared as *The Modern Cook* in 1733. It depicts a sumptuous first course featuring a pair of tureens as the pivotal objects to which one's eye is drawn from the smaller platters and dishes surrounding them. The place of honour thereby went to the soups and stews that went into them. These relied upon subtle combinations of the era's highly refined broths as their base. Unctuous broths also served as the foundation to French cuisine's growing lexicon of sauces, which glorified the roasts featured as the pièces-de-resistance of the subsequent course.

The tureen therefore came into existence not only for the practical purpose of containing liquid foods (and, as all came with covers, keeping it hot) at table but also to visually stress the importance of what went into it. Its spread to far-flung parts of the Western world maps the extent to which French cuisine and service came into use. That the object's decorative properties got watered down or creatively reinvented as it travelled hints that the foods placed in them may have been similarly simplified or reconceived from those served at the French court.

La Chapelle's seminal cookbook offers particularly rich fodder for an inquiry into the soups that went into his era's tureens. His employer, Philip Dormer Stanhope, the fourth Earl of Chesterfield (1694–1773), also assembled one of his generation's most stunning collections of silver tableware, including the so-called Chesterfield tureen, now at the Metropolitan Museum of Art in New York, which was created by England's preeminent rococo silversmith, Paul de Lamerie (1688–1751) in 1736–1737.[3] It is therefore possible to conjecture that the preparations that would have gone into it must have closely resembled those in La Chapelle's cookbook, although he by this date had entered into the service of the Prince of Orange.

In its online collection the MMA describes the tureen as being 'made to serve a spicy game stew known as oille'.[4] This distinction is made because, in French, tureens are divided into two categories: the *pot à oille*, with a perfectly round shape and the *soupière*,

Figure 3. Goose-shaped tureen and cover made of famille-rose enamelled porcelain, Qing dynasty, c. 1760–1780, produced in China for the European/colonial export market. Courtesy of the British Museum, London.

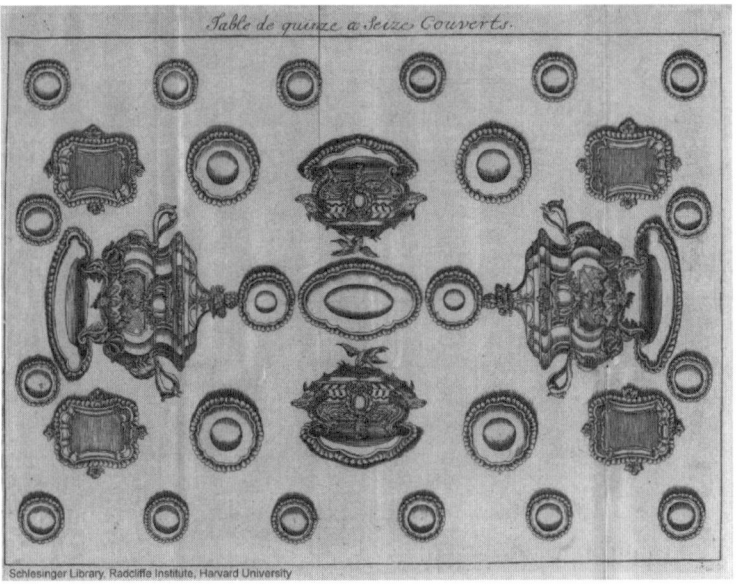

Figure 4. Table for Fifteen to Sixteen Covers, from The Modern Cook *by Vincent La Chapelle, 1733. Courtesy of the Schlesinger Library, Harvard University.*

which is oval. But in fact, decorative arts curators tend to be overly literal in insisting that these objects were only used for the foods for which they were named.

La Chapelle's *The Modern Cook* refutes this idea in its more playful suggestions about how to serve things. If his basic recipe for a French olio instructs readers to place the finished stew into an 'Olio pot', that for his Spanish olio directs them to 'serve it in cover'd *China* cups'.[5] Further on, his recipe for *Pottage à la Jambe de Bois*, which one might expect to get served in a *soupière*, tells readers to 'put it in your dish, and garnish it with all the Roots you have in your Broth'; adding as a final note that, 'If you serve it in an Olio-pot, you need not put in any greens at all'.[6] These discrepancies hint that, in spite of the fact that their French names refer to specific foods, the distinction between the oval and the round tureen was aesthetic more than anything else.

La Chapelle's French olio can nevertheless be assumed to be exactly the sort of dish to have been served in Chesterfield's tureen, and its recipe is as princely as that object. It required sweating beef, veal and mutton and then moistening it with broth.[7] A different broth was then added as well as carrots, onions, turnips, celery, leeks and a mignonette (a sachet of coriander seeds, pepper, cloves and nutmeg). Partridges, fowl, turkey, ham, and cervelas then went into the pot to boil gently. La Chappelle advised readers 'to take care your Broth be very clear and well tasted'. Grated breadcrumbs were separately soaked in some of the finished broth and put in the bottom of the tureen before more broth was poured over it. As a final flourish, two partridges were added as well as rice or pasta, which had also been cooked in the broth.

This complex dish seems quite suited to the sumptuous decoration of Chesterfield's tureen, which includes a boldly dignified lion surmounting its cover, curvaceous crayfish-shaped handles, dolphin-form feet, and exquisitely articulated foliate and classically inspired decoration on its body. The piece evinces fluency in the most sophisticated French styles of the day. Nevertheless, although its tour-de-force workmanship stands on a par with even the most regal French examples, it is, for all of its ornateness, more streamlined and restrained than analogous French examples such as those by Meissonier or Germain.

The Chesterfield tureen therefore hints that its owner had French-leaning tastes, which he nevertheless chose to reinterpret in a more toned down, English style.[8] It is impossible to know exactly which of La Chapelle's recipes his employer most enjoyed. That the author plagiarized huge swaths of François Massialot's *Nouveau cuisinier royal and bourgeois* of 1712 makes the task even more unfathomable.[9] Nevertheless, a letter of October 1728 from the Earl of Chesterfield to the Duke of Richmond entreating his friend to find him a French chef, 'who is allowed by all Paris to be at the top of his profession', confirms his desire to dine in the chicest Parisian taste.[10] However, the restraint of the Chesterfield tureen hints that perhaps he, as much as another of his friends, Thomas Pelham-Holles, Duke of Newcastle (1693–1768), may have preferred his French cuisine in a slightly simplified state. Surviving correspondence from the latter with his former French chef, Clouet, records the duke's complaints that the cook's replacement never prepared the 'plain, simple dishes such as you used to make me'.[11]

Figure 5. The 'Chesterfield' tureen and cover by Paul de Lamerie, silver, made in London, 1736-7, overall dimensions: 11⅞ x 13⅞ x 10⅜ in., 150 oz. 18 dwt. (30.2 x 35.2 x 26.4 cm, 4.694kg). Courtesy of the Metropolitan Museum of Art, New York.

Figure 6. Installation by Ivan Day based on an engraving from Joseph Gillier's Cannameliste français *for the exhibition 'Sèvres Then and Now' at Hillwood Museum and Gardens, Washington, D.C. Courtesy of Hillwood Estate, Museum and Gardens; photo. by Carol M. Highsmith.*

It seems that to be a successful French chef in England one was to bring over the most fashionable French dishes and adapt them as elegantly as Paul de Lamerie, who was the English-born son of a French Huguenot refugee, had done with his masterful tureen for Chesterfield.

The superb finesse of this object and others of its type on both sides of the Channel counter the claims of numerous contemporary authors such as Adam Gopnik and historians such as Patricia Parkhurst Ferguson that French haute cuisine was a nineteenth-century invention.[12] Certainly, it is true that it and the related field of gastronomy grew in leaps and bounds in the decades that followed the French Revolution. Alexandre Balthazar Laurent Grimod de la Reynière (1758–1838) asserted this in his lifetime.[13] His *Almanach des gourmands*, the world's first serialized food journal, constitutes a notable contribution to this phenomenon. Yet, he frequently contradicts himself to wax nostalgically about lost refinements of the good old days of the *ancien régime*.[14]

The sophistication of the tureens and other tablewares produced for eighteenth-century aristocrats is too great to imagine that the foods eaten from them were leaden glop. Those who have made the effort to prepare recipes of this period authentically, using correct equipment as well as ingredients, have repeatedly demonstrated just how on a par with the tureens was French cuisine of the period.

Gilliers and the Château de Lunéville

Ivan Day unquestionably stands out as the leader in the recreation of early European recipes and sugar sculpture. Among his astounding projects, for the 2010 exhibition *Sèvres Then and Now* at the Hillwood Museum and Gardens in Washington, D.C., Day produced an elaborate assemblage of sugar sculptures according to a centrepiece design illustrated in Joseph Gilliers' *Le Cannameliste français* of 1751.[15] (Gilliers invented the word '*cannameliste*' from '*canne*' (sugar) to imply a person who works with sugar, so his book's title might be translated as *The French Sugar-Worker*.)

Significantly, this encyclopaedia of everything to do with the *office* (the area of grand French kitchens that not only prepared desserts and pastries but which also took care of the silver, table decorations, liqueurs and salads) appeared in print the same year that Diderot and d'Alembert published the first volume of their seminal *Encyclopédie*. It has long fascinated historians for the vast range of information it provides with its clearly written, logically organized recipes and instructions for everything from how to store fruit out of season to the best methods for caring for silver. Its recipes for ice-creams, sorbets and *fromages glacées* garner special attention for their range, originality and sophistication.

Gilliers' book is, however, equally famous for its fanciful, over-the-top engravings that illustrate the most extravagant rococo table designs as well as moulds suitable for transforming any kind of ice into the shape of asparagus or a boar's head or other equally complex shapes. The most outlandish illustration depicts an enormous dessert table formed entirely out of entwined S-shaped rocaille forms, which at its central axis

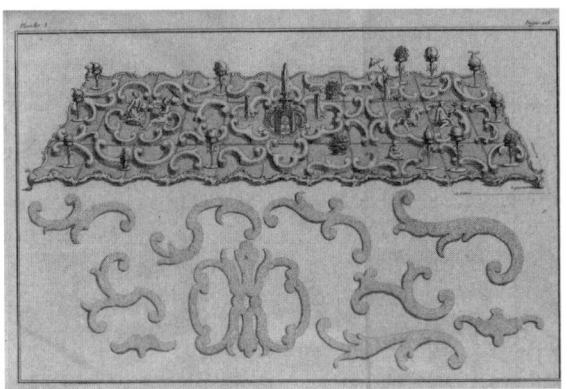

Figure 7. Image of a rococo sugar sculpture surtout-de-table *from* Le Cannameliste français *by Joseph Gilliers, 1751. Private collection.*

had an intricate central sugar sculpture composed of gods and nymphs reclining on further rocailles amidst classically inspired columns and arches, which are encrusted with floral and foliate touches for good measure.

These engravings appear so excessive to contemporary eyes that they seem entirely implausible and thereby at odds with the Enlightenment logic underpinning the book's rational organization and execution. However, in 2009 artist and professor Amy Hauft of Virginia Commonwealth University recreated Gilliers' rocaille-shaped table – albeit, even after study with Day, in considerably rougher form and without the complicated centrepiece.[16] Day's subsequent Hillwood installation more convincingly conveys the idea that Gilliers' illustrations are not only realizable but also stunning, especially if seen in the context of the objects intended to surround them.

An even deeper sense of their context can be gained by exploring the material world of Gilliers' employer, King Stanislaw Leszczyński (1677–1766). Because if Leszczyński failed miserably at politics – getting deposed not once, but twice, from the Polish throne – he excelled at hosting light-hearted entertainments in his amazing pleasure gardens, especially those at the Château de Lunéville in Lorraine, where Gilliers laboured to create the requisite sweets.

Figure 8. View of the gardens and château of Lunéville from the canal side, from the Recueil des plans, élévations, et coupes ... que le Roy de Pologne occupe en Lorraine *by Emmanuel Héré de Corny, 1750. Courtesy of the National Art Library, London.*

The Soup that Went into the Tureen

In 1737, when Leszczyński lost the Polish crown for the second time, his son-in-law, French king Louis XV, gave him the Duchy of Lorraine as compensation. Although 60 years-old, he then energetically set about transforming the gardens and châteaux to set up a court that could rival Versailles. Lunéville served as the hub of aristocratic gatherings, although Nancy, equivalent to Paris, was the region's capital. Filled with fountains, parterres and *bosquets* redolent of those created by André le Nôtre (1613–1700) for the French royal palace and which came to typify the classic *jardin français*, Lunéville nevertheless evinced the newly relaxed languor of a landscape painting by Jean-Antoine Watteau (1684–1721). In addition, Lunéville featured whimsical garden pavilions that gained it immediate fame and enduring recognition as the first *jardin anglais* in France.[17]

Although the term literally translates as 'English garden', the French *jardin anglais* did not directly imitate the famous gardens of England's great stately homes. Rather, they incorporated elements inspired from them, including asymmetry and playful garden follies that contrasted starkly with the strict linearity and formality of traditional French gardens.[18]

Sadly, many of Lunéville's most distinctive marvels got destroyed in a series of fires even within Leszczyński's lifetime or have been subsequently disassembled. However, their architect, Emmanuel Héré de Corny (1705–1763), published a magnificent, oversized, two-volume set of engravings that has preserved them for posterity and given them ongoing renown with garden historians.

Distinctive elements included cottages and a recreational kitchen garden for courtiers to play at being peasants in anticipation of the infamous hamlet that Marie-Antoinette, the wife of Leszczyński's great-grandson, Louis XVI, created at Versailles.[19]

Its myriad exotic follies included a sumptuously appointed Turkish Kiosk with a double-storied dining salon capable of hiding an orchestra in the upper gallery. In an ingenious feat of hydraulic engineering, its dining table ascended from under the floor. At its centre, a towering porcelain *surtout-de-table* sprayed jets of water. Even Gilliers' wildest creations look modest by comparison.

Lunéville's most extraordinary feature of all was a grotto filled with 86 hydraulically powered automata which created a complete mise-en-scène of village life. This included a crowing rooster, donkeys, cows and other farmyard animals; a windmill; a woodworker pausing to smoke his pipe; and villagers gathered at their table. A milkmaid churned butter not far from them while a shepherd on a hill in the distance tended his sheep. The deposed king and his courtiers purportedly spent countless hours contemplating these wonders as they sipped ices and nibbled on biscuits that may have been prepared by Gilliers himself.[20]

The desserts and the gardens went hand-in-hand, and our understanding of each benefits from looking at them together. Gilliers' grandest sugar designs merely echoed the parterres and architecture that surrounded them. His recipes for liqueurs, cakes and preserved fruits offered up the appropriately delicate treats to consume there.

Figure 9. The Turkish kiosk at Lunéville with a view of its ascending table and buffets from the Recueil des plans, élévations, et coupes … que le Roy de Pologne occupe en Lorraine *by Emmanuel Héré de Corny, 1750. Courtesy of the National Art Library, London.*

Figure Detail of the automata in the grotto at Lunéville with courtiers looking on in the foreground from the Recueil des plans, élévations, et coupes … que le Roy de Pologne occupe en Lorraine *by Emmanuel Héré de Corny, 1750. Courtesy of the National Art Library, London.*

Little is known about the *Cannameliste*'s author except that, as he explains in the preface to his book, he worked at Lunéville and reported to a M. François Richard, the Contrôleur des Offices who had worked for the deposed king since the time Leszczyński had resided at the Château de Chambord (1725–33).[21] Gilliers was merely one of six assistants, who were further aided by two kitchen boys. In addition, Leszczyński employed a full-time party planner, M. Dupuis, who held the title Dessinateur des plaisirs. All of these, not to mention an extensive kitchen staff and other servants, reported to the Duke de Tenczin Ossolonski (1666–1756), the Grand Master of the Household, to whom Gilliers dedicated his book.

Much is known, though, about Leszczyński's predilection for sweets, which was as noted as his love of garden amusements. He had, in fact, previously employed another famous Chef d'Office, Nicolas Stohrer, who had joined Leszczyński's service during the Polish king's 1719–1725 stay in Wissembourg. Stohrer left to join the queen's household when Marie married Louis XV in 1725 and then five years later opened his own pastry shop on the rue Montorgueil in Paris. It is currently the oldest in the city.[22] Leszczyński also receives credit for popularizing the madeleine.[23]

The savouries laid at Leszczyński's dinner table held equal repute, but courtiers complained that they did not have enough time to enjoy them because of their host's inordinate dislike of lengthy meals.[24] Even the eminent philosopher Voltaire (1694–1778), who visited Lunéville frequently and who completed much writing there, was rebuffed when he asked to be released from the stricture of the château's mealtimes.[25] The erstwhile king preferred to wander in his gardens, where his resident midget, Bébé (Nicolas Ferry, 1741–64), might be found resplendently dressed in his miniature carriage.[26] The competing strains of Enlightenment logic and rococo fantasy inherent in Gilliers' *Cannameliste* become more comprehensible when examined in connection to the gardens that inspired them.

Renaissance forks: a cautionary tale

Objects, engravings and paintings offer many points of entry to those seeking to understand the ephemeral foodways of previous eras. However, as with all other forms of primary evidence, they can mislead, if not outright lie. For example (to briefly summarize previously published research), one might assume by examining the tables seen in the numerous paintings from fifteenth-century Florence that depict dining, especially the popular scene of the Last Supper, that forks did not exist there at that time.[27] Whether one looks at versions by Domenico Ghirlandaio (1449–1494), Andrea del Castagno (1419–1457), or any other painter of the period, not a single fork appears. Yet inventories of Florence's leading banking families – the Medici, the Strozzi, the Pucci, etc. – show that they owned forks by the dozen.[28] This anomaly can only be interpreted by taking into account the widespread suspicion surrounding fork use at this time, especially in ecclesiastical circles. How one dines privately versus how one presents this image publicly, especially in a sacred context, can be very different indeed.

Significantly, the same Florentine banking dynasties that owned numerous forks while commissioning fork-less Last Supper paintings also sponsored the city's elaborate public banquets. Obsessively detailed records of these occasions similarly show nary a fork. Although the utensil might be fashionable for use at home in humanist circles, it was kept behind closed doors.

This was a latent echo of the vehement eleventh-century censure that St Peter Damian levelled against a Byzantine princess who had had the audacity to wield a fork in Venice. The only Florentine painting of the fifteenth-century to depict a fork is one of the four-part series of *The Marriage Feast of Nastagio degli Onesti* that Sandro Botticelli (*ca.* 1445–1510) and his workshop executed for the 1483 wedding of Giannozzo Pucci and Lucrezia Bini. It is the exception that proves the rule. Its theme derived not from the Bible but rather from Boccaccio's *Decameron*, and its intended venue was (and remains, although a related part of the series now belongs to Il Prado) the private realm of the Palazzo Pucci.[29]

About a century later, in the more pleasure-loving (by that date) Venetian Republic, Paolo Veronese (1528–1588) was called before the State Inquisitors for including, among other suspect subjects such as monkeys, dwarves, Germans and thieves, a dainty fork in the Last Supper that he painted in 1573 for the Dominicans of the Basilica di Santi Giovanni e Paolo. He dexterously circumvented this crisis by renaming the picture *The Feast in the House of Levi*, as it has been known ever since, and his elaborate defence of 'artistic licence' stands as the earliest and still unsurpassed such argument in Western society. However, that the fork still at that date drew criticism from Church officials sheds light on why the Florentine painters of the preceding generation had not included the utensil.

Material culture has much information for those seeking to study the ephemeral meals of the past. However, period images need to be interpreted in context.

Restaurant Boulanger: a final note of caution

To ignore material culture in the study of food history is to overlook a vital primary source, whether or not such research has any obvious connection to the world of objects and art. A good example of the pitfalls that can arise from ignoring such evidence can be found in Rebecca L. Spang's *Invention of the Restaurant*. The book has done much to bring new consideration to the Parisian origins of a dining institution currently so ubiquitous that its history had until then been largely overlooked. Nevertheless, her insistence that the Restaurant Boulanger never existed because she could find no evidence of the court case associated with its creation detracts from her work.[30]

Since Legrand d'Aussy's *Histoire de la vie privée des françois* of 1782 the institution had been considered the world's first-ever restaurant, which, according to this author, had opened its doors in 1765, a mere seventeen years earlier.[31] Numerous other contemporaneous mentions support this claim. Therefore, Spang went out on a rather weak limb by refuting its existence. Her apparent hope was to bolster the importance of the central figure of her book, Mathurin Roze de Chantoiseau, because with Boulanger

Figure 12. The Corner of the Rue Bailleul and the Rue Jean Tilson *by Thomas Shotter Boys, watercolour on paper, 1831. This painting depicts Paris's famed Restaurant Boulanger. Courtesy of the Musée Carnavalet – Histoire de Paris.*

out of the picture, Roze de Chantoiseau thereby laid claim to being the restaurant's inventor. This inaccuracy risks calling the rest of her work into question.

Had she taken material culture into consideration she might have avoided this unnecessary mistake. A painting by Thomas Shotter Boys (1803–1874) at the Musée Carnavalet in Paris depicts the restaurant exactly where it purported to be. Although of a later date, it corroborates the earlier stories.

Material culture offers up myriad types of primary evidence that enrich and inform the study of food history. Whether or not it is the subject at hand, it should always be taken into consideration.

Notes

1. Henry Hawley, 'Meissonier's Kingston tureen in Cleveland', *The Magazine Antiques* 151.1 (January 1997), pp. 210–213.
2. Barbara Ketcham Wheaton, *Savoring the Past: The French Kitchen and Table from 1300–1789* (New York: Touchstone Books, 1983), pp. 138–48.
3. Ellenor Alcorn, *Beyond the maker's mark: Paul de Lamerie silver in the Cahn collection* (Cambridge: John Adamson, 2006); and Marcia Schaeffer, 'Two Studies in Huguenot Silver: I. An English Rococo Sugar Box', *Proceedings of the Huguenot Society of Great Britain and Ireland*, 29.4 (2011), pp. 482–88.
4. The Metropolitan Museum of Art, 'Tureen', *British Silver* (2014) <http://metmuseum.org/exhibitions/view?exhibitionId=%7B17A658BC-6AC4-456A-B21B-EBE3734C266F%7D&oid=200583&pg=1&rpp=20&pos=17&ft=*>.
5. Vincent La Chapelle, *The Modern Cook*, 3 vols. (London: Nicolas Prevost, 1733): vol. 1, pp. 2–4.
6. La Chapelle, vol. 1, pp. 4–6.
7. La Chapelle, vol 1, pp. 2–3.
8. Matthew S. Neill, 'The 4th Earl of Chesterfield and the Presentation of Everyday Life' (unpublished thesis in the British Library, 2008).
9. Philip and Mary Hyman, 'La Chapelle and Massialot: An Eighteenth Century Feud', *Petits Propos Culinaires* 2 (August 1979), pp. 44–54 ; see also their 'Vincent La Chapelle', *Petits Propos Culinaires* 8 (June 1981), pp. 35–40 and 'Printing the Kitchen: French Cookbooks, 1480–1800', *Food: A Culinary History from Antiquity to the Present*, eds. Jean-Louis Flandrin and Massimo Montanari, trans. Albert Sonnenfeld (New York: Columbia UP, 1999), pp. 394–400.
10. Qtd. Wheaton, pp. 167–68.
11. Romney Sedgwick, 'The Duke of Newcastle's Cook', *History Today* 5 (1955), pp. 308–16.
12. Adam Gopnik, *The Table Comes First: Family, France, and the Meaning of Food*, (NY: Vintage, 2012), pp. 11–12; Patricia Parkhurst Ferguson, *Accounting for Taste: The Triumph of French Cuisine*, (Chicago: U Chicago P, 2004), p. 47.
13. Alexandre Balthazar Laurent Grimod de la Reynière, *Almanach des gourmands* 1(1803), pp. 61–64; my translation.
14. Grimod de la Reynière, pp. 43–44.
15. Ivan Day's website <http://historicfood.com/> provides a complete description of this and other projects; also see Day, ed., *Eat, Drink and Be Merry: The British at Table, 1600–2000* (London: Philip Wilson Publishers, 2000).
16. Roy Proctor, 'Re-creating a Rococo Fantasy', *The Richmond Times-Dispatch* 13 December 2009.
17. Stéphanie Chapotet, *Les jardins du roi Stanislas en Lorraine* (Metz: Éditions Serpenoise, 1999).
18. Carolin C. Young, 'Marie Antoinette's Dairy at Rambouillet, *The Magazine Antiques* 158:4 (October 2000), pp. 542–553.
19. Emmanuel Héré de Corny, *Recueil des plans, élévations et coupes tant géométrales qu'en perspective des châteaux, jardins, et dependences que le Roy de Pologne occupe en Lorraine*, 2 vols. (Paris: 1750): n.p., and for the subsequent descriptions.
20. Anne Muratori-Philip, *Le Roi Stanislas* (Paris: Fayard, 2000), pp. 192–201.
21. Joseph Gilliers, *Le Cannameliste français* (Nancy: Abel-Denis Cuisson, 1751), pp. iii–iv; Muratori-Philip, p. 176.
22. Pâtisserie Stohrer, 51, rue Montorgueil, 75002 Paris <http://www.stohrer.fr/>.
23. Muratori-Philip, p. 176.
24. Montesquieu letter to Maupertois qtd. Muratori-Philip, pp. 174–75.
25. Muratori-Philip, pp. 229–30.
26. Muratori-Philip, p. 178.
27. Carolin C. Young, 'The Sexual Politics of Cutlery', in *Feeding Desire: Design and the Tools of the Table, 1500–2005* (catalogue to the exhibition held at the Smithsonian/ Cooper-Hewitt National Design Museum, May 6–Oct. 29, 2006) (New York: Assouline, 2006), and for subsequent discussions; see also

Young, 'Depictions of the Last Supper', *Food and the Arts: Proceedings to the 1998 Oxford Symposium on Food and Cookery*, ed. Harlan Walker (Totnes, UK: Prospect Books, 1999).
28. Young, 'Catherine de' Medici's Fork', *Authenticity in the Kitchen: Proceedings of the 2005 Oxford Symposium on Food and Cookery*, ed. Richard Hosking (Totnes, UK: Prospect Books, 2006).
29. Marchese Pasquale, *L'invenzione della forchetta. Spilloni schidioncini lingule imbroaccatini pironi forcule forcine e forchette dai Greci ai nostri forchettoni*, (Soveria Mannelle (CZ): Rubbettino Editore, 1989).
30. Rebecca L. Spang, *The Invention of the Restaurant: Paris and Modern Gastronomic Life* (Cambridge, Harvard UP, 2001), p. 9.
31. Paul Levy, 'The First Restaurant in the World, Preserved in Paint', *The Telegraph* 6 July 2013.

The Future of Tableware and Cooking Vessels: Some Predictions and Practical Experiments

Ken Albala

In the five centuries since the advent of the fork as a standard eating utensil, the evolution of tableware and cutlery has been fairly stagnant. There have been periods of proliferation in the size, number and type of cutlery – witness the rigid formality of the Victorian era with its vast array of knives, forks, spoons and dishes for separate courses, or even the Baroque era with its fanciful elaborate serving vessels. There have also been periods of relative informality, when meal structures and ingredients were simplified and so too were the utensils on the table. The Arts and Crafts era, as well as the early eighteenth-century *nouvelle cuisine* movement, sought to streamline tableware by reducing the number of forms required for service and multi-purposing simple but functional items.

We are currently in another period of casualization, when, in terms of cuisine, increasingly local produce takes precedence over exotic ingredients, traditional techniques over experimental, the craft of cooking over art, and consequently our cutlery is also becoming simpler, reduced to its basic minimum, as are plates, which come in two basic sizes, and stemware, of which one or two simple forms serve for every beverage. Moreover, if we trace developments of the past few decades in the industrial food sector, it is safe to say that products are increasingly being designed which require no utensils whatsoever. There have long been pizza, hot dogs and hamburgers, which normally demand a paper plate, Styrofoam carton or paper wrapping. But the most popular new products are meant to be eaten by hand, preferably one hand, on the go, while standing or typing at one's desk, driving in the car or watching television. Hot pockets, prefabricated burritos, yoghurt in tubes, shakes in plastic cups. Not only have utensils, plastic or otherwise, become superfluous, but an entire generation may be completely bereft of the manual dexterity demanded for successful engagement of the knife and fork. Culinary historians may look back on these past few centuries as a strange anomaly in the history of table manners, the singular era when people employed unusual metal implements to convey food to their mouths.

I am not condemning these developments, only bearing witness. Nonetheless I do believe it is time for the culinary vanguard to assert their influence in curtailing the total and utter demise of tableware, and that includes the dinner table itself. It is not merely that without a table the social relations that commensal gatherings engender will likewise wither. It is not merely that waste in the form of packaging will proliferate as individuals can choose whatever they like for every meal, pop it in the microwave and

The Future of Tableware and Cooking Vessels

eat whenever they please, tossing the containers of every single meal. Nor is it merely nostalgia for proper formal service with dozens of superfluous vessels designed for single recipes, which only the wealthiest of households could afford. I am speaking here of true evolution of entirely new eating vessels, utensils and even cookware.

There have been a few fascinating new forms worthy of mention. I will ignore the flimsy plastic spork, which was really only intended to save money for fast-food restaurants and was never really good at either spearing or scooping food. But recently there is a company selling an object called the knork. It is a hefty stainless steel fork with an edge on one side sharp enough to cut food, but not so threatening that you would fear putting it in your mouth. I own a set and use them all the time. Although this is obviously only an adaptation of a regular fork, it is beautiful and well balanced and I think represents a step in the right direction. It might actually prove indispensible for one-armed people.

Another new item, brilliant in conception but an utter failure in execution, is the obol. Imagine a large bowl tilted slightly forward with a lower chamber designed to hold milk and an upper chamber that holds cereal. The idea is that you scoop cereal from the upper chamber into the lower as you eat, preventing the cereal from getting soggy. Ignore the fact that breakfast cereal is actually engineered specifically to prevent it from going soggy; this is clearly intended for slower eaters who want to avoid even the slightest chance of limp corn flakes. The only problems are that they are made of cheap plastic in garish colours and that the specially designed spoon looks very much like a baby rattle. So this, in my opinion, is only another step toward the total infantilization of consumption. It is a large baby-bowl, and would go perfectly with a sippy cup for juice.

To their credit, many experimental restaurants in the past few decades have used uniquely designed tableware to accompany their molecular creations. For example, at Alinea in Chicago a few years ago you might be served bacon on a trapeze, spun liquorice on a television antenna, or my favourite, a toilet bowl-shaped white ceramic vessel at the bottom of which were little bits of shellfish, to consume which you had to practically place your entire face into the bowl, only to realize that the whole contraption was set atop a pillow of lavender gas slowly deflating, which enveloped the diner in a fragrant cloud. Aesthetically, it worked brilliantly. But this is not the kind of utensil that will ever make it into ordinary restaurants, let alone homes.

So what I would like to present for this talk are a few ideas describing what might become new forms of cutlery, tableware and cooking vessels for the future. In all I have attempted to avoid replicating the industrial aesthetic of mass production, stark whiteness, the bland uniformity which has dominated restaurant service and made its way into private homes. Giving everyone the same exact plates and bowls, I think, gives us the illusion of democratic equality. In fact people don't want or need to eat the same amount of food. Why should portions and the vessels that hold them be uniform? These forms are executed in clay simply because that is the medium in which I work best, but – with one exception – they could be wood, glass, metal or anything else with inherent beauty and durability. Clay, obviously, is fragile, but it is an abundant and affordable natural resource. Each vessel is also designed to solve a very specific gastronomic problem for which the radically horizontal nature of contemporary vessels has obviated any possible solution.

Moreover, these objects have been designed with the fundamental premise that all material culture is a reflection of larger values, aspirations and fears inherent in culture on the whole. For example, an obsession with contamination leads to increasingly sanitary utensils designed to privatize space and shield it from the germs of others. Portable food obviously reflects a culture concerned with speed and efficiency and a work ethic that marginalizes time spent leisurely poking at food with curious implements. A culture in which shared communal feasting – and thus shared group experience – is valued will pick from a common platter, seated in a circle as equals. Thus these objects are as much a prediction about the future direction of our civilization as they are specific utensils intended to address my own idiosyncratic culinary pet peeves.

In the future, due to what I perceive as our increasing psychological need to exercise our teeth in ways that satisfy our primal urge to destroy food that resonates in our head, people will increasingly demand a device that insures long term crunchiness of fried foods. Why will crunch be psychologically more important in the future? The idea is predicated on the Freudian notion that as civilization progresses we are asked to supress a greater number of libidinal urges, among which is the hard-wired instinct to destroy and consume food. Crunching on some level replicates the advantageous behaviour that conduced toward our survival as a species: cracking open tough nuts and seeds, bones and other outer casings to get at nourishing food. Today bones are increasingly removed, food is processed so there is no need to break things open with our teeth, yet we still get satisfaction from this behaviour and at some level require it. Thus modern manufacturers have artificially put crunch back into food. Think of the way fast-food hamburgers are abetted with lettuce and squirt blood-like ketchup when chomped on. This is no accident. Or think of the ingenious engineering that devised a potato chip of the optimal size and shape to maximize resonance potential, for the loudest possible crunch.

To address this problem in the domestic setting with cooked food, I offer you the first object (overleaf). Its form is dictated first by the difficulty of keeping crunchy fried food from going soggy on a horizontal surface as moisture escapes from below. Second it prevents the food from being completely inundated by a sauce that is either on the same plate and runs into it, or even worse is dumped on top of it. The problem of maintaining the crunch is solved by keeping the food elevated above the surface of the plate, which is accomplished by a series of small wheel-thrown pointed nubbins of varying height that allow the least possible contact with the fried surface of the food. Thus steam escapes. The problem of sauce is also solved by a separate, permanently-affixed shallow bowl which holds the sauce and into which food can be dipped.

The Future of Tableware and Cooking Vessels

The object is also multifunctional. It can hold french fries or nuggets – which I believe will be the food of the future, as well as tempura-coated vegetables, panko-crusted fried shrimp, even crunchy batter-coated croquettes or fully encased miniature hamburgers or hot dogs – foods that we can expect to arrive any moment. None of these requires cutlery and the entire meal can be carried by an individual anywhere without the disastrous consequences of putting these foods and sauce on a regular plate or, even worse, eating them from an enclosed container or wrapped in paper which destroys any possibility of crunchiness. One completely unexpected use is for small pancakes which, in my opinion, become sodden and disgusting if syrup is poured over. These are eaten by hand and dipped into maple syrup. Artichokes also work nicely, as any excess water from steaming or boiling can drip down onto the plate below.

******

For my second proposal, in the interest of environmental sustainability, I decided to design a utensil that requires minimal energy input to manufacture, would be sturdy enough for a long-term use, but would also cater to the increasing desire for portability in food. Our desire to eat while going somewhere or doing something else, shows no sign of abating. This is essentially a hollow bamboo tube with an interior nodule burned out with a hot iron rod, and a spoon shape carved into the tip. The bamboo serves as a natural insulator so your fingers aren't burned. The advantage it has over thermoses is that it can't break and, if it does, it's very easy to grow in your backyard and make new ones. It also doesn't give the food a metallic flavour like most portable drinking containers. It has a strap so you can sling it over your shoulder and a cork stopper so the contents don't spill. The narrow aperture also makes sipping much easier than with a wide-mouthed rim and facilitates swallowing solid contents from the tube, which would otherwise need to be fished out with a spoon. Most importantly, the bamboo tube can be microwaved, unlike metal containers, so if it's carried to work at room temperature it can be popped in a refrigerator and then go straight into the microwave oven. Obviously you can also drink coffee or even cold beverages from it as well.

******

The third object addresses what appears to be a decided trend away from recipes that are cloudy, muddled and contain many ingredients thrown onto a plate or in a bowl where they mix into an indistinguishable mess. Eventually all the flavours mix so thoroughly that they lose their individuality. As long as the quality and texture of ingredients remains a preoccupation in gastronomic circles, a vessel that would allow them to complement each other without getting lost in a soup or stew would be an aesthetic boon.

The design also allows food to be eaten in a specified sequence of contrasting flavours from lightest to strongest, yet within a single vessel presented at the table in one course. It also contains a heating chamber for hot coals or Sterno flame below so the contents never get cold. So it is a kind of brazier soup pot, something akin to the Mongolian hot

pot, but meant for an individual diner, and not requiring the entire process of dipping ingredients one by one into the communal pot and then fishing them out. But the aesthetic effect is similar in that each course flavours and adds to the subsequent ones.

The separate courses are maintained distinct by use of several successively smaller interlocking bowls with perforations below. This allows steam to constantly rise up from soup in the base, but never lets any ingredient overcook or fall apart. In the lowest chamber is placed a stock which is kept at a low simmer with a few lumps of coal or Sterno beneath. Immediately above it is a skein of noodles which steam gently to cook. Above them is meat, cut into thin slivers, which is also cooked with steam, which drips down and flavours the noodles and eventually falls back into the base to be reheated. Above the meat are choice vegetables which require only the lightest steaming to retain integrity. The base might be beef, chicken, shellfish, absolutely any form of protein would work. Moreover the sequence can be altered or even abandoned altogether. A series of dumplings might be contained in each chamber. Or a delicate egg custard in one chamber, a whole oyster in another, a wild mushroom in another. The drama of individual ingredients gradually revealed as the diner removes each successive chamber is intended to heighten the entire experience. The fragrant steam also wafts continually before the diner, preventing the inevitable cooling and pallor that results from a bowl of soup being left open to the elements.

Nor would the chef be limited to Asian recipes. A chicken stock beneath some small steamed tamales with vegetables on the upper layers would work. So too would ravioli in the middle chamber, with perhaps fresh peas in the top. The trick would be for the chef to time how long it took to eat successive courses and to make sure each was perfectly cooked right about the time that layer was opened.

The device might even be used for a series of sweets, with perhaps a sweet almond-based stock in the base, a rice pudding above it, rose-flavoured confections above that and a small stick of cinnamon on top just for aroma. It is essentially a deconstruction into several courses of something that would ordinarily be separated.

I wondered who would want to keep such an unwieldy vessel taking up precious shelf space, when it occurred to me that each part also serves another function. The base alone could be used to keep any meal warm like a little chafing dish. Any one of the upper chambers can be used as a miniature colander, and the bottom stock chamber is simply a bowl. In other words each separate part serves another function in the kitchen. I also considered how such an implement might be produced on a larger scale and for people who don't happen to have hot coals readily available. An electric heating element of exactly the kind used to heat tea kettles would work perfectly.

******

One development in contemporary cooking that seems almost certain to continue in its steady decline is the use of a conventional oven. There are many reasons for this: time involved to heat it up, energy costs, and particularly the tendency for it to heat the whole house. This was once an added benefit, but with central heating, not to

mention global warming, the oven may well become a relic of the past. Where I live in California, the oven is completely impractical for more than half the year and in the future many other places will probably experience comparable summer heat as well.

At the same time, though, we have seen a growing interest in baking bread, not perhaps for daily consumption, but as a leisure activity for do-it-yourself types. The bread machine was a solution for some people in recent past decades, but it is entirely unsatisfying for those who want the pleasure of mixing ingredients, kneading dough and watching it rise. You basically dump the ingredients in the chamber and come back hours later to a freshly baked cube-shaped loaf. For the very same reason that in the mid twentieth century a completely idiot-proof cake mix never caught on because people wanted the illusion of having actually cooked something with the self-delusion of creative input – adding fresh eggs and oil gave the impression of cooking – it seems unlikely that the bread machine will remain a feature of our material culture in the future.

How to solve these seemingly irreconcilable tendencies: not wanting to use the oven but wanting to bake bread and enjoy the satisfaction of having actually made the bread yourself? Not long ago I would have never even suggested a promising future for the microwave oven. In fact I condemned it as the work of the devil. It obviously cannot brown food, though a few experimental models have recently attempted to do just this. They are combination toaster ovens and microwaves, so they can cook food with waves then heat with electric coils to brown food. An ordinary microwave, as it turns out, does cook vegetables nicely, bakes a potato, and even foods like eggplant or zucchini in a covered casserole. But it is hard to imagine it browning a bread crust.

Another solution presented itself to me, not with a hybrid oven, but using a very ancient technology inspired by archaeological finds. In ancient Egypt there was a very practical problem with the use of wild leavened starters for bread, and especially the use of emmer wheat. Such dough tends to absorb a lot of water at first; then, as it proves, the moisture is gradually released, making a dough much stickier than at the outset. This complicates the task of transferring the loaves into the oven on a peel. Baking many loaves at once in a wood-burning oven and shifting them around with a peel often causes them to deflate as they are moved.

These problems were ingeniously solved by baking loaves in what amounts to a small cone-shaped oven within the oven. At first these cones were probably just set into hot ashes to bake like a Dutch oven, but the long narrow cones were almost certainly used inside another oven. I think this device was perhaps suggested by what in ceramics is called a saggar, an enclosed ceramic chamber in which you put the pot to be fired, which prevents pots from sticking to each other. (These are especially helpful with glazed ceramics.) The Egyptians were the first to use copper and cobalt in their bright blue enamelled wares – which would require a saggar to stack in a kiln. The bread cone is essentially the same idea. You let the dough rise in its own clay chamber, which then is simply placed in the pre-fired oven to bake. Because it is cone-shaped, the bread can be easily slipped out afterwards.

Why not adapt this basic technology to a microwave? The advantage in my mind is that most materials that can be used in a microwave don't conduct heat well. Obviously metal can't be used at all and plastic stays cool. Glass has such a slick impermeable surface that it would prevent a crust from forming on bread. Unglazed ceramics, exactly the type you would find on an oven floor or in a clay testa, Romertopf or similar vessel, actually heats in the microwave and draws moisture from the surface of the bread. So an unglazed baking cone, shorter than the ancient Egyptian vessels, and covered so it facilitates an upper crust, was the answer.

A regular bread dough was kneaded in the vessel itself, left to rise and baked, so to speak, in the microwave on low temperature. Since it cooks from within, one need not worry about a gummy interior. And the clay did indeed draw moisture from the surface creating an exterior crust. Other shapes are also possible; a low oval shape would also fit better into a microwave well.

In any case, these are simply a few experiments that suggest ways that material culture might change in the future given evolving eating habits and social structures, cooking technologies, and the need to find more sustainable materials for tableware and cooking vessels.

Salt-pot / *Tuz Testisi*:
A Salt and Terracotta Water Cooler from Turkey

Nilhan Aras

Deriving its name from the Latin word *testa*, *testi* is the Turkish word for an unglazed earthenware water container. The original meaning of *testa* is 'a brick, an item of pottery'; the word is also used in the sense of 'clay pot'. Regardless of shape, any earthenware jug is called *testi*, but a Turkish *testi* usually has a narrow neck, a single handle (sometimes double, sometimes none), a narrow bottom, and a long, slender, amphora-like shape. While Anatolian Turkish uses of *testi* as a word for all earthenware jugs, another word, *carra* (the Arabic or Farsi word for an earthenware container), is also used in regions such as Hatay on the Syrian border and Muğla on the Mediterranean coast. The same word appears in Armenian as *carra/cerra*. In addition, there are other minor regional names such as *ırgada* in Bolvadin, Afyon; *kabalak* in Denizli; and *dodok* in Mersin on the Mediterranean coast and Eğilbaş, in Kızılcahamam, Ankara.

My focus here is on *tuz testisi*, a vessel made from clay with a very high salt content, a rare method of making traditional Turkish *testi*. In fact, *tuz testisi* means 'salt jug', a term that, in Turkish, may be mistaken for a jug to store salt; however, in this case it means made of salt. While handfuls of salt are sometimes mixed with clay to make porous containers, in this case the ratio of salt to clay is so high that the salt becomes a major component of the pot.

What is a *testi*, and how is it used?

Turkish peasants commonly carry *testi* to fields, orchards, vineyards, countryside, wilderness and forests to provide cool water or other beverages to quench their thirst. With a capacity of several litres, *testi* are not designed for table use, but rather to hold enough water for a few people working long days in the fields. It has the admirable capacity of keeping its contents cool and is often used as a shared drinking vessel for water or other beverages like *ayran* (a savoury yoghurt drink), fruit compote juices or other liquids. The iconic shape of a *testi* resembles the amphora: with a narrow bottom and wide body, the free-standing jug has a handle attached to both neck and body of the container. For other uses, some *testi* are double-handled, and smaller ones without handles are used to serve water at table.

A versatile container, the *testi* is also widely used for other culinary purposes. It can be transformed into a cooking pot to make a slow-cooked, stew-like meat and vegetable dish called *testi kebap*, or, buried in the earth, it can be used to cure cheese. *Testi* sometimes simply takes the place of other clay pots or wooden barrels used to store butter or molasses or to ferment pickles. The height, width, shape and number of handles change depending on the function. *Testi* for cooking or curing cheese have considerably wider necks and no handles, with a shape more like a jar. Even if it is used to cure cheese or to make and store yoghurt, it remains unglazed, as the porous quality aids the curing or fermentation processes by eliminating excess water. For curing cheese, the vessel is sealed with fig, bay or vine leaves or sometimes with mud and buried upside down in the ground. Cheese made this way is named after the pot, *testi peyniri*, meaning potted cheese. One noteworthy dish, *testi kebabı*, is prepared by stuffing the pot with meat and vegetables and turning it upside down on a deep tray filled with water. A little piece of meat is put in the tray as a tell-tale test piece, and the tray with the upside-down pot is placed in the oven. When the water reaches a boil, rice or bulgur is added. Once the rice or bulgur pilaf is cooked and the test meat piece is tender, the dish is taken out of the oven. The contents of the pot are arranged atop the pilaf and served.

Clay pots are used to store and transport, but another major function is the cooling effect of the container on its contents. One particular example from Central Anatolia, is unique: the famous *testi* of Şereflikoçhisar.

The source of salt: Lake Tuz

Tuz Gölü – Lake Tuz, meaning Salt Lake – is the second largest lake in Turkey, with a surface area of 1655 square kilometres (643 square miles). One of the largest hypersaline lakes in the world, it has a salt ratio of 32.4%, the source of 70% of the table salt used in Turkey. Situated in Central Anatolia, it stretches between the three provinces of Ankara, Konya and Aksaray. Lake Tuz was declared a Special Environmental Protection Area (SEPA) in 2000. The lake is very shallow, in fact the shallowest in Turkey, reaching only about 100 cm deep in May and averaging 40 cm deep. The lake has three underground salt-water basins, but during the hot, arid summer excessive evaporation almost dries the lake out, forming a salt layer about 10–30 cm thick.

Şereflikoçhisar, a district of Ankara province, lies east of Lake Tuz. In addition to being a major supplier of table salt for Turkey, their production of high salt-content earthenware pots was acclaimed regionally until quite recently. Regrettably, however, this traditional craft is in drastic decline. Only six years ago, the town was renowned for its *testi* production and, in the 1970s, at least 30 potters were active, producing tens of thousands of earthenware water jugs a year for both the local market and neighbouring towns. By 2007, only a single potter was active. In 2007 he produced 5000-6000 earthenware jugs, and that was it. Since then the *testi* production in the area has stopped.

What is a salt-pot/*tuz testisi*? How does it work?

Salt-pot/*tuz testisi* is an unglazed earthenware water jug, made with equal proportions of two kinds of clay mixed with salt and water, formed by the potter, and then baked in kilns. The history of this technique is not known; there are no historical documents about its manufacture, and archaeological evidence is not available due to lack of research in the area. However, this technique was used in the region for ages, and as far as we know the method remained pretty much unchanged.

Due to the high salt content, the Şereflikoçhisar pots are whitish in colour and relatively porous. The addition of salt makes Şereflikoçhisar's pottery quite different from other local pottery, such as that of Avanos in Cappadocia, where only red clay is used.

Due to its chemical properties, salt gives this particular *testi* two very important characteristics: cooling and purifying. Liquids stored in these containers never get warm, a tremendously useful feature in this central Anatolian region. Once the water or other liquid is put in the container, moisture is exuded through the pot as a result of a sweating process that helps cool the contents of the vessel. After liquid is added to the pot, a ring of darker colour forms at the pot's widest part. This colour change comes from miniscule water droplets that usually form within ten minutes after liquid is put in the container. The discoloration eventually spreads to the entire surface, indicating that the cooling process is complete. The cooling effect is accelerated if the jug is left in a windy spot. Besides the sweating, some of the contents are absorbed within the pot itself. As a result, yoghurt fermented in these pots has a thick dense consistency. Such pot yoghurt is spreadable like cheese, and is usually eaten wrapped in flatbread.

Through this cooling process, local peasants believe that impurities in the liquid are extracted or sieved through the porous pot walls, resulting in a more clarified content that seems both tastier and healthier. Water stored in these pots absorbs a particularly earthy taste.

Due to the absorption process the inner surface of the pot develops a thin layer of greenish moss after continuous usage of three to four months. Many households used to keep up to 25 pots for alternating use to prevent this moss formation. This phenomenon may also explain why the water first put into the pot is never drunk but poured out after rinsing the inside of the container.

What are the components?

There are four basic components to the mix used to make these pots: reddish brown and greyish white coloured clay; salt, the local grainy salt called *karınca başı* / ant's head due to its size; and fresh spring water (not saline water from the lake).

Only experienced potters can distinguish the clay ideal for a good quality pot. That around Şereflikoçhisar is alluvial. Clay for pottery needs to be free from sand to keep the body from being gritty and hurting the hands of the potter who shapes it. Though recognizing suitable clay, experienced potters still make a test batch to see whether the body will be resistant to high heat in the furnace. Only after these preliminary trials do they proceed with manufacturing pots.

The red clay contains neither salt nor lime and is not hygroscopic. Thus *testi* made with only red clay do not have a cooling effect, and even if salt is added to the body,

A Salt and Terracotta Water Cooler from Turkey

the resulting porosity is not sufficient to allow the sweating effect of the pot to cool the water. The red colour is an indicator of ferrous oxide, and the red clay makes a slick, slippery, smooth, shiny body. As mentioned above, potters in nearby regions like Cappadocia use only red clay in their ceramics and pottery.

The greyish white clay is chalky with lime, which combined with the added salt, gives the final mixture the hygroscopic qualities needed to achieve the correct porosity. It seems peculiar that these two clay types exist side by side, as if nature tells the potter to use them together.

The salt itself is the last, but hardly the least, ingredient: an addition so vital that it gives the salt-pot its name. The salt used to make the pots is table quality, with a small grain. The salt is said to crystallize within the body and explode while firing in the kiln to form miniscule air pockets. These air pockets make the pot porous, enabling its sweating, cooling and purifying properties. The villagers claim that in the past they never drank water from pots made without the salt, using salt-free earthenware only for cooking.

While not a component of the *testi*, the kiln matters too. The kiln, itself made of clay, is an egg-shaped adobe structure. Some kilns are enormous, like a kind of surreal egg, accommodating at least 500 big pots; these kilns are called *ikili*, meaning double-sized or extra-large. Most pottery masters would not even light the kiln if there were less than 600 or 700 pots ready to be fired. These gigantic kilns have two levels and are used for salt pots only. The upper level is reserved for stacking the pots, and the lower holds the fire. Access to the upper level is through two little window-like openings. The adobe floor of the upper level is slightly domed and perforated with holes to allow the hot air to circulate. Heat and smoke passes through these holes to the chimney on top. There are also two tiny windows called *gözenek,* meaning watch-hole, situated on either side of the lower level to feed the fire and facilitate air circulation. One of these windows is at a lower level, close to the ground, and is used to start the fire; the one across is at a slightly higher level to feed the fire with extra fuel.

How is it made?

Salt pots are only made in hot weather during the summer. The accumulated salt layer is only accessible during this time of the year, and the pots need to be dried before being fired in the kiln. The pot-making season starts at the end of June and lasts until the end of September.

The preparation of the body begins with the clay. Equal portions of red and grey clay are sieved to remove sand and grit – tremendous work as almost a ton of clay is prepared this way. Next, a dough, of *Guinness-Book-of-Records* proportions, is made. Equal amounts of salt and water are combined, and then poured into a well-like pocket dug at the centre of the heap; the eventual ratio of the salt-water solution to the clay mix is 1:1. Thus the final mixture is one quarter salt, a ratio that increases as the body is dried and fired. This mixture is left to 'mature' overnight. The next day when the water has been totally absorbed by the clay the 'kneading' starts. This giant salty 'dough' of clay is kneaded by treading it underfoot from the centre outwards. The trodden body is then gathered again, and the process is repeated for four to five hours until the mixture resembles a dumpling dough – one potter described the desired consistency as like the dough for *mantı*, the ubiquitous Turkish dumpling. If the body is not elastic and springy enough, it will not easily take shape on the potter's wheel and will crumble when fired. The body is left to rest another day, covered with wet clothes or plastic sheets to keep it from drying out. Before the body is shaped on the wheel, portions are cut with a wire and kneaded once again on the wheel stone. The batches of body for each pot are called *künde*, *yumak* or *beze*. When enough batches are portioned from the massive heap of pre-mixed body, the potter starts operating the wheel, turning it with his feet and shaping the body on top. (The man-powered wheels were later replaced with electric operated ones.) The initial shape is a cylinder with 4–5 cm-thick walls.

Elderly potters report that the process of preparing the body was rather different in the past. Then the salt was not mixed into the clay at first, but added later to the batches about to be shaped. This previous method required time-consuming labour and did not produce standard mixtures, resulting in inconsistent pots.

The old, experienced masters could turn a pot in two to three minutes, making eighteen to twenty double-sized pots in an hour. (The handles are stuck to the body after the pot is taken from the wheel.) The pots are left to dry, sometimes hung from the ceiling or in an airy place, for four to five days. Placing in the kiln starts when enough pots are ready for firing. After placing all the pots in the kiln, the window-like opening on the upper level is sealed with mud before the fire is started. The fuel is almost always *tezek* (formerly *kermes*), cow-dung, which is a main source of energy in rural Anatolia, especially in the arid regions. Cow dung is moulded into flat cylindrical slices, dried and stacked for future use. Wood shavings and sawdust are other fuels preferred more recently. After the fire is started, by lighting the fire through the lower watch-hole, the initial fire is kept at a low temperature, smouldering for four to five hours. More dung and sawdust is added to keep the temperature at a consistent level. The pots are blackened at this initial stage, but not thoroughly fired. This first phase is called *çeşni*, translated as savouring or seasoning, which prepares the pots for a hotter fire.

After the initial four to five hours of low fire, the lower watch-hole is sealed with mud, and the second phase is started by adding fuel from the upper watch-hole on the other side of the kiln. Taking turns shovelling dung or sawdust, the workers keep the fire burning furiously to maintain a high temperature for three to four hours. During that time, the blackened pots first turn red-hot, then become pale, attaining a whitish colour. After four hours, they allow the fire to go out. In all, the firing process lasts from early in the morning until almost sunset. The kiln cools overnight with the holes still sealed, and only at noon on the next day is the upper window opened to take the pots out. Then the pots are sold, often on the spot.

*****

A Salt and Terracotta Water Cooler from Turkey

The salt pot demonstrates an unusual use of salt, transforming this indispensable cooking element into material culture. In making *testi*, a water-carrying vessel, salt passes through fire to store and cool another food item, water.

Unfortunately the salt *testi* is in danger of extinction, sustained until recently by very few artisans. With the advance of technology, particularly refrigeration, the demand for water-cooling jars declined and manufacturing became less and less profitable until it could no longer generate a decent income for potters. Deteriorating environmental conditions in Lake Tuz also endangered the survival of this craft, as the quality of salt-clay declined and the lake became more and more contaminated. The last pottery closed in 2007. It is now hard to believe that, until a few decades ago, salt-pot making was the major industry of Şereflikoçhisar and that salt pots were found not only in the local market but also throughout central Anatolia, including the cities of Aksaray, Nevşehir and Kırşehir.

Among the last masters, two who were interviewed, Salih Doğan (born 1934) and İsmet Kargın (born 1940) insisted on the difficulty of pot making, especially of mastering the techniques to shape the body. Choosing the right clay, judging the body's consistency and understanding the nature of the fire are all skills developed through experience. Once an experienced potter could produce 150 pots in a day, now there are none. In 2004–2005, the World Bank supported attempts to open courses for young potters, but the project failed due to lack of interest. When the old masters are gone, this dying tradition will be totally lost, and this paper may be the only documentation of the story of salt pot making.

Note

Oral Sources from Şereflikoçhisar: Salih Doğan, born 1934; İsmet Kargın, born 1940; Leyla Doğan, born 1963; Ramazan Kargın, born 1965.

Mamma and the Totemic Robot: Towards an Anthropology of Bimby Food-processors in Italy

Elisa Ascione

In the age of industrial reproducibility, food and objects related to food preparation have undergone deep transformations, losing some old symbolic and cultural signifiers and gaining new meanings and associations. In this respect, contemporary Italy has experienced many changes in just one generation: there has been a real 'emancipation from the stove' in the domestic sphere with, among other things, a diminished manipulation of raw ingredients by the *massaia* (housewife) and the intensification of life's rhythms, with a strong impact on Italian cooking culture. These changes have affected the shape and function of old and new objects and even the architecture of the kitchen itself. Kitchens have become often similar to modern aseptic and efficient laboratories, populated by new objects charged with new meanings and social expectations (Vercelloni 1998).

In this paper I propose an anthropological account of the discourses and practices of owners of a famous multi-food processor, the Bimby (or, in some countries, the Thermomix). Performing thirteen different functions (cutting, mixing, weighing and so on) and even cooking food, it has had huge success in Italy. The Bimby's users describe it as a 'magic' appliance that can transform ordinary people into extraordinary chefs, able to deliver elaborate dishes with a few simple steps. People talk of Bimby as a revolutionary and amazing object, convincing friends and neighbours to buy them, organizing 'Bimby dinners' and creating a sort of 'tribal' word-of-mouth Bimby affiliation.

While there are some arguments that modern electrical equipment deskills people by replacing their cooking activities, I suggest that food preparation retains its highly symbolic functions and that people, through these machines, re-signify and re-contextualize old and new identities linked to food preparation. I believe that an anthropological reflection on the transformative power of this machine and its effect on maintaining symbolic boundaries can add an original insight to sociological theories of the impact of objects in cooking cultures: 'Forget that commodities are good for eating, clothing, and shelter; forget their usefulness and try instead the idea that commodities are good for thinking; treat them as a nonverbal medium for the human creative faculty' (Douglas and Isherwood 1979, pp. 40–41). In trying to reconstruct the 'cultural biographies' of things, we can understand cultural and cognitive processes built around commodities, in particular the ways in which kitchen machines are used and culturally redefined (Kopytoff 1986). It has been argued that, unlike other household electrical equipment that simply perform pre-existing manual skills (the vacuum cleaner, the washing machine, etc.), the kitchen robot does not refer to one specific action but contains in itself the promise of unlimited possibilities, intensifying performances rather than facilitating single tasks.

To the list of its tasks, the Bimby adds a function with strong alchemic and symbolic properties: cooking. We know from many anthropological studies that the act of cooking – the control of fire; the mediation with the stove, the oven and the pot; the direct relationship with the transformative power of heat – has always had high cultural and symbolic relevance in every human group (Wrangham 2009). If, as many anthropologists argue, the relationship with fire and food transformation has always been a key aspect of every culture, what happens when people cook through this robot?

Unidentifiable object: cooking with Bimby

Can one single object help people prepare fresh, varied, nutritious food, allowing them to try exciting new recipes and explore new culinary worlds, making them feel part of a larger community of cooks? Can one machine give people more free time, leave everything clean, provide the opportunity to become a very good chef? This is what the Bimby promises. According to some of its owners, it is a sort of 'magic pot'.

Bee Wilson (2012) shows that in Europe and North America there has always been a quest for the 'perfect pot' through innovations, inventions or rediscovery of old materials: she shows that people's expectations around pots can disclose broader cultural patterns across time. In Italy the *batteria di pentole* (a multitude of different pots and pans, each shaped for different purposes) has been an object of desire for many years. Now the Bimby has replaced this set in the list of the most desired objects: the 'ideal pot' is finally a single object – which also 'contains' some knowledge of food preparation. If the search for the perfect pot has always been part of human endeavour, discourses around the Bimby might fit into that story. In Italy, a country that has a strong sense of its cultural specificity in terms of food, cooking and 'tradition', the Bimby has had huge success: the company has recently celebrated the sale of 2,000,000 robots, more than in any other European country.

Bimby users are often enthusiastic evangelists who boast incredible stories of their newly found '*bambino*' (the name recalls the word 'child'): claims like 'it can make a dish of pasta and a tomato sauce all by itself' amaze uninitiated listeners, whereas 'purists' who oppose the Bimby as a matter of principle reject the very same idea that a machine can transform raw material into edible stuff with any cultural value.

Since the technological revolution that saw the introduction of the refrigerator, the electric oven, the espresso machine, etc., few recent inventions have had a deep cultural relevance in Italian cooking culture. For example, in Italy microwaves are used mainly to defrost and warm foods, thus performing functions that do not have high culinary and cultural status. The Bimby, however, has created a 'tribe' of enthusiasts claiming that their life has changed.

These users communicate and exchange recipes through the Internet, mailing lists and newsletters and are active agents in creating a Bimby culture. This 'culture' could be seen simply as a marketing strategy of the manufacturing company – the Bimby is sold through home-demonstrations by sales representatives (sellers and clients are mostly women) thus creating contexts in which the benefits of owning such a robot are continuously reinforced (e.g. the importance of cooking with fresh ingredients, the desirability of becoming talented in many different styles of cooking, etc.) (Truninger 2011). Nonetheless I assert that this robot has become a 'totem of the kitchen' for deeper symbolic reasons: its hybrid nature (it is neither a mixer nor a cooker, but both at the same time) defies categories, leading people to construct new expectations around it. While they can cook new things, they have to follow very detailed instructions to do so. As a result, they feel reassured about the success of their individual performances but they don't feel they are using just a 'shortcut' as if they had bought ready-made products. Thanks to this machine people define themselves as good providers for their families through the preparation of healthy home-made meals without the investment of time that has hitherto been required.

People's reaction to this kitchen robot is seldom neutral. The Bimby is either praised as the solution to culinary worries or despised as the end of the art of cooking; only rarely do people describe it as 'just an object', an instrument among many others in the multitude of modern cooking equipment. Some comments in cooking blogs openly oppose this piece of technology. A commenter named Mario, for instance, says that Bimby is the antithesis of good cooking – he thinks it has no more value than an expensive blender and that it will enter his house 'over his dead body', although his wife is thinking of buying one. Giovanna says that, for her, real cooking is doing it 'the old way' – cooking *ragù* sauce in terracotta pots, making pizza on the stone, having specific vessels for each food. Matteo, who describes himself as a very good cook, says that he likes to make risotto following very detailed processes (for example, toasting rice before adding it to the onion sauté and evaporating the alcohol of the wine he uses in order to maintain the acidity of the final dish) – putting everything inside a machine as a single '*pappone*' – a kind of undefined mush fit for animals – is not very sophisticated. Cooking good food means, to him, taking control of every single step, not delegating to a standardized machine. Among the many divergent voices, one lady says that she prefers eating foods cooked by 'human hands', since she gets from them a different feeling of 'home and warmth'. Giulia, a regular Bimby user, replies provocatively, 'What do you mean by human hands? Your hands are bound to put the food in some container, what's the difference if this vessel has also got rotating blades and produces heat by itself? I don't see the difference, they are both man-made.'

Others make very positive comments about using Bimby. Flavia describes its many functions and all the dishes she now makes (risotto, desserts, sauces, children meals, fresh fruit juices and so on) saying that, although it is expensive (it costs more than €1000), the Bimby 'gives you back' a lot. She cooks every day for her family, and she tries new things thanks to the Bimby – she even takes the robot with her on holidays, almost as another member of the family that cannot be left behind. She feels that the Bimby is like an 'ally'.

Although there are many critical views (usually from people who don't own one), many owners agree that the Bimby is a magic machine that 'does everything by itself', allowing individuals to experiment with new styles of cooking while doing other things. Although the machine has a timer and can be left unattended while cooking, the relationship between people and the Bimby is far from detached. People learn new gestures and recipes; they adjust their previous knowledge to the functions of the new machine. The majority of users actively participate in creating shared knowledge by exchanging news, recipes and information with friends and with people online.

Interviews with sales promoters and customers reveal that the majority of Bimby owners are mostly professional women, rather than *casalinghe* (housewives). It is usually women who decide to buy this machine, although often for very different reasons – some women work late but still want to be able to fix a good dinner without having to prepare the same old *fettina* (a slice of meat in the pan, a sign of culinary mediocrity). Women with food allergies want to be able to cook everything from scratch with carefully chosen ingredients. Other women have been 'terrible cooks' all their lives and they hope to gain new status and new skills thanks to this machine. Moreover people talk about a general 'return to the domestic table' – they tend to go out less, choosing instead to entertain friends and family at home. In the words of one promoter, the best clients are 'women who are successful outside the home' who want to 'rise to the occasion' inside their home too – when they invite people to dinner they don't want to *brutta figura* (leave a bad impression).

It is interesting to note that the Bimby has become a very popular gift to newlyweds – only a few years ago, the wedding list would include mostly pots and pans, but now the Bimby is replacing many of those traditional objects. Especially in Naples and in southern Italy, the Bimby has become an integral part of the wife's dowry rather than a gift for the couple; mothers invest their daughters with a sort of 'magic pan', an object endowed with an incorporated ability to transform ingredients into good food that daughters can carry with them into their new lives. Bimbys are also given as gifts to daughters and sons when they leave the maternal home to go to university or because they have found employment elsewhere.

A minority of Bimby buyers are men, although they often support the women in the house when they decide to buy them. The single men I have interviewed had a passion for cooking even before the Bimby, and they feel more confident with it because they 'have extra help' as they follow the instructions of the machine and in the recipe books: 'I can cook things that I did not dare to do, with this I know I cannot make mistakes.' Many say they don't use it as often as they would like, since social occasions are not very frequent and they tend not to use it when they eat by themselves. Although the men that cook with Bimby talk positively about this machine, they rarely attend the free cooking classes that the company offers. They tell me that they would feel embarrassed in a woman-dominated domain, and in general they tend not to share their knowledge of new recipes with other people even though they are happy to prepare food for their friends and family. One man, as a strategy to re-establish his image as 'strong', said to me during the interview, 'I would go to cooking classes, why not, only if there were plenty of good looking young women!'

Because so few men attend these cooking classes – and because the classes are such an important part of the after-sale service crucial to Bimby's marketing strategy – the company now organizes 'men-only cooking classes', trying to involve more men in 'Bimby Culture', although these sessions are not yet offered in Italy. Sales-persons responsible for follow-up meetings and 'phone calls designed to ensure that people actually use the machine sometimes emphasize their gender to reassure male clients. For example, one salesman from Germany calls himself 'the Bimby-man'; he regularly updates his Facebook profile with pictures and information about different styles of cooking. Some men play with their gendered cooking identity. John, a British Bimby user, has posted a picture of himself in front of the Bimby, with the caption 'holding a manly beer in the other hand'. The men I have interviewed tend to focus on the 'technical' aspects of the machine in their descriptions, displaying their knowledge of technology rather than focusing on culinary identities.

Most of the owners state that it is a 'magic' machine, a great object that is able to unify opposites. It is simple to use but able to deliver complex results; it is very expensive but allows you to save money by buying raw ingredients; it makes your life easier but allows you to fulfil the duties you have towards your family by providing healthy and fresh food in a tasty way. It is an object that is invested with many expectations whose aim is to 'bridge', at least symbolically, contrasting elements – efficiency and family gatherings, conviviality and rapidity. In the homes I visited during the interviews, people had the Bimby in a central position on the kitchen counter, always ready to be used. It was usually one of the only visible objects, because often fridges and dishwashers were placed inside wooden cupboards. While some people call it a simple 'facilitator', others describe their machine as an agent that changes and sometimes reinforces domestic roles, allowing people to engage and perform new and old culinary actions.

To master the Bimby, people need a constant and active relationship with it – they look for adapted recipes, they learn new habits and a new language (the cooking method is called *Varoma*, the kneading technique is called *Velocità spiga* – because different objects have new names, the cooking instructions seem incomprehensible to the uninitiated). People adapt their previous experience, often transforming old family recipes. Many of the women go to Bimby cooking classes, and some have hosted demonstrations in their homes – they say they felt 'pleasure' in sharing their new knowledge and appreciated being rewarded with a little present, a recipe book, from the manufacturing company.

Specific users' stories help illustrate the way the Bimby impacts on their lives in and out of the kitchen. At 45, Luciana lives with her son in a beautiful villa near the centre of Perugia. She has been the proud owner of a Bimby for the past five years, getting one on the recommendation of her sister. She praises the machine's 'practicality' – it both 'shortens time of cooking' and gives her control over ingredients. Her enthusiasm has led her to become a '*Padrona di Casa*', Bimby's title for women who host demonstrations in their houses. She helps the sales-person during demonstrations, and she is very skilful in using the Bimby. She has become friends with the sales-person, but often her own stories are more effective in convincing her friends – eight so far – to buy Bimbys, even though she had never before tried to convince anyone to buy electric cooking appliances.

Another woman, Silvia, a 55-year-old mother of two university students who live with her, explains that the Bimby has helped her learn to cook new things. She is constantly looking for new things to try, which she finds stimulating. For example, she now cooks savoury pastries and dishes like *spigola all'acqua pazza*, a fish recipe she had never tried before. She usually looks for new ideas in the official recipe book or online. Like Luciana, Silvia is friends with the sales-person, who gives her new recipes. Silvia uses the Bimby to try new recipes rather than reproducing traditional regional dishes. For example, she often cooks Gorgonzola and spinach risotto, a new recipe learned from the Bimby recipe book. She thinks of herself as having 'double knowledge' – one inherited from her mother (often perceived as far too time-consuming and complicated) and the new Bimby one. At the same time she is crafting her own personal knowledge, creatively using all these different registers. She shows me her many recipe books, including one handwritten by her mother, full of procedures now so 'out of fashion' that she sees it as a 'memoir' reflecting different attitudes towards cooking. (For example, her mother's book includes an instruction to whisk eggs for twenty-five minutes – 'Now we would never have all that time to do that', she says.) Another copybook holds her 'pre-Bimby' recipes, and a folder that she titled '*Ricette Bimby*' is full of printed and photocopied sheets. Although she calls her Bimby 'just a facilitator', her descriptions indicate that the machine actually changes old practices and creates new expectations about cooking performances.

That experience may explain why, while people rarely admit using pre-packaged or frozen ingredients – using frozen pizza dough or pre-cooked tomato sauce would be 'shameful' to admit – Bimby users proudly show their machines to their guests. One woman even invites friends for 'Bimby dinners', using it as a kind of slogan: 'I am confident of my choice and the food that I am able to put on my table', she says. One demonstrator explains, 'You always put some creativity in it, your actions are still important.' Another woman says, 'The merit of the final result goes to the Bimby, but it goes to me as well, because I bought it, I spent my money on it, I had the idea of it, I know how to use it, I have it and you don't have it.'

While people acquire some status as owners of an expensive piece of technological equipment, they still emphasize the personal value attached to food transformation:

they still construct a positive self-identity around cooking. Although they describe using a Bimby as an 'easy' way to cook, they don't seem to lose social benefits or the value attached to food preparation – they present this tool to their guests as almost a sacred object, able to easily gratify taste, save time and promote health. They almost become 'Bimby vestals' – the machine works for them, but they still remain the managers of the symbolic aspects linked to the 'cooking fire'. Cooking doesn't lose its sacred, alchemic properties: the magic is simply transferred inside the hidden workings of a machine.

Furthermore, people talk about the 'marvels' of creating complex dishes while leaving everything 'clean', contrary to the usual 'messy' business of food preparation. Avoiding the 'dirt', the temporary 'matter out of place' that cooking entails while still delivering a good meal to your family is heralded as an impossible accomplishment. For example, Luana says,

> You don't make things dirty, you don't have to wash. You make a mess in a controlled way, and it is very easy to clean, there are different pieces but they are not difficult to use, they are not too many and are easy to wash. You can replace industrial products and you have control over the ingredients. Some people also make butter and soap with it. It is easy to clean because you put some water in it and you make it spin quickly. You don't waste the ingredients, when you have only a little bit inside, you can pick up all the food.

People describe the Bimby as more than the sum of a blender, a grinder and a cooking vessel – having all of these properties in one single body gives it a special 'magic' quality that no other machine possesses. People constantly reassert contrasting positions – it works all by itself, but you still get the credit for the good meal; it saves preparation time, but it opens up infinite new cooking possibilities (you can even make your own ketchup, chicken stock and Nutella); you can cook like a 'real chef', but 'even an 11 year old child could use it' as well as someone with a lot of experience and cooking abilities.

******

I argue that the act of cooking is what makes this robot symbolically different from other kitchen gadgets and that this difference explains why Bimby has gained almost a totemic status for its possessors. It is heralded by people as 'magic' because it performs, in a single body, functions that are usually separated: cutting, mixing and cooking. It is this peculiar hybrid nature that makes it so extraordinary for its owners. Crossing traditional activities that have always been part of different, although related, spheres of action, this new object holds together, contains, but also mysteriously hides, processes that are usually separated, and requires new rules that challenge previous knowledge. The Bimby is thus an 'unclassifiable' object that, like Mary Douglas's pangolin, becomes almost 'sacred' because it crosses boundaries of previous separate activities (1966). By unifying in one single object a multitude of different functions, the Bimby demands reinterpretation of cultural assumptions about specific choreographies for preparing food. As a result, people either become Bimby's passionate advocates or its strenuous opponents, as if the machine represents a corruption of the 'proper way' of doing things.

Yet users of the Bimby still emphasize traditional cooking abilities and the social relevance of preparing meals. Indeed, the machine makes it easier to maintain such values through its promise of an 'easier' way to cook: by magically unifying separate tasks in a 'clean' modern system, the Bimby relieves anxieties about disorder and performance.

Cooking, with its laboratory-like nature, its alchemic transformation of elements into something else, has always been an activity at the threshold of science and magic (medicine in popular culture is often related to something to eat; magic potions are often made of cooked foods and elements) (Pizza 2012). The Bimby acquires a special status among other kitchen tools because it unifies acts that are usually symbolically separated and promises order where there is usually chaotic activity. People are mesmerized by the Bimby's 'magic' qualities (Latour 1993), not only because of its intelligent internal computer, but because it is an unclassifiable tool sitting ambiguously across that liminal time/space of food transformation that is mamma's kitchen.

References

M. Douglas, *Purity and Danger. An Analysis of Concepts of Pollution and Taboos* (New York: Routledge, 1966).

M. Douglas and B. Isherwood, *The World of Goods: Towards an Anthropology of Consumption* (New York: Routledge, 1979).

I. Kopytoff, 'The Cultural Biography of Things: Commoditization as Process', *The Social Life of Things: Commodities in Cultural Perspective*, ed., A. Appadurai (Cambridge: Cambridge UP 1986), pp.64–95.

B. Latour, *We Have Never Been Modern* (Cambridge, MA: Harvard UP 1993).

G. Pizza, 'Microfisiche del cibo tra edonismo e cultura', *Italianieuropei*, anno XII,10 (2012) pp. 40–46.

M. Truninger, 'Cooking with Bimby in a Moment of Recruitment: Exploring Conventions and Practice Perspectives', *Journal of Consumer Culture* 11 (1) (2011) pp. 37–59.

L. Vercelloni, 'La modernità alimentare', *Storia d'Italia*, Annali 13 (1998) pp. 951–1003.

B. Wilson, *Consider the Fork: A History of How We Cook and Eat* (New York: Basic Books, 2012).

R. Wrangham, *Catching Fire. How Cooking Made Us Human* (London: Profile, 2009).

Digital Gastronomy

Adrian Bregazzi

I define *digital gastronomy* as the mediation of food by means of digital technologies, or the use of digital data to inform development of new recipes. This paper does not address issues of genetic engineering, biotechnology or printing meat.

It may sound undesirable, improbable and just too much science fiction to engage digital technologies in the making of dishes for table. However, it is already happening, albeit in a trivial manner. Most recently, Choc Creator is a commercially available device that simply prints 2.5D geometric or drawn chocolate shapes from software.[1] Actually printing food, not printing on food, was first generally intimated in a technical paper as early as 1992 but has been a developing reality for seven years in consistently trivial forms.[2] Driven by innovation, exploration and sustainability, computer-engineered food will have a future notwithstanding its rather pathetic nascence.

Employing digital data in developing recipes may sound equally disturbing, but again, it is already happening. Flavour pairing, first suggested in 1992 by Heston Blumenthal and François Benzi, has become digitized and readily available online.[3] This approach can be found throughout the menus of cutting-edge chefs. The popular *Flavour Thesaurus* provides an alternative offline version.[4] Here I will focus on the physical aspects of digital gastronomy.[5]

History of the development of computer-engineered food
Conventionally, items of food are organized on a plate where they seem aesthetically pleasing, where they fit or simply where they land. There can be intended spaces between items, but it is uncommon for there to be planned or designed spaces within an item. Engineering a food item at a fundamental level can enable individual spaces to be created and individual elements to be placed in those spaces. This is food construction – something completely innovative. Alas, though there is a technology beginning to be able to offer this level of design, rarely has it been used or hypothesized.

This technology – computer-engineered food (CEF) – has been working in science fiction since at least 1934, but came to mass-audience attention with the television series *Star Trek* in the 1960s and *Star Trek: The Next Generation* in the 1980s.[6] Indeed, Jean-Luc Picard's predilection for 'tea, Earl Grey, hot' instantaneously produced by a Replicator in *Star Trek: The Next Generation* has become sub-culturally significant. However, this instantaneity was predated, indeed, highly qualified by Douglas Adams in *The Restaurant at the End of the Universe*.[7] Here, the anti-hero, Arthur Dent, on board an improbably futuristic spaceship, instructs a Nutri-Matic Drinks Dispenser in the rudiments of making a cup of tea with the near-catastrophic effect of causing the ship's computers to shut down all operations save for working out the tea problem. Herein lurks the lesson unheeded by nearly all subsequent researchers and developers: something as apparently simple as a cup of tea is far from simple.

All of these were preceded in Greek mythology by the stories of the Horn of Amaltheia, the Horn of Plenty, which could 'instantaneously become filled with whatever might be desired'.[8] More recently, Brazilian designer Bruno Oro published conceptual designs for an actual food replicator, *Home Sweet Home*.[9]

In the twenty-first century, research and development has focused on 3D printing as the technology for realizing physical CEF.[10] 3D printing is an additive process in which successive layers of an object are laid down according to data in a software model. 3D printing of food employs an extrusion deposition system in which layers of extruded food material build up the printed object. This process limits source materials to those with certain fluid properties, that is, to materials which set rapidly or can be set rapidly after extrusion and, most significantly, to food objects which can be created by an analogue layering process.

While 3D-printed food was intimated as early as 1992, an origin for this approach may be found in a 2006 NASA research proposal by the Icosystem Corporation (Cambridge MA).[11] This document outlined many salient issues and possible solutions, and proposed systems enabling 'astronauts to create familiar or novel foods from a set of basic ingredients, through a series of processing steps designed to achieve a vast selection of textures and flavors'. In 2006, 3D-printed food became a reality in experiments described in a paper by staff at Cornell University's Creative Machines Lab. Their open-source Fab@Home printer was used to create very basic patterns and 2.5D shapes using icing, spray cheese, peanut butter and chocolate. The Cornell development team were confident that the technology (solid freeform fabrication – SFF) 'allows creative and technically inclined cooks to realize food creations that would otherwise be beyond their skill level'.[12]

In 2009, the Cornell team stated that the Fab@Home SFF technology 'has the potential to drastically impact both culinary professionals and laypeople; the technology will fundamentally change the ways we produce and experience food.' And it 'has the potential to leverage its core strengths (e.g., geometric complexity, automated fabrication) and make its mark on the culinary realm by transforming the way we produce and experience food.' They go on to state that 'after molecular gastronomy, SFF promises to be the next important enabling technology in the fine dining realm, … offering fabrication of multi-material objects with high geometric complexity'. Such complexity might be suggested by '[e]xamples of future potential applications include cakes with complex, embedded 3D letters such that upon slicing the cake a message is revealed, or, even a prime rib with a hidden message.'[13]

SFF would also have the potential to save time for domestic cooks by 'end-to-end offloading of food preparation': 'If food-SFF were brought to the "set-and-forget" state, requiring minimal human labor, the average person could possibly realize time-savings of 150+ hours per year.' Furthermore, 'culinary knowledge and artistic skill of world renowned chefs can be abstracted to a 3D fabrication file and used by laypeople to reproduce famous chefs' work in the home.' And they enthuse about the potential for networking recipes to allow a 'truly global cuisine [to] evolve'.[14]

In 2007, the Fab@Home device produced simple food items directly in the device itself, requiring or receiving no further modification. In 2010, the team began using traditional cooking techniques to process items rendered in the Fab@Home device. They produced a deep-fried miniature space shuttle made from puréed scallop; a sous-vide puréed turkey flesh and bacon fat cube, interlaced with celery gel; and a small cake with the letter C embedded inside. They state, 'People are excited to have SFF solve culinary problems and allow new design spaces for food.... The key barriers to SFF's adoptation [sic] in the culinary relm [sic] are the physical limitation of the material sets printing requires and printers use, and the integration of SFF'ed food with traditional cooking techniques.' They state that their work has demonstrated 'that SFF'ed food can be prepared like traditional cuisine'.[15]

Meanwhile, several lusciously rendered design concepts for food printers were launched in Sweden, the Netherlands and the United States. Moleculaire, a free-standing food printer from German product designer Nico Klaeber, is a beautiful if rather improbable object which was one of the eight finalists in the Electrolux Design Lab 2009 competition. It features a system whereby ingredients are located in discrete recipe pods attached to the top of the device. Klaeber provides a real insight into the potential of food printing with virtual examples of very elegant small dishes. In 2013, another food printer, the Atomium, was placed second in the competition.

In the Netherlands, Philips Design published a suite of product designs for food in the company's *Design Probes* scheme intended to anticipate how we might live in fifteen to twenty years.[16] This suite included a multi-ingredient food printer; a nutrition analyser which could determine one's individual nutritional needs, as well as analyse food itself to assess its nutritional value; and a home-farming biosphere containing fish, crustaceans, algae and plants. Philips also provides a real insight into the potential of food printing with virtual examples of some interesting small dishes.

In the United States, Marcelo Coelho and Amit Zoran, postgraduate students at the MIT Media Lab, published a suite of four design concepts under the collective title, 'Cornucopia: the Concept of Digital Gastronomy'.[17] The project included the Digital Chocolatier, 'a prototype for a machine that allows users to quickly design, assemble and taste different chocolate candies'; the Virtuoso Mixer, 'a machine composed of a three-layer rotating carousel that provides cooks with an efficient way to mix multiple ingredient variations and experiment with subtle differences in taste and composition'; the Robotic Chef, 'a mechanical arm designed to physically and chemically transform a single solid food object, such as a steak, fish or a fruit'; and the Digital Fabricator, 'a personal, three-dimensional printer for food, which works by storing, precisely mixing, depositing and cooking layers of ingredients'. The project received a flurry of media attention in 2010, but unlike the Klaeber and Philips projects there were no illustrations of potential food items or dishes.[18]

Coelho and Zoran's lauding of the technologies in their Cornucopia is not effectively demonstrated by their arguments or their intended food products. For example, the Digital Fabricator process 'not only allows for the creation of flavors and textures that would be completely unimaginable through other cooking techniques, but it also allows the user to have ultimate control over the origin, quality, nutritional value and taste of every meal.'[19] Yet the recipe we see associated with this device is for lasagne; similarly, the Virtuoso Mixer makes chocolate chip cookies, and the Robotic Chef operates on a banana. There is no evidence of the vision embodied in the Klaeber and Philips project illustrations.

Computer-engineered food today

As with the MIT team, it seems clear that the evangelism of the Cornell team's writing is not matched by their products, which could seem trivial to those with a real interest in food. And while there has been a marked absence of publication on CEF from Cornell since summer 2010, Hod Lipson (director of Cornell's Creative Machines Lab, co-author of all three papers and an advisor on the Icosystem team) dedicated a chapter of his co-authored 2013 book, *Fabricated*, to 'Digital Cuisine'.[20] Notwithstanding the dearth of new achievements in this domain, Lipson's prose still reveals a missionary zeal:

> 3D printing food will change the way we eat and how we manage our health. When digital cuisine is as widely accepted as personal computing is today, our refrigerators will hold cartridges of frozen pastes of dark chocolate and pesto chicken. Amateur bakers will download a cake recipe and print out a one-of-a-kind scrumptious pastry whose complexity rivals one made by a virtuoso chef. Home food printers will have settings to allow cooks to select a food's texture, crispness, and perhaps write a custom message inside that will be revealed at first bite. Lovers or family members in distant locations will share a recipe for the same cake which they will print and eat together while they spend time on a webcam.[21]

Oddly, he immediately goes on to say, 'I'm not entirely convinced that every home will someday have a 3D printer.'[22] Stranger than this peripety is the reality that six years of research in an Ivy League university generated nothing more complex than a letter C crudely embedded within a small cake and a deep-fried space shuttle; Lipson implicitly cites these achievements as evincing 3D food printing changing the way we eat and manage our health as a kind of 'killer app'.[23] Throughout the seven years of the Fab@Home project there has been a mismatch between actual physical developments and bold claims for the future – a marked absence of any proof of the pudding, as it were.

The mission continued in *WIRED* in February 2013.[24] Here the Fab@Home technology is taken on a journey to Mars, providing astronauts with 'delicious and nutritious' custom meals as a relief from the monotony of typical packaged food, and even allows loved ones to send recipes for family favourites to cheer up lonely astronauts. Proponents claim the technology could also boost productivity at home. Michelle Terfansky, who had researched 3D printing of food in space for a masters degree at the University of Southern California, thinks that within five to ten years a single printer could produce different food items that are both flavourful and look like what they are supposed to be. Moreover, she sees a day in the future 'when most homes have a machine simple enough for a child to press a *hamburger* button and receive a meal'. And she seems to suggest that this is a good thing.

Despite such promises, doubts about a future for printed food have surfaced more recently.[25] Jeffrey Lipton, a senior on both the research and retail arms of Fab@Home, suggest how trivial early efforts could be by suggesting that wild new shapes and textures for artisanal purposes might serve as some of 3D food printing's first, albeit limited, commercial successes. 'You could see food tchotchkes find a little niche,' he says.[26]

Agreeing with Lipton, 3D-printing pioneer Janne Kyttanen concedes that fun items and novelty experiences may be the best we can expect for the moment. Illustrating the current limits of the technology, he tried printing simulacra hamburgers in plaster. His response to his own efforts, though, is revealing: 'I printed burgers just to create an iconic image and make people realize that one day we will be able to 3D-print a hamburger. And once you do, you don't want to print a traditional hamburger; you can print the weirdest thing you can imagine.'[27]

Meanwhile Kjeld van Bommel, a Research Scientist at the Dutch Organization for Applied Scientific Research (TNO), adopts a more pragmatic view: 'Making one grain of wheat is a hell of a lot more complex than doing anything with wheat flour.... If a complex structure already exists in nature, like a lettuce leaf, why would you want to print it?' Making such complex structures is more complicated than many proponents of 3D printing think: 'Obviously if you're going for universal 3D food printer, you can't have 50 million cartridges lying around for the moment you want to print a tomato, ...It sounds simple to say "we'll have a fat cartridge," but there are hundreds of kinds of fats.' Instead, there need to be sensible limits, 'maybe three types of proteins, three types of carbs.... It could happen, but we would need to know a lot about how to make different types of foods from those building blocks.'[28]

History repeated itself in late May 2013 when it was announced that NASA had awarded a $125,000 grant for a project to develop a 3D food printing system for use in space exploration, a system the designer states could end world hunger. The proposed system employs dried carbohydrates, proteins and nutrients, which are combined with water and/or 'oil' immediately prior to printing. The project's aim is to print a 'pizza' by first printing a layer of dough which is 'baked' at the same time as being laid down; this is followed by a 'tomato base'; and topped with a 'protein layer'. There is no mention of the effects of (the lack of) gravity.[29]

Computer-engineered food today

Today, CEF is limited by its means of production, the choice of materials (ingredients), objectives and imagination/innovation:

- Printing by means of extrusion deposition is the dominant means of CEF, with laser sintering playing a minor role. Extrusion deposition limits source materials to those with certain fluid properties, materials that set rapidly or can be set rapidly after extrusion. This approach limits food objects to those which can be created by an analogue layering process, roughly equivalent to what can be achieved using a conventional piping bag. Similarly, laser sintering will only work on materials with certain surface melting/solidifying properties.
- Materials have hitherto been of minimal culinary interest: spray cheese, peanut butter, scallop purée, cookie dough, granulated sugar, etc. However, TNO is producing laser-sintered shapes composed of granulated mealworms.[30]
- Objectives have been innovation for sustainability in TNO's work; design innovation from Philips, Nico Klaeber, and Coelho & Zoran; and simply endeavouring to find a purpose for a technology.[31]
- Imagination/innovation characterize the work of Icosystem Corporation, TNO, Philips, and Nico Klaeber, which all score highly in terms of actual or conceptual food, whereas mainstream news, aggregation and blogs seem to favour the familiar burger, lasagne and pizza.

What could be achieved in the very near future

Considerable research is being undertaken into developing new materials from algae.[32] Structural materials may be developed which offer a wide range of properties essential for real CEF innovation (stiffness, absorption, texture, opacity, etc.) and which can be employed in existing extrusion deposition and printing/assembly technologies. Such materials could be used to create cellular entities which could take on natural flavours and colour; they could be used to create architectural spatial structures within/around ingredients in which wholly innovative dishes could be constructed; and they could be used to create self-sufficient dishes requiring no conventional tableware.

Such developments will most likely open up a future for pure innovation at limited-edition levels rather than those of common domestic use. Dreams of 3D food printers producing commonplace fast-food or chef dishes at the touch of a button in every home are unlikely to be realized; the required levels of system and material universality are probably decades away. CEF will necessarily remain specialized or industrial for a foreseeable future.

But let us return to those new material possibilities. The juice vesicles in citrus fruit are natural cellular entities with flavour and colour that can provide initial inspiration for what could be achieved with CEF cellular entities. Simply emulating them could create a dish of elliptical (or spherical, or polyhedral) cells with a carefully selected mix of fruit flavours, lightly bound in a fruit sauce. Or a single level soft-bonded matrix of cells containing (say) lime juice, tequila and Cointreau which, when placed in the mouth, could slowly release a margarita with its distinct flavours. Or a multi-level soft-bonded matrix of flavours and colours (say) redolent of a summer pudding. These concepts also require new thinking in terms of tableware and delivery to mouth – could the margarita matrix be delivered to your mouth by another person, and should this person be another table-guest or it could be a waiter? A softer cell base could be used to create a semi-liquid cocktail, delivering different flavours in sequence. These ideas employ the assembler function of many current 3D printers. These may seem contrived as simple verbal descriptions, but they could take on a new life in visual form.

Edible micro-architectural structures could be made around/within other ingredients to create fully edible quasi-sculptural dishes in which internal spaces are integral, as demonstrated by Philips Design. Flowers might provide a starting point for design, not as edible facsimiles but as forms. The forms of (say) sunflowers, peonies, lotus, chrysanthemums, bluebell florets, even over-the-top baobab flowers can all offer valuable starting points. And elements of *trompe l'oeil* could be dazzlingly effective. Reversing the familiar, an edible shell might contain a miniature rock pool of virtual seaweeds, anemones and shellfish. It is important that consideration be given to the intrinsic nature of these architectures as they must be integral to the eating of the dish, not merely a gimmick.

The architectural potential could also be extended to develop self-sufficient dishes which could avoid the need for conventional tableware, even requiring its own dedicated 'cutlery', and thus, along with the margarita matrix and its ilk, could disrupt conventional manners of eating. Taking this a stage further, dishes might even be designed to be difficult to eat.

The missed opportunity

In Spring 2006, when the Icosystem Corporation outlined its view of CEF for extended space missions, its research proposal to NASA contained five bullet points that realized a wholly data-driven and digitally-delivered view of the future for food in space:

- develop a *food grammar* using ingredient combinations and transformations
- identify and design *elementary building blocks* ('food phonemes')
- determine necessary *physical and chemical specifications* for implementation
- discover *reverse mapping* from desired food to generative description
- create *novel foods* with desirable properties (texture, taste, nutrition…)[33]

This digital paradigm is in contrast to current digital-analogue CEF technologies. Here is a complete system of unique objects (blocks/phonemes), properties (texture, taste, nutrition…), procedures (generative description, reverse mapping) and an abstract language (food grammar). It rejects then existing SFF technologies as not being immediately applicable and, critically, states, 'It is better to make something new, rather than do a mediocre job of replicating something familiar.' Notwithstanding that this was a special case dealing with astronautics, I believe that the elements of this system are crucial to the development of effective terrestrial CEF, and that in the last seven years the current preference for extrusion deposition systems have demonstrated that it is severely limited in its ability to deliver a coherent repertoire.

A cuixel future

The future of CEF may well be elementally simple and native to the technology – object-based and synthesized. *Star Trek*'s Food Synthesizer employed twenty-third-century 'protein sequencing' technology to create food to order. In *Star Trek: The Next Generation* the Replicator employed twenty-fourth-century 'transporter' particle technology to create almost anything to order. Both technologies manipulate very small objects at ultra high speeds. Given that there are some ten billion molecules in the average burger, it would take in excess of 160 million sequential physical operations per second to create an uncooked burger, at speeds in excess of 55,000 metres per second. And given that there is more instantaneity in these science fictions, with requests met without delay, such technologies may well not be available until the twenty-third century.

However, if we move up several orders of magnitude to the visible, it is possible to envisage a building block system such as proposed in the visionary 2006 Icosystem project. Thus, I have devised the word 'cuixel' to describe a small discrete unit of edible matter.[34] Imagine these as visible physical building blocks whose size is determined primarily by technology and thence by the desired level of granularity. And unlike the basic Lego building block, cuixels could bond with each face.[35]

Now, imagine what new food items could be achieved at even a relatively granular level! I suspect that the major problem will be finding appropriate names for these new dishes. And, when development achieves a stage where a large number of options are available (flavours, colour, texture, nutritional values, etc.), it would then be possible to create an interactive food system wherein a user would communicate some broad requests directly with the system and it would proffer potential dishes.

With notable exceptions, most outcomes from developing 3D food printing technology have been made without the necessary input of even a basic knowledge and experience of cooking food. The predilection for achingly familiar fast-food (burgers, pizza, lasagne) and naïve tricks (letters in a cake, a message in a steak) clearly demonstrate this limitation. There is an exciting future for CEF if we move away from doomed-to-failure replication of what already exists and think beyond existing repertoires.

The input of cooking experience and left-field thinking – and the abandonment of claims to solve world food problems, to save everyone's labour, or to place a food printer in every home to produce burgers – should lead to a brighter future for both existing and soon-to-be-developed technologies.

Notes

1. Chocolate printer to go on sale after Easter', *BBC Technology News*, 6 April 2012 <http://www.bbc.co.uk/news/technology-17623424>; 'Chocolate Choc Creator vi', *Chocedge* <https://chocedge.com/choc-creator-vi.php>. Retail price £2888. This device is a commercial spin-off from a project led by Dr Liang Hao of the University of Exeter in collaboration with Brunel University and software developer Delcam. It was funded as part of the Research Council UK Cross-Research Council Digital Economy Programme and managed by the Engineering and Physical Sciences Research Council (EPSRC) on behalf of ESRC, AHRC and MRC.
2. Marshall Burns, *Perspectives on StereoLithography*, StereoLithography Users Group Annual Meeting, San Francisco CA, March 1992 <http://www.ennex.com/~fabbers/publish/199203-MB-SLAPerspec.asp>; Dan Periard et al., 'Printing Food', *Proceedings of the 18th Freeform Fabrication Symposium* (Austin, TX: August 2007) <http://creativemachines.cornell.edu/papers/SFF07_Periard2.pdf>.
3. Liz Roth-Johnson, 'The Flavor Network', *Science and Food*, 26 February 2013 <http://scienceandfoodu-cla.wordpress.com/2013/02/26/the-flavor-network/>; *Foodpairing* <https://www.foodpairing.com>.
4. Niki Segnit, *The Flavour Thesaurus* (London: Bloomsbury, 2010).
5. Illustrations of developing technologies and new designs can be found on Adrian Bregazzi, *Digital Gastronomy* <http://digitalgastronomy.net/>.
6. In 1934, John W. Campbell's 'Twilight', (*Astounding Stories* November 1934) included machines that made food 'synthetically...and perfectly'; 'Food Synthesizer', *Memory Alpha* http://en.memory-alpha.org/wiki/Food_synthesizer; 'Replicator', *Memory Alpha* <http://en.memory-alpha.org/wiki/Replicator>.
7. Douglas Adams, *The Restaurant at the End of the Universe* (New York: Ballantine, 1980).
8. William Smith, 'Amalthea', *Dictionary of Greek and Roman Biography and Mythology*, 3 vols, (Boston: Little, Brown, and Company, 1867): vol. 1, p. 136.
9. Bruno Oro, *Home Sweet Home* <http://www.coroflot.com/bruno_oro/Home-Sweet-Home>.
10. Periard.
11. Burns; Daphna Buchsbaum, Eric Bonabeau and Paolo Gaudiano, 'Customizable, Reprogrammable, Food Preparation, Production and Invention System' (NIAC Phase 1 Contract Final Report) <http://www.niac.usra.edu/files/studies/final_report/1072Bonabeau.pdf>.
12. Periard, 'Conclusion'
13. Daniel L Cohen et al., 'Hydrocolloid Printing: A Novel Platform for Customized Food Production', *Proceedings of the 20th Freeform Fabrication Symposium* (Austin, TX: August 2009) <http://creativema-chines.cornell.edu/sites/default/files/SFF09_Cohen1_0.pdf>.
14. Cohen.
15. Jeffrey Lipton et al., 'Multi-Material Food Printing with Complex Internal Structure Suitable for Conventional Post-Processing', *Proceedings of the 21st Solid Freeform Fabrication Symposium* (Austin, TX: August 2010) <http://creativemachines.cornell.edu/sites/default/files/69-Lipton-Mutlimaterial%20food%20printing%20Final.pdf>.
16. 'Food Probe by Philips Design', in *Dezeen Magazine*, 9 September 2009 <http://www.dezeen.com/2009/09/08/food-probe-by-philips-design/>
17. Marcelo Coelho and Amit Zoran, 'Cornucopia: The Concept of Digital Gastronomy', *Leonardo* 44.5 (October 2011): pp. 425–31 <http://fluid.media.mit.edu/sites/default/files/44.5.zoran%20%281%29.pdf>.
18. This article is typical of media enthusiasm for the Cornucopia project: Loz Blain, 'Cornucopia: Digital Gastronomy – Could 3D Printing Be the Next Revolution in Cooking?', *Gizmag*, 14 January 2010 <http://www.gizmag.com/cornucopia-digital-gastronomy-3d-food-printer/13873/>.
19. Coelho and Zoran, p. 429.
20. See, however, Bregazzi, 'Shrödinger's Cake', *Digital Gastronomy*, 2013 <http://www.digitalgastronomy.net/schroedingers_cake.php>; Hod Lipson and Melba Kurman, *Fabricated: The New World of 3D Printing* (Indianapolis, IN: John Wiley & Sons, 2013).

21. Lipson and Kurman p. 150.
22. Lipson and Kurman p. 151
23. The choice of a space shuttle as a model to demonstrate the level of detail that could be achieved in SFF food, and its subsequent detrimental deep-frying, seems in remarkably bad taste given what happened in 1986 to the space shuttle Challenger; Lipson and Kurman, p. 151
24. Adam Mann, 'Feeding the Final Frontier: 3-D Printers Could Make Astronaut Meals', *WIRED Science*, 6 February 2013 <http://www.wired.com/wiredscience/2013/02/3-d-food-printer-space/>.
25. Adam Hadhazy, 'Will 3D Printers Manufacture Your Meals?', *Popular Mechanics* 25 March 2013 <http://www.popularmechanics.com/science/will-3d-printers-manufacture-your-meals-15265101?click=pm_latest; Bianca Bosker, '3D Printers Could Actually Make Donuts Healthy', *Huff Post Tech* 24 April 2013 <http://www.huffingtonpost.com/2013/04/24/3d-printed-food_n_3148598.html>.
26. Hadhazy.
27. Ben Hobson, 'Food Is the Next Frontier of 3D Printing', *Dezeen* 27 March 2013 <http://www.dezeen.com/2013/03/27/food-is-the-next-frontier-of-3d-printing-janne-kytannen/>.
28. Hadhazy. It should be noted that he did feature lettuce leaves in a presentation at TEDxBrainport 2012 <http://www.youtube.com/watch?v=3iwD1P_7vxo> and <http://www.tno.nl/downloads/tedx_brainport_food_printer.pdf>.
29. Christopher Mims, 'The Audacious Plan to End Hunger with 3-D Printed Food', *Quartz* 21 May 2013 <http://qz.com/86685/the-audacious-plan-to-end-hunger-with-3-d-printed-food/>.
30. Mims.
31. Lipton et al.
32. Corjan van den Berg, 'Algae for a Sustainable Future', *TNO: Innovation for Life* <http://www.tno.nl/content.cfm?context=thema&content=prop_case&laag1=892&laag2=908&laag3=87&item_id=1758&Taal=2>.
33. Buchsbaum, Bonabeau and Gaudiano.
34. The word 'cuixel' is based on a 'voxel' – a volumetric picture element; which itself based on 'pixel' or picture element. I opted for cooking's predilection for French rather than opt for 'foxel' or 'fooxel' http://www.digitalgastronomy.net/cuixels.php.
35. If the cuixel is a cube it will have 6 faces, any of which could bond with a contiguous cuixel. Technically, they have R3 tessellation and rotation invariance.

The Shape of Things to Come: Bottles, Glasses and Contrasting Beer Cultures in Belgium and the United States

Anthony F. Buccini

Opgedragen aan wijlen Lucas Van Langendonck, vriend en baas van mijn oude staminee te Leuven, den Amadee.

Bud's bowtie can and Stella's chalice[1]

'This can is incomparable.' In the spring of 2013, on billboards across America, there appeared an advertisement announcing as noteworthy news from the greatest brewery in the United States the arrival of a revolutionary and long-awaited new product: the 'Bowtie Can' for Budweiser beer. What is novel and noteworthy about this new product has nothing whatsoever to do with the quality or flavour of the actual beer involved, which is nothing more nor less than the Budweiser beer of a now long-standing recipe. Rather, it is the can itself, the new container in which the beer will now be offered.

This 'Bowtie Can' is indeed both novel and noteworthy in several ways, especially according to the press releases from Anheuser-Busch, the proximate parent company that produces Budweiser. Pat McGauley, the company's 'vice president of innovation', does not spare hyperbole in discussing it: 'This can is incomparable, like nothing you've ever seen before…. The world's most iconic beer brand deserves the world's most unique and innovative can. I think we have it here' (Vanderborg 2013). What makes this can so different from others is that it pinches in toward the middle at an angle of ten degrees – hence the 'bowtie' name – and that, in order to achieve this form, the can requires a far more complex manufacturing process (involving sixteen steps), as well as twice as much aluminium as is required for the conventionally shaped can. Nonetheless, the new packaging is economically advantageous to Budweiser, as the bowtie cans are priced like the old cans but contain 0.7 ounces less beer.

While most, if not all, of the major breweries that sell beer in the United States regularly make all manner of claims regarding their respect for and place in time-honoured tradition, at the end of the day the main thrust of their marketing routinely touts not tradition but novelty. Indeed, over the past several decades, the American beer market has been dominated by two key strategies: 1) the introduction of novel kinds of beers, first offered by one of the breweries but soon after imitated by their competitors; 2) the introduction of novel or eye-catching forms of packaging. Among the former, the most notable was the first such new style of beer, the category of 'light' beers, which first gained mass popularity in the early 1970s; among the latter, the Bowtie Can is but one of a number that have appeared with considerable frequency over the years.

'It's a chalice, not a glass'

There is perhaps some touch of irony in the fact that Anheuser-Busch, a beer company that has for so long been thought of by so many as producer of the quintessential American brew, has been since 2008 a subsidiary of an even larger brewing and beverage conglomerate, AB InBev, which is in large measure a Belgian (and Brazilian) corporation, based in the ancient brewing centre of Leuven and most closely identified with the brand Stella Artois, which is itself still produced in that Flemish city. That under AB InBev Anheuser-Busch continues to market its American products such as Budweiser in a manner consistent with established American marketing strategies is in no way surprising. For those who are at least somewhat familiar with Belgian beer culture, it is perhaps also not surprising that AB InBev's marketing strategy in the United States for its flagship beer, Stella Artois, draws in good measure on one of the most striking aspects of modern Belgian beer culture, namely, the prominent role given to glasses which are more or less specific in form to each beer and which bear the brand's logo. Indeed, though many beers sold in the United States – both foreign and domestic – have over the years offered special glasses festooned with the brand's logo, the offerings have been on a limited basis, and to my knowledge no other brewery has ever made the glass itself the focus of the advertising in the US in the way that Stella has in the years since AB InBev became a major player in the American market, with billboards and television spots featuring the elegant tulip glass with its long stem, accompanied in some cases by the comment: 'It's a chalice, not a glass'.

Yet, while it is certainly true that the offering of a distinctively shaped and decorated beer glass for a specific brand of beer is something very much normal in Belgium and very much out of the ordinary in the States, AB InBev's prominent use of the Stella 'chalice' in its American advertising is itself not very Belgian at all, but rather a sort of new twist on a long-standing marketing strategy in the US. Specifically, we note that these chalice advertisements put the primary focus not on the beer itself but rather on the material object most closely related to the serving of the beer, giving the Belgian-style glass a role played for other beer brands in the States by the bottle or the can. Of course, the elegant Stella 'chalice' is a decidedly Belgian object and it can thus bear several semiotic functions at once in AB InBev's American advertising: it becomes iconic for the Belgian origin of the beer and generally for the quality of the beer as an import from Europe; the elegance of the glass itself further strengthens the idea that Stella beer is a luxury item to be appreciated by sophisticated consumers willing to pay its higher price; indeed, this drinking vessel is so special that it is no mere 'glass' but a 'chalice' and by extension its use takes on an almost sacral air; and last but certainly not least, the Stella glass finds its own especially novel and noteworthy place not alongside but well above the usual American beer bottles and cans.

What we see in the marketing of Stella in the United States may seem a trivial adaptation and introduction of a minor element of Belgian beer culture, the specially formed and branded drinking glass, into the context of the American beer market. But it is this writer's belief that the contrast between the 'fancy' Belgian beer glass and the American bottle and can is not in the least trivial; rather, it is a contrast that reifies the enormous differences between the beer cultures of the two countries, two beer cultures which represent extreme opposites along a continuum of modern Western beer cultures. The initial focus of this paper is on the contrasting material aspects of these beer cultures, but ultimately we argue that the seemingly superficial differences in the material aspect are in fact reflections of fundamental differences at several other levels, to wit, the aesthetics of beer, attitudes toward alcohol consumption in general and attitudes to beer in particular with regard to its relationship to culinary culture. Finally, we consider these deep differences in connection with certain socio-historical developments in the early twentieth century.

Belgian and American beer cultures: a study in contrasts

General trends in the brewing industry. The modern American and Belgian beer industries are not only now intimately connected at the corporate level as a result of the purchase of Anheuser-Busch by InBev, but they also resemble each other in some general ways. Through the same movement that brought these mega-breweries together, there have been many large and small corporate mergers and brewery buy-outs leading to the current situation in which the overwhelming majority of beer production and sales in both countries has come under the control of less than a handful of giant beer and beverage concerns. Each of these large-scale brewers offers to the public a range of different beers and beer styles, many of which continue more or less faithfully the products of the formerly independent businesses which the survivors have absorbed.

While the process of concentration of the industry started earlier and has proceeded further in the US than in Belgium, the current state of affairs in Belgium – allowing for the considerable difference in overall scale – has developed in an analogous way, especially with respect to the production of the most popular and, in a sense, basic beer style, pilsner, where concentration has been greatest. Independent brewers of other speciality beers have been better able to survive in Belgium and – as in the US, where microbreweries have flourished in recent decades – there has been considerable growth in the sector of these craft (as opposed to 'industrial') breweries who make styles of ales and lagers that appeal to small but passionate audiences.

The American bar and the Belgian café. As globalization also involves the brewing industry, it is inevitable that similarities as well as direct connections between the American and Belgian businesses develop. But while such convergence is already important and seems to be the vanguard of continued and far-reaching international homogenization, the fact remains that in many important respects, the beer cultures of the two countries are very different, and these deep differences are reflected in aspects of the material attributes of the basic venues where beer is habitually consumed, the American bar and the Belgian café.

In both countries, the basic kind of drinking establishment or, for simplicity's sake 'tavern', is by no means monolithic.[2] Indeed, even if one categorizes and sub-categorizes kinds of drinking establishments, there still is a considerable amount of variation within those categories involving any number of geographic and demographic parameters. In addition, one occasionally finds taverns in Belgium which consciously imitate kinds of American bars and increasingly there are upscale American bars that consciously imitate Belgian cafés, at least with regard to certain features. There is, moreover, a tendency in both countries for many older taverns that formerly served little or no food to make such offerings an important part of their business; newer taverns increasingly tend to open as mixed tavern/restaurant gastro-pubs, and in many localities the pure drinking establishment is disfavoured or outlawed by governments.

Be that as it may, anyone who has had occasion to visit many drinking establishments in the two countries will recognize that there are certain norms for both and that in many instances they stand in contrast to one another. Among the most notable differences are the following:

The size and prominence of the counter or bar (in the narrow sense) at which patrons can stand or be seated on a stool or raised chair and which forms both a serving space and a physical barrier between the patrons' space and the workspace of the bartender: in the typical American tavern, the bar is especially long and prominent and serves as the primary location for patrons to be stationed. In the typical Belgian tavern, the bar is significantly smaller and often not the primary location for patrons.

Given the differences in degree of prominence of the bar counter, Belgian cafés provide relatively more space at tables with chairs than their American counterparts. In older and more traditional cafés, the tables are usually like tables suited for dining, with both tables and chairs made of wood and resembling simple home furnishings. In American taverns, tables are very often of special design for the bar setting, raised up high and accompanied by stools or high chairs of the same sort as those set along bar counters.

Size and composition of beverage displays: on the wall behind the bar counter, thus facing out toward the patrons' space at the bar and beyond, both Belgian and American taverns typically have on prominent display many of their beverage offerings. The difference here lies in scale: in American bars, even small ones, there are multiple shelves bearing scores of bottles of distilled spirits, liquors, fortified wines, etc., whereas in the typical café, the number of such bottles on display is vastly smaller and, in old-fashioned, small cafés, there may be just a handful of bottles of the most commonly requested strong drinks. Conversely, in a café there is necessarily shelf-space devoted to the storage and display of the many branded beer glasses which are habitually used, while in American bars, such displays are non-existent outside the context of newer upscale bars featuring imported and domestic speciality beers.

Prominence/intrusiveness of electronic entertainment: an immediately striking difference between American bars and Belgian cafés resides in their use of televisions. In the US, almost all bars have televisions, and nowadays most have multiple high-definition screens arranged on the walls throughout the public space, including high up on the wall behind the bar counter, so that patrons seated at the bar are given, if not forced to have, direct views of one or more of the screens. It is, moreover, routine and clearly expected by the public that television will be on throughout a bar's opening hours. When sporting events of interest to the clientele are broadcast (and in the US there are a great many televised sporting events), it is expected that those events will be shown, but when no sporting events are on, the televisions are set to any sort of programming, providing a constant source of noise. When music is being played, televisions always remain on with the sound turned down. It is also exceedingly common in US bars for television audio and especially jukebox music to be played at very high volume, often rendering conversation among groups difficult or impossible.

The majority of Belgian cafés these days also have television sets but typically there is but one and it is used sparingly, to show, for example, a match of the local football team or some sporting or news event that is of national or international significance. A television in a café being left on throughout the day is something that I have never encountered in my many years of fieldwork. With regard to the use of music, there are certainly cafés that have jukeboxes but there are also many where the music is, in effect, programmed by the café owner or bartender to his or her own tastes and to those of the regular guests. Though music can at times be loud in certain kinds of cafés (e.g. student cafés) and at certain times of day (e.g. late evening), it is not normally at such a volume as to drown out group conversation.

Lighting and advertising: the two must be mentioned together because in the US, bars are intentionally dimly lit in the main public spaces, with brighter lighting limited to areas where it is needed for recreational games, such as billiards or darts; consequently, a significant portion of the lighting is provided by bright electronic advertising (neon or otherwise) which calls attention to products on sale in the establishment. In such spaces, reading or writing is rendered impossible. By contrast, traditional Belgian cafés are fairly well lit, and reading is quite possible and regularly carried out by patrons; in those cafés which are dimly lit, there are often at least some spaces where focussed lamps provide good light. Though electronic advertising is present, it stands out less and shares its role with old-fashioned metal signs and paper posters.

All these points of contrast can be considered elements in creating the overall ambience of the drinking establishments of interest here and as such they should also be seen in relation to the broader physical context provided by the architecture and building materials of the spaces housing these establishments. Older buildings with interesting layouts and brick walls, fireplaces or stoves, wooden timbers, wainscots, etc., are appreciated in both countries as forming cosy settings for drinking, but such considerations lie outside our primary focus.

What is relevant here are the overall effects of the environmental elements of the archetypical American bar and Belgian café. In the former, we have a public institution that is more overtly and intensely commercial, in which a common experience is demanded through the inescapable television or loud music and the dim lighting; in a way, the prominence of the bar and the display of bottles and television screens on the wall behind it form a sort of pre-Vatican II-style altar, the focus of attention for those in attendance. And yet one is also pushed by these same environmental attributes in the direction of easily being alone or in the minimal group of two, unseen, unheard, unnoticed by others, if one so wishes. In the café, without the incessant interference of television or loud music, the public space is more easily shared, though the orientation toward tables allows for considerable private or small group escape. In a sense, though the archetypical café is absolutely a public space, it has an air of domesticity to it, a sort of shared living room, where people gather to talk or play cards or to sit alone with a newspaper or book, but with the added advantage of having beer on draught.

Of course, we are talking here of archetypical, if not idealized, forms of the bar and café, but while there are all kinds of drinking establishments in both countries and a great deal of overlap across the divide, the two kinds of national taverns do tend to differ strongly as described above: the archetypes are well represented in both lands.

Drinks and drinking vessels

Within the ambient framework of the tavern, one drinks but again, while there is much overlap of what is consumed in US bars and Belgian cafés, there are very different tendencies and preferences. Of particular interest here, however, is the relationship between the beverages themselves and the vessels out of which they are consumed. With specific regard to beer, the vessels themselves constitute a striking difference in the material aspects of beer culture in the two lands and they have, moreover, played an especially important role in the formation of those cultures.

Although an enormous quantity of beer is consumed each year in the United States, the amount of the total of ethyl alcohol from beer consumed per capita by Americans breaks down roughly to half, with the remaining half being split approximately to one third from wine and two thirds from distilled spirits. For the year 2005, the figures were approximately 53% from beer, 16% from wine, and 31% from distilled spirits; for Belgium that year the percentages were roughly 56% from beer, 36% from wine and a mere 6% from spirits.[3] In other words, Americans drink a very considerable amount of distilled spirits, as one could guess from the prominence of the bottle displays in bars, whereas Belgians drink relatively little strong liquor.

The importance of distilled spirits in American drinking habits is reflected not only by the altar-like display of their bottles in bars but also by the creative energy put into the development of spirit-based mixed drinks and additionally by the variety of glasses designed specifically for the serving of these cocktails: cocktails are designed not only to taste good but also to look good, with the visual aesthetics not being required but in general much appreciated.

In stark contrast to the variety of forms and the elegance of particular cocktail glass types is the extreme lack of variety of American beer glasses and the utter simplicity of commonly used forms. In most bars these days, there are two basic beer glasses in regular use. The 'shaker glass' (used in preparing shaken cocktails), which holds a pint of liquid, is the most common glass used for draught beers but then it is also put into service for soft drinks from the bar fountain and additionally for serving some voluminous cocktails, such as Bloody Marys. Another, smaller glass in the form of a straight cylinder is available – usually given only on request – for patrons who are drinking bottled or canned beer. Also reasonably common is the 'stein', with a heavy base and a handle on the side, which depending on size may be used either for draught beers or offered alongside bottled or canned beers.

Perhaps what is most striking to a first-time Belgian visitor to a US bar – aside from the ubiquitous and constant use of the television – is the fact that an extremely high percentage of the patrons drink their beer not out of a glass at all but rather out of a bottle or can. There are two observations to make in this regard. First, this common use of a bottle or can as the drinking vessel in a bar is only possible for the obvious reason that American consumers, including those visiting taverns, drink considerably more packaged beer than they do draught beer. Indeed, in 1960 total packaged sales had already exceeded 80% of total beer sales and by 1988 packaged sales had reached 88% of the total compared a paltry 12% for draught beer (Stack 2010) and in the specific context of on-premise beer sales, draught beer accounted for only 38% of total sales in 2001.[4] While in the intervening years the overall consumption of draught beer may well have risen on account of increased sales of microbrew and imported beers, mainstream domestic American beers surely continue to be strongly preferred as packaged items, even in bars. Second, extremely high percentages of overall packaged sales in the States reflect a weaker attachment of beer consumption to tavern life and a concomitant greater association with other activities – Americans drink much of their beer at sporting events, at cookouts, at the beach and, of course, at home, all places where draught beer is less commonly or not at all available.

American and Belgian patterns of beer consumption differ in degree but the order of difference is sufficiently great as to bespeak a difference of basic attitude. For example, the overall percentage of draught beer consumed in Belgium through the 1990s on to 2001 remained roughly steady around 40% while the overall amount of beer consumed at home was also about 40%, leaving approximately 60% to on-premise consumption.[5] American on-premise beer sales comprise only some 25% of the total. In short, Belgians drink much more of their beer in taverns than Americans and, of the beer they drink there, a significantly greater amount is draught beer.

But it is not only draught beer that Belgians drink in their cafés: they also consume prodigious amounts of bottled beer on premise as well as at home. It is all but inconceivable, however, that a Belgian in a café would drink his beer straight from the bottle, as his American counterpart typically does. Indeed, an integral part of Belgian beer culture is the aesthetic relationship between beer varieties and their associated forms of glassware, associations that go back in time at least to the early twentieth century and in some cases before that. In addition now, as a marketing tool used by breweries but very much in harmony with the public's aesthetic expectations, the vast majority of Belgian brewers provide distinctive branded glasses for their products, something that has no full parallel elsewhere in the beer world.

Tastes great vs. less filling: an historical account

How did Americans come to care so little about glassware for beer and even prefer to drink straight from the bottle or can, while Belgians have taken an older tradition of matching beer styles to glass shapes and developed it further into a central aesthetic expression? Somewhat counter-intuitively, the answers to both of these questions crucially involve the effects of temperance movements in the early twentieth century. Space limitations require that this discussion be brief, but we can highlight the central points.

At the time when the Volstead Act, by which the manufacture and sale of all alcoholic beverages was prohibited, went into effect in 1920, there existed in the United States a robust and varied brewing industry, driven largely by the efforts and tastes of northern European and especially German immigrants. Though Prohibition was by no means successful in halting the consumption of alcohol in the US, it had an enormous and lasting impact on the drinking culture of the country. One important effect that arose from a number of logistical considerations was an increase in the popularity of distilled spirits, and, given that the available spirits were often of decidedly poor quality, the already existing but relatively minor practice of making mixed drinks blossomed into the cocktail culture that remains popular to this day. The same logistical considerations that made distilled spirits more easily available rendered beer a less practical commodity. And again, of the beer that was available in the years of Prohibition, much was of poor quality.[6]

When Prohibition was finally repealed in 1933, it took but little time until beer was again produced on a significant scale, but the thirteen-year interruption altered the nature of the brewing industry fundamentally. First, many smaller local and regional breweries simply vanished, leaving only a small number of the biggest pre-Prohibition breweries in a position to take up the business again. Second, the hiatus in the public's enjoyment of beer, together with the concentration of brewing in a far smaller number of more nationally oriented brewing companies reduced drastically the range of beer styles and beer quality on offer: the American beer market became utterly dominated by beers which were all of the same style – American pale lager – and barely distinguishable from one another in taste. This concentration of beer production also disfavoured the sale of draught beer; with the major breweries shipping beer long-distance to points all over the country, bottled and ultimately canned beer was favoured by the producers and marketed heavily to consumers. In addition, from the bar owner's standpoint, draught beer entails more work than packaged beer. There also arises a sort of downward spiral: the less draught beer is sold, the less fresh it is and the less consumers will want to buy it. Finally, from the large producers' standpoint, who – given the minimal differentiation of actual products – increasingly relied on marketing gimmicks to drive sales, draught beer, served in an anonymous glass, was far less attractive than bottled or canned beer that is conveyed to the consumer in its own small-scale advertisement.[7] And the more beer came to be drunk straight from the bottle and can, the beer glass became even more marginalized and uninteresting.

There was also a strong temperance movement in Belgium in the decades before the First World War, and in just the same year of 1920 that National Prohibition came into effect in the US, the Belgian temperance law (*Wet Vandervelde*) was enacted. But in Belgium the prohibition of alcoholic beverages was only partial and intended specifically to curb the consumption of distilled spirits among the lower economic strata of society: the sale of distilled spirits on premise was forbidden, as was the sale of distilled spirits in quantities less than two litres.

As demonstrated by American Prohibition, if people want to drink, they will find a way to do so. And if they are prevented from enjoying one form of alcohol, they will be inclined to enjoy other forms a little more, as demonstrated both by the disastrous Icelandic temperance law (prohibiting beer and resulting in the massive abuse of distilled spirits) and the Belgian *Wet Vandervelde*. Clearly, this law was successful in curbing consumption of distilled spirits, given the low quantities consumed by Belgians even today, decades after the final repeal of the prohibition of the on-premise sale of spirits in 1983. But this law ironically had a very positive influence on Belgium's beer culture, for in removing spirits from the mix, the alcohol-related creative energies of the country became more purely focussed on beer. It is surely for this reason that so many local styles of beers have survived in the country and why, through the twentieth century and on to today, Belgian brewers produce such a remarkable variety of beer styles, including many strong beers that offered a way to, in a sense, circumvent the sobering effects of the *Wet Vandervelde*.

And to return to the question of bottles and glasses, we find that in contrast to the logistical and market forces that led to the relative marginalization of draught beer and beer glassware in the US, Belgian brewers, faced with their own problem of marketing their products to a public that was very attached to draught beers, as well as to bottle-fermented beers, chose the simpler and infinitely more elegant solution of making the glass the bearer of their advertising.

One final comment: perhaps the saddest effect of Prohibition on American beer culture was that it led to beer being almost totally divorced from one of its basic functions, namely, as a food. This divorce is most clearly seen in the striving of the mainstream American brewing industry to minimize flavour and especially to reduce caloric content of their products. But in Belgium, beer continues on to this day with its full range of functions: refreshment, social lubricant, intoxicant, and food.

Notes

1. Research for this project has involved the usual extensive reading but additionally more than thirty years of the most pleasant field work imaginable. Many thanks to Tamás Bősze, Paul Stuyven, Tie Vanbeselaere, William Gisgand, Kurt Zarris and Amy Dahlstrom.
2. Here I use 'tavern' as an overarching term (cf. Clinard 1962: 271) alongside 'bar' as the term denoting the basic kind of public drinking establishment in the US and 'café' as its Belgian analogue. My definition of 'tavern' follows that of Clinard 1962 but differs in detail. We take as basic characteristics of the tavern: a) the sale of alcoholic beverages is the central feature of the business, even if food is served and represents an important source of revenue; b) the establishment is not a private club but offers open and public access, admitting in principle anyone of the appropriate age; c) the primary space of the establishment is an open space, so that patrons are in some sense drinking together; d) the establishment has one or more functionaries (bartenders, waiters, etc.) who interact with the patrons; e) as Clinard (p. 271) says, 'it has a physical structure and a set of norms. Patrons are served at a bar, tables, or booths, in specially decorated surroundings, with entertainment or recreational facilities like cards, darts, and shuffleboard available… Certain norms are also well established, including certain hours of drinking and appropriate drinking behavior.'
3. These figures are based on those from the World Health Organization, as cited in the Wikipedia article 'List of countries by alcohol consumption' (accessed 17 Jan. 2013).
4. SABMiller online publication of beer sales statistics from 2003: <http://www.sabmiller.com/files/presentations/2003/000503/may03_ontradeofftrade_slides.pdf> [accessed May 2013].
5. See 'European Beer Statistics' with statistics gathered from a wide variety of brewing industry sources <http://www.europeanbeerguide.net/eustats.htm>.
6. For an overview, see Okrent 2010.
7. On the history of marketing in the American beer industry, see Van Munching 1979.

Bibliography

Marshall B. Clinard, 1962, 'The public drinking house and society', in *Society, Culture, and Drinking Patterns,* ed. Pittman, D. & C. Snyder (New York: John Wiley), pp. 270–92.

Daniel Okrent, 2010, *Last Call. The Rise and Fall of Prohibition* (New York: Scribner).

Martin H. Stack, [2010?], 'A Concise History of America's Brewing Industry' <http://eh.net/encyclopedia/article/stack.brewing.industry.history.us>.

Carey Vanderborg, 2013, 'Budweiser Bowtie Can Shape Mirrors Brand's Longtime Logo, Release Date Set for May 6, 2013', *International Business Times* <http://www.ibtimes.com>.

Philip Van Munching, 1979, *Beer Blast. The Inside Story of the Brewing Industry's Bizarre Battles for Your Money* (New York: Random House).

The Bamboo Tea Whisk in Japanese Tea Tradition

Voltaire Cang

Chado – the Way of Tea, otherwise known as the tea ceremony – is well known as a symbol of Japanese culture.[1] It belongs in the élite company of *ikebana* (flower arrangement), Kabuki theatre and sumo wrestling, which are frequently referred to by Japanese and non-Japanese alike as unique cultural representations of Japan. The spiritual development of the practitioner is the ostensible goal of these traditions, and for *Chado*, the way through which this goal is achieved is deceptively simple:

> [The Way of] Tea is naught but this;
> First you heat the water,
> Then you make the tea.
> Then you drink it properly.
> That is all you need to know.[2]

This poem is attributed to Sen Rikyu (1522–1591), a former merchant from Sakai in Osaka who is generally acknowledged as the official founder of *Chado*.[3] His poem is taught to practitioners of the tea tradition to help them achieve its aim, as well as to have them learn, or at least be able to ponder, its essence.

However, even the casual spectator of *Chado* will immediately realize that this supposed aim requires the participants, the host and guests, to act out a series of complicated moves that appear to follow rules which are not always obvious. Any spectator of the ritual will also observe that many utensils are required in its performance. These utensils include those for serving the tea, such as ceramic tea bowls, lacquered tea caddies, bamboo ladles, tea scoops and water containers, as well as those not directly related to the tea service but needed for the tea room setting, like the hanging scrolls, flowers in vases or baskets and containers for incense, among others.

Many of the utensils are specific to the *Chado* tradition and are rarely used outside its context. Nonetheless, almost all of them may be substituted for more everyday items whenever the prescribed ones are difficult to procure. Hence, breakfast bowls may be used instead of the usual tea bowl, or silver spoons instead of the bamboo tea scoop.

There are, however, two elements in *Chado* that cannot be substituted by anything else. First, there is the tea itself. *Chado* always uses powdered green tea, or *matcha* (*matsu*=to rub/grind, *cha*=tea). This distinctive type of tea is made from freshly picked, young tea leaves that are steamed first and dried immediately to retain their colour then ground to a fine powder in stone mortars. It is distinct from other types of tea in that it is prepared by whisking, not infusing or steeping it in hot water. *Matcha* is the only type of tea used in *Chado*.

The Bamboo Tea Whisk in Japanese Tea Tradition

The second indispensable element is the bamboo tea whisk, or *chasen* (*cha* = tea, *sen* = whisk). Tea in *Chado* is regularly served in either of two ways: thick, with a consistency similar to rich espresso coffee; or thin and frothy, like cappuccino. In both cases, *matcha* is suspended, not dissolved, in hot water, a condition that is easily achieved through the use of the bamboo whisk with its numerous tines. A *chasen* with eighty or more tines is said to be ideal for making the thin, frothy type of *matcha* tea, which may be whipped up in mere seconds.

The bamboo tea whisk's primary role in *Chado* is widely acknowledged; websites and media articles frequently speak of the *chasen* as the most important utensil in the Way of Tea. Such a role may well be taken for granted too often, however, as the *chasen* is hardly mentioned in scholarly literature. Although it is perfunctorily described, often in passing, in a few of the extensive academic studies on the Way of Tea tradition, none of these studies have dealt with the *chasen* specifically. As for studies outside those devoted to the Way of Tea, very few papers have attempted to study the *chasen*; such studies mainly deal with its history, and are available only in Japanese. This paper, perhaps the first of its kind in English, constitutes a preliminary study of the bamboo tea whisk in the context of the Japanese tea tradition. It aims to provide a background and prolegomenon for research on this most important of implements in the Way of Tea.

Material and method of production

All *chasen* are made from bamboo, as it is considered the most ideal material for mixing *matcha* for several reasons. One is bamboo's flexibility. When shaped into tines, the material bends against rather than pierces the bowls in which the tea is made, protecting the bowls that are in many cases unique and very costly vessels, even works of art. Bamboo is also durable, so the whisk retains its shape despite vigorous and constant use. (Although durable and long lasting, in the past, and sometimes today, new whisks were mandatory at every tea gathering; after each event, used whisks were disposed of even if they remained in perfect shape.) Moreover, after bamboo is dried and processed into whisks, it does not give off any odour or taste that would affect *matcha*; neither does it absorb other smells or flavours.[4]

At first glance, the *chasen* looks like a sculpted shaving brush about ten cm tall. A closer inspection reveals that all of it, including the handle below the node and the finely curved, hair-thin tines on top, is shaped from a single, slim bamboo cane. The size of the whisk, the number of tines (most have between 60 and 240), and other specifications are exactly determined according to the type of tea to be made and the venue of the tea gathering. Different schools and lineages of *Chado* also have unique requirements for the size, colour and shape of the whisks.

The *chasen* looks like something only very skilled craftspeople can make because it is. Its production usually involves a single person from start to finish, and generally follows an eight-step procedure:

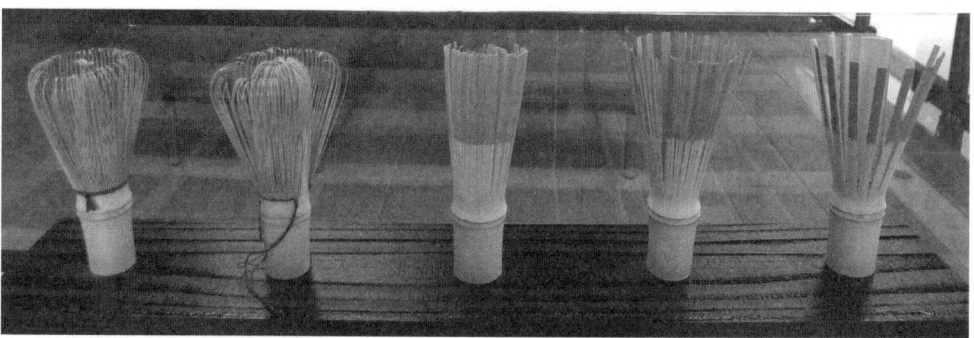

Figure 1. The stages of chasen *production. (Photograph by the author)*

1. First, bamboo that has grown to the appropriate size is harvested during late autumn and winter. These are de-oiled in boiling water, wiped free of dirt, and bleached in the winter sun, when the air is at its driest, for around one month. They are subsequently cut into shorter lengths and matured further in storage for two to three years.
2. Matured bamboo is selected and cut to the desired length of the whisk based on the position of the node. The skin above the node is stripped, and the cane (or culm) that remains is split into sixteen (or twelve, eighteen, twenty, or twenty-four, depending on the size of the final product) preliminary, crude tines. A splitting knife is inserted into each tine to separate the outer wood, which eventually becomes the actual tines, from the inner layer, which is removed.
3. Each tine is split further into an even number of thinner tines, half of which will form the outer layer or rim of the whisk and the remaining half the inner, bunched layer. The tine count always refers only to the outer layer, so that the typical eighty-tine *chasen* actually has 160 tines in all. To make the eighty-tine *chasen*, then, the preliminary tines (the initial sixteen) have to be split evenly into ten thinner tines each (totalling 160), half for the outer and half for the inner layers.
4. The tines are dipped in hot water and the inner bark is whittled off, as the tines are thinned towards the tip. The tips are often curled inward: The degree of the curl is dictated by the conventions of the *Chado* school and the type of tea (thick or thin) for which it is to be used.

Figure 2. A completed chasen.*(Photograph by the author)*

5. The tines are smoothed and planed (chamfered) one at a time. This is an essential and very important process, as it prevents powdered tea from sticking to the tines when whisking the tea.
6. The tines are then divided into the two layers. The outer layer is extended out and forms a ring around the inner layer, which is bunched together in the centre. A thread is woven once around the outer layer to secure its shape, and twice around the inner layer to keep it separate and also to fortify the base of the tines.
7. A thin bamboo spatula is used to adjust the threading and push the inner layer further inward, in order to fix the final shape and size of the whisk.
8. Final adjustments are made to ensure that the tines are of even length and curve, and that the gaps between them are equal. The final product, a fully handmade piece of bamboo art, is then boxed, ready for sale and use.

Chasen's status in the Way of Tea tradition

As a *Chado* implement, the whisk belongs to the category of bamboo utensils that includes ladles, tea scoops, flower vases and baskets, among others. Except for the *chasen*, bamboo utensils have been produced by a single family of bamboo craftsmen, the Kuroda lineage, which has been accredited as the main supplier by the major schools and families of *Chado* since the sixteenth century. The Kurodas are part of a select official group of 'ten craftsmen families' whose products are considered the standard implements for use in the tea tradition.[5] These families include the makers of *raku* ceramic bowls (Raku family), iron kettles (Onishi family) and lacquer ware (the Nakamuras).

The official crafts families form a union not unlike that of an accredited crafts guild; they are the purveyors to the major schools of almost all the necessary implements required in the practice of the Way of Tea. Although they had been constantly supplying *Chado* schools with their products from the time of Sen Rikyu, they became the ten official suppliers only relatively recently, around the middle of the eighteenth century. The heads of the major *Chado* schools (Rikyu's descendants) had seen fit to standardize many aspects of the tea tradition, including the tools of the trade.[6]

However, despite producing every other bamboo implement for *Chado*, the Kuroda family does not make tea whisks in their workshop. Of all the implements in *Chado*, only the *chasen* is not supplied by one of the ten craftsmen families. The Kurodas rely on other bamboo craft products such as tea scoops and vases for the majority of their production and, consequently, their income. For whisk production, the family defers to the *chasen* makers of Takayama, a small town in Nara Prefecture. Today, in this quiet town where *chasen* have been traditionally manufactured, 90 per cent of all bamboo whisks produced in Japan are made.[7]

There are several reasons for the absence of this most essential of bamboo utensils from the Kuroda workshop. Bamboo vases, baskets, ladles and tea scoops for *Chado* fetch much higher prices than tea whisks, so it makes good business sense to concentrate more on manufacturing higher-earning products. Despite its relatively cheaper price, the *chasen* requires more time, not to mention skill, to make; hence its cost performance is much lower than the other bamboo implements. (A professional *chasen* maker is said to be able to make only ten whisks in one day.[8]) Whisks are also more troublesome to make. Vases and scoops, for example, may be fashioned in different ways depending on the qualities of the raw material, while the *chasen* must be crafted into a precise and specific size and shape. And while other bamboo products can be fixed easily when, for instance, a careless cut is made in the material, this is not the case for *chasen*. One bent or broken tine immediately renders it useless.

Early development

However, the absence of *chasen* from the workshops of the accredited crafts families is also due to more significant factors than the lower profit potential and the hard work involved in its production. The most important is simply historical. That is, the tea whisk has the oldest credentials among all the tea implements, bamboo and otherwise.[9] *Chasen* were already standard implements for the ritual serving of tea in Buddhist temples and other places when they were appropriated for use in *Chado*. Tea whisk production existed in Takayama long before the Way of Tea itself was established as a ritualized art form.

Takayama is also well placed geographically. It lies within the triangle formed by Nara, Kyoto and Osaka, three of Japan's most important cities in the early modern period (from the sixteenth century) when the *Chado* tradition was also established and fully developed. This geographical position made the town a natural conduit for the supply and transport of raw materials – invariably including bamboo – and finished products to these major city centres.[10]

Hachiku bamboo (*Phyllostachys nigra* f. *henonis*), the species considered most suitable for tea whisks, also grows plentifully in Takayama. Mature *hachiku* have narrower canes, making them easy to transform into handles, and their skin can be stripped easily and split into thin strips. *Hachiku* also have short internodes, so that more whisks may be made from a single cane.[11]

Despite these advantages, the first *chasen*, or at least its prototype, was not a Takayama invention. Bamboo 'tea stirrers' were already made in China and other parts of Japan before Takayama monopolized the industry. The first reference in literature to such stirrers is found in China's *Treatise on Tea* written by Song Dynasty Emperor Huizong in 1107.[12] The section that prescribes the proper method for preparing tea offers the following advice:

> The bottom of the cup should be deep and somewhat wider. A deep bottom allows the tea powder to rise up for suspension in the liquid, so that the milky froth is readily produced. A wide bottom allows the stirrer to be moved freely in a circular motion, so that there is no interference.[13]

The Bamboo Tea Whisk in Japanese Tea Tradition

In this passage, the character for 'stirrer' in Chinese is the same one used for *sen* in *chasen* in the Japanese. However, these early stirrers from China were more likely in the form of a brush made of several thin strips of bamboo tied together at one end of a short cane.[14] This type of tea implement eventually found its way to Japan, where it developed into its present form and came to be used exclusively for *matcha*. The custom of drinking powdered tea, though Chinese in origin, has since disappeared in China. In Japan, due mainly to *matcha*'s central role in *Chado*, it has survived into the present day.

Chasen appears in Japanese literature from the late Kamakura period (late thirteenth century), and the earliest drawing is found in an illustrated scroll from 1351, the *Bokie kotoba*, from the Honganji Buddhist temple in Kyoto.[15] Buddhist temples in Japan were the earliest consumers of powdered tea drinks, as it was found useful as both medicine and meditation aid; then, as now, it was said to prevent drowsiness. And it was a Buddhist priest, Murata Shuko, born in Nara near Takayama, who is frequently credited today with creating – or at least commissioning – the first *chasen* and promoting its use in the tea ritual.

Shuko (or Juko) (*c.* 1422–1502) had developed a ritualized 'cold and withered aesthetic' style of serving tea in his temple.[16] This style was said to be his reaction against the more flamboyant tea gatherings that were common in his day, which were essentially tea parties that involved the consumption of large amounts of food and alcohol as well as tea.[17] Shuko's spare style of serving tea was subsequently transmitted by his followers, and their followers in turn, eventually reaching Sen Rikyu, himself a student of Zen, three generations later.

While he was the head priest of Shomyoji (Jodo sect) temple in Nara, Shuko became acquainted with a fellow priest, Sozei, who was the second son of the warrior lord of the neighbouring castle town of Takayama. Sozei's family patronized the bamboo industry that was a major source of income for many of Takayama's samurai families at the time. It is assumed by several historians (and disputed by others) that it was to Sozei that Shuko turned to for help in producing a whisk that he could use to make the *matcha* tea that he was already serving in his temple.[18] Sozei, through his personal connections with the bamboo craftspeople of Takayama and perhaps through his own skills as well, was able to create the first *chasen* prototype based on Shuko's request.

No historical record confirming this collaborative relationship between Shuko and Sozei has been found. However, it is indeed plausible that such a relationship existed, not the least because of the two individuals' high-ranking professional roles as Buddhist priests in neighbouring parishes in Nara during the same period. There is also an official account of Shuko offering a set of bamboo tea whisks to the Emperor Gotsuchi (1442–1500) in Kyoto; these *chasen* were described as having been made in the workshops of Takayama in the period when Sozei and his family were administrators of the town and its bamboo industry.[19]

Shuko later left Nara to pursue studies in Zen Buddhism in Kyoto. (Shuko would eventually leave his own Buddhist sect and become a Zen priest.) In the capital city, he promoted his ascetic and esoteric style of serving tea, bringing his Takayama-made whisks with him.

Zen's deep influence in the Way of Tea is evident even today. For example, *Chado* teaches the importance of the concept of the present moment, or the 'eternal now', and its underlying 'four basic principles of harmony, respect, purity, and tranquillity'.[20] These concepts are central to *Chado*; they also dictate the way the tradition is practised, as they are also expressed in the ritualized movements and in the choice and use of tea implements. The *chasen*, for instance, is used not only because it is the most efficient tool for whisking powdered tea and hot water into a delicious froth, but also, and perhaps more importantly, because of its symbolic aspects. Bamboo has long been a symbol of purity in Japan, and its use as material for the whisk and other implements is not unrelated to the 'basic principle' of purity mentioned above.[21] The practice of discarding *chasen* after each tea gathering is based on the same principle: the new *chasen* is unblemished; in this case, the emphasis on purity trumps any concern for wastefulness.[22]

While Shuko and succeeding generations of his followers were establishing the tea ritual, Japan was being unified by a series of political strongmen, Oda Nobunaga (1534–1582), Toyotomi Hideyoshi (1536/37–1598) and Tokugawa Ieyasu (1543–1616). These most famous of Japanese warlords also became practitioners of the fledgling tea tradition, as well as passionate collectors of prized tea utensils. As connoisseurs, they recognized the significant role played by the *chasen* makers of Takayama, and they supported the whisk industry of the town.

Upon assuming power, Nobunaga wrested the administration of Takayama from its castle lords and confiscated their lands, but he permitted the local (non-landed) samurai families to continue producing *chasen*. He had realized that Takayama *chasen* were already unmatched in their technical and design qualities, a level reached through continuous development of the techniques of the craft by generations of whisk makers.[23] These techniques had been kept strictly secret from outsiders through *isshi soden* (literally, one child, one inheritance), the cultural practice that ensured Takayama's monopoly on making the best *chasen* in the country.

Isshi soden is a term frequently used to describe the teaching style in many Japanese arts and crafts traditions, including *Chado*. Under this system, the master – in most cases the male patriarch – hands down the secret methods of the art or craft to only one disciple, his appointed heir. Such was the case for the Takayama *chasen* makers: Throughout upheavals in the Nara political landscape and the breakup of family networks in later generations, this style of transmission of techniques continued until the twentieth-century postwar period in Japan.[24] Some families in Takayama still continue to practise it today.[25]

Nobunaga's successor, Hideyoshi, was another devoted student of *Chado*. He once held a now-legendary tea gathering in the grounds of the Kitano Tenmangu temple in Kyoto in 1588, with more than 1000 participants coming from all over the country. At this huge event, guests and record keepers noted that Takayama makers offered 100 *chasen* to be used for the occasion.[26]

By the time the Tokugawa shoguns were entrenched as leaders of Japan in the early eighteenth century, thirteen families of *chasen* makers in Takayama were officially appointed as purveyors of tea whisks to the shogunate.[27] This appointment would enable Takayama *chasen* to become the de facto standard whisk favoured by the élite, including the Imperial household and the rest of the aristocratic and priestly nobility. They became the most coveted among bamboo tea whisks in Japan, and consequently elevated the status of their makers in Takayama, particularly the purveyor craft families. The appointment also saw the further entrenchment of *isshi soden*, as the system helped assure the continuity of the families and their monopoly of the techniques as well as the corresponding income from their craft.

The period in Japanese history when Tokugawa shoguns ruled the country corresponds to the Edo period (1603–1868), which is also the time when Japan was largely closed to foreign contact. This period of isolation resulted in a great flourishing of local arts and traditions; many of the art forms that Japan is famous for today, including *Chado* and *ikebana*, were developed into distinct traditions during this time.

Recent development

The Tokugawa regime ended with the so-called 'Meiji Restoration' of 1868 and the beginning of the Meiji period (1868–1911), which is particularly notorious for the Japanese people's ardent embrace of Western culture and civilization – in education, clothing styles, government systems, architecture and so on – to the detriment of Japanese ways and traditions. *Chado* initially suffered along with the other Japanese art traditions; in particular, it suddenly lost the patronage of the former ruling class (the Tokugawas and their network of ruling samurai families) through the abrupt change of government. However, the leaders of the Way of Tea schools managed to have their tradition introduced into the school curricula, especially in women's schools, as it was considered good training for etiquette and deportment.[28] This resulted in *Chado* emerging from its background in the Japanese modern period as a Zen-based ritual for spiritual development involving mostly men, into its present incarnation, a tradition still based on Zen but engaged in by an overwhelming number of women mainly as etiquette and deportment lessons.

Chasen today

Chado's development and continuing popularity was good for Takayama, and the town's specialization in the production of *chasen* has served it well, sustaining it for most of its modern history. In recent years, though, it has experienced setbacks that are poised to threaten its long, unique role in the tea tradition in Japan.

One threat is economic: some businesses in China have recently succeeded in producing whisks similar to those made in Japan using Chinese bamboo and cheap labour. Although the material is flimsier and the workmanship less precise, the whisks sell well because they are less expensive and look the same as the Takayama-made *chasen*, at least to the untrained eye. Chinese-made *chasen* are not as durable, either, but they are more than functional – the tea looks and tastes as good as the ones whipped with locally made *chasen*. The workshops of Takayama are understandably worried, and some have taken to the Internet to voice their concerns regarding, and opposition to, this foreign (Chinese) threat.[29]

Another threat is even more pressing: like the rest of Japan, Takayama is an ageing society with falling birth rates, and many of the *chasen* craft families are finding themselves without successors. One generation ago, there were 50 workshops in the area; there are only 23 today.[30] The thirteen official purveyor families during the Tokugawa era increased to sixteen in the Meiji period, only to dwindle down to but three in 1997.[31] These families, however, branched out into sub-family networks, forming the present Takayama community of *chasen* workshops.

The ways in which Takayama is coping with these threats is a subject well worth intensive discussion and analysis. It will be meaningful, not to mention important, to continue to investigate the prospects for Takayama and its singular product, the *chasen*, in a future study.

Notes

1. Practitioners prefer the term *Chado* or *Sado* [*cha*/*sa*=tea, *do*=way] to refer to what is commonly called the 'tea ceremony' in English. They are said to 'dislike' the rendering of their practice as a 'ceremony' due to the ritualistic and religious connotations of the term. See Takeshi Watanabe, 'Breaking Down Boundaries: A History of Chanoyu', in *Tea Culture of Japan*, ed. S. Ohki (New Haven, CT: Yale University Art Gallery, 2009), p. 47. This paper, by a Way of Tea practitioner, uses *Chado* interchangeably with the Way of Tea, and avoids the term 'tea ceremony'.
2. Soshitsu Sen XV, *Tea Life, Tea Mind* (NY: Weatherhill, 1979), p. 79.
3. Japanese names appear in the traditional order, e.g., family name (Sen) followed by given name (Rikyu).
4. Nancy Moore Bess, *Bamboo in Japan* (Tokyo: Kodansha, 2001), p. 80.
5. Conventional translation of *Jisshoku* [*ji*/*ju* = ten, *shoku* = craft/work], as the families are referred to in the Way of Tea tradition.
6. Isao Kumakura, 'Waza wo tsutaeru kiseki no shudan' [A Phenomenal Group of Emissaries for their Art], in *Senke jisshoku* [Ten Craftsmen Families of the Sen Family] (Tokyo: Sekai Bunkasha, 2012), p. 43
7. Asako Miyasaka, 'Artisans Hand Down Tea-whisk Tradition', *Asahi Shimbun*, 28 May 2010. <http://www.asahi.com/english/TKY201005270376.html> [accessed 5 May 2013].
8. 'A Weighty Tradition', *The Association for the Promotion of Traditional Craft Industries*, 2009 <http://kougeihin.jp/en/crafts/introduction/bamboo/2915?m=cu> [accessed 15 April 2013].
9. Asao Kozu, *Chanoyu to Nihon bunka* [Way of Tea and Japanese Culture] (Kyoto: Tankosha, 2012), p. 104.

10. Yasuo Miyakawa, 'Evolution of Bamboo Craft and Metamorphosis of Tea Whisk Production Area', *Bulletin of the Graduate School of Social and Cultural Studies, Kyushu University*, 4 (1998), p. 71.
11. Bess, p. 35.
12. Masao Kikawa, 'Chasenjo take seihin no keifu' [Genealogy of *chasen*-shaped bamboo products], *Aichi Prefectural Center for Archeological Operations Research Bulletin*, 1 (2000), p. 60.
13. Ronald Egan, 'Huizong's Tea Manual: A Discourse on Tea from the Daguan Reign Period', *Food and Culture at Court Conference*, UCLA, n.d. <http://evc.ucla.edu/conference-papers/food-and-culture-at-court/Egan> [accessed 15 April 2013].
14. Kikawa, p. 59.
15. Kikawa, p. 60.
16. Theodore Ludwig, '*Chanoyu* and Momoyama: Conflict and Transformation in Rikyu's Art', *Tea in Japan: Essays on the History of* Chanoyu, ed. P. Varley and I. Kumakura (Honolulu, HI: University of Hawaii Press, 1989), pp. 71–100 (p. 79).
17. Soshitsu Sen XV, *The Japanese Way of Tea: From its Origins in China to Sen Rikyu*, trans. by V. Dixon Morris (Honolulu, HI: University of Hawaii Press, 1998), p. 129.
18. Miyakawa, 'Evolution of Bamboo Craft', p. 71. See also Fukutaro Nagashima, '*Takayama chasen ga kataru sado no rekishi* [History of the Way of Tea as Told Through the Takayama *Chasen*]', *Takayama chasen no okori* [The Emergence of the Takayama *chasen*] (Osaka: Naniwa Linden Books, 1998), p. 9.
19. Miyakawa, p. 71.
20. Sen, 'Tea Life', p. 13.
21. Bess, p. 23.
22. The same practice is also associated with Shinto purification rituals. See Jennifer Anderson, *An Introduction to Japanese Tea Ritual* (Albany, NY: State University of New York Press, 1991), p. 188.
23. Miyakawa, p. 72.
24. Tango Tanimura, 'Takayama chasen nitsuite' [On the Takayama *Chasen*], in *Takayama chasen no okori* [The Emergence of the Takayama *Chasen*] (Osaka: Naniwa Linden Books, 1998), p. 34.
25. Miyasaka.
26. Miyakawa, p. 72.
27. Tanimura, p. 34.
28. Paul Varley, 'Chanoyu from Genroku to Modern Times', *Tea in Japan: Essays on the History of* Chanoyu, ed. P. Varley and I. Kumakura (Honolulu, HI: University of Hawaii Press, 1989), p. 189.
29. See <http://www.chasen.jp/history>.
30. Miyasaka.
31. Tanimura, p. 35.

Trench Fare: Cooking under Fire, France 1914–1918

Kyri W. Claflin

Feeding the troops was a priority for every combatant nation during the First World War.[1] For the French, like the others, securing proper food for fighting men was a principal consideration when making provisioning policies that affected civilians. A crucial consideration in the planning and management of military meals was maintaining what we may call Frenchness. Cuisine is one of the practices by which we connect to and express group identity. In wartime, the daily confirmation of shared identity through food and cooking provided points of contact to keep French soldiers connected to the idea of the nation, to the sense of belonging to French tradition, and to home.

The First World War was a period of intense nationalism, and this was often expressed through the medium of food. French standards in cooking and eating, whether assumed or stated to be superior, were prominent themes in French wartime nationalism. The culinary trope was particularly pronounced in the discourse of cultural superiority. Ridiculing food habits called attention to the uncivilized character of the enemy. For the French gastronomic community writing during the war, German crimes against humanity occurred both on the battlefield and at the table. According to the French the Germans recklessly disregarded human life, and their cooks were, no less, assassins of innocent fruits of the land. In a 1915 article entitled 'Barbarians at Table', one contributor to the professional culinary journal *L'Art culinaire* wrote that, 'Germans are notoriously preoccupied with quantity rather more than quality. Whoever has lived or worked in hotels with a cosmopolitan clientele has been in a position to notice this. There is little importance to what is on the menu, however badly prepared, provided it is on the table at the correct hour.' The author continues, '*La cuisine est un art bien français, qui est inné chez nous.*'[2]

Wartime writers pursued the theme that the Germans were jealous of the French gift of *la bonne chère* – taking pleasure in good food and wine – even if they did not have the capacity to truly engage in it.

From the beginning of the war, the Paris daily newspapers demonstrated indefatigable interest in reporting on the horrible things the Germans had been reduced to eating due to the effects of food shortages caused by the allied blockade.[3] There was outright glee over the German K-bread (*Kriegsbrot*, or war bread) made with five to ten per cent potatoes (even worse, it was rationed): reporters remarked that this was evidence of the enemy's 'kulinary' barbarism.[4] The French, Parisians particularly, believed that keeping white, pure wheat bread on the table signalled their superiority.[5] Such articles demonstrate what may be a natural tendency toward *Schadenfreude* in such circumstances, as well as what Priscilla Ferguson calls the 'politics that lurk behind the culinary'.⁶ The politics of the culinary operated in the theatre of war as well as on the home front. And so, by contrast, the provision of good French food itself was important to keeping the troops' spirits shored up and essential in reinforcing identity and traditions that each Frenchman was believed to embody by virtue of his belonging to the nation.

This paper focuses on two wartime projects of Prosper Montagné (1865–1948) to get a glimpse into the material culture of military cooking and eating. These projects help us understand ways that food and culinary objects facilitated a positive connection between the soldiers and the nation. Montagné is known as a Paris restaurateur, cookbook author, and the first editor of *Larousse gastronomique* (Paris, 1938). One of his many passions included helping to improve the quality of wartime food for both civilians and soldiers. This paper focuses on two examples of his wartime culinary activities that bear on his devoted interest in the food of the troops on the Western Front. The first is a cookbook and the second is an innovation.

Manuel du bon cuistot et de la bonne ménagère (1918)

Montagné published a book in 1918 entitled *Manuel du bon cuistot et de la bonne ménagère*. As the title indicates, the primary purpose of the recipes in this book was to help the army cook, called a '*cuistot*', which is a shortened form of military slang for cook, *cuistancier* (derived from the word for male cook, *cuisinier*). When the recipes were collected for the book, having been originally published in Montagné's regular column in the *Army Bulletin*, housewives (*ménagères*) were appended to the intended audience. The word '*ménagère*' means more than simply a housewife; it is typically used in reference to a working-class and/or a lower-middle-class housewife. The *ménagère* is included, says the introduction, because these recipes are economical, which is what women needed: after four years of war the cost of foodstuffs in France had risen at least 200–300 per cent. It isn't clear what housewives were supposed to do with recipes calculated to serve 50 or a 100 men. The home cook may have been an afterthought for broadening the book's audience. However, throughout the war, the categories of troop food and food suitable for working-class families were couched as interchangeable.

While Montagné created the structure of the book and wrote some of the recipes, army cooks themselves had contributed quite a few of the recipes. Through these formulas, *cuistots* shared clever ideas and tricks of the trade that they had learned during their wartime cooking experiences. Similarly, many of the wartime recipes in *L'Art culinaire* were created in front-line and home-front chef collaborations, in addition to menus and recipes that the *poilus* sent in to the journal. (The word *poilu* is slang for a French soldier. It comes from the word for hair (*poil*), because being hairy was associated with masculinity. I use it because it underscores that the soldiers we are talking about here were by and large the rank and file troops and non-commissioned officers (e.g. corporals), not higher level commissioned officers, who usually ate together separately from the soldiers.)

Figure 1: A military bakery. Not far from the Western Front, the military constructed bakeries to supply bread to be sent up to the poilus *fighting in the trenches.*

Figure 2. Soup's on, 1914. A line of cuisines roulantes, *or rolling cookers, near the Western Front being used by the* cuistots *to prepare meals for the soldiers.*

Cooking under Fire, France 1914–1918

Bon cuistot was intended for cooks near the front lines of trench warfare as well as in the encampments further to the rear of the army zone. Montagné had visited army kitchens (*cuistances*) and he remarks in the introduction that the material conditions military cooks are working in are hardly easy. He writes that, 'They will have to strive to overcome difficulties without number in order to be able to serve their comrades food as good as the circumstances will permit.'[7] Montagné says that the foodstuffs delivered to them by the military *Intendance* (Supply Group) and the foods that the troops buy for themselves are good in quality and variety – actually, he writes 'as good *as possible*' [my emphasis]. The army supplied each man with a daily bread ration of between 600 and 750 grams; 300 to 350 grams of meat (this had been reduced from an early war high of 400 to 500 grams per day); dried legumes averaged around 250 to 300 grams per week; potatoes varied from 900 grams per man per week up to 2.3 kilos; the amount and selection of green vegetables varied quite dramatically, as did fruit. Rice or pasta were at times substituted for vegetables. Wine was rationed at a minimum of half a litre per day, but whenever possible twice this amount was distributed; men were also given *eau-de-vie* (six centilitres per day), coffee and sugar. Troops purchased preserves, jams, chocolate, cheese and more wine in army cooperative stores and in village markets.[8] Families sent parcels of foods (foodstuffs to be cooked and prepared items), alcohol, warm clothing and other necessities. One wife in the Dordogne sent her husband a package containing two rabbits and some cooking fat so that he could prepare the meat in the style of his home region. She sent a bottle of wine, too. During the war the French postal service handled an astonishing 200,000 packages daily.[9]

Cuistots lacked a lot of ingredients that they would have had access to on the home front, such as seasonings, condiments and many other things that normally allow the home cook to enhance the flavour of dishes. Montagné says that the material conditions of cooking in the encampments are somewhat rudimentary, even after four years of improvements. In a 1918 meeting of the Commission Sanitaire des Pays Alliés, the French delegates reported that there had been 'real progress' in the area of army cuisine as cooking classes had been made available to *cuistots*.[10] And finally, the *cuistot* must at times provide meals in dangerous places. Montagné stresses that the military cook must realize that what he feeds the troops will also give them courage and strength to continue the fight.

Regardless of the rustic conditions in which a *cuistot* worked, Montagné opens his cookbook in traditional French culinary fashion, with the stocks, the *fonds de cuisine*. He passes through *roux* and other liaisons on his way to sauces. I think this is just more evidence that stocks and sauces are incontrovertibly at the heart of what makes French cooking French, war or no war. What comes next in the book is also a feature of French cuisine that makes it identifiable whenever you smell or taste it – the traditional condiments and seasonings (e.g. aromatic herbs, shallot, garlic) that contribute to the distinct French flavour profile. It would hardly be a cookbook of the era without a list of the necessary *batterie de cuisine*, or kitchen tools. The equipment consists mostly of different size pots and covers and mess-kit type containers (*gamelles*) that four men can eat from as well as individual *gamelles*. The text proceeds to the *mise en place*.

For the benefit of *cuistots* and troops on the move, a number of the recipes are suitable for the *cuisine roulante*, which was a rolling kitchen or rolling cooker similar to Alexis Soyer's Crimean War field kitchen invention of the 1850s.[11] This piece of equipment was of great importance in feeding troops, and it was pressed into service again at the beginning of the Second World War in 1939. The *cuisine roulante*, constructed of sheet-iron, held two or four deep wells for large pots and a space for coal or wood fire underneath. The larger ones had an oven as well. All of the French ones I have seen are on wheels, while British field kitchens are often free-standing. Soyer's Crimean illustrations show both kinds. Depending on its size, a small cooker could probably be manoeuvred by a couple of soldiers. Most were hooked up to be pulled by a horse with a bench seat for the driver.

A corporal of the Eighth Army wrote to Montagné that he had fed his unit for five months in the woods using only a two-cauldron *cuisine roulante* without an oven. For breakfast he made soup and beef which he simmered slowly for never less than three hours. For the evening meal he made braised beef *à la 'roulante'* with rice, pasta or potatoes. Montagné lists fourteen beef dishes that work well in the *cuisine roulante*, six braised mutton dishes and four pork dishes. All are ragouts, braises or something similar. Long cooking techniques were necessary for the second-quality cuts of meat the Army supplied. Occasionally, unforeseen events could happen to foil even a good system. The 280th Infantry was passing through a village in northern France when a shell landed on their *cuisine roulante*, seriously injuring four cooks. One soldier wrote: 'nothing to eat that day'. They marched eight hours on nothing but a cup of coffee.[12]

While on the move, sometimes one soldier would be chosen by his comrades to cook for the group, although he was not necessarily a *cuistot*. Hopefully he might have had some culinary training or ability in his civilian life. Montagné supplies suggestions such as improvising the flavour of soups with wild field herbs common to northern France. There are two recipes for escargots sent in by soldiers; I like to imagine this would have been an opportunistic meal after the *poilus* had stumbled upon a cache of snails, nursed them along for a few days until they had released their impurities, and then prepared a great Burgundian feast to celebrate their good fortune (according to the recipe 100 escargots will serve five or six *poilus*).

The cookbook includes ideas, with illustrations, for improvising field kitchens, i.e. cook stoves and ovens. Instructions say to position two or four stones on the ground on which the cook would place the cooking pots high enough to build a fire underneath. Louis Barthas's war notebook attests that this method worked handily for his squad's '*habile cuisinier*', who assembled stones into a row of squares to accommodate multiple pots for the daily soup.[13] Montagné suggests that alternatively the cook can dig a small trench in the ground to contain the fire and use the surrounding ground to position and support the pots at the correct height. These two solutions are particularly recommended if the group is only going to be in one place for a short time. Montagné is enthusiastic about the ingenuity of the *cuistots* and how much improvement he has seen since the beginning of the war. One elaborate design involves two perpendicular trenches dug so that there is an intersection. Pots are placed on the banks over the trenches on four sides; at the intersection there is a chimney constructed of empty food cans that directs the smoke from the fires up and away from the cook.

Soldiers moving through the countryside of northern France were often billeted in a village. There might be a grocery store still operating selling wine and other items; soldiers could borrow equipment from women in the town (Montagné suggests this); troops might even luck into an abandoned house with a real kitchen and other comforts of civilian life. Infantry soldier Barthas writes that his group was lodged for a short time on a farm where they were not at all welcomed. The residents 'refused to lend us some utensils, such as plates, pails, frying pans, to supplement our cooking equipment.'[14] A group of soldiers in the novel by Henri Barbusse, *Under Fire*, come upon a village where they are to spend several nights. They rent a barn belonging to a couple who do this to make up for income lost to the events of the war and the corporal is forced to haggle over the price of everything they want to use. Of the greatest importance to the group is that they will have a table and chairs for their meal, referring to the barn as 'our new dining room'. They fill up with food and wine while 'savouring the pleasure of enjoying it sitting down'.[15] Eating hot food at a proper table in the midst of total war signifies that they are still civilized men.

The easiest type of ration to send with men on the move was canned beef, which had earned the epithet '*singe*' (French for monkey) in the earlier Moroccan campaign. There are a number of recipes in *Bon cuistot* for this lowly ingredient. Auguste Escoffier developed some that were published in *L'Art culinaire* as well. The goal was to help *cuistots* create the greatest variety of preparations and tastes possible with this one less-than-ideal foodstuff. There are, unsurprisingly, recipes for sauces (e.g. *Sauce indienne*, a curry-flavoured sauce). Boiling the contents of the can in seasoned water makes a bouillon. Vegetables may be cooked in the bouillon. Then the meat, vegetables and bouillon are separated and served like a rough *pot-au-feu*. *L'Art culinaire* devised a fairly ingenious onion soup recipe using bouillon made this way and then adding the one vegetable most reliably on hand.[16] One army cook devised a recipe for stuffed cabbage using canned meat. *Cuistots* who sent these recipes to Montagné were clearly pleased that they could make a decent French meal from *singe*. The military did try to limit the amount of canned beef in the soldiers' diet, which ideally featured a lot of fresh-killed meat. Troops in fact had far too much meat in their diets, causing a panoply of digestive ailments.[17] But that story is to be saved for the Oxford Symposium on Wretched Diets.

Montagné writes that when troops are ordered to move to the front or take up a new position each man should be able to cobble together a meal for himself. Men carried

Food and Material Culture

Figure 3. Poilus *cooking. A group of soldiers have set up an impromptu kitchen in the cellar of a partially destroyed building.*

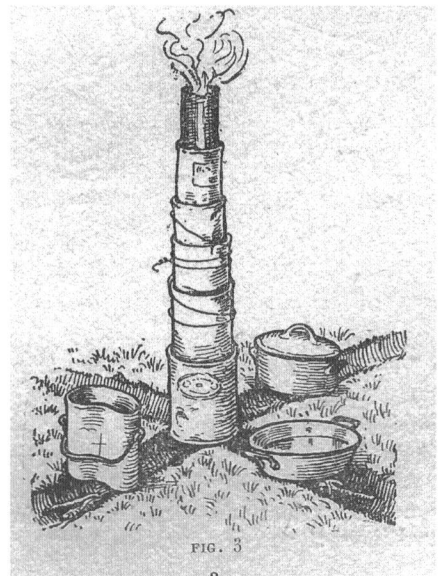

Figures 4 & 5. Débrouillardise. *Two illustrations from* Bon cuistot *showing very clever ways to cook while camping away from more orthodox equipment. These cookers could be made of any scrap metal the* cuistots *could find.*

some food rations and a small ration of cooking fuel. While the book touches on troops cooking on the front lines, novels and diaries suggest that frequently there was not much to work with by way of ingredients or heat sources in the trenches. One soldier wrote to his wife in the winter of 1916 that during the 60 hours it took his battery to dig into their position they had no hot food whatsoever.[18] The trenches, at times, were not an appetizing environment either, penetrated as they often were with the stench of dead men and bloated horse cadavers that could not be removed from 'no-man's land' (the area between the trenches of the opposing armies) until a temporary truce was declared for this purpose.

What is different in the *Bon cuistot* cookbook – different from the regular army cooking manuals and the home-front wartime cookbooks – is that Montagné has established and put into print an on-going dialogue between himself, a renowned chef, and army cooks. A *cuistot* who was a chemist in civilian life, for example, was no doubt grateful for some culinary guidance.[19] But beyond that Montagné's writing created a human connection as well. Like the articles in *L'Art culinaire* during the war, food talk in this community of cooks, male cooks, was about being in the club and being in this ordeal together. True, Montagné nominally included housewives, and *L'Art culinaire* similarly notes that some of the simple and economical recipes for *cuistots* are appropriate for the working-class table; yet these references to women, who are outside of the chef brotherhood, are fleeting. We might go so far as to say that, in many ways, this cookbook is about male bonding in wartime.

Bon cuistot is also about equality, the great chef and the *cuistot*, their recipes together on the same playing field with no distinction as to one being better than the other, and all contributions are credited. Someone who had spent time near the front lines and in army camps, as Montagné did, would know that this is precisely what *cuistots* and *poilus* needed, just as much as they needed to be cooking and eating as Frenchmen. Montagné evokes in this book a community of equals, an imagined community of French male cooks. This cookbook was one of the ways in which people in this community were talking to each other.

With this publication, Montagné created a vehicle for infusing the troops with Frenchness, a booster shot of national identity in the form of traditional recipes and food talk, and a sense of being connected to the larger communal effort, which was, after all, saving the French way of life from those 'Barbarians at the table'.

Plats cuisinés – Système Montagné

During 1917, the third year of the war, Montagné proposed a novel culinary idea to the French military. He suggested setting up a central army kitchen to produce large numbers of what he called '*plats cuisinés*' for the troops. *Plat cuisiné* meant essentially a pre-cooked meal, perhaps an early proto-type for today's military MREs ('meals ready to eat'). *Plats cuisinés* were intended to replace the canned meat rations for troops in the trenches and other places where getting hot food was difficult.[20] The meals could also be eaten cold when necessary. Montagné mentions his *plats cuisinés* in the *Bon cuistot* cookbook and briefly notes how to prepare them in the field. I'll return to this below.

A central kitchen of Montagné's design was set up just outside Paris to make *plats cuisinés* for the army. Also called the experimental kitchen (*la cuisine d'essais*), the central kitchen was likened to a 'sort of military gastronomic laboratory'.[21] The 1300 square metre space was located in a compound of military buildings on an island in the River Seine that also housed an army bakery (at least there were bread ovens according to a schematic drawing of the facility).[22] Thirty male cooks prepared the main (meat) part of the meal and twelve female workers prepared the vegetable garnishes. They cooked with ten pots, each with a capacity of 300 litres, on a wood-burning stove. In twenty-four hours the central kitchen could produce 16,000 portions of *plats cuisinés*.[23] Each portion (one *plat cuisiné*) was one meal and included half the daily meat ration of 350 grams. The soldier's second meal, even if it were another *plat cuisiné*, was supposed to have the other 175 grams of meat.

The components of each pre-cooked meal were made up in moulded loaves of seven rations, wrapped in parchment paper, and bundled together in small crates containing two of the loaves. They were delivered up to the army zone in trucks. To prepare them the loaves were heated on low heat with a little water added to reconstitute them. The loaves could also be sliced into seven sections and heated individually. Vegetables, such as carrots or lentils, might be incorporated with the meat. If vegetables were a separate garnish, they were pre-cooked with agar-agar, which acted like a gelatin that dissolved when the vegetables were heated with a little water. Separate vegetable portions could also be made into soup. Because soldiers often did not eat the vegetables, they were increasingly included with the meat and sauce. Other components of *plats cuisinés* were pasta and rice, neither of which was popular. Rice, in particular, was not typical in French cuisine (aside from sweet dishes), and the soldiers' refusal to eat it was legendary.[24] Moreover, when home cooks made rice, the preference was for the best quality Carolina rice. The military purchased low-quality rice from colonial Indochina, which became sticky and mushy when cooked.[25] Potatoes were not used in the pre-cooked meals because they tasted terrible when reheated.[26] Because *plats cuisinés* were introduced near the end of the war, they were only on the *poilus*' menu for a short time. Afterwards, they continued to be made and were sold in municipal grocery shops and consumer cooperatives as a low-cost, quick working-class meal.

In the foreword to *Mastering the Art of French Cooking*, Julia Child wrote that the French are most pleased with a 'well-known dish impeccably cooked and served'. While for *cuistots* the impeccable part was near impossible, the recipes for trench fare discussed in the previous section were at least a representation – or simulacrum – of well-known dishes of French home cooking that could impart to soldiers taste memories of home and tradition. So it was as well with the *plats cuisinés*. The most common prepared meals were *Boeuf bourguignonne, Boeuf fermière, Boeuf à la mode, Boeuf braisé, Boeuf à la bourgeoise, Estouffade de boeuf aux haricots* and *Boeuf aux lentilles*. Other meals that were said to be popular included *Tripes à la mode de Caen* made from white offal and *Paté de foie* made of red offal.

What Montagné created both in the cookbook and with *plats cuisinés* is comfort food (i.e. 'well-known dishes'). Of course the military must feed the soldiers something they will want to eat, which is to say familiar foods. However, the psychological effect of these types of dishes should not be minimized for men living amid destruction on such a massive scale. Barbusse writes about spare moments in the trenches: 'Letter-writing time is the moment when we are most and best what we were. Several of the men abandon themselves to the past and the first thing they speak about is food.'[27] This was a mechanized war, a greatly dehumanized war. Wounded soldiers, once recovered, were sent back to the front, sometimes to the same area, as many as three or four times.[28] The scale of death and the bodily violence from shells and shrapnel that the living witnessed caused tremendous psychological damage to all but the most hardened of men. Comfort food, regional French cuisine, women's cooking – all interchangeable terms for these dishes – would have offered, at least sometimes, moments of respite and escape to, as Barbusse says, 'what we were' in the way that Marcel Proust's famed taste of the madeleine cookie dipped in tea conjured up intense memories of Combray, the village of his childhood home.

Notes

1. My thanks to Jeri Quinzio for reading and commenting on an earlier draft of this essay.
2. H. Heyraud, '*Les Barbares à Table*', *L'Art Culinaire*, December 1915, p. 18, 'Cooking is really a French art that is innate in the French people'.
3. The Gallica website of the Bibliothèque Nationale de France has digitized most of the major Paris newspapers for every day of the war. They can be accessed at gallica.bnf.fr.
4. Many writers substituted 'k' for 'c' whenever possible to mockingly Germanize non-German words.
5. This point has been analysed extensively in the books of Steven L. Kaplan.
6. Priscilla Parkhurst Ferguson, *Accounting for Taste: The Triumph of French Cuisine* (Chicago: U Chicago P, 2004), p. 127.
7. Prosper Montagné, *Manuel du bon cuistot et de la bonne ménagère* (Paris: Librairie Chapelot, 1918), p. 1.
8. *Revue d'hygiène et de police sanitaire*, no. 40 (1918) 581. Men shopped in villages and in the cooperative shops that were set up at the rear (about fifteen miles from the front) where the stationary bakeries, cattle parks, and abattoirs were located.
9. Martha Hanna, *Your Death Would Be Mine* (Cambridge: Harvard UP, 2006), p. 58.
10. 'Alimentation des Troupes', *Revue d'hygiène et de police sanitaire*, no. 40 (1918) 582.
11. According to Dan and Jan Longone, the French army developed something slightly different from Soyer's Crimean field kitchen that was based more on Denis Papin's '*Digester*', or pressure cooker. The Longones write that the US Army may have had something similar to the French version during the American Civil War. Dan and Jan Longone, 'Camp Cookery in the American Civil War: The Florence Nightingale and Alexis Soyer Connection', in *Public Eating: Proceedings of the Oxford Symposium on Food and Cookery 1991*, ed. Harlan Walker (London: Prospect Books, 1992), p. 187.

12. Louis Barthas, *Les carnets de guerre de Louis Barthas, tonnelier, 1914–1918* (Paris: La Découverte/Poche, 2003), pp. 156–57.
13. Barthas, *Les carnets de guerre*, p. 107.
14. Barthas, *Les carnets de guerre*, p. 107.
15. Henri Barbusse [1916], *Under Fire* (New York: Penguin Classics, 2004), pp. 67–68.
16. *L'Art culinaire*, 'Recettes diverses pour accommoder le boeuf de conserve autrement appelé "le singe" (terme militaire)', December 1915.
17. Rachel Duffett details the similar plight of rank and file soldiers in the British Army in her book *The Stomach for Fighting: Food and the Soldiers of the Great War* (Manchester: Manchester UP, 2012).
18. Hanna, p. 87.
19. Samuel Chamberlain joined the American Field Service in France to drive an ambulance. He was attached to Section 14 of the army and this unit's cook had been a chemist before the war. Chamberlain wrote that from 'dubious cuts of beef' and some vegetables the crafty cook created a classic *pot-au-feu*. Favorite 'standbys' were *poule au pot*, *navarin* and *boeuf à la mode* 'accompanied by great platters of *pommes frites*'. *Etched in Sunlight: Fifty Years in the Graphic Arts* (Boston: Boston Public Library, 1968), p. 7.
20. 'Cuisine Centrale, d'après le système Montagné', [n.d. 1918?], Archives de Paris (AP) Series DR7 box 341 (Conseil Municipal de Paris).
21. 'Proposant la création d'une cuisine centrale d'essais dans le gouvernement militaire de Paris', n.d. AP DR7/341.
22. 'Petit atlas des batiments militaires – Etablissements de l'Ile St-Germain à Billancourt, Plan d'ensemble', n.d. AP DR7/341.
23. 'Suite au rapport de l'officier d'administration de l'Inspection Générale des Cantonnements sur sa visite de la cuisine centrale d'armée'. AP DR7/341.
24. Erica J. Peters, 'Indigestible Indochine: Attempts to Introduce Vietnamese Food into France in the Inter-war Period', in *Empire and Culture: The French Experience, 1830–1940*, ed. Martin Evans (New York: Palgrave, 2004), p. 93.
25. Lauren Janes, 'Selling rice to wheat eaters: the colonial lobby and the promotion of *Pain de riz* during and after the First World War', *Contemporary French Civilization*, vol. 38, no. 2: p. 185. Doi: 10.3828/cfc.2013.9.
26. 'Installation de la cuisine centrale, rapport de l'officier d'administration Vrel', n.d. AP DR7/341.
27. Barbusse, p. 38.
28. Stéphane Audoin-Rouzeau and Annette Becker, *14–18: Understanding the Great War*, trans. Catherine Temerson (New York: Hill and Wang, 2002).

The Significance and Symbolism of Sugar Sculpture at Italian Court Banquets

June di Schino

The Renaissance, the golden age of the table in Italy, heralded the birth of Italian gastronomic literature and created a position of unparalleled culinary hegemony in Europe. The banquet feast resembled *il giardino delle delizie,* the garden of delights, with the most spectacular exhibition of opulence imaginable. Lavish trappings abounded on walls hung with fine damasks and splendid tapestries often depicting banquet scenes. The *credenza* presented a sumptuous multilevel showcase of glittering silverware, rock crystal bound with gold for precious wines resplendent as jewels and elaborate delicacies nestled in lustrous polychrome majolica. The table became a spectacular stage for all the arts: music, dance and poetry contributed to create a feast for both the spirit and the palate, exemplified by the banquet of 796 dishes served to Charles V in Rome.[1]

Clearly the complexity of the convivial ceremony required new techniques and innovative professions known as *offitiali della bocca: lo scalco,* the grand supervisor, and *il coppiere*, the cupbearer, but perhaps prominence should go to *il trinciante*, the carver, an extraordinarily theatrical figure who performed an acrobatic act with a formidable range of knives. He would dextrously slice, cut and chop all manner of foods in the air – a suckling pig, an artichoke, a pike, even an egg. If he carved on a plate, he would be instantly recognized as second-rate, a judgment that would reflect on the prince's prestige.

Every detail was invested with ingenious creativity, like the art of napkin folding, which required snowy white linen to be carefully starched and ironed, then folded a 1000 times to form a myriad of fantastic castles, towers, unicorns and lions.[2]

The table was pure theatre. One gorgeous display was described as 'Arches, Castles, Galleries and works of art which put Nature to shame'.[3] The key word to this wealth of imagery was *magnificence*. Such carefully choreographed construction was part of a strategy to enthral the guests caught in a web of enchantment that proved yet another expression of princely power.

The chronicler Sforza Pallavicini describes the food of these banquets as 'an extraordinary array of dishes dressed with pomp and splendour, luxury and wealth'.[4] During the Renaissance the concept of taste was completely different. Today we have a clear-cut distinction between flavours; generally the meal begins with the savoury and ends with dessert. During the sixteenth and seventeenth centuries, however, flavours blended together in an intense stratified adventure of the palate. Elaborate dishes were prepared with subtle alchemy redolent of exotic lands, with spices like grains of paradise, musk, cinnamon and amber. Sweet and sour flavours were infused with aromatic vinegars, figs and candied fruit. Particularly fashionable at the time were rose and other perfumed waters, which left a distinct flowery aftertaste.

However sugar was considered the pinnacle of all palatable pleasures, the most sublime edible substance. Exceedingly costly, it was the icon of aristocracy, and sugar sculpture represented the peak of all ephemeral art forms. In Italy sweetness became a princely passion that represented both wealth and power: for over two centuries sugar defied all sumptuary laws to reign supreme on the table.

The significant role of Venice brought about sugar importation in many forms: loaves, cones, crystals and fine powder are recorded in such archival documents as the *Statuto Capitolare Nauticum*, which dates back to 1255. Venetian merchants and *speziali* sold numerous varieties of sugar, perfumed with violets or roses, coloured with vegetable dye and cochineal and shaped in various sugar loaves called *caphetino, campanon* or *panon* and pyramids called *babilonia*.[5] Indeed, sugar came in many varieties and forms:

> *Muscabà*: ordinary, low quality sugar;
> *Zucarum album*: plain granulated sugar;
> *Tre cotte*: refined quality sugar;
> *Fioreton*: high quality, very white sugar;
> Fine white powdered sugar from Cyprus;
> Crystallized white sugar from Candia;
> *Capheton, campanin, panon*: rounded sugar loaves;
> *Babilonia*: sugar pyramids;
> Sugar cones to be grated;
> *Rosatum e violatum*: rose and violet perfumed sugars;
> Coloured sugars in saffron-yellow or spinach-green.

Sweetness, the epitome of tastes, took on at least five different roles in cuisine. Sugar was ever-present in all dishes: meat, *pasticcio*, fish, soup, vegetable and *biancomangiare*. Renaissance gastronomic literature abounds with recipe collections in which we continuously read *et zuccaro sopra* – sprinkled with sugar on top to form a crystalline crust.[6] Platina da Cremona, the first librarian of the Biblioteca Apostolica Vaticana, wrote in *De Honesta Voluptate et Valetudine*, 'There is no dish which cannot be improved with sugar.'[7]

Sugar was used to glaze all kinds of foods, while *pasticci* and tarts were bedecked with strips of trellis work. Banquets ritually opened with a galaxy of sweetmeats such as sugared strawberries, marzipan delights, fine *mostaccioli* and *pisani biscottini*. And banquets concluded with a wonderful array of almond paste desserts, candied fruits, jellies and a surfeit of '*confetti*' – sugar-covered comfits ranging in size, coating and filling.[8] In fact, during the Italian Renaissance the art of confectionery, which involved the mastering of boiling sugar, was perfected.

Sugar Sculpture at Italian Court Banquets

Figure 1. Bartolomeo Platina, De Honesta Voluptate et Valetudine, *frontispiece.*

Sugar had unexpected uses. During religious festivities, despite the prohibition of meat, illusory foods like giant hams would appear on the table made from pink marzipan masquerading as the real thing! Everything on the table could be embellished with sugar. Even small game birds were dressed up in shirts of shiny pistachio sugar paste. Sometimes sugar was moulded into architectural supports such as the two giant sea horses which upheld a majestic *mortadella* cooked in wine presented at an official banquet offered by Clement IX.[9] The table was also exquisitely decorated with beautiful sugar flowers and gilded festoons.

Fortunately, the well-documented feasts of the Venetian *Serenissima Repubblica* recount the profuse presence of sugar both in cuisine and as a showpiece. For example, to honour Francesco Maria della Rovere, duke of Urbino and chief captain of the Venetian troops, the *Compagnia della Calza 'I Valorosi'* offered a sumptuous banquet in July 1524 with numerous allegories and symbols made of sugar representing both states and ambassadors. According to Marin Sanudo's detailed diary, the states, including Urbino, Milan and Mantua, were presented in a triumphant chariot of finely wrought gilded sugar – 'un caro triumphal lo presentò al Signor duca di Urbin, et una aquila di zucaro all'orator cesareo, et un bisson a l'orator dil duca di Milan, et uno altro presente a l'orator di Mantoa'.[10]

Sugar represented such a socially predominant phenomenon that a special new repast composed exclusively of sweetmeats and confectionery was invented to satisfy the insatiable desire for all things sweet. This was known as the exceedingly fashionable *'collazione'* at the time. One splendid example was the elaborate reception the *Compagnia della Calza 'I Reali'* held to honour Francesco Sforza, Duke of Milan, in October 1530. Before the dinner at Palazzo Ducale, there was a public parade through the city of the extraordinary sugar showpieces carried by 460 *servitori*. The populace was astounded at the vision of the gods like Venus, Neptune, Mercury and others made of sugar that appeared in giant silver bowls, and it was *cosa molto dilectevole da vedere*.[11]

The continual ostentation of '*saccaromania*' caused the Venetian Senate to act against 'the sinful excesses' of princes and prelates, and, on 8 October 1562, a sumptuary law was promulgated forbidding confectionery and sugarcraft during weddings as well as public and private receptions.

Significantly, this law was completely ignored, as the wealthy and powerful were not willing to renounce sugar, a status symbol *par excellence*. In June 1564 the *Compagnia della Calza de Gli Accesi*, organized a most sumptuous *collazione* close to the Rialto bridge, where over a thousand servers carried more than a 1000 trays of gilded sugar statues, figures and superb sweetmeats made of pistachio, cinnamon, *pasta reale*, candied melon, peaches, figs, pears and apricots to the eagerly waiting guests.

Such extravagance had begun much earlier. Archival documents show that, in May 1493, a '*collazione*' was organized by the *Compagnia della Calza de 'I Potenti*' at Maggior Consiglio di Palazzo Ducale in honour of Beatrice Este, wife of Ludovico il Moro where 300 marvellous compositions of sugar decorated with gold leaf were presented to the enraptured guests; the sugar sculptures depicted a multitude of figures such as the pope, the prince and duke of Milan with their respective heraldry and St. Mark (patron saint of Venice), followed by many other fantastic figures in a *bellissimo spectaculo*.[12]

A similar spectacle followed the presentation of the melodrama *La Vita Umana*, written by Giulio Rospigliosi for Christina of Sweden, featuring a spectacular selection of 76 different varieties of confectionery, preserves, candied fruit, vegetables and *biscottini*.[13] The documents recorded in the Vatican secret archives indicate that the artist Giovan Francesco Grimaldi, who created the scenery, did not receive complete payment despite his letters of protest, yet the exorbitant accounts for the dulcet delicacies were paid in full, a discrepancy that clearly shows their social significance.[14]

Further testimony of the importance of confectionery comes from the accounts of the banquet offered by Giovan Battista Borghese to Innocent XII in 1687.[15] In the open countryside near Carroceto, an extraordinary fake setting made out of wood and plaster with painted cloth for frescoes, was erected to host a grand luncheon for the pope and his retinue of 400. This film set-like setting required four months of organization and transportation of foodstuffs, materials and professionals from Rome. The confectionery included candied fruit, cinnamon, aniseed confetti, preserves, '*folignati*' (from the city of Foligno) and quince jelly; accounts indicate the cost amounted to the enormous sum of 131.42 *scudi*.

The era between the sixteenth and seventeenth centuries represented the triumph of sugar sculpture. Not by chance are these known as *trionfi* in Italian, to evoke the element of superiority by emulating the victorious conquests of Ancient Rome. Sugar showpieces signified social prestige and frequently involved the design of great court artists and the expert workmanship of the *credenziere*. Sugar sculpture symbolized wealth and power, and it was imbued with many forms of subtle communication – political, allegorical and religious. This much neglected aspect of the table, one of the finest forms of decorative art, deserves recognition for its aesthetic value, expert craftsmanship, social and economic significance and wide ranging symbolism. It probably originated with the early presence of *sotleties*, or subtleties, fashioned according to the theme of religious occasions, such as the coronation of an archbishop of Canterbury in 1433, or as heraldic representations at medieval feasts. The objective of these creations was to induce contemplation of subjects either inspiring or pertinent to the event. The earliest documentation I have found dates back to 1474 with the theatrical marriage Sforza-Aragona when the Sun brought down *la cucina*, the hot dishes, from heaven, and the Moon descended with *la credenza*, the cold dishes. For the wedding celebrations of Roberto Malatesta and Isabetta in Rimini (1475) the *Tempio Malatestiano* was reconstructed in sugar and presented with horses, cupids, elephants and sugar statuettes.[16]

Great artists such as Leonardo da Vinci, Giulio Romano and Tiziano paid homage to the table, and Jacopo Sansovino and Gian Lorenzo Bernini dedicated their talents to these exceptional centrepieces. For an official dinner at Casa Falconieri offered by the Spanish Embassy on 30 October 1668, Pietro da Cortona designed all the *apparati effimeri* for the table which were subsequently sent as special gifts to important guests. For the wedding celebrations of Maria de'Medici and Henry IV of France in Florence in 1600, the groom was not present, but his image arose from the table as an impressive equestrian *pièce montée* created out of sugar by Pietro Tacca, chief apprentice to Giambologna. Subsequently the artist also sculpted a bronze equestrian statue of the king that was sent to Paris but destroyed in 1703.

After the death of Giambologna, his successor Pietro Tacca became the grand ducal sculptor and was commissioned to create 40 fantastic *trionfi di zucchero* for the 1608 marriage celebration of Cosimo de Medici to Maria Maddalena, arch-duchess of Austria.[17] He became an outstanding artist of his time, and among his numerous achievements were several works on Hercules which appealed immensely to Ercole d'Este.

While serving the Estense court, Cristoforo da Messisbugo wrote an early masterpiece of gastronomic literature that abounds with references to sugar sculpture, such as twelve naked Moors created out dark *mostaccioli* biscuits with their private parts covered with foliage and twelve similarly attired Moorish ladies.[18] Messisbugo's account ledgers were richly illustrated with the 25 labours of Hercules, which must have closely resembled the versions in sugar which graced his patron's table.[19]

A collection of drawings of the Estense court reveals interesting information about various table sculptures in sugar and gelatine.[20] These depict several subjects such as Neptune slaying a marine monster, an ornamental fountain and a vineyard scene. Attentive reading of the documents concerning these dinners reveals that these showpieces were not created for hundreds of guests, but for ten and even six, showing that even for small occasions in everyday life these exceptional ornaments were deployed.

Figure 2. Drawing of an ornamental centre-piece for the Estense table in sugar and gelatine.

The study of sugar sculpture involves both documentary and iconographic sources. The *relationi* of numerous historical banquets eloquently portray these exquisite masterpieces and offer much information. Authors of gastronomic literature such as Messisbugo, Scappi and Rossetti also provide innumerable examples of *trionfi da tavola*. Antonio Latini excels in *Lo scalco alla moderna* (1692), dedicating a complete chapter to the enormous range of subjects for table sculpture. In just 26 pages, 'Varii Trionfi da mettersi sopra le Tavole' describes 167 ornate showpieces, including, to name just a very few: imperial eagles highlighted in gold; a triumphal chariot on a gold pedestal with figures adorned with coral and pearls; four shepherds in marzipan tending sugar lambs and garlanded nymphs; Alexander the Great on horseback; two giants in combat; a silver whale with gilded sea horses; a snowy white peacock with a gold crown and tail outspread; a chariot full of sweetmeats such as *cialdoncini, ciambeletti*; quince jelly and pasta reale drawn by two turkeys; Abundance with a cornucopia and a sheaf of wheat; America as a beautiful naked maiden with mermaids.

Insight into the sublime character of *trionfi di zucchero* can be gained from various illustrations as well, such as the outstanding representation of the wedding feast of Johann Wilhelm, duke of Jülich and Jacoba of Baden in Düsseldorf in 1585, which depicts the table as a grandiose landscape of castles, towers and cavorting animals while the admiring guests provide a sense of scale.

The drawings of sugar sculpture illustrate their extreme complexity, indicating the enormous difficultly involved in creating these fragile works that required, not only specific knowledge and dexterity, but considerable good fortune. White crystals were magically transformed into a flexible artistic medium for a myriad of inventive figures.

The oldest method of manufacturing these ornaments was to pour molten concentrated sugar syrup into moulds generally made of plaster, terracotta, or wood. It was essential to move the mould around gently to distribute the syrup into all the curves and angles and to tightly bind the parts together for the complete solidification of a successful showpiece. In *Lo Scalco alla Moderna* (1692), Antonio Latini gives a recipe for moulding figures in sugar:

Figure 3. F. Hegenberg, banquet table with castles, coats of arms and sugar sculpture (Dusseldorf, 1587).

> According to the size and shape of the figures that you intend to make, take approximately three pounds of sugar, clarify it, sieve it, then boil it to the point of cassé, taking care the temperature is correct. Prepare a well cleaned and oiled mould and check that there are no openings whatever except on top. Check the mould closes properly and have string ready to bind it efficiently. Hold the mould with the left hand covered with a protective cloth, and with the right pour in the molten sugar taking care to move it around gently. The sculptures must be transparent and hollow inside, hence the mould must be turned continuously to perfectly distribute the sugar. Leave the mould until the substance is perfectly dry and take great care on opening the mould.

The other method involved moulding sugar paste pieces that were often assembled together to form more complex creations. Some details come from Rosselli, a noted apothecary from Florence, who left a series of family documents on confectionery and recipes such as one for making small missals, caskets, cups and vases and similar things such as lutes, shoes and slippers out of sugar:

> Beginning with the paste take white tragacanth, cleaned of all impurities, in the amount required then add a good amount of rose and orange flower water and leave to soak. Sieve carefully and place in a clean bronze mortar and while gradually adding fine white powdered sugar so that the paste increases in size. Then add 4 g of musk for each lb of sugar with the same amount of starch and continue adding fine sugar until the paste is ready. The paste should not be too stiff to avoid cracking and as pliable as dough for maccheroni. To make a missal, a small wooden book mould is required with single sheets of paper, buckles and binding. Once finished, trim well with a knife, leave to dry. Finish all pieces with a fine line of gold, small leaves and arabesques to make it beautiful.[21]

Of primary importance for this method was the use of gum tragacanth, a viscous, odourless, water-soluble mixture of polysaccharides drained from the sap of *Astragalus genus*. When steeped in water, gum tragacanth formed a thick mucilage able to absorb any powdered material such as sugar, transforming it into a pliable, plasticine-like material. This paste lent itself perfectly to creating figures and objects, as it could be sculpted, rolled out thin, finely pleated, fashioned into delicate petals, or pressed into carved moulds to form a cherub's wings, scrolls for columns or limbs for statues. The diverse pieces were carefully assembled to form statues similar to *Cupid, Fortune with a cornucopia* and *Roma sedente* that were created by the artist Rolf Stalberg for the recent exhibition *Magnificenza a tavola: Le arti del Banchetto Rinascimentale*.[22]

Once dry, sugar paste became a fine, whitish material, often decorated with gold leaf or coloured, which was highly appreciated for its ornamental potential. Complex inventions were made by using wire or wooden frameworks to create three-dimensional or multilevel showpieces. My forthcoming book on the art of confectionery at the papal court, *arte dolciaria*, contains numerous rare recipes for creating superb *trionfi* from an unpublished manuscript. There is also one for making sugar paste written by the *credenziere* to Alexander VII, although painstaking research reveals that he copied word for word from an earlier recipe for gum-paste dating back to 1557.[23]

The drawings for sugar ornaments underline their extreme fragility and the finesse of their detail. For *Il Convito* (1693), offered by Francesco Ratta at Bologna, we have superb woodcuts of the single decorative elements and a spectacular circular table of sugar arabesques that surrounded a monumental creation of the continents. Below, large trays of delectable sweetmeats adorn the base. This is perhaps the most breathtaking illustration of a truly awe-inspiring art.

Figure 4. F. Ratta, Trionfo di zucchero from Disegni del convito *(Bologna, 1693).*

Sugar Sculpture at Italian Court Banquets

Such illustrations show why sugar sculpture was considered the epitome of grand hospitality that was so highly valued as a refined form of communication at official banquets. In 1574 Venice received Henry III of France with regal splendour, and during *la festa del Bucintoro* church bells rang, cannons resounded and a procession of 40 gondolas bedecked in blue and gold damask followed the majestic barge. For the exceptional reception at the Arsenale, 'ogni cosa maravigliosa et extraordinaria era di zuccaro': every piece of cutlery, glass and dish on the table was wrought out of sugar to stupefy the king. Francesco Sansovino describes this memorable event in his work *Venetia città nobilissima et singolare* (1581).[24] However an even grander banquet was offered to the king at the Palazzo Ducale, where the *speziale della pigna*, Nicolò della Cavaliera, was commissioned to create over 300 statues in sugar that had been designed by the famous Jacopo Sansovino.[25] These represented both sacred and secular themes with a glorious parade of popes, saints and Saint Mark, patron of the city, accompanied by King David, the doges and the princes. Then the gods of Mount Olympus – Pallas, Hercules, Jove, Mars, Mercury, Pegasus and Diana appeared, followed by dancing nymphs – Fame, Justice, Prudence and Peace and the Seven Virtues. The triumphant moment was the most incredible creation of a crowned queen, regally seated between two tigers that held two crowns with the coats of arms of France and Poland in eloquent praise of the guest of honour. The imposing statue was surrounded by lions, gryphons, eagles and small figures holding bouquets and fruit cornucopias. The king was so enraptured by this astounding exhibition that he immediately commissioned a certain Pietro Vicentino to create 39 superlative works of art in sugar to take back to France, indicating how highly *trionfi* were treasured.

The drawings by Pierre Paul Sévin, a French artist who lived in Rome, recorded *trionfi da tavola* from 1666–68, providing us with exceptional evidence. One illustrates a celebration for Maundy Thursday offered by Clement IX with the papal coat of arms in the centre of the table surrounded by a religious scenario depicting the stations of the cross and the last supper. Two years later the same feast table was dominated by

Figure 5. Sugar sculpture for the banquet of Lord Castlemaine. A. van Westerhout from the drawings of G.B. Lenardi.

an architectural model of Bramante's *Tempietto*, surrounded by *trionfi* of the cardinal virtues. In the most outstanding banquet scene we can admire Pope Clement IX and Queen Christina surrounded by the stunning display of about twenty arabesqued sugar sculptures on the table. Such creations were even celebrated in song – I found an unknown madrigal that extols the virtues of Luigi Fedele, celebrated creator of *trionfi di zucchero* for the queen.

What Christina really loved was the pomp and pageantry, the theatre. The master organizer of the lavish decorations for Alexander VII's banquet to welcome Christina was Gian Lorenzo Bernini. The table drawings of Mercury and Pegasus have been attributed to him and Johann Paul Schor, as was that of the Sun, associated with the phoenix, an alchemical emblem favoured by the queen, who had a medal struck with her profile and a human-faced Sun.

During this period, all-important receptions for foreign monarchs or ambassadors featured a dazzling array of *trionfi da tavola*, usually with of a specific allegorical or political communication. For the banquet offered by Alexander VII to the Venetian Ambassadors in 1660, the table was adorned with a most exquisite sugar sculpture, created by the artist Anthoine Fournier, which emanated a precise diplomatic statement. On one side there was the personification of *Roma Sedente* on the other, *Venezia Sedente*. In the centre was a large statue of Victory with three lions and three wolves, symbols of Venice and Rome respectively, on both sides. Two cherubs bridling a whale, three cherubs holding stars and a tree surrounded by cherubs completed the splendid scenario.

Such extravagance sometimes required more display than possible at a single event. For example, the spectacular banquet offered by Roger Palmer, Earl of Castlemaine and ambassador to Pope Innocent XI in 1686, presents both exceptional visual evidence of sugar sculpture created by the engraver, Arnold Westerhout, and the artist, Giovan Battista Lenardi. In written testimony recorded by John Michael Wright, it is said that the superb display was on view for several days for the Roman nobility to admire the 80 superb sugar sculptures, almost life-sized and 'modelled to the utmost skill of statuary' representing the elements and mythological allegories in praise of James II.

In *Lo Scalco alla Moderna* (1692), which heralds the end of a celebrated epoch, a foldout illustration shows the acme of magnificence at the table. Six superb sugar sculptures frame a glorious Sun Chariot driven by *La Chiarezza*, with Clarity holding the bridle of four rampant lions. The guests were ecstatic to see the golden light emanating from Apollo's shining chariot, which was described as an impressive aura of almost divine beauty.

The table is always a mirror of society. The Italian humanist movement that characterized this era revived classical antiquity, linking philosophical and moral issues in ways that permeated all the arts. Humanism emerged along with a profound enthusiasm for classical studies in an attempt to imitate a world centred on Protagoras' concept that 'Man is the measure of all things'. The return to classical mythology is perfectly reflected at the banquet table where sugar sculptures of the gods Apollo, Bacchus, Venus and Diana paraded around in the golden candlelight creating a highly evocative atmosphere in which the guests perceived a numinous presence:

> Tell me of the highly praised banquet of the gods; where, though the divinities did not dine, there were to be found: the generosity of Jove, the knowledge of Athena, the sagacity of Mercury, the mastery of Vulcan, the richness of Juno in luxury, and everywhere were flowers, perfumes, beauties, delights. A Diana served pheasants, grey partridges, and game birds of every kind, Neptune with oysters and seafood, and finally Saturn brought in the Age of Gold.[26]

Ultimately, we can recognize an archetypal image of the Banquet of the Gods, the Land of Cockaigne, in the scintillating *cosmos* of the convivial ceremony.

The banquet feast is the symbolic form of these two centuries reflected in the dynamic of techniques, the theory of elements, the magic of metamorphosis and the marvellous. Here water is changed into wine, artifice becomes nature and sugar is transformed into sculpture. Sugar sculpture expresses the most eclectic and ephemeral art form of the banquet.

Notes

1. J. Di Schino and F. Luccichenti, *Il cuoco segreto dei papi. Bartolomeo Scappi e la confraternita dei cuochi e pasticceri a Roma* (Rome: 2003).
2. M.M. Giegher, *Li tre trattati* (Padova: Paolo Frambotto, 1639). Cf. E. Garbero Zorzi, *Cerimoniale e spettacolarità: il tovagliolo sulla tavola del principe* (Milan: Bompiani, 1985).
3. C. Sforza Pallavicini, *Descrizione del primo viaggio di Christina di Svezia* (Rome: 1838).
4. Pallavicini.
5. *Speziale alla grassa* was a sort of apothecary that sold spices herbs and sugar
6. B. Scappi, *Opera* (Venice: Tramezzini, 1570).
7. B. Platina, *De Honesta Voluptate et Valetudine* (Ulrich Han, ca. 1475), p. 82.
8. Up to a dozen coats of syrup were needed before the nuts and seeds were satisfactorily encrusted.
9. J. Di Schino, *Tre banchetti per Cristina di Svezia,* (Rome: Accademia Italiana della Cucina, 2000).
10. M. Sanuto, *Diarii di Marino Sanuto* (Stabilimento Visentini Federico Editore, 1879–1902).
11. 'Taza d'argento con dentro cose fatte di zuchoro, alcuni un Cupidine, altri una Venere, molti Neptuno et un Mercurio, et altri altre diverse figure, così de Dei come de homini et de diversi animali', A. Latini, *Lo scalco alla moderna* (Naples: Parrini, 1692), p. 86.
12. 'Prima comparse sopra d'uno asse lo papa, el principe et lo duca di Milano cum le arme loro et quelle de la signoria vostra, poi santo Marco, altre representazioni de diverse cose', P. Molmenti, *La storia di Venezia...nella vita privata...*, vol II (Venice: 1895), p. 498. The letter was written by Beatrice d'Este to her husband Ludovico il Moro.
13. J. Di Schino, *Tre banchetti per Cristina di Svezia.*
14. 528 *scudi* and 81 *baiocchi.*
15. J. Di Schino and F. Luccichnti, *Il viaggio di Innocenzo XII da Roma a Nettuno* (Rome: Viviani, 1998).
16. *La cucina*: hot dishes; *la credenza*: cold foods, confectionery.
17. *Descrizione delle feste fatte nelle reali nozze dei... Cosimo de Medici e Maria Maddalena Arciduchessa d'Austria* (Florence: Giunti, 1608).

18. C. Messisbugo, *Banchetti vivande e imbandigione...* (Ferrara: 1540).
19. Archivio di Stato di Modena.
20. Biblioteca Universitaria Estense Fondo Campori.
21. Stefano Francesco di Romolo Rosselli, *Secreti à Florence* (Florence: 1593).
22. J. Di Schino and M. Cogotti, *Magnificenza a tavola. Le arti del Banchetto Rinascimentale* (Rome: De Luca, 2012.)
23. Alexius Piedemontanus was a pseudonym used by the writer and cartographer; Ruscelli's work has been translated into German, French and English.
24. 'Apparecchiata una bellissima colatione di confettini et di frutti di zuccari, co i cortelli, con le tovaglie, co i piatti et con le forcine fatte di zuccaro' (*Relatione della festa offerta a Henrico III di Francia a Venezia 1551*).
25. John Varriano points out that Sansovino was dead by this time, in *Tastes and Temptations* (Berkeley, CA: University of California Press, 2009). Perhaps the drawings came from his school, as was often the case.
26. Di Schino, *Tre Banchetti per Christina di Svezia*.

Cultures on Ice: Refrigeration and the Americanization of Immigrants in the First Half of the Twentieth Century

Betsey Dexter Dyer and Jonathan Brumberg-Kraus

The introduction of refrigeration in the early twentieth century played a dramatic role in shaping American kitchens, determining thresholds of acceptance of various types of stored foods and framing an American attitude toward 'ethnic' food odours and tastes. That kitchens have refrigerators is assumed in developed countries today, and that refrigeration is essential for safety and health. However it was not always so. We explore here how the emergence and marketing of new technologies to refrigerate foods, especially 'fresh' meats, dairy products, fruits and vegetables, converged with the 1880–1920 influx of US immigrants from eastern, central and southern Europe to become crucial components of social programs to Americanize the new immigrants and of marketing strategies to sell refrigerated foods and electric refrigerators to them.

In 1927 the General Electric Refrigerator Company published a little hard-covered book, *Electric Refrigerator Menus and Recipes*, dedicated to 'the modern American homemaker'. The author, Alice Bradley, was a principal of Miss Farmer's School of Cookery and cooking editor of *Woman's Home Companion*. Miss Farmer's school was also a laboratory for scientific approaches to nutrition and food, the foundation of a growing home economics movement. This book of refrigerator recipes is surprisingly cautious and circumspect. Bradley, born in 1875 without a refrigerator, since the first household model appeared in 1914, seems to struggle with the very idea of what the device is for. In fact 1914 is conservative as a beginning for household refrigerators; the first ten years or so of modern electric household refrigeration were characterized by a leakage of harmful chemicals, the retention of disturbing odours and the need for frequent repairs. By the 1920s, some of the bugs were worked out, and aggressive marketing of refrigerators commenced (Cowen 1983; Nickles 2002). Alice Bradley's book conveys no particular urgency for acquiring a refrigerator. There is no indication that any normal kitchen would be considered non-functional and unsanitary without it. That rhetoric comes later. Rather, Bradley suggests that 'some family food problems and perplexities about entertaining' might be solved. She describes having an electric refrigerator as having 'an Aladdin's lamp and not knowing the right way to rub it' and notes that the 'total sum of its usefulness has not in any way been solved'. One of the family food problems that Bradley offers to solve centres on frozen desserts. One chapter describes preparing blocks of ice both 'plain and fancy'. Two chapters encourage starting meals with frozen salads, cold soups and aspic jellies. Another chapter entices invalids to enjoy food by freezing it; items for the sick include frozen chicken broth and clam juice.

The image conveyed is that a household refrigerator is an elaborate dessert-making machine with some additional highly specialized uses (Bradley 1927; Allen 1926). *Electric Refrigerator Menus and Recipes* also ventures, briefly and cautiously, to consider more basic practicalities. Bradley actually feels the need to ask 'Why a refrigerator?' and then attempts to convince the reader by citing the United States Department of Agriculture. According to the USDA, neither milk nor butter is palatable and safe except maybe in winter when 'nature can furnish you with adequate refrigeration'. Bradley notes that 50 degrees Fahrenheit is a 'danger line' above which bacteria proliferate. Conveniently, the typical temperature kept by early electric refrigerators was about 45 degrees; thus it seemed to be a perfect solution for keeping bacteria in check. (Today we know that cold-loving bacteria decompose food below 45 degrees.) Bradley also suggests that daily shopping trips become unnecessary when meat, fish, fruit and vegetables are chilled. And because fish and meat odours might taint butter and milk, she recommends refrigerator dishes with tight lids.

The various 1920s editions of the *Boston Cooking School Cook Book* (at which Bradley taught) seem to consider refrigeration optional in a typical kitchen (Farmer 1921, 1923, 1926; Fishkoff 2010). For example, butter could be kept, covered, in a cool place and salted to preserve it. Refrigeration was listed as merely one of many ways to preserve food including salting, drying and pickling. Even in 1944, *The Alice Bradley Menu Cook Book* maintained a very short list of what requires refrigeration; all else may be kept in a 'cool' or 'dry and cool' place in a cabinet or pantry.

When making frozen desserts alone was not enough to get refrigerators in most kitchens, a scientific approach turned out to be more successful. To broaden the market, refrigerators had to be heavily promoted using the authority of credentialed experts in white coats. The influential home economics movement provided exactly that. The campaign entailed convincing people that the food at ambient room or cellar temperature eaten by hundreds of generations of their ancestors was in fact unsafe unless kept at the somewhat arbitrary temperature maintained by early refrigerators.

At the time, microbiology was developing into a major topic in biology, driven by the study of disease organisms. As a result microbes became equated with pathogens, and all were viewed with suspicion, distrust and even fear. Fermenting microbes (food preservers and flavour enhancers for millennia) were categorized as food spoilers and even potential pathogens. The American Home Economics Association (named in 1899 and founded in 1909) maintained an objective stance on the serious business of keeping a household, using the latest information from biologists, chemists and sanitary engineers. Soon however, the manufacturers of appliances saw a great opportunity and some home economists succumbed to a much more subjective stance on behalf of particular foods and devices. In the field, whether to remain neutral or to participate in lucrative marketing campaigns became controversial (Zimmerman 2003).

Refrigeration companies quickly hired home economists (often dressed in lab coats) to put a scientific spin on the necessity of refrigeration. The phrasing of refrigerator advertising switched from 'You could make dessert!' to 'You should keep your family hygienically safe from invisible microbes'. 1920s advertising for Kelvinator refrigerators (named for the scientist whose temperature scale included absolute zero) referred to the protection of the 'zone of kelvination'. Even frozen desserts made in a Kelvinator acquired the safe-sounding name of 'kelvinated desserts'. White Mountain refrigerators of the 1920s were advertised as 'scientifically right' (Lifshey 1973; Waggoner 2007).

In 1923 the 'Household Refrigeration Bureau', initiated by the National Association of Ice Industries, hired a biological chemist, Mary Engle Pennington (Stephan 1996; Snodgrass 2004). The ice industry was concerned about perishable foods spoiling while being transported by rail. Pennington helped establish standards for industrial refrigeration to keep foods 'fresh' for weeks. That required a redefinition of the word 'fresh' (Freidberg 2009). Pennington also published 'Household Refrigeration Bulletin' brochures to promote the industry to home economics teachers. Her goal was an unbroken chain of chilled food from stockyard or field to market and then to home refrigerators (Stephan 1996). While long distance transportation of otherwise unpreserved food absolutely requires cold, the interesting extension of the idea was that households should expect their food supply to come from far away and arrive cold, that industrial cold storage ought to continue in grocery stores and even their own kitchens to keep food 'fresh'.

Keeping fresh foods 'fresh' on ice for days or even weeks (as though in a mausoleum) did not seem like a good idea to anyone who shopped daily: it was viewed suspiciously as a scheme to sell old meat, old milk, old eggs, etc. And indeed it was! Refrigeration on this grand scale enabled foods to be shipped from far away in railroad cars and required a project to convince consumers that these foods were not technically 'old'. Rather, after being held for weeks at chilled temperatures, it was 'fresh' (Freidberg 2009; Wilson 2012). This fact is still not obvious to most of the world where food is still local and purchased daily. Throughout the twentieth century, the refrigerator industry was mostly unsuccessful in France, where people chose to shop for fresh food regularly, kept it on countertops, and somehow managed with tiny refrigerators while maintaining admirable good health and a delightful cuisine. Even terminology referring to refrigeration entered the French language with confusion and ambiguity. In an earlier Symposium paper, Kyri Claflin calls the French view 'frigophobia'. Susanne Freidberg notes that the French engineers coined *'frigoriphobie'* to describe the stubborn recalcitrance of their hoped-for buyers (2009: 30). Contemporary chef Marcus Samuelsson describes his Swedish grandmother not trusting refrigeration because she was never sure of how old the chicken really was (2012: 24). In Agatha Christie's mystery, *4:50 from Paddington Station,* Alice notes, after reading about 40 people getting food poisoning at a hotel, 'All this refrigeration is dangerous, I think. People keep things too long in them' (1957: 242). In the early 1900s, a Jewish doctor voiced similar distrust of refrigeration to defend kosher dietary laws on medical grounds:

Meat kept over three days is very rarely used by the Jews, unless the same has been well washed and salted, and then only in exceptional instances and with much misgivings on the part of the consumer as well as the butcher. No such thing as indefinite or prolonged refrigeration or cold storage is permitted, so universally in vogue among Gentile packers and butchers. The meat that comes to the Jewish table is fresh, clean, wholesome, and free from patogenic [*sic*] organisms, in short, it is 'kosher'. (Aronstam 1912: 20–21)

Ironically, food purchased regularly and locally, preserved through traditional methods, does not typically become a teaming culture of pathogenic bacteria: fermenting bacteria prevent pathogens from growing. However food processed far away, handled in great industrial quantities by many middlemen, and transported and stored for weeks could contain pathogens. In fact it would be best held at chilled temperatures and then thoroughly cooked. In his 1906 novel *The Jungle*, Upton Sinclair exposed the unsanitary industrialized meat packing plants that shipped meat all over the United States. Around the same time industrialized milk production in crowded urban dairies (often in dank basements), where cattle were fed garbage, increased the incidence of tuberculosis bacteria in milk. Milk pooled from many such sources, stored in vast quantities, and then distributed long distances requires an unbroken chain of refrigeration. Any negligence around refrigeration endangered the health of the household. So keeping food cold, even at home, became an ethical mandate, no longer a luxury but an absolute necessity (Nickels 2002; Levenstein 1988, 2012).

Inconveniently for marketing refrigerators as ethical necessities, much of the United States was not electrified until the 1930s or even later. Therefore household advice continued to be circumspect. In *The Healthful Farmhouse*, Helen Dodd, 'a farmer's wife', tells us we need an isolated, sunny 'milk room' with a tank of cool spring water (1906: 22–23). The room is depicted with not only without the as-yet-uninvented refrigerator but even without an ice box. The cellar of the farmhouse is described containing the kind of fruits and vegetables that keep well there. Ellen H. Richards, the noted early founder of home economics, wrote the introduction for this book, presumably approving this handling of the milk. Richards was in no position to insist on ice. In 1929, after refrigeration was established and when marketers began appealing to science, the Women's Institute of Domestic Arts and Sciences of Scranton, Pennsylvania wrote *Buying and Preparing Foods: Cookery, Equipment, Selection, and Use of Equipment, Purchase of Foods, Preparation of Foods*. This exhaustive treatment by experts would surely promote a refrigerator in every kitchen! Yet it acknowledged the difference between the electrified cities and the rest of the rural country, and did not tout refrigeration as a necessity but rather as a nice labour-saving device.

Another book, *Dairy Products*, written in 1929 by the same women's institute, develops a different sort of concern. Butter readily absorbs odours. In long-term cold storage it might pick up odours from other foods. Refrigeration might co-mingle the smell of older rancid butter with fresh batches. From the very beginning of household refrigeration design, there was a concession to the special needs of butter. To this day, most refrigerators have a butter compartment where temperatures are supposedly less cold and from which odours are kept. Butter storage still divides families, with some preferring spreadable butter kept on the counter while others prefer cold, hard butter stored in the refrigerator. Such divisions have even spurred development of highly modified, ice-cold yet strangely spreadable butter-like products.

Meanwhile in the 1920s, another branch of the home economics movement strictly defined 'sanitation' to exclude just about everything that was not thoroughly scrubbed, well chilled, and tightly packaged. At the same time, newly-arrived immigrants were transforming American cities. Some initiatives around those arrivals comprised controlling their cuisines (deemed unhealthy) and household habits (deemed unsanitary). Fermented foods, especially odoriferous ones, kept at room temperatures were among the targets of well-meaning social workers and home economists. The refrigeration industry was also quick to see opportunity. Professionalization and the 'science' of homemaking became rationales for sanitizing the habits of immigrants, and insisting generally on a new regime of refrigeration for everyone.

Ellen H. Richards, who had written the introduction to Dodd's book, was a chemist with a degree from MIT. The original name she coined for the home economics movement – 'euthenics' or 'the science of controlled environment' – did not catch on. Richards was particularly concerned with outbreaks of disease and general unhealthy living that could be easily avoided by common-sense sanitation and, most importantly, education (Richards 1912; Hunt 1918). Early twentieth-century America was becoming more heterogeneous with the influx of immigrants, so the times were right for education and reform movements. Indeed a more homogeneous society would not have provided as much impetus for reform, since ordinary customs and foodways taken for granted as 'normal' would be overlooked. Cultural differences stood out, demanding assimilation to some idealized American standard.

Impoverished, newly-arrived Jewish families living in squalid tenements were a favourite subject. In *97 Orchard*, Jane Ziegelman describes some of the conditions: unsanitary foods (at ambient temperature) sold by pushcart vendors were supposedly a leading cause of death among Lower East Side children. According to Bertha Wood, Jews ate highly seasoned food and not enough fresh milk and that is why they were so nervous; Jews ate far too many pickles and other fermented foods which 'renders assimilation more difficult' (1922: 90). Indeed Jewish children were known to spend their precious lunch money on pickles. Other assessments of the stench of Jewish immigrant markets and pushcarts were even harsher. One reporter describes a 'slatternly young [pushcart] woman who had a scarcity of clothing' selling cheese upon which 'it did not require a microscope to detect the mites … for they were large and lively.' The ethnocentric journalist stated he 'received such a shock from the powerful odour thrown out that [I] almost had a spasm. Phew! How that cheese did smell. Yet the long-whiskered descendants of Abraham ... put their fingers in it and then suck them with great and evident relish.' Another 'Times reporter maintained that a "writer might go on for a week reciting the abominations of these people. This neighbourhood ... [is] perhaps the filthiest place on the Western Continent. It is impossible for the Christian to live there, because he will be driven out ... by the dirt and the stench. Cleanliness is an unknown quantity to these people. They cannot be lifted up to a higher plane because they do not want to be"' (Burnstein 1996). Nevertheless, what repulsed some critics attracted some Jews. Even wealthy Jews were observed travelling by chauffeur from Fifth Avenue to the Lower East Side to buy odoriferous fermented herring and sauerkraut.

To help immigrants adjust to their new country, Settlement Houses were established. These sometimes included demonstration or model kitchens (often with refrigerators.) These were laboratories of a sort where immigrants might try the newest ideas in household management and nutrition (with controlled conditions and guidance) (Levenstein 1988: 104–07; Leavitt 2002: 76–82). Not only was the immigrant diet deemed unhealthy and unsanitary but also uneconomical because it was concocted from mixtures of foods purchased from various sources, which 'required uneconomical expenditures of energy to digest': 'one whiff of the pungent air in the tenements or a glance into the stew pots was enough to confirm that the contents must wreak havoc on the human digestive system' (Levenstein 1988: 104). A bland, white-sauced diet with surprisingly large quantities of fresh (presumably chilled) milk was considered superior. What immigrant women living in crowded apartments with no appliances were to do with their new cooking skills was another problem.

Many unforeseen consequences resulted from the campaign to sanitize the foods of immigrant Jews. Refrigeration provided the material circumstances for two significant shifts in first- and second-generation American Jewish immigrant eating habits in the first decades of the twentieth century. According to Joselit and Diner, these were the 'steady irrevocable decline' of *kashrut* (observance of the Jewish dietary laws), and the rise of Jewish restaurants and delicatessens and the Jewish predilection for eating-out (*oyesessen*) (Joselit 1994: 177; Diner 2001: 200). Since neither Joselit nor Diner trace these shifts specifically to refrigeration, it is worth showing how refrigeration in early twentieth-century American food culture shaped American Jewish immigrant food preferences.

Refrigeration of meat made it much less expensive and more readily available than it had been in the new immigrants' countries of origins (Friedberg 2009). For Eastern European Jews, 'where food was sacred for all, but in which scarcities loomed for most [it] was a rare text – novel, poem, short story, personal memoir – that failed to connect the sanctity of Jewish food to the inequitable distribution of resources' (Diner 2001: 147). For such Jews, America's food abundance was tremendously alluring. Diner describes how Jews' particular 'hunger for America' had,

Refrigeration and the Americanization of Immigrants

its roots in Eastern European Jewish foodways ... [which] connected food, sanctity, community, class, and the gendered nature of everyday responsibilities Jews bore to each other. These realities played a shaping role in the migration to America, an act best understood as a search not just for bread, but for *meat* and fish, noodles and soups, and all the sweet stuffs that the less well-off only got only at sacred time. (2001: 176)

In stories and lullabies Eastern European Jews fantasized about America's abundant food, especially meat, as in Leon Kobrin's *Lithuanian Village* (1927): 'on the very sidewalk lay precious things such as I could only wish you could have on your table for the holidays. ... [T]hey eat of the very best here. They don't lack even bird's milk! Roast hens in the middle of the week and so many other dainty dishes that I don't know how to name them' (Diner 2001: 176). In Sholem Aleykhem's lullaby, a mother sings to her child that they'll soon be able to join husband and father in America, 'where as everyone knew, they could have chicken soup and challah in the middle of the week' (Diner 2001: 177). This common conceit of eating holiday foods on weekdays became a reality for new Jewish immigrants that deeply affected their food expectations and preferences. The general accessibility of food outside the home, especially in delicatessens and restaurants,

> complicated the meaning of food to people who had once lived with hunger. ... By eating foods once the reserve of the Jewish upper classes, they engaged in an act of class reversal. The formerly poor started to eat *blintzes, kreplach, kasha-varnitchkes, strudel,* noodles, *knishes,* and most importantly, meat every day. Their once meager cabbage or beet *borschts* now glistened with fat pieces of meat. (Diner 2001: 179–80)

Thus one Romanian Jewish immigrant exclaimed, 'In New York, every night was Friday, and every day was Saturday, as far as food went' (Diner 2001: 180). None of this would have been possible without refrigeration in processing, storage and transportation that made meat inexpensive enough to become everyday food.

Jewish delicatessens, small shops, cafés and restaurants were venues where Jews purchased this plentiful supply of meat inexpensively. Refrigeration played a special role in the production of two staples of these institutions: corned beef and pastrami. Corned beef originally referred to a medieval English way of dry-salting meat, which gave it the consistency of salt cod, and so took hours of soaking and boiling before it was edible. But later, according to Gil Marks:

> in the mid-nineteenth century, artificial refrigeration allowed the substitution of a much weaker salt-water brine, which also contained less sugar that could be used for curing meat any time of the year and produced milder and tender meat. Toward the end of the nineteenth century, central European immigrants in America, including German Jews, popularized [this so-called] *pickelfleisch* made

from brisket … typically flavored with peppercorns and bay leaves, … cured using the lighter brine and the refrigeration method available in America.… Home kitchens and small stores, some called delicatessens, began selling food catering to Jewish immigrants, many of them males who were either single or attempting to save up enough money to bring over their families from Europe. These eateries commonly served the less expensive pickled and cured meats and much of it kosher, between slices of rye bread – the simple dish was a filling meal. Sandwiches were also more portable than plain meat and could be taken home or to work. (Marks 2010: 449)

Marks also suggests that Irish immigrants probably adopted this 'Jewish' corned beef in America as a substitute for Irish bacon. Similarly, '[m]odern pastrami is a relatively recent American innovation – to be precise, it emerged in New York City. As with corned beef, in the late nineteenth century, the advent of artificial refrigeration allowed for the use of a weaker salt brine for curing, leading to the development of a softer form of pastrami' (Marks 2010: 450). These refrigeration-aided curing processes made inexpensive cuts of meat palatable and convenient, especially for immigrant adult males, but also for school children who had neither time nor inclination to eat food cooked at home.

Presumably, it wasn't the refrigeration *per se,* but rather the pungent, aromatic spicing of these cold cuts that made them particularly palatable to their Jewish immigrant clientele. While corned beef tended to be flavoured with peppercorns and bay leaves, pastrami possessed a particularly 'heady mix of spices – including allspice, bay leaves, cinnamon, cloves, coriander, ginger, juniper berries, paprika, pepper, and garlic' (Marks 2010: 450). Jewish immigrants' taste for these spicy, pickled, smoky flavours typical of deli and restaurant food was noted both in the fond reminiscences of their consumers and in the criticisms of well-intentioned nutritionists who sought to 'cure' them of these unhealthy preferences (Diner 2001: 214–19). So on the one hand, we have Alfred Kazin remembering the delicatessen food in his Brownsville neighbourhood as 'our greatest delight in all seasons …hot spiced corned beef, pastrami, rolled beef, hard salami, soft salami, chicken salami, bologna, frankfurter "specials" and the thinner wrinkled hot dogs always taken with mustard' (Diner 2001: 201).

On the other hand, we have Jewish nutritionists in the home economics movement, like Mary L. Schapiro, identifying 'high seasoning' as one of the major 'Jewish Dietary Problems'. She observes 'the limitations of the diet, when unchanged by instruction, are evident. It is inadequately balanced, over-rich, and over-seasoned' (Schapiro 1919). Yet the fact that Mary Schapiro, S. Etta Sadow and other Jewish women themselves embraced 'American nutrition culture' suggests the relations between new Jewish immigrants and the home economics was not as one-sided as it may have first appeared. Indeed Jewish nutritionists like Schapiro and Sadow played an important role explaining Jewish foodways to their Gentile colleagues, and advocated accommodations to

Refrigeration and the Americanization of Immigrants

Jewish kosher rules (like respecting the prohibitions against pork and mixing milk and meat) and tastes for pickles and highly seasoned food over fresh vegetables, in order to be win over their Jewish clients to adopt what contemporary science viewed as more nutritional and hygienic diets (Diner 2001: 214–19). Ultimately, the home economists successfully persuaded many Jewish immigrants to change their diets, ironically at the cost of the very kosher rules for which they urged respect.

The 'steady irrevocable decline' of *kashrut* in this period was made possible by the home economics movement and Jewish deli/restaurant culture, both dependent on refrigeration technology. First, easy access to inexpensive meat enticed many Eastern European Jews to America, and many of those immigrants were already less observant than those who remained (Diner 2001: 158–77). Second, the autonomy of 'rational consumption' advocated by the home economists appealed to Jewish women. 'Rational consumption' that 'embraced the values of sanitation, health, cleanliness, economy, and efficiency [were] hallmarks of new identity, secure points of reference through which to demonstrate that they belonged to this social group' of 'modern *American* homemakers' (Goldstein 2012: 13). *Kashrut* often opposed these values, like making milk part of every meal (especially children's), storing it next to meat in one's home refrigerator or purchasing meat economically (Schapiro 1919; Goldstein 2012: 126). Jewish women organized protests against kosher meat's high cost (Diner 2001: 206–07). Dr Noah Aronstam's defence of *kashrut* on microbiological grounds acknowledges the adoption of home economical values by Jewish homemakers. Jewish women's insecurity about home-cooking may also have weakened attachment to old kosher ways. A running joke in the Jewish community was that Jewish men deserted their wives because of bad cooking (Diner 2001: 215). In any case, home economics culture empowered Jewish woman to make decisions about diet traditionally made by male Jewish authorities.

Finally the options the new Jewish delicatessen/restaurant culture offered Jews to eat-out *(oyesessen)* resulted in new ways to express their American Jewish identity: 'selectively *treyf*' and 'selectively kosher'. As Joselit explains, American Jewish immigrants:

> display[ed] what has [been] called 'selectively *treyf*' behavior, American Jews, as a group, avoid[ing] pork and patently non-kosher food products while vigorously indulging an appetite for chop suey and ballpark hot dogs whose *treyf*-ness was less overt. [Yet] they held on to their affinity for gefilte fish, brisket, and blintzes, chipping away at the identification between 'Jewish' and 'kosher' in the process…. Following the dictates of convenience rather than those of tradition, American Jews became 'selectively kosher' or 'kosher style.' This singularly American Jewish invention[,] … [t]he gastronomic equivalent of ethnicity, 'kosher-style' enabled its adherents to practice kashruth 'without pain or effort' by disentangling food from the traditional restrictions governing its use, a Judaized version of having your cake and eating it too. (Joselit 1994: 172–174)

Refrigeration made these options possible by providing the material conditions for Jewish deli and restaurant culture, and by weakening Jewish immigrants' *kashrut* observance.

However, refrigeration's role in the development of the supermarket and 'big box' stores in more recent decades has had the reverse effect. That these stores now carry kosher meat alongside other foods, including different ethnic foods, has driven most smaller Jewish delis and markets out of business, and has expanded the market for kosher food beyond observant Jews to a much broader consumer base. The consumption of kosher food has become widespread enough to make kosher certification profitable (Fishkoff 2010).

Freezing and chilling have become the preferred way to offer ethnic foods in a modern supermarket. Previously for the Oxford Symposium, we wrote about the emphatic odours of well-fermented cuisines as shibboleths to unite an ethnic group around celebratory foods and distinguish their foods from those of other groups. Cultures of microbes build food cultures in both microbial and sociological senses of the word. So we lament the olfactory contrast between American style grocery stores and open-air markets, traditional delicatessens and small ethnic food markets. A shopping cart gliding down the 'International Foods' aisle in a well-chilled grocery store passes seamlessly through a dozen ethnic neighbourhoods, each occupying a sliver of frozen shelf space. Thus the title for this paper: 'Cultures on Ice'. If all is well (that is, no package or jar broken open) you should smell exactly nothing. Nor should you smell anything in the refrigerated aisle where a selection of more labile ethnic foods (cheeses, sauerkrauts, pickles) may be found, tightly packaged and briskly cold to suppress volatile emissions. A modern grocery store seems to protect us from encountering those intriguing olfactory shibboleths, and maintains an illusion of olfactory neutrality, a uniform harmony or truce of sorts.

When we don't smell food, we forget much of what makes the smell. Microbes. For most of the twentieth century one could scarcely find a grocery store pickle or home-pickling recipe in the United States that acknowledges lactic acid bacteria's role in food preservation (Pollan 2013: 291–305). However, recently in developed countries including the US, there is a popular new movement to revive authentic, ancestral recipes. Pickling with microbes has been cautiously rediscovered; in Sandor Katz's case, not so cautiously. In *The Art of Fermentation*, he envisions a future where 'the refrigeration bubble could burst' (due to a greater need to conserve energy), necessitating a return to fermented foods. Certainly Katz has paved the way with his exhaustive research, writing and speaking on fermentation (2012: 32).

Many modern American and European refrigerators are designed as behemoths crammed full of a couple of weeks' worth of groceries. Yet there are subtle changes in attitude about what must be refrigerated and what is better at ambient temperatures. Internet movements are afoot promoting anti-refrigeration, e.g. Nicola Twilley's post 'The Anti-Fridge' on her blog 'Edible Geography'. Throughout the twentieth century, a wistful nostalgia has developed for the pantry as a keeping place. In *The Pantry*, Catherine Seiberling Pond illustrates her book with gorgeous still-life photographs of foods at ambient temperature. Some of this nostalgia fuels the trend in eating locally and shopping more mindfully and regularly.

Home economists are great list- and rule-makers, yet there has never been a strong consensus on exactly what should be on the list for refrigerator storage besides perhaps fresh meat and milk for the next several days. A refrigerator could hold a special, fragile, invented-for-refrigeration dessert, as it did originally as a dessert-maker. The list is getting shorter. Do not refrigerate most cakes and breads nor root, tuber and bulb vegetables. Both cabbage and apples are 'keepers' according to our ancestors. Keep tropical fruits and vegetables including eggplant, tomatoes, and mangoes in a fruit bowl to be eaten soon. Other fruits like pears, plums, and bananas do not ripen well in the refrigerator. Savoury, salted cured meats and cheeses taste better at room temperature. Eggs fresh from your backyard chickens can stay in a bowl on the countertop. Even last night's stew may remain well covered on the cool stovetop and then brought to a boil before making it lunch the next day. It should go without saying that food already preserved such as condiments, pickles, jams, chutneys and the like belong in pantries. Butter remains a huge dilemma, though a growing Internet presence encourages us all to relax and leave it out on the counter as long as it takes for the family to eat it.

The marketing of refrigeration took many convoluted paths and unexpected detours. We take for granted the ubiquity of refrigeration. Yet without explicit advertising, the new appliance might not have become a necessity. The cultural heterogeneity of the US in the early twentieth century was a perfect storm. Electric refrigeration then evolved its own uniquely American foodway inventions: the delicatessen, corned beef, and pastrami; 'selective *treyf*' and 'selective kosher'; and 'rational consumption'– with the women of the home economics movement leading the way to shape uniquely American immigrant food identities. The technology of refrigeration was the unexpected catalyst.

References

A.C.B. Allen 1926, *The Kelvinator Book of Frozen Delicacies* (Kelvinator Corporation, 1926).
N.E. Aronstam 1912, The Jewish Dietary Laws from a Scientific Standpoint (New York: Bloch, 1912).
A. Bradley 1927, *Electric Refrigerator Menus and Recipes* (General Electric Company, 1927).
A. Bradley 1944, *The Alice Bradley Menu Cook Book* (MacMillan, 1944).
J. Brumberg-Kraus and B.D. Dyer 2011, 'Cultures and Cultures: Fermented Foods as Culinary "Shibboleths", *Cured, Fermented and Smoked Foods: Proceedings of the Oxford Symposium on Food and Cookery*, ed., Helen Saberi (Totnes, UK: Prospect Books, 2011), pp. 56–65.
D. Burnstein 1996, 'The Vegetable Man Cometh: Political and Moral Choices in Pushcart Policy in Progressive Era New York City', *New York History* 77:1 (January 1, 1996) 47-84.
A. Christie 1957, *4:50 from Paddington* (New York: Dodd, Mead and Company, 1957).
K.W. Claflin 2008, 'Les Halles and the Moral Market: Frigiphobia Strikes in the Heart of Paris', *Food and Morality: Proceedings* of *the Oxford Symposium on Food and Cookery 2007*, ed. Susan Friedland (Totnes, UK: Prospect Books, 2008), pp. 82-92.
R.S. Cowen 1983, *More Work for Mother: The Ironies of Household Technology from the Open Hearth to the Microwave* (New York: Basic Books, 1983).

H.R. Diner 2001, *Hungering for America: Italian, Irish, and Jewish Foodways in the Age of Migration* (Cambridge, MA: Harvard UP, 2001).
H. Dodd 1906, *The Healthful Farmhouse* (Boston: Whitcomb and Barrows, 1906).
F.M. Farmer 1921, 1923, 1926, *The Boston Cooking-School Cook Book* (Boston: Little, Brown, 1921, 1923, 1926).
S. Fishkoff 2010, *Kosher Nation: Why More and More of America's Food Answers to a Higher Authority* (New York: Schocken Books, 2010).
S. Freidberg 2009, *Fresh: A Perishable History* (Cambridge, MA: Belknap Press, 2009).
C.M. Goldstein 2012, *Creating Consumers: Home Economists in Twentieth-century America* (Chapel Hill, NC: U North Carolina P, 2012).
C. Hunt 1918, *The Life of Ellen H. Richards* (Boston: Whitcomb and Barrows, 1918).
J.W. Joselit 2013, 'Then and Now, Trying to Demystify Kosher Rites', *The Jewish Daily Forward* <http://forward.com/articles/165230/then-and now-trying-to-demystify-kosher-rites/?p=all> [accessed May 28, 2013].
J.W. Joselit 1994, *The Wonders of America: Reinventing Jewish Culture 1880–1950* (New York: Henry Holt, 1994).
S. Katz 2012, *The Art of Fermentation* (White River Junction, VT: Chelsea Green Publishing, 2012).
S. Leavitt 2002, *From Catherine Beecher to Martha Stewart* (Chapel Hill, NC: U North Carolina P, 2002).
H.A. Levenstein 1988, *Revolution at the Table: The Transformation of the Ameican Diet* (Oxford: Oxford UP, 1988).
H. A. Levenstein 2012, *Fear of Food: A History of Why We Worry about What We Eat* (Chicago: U Chicago P, 2012).
E. Lifshey 1973, *The Housewares Story* (Chicago: National Housewares Manufacturers Association, 1973).
A. Mack 2010, '"Speaking of Tomatoes": Supermarkets, the Senses, and Sexual Fantasy in Modern America', *Journal of Social History* 43: 4 (2010) 815-42.
G. Marks 2010, 'Pastrami', *Encyclopedia of Jewish Food* (Hoboken, NJ: John Wiley & Sons, 2010), pp. 449–50.
S. Nickles 2002, 'Preserving Women', *Technology and Culture* 43 (2002) 693-727.
M. Pollan 2013, *Cooked: A Natural History of Transformation* (New York: Penguin, 2013).
C.S. Pond 2007, *The Pantry: Its History and Modern Uses* (Layton, UT: Gibbs Smith, 2007).
E. Richards 1912, *Euthenics* (Boston: Whitcomb and Barrows, 1912).
M. Samuelsson 2012, *Yes Chef: A Memoir* (New York: Random House, 2012).
M.L. Schapiro 1919, 'Jewish Dietary Problems', *Journal of Home Economics* II 2 (1919) 47-59.
U.Sinclair 1951, *The Jungle* (New York: Harper, 1951).
M.E. Snodgrass 2004, 'Refrigeration', *Encyclopedia of Kitchen History* (New York: Fitzroy Dearborn, 2004), pp. 803–12.
K.D. Stephan 1996, 'Mary Engle Pennington, Food Refrigerator Engineer', 1996 *American Society for Engineering Education Annual Conference Proceedings*.
N. Twilley 2010, 'The Anti-Fridge', *Edible Geography* <http://www.ediblegeography.com/the-anti-fridge/> (2010)
S. Waggoner 2007, *Classic Household Hints: Over 500 Old and New Tips for a Happier Home* (New York: Stewart, Tabori and Chang, 2007).
B.Wilson 2012, *Consider the Fork* (New York: Basic Books, 2012).
P.A. Scranton 1929, *Dairy Products* (Women's Institute of Domestic Arts and Sciences, 1929).
P.A. Scranton 1919, *Buying and Preparing Foods* (Women's Institute of Domestic Arts and Sciences, 1919).
B.A. Woods 1922, *Foods of the Foreign-born in Relation to Health* (Boston: Whitcomb & Barrows, 1922).
Ziegelman, J. 2012. *97 Orchard: An Edible History of Five Immigrant Families in One New York Tenement* (Washington, DC: Smithsonian Books, 2012).
J. Zimmerman 2003, *Made from Scratch: Reclaiming the Pleasures of the American Hearth* (New York, Free Press, 2003).

Shaken, not Stirred: The Story of Mixers and Mixing

Len Fisher, Janet Clarkson and Alan Parker

For once, James Bond got his science right.[1] A Martini should be shaken, not stirred, because the aim is not so much to mix the ingredients as to get them cold through contact with ice.[2] Shaking is much more efficient because it creates a turbulent environment where more of the liquid can come into contact with the ice surface over a given time. But what of other foods – believing, as we do, that Martinis are a food? Why do we shake, stir, or otherwise manipulate them during preparation? How should we do it? What tools should we use to assist us? In this brief survey of gastronomic materials, techniques and gadgets, we examine these three questions in turn, providing a relatively detailed background to these common tasks.

Mixing

Mixing is one of the basic processes in cookery although, as Peter Hertzmann points out in his excellent on-line video 'Stirring Conclusions', cookery students rarely understand just why they are doing it.[3] When we stir the ingredients of a cake batter together, for example, our aim is to ensure that they are uniformly mixed before baking, as in the following nineteenth-century recipe for an Adelaide cake:

> Beat with the hand, in an earthenware basin, one pound of butter, and the same of sifted loaf sugar; beat separately the yolks and whites of ten eggs; add the yolks first, along with one pound of flour and two ounces of rice flour, add the whites, and one pound of nicely cleaned currants; flavour with essence of nutmeg and lemon, and bake in a tin.[4]

By beating with the hand, the cook uses the heat of the hand to warm the butter in contact with the skin so as to help it flow more easily as it becomes mixed with the sugar. The cook can also feel how the hard butter and the gritty sugar become blended into a soft mass, how the egg components and the flour become incorporated to produce the very different texture of the batter, and whether the currants are distributed uniformly throughout the mass before cooking.

On other occasions we wish to mix not only the physical ingredients but also the heat that they carry. When we 'stir-fry', for example, the stirring process ensures that the heat of frying is distributed uniformly throughout the mixture and that the ingredients that initially absorb the heat from the pan are not overheated while the rest remain cold. Similarly, when we add milk to our coffee, we stir to ensure that the liquids are mixed uniformly and also that the heat is distributed uniformly. If we do not stir, convection processes break the liquid up into discrete units called Bénard cells, evidence of which can be seen in the patterns that appear at the surface.[5]

The achievement of uniformity is not always as easy as it seems. To take one example, if we were to 'stir' a mixture of dry ingredients by shaking it in a container rather than using a spoon or other 'paddle' stirrer, the larger particles would rise to the top through a phenomenon called the 'Brazil nut effect'. The name comes from the tendency of the largest nuts (usually Brazil nuts) in a shaken container of mixed nuts to rise to the top (it is also called the 'muesli effect' because the nuts and pieces of fruit in a packet of muesli tend to rise to the top as it is shaken). One simple explanation is that smaller particles fall into the voids under the larger particles after each shake, so the larger particles gradually rise. (One simple way to overcome the Brazil nut effect when stirring powders is to use a rotary stirring motion that involves moving a spoon or other implement in a vertical circle about a more-or-less horizontal axis, so that the smaller particles are lifted from the bottom and put on the top again.) This is not the only process at work, however.[6]

Changing the character of the mixture

A second reason for stirring is to change the physical characteristics of the mixture. This may sometimes be achieved simply by mixing, as in the Adelaide cake recipe above. We may also stir by beating or whipping to incorporate air, as in making a soufflé.

More often, though, we achieve texture changes by breaking up droplets, particles and even molecules, forcing them to combine into new structures. When we make mayonnaise, for example, we beat an oil and water mixture vigorously to create and break up oil droplets, making them ever tinier. When we knead bread dough, we are working at an even smaller level, forcing glutenin molecules to stretch and cross-link with gliadin in a network that conveys elasticity to the dough.

Whether we stir for mixing, or stir for texture, or both, we still need to stir in the right way to achieve our goal. Here we examine more closely just what happens when we stir, and how our stirring technique can sometimes vastly affect the outcome through generating different flow patterns in our mixtures.

Stirring for uniformity

Some recipes (especially those from the nineteenth century and earlier) specify slow stirring in one direction only – usually clockwise, as in the medieval belief that one should only walk 'widdershins' around a church. To modern ears, it sounds like unsupported superstition, but strangely it has a scientific basis when what we are stirring consists of droplets of one liquid suspended in another.

The flow pattern that we generate by such slow stirring is called laminar flow. It may be visualized as being like the lazy flow of a slowly moving river, where bits of floating debris may pass each other, moving fastest in the centre and more slowly towards the banks, but do not intermix laterally.[7] In fact, such a flow pattern may be reversed by reversing the direction of stirring. So stirring slowly in one direction appears to make sense.

But it doesn't, because even though the liquids may appear to mix, in fact they don't. As James Bond understood instinctively, the key to effective mixing is to avoid laminar flow, and instead to create turbulence. We may do this, for example, by stirring in a figure-of-eight pattern, criss-crossing and mixing up the flow lines.

Better still, we can speed up the stirring, and also choose an implement that generates turbulence through its design. One such implement is the *spaddle*, described in *Miss Leslie's New Receipt Book* (1850) as 'a [round wooden stick] about a foot long, and flattened at the end like that of a mush-stick, only broader'.[8]

The spaddle is a forerunner of the modern paddle-blade mixer, and works in a similar way by producing turbulence at the edges of the blade. Such turbulence has been studied extensively by engineers, who have devised a number of simple rules that can be useful in considering just how we should stir different food mixtures.[9]

One fairly obvious rule is that, for the most effective mixing, keeping the plane of the blade or spoon that you are using square-on to the direction of motion as you stir forces the maximum amount of material past the edges and at the highest speeds.

Another, slightly less intuitive, observation is that that the highest turbulence occurs near the wall of the container when the blade or spoon is kept close to it. Annoyingly, though, studies have shown that mixing in the rest of the liquid (away from the zone of motion of the stirring implement) is correspondingly less effective when the implement is kept close to the walls of the container while stirring. The answer is to stir in a spiral or figure-of-eight motion, bringing the implement close to the pan edge for some of the time but then bringing it towards the centre and back again.

One further observation is that multiple edges are multiply effective in producing turbulence, so for thorough mixing a slotted spoon beats an ordinary spoon hands down.

Stirring for texture.

Most of the complex, multi-component food mixtures that we stir are non-Newtonian, which means that their flow properties change with the speed of stirring. A spectacular example is corn starch-based custard, which can be poured slowly as a liquid, but which becomes solid under a sudden impact, so that it is possible to walk or run across the surface of a large pool of it.

A contrary example is tomato ketchup, which can be very thick and virtually un-pourable until the bottle is shaken, when it becomes much less viscous and easier to pour – hence the old rhyme:

> Shake, shake the tomato sauce bottle,
> First none'll come, and then a lot'll.

Such changes occur because stirring affects: the size, shape and distribution of the long macromolecules (e.g. proteins and polysaccharides) in the food; the size, shape and distribution of the solid particles in the food; the size and distribution of liquid droplets such as oil droplets.

The scientific complexities involved in these questions are well beyond the scope of this talk, but from the point of view of the practical cook, there are three simple questions that we can ask: do we want to break up particles, lumps or droplets, or merely disperse them uniformly? Do we want to align large molecules such as proteins and polysaccharides, entangle them, or even break them? How fast should we stir, and what implement should we use, to achieve these effects?

Here we offer some answers to these questions, along with their basic rationale.

Slow stirring

Slow stirring tends to create flow fields consisting of parallel streamlines (scientifically known as shear flow). Adjacent streamlines move at different speeds, so that molecules or particles that lie across them will be stretched and rotated, thus changing the properties of the mixture.

Tomato ketchup, for example, contains stringy, thread-like particles of cellulose and other material. These particles are normally tangled together to create a semi-solid mixture. When we shake or stir the mixture, adjacent streamlines undo the tangles, rotating and aligning the particles so that they can more easily slide past each other and allow the mixture to flow.

The stirring of porridge provides a different example.[10] As cooking proceeds, the starch granules in the individual flakes absorb water, swell, and sometimes burst, releasing starch molecules. These molecules can act like glue, sticking the swollen flakes together and making the porridge lumpy.

To nullify this process, we must stir the porridge. We do not have to go to the lengths of three-time World Porridge Making champion Duncan Hilditch, who immersed himself naked in a bath full of porridge and used his legs and hands as stirrers. As Duncan himself pointed out, it is sufficient to use the traditional spirtle – a wooden rod roughly one centimetre in diameter. The aim is to provide sufficient force to separate the sticking flakes, without breaking the swollen flakes, which releases free starch and causes the porridge to become gluey. Calculations show that optimum shear forces are achieved by stirring at around one revolution of the pan per second.[11] As with many stirring problems, centuries of experience have produced the optimum outcome. A whisk produces much higher shear rates at its boundaries, and would be much less suitable.

A whisk, however, is a much better implement for whipping cream, because in this particular case high shear rates actually force particles to stick together, rather than tearing them apart. The 'particles' in this case are fat globules, suspended in water. The globules have small sharp crystals protruding from their surfaces (these crystals only form when the cream is sufficiently cold), which are otherwise covered with a protective protein film. When the globules are caught in a shear field, they are pushed up against each other and forced to roll around each other. At sufficiently high shear forces, the crystals can pierce the protective films of adjacent globules, causing them to clump together.[12]

Finally, in this brief survey of the effects of relatively slow stirring, we note that slow stirring may sometimes result in the separation of the stirred material into layers in a process known as shear banding.[13] We are unaware of particular gastronomic examples, but would be very interested in hearing of such.

Fast stirring

Fast stirring creates very complex flow fields, where streamlines, vortices, eddies and a host of other flow patterns exist simultaneously. This is very good for mixing, and can have profound effects on texture, which arise in part because there are many points (called 'stagnation points') from which material is rushing away in opposite directions.

Physicists call this 'extensional flow.' Its effect on long molecules, such as proteins and polysaccharides, is that they become untangled and stretched, like the rope in a tug of war competition.[14] When we stir egg white in this way, for example, the albumin molecules that are normally curled up into a ball become stretched out like pieces of string, which are then able to cross-link with other molecules at specific active points (normally safely hidden within the balls), thus forming a three-dimensional network.

When we stir more complex mixtures, such as that required to produce a chocolate ganache, the effects can be equally complex. A typical (abbreviated) chocolate ganache recipe consists of: 200g dark chocolate, 200g butter and 1 tbsp instant coffee dissolved in 125ml cold water, all mixed together and warmed until melted. Then a powder mixture consisting of 85g self-raising flour, 85g plain flour, 200g muscavado sugar, 200g caster sugar and 25g cocoa powder is stirred with 3 medium eggs and 75ml buttermilk. The melted chocolate mixture and the egg mixture are then stirred together until smooth and runny.[15]

So far, so apparently simple. But if we keep beating the mixture, it will first become thinner, and then thicker, eventually ending up as a fondant!

Scientists are only now beginning to understand how stirring affects such complex non-Newtonian mixtures, and there is a long way to go before definitive predictions can be made. From the point of view of the practical cook, though, there are four simple messages: (1) choose the appropriate implement for the job; (2) use the implement so as to generate the desired flow pattern; (3) start stirring slowly, and gradually speed up until you achieve the desired effect; (4) don't over-stir, or you may undo all of your good work.

Happy stirring!

Notes

1. H. Lois, Gresh and Robert Weinberg, *The Science of James Bond: From Bullets to Bowler Hats to Boat Jumps, the Real Technology behind 007's Fabulous Films* (London: Wiley, 2006).
2. The original ingredients comprised three measures of Gordon's gin, one of (unspecified) vodka, and half a measure of Kina Lillet (a vermouth-like aperitif with quinine as the bitter ingredient (Ian Fleming, *Casino Royale*, reprint ed. (Las Vegas, NV: Thomas & Mercer, 2012), p. 44). Kingsley Amis describes this recipe as 'the great Martini enormity' on account of the substitution of Kina Lillet for the more traditional dry vermouth (*The James Bond Dossier* (London: Jonathan Cape, 1965), p. 123). The Bond recipe, however, still appears on cocktail menus as a 'Vesper', with Cocchi Americano replacing the Kina Lillet, which is no longer available <http://chanticleersociety.org/forums/p/1116/6670.aspx>.
3. Peter Hertzmann, 'Stirring Conclusions', *à la carte*, 2008 <http://www.hertzmann.com/techniques/index.php?Stirring_Conclusions>.
4. Mary Somerville, *Mrs. Somerville's Cookery and Domestic Economy* (Glasgow: George Watson, 1862), p. 156.
5. Len Fisher, *How to Dunk a Doughnut: The Science of Everyday Life* (London: Penguin, 2002).
6. The Brazil nut effect poses a particularly serious problem in the pharmaceutical industry, where pharmacologically active materials in powder form must be mixed uniformly with other 'carrier' powders, whose particles may be quite different in size and shape; see 'Cracking the Brazil Nut Problem', *Physics World* (11 April 2001) <http://physicsworld.com/cws/article/news/2001/apr/11/cracking-the-brazil-nut-problem>.
7. While on the subject of stirring in a spiral motion, we note that wine swirling involves a similar sort of motion. Recent studies have shown that the swirling process not only increases the speed of air flow over the wine surface, thus aiding the release of vapours, but also generates complex wave patterns that increase the surface area and further enhance the release process (Martino Reclari et al., 'Oenodynamic: Hydrodynamic of Wine Swirling', *arXiv.org* (Cornell University Library), 2011 <http://arxiv.org/abs/1110.3369>).
8. Eliza Leslie, *Miss Leslie's New Receipt Book: A Useful Guide for Large or Small Families* (Philadelphia: A. Hart, 1850), p. 194. Leslie maintains, '[f]or stirring butter and sugar together, nothing is equal to a wooden spaddle'. Mrs Beeton sees the spaddle as more of a scraper: 'The spaddle is generally made of copper, kept bright and clean. […] The use of the spaddle is to stir up and remove from the sides of the freezing-pot the cream, which in the shaking may have washed against it, and by stirring it in with the rest, to prevent waste of it occurring' (*The Book of Household Management* (London, 1861), p. 761).
9. Douglas Bohl et al., 'Characterization of Mixing in a Simple Paddle Mixer Using Experimentally Derived Velocity Fields' <http://people.clarkson.edu/~ebollt/Papers/BohlMixerPaper.pdf>.
10. For Len Fisher's choice for the perfect porridge, see Amy Vickers, 'The New Oat Cuisine' *Daily Express* 4 September 2004, p. 27.
11. Simon Rookyard, 'The Physics of Porridge' (T-shirt design for the 2010 'Golden Spurtle' World Porridge Making Championships) <http://www.flickr.com/photos/bobsredmill/5096634651/>.
12. Pieter Walstra, *Physical Chemistry of Foods* (Boca Raton, FL: CRC Press, 2003), p. 548.
13. Robyn L. Moorcroft and Suzanne M. Fielding, 'Criteria for Shear-Banding in Time-Dependent Flows of Complex Fluids', *Physical Review Letters* 110 (2013).
14. These forces can be so severe that the 'rope' actually breaks (J.A. Odell and A. Keller, 'Flow-induced Chain Fracture of Isolated Linear Macromolecules in Solution', *Journal of Polymer Science B* 24 (1986), pp. 1889–1916). The practical outcome is that the mixture can become thinner, or less viscous, the longer it is stirred because, as these long molecules become shorter, their contribution to the viscosity becomes less. This actually happens during our lifetime with the long molecules in the synovial fluid that protects our knee joints, where the molecules gradually become broken and degraded, and are not replaced.
15. Angela Nilsen, 'Ultimate Chocolate Cake', *Good Food* April 2004 <http://www.bbcgoodfood.com/recipes/3092/>.

'To lick thy fingers greasy or to dry them upon thy clothes be both unmannerly': Napkins and Handkerchiefs in Early Modern Drama

Joan Fitzpatrick

What role do napkins play in early modern drama and what might it mean that napkins, so closely associated with food and good manners at table, are also used repeatedly in plays to signal the most heinous and uncivilized deeds? Might there be some acknowledgement in the plays that napkins mark the fine line between man and beast, their adoption being part of what Norbert Elias termed 'the civilizing process'?[1] For the early moderns the napkin was apparently synonymous with the handkerchief, reputedly invented by King Richard II.[2] The handkerchief was, ostensibly, a small piece of cloth a gentleman or lady would carry about their person to wipe the face, eyes, nose or lips at meal-times. Napkins were especially important before forks became common. Knives and spoons would be provided for guests in wealthy households and sometimes napkins too. These niceties are inter-connected, because cutlery helped keep hands clean; it appears that the only distinction between the handkerchief (meaning 'hand cloth') and napkin (meaning 'little cloth') is the context.

Travelling across Europe, the early modern Englishman Thomas Coryate was impressed by the use of the fork in Italy:

> I observed a custome in all those Italian Cities and Townes through the which I passed, that is not used in any other country that I saw in my travels, neither doe I thinke that any other nation of Christendome doth use it, but only Italy. The Italian and also most strangers that are commorant in Italy, doe alwaies at their meales use a little forke when they cut their meat.... The reason of this their curiosity is, because the Italian cannot by any means indure to have his dish touched with fingers, seing all mens fingers are not alike cleane.[3]

Forks were expensive; an unusual find during recent excavations of the Rose Theatre was a brass-topped iron fork, from between 1587 and 1606, which reflects ostentatious consumption at the playhouse. In Ben Jonson's *The Devil is an Ass*, first performed in 1616 and printed in 1631, Merecraft (a spiv character) proposes a monopoly on the use of forks, which he envisages 'Brought into custom here, as they are in Italy', and that will be 'A mighty saver of linen through the Kingdom' (5.4.19, 26).[4] In his influential book on manners, first published in 1530 (English translation 1532), Erasmus stipulates that the napkin should be laid on the shoulder to wipe greasy fingers, and if none is provided the table-cloth may be used.⁵ With no forks on the table, early modern English people would have had dirtier fingers than Italians.

To see if and how the nomenclature changed, I've searched Literature Online (LION), which contains all English literary texts up to 1910, for plays first performed between 1580 and 1610 containing both the word 'napkin' and the word 'handkerchief' (in all their possible spellings) to see if they are distinguished and if either is more commonly associated with food.⁶ Here are the plays:

Non-Shakespearian
Thomas Kyd, *The Spanish Tragedy* (first performed 1585–1589; first printed 1592)⁷
Anon, *Arden of Faversham* (first performed 1588–1592; first printed 1592)
George Chapman, *An Humorous Day's Mirth* (first performed 1597; first printed 1599)
Anon, *A Warning for Fair Women* (first performed 1596–1600; first printed 1599)
Thomas Dekker, *The Shoemaker's Holiday* (first performed 1599; first printed 1600)
Thomas Heywood, *The Wise Woman of Hogsdon* (first performed c. 1604 (?); first printed 1638)
Ben Jonson, *Volpone* (first performed 1605–1606; first printed 1607)
Francis Beaumont, *The Woman-Hater* (first performed 1606; first printed 1607)
Nathan Field, *A Woman Is a Weather-Cock* (first performed 1609–10; first printed 1612)

Shakespearian
3 Henry 6 (first performed 1591; first printed 1595)
The Merry Wives of Windsor (first performed 1597–1598; first printed 1602)
As You Like It (first performed 1598–1600; first printed 1623)
Othello (first performed 1603–1604; first printed 1622)⁸

Forks occur in just one of these, *Volpone*, when Sir Politic Would-Be offers Peregrine advice for 'your crude traveller', including how to talk and eat:

> Then must you learne the use
> And handling of your silver fork, at meals,
> The metal of your glass – these are maine matters
> With your Italian – and to know the hour
> When you must eat your melons and your figs. (4.1.27–31)⁹

This confirms that the fork was an exotic and expensive implement that an Englishman would encounter abroad. Napkins are used at dinner in early modern plays set at home and abroad and to wrap and carry pieces of food but most curiously they are also recurrently produced as evidence of lust, violence, adultery and murder.

Napkins and Handkerchiefs in Early Modern Drama

In Thomas Kyd's *The Spanish Tragedy* from the 1580s, Hieronimo, having found the body of his son Horatio stabbed and hanging in an arbour, tells his wife Isabella, 'Sees't thou this handkercher besmeared with blood? / It shall not from me till I take revenge' (2.5.51–52).[10] In the next act, sympathizing with Bazulto, whose son has also died, Hieronimo says, 'Here, take my handkercher, and wipe thine eyes', and the accompanying stage direction indicates that Hieronimo 'draweth out a bloody napkin', an act that reminds him of his earlier oath to avenge his son's murder (3.13.86–89). In the play's denouement, having stabbed those who murdered his son, Hieronymus proclaims, 'And here behold this bloudie handkercher, / Which at Horatio's death I weeping dipped / Within the river of his bleeding wounds' (4.4.122–24). The terms 'handkercher' and 'napkin' are clearly synonymous in this play – although 'napkin' occurs only in the stage-direction – and nowhere is either term used specifically in relation to food. Although Hieronimo is present at a banquet in Act 1, scene 4, when he finds Horatio's body he has come straight from bed, the stage direction indicating that he is 'in his shirt' (2.5.0), meaning his nightshirt, and so it is unlikely that he would still have a dinner-napkin on him. The handkerchief/napkin that he dips in Horatio's blood is never connected with dining or good manners of any sort but immediately becomes a symbol of murder and revenge.

In the anonymous play *Arden of Faversham* from the late 1580s or early 1590s, Thomas Arden's adulterous wife Alice plots her husband's death but is unwittingly foiled by Franklin, Arden's friend, as the servant Michael explains to the would-be murderers Greene, Will, and Shakebag:

> I did perform the outmost of my task,
> And left the doors unbolted and unlocked.
> But see the chance: Franklin and my master
> Were very late conferring in the porch,
> And Franklin left his napkin where he sat,
> With certain gold knit in it, as he said.
> Being in bed, he did bethink himself,
> And coming down he found the doors unshut.
> He locked the gates and brought away the keys,
> For which offence my master rated me. (7.6–15)[11]

This might be a culinary napkin, as Franklin and Arden stayed up late talking after dining at a nearby ordinary. Later in the play, whilst making their way to Faversham, Franklin tells Arden the story of a wife discovered in adultery who 'softly draws she forth her handkercher, / And modestly she wipes her tear-stained face' (9.83–84). Perhaps we are to think that Franklin illustrated this action by pulling out his own purely decorative napkin, since it would not be easy to remove food stains from cloth sewn with gold.

In George Chapman's *An Humorous Day's Mirth* from the late 1590s, old Labervele believes his wife to be passing his test of constancy by resisting the advances of Lemot.[12]

He says, 'Hark you, wife, what sign will you make me now, if you relent not?' to which she replies, 'Lend him my handkerchief to wipe his lips of their last disgrace' (6.108–11). Labervele is being fooled since his wife has already pledged her love to Lemot. Here the use of the handkerchief is clearly figurative: what should be wiped is the love-making that issues from the mouth of Lemot. Later in the play the action moves to Verone's ordinary and we have the stage direction '*Enter* VERONE *with his napkin upon his shoulder, and his man* JAQUES *with another, and* [*a* BOY], *his son, bringing in cloth and napkins*' (8.0), recalling Erasmus about where diners should place their napkins. Amongst themselves the servants complain of the diners' behaviour, with the Boy noting: 'if there be any chebules in your napkins, they say your nose or ours have dropped on them, and then they throw them about the house' (8.11–13). Chebules, a prune-like fruit (*OED* chebule, n.), was also a euphemism for snot.[13] Here food and bodily effusions are interchangeable, and I think that overlapping functions of the napkins and the handkerchief lie behind this arresting image. As we shall see, in later drama the two functions were distinguished, and the uses of napkins and handkerchiefs ceased to overlap. In a subsequent scene in this play Catalian, one of Lemot's friends, who has been playing tennis, asks the Boy to 'call for a coarse napkin' (8.109), and, as the editor of the Revels edition observes, this must mean 'a small towel (*OED* n. Ib)'[14] to absorb sweat.

Echoes of Kyd's play *The Spanish Tragedy* resound through later plays, including the anonymous *A Warning for Fair Women* from the late 1590s.[15] After murdering George Sanders, Captain George Browne dips his handkerchief into the man's blood to make a love-token he can send to the deceased's wife, Anne (8.1385–86). John Bean, the servant of a business associate of Sanders, has been injured in the attack and his neighbour Old John instructs his maid Joan to 'take my napkin and thy apron, and bind up his wounds' (8.1465–66). Earlier in the play Joan tells Bean of a prophetic dream: 'me thought your nose bled, and as I ran to my chest to fetch ye a handkercher, me thought I stumbled and so waked: what do's it betoken?' (6.1032–33) In this rather old-fashioned play, the handkerchief and napkin are not distinguished, and these pieces of cloth are mentioned exclusively and repeatedly for their function in soaking up blood.

In Thomas Dekker's slightly later but much more modern *The Shoemaker's Holiday* from 1599, Hamond, who is in love with Jane (another man's wife), enquires about certain items, including a handkerchief, that Jane has been working on.[16] The scene takes place in a sempter's shop, and there is a sense that the handkerchief is ornately decorated by Jane, not least because Hamond comments, 'How prettily she works! O prettie hand!' (12.13). Although Jane says that she will sell it 'cheap', it is one of many other delicate items in the shop, including 'Fine cambric shirts' (12.23). Later in the play the Shoemaker Eyre, newly made Mayor of London, holds a feast for the king at which his employees will officiate. The culinary specificity of the napkin is indicated in the stage direction '*Enter* AYRE, HODGE, FIRK, RALPH *and other shoemakers, all with napkins on their shoulders*' (20.0), and these cloths are quite distinct from the fine work being constructed by Jane. As Will Fisher has pointed out, the handkerchief was 'a relatively new cultural artifact, and therefore its social connotations and the rules governing its use were still in process of being defined', but, increasingly, the handkerchief played an important role 'in materializing early modern notions of femininity, and the female body'.[17] Referring to the work of Stephanie Dickey, Fisher observes that that the handkerchief itself is a strangely contradictory artefact; as Dickey pointed out, 'to employ a costly, elaborately decorated article like the embroidered handkerchief … for actually blowing the nose would be … unthinkable.'[18]

'Unthinkable' is perhaps a bit strong, since the significant taboo is in retaining bodily effusions after use of the cloth. Today we certainly do not expect the handkerchief protruding from a well-dressed man's top pocket to be blown into and replaced, but, as with the myth of the Earl of Essex laying down a valuable cloak to keep Queen Elizabeth's feet from the mud, the willingness to use a cloth that has become decorative for its original practical purpose strongly connotes gallantry. The brief encounter that initiates the affair in David Lean's 1945 film is Trevor Howard's use of his handkerchief to remove a piece of grit from Celia Johnson's eye, and his returning the soiled cloth to his top pocket adds to the symbolic intimacy of the moment. In the plays from the period I'm concerned with, 1580–1610, we see first emergence of the handkerchief as something primarily decorative and not ordinarily to be used to collect grease from food or bodily fluids. Five years after Dekker's *Shoemaker's Holiday* made the napkin/handkerchief distinction, Thomas Heywood's *The Wise Woman of Hogsdon*[19] of around 1604 confirmed it with a scene of similarly delicate labour: '*Enter* LUCE in a sempster's shop, at work upon a laced handkercher' (1.2.0). Handkerchiefs come up again later when the rogue Chartely says of his father-in-law and Luce, 'Here's such wetting of handkerchers./ He weeps to think of his wife, she weeps to see her father cry' (3.3.136–37). The handkerchief is not solely decorative here, being used to wipe tears, but it is entirely distinct from the food-related napkins that are mentioned during the preparations for Chartley's marriage to Grantiana in the stage direction '*Enter* TABOR and SIR BONIFACE with a trencher, with broken meat and a napkin' (4.5.0). Later in the same scene two more stage directions confirm the handkerchief/napkin distinction: '*Enter* TABOR with a bowl of beer and a napkin' (4.5.27) and '*Enter* CHARTLEY with his napkin as from dinner' (4.5.36). The distinction between the lust of the play's young men and the finer feelings of its young women is emblematized in the difference between napkins used at meals and the 'laced handkercher' that Luce works on.

Ben Jonson's *Volpone* of 1607 sharply distinguishes between the napkin as a practical cloth and the handkerchief as a decorative and symbolic one.[20] Pretending to be the mountebank Scoto of Mantua, Volpone describes the use of a napkin 'To fortify the most indigest and crude stomach' by 'applying only a warm napkin to the place, after the unction and fricace' (2.2.102–05). Still in the guise of the mountebank, Volpone puts on a show beneath the window of Celia, the pretty young wife of Corvino, telling the crowd who have gathered to 'toss your handkerchiefs cheerfully' (2.2.220–21). In response to this, 'Celia at the window throws down her handkerchief' (2.2.226). Brian Parker points out that 'It was usual to throw mountebanks money tied in handkerchiefs, which were then returned wrapped around the purchase … so this in no way suggests flirtatiousness in Celia.'²¹ In this context, however, it does emphasize her femininity. Dickey considers the early modern handkerchief 'almost exclusively a female attribute' and although Fisher argues that 'the handkerchief was a detachable part and as such could not be tied exclusively to any one particular group or person' he acknowledged 'the ideological work' – in the paintings and plays mentioned by Dickey – 'to make it seem as if handkerchiefs were simply a female attribute.'²² Fisher begins his essay with Thomas Randolph's account of a story about Queen Elizabeth's napkin, namely how the Earl of Leicester annoyed the Duke of Norfolk by taking her napkin to wipe the sweat from his face after a game of tennis.²³ Fisher does not seem to notice that the affront here was in the misuse of the cloth: even if called a 'napkin' a lady's personal cloth had acquired the status that we now attach to a handkerchief, and, as we have seen, the plays of the period were beginning to make this distinction overtly and to separate the terminology.

In Francis Beaumont's comedy *The Woman-Hater* of 1606, Lazarello 'the Hungrie Courtier' who 'doth hunt more after novelty, then [than] plenty' (1.2.77, 83–84), pursues not love but, rather, a particularly choice fish-head that has been prepared for the Duke:

> Thither must I
> To see my loves face, the chaste virgin head
> Of a deere Fish, yet pure and undeflowred,
> Not known of man, no rough bred countrey hand,
> Hath once toucht thee, no Pandars withered paw,
> Nor an un-napkind Lawyers greasie fist,
> Hath once slubbered thee: no Ladies supple hand,
> Washt o're with urine, hath yet seiz'd on thee
> With her two nimble talents: no Court hand,
> Whom his own naturall filth, or change of aire,
> Hath bedeckt with scabs, hath mard thy whiter grace:
> O let it be thought lawful then for me,
> To crop the flower of thy virginitie. (1.2.216–28)²⁴

The lawyer's 'un-napkind' greasy fist is all the more disgusting because he cannot even wipe it clean. Chasing his object of desire across the play's scenes, Lazarello even considers the drama's favourite trick of cross-dressing, and he thinks a handkerchief would make the switch in clothing more convincing: 'My Lord, what doe you thinke, if I should shave my selfe, put on midwives apparell, come in with a hand-kercher, and beg a peece for a great bellied woman, or a sick child?' (3.2.92–94).

Three or four years later, Nathan Field's play *A Woman is a Weather Cock* has the familiar use of napkins when refreshments are brought in: 'Enter with Table Napkins. Count, Worldly, Neuill, Pendant, Sir Innocent, Lady, Sir Abraham, Seruants with wine, Plate, Tobacco and pipes' (E3v).[25] Later in the play, we see the entrance of Sir Abraham 'knawing [gnawing] on a Capons Legge' (H2v). Nevill tells him, 'Soule man, leaue eating now, looke, looke, you haue all dropt a your sute', to which Abraham replies, 'Oh Sir, I was in loue to day, and could not eate, but heere's one knowes the case is alter'd, lend mee but a Handkerchiefe to wipe my mouth, and I ha done' (H2v). This might look like evidence against my thesis that the culinary napkin and the decorative handkerchief were increasingly distinguished, but here the capon-gnawing Sir Abraham is a fool and a boor: it is a mark of his poor manners that he does not know to ask for a napkin rather than a handkerchief. The point would be made all the more clearly in performance if Nevill daintily gives him what he asks for and looks on in disgust as it is misused.

Finally we come, as all such surveys must, to Shakespeare's habits. Shakespeare uses the term 'napkin' and 'handkerchief' without distinction in his plays. In *3 Henry 6* from the early 1590s, audiences would have been reminded of Kyd's *Spanish Tragedy* when Queen Margaret tauntingly rubs in the Duke of York's face a 'napkin' dipped in his son Rutland's blood (B1v), and York replies that his tears 'wash the bloud awaie' (B3r).[26] When a messenger later reports this scene to Richard Gloucester he calls the cloth a 'handkercher' (B4r). Behind the apparent synonymy of napkin/handkerchief lies a tension between the vulgar and the delicate mopping of bodily effusions. Put to its right purpose of mopping tears, says York, the cloth will be cleansed of the child Rutland's blood and so symbolize the triumph of remorse over blood-lust. Shakespeare takes Kyd's image of the bloodied cloth and makes it bear additional symbolic freight as a token of repentance. He does the same with the napkin/handkerchief in *As You Like It* from the end of the 1590s, which a reformed Oliver brings from Orlando to excuse his lateness.[27] Although here Shakespeare seems to use the terms interchangeably (4.3.94–98, 4.3.139–56), Rosalind's mask of masculinity slips when she faints at the sight of the bloodied cloth, and in explaining this itself as a pretence of femininity she perhaps betrays herself further by using its feminine name: 'Did your brother tell you how I counterfeited to swoon when he showed me your handkerchief' (5.2.25–26).

In the quarto of Shakespeare's late-1590s play *The Merry Wives of Windsor*, foolish Slender swears that Pistol has picked his purse: 'I by this handkercher did he. Two faire shouell boord shillings, besides seuen groats in mill sixpences' (A3v).[28] It is likely that the affectatious Slender carries the handkerchief as a kind of stylish accessory. Later in the play the failed seducer Sir John Falstaff complains that, hiding in a laundry basket, he endured 'foule shirts, stokins [stockings], greasie napkins,/... a compound of the most/Villanous smel, that euer offended nostrill' (E3v). In Shakespeare, grease may come from food or the human body, although Sir John's gluttony would make culinary napkins a particularly suitable punishment.[29] Picturing his wife soiled by Sir John and himself cuckolded, Ford imagines himself humiliated by the horns growing on his head serving for others' convenience: 'they may hang hats here, and napkins here/Vpon my hornes' (E4r).

The most famous dramatic handkerchief must be the one that in 1603 or 1604 Othello first gave to Desdemona.[30] Its loss stands for the soiling of Desdemona: it passes through hands that should not touch it, and it gets called a napkin in the play. To emphasize the crude misuse of this strawberry-spotted cloth, Iago claims to have seen Cassio 'wipe his beard' with it (3.3.439). Unlike the chebules in napkins mentioned in Chapman's *An Humorous Day's Mirth*, strawberries were not vulgar, but, as critics have noted, they carried sexual connotations and suggested hymeneal blood.[31] We see here the blurring of boundaries between food and bodily effusions that we saw in Chapman, but with tragic rather than comic significance.

In Kyd's early and influential play *The Spanish Tragedy*, the napkin and handkerchief are used synonymously, and the bloody cloth is a symbol of murder, something that occurs also in Shakespeare's *3 Henry 6* and the anonymous *Warning for Fair Women*. In later plays there emerges a distinction between the napkin as an item specifically associated with food, grease and practical applications and the handkerchief as an ornate, delicate and specifically effeminate item, carried about the person and intended primarily for intimate use or decoration. There is less clear evidence of this distinction in Shakespeare. Why might this be? In Shakespeare's collaborations with other playwrights, for example John Fletcher, it is possible to attribute particular scenes to a specific author. As Jonathan Hope points out, Fletcher and Shakespeare emerged from very different socio-economic backgrounds: Fletcher was 'born in 1579 in the south-east and brought up in an upper-class, urban environment ... and [probably] attended Cambridge University', whereas Shakespeare was born 'fifteen years earlier in the rural south-west midlands', with a 'lower class status, and lack of higher education'. The co-authored plays reveal differences in word-usage; as Hope puts it, 'Fletcher will use more in-coming prestige variants than Shakespeare'.[32] It is perhaps not surprising, therefore, that Shakespeare would be behind his colleagues in the latest and most fashionable terminology, for example using 'napkin' instead of 'handkerchief'.

Notes

1. Norbert Elias, *The Civilizing Process: Sociogenetic and Psychogenetic Investigations*, trans. Edmund Jephcott; revised edition, ed. Eric Dunning, Johan Goudsblom and Stephen Mennell (Oxford: Blackwell, 2000).
2. George B. Stow, 'Richard II and the Invention of the Pocket Handkerchief', *Albion: A Quarterly Journal Concerned with British Studies*, 27 (1995) 221–35.
3. Thomas Coryate, *Coryats Crudities*, STC 5808 (London: W[illiam] S[tansby for the author], 1611): sig. I6v–I7r.
4. All quotations from early modern plays will be from a good modern edition where available.
5. Desiderius Erasmus, *[De Civilitate Morum Puerilium]. A Lytell Booke of Good Maners for Chyldren... [Translated] By Robert Whytyngton*, STC 10467 (London: Wynkyn de Worde, 1532).
6. To find the first performance and publication date for these plays I have used the electronic resource

Database of Early English Playbooks or 'DEEP' <http://deep.sas.upenn.edu/>. Where DEEP gives both a precise date and a date range in square brackets, the latter showing a degree of uncertainty, I have used the latter.

7. The 1592 text of *The Spanish Tragedy* is the sole authoritative text of the play (Thomas Kyd, *The Spanish Tragedy*, ed. J. R. Mulryne, The New Mermaids (London: Ernest Benn, 1970), p. 33. It was enormously popular and reprinted in many times; curiously, the words 'napkin' and 'handkerchief' do not appear in the 1602 edition that reflects the play after revision by Ben Jonson.
8. In *3 Henry 6* the words 'napkin' and 'handkerchief' occur together only in the Octavo of 1595 and not in the 1623 Folio text; in *The Merry Wives of Windsor* they occur together only in the 1602 Quarto, known as the 'bad quarto', not the Folio of 1623; *As You like It* appears only in the 1623 Folio text and both terms occur together; in *Othello* both terms occur together in the Quarto and Folio texts.
9. Ben Jonson, *Volpone, or The Fox*, ed. Brian Parker; revised edition, The Revels Plays (Manchester: Manchester UP, 1999).
10. Kyd, *The Spanish Tragedy*.
11. Martin Wiggins, ed., *A Woman Killed with Kindness and Other Domestic Plays: The Tragedy of Master Arden of Faversham, A Woman Killed with Kindness, The Witch of Edmonton, The English Traveller*, Oxford World's Classics (Oxford: Oxford UP, 2008).
12. George Chapman, *An Humorous Day's Mirth*, ed. Charles Edelman, The Revels Plays (Manchester: Manchester UP, 2010).
13. Chapman, p. 116n11.
14. Chapman, p. 122n109.
15. Anon, *A Warning for Fair Women: A Critical Edition*, ed. Charles Dale Cannon (Paris: Mouton, 1975), pp. 28–43; Jeffrey Kahan, 'The 1597 Additions to *The Spanish Tragedy* and Its Subsequent Influences on *A Woman Killed with Kindness*', *ANQ*, 17.2 (2004), pp. 20–4.
16. Thomas Dekker, *The Shoemaker's Holiday*, ed. Anthony Parr, New Mermaids (London: A&C Black, 1990).
17. Will Fisher, 'Handkerchiefs and Early Modern Ideologies of Gender', *Shakespeare Studies*, 28 (2000), p. 201.
18. Fisher, p. 205; Stephanie Dickey, 'Women Holding Handkerchiefs in Seventeenth-Century Dutch Portraits', *Image and Self-image in Netherlandish Art, 1550–1750*, ed. Reindert Falkenburg, Jan De Jong, Herman Roodenburg and Frits Scholten Scholten, Netherlands Yearbook for History of Art (Zwolle: Waanders, 1995): IV6, p. 336.
19. Thomas Heywood, *Three Marriage Plays: The Wise Woman of Hogsdon, The English Traveller, The Captives*, ed. Paul Merchant, The Revels Plays Companion Library (Manchester: Manchester UP, 1996).
20. Jonson.
21. Jonson, p. 153n220. Parker adds that 'Handkerchiefs were invented in Venice in the fifteenth century, and were still used more for fashion than hygiene' but provides no evidence for this assertion, whereas Stow makes a compelling argument for its invention by Richard II at the English court.
22. Dickey, p. 340; Fisher, p. 205.
23. Fisher, p. 199.
24. Fredson Bowers, ed., *The Dramatic Works in the Beaumont and Fletcher Canon, The Woman Hater*. Ed. George Walton Williams, 10 vols (Cambridge: Cambridge UP, 1966), I: *The Knight of the Burning Pestle; The Masque of the Inner Temple and Gray's Inn; The Woman Hater; The Coxcomb; Philaster; The Captain*.
25. Nathan Field, *A Woman is a Weather-cocke*, STC 10854 (London: Printed for John Budge, 1612).
26. William Shakespeare, *[3 Henry 6] The True Tragedie of Richard Duke of Yorke, and the Death of Good King Henrie the Sixt*, STC 21006 (O) BEPD 138a (London: P[eter] S[hort] for Thomas Millington, 1595). Shakespeare, *The Third Part of King Henry VI*, ed. Andrew S. Cairncross, The Arden Shakespeare (Harvard: Methuen, 1964), p. 184; Shakespeare, *Henry VI, Part Three*, ed. Randall Martin, The Oxford

Shakespeare (Oxford: Oxford UP, 2001), p. 52. In his 1765 edition of the play Samuel Johnson adds a note clarifying Queen Margaret's actions: 'A napkin is a handkerchief' (*Mr Johnson's Preface to His Edition of Shakespear's Plays* (London: Printed for J. and R. Tonson, H. Woodfall, J. Rivington, R. Baldwin, L. Hawes, Clark and Collins, T. Longman, W. Johnston, T. Caslon, C. Corbet, T. Lownds, and the Executors of B. Dodd, 1765), p. 136 n.2).

27. Shakespeare, *As You Like It*, ed. Alan Brissenden, The Oxford Shakespeare (Oxford: Oxford UP, 1993). In his 1778 edition of the play George Steevens adds a note, 'napkin, i.e. handkerchief', and directs the reader to the use of the word in *Othello*: 'Your napkin is too little' (Shakespeare, *The Plays of William Shakespeare. In Ten Volumes. With the Corrections and Illustrations of Various Commentators; to Which Are Added Notes By Samuel Johnson and George Steevens*, 2nd edn. Revised and Augmented (London: C. Bathurst [and] W. Strahan [etc.], 1778), p. 363 n.1).
28. Shakespeare, *[Merry Wives of Windsor] The Most Pleasaunt and Excellent Conceited Comedie, of Syr Iohn Falstaffe, and the Merrie Wiues of Windsor*, STC 22299 (Q1) (London: Thomas C[reed], 1602).
29. Joan Fitzpatrick, *Shakespeare and the Language of Food: A Dictionary*, Arden Shakespeare Dictionaries (London: Bloomsbury, 2010): 'grease/greasy'.
30. Shakespeare, *Othello*, ed. Michael Neill, The Oxford Shakespeare (Oxford: Oxford UP, 2006).
31. Marion Lomax, *Stage Images and Traditions: Shakespeare to Ford* (Cambridge: Cambridge UP, 1987), p. 36; Andrew Sofer, 'Felt Absences: The Stage Properties of *Othello*'s Handkerchief', *Comparative Drama*, 31 (1997), pp. 381, 392 n.33.
32. Jonathan Hope, *The Authorship of Shakespeare's Plays: A Socio-linguistic Study* (Cambridge: Cambridge UP, 1994), p. 8.

Kitchen Knives: the New Bling

Peter Hertzmann

At another time, this guy would have been called a dandy, or even a macaroni, but instead of an outlandish eighteenth-century powdered wig, his hair was bleached to an albino shade of yellow and spiked with gel. And, this being the first decade of the second millennium, his shirt of crushed, brown silk, with a top button closer to his navel than his neck, revealed more bleached hair behind a number of heavy-looking gold medallions suspended from equally heavy-looking gold chains. The fingers on his hands were spread gently outward due to the rings on each one except for the ring finger on his left hand, which appeared conspicuously naked. During class, I had pleaded with him to remove the rings for both safety and sanitation reasons. Now each was back on its perch. He spoke with a pleasing southern, probably Texas, accent in a soft voice that was barely audible at times.

The class he attended was basic knife skills. It was taught in a cookware store that is part of a large chain in the United States. Although the class was presented to the students as a learning experience, it was organized by the corporation to bring more potential customers through the front door. As an instructor, I was told what products to push and how a significant portion of the class time should be devoted to the students perusing the sales floor instead of being in the kitchen learning the day's subject.

Now the class was over, and this gentleman was about to help the store manager meet her sales quota for the day. He stood on the customer side of a countertop-high display case. I stood behind it. Behind me, in a locked, glass display, was a selection of knives ranging in price from expensive to more expensive. The store did carry a small selection of inexpensive but good quality knives. These were sealed in plastic and hung from a rack close by, but out of view from where my current customer stood. It didn't matter. It was obvious that his intention was to purchase the fanciest looking knife in the cabinet. The fact that it was the most expensive was inconsequential. I removed the knife from its current position in a knife block and handed it to him. I suggested that he use the techniques he had just acquired in class to dissect the carrot that sat on the counter in front of him.

As he sliced with the knife, demonstrating that he grasped the techniques taught during the previous two hours, I decided to talk him out of that dandified knife. I knew from the outset that I wouldn't be successful, but it seemed like something I should try. One after another, I presented him with knives that were only slightly plainer and had smaller price tags. He politely tried each one, anyone of which would have been a better knife to use for slicing and dicing a few vegetables. I pointed out differences in each handle, curve of the belly, feel of the spine and weight and balance. As my supply of alternatives ran out and the evening ran on, he politely insisted on purchasing the fancy knife he originally requested. Since he was receiving a small discount as a class member that evening, he requested a second knife that was almost as expensive as the first. In the end, his bill for the two knives ran to over £500 ($800).[1] He now had two knives that matched the bling that hung around his neck and adorned his fingers.[2]

That night, I began to notice that many of the knife customers I helped, although not dressed as gorgeously as the customer that evening, still were more interested in the appearance of the knife they were purchasing rather than its functionality.

As a self-styled knife evangelist, I am often asked: 'Which knife is best?' or 'Which knife should I buy?' My answer goes towards each individual's unique need for the knife: 'Buy the one that feels the best to you.' I want people to take a knife for a 'test drive', but all too often, the purchase decision is made by the eyes and the mind, not the hand.

The bling-buying customer described previously, when asked if he would like to purchase a pair of inexpensive plastic sleeves to protect his new investment, politely declined. It seemed that he had a magnetic bar on his wall, and that he planned to put the knives on display. I thought that it would be like sculpture art for his guests to enjoy. They wouldn't need to ask the price since these knives looked very expensive.

Looking at a wall of knives for sale in a modern cookware store, it is easy to see how different styles of knives could attract different personalities. German-made knives designed to look traditional, with their squared-off edges and massive bolsters, tend to imply the same precision that car buyers may visualize when considering a Mercedes-Benz or BMW.[3] Japanese-made knives intended for the American market may imply softness and artistic intentions. In these knives, aesthetics may be as important as performance.[4] Knife manufacturers are well aware that two important factors in customer appeal are sex appeal and uniqueness.[5] I wonder how many customers pick up this knife or that one and have Walter Mitty-like visions of using the knife on food television. Maybe not in Ikea where the knives are displayed in a utilitarian, hands-off manner and sold for typical Ikea prices, but when handling one of the fancier models gently removed from the wall of cutlery by a sales 'consultant' at Williams-Sonoma, it's hard not to imagine the knife doing something more heroic than slicing carrots.

I've even observed this fantasy-producing effect in line-cooks and chefs when they ogled a fancy knife at a commercial exhibition or even in the knife roll of the next person down the line. With professionals, as they bounce the dream knife in their hand, it is almost as if having this big beautiful example will move its owner higher up the professional ladder. I remember querying one *chef de cuisine* after he handed me, still housed in its handmade wooden sleeve, his custom-made, Japanese *gyuto* (牛刀) to use.[6] The knife was in very poor condition with a number of large voids in the cutting edge. The blade was badly stained. He had used it one day to chop some bones when he couldn't find a cleaver. He said that he bought the knife just out of cooking school

Kitchen Knives: The New Bling

with a fantasy that the knife would help him succeed, but he found that an inexpensive, plastic-handled knife of the same size was more appropriate for his career. The knife had become bling.

I frequently experience a similar situation with my students. I teach knife skills in many different situations, but one location that I have been at for many years is a vocational school where new students start the first Monday of each month.[7] I show up the following Wednesday or Thursday to provide their basic knife-skill training. It takes about four months for the students to complete the 350 hours required for fulfilment of the programme, so I see the same students in the school's kitchen for a few of my visits. As these students approach the end of their training and start working in commercial kitchens, they'll often ask me for advice regarding what knife they should purchase. My advice is always the same: 'Buy the one that feels the best to you'. For these students, I will go on to suggest that they seriously consider a certain Swiss-made chef's knife that can be obtained online for less than £20 ($30).[8] It's an excellent knife and well suited for commercial use. Alas, the knife they purchase is some fancy, high-end knife that looks impressive but isn't suitable for their work environment. Their new possession will not serve them well on the job, but it works great as bling.

My experience after many years is that professionals are often no better than amateurs when it comes to knife purchases. They may actually use the knife they buy, but then again, maybe not. One of the chefs I was a *stagiaire* for in France used to keep a super-sized chef's knife on the magnetic bar above his work station. The blade was 30 cm (12 in) long. Most cooks have either a 25 or 20 cm (10 or 8 in) long knife. One day I asked him why he never used the knife. He initially gave me a song-and-dance about how the carbon steel discoloured onions, but one night, after some serious imbibing of *eau de vie,* he admitted that he kept it around as a symbol that he was the chef and everyone else were cooks.[9] It was his symbol of office. It hung on the wall as a warning. He was the big kahuna. It was bling.

This chef may have been the head of his kitchen and even well known in his region, but he was no celebrity chef. For those we need to check our local television listings. Here we find a slew of celebrity chefs that have rented their name and image to a knife or housewares manufacturer. There are knife products bearing the names of Martha Stewart, Emeril Lagasse, Rachael Ray, Alton Brown, Paula Deen, Cat Cora, Guy Fieri, Giada DeLaurentis and Masaharu Morimoto in the United States and Nigella Lawson, Gordon Ramsay and Jamie Oliver in the United Kingdom.[10] Some products are only available through select outlets, such as the shopping channels on cable television or certain stores such as Martha Stewart's line of products at Macy's. Most of these celebrity-created and/or endorsed knives are crap.[11] Also, most are quite inexpensive. Macy's sells a Martha Stewart sixteen-piece set for under £50 ($80), thirteen of which are knives.[12] This is an average of about £4 ($6) per knife. There are exceptions to the poor quality and low price of most celebrity-chef knives, but not many. Myabi-brand knives with Morimoto's name are a significantly better quality with an appropriately higher price. At the high end are the knives manufactured by Shun with the name of Michel Bras, not a well-known celebrity in the English-speaking world. The complete set of ten knives is a mere £2194 ($3376).[13] Those on a budget can buy an 8 cm (3 in) paring knife for £220 ($338).[14]

Why do people buy these poor-quality celebrity-endorsed knives? First, most customers don't understand knives or how to use them. Second, price may be an issue. I contend that people buy knives pushed by celebrities because they want to be, if only vicariously, associated with the celebrity. The same people that watch Paula Deen create fat-filled fantasies on the Food Network want a bit of Paula in their kitchen. If it's a knife that they are interested in – there's a whole range of other types of housewares available from Paula Deen's online store – they can choose between a red or blueberry-coloured set of three for less than £16 ($24).[15] Each time a customer uses one of these knives they can pretend that Paula is there whispering in their ear. Or better yet, they can leave the knives sitting on the counter for their friends to see and hopefully draw the association between the knife owner and Paula Deen.

Another type of celebrity that peddles knives is the celebrity knife designer. Two designers to come over to the dark side of commercial endorsements are Bob Kramer and Ken Onion. Knives available under the name of either of these two gentlemen are relatively expensive and seem to be of interest more to the men than women. These designs are for fairly hefty knives. I've seen a number of professional cooks using Ken Onion's original chef's-knife design.[16] To a man, they've each talked about how well the knife felt in their hand and how well it works, but also to a man, the fancy Ken Onion knife was not the knife they used on a regular basis. They liked having it around, but that can be a problem. The unique profile makes it difficult to store without the blade getting damaged. The Ken Onion chef's knife comes with a wooden stand that's ideal for displaying the knife as an *objet d'art* on the countertop (Figure 1). This would protect the blade when not in use, but is really only useful in a home environment.

Bob Kramer knives are real 'lookers'. The version made by Shun was the knife that the blonde gentleman bought in the beginning of this essay. Kramer, who also makes custom knives in his own shop, has since switched his allegiance to Zwilling J. A. Henckels (Figure 2).[17] There are now multiple styles, all expensive, of his designs. There's a limited edition of 250 knives that sell for £1170 ($1800) each.[18] Very pretty, not particularly practical, and a steal considering the price and waiting time for Kramer's knives made by his own hand. It may be the ultimate knife bling – expensive and scarce.

There's a third type of celebrity knife that appeared briefly and now seems to be on the wane. The knives were designed by F.A. Porsche, manufactured in China, and sold by the Chroma USA as the Chroma Type 301 (Figure 3).[19] They appear to be designed from ground up: they look the least like the kitchen knives that everyone is used to seeing. They have a unique handle design that includes a post on each side to indicate to the user's hand the intersection of the handle and the blade. They are marketed to

Kitchen Knives: The New Bling

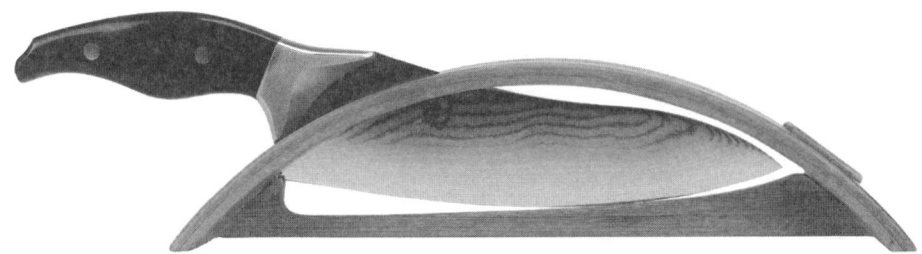

Figure 1: Ken Onion-designed 20-cm (8-in) chef's knife sold under the Shun brand. (Photo. © Kai USA, Ltd. Used with permission.)

professional cooks and showed some success in that market for a few years. Referring to professional cooks, one knife-seller who no longer sells the Type 301 knife commented, 'They buy shit, even if they don't need it'.[20]

A sizeable percentage of the knife purchases in the United States are sets selected by future couples and added to their bridal registries. Depending on the paperwork, people accessing the registry can buy a single knife or the whole set. I've lost count of the number of former brides who asked me in a knife-skills class what they should do with each of the knives. I have a difficult time answering this question tactfully since I believe you only need three knives at the most. As one knife developer sarcastically asked me in passing, 'You need a special knife to cut a sandwich?'[21]

The selection of one knife set versus another is often made by the young couple without ever looking at any of the knives in the set. Instead, the decision is made by looking only at the handles.[22] The sets are generally displayed as knife blocks with all available slots filled with knives. The couple can imagine each set as it will look on their countertop. Even if the set is to be displayed as separate knives on a magnetic bar on the wall, the decision is often made based solely on looks.[23] To take better advantage of this selection process, one German manufacturer will be introducing a knife block with 36 slots in it.[24] Other than the two slots occupied with the steel and scissors, the remaining slots will be for knives. I wonder if a couple considers how much counter space they need to give up to support a knife block of this size?

Figure 2: Bob Kramer-designed 20-cm (8-in) chef's knife by Zwilling J. A. Henckels (Photo. © Zwilling J. A. Henckels. Used with permission.)

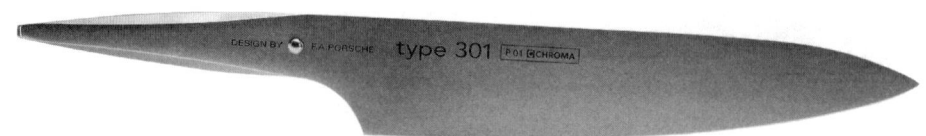

Figure 3: F.A. Porsche-designed 26-cm (10-in) chef's knife by Chroma USA. (Photo. © Chroma USA. Used with permission.)

This attraction to knives as bling is relatively new, and pretty much confined to the United States. In most countries, if guests are invited to dinner, they are not welcomed into the kitchen. The reason for this can be cultural or just that the kitchen is small. In the United States, middle-class houses in the nineteenth century, especially farmhouses, were often built around the kitchen, which may have been the only room with heat in the winter. Even today, where some form a living room exists, it is not uncommon for Americans to say they entertain in their kitchens.[25] The kitchens usually are not large enough to eat in, but the guests will gather there until dinner is ready. Whether consciously or not, many purchase decisions in the United States, when it comes to items for the kitchen, revolve around appearance and perceived intrinsic value rather than function.[26] This attraction has lead to the development of modern kitchen knives, some of which are so fancy they almost become ceremonial.

The sixteenth-century cook's knife illustrated in Scappi's *Opera* looks essentially the same as the early nineteenth-century cook's knife illustrated in Jules Gouffé's *Le Livre de cuisine*.[27] Two decades later, the three-piece knife construction shown in Hatfield's 1886 patent, a minor change to the then current design, became the standard for many European manufacturers for the next century.[28]

Texts of the era that specify which tools a cook needs in the kitchen generally call for a large cook's knife, a paring knife, a bread knife and a cleaver.[29] Some also call for a chopping knife and wooden bowl.[30] The detailed names of the knives occasionally change, but the total quantity is about the same. They also specify a carving knife and fork, but normally for table-side use rather than in the kitchen.

Figure 4: Global 27-cm (10.6-in) cook's knife illustrating Yoshida Metal Industry's unique handle design. (Photo. © Scanpan USA Inc. Used with permission.)

Kitchen Knives: The New Bling

Checking out some of the housewares catalogues of the day, we find only a limited number of knives available to the cook in the home, whether an employee or a member of the family. The 1895 Montgomery Ward & Co. catalogue shows many butcher and bread knives, but only a single 'French Cook Knife' in three lengths.[31] There's also half a page of carving knives, singularly and in sets, three chopping knives and three paring knives.[32] The 1897 Sears Roebuck & Co. catalogue has a smaller selection of the same types of knives except for no cook's knives.[33] The 1898 catalogue for Au Bon Marché displays a cook's knife in seven lengths and a matching paring knife in two.[34] There's also a cleaver and a chopping knife.

Knife sets start to appear in American magazine advertisements just after the Second World War. The typical set contains four knives for use in the kitchen: a French cook's knife, a utility knife, a paring knife, and a bread knife.[35] There are also a number of knives intended for use at the table such as a roast slicer, a steak slicer, a ham slicer and a beef slicer.[36] The utility knife is a somewhat new addition and is essentially a lengthened paring knife. The slicers are all slight variations of the same knife, something many modern producers are doing today. Bringing a bread knife into the set may have been new, but knives have been used for bread for centuries. Bread knives with thickness gauges go back at least as far as 1874, and the serrated knife that we commonly picture as a bread knife dates back to at least 1893.[37] Only the Sears catalogue shows a knife with a wavy edge, which is not the same as serrated.[38] The three wavy-edge knives are specified individually as being for bread, cake, or carving.

Throughout much of the first half of the twentieth century, people displayed their status not with kitchen knives but with carving knives. In middle-class homes, roasts were carved at the table in front of the guests. One just couldn't use a kitchen knife for the job. Although these carving knives served a utilitarian purpose, they also were often highly decorated. Handles were fashioned out of deer antlers or made of silver-plated metal. There are numerous design patents for carving knives during this period, and often the handles are what make a design special.

The expansion of the knives available to cooks really starts in the 1960s with the principle German manufacturers expanding their lines with both increases in patterns and increases in styles.[39] Today, Wüsthof produces fifteen different sizes and weights of cook's knife in their 'classic' style. In all, the company produces almost seventy different knives in the same style – more than any individual could ever need or use.[40]

In the late 1980s, Wüsthof introduced their version of the Japanese santoku, sold exclusively by Crate & Barrel.[41] Being lighter and slightly smaller than most cook's knives of the period, the Wüsthof santoku was a big hit.[42] Today, almost every knife manufacturer has their version of the santoku.

One version of the santoku sported oval-shaped depressions, called kullens, on each side of the blade.[43] The little depressions have become so popular that, even though there is a debate as to whether they work to reduce knife drag, Wüsthof is adding them to more knives.[44] Apparently, some people find the little darlings a bit sexy.[45]

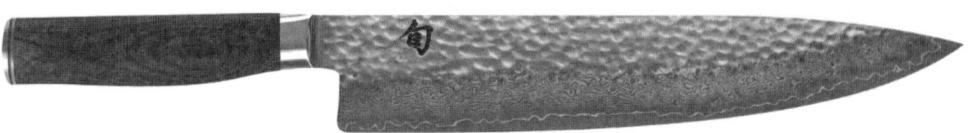

Figure 5: Shun-brand, Premier-style 25-cm (10-in) chef's knife by Kai USA illustrating an elaborate, Japanese design. (Photo. © Kai USA, Ltd. Used with permission.)

Slightly prior to the introduction of the Western-style santoku, in 1983, the Yoshida Metal Industry Company introduced Global knives to the west (Figure 4).[46] These knives featured a lightweight design with an all stainless steel construction. They've won numerous design awards, and led the way for the other Japanese knife companies to enter the U.S. market. Numerous people have told me that they originally purchased their Global knives because of their looks, and that they have many Global knives that people admire but that they never use. Global knives may have been the start of knives as bling.

Global-brand knives are the direct antecedent the today's ultra-fancy Japanese knives directed towards the high-end market (Figure 5). The newer Japanese knives are principally produced by Shun and Miyabi.[47] In contrast to these knives with rounded edges and sweeping lines are the traditional German-style knives with their square edges and clean-looking surfaces (Figure 6). The principle producers of these knives are probably Wüsthof and Henckels.[48]

Although I have tried to make the point that many of these knives are bought as bling, I will concede that that is not always the case. There are people who purchase fancy knives and only bring them out of the drawer when they use them to cut food. I will also concede that storing the knives in a knife block or on a magnetic bar may be the best approach in some kitchens, and the knives' owners seriously use every knife at their disposal. But I would still contend that a significant portion of the knives purchased see more time as bling than as useful tools.

Figure 6: Classic-style 26-cm (10-in) cook's knife by Wüsthof illustrating a classical, clean, German design. (Photo. by author.)

Kitchen Knives: The New Bling

Notes

1. US dollars have been converted the UK pounds at the rate of 0.65 £/$, the rate at noon on 5 April 2013. No attempt has been made to reflect the actual cost of purchasing the products at the prices quoted in pounds from a United Kingdom location. Where the exact amount of currency was not important, liberal rounding has occurred.
2. A slang term popularized in hip-hop culture, referring to 'ostentatious jewellery. Hence: wealth; conspicuous consumption' (*OED*).
3. Rick Rodgers (cookbook author and teacher), in discussion with the author, 18 March 2013.
4. Tommie Lucas (product developer, Kai (Shun) USA), in discussion with the author, 18 March 2013.
5. Todd Myers (vice-president of sales, Wüsthof-Trident of America), in discussion with the author, 18 March 2013.
6. A *gyuto* is a Japanese version of western-style chef's knife <http://zknives.com/knives/kitchen/misc/type/Gyuto.shtml> [accessed 20 March 2013]. This conversation took place one morning in the spring of 2009 in the basement prep kitchen of Cowbell Restaurant in Toronto, Canada. I don't remember the name of the chef.
7. JobTrain is a vocational school that provides training in entry-level jobs, primarily for disadvantaged students. <http://www.jobtrainworks.org> [accessed 20 March 2013].
8. Both 'chef's knife' and 'cook's knife' refer to the same knife pattern and are used interchangeably in this paper.
9. Frédéric Médigue (chef-owner, Château d'Amondans), in discussion with the author, May 2002.
10. This is not a complete list of knives with celebrity names.
11. Celebrity Knives Review from Consumer Reports, 16 June 2009 <http://www.youtube.com/watch?v=Gnbstb4kPss> [accessed 21 March 2013].
12. Macy's item 731816 <http://www1.macys.com/shop/product/martha-stewart-collection-stainless-steel-cutlery-16-piece-set?ID=731816&CategoryID=30194> [accessed 20 March 2013].
13. Williams-Sonoma item 41-7246218. <http://www.williams-sonoma.com/products/michel-bras-10-piece-knife-set> [accessed 21 March 2013].
14. Williams-Sonoma item 41-8137895. <http://www.williams-sonoma.com/products/michel-bras-3-inch-paring-knife> [accessed 21 March 2013].
15. Paula Deen Store item 415252. <http://www.pauladeenstore.com/Product/detail/Paula-Deen-Signature-Cutlery-3-pc-Chef-s-Set-Red/415252> [accessed 20 March 2013].
16. Amazon item DM0507. <http://www.amazon.com/Onion-Shun-DM0500-8-Inch-Chefs/dp/B0007IR2MO> [accessed 21 March 2013].
17. Kramer Knives website. <http://kramerknives.com> [accessed 28 March 2013].
18. Sur la Table item 893461. <http://www.surlatable.com/product/PRO-893461/Bob-Kramer-Carbon-Damascus-Chefs-Knife> [accessed 22 March 2013].
19. 'Ferdinand Alexander Porsche, nicknamed 'Butzi', son of Ferry Porsche, grandson of Ferdinand Porsche, was a German designer whose best known product was the first Porsche 911'. <http://en.wikipedia.org/wiki/Ferdinand_Alexander_Porsche> [accessed 28 March 2013].
20. Mike Solaegui (owner, Perfect Edge Cutlery), in discussion with the author, 28 March 2013.
21. Lucas, discussion.
22. Tula Gieseker (sales associate, Williams-Sonoma), in discussion with the author, 25 March 2013.
23. Sima Thomas (former bride), in discussion with the author, 16 March 2013.
24. Myers.
25. In other English-speaking countries, the living room is often called the lounge or, in former times, the parlour or drawing room.
26. Gieseker.
27. Bartolomeo Scappi, *Opera di M. Bartolomeo Scappi, cvovo secreto di Papa Pio V.* (1570?): Plate XIII; Jules Gouffé. *Le Livre de cuisine* (Paris: Librairie de L. Hachette et Cie, 1867), p. 17, pl. 12; Jules Gouffé, *The Royal Cookery Book (Le Livre de cuisine)*, trans. Alphonse Gouffé (London: Sampson Low, Son and

Marsten, 1869), p. 13.
28. US Patent 336,314. 16 February 1886. W.B. Hatfield, *Knife*.
29. Gouffé, *Le Livre de cuisine, op. cit.*: 17, 20. Gouffé; *The Royal Cookery Book*: pp. 12, 14; Janet McKenzie Hill, *Cooking for Two: A Handbook for Young Housekeepers* (Boston: Little, Brown and Company, 1919), p. 22; Juliet Corson, *Cooking School Text Book; and Housekeeper's Guide to Cookery and Kitchen Management* (New York: Orange Judd Company, 1883), p. 265; Mary Johnson Bailey Lincoln, *Mrs. Lincoln's Boston Cook Book* (Boston: Roberts Brothers, 1884), p. 509.
30. These knives are similar in appearance to the *mezzaluna* sold today.
31. *Montgomery Ward & Co. Catalogue and Buyers' Guide, No. 57, Spring and Summer, 1895* (New York: Dover Publications, 1969 [facsimile]), pp. 436, 446–48.
32. The paring knives were available either individually or by the dozen. The simplest one cost a nickel (5¢) for one or four bits (50¢) for a dozen.
33. *1897 Sears Roebuck & Company Catalogue* (New York: Skyhorse Publishing, 2007), p. 122.
34. *Catalogue des Articles de ménage* (Paris: Au Bon Marché, 1898), p. 8.
35. *Life Magazine*, 3 May 1948, p. 88.
36. *Life Magazine*, 24 November 1947, p. 8.
37. US Patent 157,516. 8 December 1874. Eva Heineman, *Improvement in bread knives*; US Patent 495,110. 11 April 1893. Francis Hayes & Fred J. Lewis, *Knife*.
38. *1897 Sears Roebuck & Company Catalogue*, p. 122.
39. 'Patterns' refers to the knife profile. Cook's knives, paring knives, utility knives all have different profiles, but may be designed with the same handle and overall visual style. 'Styles' refers to the different overall visual appearance that one set of knives will have as opposed to another, usually a function of the handle design.
40. Myers.
41. Myers.
42. At the same time, many professional chefs were experimenting with Chinese slicing cleavers as an alternative to the cook's or chef's knife. Other than among serious cooks of Chinese cuisine, the cleaver never achieved much popularity.
43. 'A similar design, *kullenschliff* (*kulle* is Swedish for hill (or – more likely – a misspelling of the German word 'Kuhle' meaning 'hollow' or 'deepening'); *schliff* meaning 'cut' or grind in German), has oval scallops (*kuhlen*) hollowed-out of one or both sides of the blade above the edge'. <http://en.wikipedia.org/wiki/Kitchen_knife> [accessed 24 March 2013].
44. The purpose of the kullens is to create air pockets on the side of the blade so there is less drag. Their effect is a subject of much debate in some circles.
45. Myers.
46. Yoshida Metal Industry Company http://www.yoshikin.co.jp/w/company/index.html [accessed 24 March 2013].
47. Shun is made by Kai USA Ltd, a division of the Kai Group, Tokyo, Japan <http://www.kai-group.com> [accessed 24 March 2013]; Miyabi is a brand name owned by Zwilling J.A. Henckels AG, part of the Zwilling Group, Solingen, Germany. The knives are manufactured in Japan <http://www.zwilling.com> [accessed 24 March 2013].
48. Ed. Wüsthof Dreizackwerk KG <http://www.wuesthof.de> [accessed 24 March 2013]; Zwilling J.A. Henckels AG <http://www.zwilling.com> [accessed 24 March 2013].

Tsatsal: the Symbolism and Significance of Mongolian Milk Spoons

Sharon Hudgins

Nomads of the steppes

Mongolia is a sparsely populated, landlocked nation in East-Central Asia, bordered on the north by the Russian Federation (Siberia) and on the east, south and west by the People's Republic of China, (including the Chinese autonomous region of Inner Mongolia). Covering 1.5 million square kilometres, Mongolia is a land of desert, semi-desert, forests and grassy steppes, with mountains in the northwest, west and southwest, and the Gobi Desert in the south. The climate ranges from arid desert to continental (with large daily and seasonal temperature ranges).[1]

Mongolia's economy is based on mining (coal and many industrially important minerals), the rapidly growing service sector and animal husbandry, the traditional mainstay of its economy in the past. Only a century ago, most of the population was classified as nomadic animal herders. Today, one-third of Mongolia's population of 3.2 million is engaged in herding and agriculture (primarily herding), a number that has recently declined from higher levels after an unusually severe winter in 2009–2010 destroyed nearly a quarter of the country's livestock. In recent history, prior to that disaster, Mongolia had a population of about 30 million herd animals, or ten times its human population, and a larger percentage of its people lived as nomadic herders.

Today, one-third of Mongolia's people live in the capital, Ulaanbaatar, and 62 per cent of the total population is urban. Those Mongolians still engaged in herding and agriculture live in rural areas and are considered either nomadic or semi-nomadic depending on how often they move their households and whether they plant any crops (possible in only a small part of the country, since most of the land is not arable).

Both nomadic and most semi-nomadic people live year round in *gers* (yurts), portable, circular-shaped, one-room houses made of wooden latticework covered with a thick layer of wool felt and an outer layer of canvas. These traditional Mongolian *gers* can be quickly and easily disassembled and packed for transport, along with the owners' other household goods, for reassembly in another location. In the past, some Mongolian nomads moved their households and herds as many as eight to ten times a year. The method of transport was pack animals and carts: camels and yaks loaded with packs, and/or wooden carts with wooden wheels, pulled by cattle. Today, Mongolian nomads might relocate only twice, to winter and summer pastures, unless there is a need to move to better pasturage at other times during the year. Their household possessions and disassembled *gers* are usually packed onto small trucks and sometimes loaded onto motorcycles, too. Wealthier nomads might even need to transport their satellite dish, solar-powered electric generator and modern television set to their new location.[2]

The traditional Mongolian *ger* 'kitchen'

Nomads tend not to accumulate as many material possessions as settled populations (especially those living in wealthier, high-consumption societies). Most of their possessions are functional (although sometimes also highly decorated), and they often serve more than one purpose. However, nomads' material possessions can also include personal items of purely decorative or sentimental value, as well as a few items of spiritual significance only, such as small items associated with the veneration of 'house gods' and 'pasture gods' if the family subscribes to animist/shamanist beliefs, and/or a small shrine if they are Buddhists.[3] In addition, among the few ritual objects in their possession is often a *tsatsal*, a specially shaped wooden spoon used for specific offerings of milk (or milk-based liquids) to the deities in the Mongolian pantheon and for ritual supplications, blessings and expressions of good will.

Every *ger* is assembled with its single door facing south (which a young local described to me as 'Mongolian GPS'). In the centre of each *ger* is a small, round, sheet-iron stove (usually fuelled by dried animal dung), with a stovepipe leading up to an opening in the centre of the *ger*'s top; this stove is used for both heating the *ger* and preparing food indoors. On the north wall, opposite the south-facing entry, is sometimes a religious shrine (Buddhist, or animist/shamanist, or both, depending on the owners' beliefs). Arranged around the curving walls of the *ger* are single beds (which double as seating during the day), wooden chests for clothing and perhaps a small set of shelves (often just the wooden boxes used for transporting household goods) for the kitchenware (mostly cookware, some of which doubles as tableware). Some, but not all *gers*, also have a low wooden table and small, short, backless wooden stools, placed in the middle of the room between the central stove and the north wall. Just inside the door, a barrel of fermenting *airag* (kumis, made from mares' milk) occupies the space to the right (south-west side) of the door, as you face outward from inside the *ger*. Traditionally this kumis container was a large bag made of leather; today it's likely to be an industrial heavy plastic barrel with a plastic lid.

The *ger* is divided into the male section, on the west side, and the female section on the east where most of the utensils for food preparation are kept.[4] Kitchenware consists of a few metal bowls, pots, pans, jugs and kettles (usually made of inexpensive, lightweight aluminium), along with metal ladles and large wooden or metal spoons, all used multi-functionally for cooking, processing milk products and serving foods. Smaller bowls (wood, metal, sometimes ceramic) are used for serving liquid milk products and the numerous tea concoctions and soups favoured by the Mongols. Some families also own a few ceramic and/or metal plates (often used only as serving platters). Many foods are simply eaten by everyone from a single communal bowl. There are also wooden milk churns, metal milk cans, wooden racks and trays for drying meats and

The Symbolism and Significance of Mongolian Milk Spoons

milk products and wooden, metal or plastic buckets that are sometimes turned upside down to double as stools. Metal and wooden boxes, containers made of birch bark, and bags made of burlap or animal skins hold food supplies such as tea, rice and flour.

In the past, ancient Mongolian nomads ate with their fingers and with knives (all men carry hunting knives); spoons were a later addition. Food is prepared in such a way that it can be eaten with only those implements: knives for cutting large chunks of meat into smaller ones and for lifting meat to the mouth; fingers for eating meat (on and off the bone), as well as steamed dumplings, fried dumplings and some solid milk products (cheese, dried yoghurt); and spoons for liquids such as soups (although many soups and other liquids are sipped directly from bowls). Although William of Rubruck reported the Mongols' use of a two-pronged fork in the mid-thirteenth century, and chopsticks were later introduced by the Chinese, in the modern era fingers, knives and spoons are still the most common eating implements in a nomad's *ger*.[5]

The only 'spoon' that is not used for cooking, serving or eating, but is intimately connected with food, is the ceremonial *tsatsal*, used for making libations of milk, *airag*, or milk-tea.[6]

White foods (*Tsagaan idee*)

Meat and milk are the mainstays of the Mongolians' diet. Both foods are products from the same domestic animals (along with useful hides, fleece and wool, including cashmere from goats, as well as transportation provided by some animals). The Mongolians refer to these animals as 'the five muzzles': horses, cattle (cattle and yaks together, as well as hainags, a cow/yak cross), sheep, goats and Bactrian camels.[7] People living in the north-western regions of Mongolia, bordering on Russian Siberia, add a sixth muzzle to the herd: reindeer, which are also raised for their meat, hides, milk and used for transport.

Nomadic Mongolians subsist primarily on meat (and some preserved milk products) during the winter season from October to April, whereas milk (in many forms) makes up the majority of their diet in the summer season from April to October, the six months between the birth of new animals and the end of the prime milking period.[8] Through thousands of years of experimentation, Mongolians have learned to make a surprisingly large variety of milk products – boiled, curdled, fermented and/or dried, as well as distilled – many of which are little known in the West. Milk is turned into many forms of cream, butter, 'milk skins', soured clotted milk, buttermilk, yoghurt, sour cream porridge, cheeses, 'milk vodka', kumis and several other variations on this same lacteous theme. Milk from all of the 'six muzzles' is used for dairy products, although milk from certain kinds of animals is often preferred for a specific product, such as mares' milk for kumis, and sheep, goat, camel and yak's milk for a variety of fat-rich cream products.[9]

Mongolians consider dairy products to be 'white foods' (*tsagaan idee*), a special category of food. The colour white has long had a sacred role in Mongolian culture. Traditionally whiteness has been associated with women, and white is considered to be the 'mother' of all colours, which descend from it. White also has a number of positive attributes: light (as opposed to darkness), innocence, purity, nobility, kindness, honesty, happiness, prosperity, respect, high social status – and all naturally white-coloured things, from milk to clouds, are considered to possess these properties.[10] In addition, the word milk (*sü*) itself connotes warm and pleasant feelings to Mongolians.[11]

Mongolian milk rituals

Milk holds such an important place in Mongolian life that it is used in many sacred rituals rooted deep in Mongolian history and culture.[12] Women are usually, but not exclusively, the people who offer these libations, because women are the family members who milk the animals and process the dairy products, and because of milk's (and whiteness's) symbolic association with women. Certain liquid milk products are offered as a gift to honour several spirits of the earth and sky; as supplications for protection of the family and the herds; to ask for an increase in the herds and an abundance of milk; and as blessings and expressions of good wishes towards a person, animal or inanimate object.

Every morning, after the animals have been milked and before breakfast is eaten (sometimes in the evening, too), a female member of the family (usually the herder's wife) steps outside the *ger* and tosses an offering of fresh milk, *airag*, or milk-tea, one to three times in each of five directions: upward to the sky (to the great eternal god Tengri who lives in the blue sky, or to the many *tengris* in the heavens) and then in the four directions of the compass ('the four directions of the wind', although the number of directions can vary from four to eight). Traditionally the woman is dressed in a respectful manner (not casual clothing), and her head is covered with a hat or scarf. She holds the libation spoon in her right hand and the container of milk in the left.[13] A modern urban manifestation of this ritual is the tossing of milk off the balcony or out the window of a Mongolian's apartment in a high-rise building in the city. Shamans (male or female) also offer libations in several ceremonies where milk is sprinkled into the air or onto an object, as do adherents of Burkhanism, a belief system influenced by Mongolian Buddhism, which includes some shamanistic aspects.[14] Many Mongolians also believe that an offering tossed into the air multiplies many times in its strength and effectiveness as it reaches upward to the spirits.

A dance performance by Gankhuyag Natsag's Mongolian Tsam Dance Troupe depicts this ritual performed by a woman in traditional Mongolian clothing, with the following narration:

> For hundreds of years
> With rising sun in the morning
> Mongolian mothers offered milk to the Nature
> To the Sky
> To the Land

The Symbolism and Significance of Mongolian Milk Spoons

> To the Masters and Spirits of Nature
> As milk is a symbol of love and respect.
> Mongolians believe in strong connection with Nature
> Giving mother's love, care, warmth
> From the drops of milk to the Gods
> Father Sun
> Mother Land
> Masters of Nature.
> From the drops of the milk
> Pour back to the humankind
> The rain that will wash away our pain
> The wind that will blow away our suffering
> The sunshine that will blossom our lives.[15]

An especially important occasion for ceremonial libations is the Mongolian Lunar New Year that starts on the first day of the Tsagaan Tsar (White Month, White Moon), which occurs in late January or early February, when many people (both men and women) go at sunrise on the first day of the new year to designated sacred places, or even just outside their own *ger*, to greet the new year (and by extension, the beginning of spring) by tossing milk into the air toward the rising sun. At the beginning of spring the herder's wife also goes outside to the back of the family's *ger* to toss milk in the direction of north, to signify that the hard winter is over and better times are to come.

Another milk sprinkling ritual in the spring occurs after most of the animals' new offspring have been born:

> A prayer of sprinkling is told and an incense made of butter, cream and juniper branches is burned at the west side or in the four directions of the camp. The milk of the first mother animal that delivered its baby that spring is offered to the nature... This ritual is done by two women, of whom one holds the vessel with the milk and the other sprinkles with a sprinkling spoon. They offer the milk to the 99 skies, 77 earth spirits and to the lords of mountains and rivers while going around the camp in a clockwise direction.

This same source cites the prayer spoken when sheep's milk is offered to nature in this sprinkling ritual:

> To the high king, Eternal Blue Sky
> To the Mother Earth and billion stars
> The Golden Sun and Silver Moon
> On this good fortune day
> We offer this ritual of sprinkling

The milk of black sheep
Not tasted, no one touched
To ask for blessing and
To protect the sheep herds
When milking sheep:
Let the milk fill the vessel
Let your wish come true as you hope or
May the vessel be full
Milk be affluent
Livestock be many.[16]

When a guest or family member sets off on a journey by horseback or camel, milk is splashed onto the muzzle, mane, tail, rump and sometimes flanks of the animal, as well as the stirrups of the saddle, as a blessing to protect the person on his journey. Modern modes of transportation (and their riders) are blessed similarly, with a splash of milk on the headlights, tail-lights, tyres and windshields of the truck, automobile or motorcycle. Likewise, milk can be splashed onto the carriage of a train when someone is departing by rail. People standing on the ground even toss milk into the air as an airplane takes off from the runway, to protect the passengers on the flight.

Many other situations also occasion the ritual sprinkling of milk as a blessing or an offering: when making wool felt; when a new site for the family's *ger* is chosen; on the felt covering of the *ger* after it has been erected in a new location; when a burial place has been selected (but before the burial begins); when a child's hair is about to be cut for the first time; on the first day of milking the mares; on the heads of male animals before castration; on the young male animal newly selected as the future sire of the flock or herd; at the beginning of a horse race, and afterward upon the winning horse. Milk is also splashed onto sick animals to make them well.[17]

Although other liquids such as *airag* (kumis), milk-tea, 'milk vodka' (clear spirits distilled from milk) and commercial vodka (distilled from potatoes or grains) are sometimes used in these sprinkling or tossing ceremonies, milk is the favoured liquid for many rituals because of its positive attributes and its deep significance in Mongolian culture. Numerous written and photographic documents show that the milk can be sprinkled or tossed into the air using the fingers, a bowl (wood, metal, plastic), a ladle (wood or metal), a soupspoon or large kitchen spoon (metal or plastic) or a wooden spoon (such as a spoon with a deep oval bowl at one end and a horse's head or wild goat's head carved at the other end of its handle). But the traditional ceremonial spoon most often used for certain milk libation rituals – particularly those made by women – is the *tsatsal*, a uniquely shaped spoon, usually carved from wood, which is employed solely for this purpose.

The Symbolism and Significance of Mongolian Milk Spoons

The Mongolian milk spoon (*tsatsal*)

These special libation spoons are among the material possessions that nomadic Mongolians carry with them as they move across the steppes. The family's single milk spoon is a treasured family heirloom, passed down from one generation to the next. Its sole function is to transfer milk from another receptacle (bowl, jug, kettle) into the air, thus transforming the milk (or sometimes *airag* or milk-tea) into a sacred offering or a supplication to the gods, or into a blessing upon other people, animals and objects.

Most of these spoons are carved out of a single piece of wood that is sometimes oiled or varnished, but left its natural colour, although a few of the carved spoons also have painted handles. (More rarely, these libation spoons are carved from soapstone or made from silver or brass.) The characteristic shape of the spoons is spatulate, with long handles decorated with a variety of carved symbols: mythical, animistic, Tibetan Buddhist, zodiacal, nationalistic, naturalistic, realistic, purely ornamental geometric or floral, often in combination. The 'bowls' of the spoons are most often flat squares or rectangles (or occasionally trapezoids), not the concave rounds or ovals characteristic of common spoons used for eating. The carving on these flat 'bowls' looks much like a waffle iron, with nine symmetrical square or rectangular indentations (hollows or wells) forming a grid of three rows of three hollows each (although some *tsatsal* have four, eight, ten or thirteen hollows or 'eyes' as they are sometimes called).[18] Each of these indentations is an inverted four-sided pyramid (or, less often, a small, circular, concave hollow), into which the milk is poured. Most of these spoons are carved only on the front side, although some are also carved, less extensively, on the back of the handles and/or on the back of the flat bowls.[19]

The flat bowl with its three-by-three grid pattern of hollows is the only element common to most of these spoons. The nine hollows (three down multiplied by three across) represent a sacred and auspicious number to Mongolians, as do other multiples of three (which are computed by also counting the two diagonals of three hollows on the grid). Three and nine are also significant numbers in Buddhism – and indicate the direct influence of Buddhist symbolism on many of these milk spoons. To Mongolians, the number three has several symbolic meanings:

> Past – present – future
> The three stages of life: youth/childhood – adulthood – old age/wisdom
> Heaven – Earth – the Lower World/Underworld
> For Buddhists: the three pillars of Buddhism

Hence the carving on this grid, with its pattern of threes and nines, and the offering of milk from this grid, brings into play all of these symbols, with meanings that resonate deeply with many Mongolians.

All of the 43 *tsatsal* (contemporary and antique) that I have examined range in length from 18 to 40 cm and in width from 1.25 cm at the narrowest end to 8 cm at the widest. With the exception of one very plain, crudely carved milk spoon and a few that are also not very skilfully carved, most of the handles of the other spoons are intricately carved by very good craftsmen. All of them display one or more of the following symbols, in various combinations, usually with several symbols depicted on each spoon:[20]

- Yin-yang symbol, representing the interconnectedness and interdependence of seemingly opposite forces, including light and dark, good and evil, masculinity and femininity; the unity of complementary opposites.
- Two fishes intertwined in a yin-yang configuration, representing an animal that never closes its eyes and hence is always vigilant; also symbolizing the unity of men and women, with the masculine and feminine uniting to reproduce human beings. Two fishes in a parallel vertical or horizontal position are an ancient pre-Buddhist symbol, as well as a Buddhist symbol of happiness, conjugal fidelity and unity, fertility and abundance.
- The endless knot (eternal knot), a geometric diagram symbolizing Buddha's endless wisdom and compassion, without beginning or end; the union of wisdom and compassion; the continuity and the interrelatedness of all phenomena, despite the interaction of opposing forces; presumably also suggesting the intertwining of husband and wife as the cornerstone of the family. The spaces created by the intertwining of the knot's element can also have numerical significance.
- The three precious jewels (the triple gem), representing the three pillars of Buddha: Buddha himself, the Dharma (Buddha's teachings) and the Sangha (Buddhist monks and nuns and the community of people who have attained enlightenment).
- Eight jewels within a flame nimbus, symbolizing the granting of wishes or bringing of wealth; eight is an especially auspicious number in Buddhist iconography.
- The begging bowl, a symbol of Buddhist humility; on these spoons it might also represent the bowl in which milk products ('white foods') are offered to guests or as libations.
- The soyombo ideogram on the Mongolian national flag, representing the freedom and independence of the Mongolians. The three flames at the top symbolize prosperity in the past, present and future. The round sun and crescent moon are ancient Mongolian symbols representing the origin of its people. In the lower part of the ideogram, the triangles at the top and bottom symbolize the spear and the arrow, both pointing downward to indicate the defeat of Mongolia's enemies. Two horizontal rectangles and two vertical rectangles (the latter representing firmness and strength) are said to enclose and stabilize the round motif (an unstable form), which also contains the fish yin-yang symbol, with its attendant meanings. (Sometimes the 'three flames', or even a single flame, are carved on these spoons separately, independent of the Soyombo national ideogram.)
- Mongolian calendar animals, the twelve animals of the Mongolian twelve-year calendar (based on the Chinese zodiac and representing the twelve different

The Symbolism and Significance of Mongolian Milk Spoons

Figure 1. Tsatsals *with yin-yang fishes, eternal knot and three flames motifs (Sharon Hudgins).*

Figure 2. Tsatsal *with yin-yang fishes, eternal knot and Soyombo ideogram motifs (Sharon Hudgins).*

Figure 3. Tsatsal *with motifs of the eternal knot, three precious jewels and 'five muzzles', depicting the five animals from which milk is obtained (Sharon Hudgins).*

Figure 4. Tsatsals *with motifs of two stylized elephants, yin-yang fishes and a 'torch dragon' with a flaming tail (Sharon Hudgins).*

Figure 5. The indentations in the 'bowl' of the spoon hold the milk for ritual libations. This spoon is decorated, above the bowl, with Buddhist motifs of the begging bowl and the three precious jewels (Sharon Hudgins).

Figure 6. Tsatsal *with motifs of the three flames, the sun and the moon at the top and Buddhist motifs of the begging bowl and the three precious jewels at the bottom (Sharon Hudgins).*

The Symbolism and Significance of Mongolian Milk Spoons

Figure 7. Tsatsals *with similar geometric motifs (Sharon Hudgins).*

Figure 8. Tsatsal *with the three flames motif above the twelve animals of the Mongolian calendar (Sharon Hudgins).*

animals associated with the cycle of individual years): rat, ox, tiger, rabbit, dragon, snake, horse, sheep, monkey, rooster, dog and pig, in that order. One spoon, probably crafted for the tourist trade, depicts all these animals on the front of the handle, with the backside also highly carved: the large flat 'bowl' is completely decorated with a scene of grassy steppes, peaked mountains, a full moon, stars in the sky, two camels and two *gers*, and the handle is ornamented with two large leaves enclosing the word 'MONGOLIA' in English.

The 'Five Muzzles', the domestic animals from which milk is obtained: camel, horse, cow/yak/hainag, sheep and goat. Spoons carved with these five motifs also give a clue to the probable regional nature of these artefacts; had they been carved by, or for use by, Mongolians living in the north-western part of the county, they might also have included the 'sixth muzzle', a reindeer.

Two elephants, a Hindu symbol associated with wealth and fame. I have seen

elephants carved on only two spoons, in conjunction with a yin-yang symbol and a dragon with a flaming tail.
- Dragon with a single flame at the point of its tail; a serpentine Chinese-style dragon with a distinctive face, suggesting that it might be a 'torch dragon', the mythical creature responsible for creating day and night, seasonal winds and the aurora borealis.
- 'Left-hand' swastika, in Buddhism a symbol of the footprints of Buddha, as well as prosperity, long life and eternity; sometimes highly stylized and depicted as an interlocking pattern of repeated swastika motifs, representing unending life.
- The mandorla (two interlocking circles), symbolizing the unity of complementary opposites (heaven/earth, life/death, good/evil, light/dark, man/woman); traditional Mongolian symbol of a married man, also often depicted on a man's wedding ring.
- Two interlocking diamond shapes, traditional Mongolian symbol of a married woman, also often depicted on a woman's wedding ring.
- Lotus flower, one of the eight auspicious symbols of Buddhism, representing spiritual and mental purity.
- General floral motifs, probably representing stylized depictions of wild plants found in Mongolia.

Three of the milk spoons I examined are very different from the others: longer, wider and very flat, with five, seven or eight distinct divisions on the handles, each division framing a specific symbol carved in bas relief, with an additional floral motif at the top or bottom of each handle. (The nine indentations for the milk are more simply carved, unpainted and unvarnished.) The motifs on each of the spoon handles are painted in bright colours (green, yellow, red, pink, blue, orange, white, black; one also has highlights of metallic gold paint), whereas most milk spoons are unpainted and simply oiled, varnished, or left untreated.

These three painted spoons (which look like they were made by the same hand) all have one motif in common: the endless knot (which appears on many other *tsatsal*). Two of them also depict the right-turning conch shell, representing the spread of Buddha's teaching in all directions, like the sound from a conch shell trumpet, and the consequent awakening from ignorance, as well as the Mongolian symbolism of victory in battle. Other symbols on these painted milk spoons include:

- The wheel, one of the most important Buddhist symbols, representing the teachings of Buddha, as well as transformation and rebirth; the wheel of life.
- A bowl filled with grain, being nibbled by two white rats, symbolizing wealth or abundance.
- A rat, horse, rabbit, ox, rooster and snake – all animals associated with specific years on the Mongolian twelve-year calendar, as well as with Buddhist legends.

The Symbolism and Significance of Mongolian Milk Spoons

The sun, moon, stars, mountains, flowers, grasses, foliage and blue sky – all natural images important to nomadic herders and believers in animism.

All of these libation spoons convey a sense of the individual carver and the spiritualism inherent in each piece – Buddhist, animist and shamanist beliefs, as well as the direct link between the animals and landscapes that produce the milk and the sacred uses of that milk in many Mongolian rituals. En route from bowl to sky, tossed from the carved hollows on these spoons, milk is transformed from a common material substance, essential for daily life, into a form of worship, a supplication, a blessing, each drop of which transcends the boundaries of matter and attains a spiritual significance of its own. No wonder that Mongolian nomads count these spoons among the most precious of their material possessions.

Acknowledgements

Much of the information in this paper comes from my own experience during five trips to Mongolia with National Geographic Expeditions in 2006–2008, including visits to the National Museum of Mongolia, interviews with Mongolians living in the capital city, Ulaanbaatar, and visits to nomads living in *gers* in the Gorkhi–Terelj National Park near Ulaanbaatar. Subsequent interviews and correspondence with scholars who study Mongolia have added greatly to my knowledge of this subject. I am especially indebted to Mette M. High, Anett C. Oelschlägel, Isabelle Bianquis, Gaby Bamana, Gankhuyag Natsag and B.A. Baasankhuu (with translations by Enkhtsetseg Tumurbaatar) for the information from their field research that they so generously shared with me.

Notes

1. Statistics in this section are from *CIA World Factbook Online: Mongolia* <https://www.cia.gov/library/publications/the-world-factbook/geos/mg.html>.
2. 'Nomadic Life' <http://asiarecipe.com/monnomad.html>.
3. Mongolians were originally animists/shamanists. After Buddhism (especially Tibetan Buddhism) spread into Mongolia, it eventually became the dominant religion there. Mongolian adherence to Buddhism has waxed and waned over several centuries, for a number of reasons, but has been experiencing a revival in the recent post-Communist period. Today, approximately half of Mongolians identify themselves as Buddhists, whereas a much smaller percentage claims to be shamanists. However, many people apparently adhere to both belief systems simultaneously, and practice rituals belonging to both religions.
4. Eric Thrift, *The Cultural Heritage of Mongolia* (Ulaanbaatar: Naranbulag Printing, 2001), p. 8.
5. Peter Jackson (trans.), *The Mission of Friar William of Rubruck: His Journey to the Court of the Great Khan Möngke: 1253–1255* (London: Hakluyt Society, 1990), p. 79. Mary Ellen Snodgrass (ed.), in the *Encyclopedia of Kitchen History* (New York: Taylor & Francis, 2004), p. 212, makes the point that Mongolians, among certain other Asians, 'use fingers, spoons and chopsticks, according to family custom and the type of food served'.
6. For a description of a variety of Mongolian milk-teas and how they are made, see Sharon Hudgins, 'Raw Liver and More: Feasting with the Buriats of Southern Siberia', *Food on the Move: Proceedings of the Oxford Symposium on Food and Cookery 1996*, ed. Harlan Walker (Totnes, Devon, UK: Prospect Books, 1997), pp. 138–39, 151–52.

7. Natasha Fijn, *Living with Herds: Human–Animal Coexistence in Mongolia* (Cambridge, UK: Cambridge UP, 2011).
8. Natalia Zhukovskaya, 'The Milk Food of the Mongolian-Speaking Nomads of Eurasia in a Historical and Cultural Perspective', *Acta Ethnographica Hungarica* 53.2 (2008), pp. 307–14.
9. Badarch Dendevin et al. (eds.), *Mongolia Today: Science, Culture, Environment, and Development* (London: RoutledgeCurzon, 2003), pp. 69–85. Traditionally, milk and meat constituted the entire nomadic diet, except for a few wild berries, fruits, pine nuts, onions and garlic foraged from the land. Contact with the Chinese, and later the Russians, eventually brought root vegetables, cabbages, cucumbers, bell peppers, grains (wheat, rice, barley) and a few spices (black pepper, red pepper) into the Mongolians' diet.
10. Zhukovskaya, pp. 312–13.
11. Choi Lubsangjab, 'Milk in the Mongol Customs: Some Remarks on Its Symbolic Significance', *Etnografia Polska* 24.1 (1980), pp. 41–43.
12. Dendevin, p. 84.
13. Author's interview with Gankhuyag Natsag, 23 October 2013. See also Andrei Vinogradov, 'The Phenomenon of "White Faith" in Southern Siberia', *Anthropology & Archaeology of Eurasia* 45.3 (2006–2007), pp. 73–88.
14. V.K. Kos'min, 'Mongolian Buddhism's Influence on the Formation and Development of Burkhanism in Altai', *Anthropology & Archeology of Eurasia* 45.3 (2006–2007), pp. 43–72.
15. Gankhuyag Natsag's Mongolian Tsam Dance Troupe's performance at the beginning of *Mongolia!*, John F. Kennedy Center for the Performing Arts, Washington, D.C., 12 March 2013: <https://www.youtube.com/watch?v=iUdtURmlRlA> (segment 0:03:00–0:04:20). Narration transcription by the author.
16. 'The Traditional Cuisine of Mongolia: White Essen: Mongolian Milk' <http://www.legendtour.ru/eng/mongolia/informations/mongolian_milk.shtml>. It is unclear why the milk of a black sheep is used; perhaps the reference is to duality in nature: black sheep, white milk.
17. Lubsangjab; Zhukovskaya, p. 312; 'The Traditional Cuisine of Mongolia: The White Food of the Mongol' <http://www.legendtour.ru/eng/mongolia/informations/white_food.shtml>.
18. B.A. Baasankhuu, with Enkhtsetseg Tumurbaatar (trans.), personal communication with the author, 11 November 2013.
19. Since very little has been published about the actual form, decoration and symbolism of these ceremonial spoons, much of the information in this section is based on (a) my own collection of Mongolian milk spoons; (b) those I have seen in Mongolia and in photographs (mainly from owners of these spoons); (c) personal communications to me from B.A. Baasankhuu with Enkhtsetseg Tumurbaatar (trans.), October–November 2013; and (d) interview with Battsetseg Chagdgaa in Ulaanbaator, Mongolia, September 2008.
20. Much of the information about the meaning of these symbols comes from Thrift, pp. 49–53, and Robert Beer, *The Encyclopedia of Tibetan Symbols and Motifs* (Boston: Shambhala, 1999).w

Katai: Coconut Scrapers

Phil Iddison

Coconut is an essential and versatile ingredient in south and south-east Asian food. The fruit of the coconut palm *Cocos nucifera*, a nut, is used in various stages of its growth for human consumption. Coconut water and the gelatinous flesh from the immature nut; the grated or shaved fresh mature flesh; coconut milk and cream extracted from the fresh grated flesh; coconut oil derived from copra, the dried nut flesh; and desiccated coconut all have rolls to play in local food in the diverse area that stretches from East Africa to Indonesia, into the Melanesian region and also around the tropical world. The coconut has been widely distributed by nature and exploited by man. Coconut milk in particular is an essential component and common theme in the cuisines of these regions.

Extracting the flesh from a mature and fresh nut is not straightforward. The coconut shell is extremely strong, and the coconut flesh inside is dense and conforms tightly to the inside face of the shell. There is a thin dark brown membrane that separates the flesh from the shell but the tight fit within the shell means that considerable physical effort is required to prize out sections of flesh once a nut has been opened. This is certainly the case with any fresh coconut worthy of human consumption.

Given the ubiquity of the coconut it is therefore no surprise that specialist tools have evolved to extract the flesh. These are generally based on the mechanics of extracting the flesh from the halved nut.

They can be simple pieces of serrated metal attached to a wooden handle to scrape out the flesh. In this form they are similar to tools for shredding other fruit and vegetables such as unripe papaya and green mango.

Mounting a scraper on a strong support that can be anchored allows two hands to be applied to the scraping process, significantly improving productivity. If the support is large enough to sit on, bodyweight will anchor the combined tool to the kitchen floor or ground, often the kitchen workplace in the tropics.[1] This eminently practical solution is the focus of this paper.

In Thailand the resulting tool is called a *katai*, often translated as a rabbit. At its simplest it is merely a plank of wood with a metal scraper at one end and short foot near the scraper to provide clearance under the scraper to scrape the nut and for a receptacle to collect the shredded coconut. More stylish examples are often carved from wood with a cranked iron 'tongue' attached to scrape the coconut flesh from the shell. They can be highly decorated craft objects. These artisanal characteristics together with the search for convenience or the desire to have a new kitchen gadget have consigned many of them to be re-cycled as curios for the tourist trade.

From personal experience, and without the benefit of a locally developed tools, the flesh can be loosened somewhat by repeatedly striking the whole nut with a blunt object (the back of a cleaver or hammer for instance) until the shell audibly cracks and can finally be broken open, frequently into randomly shaped pieces of solid flesh. This also has the effect of breaking the 'surface tension' of the membrane to the shell surface. These random fragments of shell flesh can be processed but do not lend themselves to a logical or efficient production process. The pieces of coconut flesh can be grated individually for preparing coconut milk or can be pared to make coconut crisps. This was my modus operandi to prepare coconut, for instance for pan toasted coconut shavings, a delicious way of enjoying the nut flesh.

Can we assume that cooks are always in search of efficiency? The process that is described above does succeed, but is not efficient. Despite owning traditional coconut scrapers, I did not appreciate their inherent efficiency until I carried out a practical experiment to marry a Thai *katai* to a coconut purchased on a London high street. With a little skill in directing the knife blows along the equator of the shell the nut was split into two hemispheres. Working a half nut backwards and forwards over the metal tongue of the *katai* produced a reasonably uniform pile of grated coconut. It was a short learning curve to assess the best angle to hold the coconut shell and to choose whether to scrape in both directions of motion. I could appreciate that in experienced hands these tools could quickly prepare the flesh for preparation of coconut milk.[2]

I came across references to these implements before visiting Thailand. On an early visit I obtained a copy of *Modern Thai Cooking*, published in 1977,[3] this had several line drawings of *katai* in animal forms and a photograph with two such examples. On these holiday visits I never found a carved *katai* but did see the simple plank versions and hand tools in the food markets. When I went to work in Thailand I was determined to find a *katai*. I ended up with a collection of more than twenty! Travels in the region added examples from Malaysia and Indonesia. A subsequent return to work and travel in Asia extended my collection with examples from Zanzibar, India and Cambodia.[4]

Markets in these areas usually have a vendor operating a commercial coconut scraper, to meet the demand for freshly grated coconut. This is typically a fearsome toothed spherical grinding head attached to an electric motor onto which the coconut halves can be forced to ream out the white meat. This usually takes place in a potentially hazardous manner with no safeguards whatsoever apart from the hard coconut shell itself. This commercial availability has contributed to the redundancy of the traditional tools and has also now been hastened by the ready availability of canned coconut milk.

I have seen machines of this type operated in Thai and Cambodian markets and even in a small supermarket in Al Ain in the UAE. In the latter case the shredded coconut was on sale to satisfy the needs of the expatriate south Indian community as coconut milk is not generally used in traditional Arabian food.

There are few basic kitchen utensils that have become art objects in their own right. Function normally determines form, and, whilst a sieve finely crafted from basketwork

Katai: Coconut Scrapers

may be a beautiful object to Western ethnic taste, it is still essentially a sieve. Spoons may be carved with plant or animal motifs, and a serving tray may have intricate decoration chased into its surface. However both these examples would naturally be part of the public display of a meal and not something that was essentially a tool confined to food processing in the relative privacy of the kitchen as is the case with the *katai*.

These simple tools have achieved a status well above their basic utility because of the coconut's importance. An analogy can be drawn with the status of key ingredients in other cuisines. The olive has a similar role and importance as a cooking medium in Mediterranean food and has iconic cultural status. It is produced, marketed, depicted and consumed with a high profile as a desirable and key ingredient. The coconut inhabits a similar niche in Asian food cultures. Processed coconut flesh is a binding ingredient across a large number of dishes from savoury to sweet. The *katai* is the marker for start of the detailed process to produce coconut milk as the cooking medium. In turn this is often the start of the process to create a meal.

This range from utilitarian simplicity to highly decorated examples leads me to believe that they may also have reflected their owner's status and aspirations, a utensil to own and use with pride. The carved wood, lacquer and paint are not essential to the function of these tools which do not appear in the final presentation of the meal.[5]

There are several distinct morphologies of these tools that reflect the cultures in which they are used. In Thailand the carving and decoration are most often in the form of a stylized animal. I have collected examples carved as a rabbit, a dog, a snake, a rat, a cat, a lion, a lizard or dragon, a turtle and in one case a cross between a pig and an elephant. Whatever form is chosen, the head or mouth supports the metal scraping tool and the back supports the cook who is scraping the coconut. The animal is often carved out of a sawn piece of wood but in one case in my collection it is formed from a suitable array of forked branches that achieve the required function. Sometimes it can take imagination to recognize the intended animal form in a display of the carver's ingenuity. One example has a creature swallowing the tail of the rather amorphous animal that supports the scraper.

In Cambodia the animal form is also used. The scraper that I purchased also shows the modest decoration of the bare wood that is rare in my experience. I have seen one Thai *katai* that was painted in a rather garish temple decoration style.

Examples from Malaysia and Indonesia have more varied and complex forms and often work in local carving styles such as animism and also with specific depictions of gender.[6] The Malay term for this tool is *kukur kelapa*, and I believe that this name is also used in Indonesia. An example collected in Malacca has a sturdy body with side panels decorated with vegetal detail in low relief carving. When I found it, it had lost its tongue but there was the characteristic hole for installing the metalwork. I had no difficulty purchasing a replacement forged iron tongue from a Thai market. Their ready availability indicated that the traditional *katai* were still in use and there was a demand for replacement tongues.

Food and Material Culture

Figure 1. A small carved rat katai *from Thailand with a skilfully formed tongue scraper and a small lidded box in the back for an unknown purpose!*[7] *The rat tail is wrapped round the back of the animal in the photo.*

I do not have extensive experience of the Indonesian equivalent of the *katai*. Two examples in my collection do exhibit characteristics that I understand are in the Indonesian style, but only one was collected in Indonesia. This one comprises a substantial slab of wood with a human figure extending at an angle from one end. The metal tongue projects from the top of this figure's head. The second one is an example of a 'boxed' *kukur kelapa*. The carved box conceals a hinged scraper that lifts out of the box to be secured by the lid for operation as a scraper. The carved decoration on the box includes a scorpion.

In contrast the scrapers that I found in Zanzibar are far more restrained as befits the coastal culture's Islamic influences. Some are in the form of a folding stool that is very characteristic of the local carving tradition and is also the basic form of folding bookstands used for instance for supporting a Koran. The Swahili name is *mbuzi*. These are carved from a single plank of wood and the hinge enables the height of the scraper to be adjusted.

I also found a larger and more stylish *mbuzi* in Zanzibar. The joints in the woodwork are pegged and wedged in a competent manner to match the quality of the simple carved detail. The ferrule around the tip of the neck to prevent the wood splitting is also a mark of quality construction. The carved detail around the base of the scraper and the support for the scraper itself look suspiciously like a depiction of male genitalia, possibly reflecting earthier local cultures.

Indian examples have considerable variety, ranging from carved wood to brass and copper constructions. Sometimes animal depiction still dominates although more

Katai: Coconut Scrapers

Figure 2. A Thai katai *formed from a piece of naturally branched timber with minimal carving. The back legs are fused together and despite its appearance it is quite stable in use. The form is a mix of dragon and lizard.*

restrained geometric examples are also found.

Two all-metal graters that I purchased from an antique dealer in London are examples from the west coast of India. They have a stylized animal form with quite short legs and may have been used on a low table to provide working space for the grating process. They are quite intricate examples of metal work combining a number of techniques, casting, sheet metal work, punching and riveting. Both have an auxiliary grater formed in the brass sheeting which forms the top surface. On one this has two sizes of holes punched into the metal to create the grater; the fine holes would be ideal for grating ginger or garlic. Both have hanging loops to store them out of the way or possibly for the purpose of display.

The final example comes from Kerala and shows yet another variety of this basic tool. In this form the carving includes an integral bowl to collect the grated coconut flesh.[8] This one is again very restrained in shape, a simple rectangle on short feet with the iron tongue driven through the whole thickness of the scraper to ensure a robust tool. The only decoration is an ogee indentation on each long side. The back edge of the steel support for the tongue is formed into a vertical sharpened edge which could have been used for slicing food as a secondary function similar to a Bangladeshi *bonti*.

A web search for coconut graters yields old specimens for sale to collectors and specimens in ethnographic collections. There are also modern hand and electrical scrapers to purchase. The modern tools are surprisingly uniform in appearance, and whilst they may be more efficient they lack the charm and interest of the traditional scrapers with their wide range of forms and finish.

Figure 3. A Cambodian scraper that is obviously a rabbit with whiskers, lop ears and a bob tail. The wood is treated with a matt varnish and highlighted in gold paint. The everted edge of the finely wrought tongue is furnished with very sharp teeth.

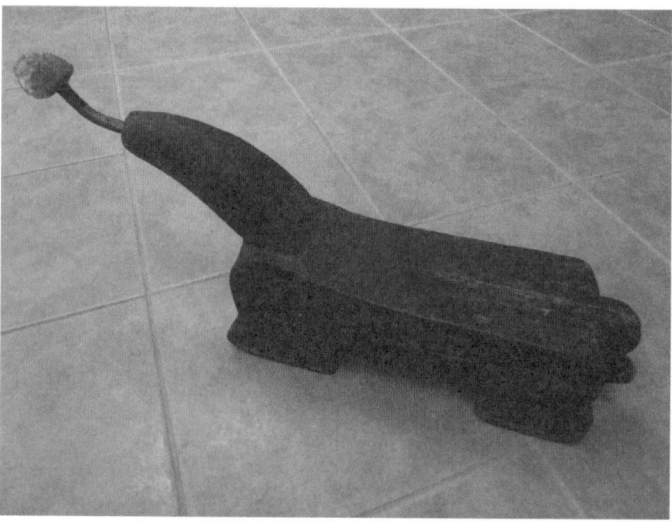

Figure 4. This Malay coconut scraper is finished with a dark wood dye to highlight the carved side panels and also some carved detail around the base of the neck.

Katai: Coconut Scrapers

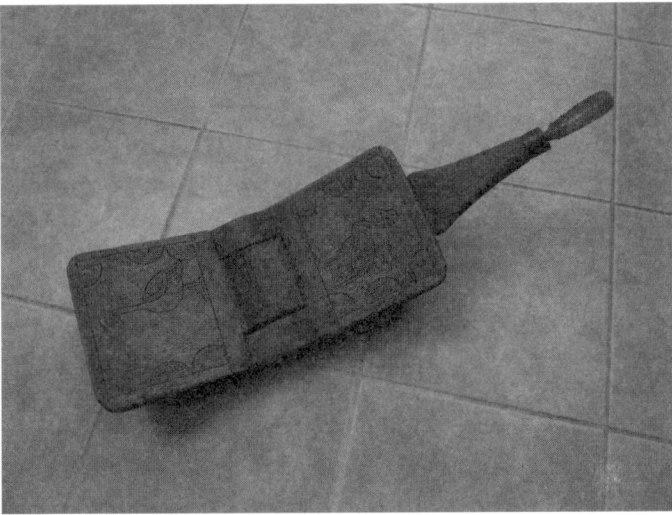

Figure 5. Zanzibar folding scraper. This example is decorated with two incised ostriches. Another example has simple vegetal decoration.

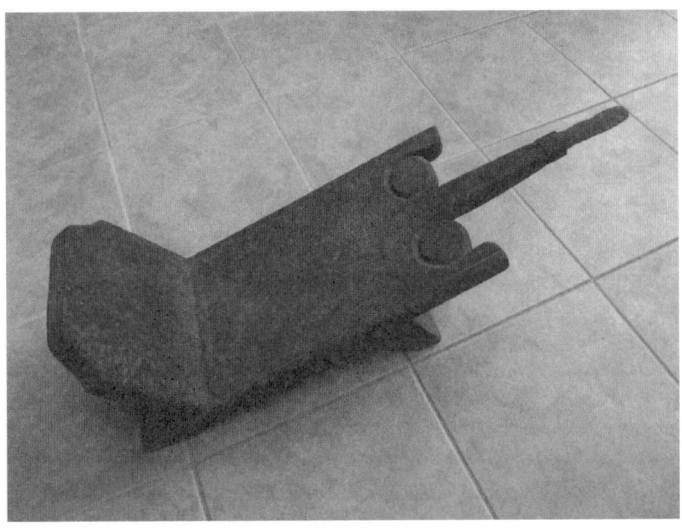

Figure 6. A well-constructed mbuzi *from Zanzibar. It is also the largest specimen that I have seen.*

Figure 7. Indian coconut scraper, called a peeta. *The frame is cast brass and the punched brass sheet of the auxiliary grater is secured with brass rivets*

Figure 8. A Keralan peeta, *the wood carving is rather coarse, there are adze marks on the surface or they could be cleaver marks from the surface being used as a chopping surface, quite a common fate for these objects.*

Katai: Coconut Scrapers

The requirement to shred coconut flesh to be processed for food has led to the development of tools for the process. In turn these have led to ethnic styles of scrapers that reflect local artistic traditions. The investment of effort and ingenuity perhaps reflects the importance of the prime ingredient, coconut flesh, and the need to process it into coconut milk as a key ingredient of traditional food. The availability of mechanical equipment to replace these simple artisanal tools of a food culture is part of an on-going transfer to modern technology. Their cultural significance is attested by web postings fondly remembering the presence of these stylish and efficient tools in the kitchens of previous eras.

Notes

1. One other similar floor mounted culinary tool from Bengal can be referenced. The *bonti* is a knife blade mounted vertically on a wooden board that is used for peeling, cutting and shredding food in Bengali cuisine. Like the *katai* the user sits on the board and thus has both hands free for working with the food.
2. Video clips of coconut scraping contests in which participants scrape against the clock can be found on the internet.
3. M.L. Kritikara and M.R. Pimsai Amranand, *Modern Thai Cooking* (Bangkok, Thailand: Editions Duang Kamol, 1977).
4. All photos are by the author and are of coconut scrapers in his collection.
5. The book *Thai Style* by Lucca Invernizzi Tettoni and William Warren (Bangkok: Asia Books, 1988) has photographs of a collection of Thai *katai* that includes specimens with paint and lacquer finishes (pp. 120–21).
6. The website of the Art Gallery of New South Wales <www.artgallery.nsw.gov.au> illustrates a splendid grater from Nias, Indonesia. It is carved with male genitalia and breasts on the underside between the legs and also sports a male figure carved in high relief at the base of the neck with a large headdress.
7. This is my smallest *katai*, which made me wonder whether it was practical and had ever been used. However I have seen illustrations of children grating coconut and many Thai are slightly built.
8. I also have a Thai *katai* with an integral bowl and have seen references to examples from other countries.

Moulds for Shaping and Decorating Food in Turkey

Priscilla Mary Işın

Making food look good as well as taste good is an age-old way of entertaining guests and attracting customers, and moulds have been used to decorate food by creating patterns or forming it into shapes in many cultures around the world. The Egyptians, Romans, Chinese and Arabs all used food moulds: the Egyptians moulded bread in the form of cones to place in temples or eat at celebrations; the Romans had bronze moulds in the shape of suckling pigs and hares; the Chinese moulded sugar into the shape of human figures, tigers and lions; and the Arabs shaped stuffed biscuits in carved moulds (Dalby 1996: 19; Schafer 1985: 153; Nasrallah 2007: 426).

Demir tatlısı: fritters shaped with irons

Turkish cuisine continued the tradition of shaping and decorating foods with a variety of wooden and metal moulds. One example is fritters made with shaped irons and known as *demir tatlısı*, 'iron pudding', which is made in Erzurum and several other Turkish provinces. The mould is either cast or made of sheet iron strips bent and curved into a variety of geometric shapes and attached to a beaten iron handle (Fig. 1). The batter is made of flour, eggs, salt, and sometimes yogurt. The fritter iron is first heated by plunging into boiling clarified butter or oil then dipped into the batter and again into the hot fat. In less than a minute of fritter slips free of the iron mould and when golden brown is removed from the pan with a draining spoon and soaked in sugar syrup or sprinkled with powdered sugar.

This type of fritter, shaped by dipping a heated iron mould into batter, dates back at least five centuries and probably far longer. It is first mentioned and illustrated in 1570 by the Italian Renaissance chef Bartolomeo Scappi, who calls them *fritelle* and says the moulds are in the form of 'lions, eagles, knots and other fanciful shapes' (Scappi 2009: 532, 650). A similar German recipe is found in Marx Rumpoldt's *Ein new Kochbuch* dated 1581, with the difference that after frying in hot fat the fritter is held close to a fire to dry it.

The origin of these decoratively shaped fritters is hard to pin down, especially since they have spread to so many parts of the world, including Iran, Syria, Afghanistan, Tunisia, Indonesia, Scandinavia, the United States, Mexico and Hong Kong, and are known by a variety of names, such as *rosetti* in Finland, *struvor* in Sweden, *rosetbakkelser* in Norway and *buenellos* in Mexico. This extraordinary range is testimony to their universal appeal. In Spain, where they are known as *hojuelas*, 'leaves', they were associated with Jews in the early modern period and feature as evidence against the defendant in Inquisition interrogations of crypto Jews (Hayward 2011). Vicky Hayward remarks that the Jews may well have adopted this dish from the Spanish Muslims, and an origin in the Islamic world is more likely in view of its wide dispersal in provincial Turkey, which cannot easily be explained by the influence of Jewish cuisine. The fritters may have developed from the *zulbiye/zalabiye* of medieval Arab cuisine made by pouring a stream of batter into hot oil to form decorative shapes. This is still made in Iran and India by the name *jalabi* and *jelebi* respectively, and was made in Turkey by the name *zülbiye* until the nineteenth century. Even if *zulbiye* is the origin, it leaves us with the question of how and where the leap from just pouring batter to using a shaped iron occurred. One tentative idea is that fritter irons were inspired by branding irons for livestock. Antique examples *circa* 1900 bear a remarkable resemblance to antique Turkish fritter irons. In the past families in Van each had a distinctively patterned fritter iron (Dr. Münevver Ünsal, personal communication), which suggests a parallel with the past use of branding iron motifs known as *tamga* that identified each family, a long-standing tradition in pastoralist culture (Fig. 2).

One of the earliest known shapes is that illustrated by Scappi, a square divided into four smaller squares, which is the same as the traditional Iranian fritter, called *nân-ı panjara* 'window bread' (Neyzi). However, as we have seen, Scappi also mentions irons in 'fanciful shapes'. Apart from the examples given by Scappi, some other shapes of fritters 'in the Italian fashion' – a fish, escutcheon and carnation – are illustrated in a seventeenth-century English cookbook by Robert May (May 1685: 172). According to May, the fritters were used to garnish boiled fish or stewed oysters, not steeped in honey or sprinkled with sugar as described by Scappi, which is more suggestive of the Middle Eastern tradition of pastries soaked in syrup. Despite the publication of May's recipes, these fritters do not seem to have got past the novelty stage in England, as demonstrated by Mrs Beeton, who includes drawings of two fritter irons but instead of explaining how to use them gives a recipe for spooning the batter into hot fat (Beeton 1861: 741–742). Evidently no fritter irons were available in England.

In Turkey fritter irons come in diverse shapes, usually geometric, although some antique examples resemble a stylized fish, which possibly indicates a Christian influence. They are – or were until recently – made by blacksmiths in a number of provincial towns and cities, in whatever shape they or their customers fancied (Fig. 1). One of the last makers today is an 80-year-old craftsman named Talat Dürüst in Erzurum.

The earliest Turkish recipe we have is in a cookery book written by Mahmud Nedim bin Tosun, an infantry lieutenant in the Ottoman army, published in Istanbul in 1900 (Mahmud Nedim 1998: 110). He was serving in Erzurum in eastern Turkey at the time he collected the recipe and remarks that the best fritter irons were made in that city:

> As for the irons, since they have traditionally been made in Erzurum, they produce them in many well shaped forms that depend on the skill of the craftsmen. Although they are imitated elsewhere, none hold the batter like an

Erzurum fritter iron. Even if they work the first time, they are no good on the second occasion.

His assumption that *demir tatlısı* originates in Erzurum and has been 'imitated elsewhere' is impossible to confirm. People from Erzurum would like to think so, and of course it is possible, but so far nothing is known about how or when *demir tatlısı* spread through Turkey. However, the fact that these fritters were regarded as traditional in Erzurum in 1900 and are widely known elsewhere in Turkey suggests a history here going back a considerable way. They are used in several provincial cuisines across the country, not just in provinces close to Erzurum such as Bitlis, Erzincan and Malatya, but also in Gaziantep in south-eastern Turkey; Zonguldak and Kastamonu in the Black Sea region; and Uşak, Bursa and Eskişehir in western Turkey. Interestingly there is no evidence for *demir tatlısı* ever being known in cosmopolitan western Turkish cities like Istanbul or İzmir, which suggests an eastern rather than western origin (Fig. 3).

Animal lollipops

Another use of moulds is to make hollow lollipops known as *horoz şekeri*, 'cockerel sweets', since the cockerel is the most popular shape. These double moulds are mainly figures of various animals, with some exceptions such as train locomotives, pistols and baskets. The oldest reference to these animal-shaped lollipops is by the early sixteenth-century Turkish writer Lâtifî, who in 1525 describes sugar models of elephants, horses, partridges and vultures being sold in the streets of Istanbul (Lâtifî 1977: 54; Işın 2013: 53). The oldest illustration dates from the middle of the seventeenth century and shows a street seller with his lollipops ingeniously displayed by inserting the sticks into holes in a bottle gourd attached to a stick. These lollipops are in the form of birds and flowers on sticks (Fig. 4).

Hollow lollipops were popular all over Turkey until recent decades, made by itinerant confectioners who produced them at home and sold them in the street, often outside schools, or at weddings, when parents bought them as a treat for children. Since it is now forbidden to sell street foods outside school gates, the tradition of buying them at weddings is the main reason for their survival. They have also suffered from the encroachment of modern sweets, particularly chocolate bars, and I have only been able to trace two people who still make them. One of the last *horoz şekeri* makers is İbrahim Denizci who lives in Bergama in western Turkey and sells the majority of his lollipops to tourists and at weddings. Today he uses barbecue sticks that he buys in packs, but before these were available the lollipop sticks were made from vertical segments cut from the hollow stems of the giant cane (*Arundo donax*). When I visited his home, İbrahim's brother gave a demonstration of how they used to make these sticks, each one carefully smoothed off so that there was no risk of injury from splinters. It was a laborious task.

İbrahim Denizci's collection of moulds, inherited from his father, includes over twenty different shapes, including a mermaid, horseman armed with a sword, lion, giraffe, cow, rabbit, hen, small bird, donkey, horse, fish, bear riding a bicycle, train, basket, vase and pistol. He no longer uses the large-sized moulds, such as the mermaid, horseman and train, since he would have to charge a higher price than customers are now willing to pay. Anyway most children prefer the traditional cockerel and other smaller figures. He makes the lollipops at home in his sitting room, helped by his wife. He boils the sugar syrup on a small portable gas cylinder, wearing thick gloves to protect his hands. His wife rubs vegetable oil on the inside surface of each mould. The sugar syrup, usually dyed red, is boiled to crack then poured into the mouth of the oiled mould, whose two parts are gripped firmly together in one hand. When full the mould is turned upside down to pour the excess back into the sugar pan and a stick is pressed onto the rim. After the lollipop has cooled the two parts of the mould are carefully removed. Today for reasons of hygiene the finished lollipops are wrapped in squares of cellophane. The lollipops are very fragile and do not travel well (Figs. 5, 6, 7).

Another hollow lollipop-maker who still manages to scrape a living is Rahmi Tütüncüoğlu who lives in Bursa, a city south-east of Istanbul. He too works at home, helped by his wife and daughter. He sells the sugar figures on Mount Uludağ in the skiing season, at weddings during the summer, and also sells them to grocery stores and street vendors of *simit* (bread rings with sesame seeds). He justly asserts that since the lollipops contain no artificial additives they are healthier than modern sweets. Tütüncüoğlu colours his lollipops with natural colouring made from sour cherries or blackberries. He uses poplar wood sticks, square in section, cut from leftover wood by carpenters in the town of İznik. He says they can also be made of pine, which has a pleasing resinous scent.

These lollipops often incorporate sugar whistles, which are moulded separately and then attached to the lollipop, so that they double as toys, as emphasized in the poem 'Childhood' by Cahit Sıtkı Tarancı (1910–1956):

> My kite high above the clouds
> My marbles shiny and bright
> My splendidly spinning hooş
> I wish my cockerel lollipop would never end!

Whistles are made separately in one mould consisting of a row of five whistles. When these have solidified and cooled small holes must be cut out for the air to pass through so that they emit a whistle when blown. Then they are stuck onto the lollipop using a dab of melted syrup. While Rahmi Tütüncüoğlu still attaches sugar whistles to his lollipops, İbrahim Denizci says it is too fiddly and not worth the trouble (Figs. 8, 9).

In the early seventeenth century Sir Hugh Plat describes making hollow sugar fruits in plaster moulds by the rather eccentric method of swinging them up and down to make the sugar form a coating around the inside (Plat 1609: recipe 44). In 1865 the English confectioner Henry Weatherly describes the method used in Turkey for 'Boiled

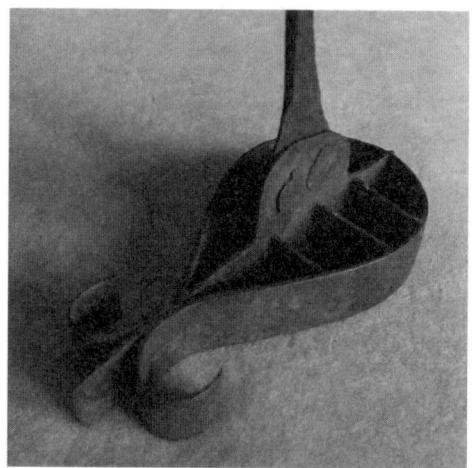

Figure 1. Turkish fritter iron, early 20th century. Photo. Mary Işın.

Figure 2. Antique branding iron from Texas illustrating the similarity with fritter irons. Photo. Andreas Praefcke.

Figure 3. Fritter irons used in the village of Keramet southeast of Istanbul. Photo. Füsun Ertuğ.

Moulds for Shaping and Decorating Food in Turkey

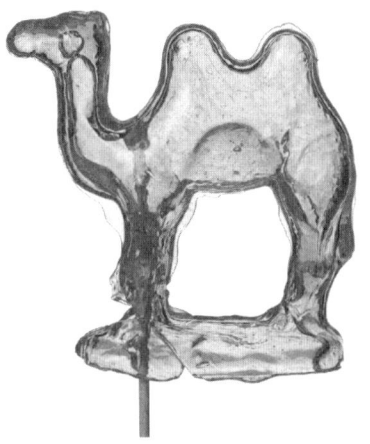

Figure 4. Lollipop in the form of a camel made by İbrahim Denizci. Photo. Hakan Ezilmez.

Sugars in Moulds' made with cast iron moulds 'of all shapes' (Weatherly 1865: 56), and in 1881 another English confectioner, E. Skuse, gives a more detailed description of what he calls 'Boiled-Sugar Figures' in the form of 'all kinds of figures, such as dogs, cats, elephants etc. etc.' (Skuse 1881: 82). This type of lollipop is still made in Germany, but exclusively in the shape of hares, hence the name *roter zuckerhase* (red sugar hare), and is a traditional Easter sweet (Fasolt 2010; Anlicker 2012). They are still made in the United States by the name barley toy or clear toy. The same type of double mould in mainly animal shapes is used, but without emptying out the syrup, so they are solid instead of hollow (Fasolt 2010; Dorothy Timberlake Candies). In the past when sugar was more expensive this would have made them a luxury item that working-class parents could not afford as a treat for their children, so I assume they too were originally hollow. Probably these lollipops were known in other countries as well, although I have not yet come across any references to them.

Making *horoz şekeri* was a cottage trade that anyone could learn so long as they had a set of moulds, which were the most costly piece of equipment required. Both of the surviving *horoz şekeri* makers in Turkey learned the trade from their fathers. In the 1950s Rahmi Tütüncüoğlu's father was unemployed and asked an elderly lollipop maker to teach him how to make them. The old man not only did that but also gave him his moulds as a gift. İbrahim Denizci's father began in a similar way, taught by an elderly woman in the town of Soma who used to help her father. She presented him with her father's moulds.

Wafer Irons

Another type of metal mould is wafer irons with incised designs. Orthodox Christians use leavened bread for the Eucharist rather than the unleavened communion wafers used in Europe, so the Turkish variety is possibly a late introduction by Istanbul's Catholic communities. In Istanbul they became a popular sweetmeat made by spreading the

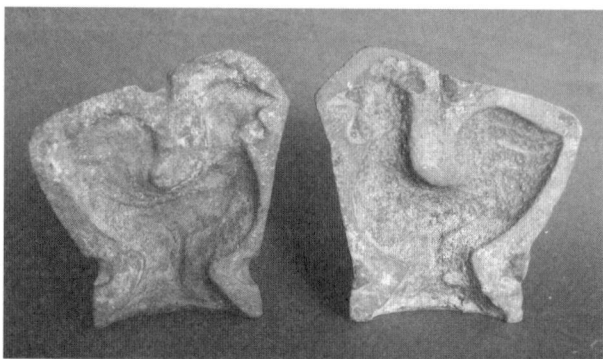

Figures 5, 6, 7. Lollipop moulds in the form of a cockerel donkey and pistol. Photos Mary Işın.

wafers with soft nougat and sticking several together in layers. The earliest reference to wafers, called *kağıt helvası*, 'paper helva', in Turkish, is in a mid-eighteenth century recipe manuscript (Ünver 1948: 16–17). There are several wafer moulds in the Topkapı Palace kitchen collection. These have a Seal of Solomon star motif on one side and a hatched design on the other. Ships, birds and stars were other popular motifs on wafer irons. Restaurateur Murat Kargılı comes from an Albanian family who used to make a

Figure 8. Mould for making sugar whistles. The curved nails create the air hole that produces the sound. Photo. Mary Işın.

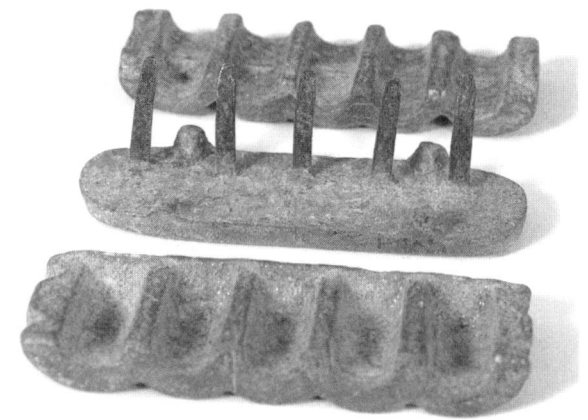

Figure 9. Cockerel lollipop with a sugar whistle attached made by Rahmi Tütüncüoğlu. Photo. Mary Işın.

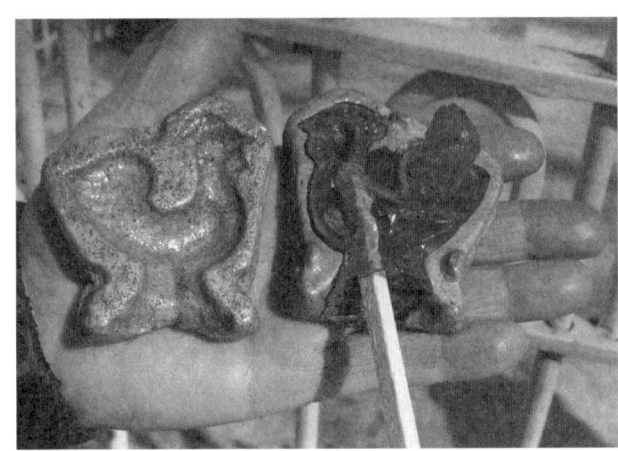

Figure 10. Bird motif on a Turkish wafer iron signed by the blacksmith 'Sali Usta' and dated 1931. Photo. Mary Işın.

Figure 11. Ship motif on a Turkish wafer iron dated 1931. Photo. Mary Işın.

Figure 12. Turkish wafer with a bird motif made in a traditional mould belonging to Murat Kargılı. Photo. Mary Işın.

Figure 13: Carved wooden mould for decorating kete *in Erzurum. Photo. Mary Işın.*

Moulds for Shaping and Decorating Food in Turkey

Figure 15. *Carved wooden mould for decorating kete in Kayseri. Photo. Mary Işın.*

Figure 14. Gerebiç (ma'moul) *mould made in Antakya. Photo. Mary Işın.*

Figure 16. *Tithe mould (çeç mühür) used in Erzurum. Photo. Mary Işın.*

Figure 17. *Tithe mould (çeç mühür) used in Sivas. Photo. Mary Işın.*

living by preparing *kağıt helvası* and ice-cream to sell in the street. He remembers his uncle and aunt wielding the heavy wafer irons, which weigh up to nine kilograms, in the process of making five kilograms of wafers a day in the workshop behind their small one-storey house in Pendik, a former village now a suburb east of Istanbul. His uncle and aunt continued to make the traditional wafers spread with layers of soft nougat made with sugar and a decoction of helva root (*Gypsophila*) until 1985. As well as selling them in the street they used to sell them at weddings in the village of Kurtköy. The *kağıt helvası* still widely sold in the streets in Turkey today is now a tasteless factory-made variety (Figs. 10, 11, 12).

Wooden moulds

Wooden moulds with carved designs are used in the province of Kayseri to create patterns on pastries known as *kete*. These moulds are of two types, either circular or in the form of a rolling pin. Housewives who do not have a mould use the prongs of a fork to create hatched patterns (Figs. 13, 15).

Another type of wooden mould is used in south-east Turkey for biscuits stuffed with walnuts known as *gerebiç* or *mamul* (*ma'moul*). In the province of Kilis these are made for the Ramazan *bayram* (Serkant 1990: 123). In other countries of the Middle East they are known as *ma'moul* and stuffed with nuts or dates. These can be traced back to the tenth century, when they were known as *halwâ mahshuwwa* and made in 'a concave mold (*qâlab*) carved with decorative shapes' (Nasrallah 2007: 426). In the thirteenth century Baghdadî gives a recipe under the name *urnin wa-khubz al-abâzîr* (Perry 2005: 102–03) (Fig. 14).

A type of wooden mould called *çeç mühür*, 'heap of grain stamp', or *döşüm* has an agricultural rather than culinary function. These were used in past centuries to mark piles of grain when government tithe collectors came round. Each farmer had his own distinctive carved mould, and after the tithe collector had made his calculations the mould would be pressed onto the side of the heaps owing as tax. Any attempt by the farmer to remove grain from the base of a heap after inspection would cause the indented pattern made by the mould to disappear (Figs. 16, 17).

Carved wooden bread stamps with sacred motifs and writing were used by members of the Greek Orthodox Church to mark the top of loaves used for the liturgy and special religious occasions.

Drop rollers

In the first half of the nineteenth century, French drops became popular in Istanbul. Although these were essentially the same as the Turkish *akide şekeri* (boiled sweets), it was the fancy shapes of the French version that caught the imagination. These were made using small machines called drop rollers with a handle that was turned by hand while a sheet of semi-solidified sugar syrup was fed through two cast brass rollers with intaglio designs such as balls, fish and flowers. At some point metal workers began to

Moulds for Shaping and Decorating Food in Turkey

Figure 18. Cast brass drop roller made in Turkey, 19th century. Photo. Sinan Çakmak.

make these locally, at first of brass and later of iron, and they became known as *gırgır*. Artisans continued to produce these for Turkish confectioners until around twenty years ago, the last being Harolombos Usta, Akistekolos Usta and Minür Usta, who had workshops in Kasımpaşa and Tahtakale (Erol and Erdoğan) (Fig. 18).

Despite the fact that moulds are not easy or cheap to make, it is interesting to see how widely foods shaped by moulds spread, the ultimate example being fritters made with irons, which have been embraced in more than a score of countries across the world. Universal fascination with attractively shaped foods is one reason for this popularity, but often shapes and patterns also reflect the spiritual and celebratory function of food. In the Turkish villages of Keramet in Bursa and the town of Ulubeyli in Uşak, fritters made with irons are a speciality of engagement celebrations (Aras 2011: s. 12) and similar examples of association with special or religious occasions are Germany's red sugar hares, patterned communion wafers and the *gerebiç* made for Ramazan.

References

Alexander Anlicker, 2012. 'Mit 'Zuckerhase' getaggte Beiträge', *Neues aus dem Markgräflerland* <http://markgraefler.wordpress.com/tag/zuckerhase/>.

Nilhan Aras, 2011. 'Âşıkların Mutfağı Uşak', *Metro Gastro* 62: 8–45.

Isabella Beeton, 1861. *Beeton's Book of Household Management*, facsimile edn. (London: Jonathan Cape, 1968).

Andrew Dalby, 1996. *The Classical Cookbook* (London: British Museum).

Dorothy Timberlake Candies. *Dorothy Timberlake Candies* <http://www.timberlakecandies.com/from_dnt.html>.

Erol, Nurtekin, and İsmail Erdoğan. Personal communications with the author.

Nancy Fasolt, 2010. *Clear Toy Candy* (Philadelphia: Stakepole Books).

Vicky Hayward, 2011. Personal communication with the author.

Priscilla Mary Işın, 2013. *Sherbet and Spice: The Complete Story of Turkish Sweets and Desserts* (London: I.B.Tauris).

Lâtifî 1977. *Evsâf-ı İstanbul*, ed. Nermin Suner (Pekin) (İstanbul: İstanbul Fetih Cemiyeti).

Mahmud Nedim bin Tosun, 1998. *Aşçıbaşı*, ed. Priscilla Mary Işın (İstanbul: Yapı Kredi Yayınları).

Robert May, 1685. *The Accomplisht Cook* (London: Obadiah Blagrave).

Nawal Nasrallah (ed. and tr.), 2007. *Annals of the Caliph's Kitchens, Ibn Sayyâr al-Warrâq's Tenth-Century Baġhdadi Cookbook* (Leiden: Brill).

Leily Neyzi. Personal communication with the author.

Charles Perry (trans.), 2005. Muhammad b. al-Hasan b. Muhammed b. al-Karîm, *A Baghdad Cookery Book: The Book of Dishes (Kitâb al-Tabîkh)* (Totnes, UK: Prospect Books).

Hugh Plat, 1609. *Delightes for Ladies* (London). Rpt. *A Collection of Medieval and Renaissance Cookbooks*, vol. 1, 4th edn. eds. Duke Cariadoc of the Bow and Duchessa Diana Alena (Duke Cariadoc of the Bow: 1987).

Marx Rumpoldt, 1581. *Ein new Kochbuch* <http://www.uni-giessen.de/gloning/tx/rump-gbk.htm>.

Bartolomeo Scappi, 1570. *The Opera of Bartolomeo Scappi (1570): The Art and Craft of a Master Cook* (Toronto: U Toronto P).

Edward H. Schafer, 1985. *The Golden Peaches of Samarkand, A Study of T'ang Exotics* (Berkeley: U California P).

Ahmet Serkant, 1990. *Annemin Kilis Yemekleri*, 2nd edn. (Istanbul: Birsen Yayınevi).

E Skuse, 1881. *The Confectioners' Handbook*, 3rd edn. (London: n.p.).

Gonca Tokuz, 2002. *Gaziantep ve Kilis Mutfak Kültürü* (Gaziantep: Gaziantep Üniversitesi Vakfı).

Süheyl Ünver, 1948. *Tarihte 50 Türk Yemeği* (İstanbul: İstanbul Üniversitesi Tıp Tarihi Enstitüsü).

Henry Weatherly, 1865. *A Treatise on the Art of Boiling Sugar* (Philadelphia: Henry Carey Baird).

'I have no mind to buy more Pewter': an Examination of Elite Consumption Trends in Ceramic Tableware in Georgian Ireland

Tara Kellaghan

The shift towards chinaware[1]

Examination of the 'things' that are the focus of material culture can provide an entrée into hidden elements of past worlds. Details about the individuals who fabricated, purchased and used them come to light, providing tantalizing glimpses into the lives of those long dead (Barnard 2005: 11). In this context, this paper considers the growing desire for ceramic tableware amongst members of the privileged minority in eighteenth-century Ireland. The demand for an expanding array of porcelain and earthenware serving, dining and drinking vessels was driven by factors such as improved techniques in European pottery manufacture (predominantly in imitation of Chinese imports); a burgeoning of the overall luxury goods market; the increasing consumption of chocolate, coffee and, particularly in England, tea; and refinements in food preparation and service, which, in turn, were linked to changing dining practices that increased the importance of the dining room as the sphere of commensality.

Mirroring trends in England and continental Europe, ceramics started to replace pewter serving and dining ware in late seventeenth- and early eighteenth-century Ireland. In England, up until the mid-eighteenth century, pewter vessels were more commonly used than those made of china (i.e. porcelain) or earthenware. The high cost and relative scarcity of these materials militated against their general usage (Weatherill 1996: 8). By the 1740s, however, as tea steadily usurped beer as the most popular form of liquid refreshment, pewter drinking-vessels gradually fell into disuse (Rock 2006: 39–40). Owing to their heat-resistance capacity, porcelain and earthenware were more desirable than pewter for the manufacture of vessels in which to serve the increasingly fashionable hot beverages of tea, coffee and chocolate. Certain pottery warehouses actually sold these three commodities in conjunction with appropriate ceramic wares (Dawson 2010: 15). Pewter manufacture in Ireland was said to be 'at a standstill' by 1753, due to significant importation of French earthenware (Westropp and Delamain 1913: 8).

Chinese porcelain and European-made copies

The popularity of pewter as a material used for the serving of food and beverages declined steadily as European-made alternatives to Chinese porcelain improved in quality, became more affordable and, consequently, more widely available. True Chinese porcelain (which dominated the luxury ceramics market in Europe until the introduction of hard- and soft-paste porcelain and bone-china manufacture there in the eighteenth century) graced solely the tables of the very wealthy. After its production began in England in the 1740s, soft-paste porcelain was the only 'china' that could be imported into Ireland without attracting punitive duties. Inevitably, illicit means were employed to avoid the latter. Smuggling and the plundering of shipwrecks helped speed bargain-priced porcelain into the hands of fashionable, acquisitive locals. The arrival at Kinsale, in 1756, of an East Indiaman returning to England with a hold replete with luxuries was followed by feverish, unregulated, quayside sales activity. It was subsequently observed that 'never [had] such a sight of fine and coarse china ware' been seen in Cork (Wight, qtd. in Barnard 2004: 132). For those in the upper echelons of society, orders for true Chinese porcelain could be placed with well-connected retailers in Dublin (Barnard 2004: 127). Those aspiring to 'make the grand figure' on a tighter budget could opt for more affordable copies fashioned in tin-glazed earthenware.

Delftware

Tin-glazed earthenware or pottery production in England dates from the sixteenth century. By the eighteenth century, however, the high-quality, distinctive blue and white pottery (in imitation of Chinese blue and white porcelain) produced in the Dutch city of Delft was so widely imported into England that the terms 'delft' and 'delf' were eventually adopted as generic descriptors of virtually any ware of this type – regardless of coloration or point of origin. In France, *faïence* was the term applied to tin-glazed earthenware. There was a vogue in mid-Georgian Ireland for the *faïence* of Burgundy, Marseilles and Rouen, with the latter sometimes misspelt or Anglicized as Roan or Rohan ware (Westropp and Delamain 1913: 8).

Affluent consumers in the kingdom of Ireland were obliged to pay unreasonably high tariffs on most foreign imports such as china and delft. Since the raw materials and expertise were locally available, it is easy to see why attempts were made to establish an Irish delftware industry in the late seventeenth and the eighteenth centuries. For a period of roughly seventy-five years (dating from 1697), locally produced delftware was the only alternative to genuine china manufactured in Ireland (Francis 2000: 7, 9). The entrepreneurs responsible for the brief flowering of an Irish delftware industry hoped to lure local custom by emphasizing the lower price of Irish-produced wares relative to imports. In 1737, a Dublin journal assured consumers that the earthenware made at the 'White Pothouse' was in every way equal to English and Dutch delftware, but retailed for twenty-five per cent less than those products (Francis 2000: 35).[2] The market in Ireland alone was – even at its mid-to-late Georgian peak – sufficient to sustain only one commercial-sized pottery. Attempts to (legally) export Irish delftware were stymied by legislation. A series of English navigation acts in this period amounted to 'an ad hoc assemblage of prohibitions inspired by particular interests in England' and were designed to ensure that exports from Ireland were disadvantaged in relation to those of

England. The result for Irish merchants was severe circumscription of their ability to trade freely (Livesy 2013: 108–09).

It is evident that a finite market and government-imposed obstacles to trade were determining factors in the failure of Irish delft manufacture to develop on an industrial scale in Georgian Ireland. Notwithstanding impediments to trade, Irish-manufactured delft did cross the Atlantic, as excavations at sites along the Eastern seaboard of the United States have proven. The absence of custom records detailing any such exports, however, leaves the manner of their arrival in the American colonies open to speculation (Francis 2000: 56).

Georgian pothouses

The Dublin Society offered premiums to encourage the establishment of delftware manufacture in Ireland.[3] As early as 1738, the Society encouraged the improvement in standards of pattern drawing for industrial applications such as delftware production, underscoring its enthusiasm for the latter (Turpin 1986: 40). Nature also provided an impetus to pottery making, with clay deposits at Carrickfergus, in the north of the country, proving especially favourable to delftware production. These deposits facilitated the establishment of what has been identified as probably the first earthenware manufactory in Ireland, the Belfast 'Potthouse' (Francis 1994).[4] It appears to have been in operation as early as 1699 and turned out delftware continuously for a period of roughly twenty-five years (Francis 1997: 89). A number of pottery-making enterprises sprang up in Dublin between the 1730s and the early 1750s, and there is evidence of further small-scale attempts at delftware manufacture in the provinces, e.g. Limerick, Doneraile (Barnard 2004: 128).

Irish delft manufacture: an entrepreneur's tale

Captain Henry Delamain (1713–1757) was one of the enterprising individuals to benefit from the Dublin Society's benevolence, and, in terms of Irish delftware manufacture, possibly the most significant. The story of his essay into pottery manufacture, in mid-eighteenth-century Dublin, illustrates the highs and lows of that short-lived industry in Ireland. Delamain, once a captain in the service of the Prince of Saxe Gotha, established himself in Dublin as a dealer in Chinese porcelain and tea, after which he purchased and modernized a defunct pottery manufactory situated at the evocatively named World's End in 1752. Delamain threw himself and his capital into improving the quality of Irish delft and expanding his Irish Delft Manufactory (Francis 2000: 47, Rynne 2006: 175–76, Westropp & Delamain 1913: 7–14). He not only developed a new type of kiln (fired by coal rather than wood), but he is very likely the same Delamain who, in 1753, established the Battersea Enamel Works with Stephen Theodore Janssen (Lord Mayor of London in 1754) and John Brooks. The latter, a talented engraver born in Dublin, is credited with inventing the process of transfer printing onto a variety of ceramics, including delft (Berg 2010: 136, Francis 2000: 48). Delamain's Herculean efforts to make a success of his pottery-manufacture could not outweigh serious obstacles to business such as onerous trade tariffs and a miniscule local market. He died suddenly in 1757, and the manufactory was quickly taken over by, first, his female companion and, second, his brother William. Nevertheless, by 1766 the business was terminated.

Henry Delamain's name is now synonymous with fine Irish ceramics of the Georgian period, with relatively few examples of Delamain Irish delft surviving in private collections and museums. Reflecting the rarity and desirability of such items, a single, polychrome candlestick from the Henry Delamain Factory realized £12,500 at a sale at Christie's London auction house in June 2010.[5]

Rare and difficult to identify: Irish delftware

Potters working in earthenware manufactories in Georgian Ireland tended not to mark their products, rendering identification of seventeenth- and eighteenth-century Irish-made delftware difficult (Godden 1979: 197). Applying the practices of archaeological excavation at sites where relevant discoveries have been made, however, has facilitated the attribution of assorted earthenware shards and pieces to specifically located eighteenth-century delftware potteries, e.g. at Belfast, Rostrevor, Youghal, Limerick and Dublin (Francis 1997: 88; Rynne 2000: 175). Delftware originating from the aforementioned Belfast Potthouse has, nonetheless, proven markedly difficult to differentiate from examples produced at a London delft manufactory of the same period due to strong stylistic similarities. Certain Belfast pieces do, however, exhibit distinctive shapes, thereby assisting in their attribution to local manufactories. Porringer handles, in particular, have exhibited moulded designs that appear unique to Belfast (Francis 1997: 90, 92).

French *faïence* was greatly esteemed by prosperous householders, and local Dublin potters were well aware that their products were competing directly against the popular imports. Doubtless, this factor inspired them to copy French models in terms of both style and decoration. Experts in the field of eighteenth-century ceramics have had recourse to the French influence in an attempt to explain the seemingly unique (in the British Isles) manufacture of five large delftware wine or brandy barrels in Ireland. It is noteworthy that Henry Delamain had close relatives who were cognac producers, and four of the five barrels have been attributed to his pottery.[6] Ceramics specialists continue to remain perplexed by the apparent absence of any similar examples of English manufacture (Francis 1997: 90, Francis 2000: 108–09).

The bishop's chinaware

Glass and chinaware have been identified as principal components of 'the grammar of the polite table' in the eighteenth century (Berg 2010: 117). The polite table appears to have been a matter of particular concern to Edward Synge, Bishop of Elphin.[7] The battery of missives he dispatched to his only daughter, Alicia, between 1746 and 1752, include numerous and very specific instructions relating to the purchase, use and transport of his chinaware which, in fact, appears to have comprised Dublin-made delft combined with French *faïence* or 'Rohan ware'. Though Synge claimed that he had 'little use of China, since Plate came in fashion with me', he made either direct or oblique reference to chinaware in over twenty letters written to Alicia in the summer months over a six-year period (Legg 1996: 180). An extract from a letter of 9 May 1747 illustrates a remarkable degree of pernicketiness on the part of the ceramics-obsessed Bishop:

> Tell Mrs Jourdan that between her and Wilkinson, I have the poorest pimping Soop-dish, that I ever saw. It is less than the one I complain'd of … [the cook] has measur'd the new Soup dish, and the old one of which I complain'd last year, which, it seems, is still here – I have order'd him therefore to lay the new one by, in order to return it … Desire Mrs Jourdan to send for him [Wilkinson] immediately, and order him to make one out of hand, that will hold a Pottle or more. He must not make it broader, but deeper, and the Rim broader. He'll say perhaps he has no mold. But he must find one or Some one else must be apply'd to. I must have this as I direct, if Dublin will give it me. (Legg 1996: 11)[8]

The bishop's exacting instructions appear to indicate that Wilkinson was an actual potter working in Dublin in 1747. Wilkinson is not a name that appears amongst those awarded premiums for delftware production by the Dublin Society between 1747 and 1751. After the death of Henry Delamain, however, one Samuel Wilkinson, in conjunction with William Delamain (brother of the deceased), petitioned the Irish Parliament in 1761 for grant aid to keep the Delamain manufacture operational (Westropp & Delamain 1913: 7, 15). This could be the very Wilkinson whose original 'pimping Soop-dish' so discombobulated Bishop Synge. If so, it is possible that in 1747 Wilkinson was employed by John Crisp & Co., a manufactory that had been awarded a premium by the Dublin Society in that same year for 'the best dishes and plates of earthenware … their ware seems to be as good as any imported for colour, size and paint' (Westropp and Delamain 1913: 6).

Whatever the true identity of Synge's Wilkinson, his unsatisfactory work is still exercising the bishop's patience ten days later, as on 19 May 1747, Synge advises Alicia that he is sending 'the new pityfull Soup-dish' back to Dublin by a 'Carr-man' named Noon, to be returned to the hapless Wilkinson (Legg 1996: 27). This particular soup-dish is fated to be a source of on-going vexation for Bishop Synge. On the first of July, he expresses his surprise that Alicia has 'no account of Noon, or the Soop-dish. For he has been here and told … that He had deliver'd it …. The dish you sent me down is perfectly right' (Legg 1996: 46).

The relief must have been palpable for all concerned when the bishop's exigencies regarding chinaware were satisfied. Even Synge himself tacitly acknowledges this on 6 June 1749:

[The cook] is short in China Dishes .... Those he wants ... are about the size of the Small ones of the Burnt China. It matters not if they be a little larger. Four will do; and there must be a dozen China Plates got, as like the few old ones blew and white which you have .... Desire Mrs Jourdan to have no palpitations about these, but chuse as she likes. I promise beforehand that I will like them. (Legg 1996: 98)

Alicia clearly remained unconvinced about her father's indifference to this purchase, as he takes pain to assure her on 15 June 1749 that 'It is no great matter whether the Plates you have bought, be like the old ones you have, or not ... what signifys it, if there be a new one added; provided they be pretty and strong' (Legg 1996: 108).

Finally, any fear on the part of the Dublin ladies (Alicia and Mrs Jourdan) is extinguished when the Bishop writes on 28 June, 'I like the China-dishes, and plates greatly. You said there was a third of one kind of Dish. Secure it' (Legg 1996: 120). *Faïence* from Rouen is on Synge's mind in June of 1751. He expresses concern that his supplier, a Mr. Sullivane, may send him more dishes 'margen'd blue' when what he desires are dishes like 'the plates with other Colours'. He specifies that he has 'added more dishes, some round, some Tirrenes, and other things' (Legg 1996: 294).

Bishop Synge's letters to his daughter reveal him as a man with a seemingly limitless interest in the minutiae of the material culture of his homes, as his preoccupation with chinaware alone demonstrates. Lest we view Bishop Synge's concentration upon crockery-related matters as an aberration, ample period evidence suggests that his preoccupation with this aspect of material culture was widely shared by his social peers, and that other gentlemen were 'bewitched' by contemporary porcelain and delft. In 1742, an Irish member of parliament, seeking out fine tableware for a friend in a Parisian retail establishment, observed that he 'never withstood so much temptation as in that shop' (Barnard 2005: 131).[9]

Affluent consumers of ceramic tableware in Georgian Ireland

Concerning material objects, it has been observed that people use them 'as vehicles of meaning through which [they] negotiate relations with each other and the world at large' (Attfield 2000: 75). They also purchase specific goods in relation to their needs and their sense of self. Regarding the purchase of luxury goods, self-image and the image an individual wishes to present to society are fundamental drivers in the selection process. The historian Toby Barnard (2004) has compellingly demonstrated the Irish predilection, in the eighteenth century, for 'making the grand figure'. In the quest to vaunt their goods, and, by implication, their status, members of Ireland's élite mirrored the behaviour of contemporaries in Europe and Colonial America. As early as the late seventeenth century, in Holland, 'the wealthiest members of the bourgeoisie began to favour porcelain over pewter .... The former had the prestige of being an exotic and expensive product' (Zumthor 1994: 65). In eighteenth-century France, the crucible of

European fashion, domestic life (for the privileged) was becoming increasingly elegant, especially in the realm of dining. An ever-expanding array of fine wares started to replace traditional pewter, 'though only the wealthy used china dishes, their social subordinates had … dining sets that included such social refinements as terrines, serving platters, salad bowls and salt-cellars' (Maza 2005: 48).

In Colonial America, Benjamin Franklin observed that his changing breakfast-table settings emphasized the social and cultural significance of fine tableware while simultaneously providing a metaphor for the course of his own social ascent. He reflected that 'breakfast was a long time bread and milk (no tea)' which he ate 'out of a two-penny earthenware porringer with a pewter spoon. But mark how luxury will enter families, and make a progress, in spite of principle: being call'd one morning to breakfast … I found it in a China bowl, with a spoon of silver!' (Breen 2004: 154). Bishop Synge, by 16 June 1750, appeared to have developed a similar disdain for pewter ware, commanding his daughter to send 'two dozen plates to be provided immediately and sent down hither with the baking dishes. I hope the old and useless pewter you have will provide these' (Legg 1996: 200). The disregard for pewter now articulated by the bishop appears bewildering since he had previously asserted that he had 'little use of China, since Plate came in fashion with me'. Taken in context, however, that remark is clearly facetious. Two sentences earlier, in the same paragraph, Synge discusses the relative merits of 'the Blew and White kind' (of dishes) versus 'what they call the burnt ones', opining that the latter are 'finer than they [the blue and white], but not fine enough to be laid by as a rarity' (Legg 1996: 180). The quality of material goods was of profound importance to Ireland's élite, but not to the extent that style would ever be sacrificed to substance. Bishop Edward Synge, in addition to fretting that he had every item of delftware necessary to his households, was equally anxious that such items were sufficiently decorative to impress guests, reminding his daughter in 1751 that 'my shew day is july 3. It would please me much to have them [new Rouen ware dishes and tureens] here for that Occasion' (Legg 1996: 295).

The proprietors of a provincial pottery clearly studied how they might best cater to potential customers' requirements. In the *Dublin Journal* of 10 April 1742, they advised gentlemen that they could 'bespeak sets of dishes and plates [that] may have their coats of arms or any other pattern they please done on them in the best manner'. If this appeal to personal vanity proved insufficient, further ones to thrift and patriotism could be invoked for marketing purposes. The sought-after clientele was assured that all bespoke products were made 'by natives of this kingdom only', and that they 'humbly hope to meet with proper encouragement, and propose to sell at the most reasonable rates', providing the example of the Lord Chancellor as a satisfied customer (Westropp & Delamain 1913: 23). A set of East India china, bearing his personal armorials, was deemed a fitting gift for a prominent Anglo-Irish aristocrat at century's end, highlighting the desirability and significance of ceramic tableware in the register of luxury goods in that era (O'Connor 1987: 58).[10]

The Anglo-Irish estate owner Richard Lovell Edgeworth struck up a friendship with Josiah Wedgwood (1730–1795), the renowned English potter, through a shared interest in science.[11] In correspondence between the two men, Edgeworth is revealed not only as a discerning client of Wedgwood's ceramics, but also as an individual preoccupied with the elements of design and practical usage that may be assigned to pottery. One lengthy order placed by Edgeworth, dating from 7 October 1788, articulates his requirements on both counts:

> I wished to have a Dozen more of the same plates – Two Lapis lazuli Sugar Bowls, with white figures & Two Cream Ewers D° – Two Green Edged Sallad bowls – and a d° cheese plate … The Stands for butter boats if made heavy will … answer very well & perhaps a similar Stand for a Sallad Dish would be approved, if the stands were Lapis-lazuli with dancing hours round them in white this would be very elegant. (Doherty 1986, 259)

Though Edgeworth may not have been the actual inventor of the pottery pie-dish, he was certainly an early enthusiast in perfecting its design and promoting its manufacture. In response to a suggestion from Edgeworth on the modelling of a pottery pie-dish with a detachable lid, Wedgwood advised, on 24 December 1786, 'I made a clay pye and shewed it to my children … but they, not knowing what it was intended for, convinced me at once that it was wrong, & I have not yet made another essay' (Doherty 1986: 253). A nineteenth-century tax on flour apparently finally prompted the Wedgwood firm (and others) to manufacture ware that could enable a cook to make pies without being obliged to make pastry (Doherty 1986: 253). Richard Lovell Edgeworth appears to have played a role in the innovation of piecrust ware – a product that evolved into modern oven-to-tableware. Certainly, he is another example of an Ascendancy gentleman fascinated by the possibilities provided by constantly improving techniques of pottery manufacture for the expansion of the variety of wares used in dining, serving and baking.

The role of chinaware in the construction of 'the grand figure'

Historically, the Anglo-Irish perceived the Irish natives' adherence to modes of hospitality that were part of the Gaelic tradition as a negative characteristic. Yet, by the Georgian era, the assimilated élite had adopted these very modes of exaggerated hospitality (Mac Con Iomaire 2009: 69). This ostensibly pleasing development did not meet with universal approval. In 1769, one English visitor summed up the views of fellow prigs, opining that the Irish 'pique themselves much on their hospitality in all parts of the kingdom …. I am afraid, indeed, that too much of their boasted hospitality in every province has a greater right to be denominated ostentation' (Bush 1769: 14–15). Such criticism, by strangers, of the extravagant mode of living favoured by Ireland's élite was virtually routine, but it did not deter the latter from enjoying its oft-precarious lifestyle to the full.

Incessant entertaining required an endless supply of elegant tableware, and the well-heeled were not remiss in keeping abreast of the latest trends. Delft, whether imported or Irish-made, was *de rigueur* for those of the middling ranks and upward, with fine porcelain remaining the preserve of those at the apex of society (O'Connor 1987: 58, Barnard 2004: 133). Numerous references to delft and china, in the late eighteenth-century inventory of a northern lady's effects, attest to the ubiquity of such items in gentry households of the period (Clarkson & Crawford 1985: 73–82). Clearly, the 'grand figure' could not be made haphazardly, and ceramic tableware was a significant constituent element of the material culture of privileged households in Georgian Ireland.

Conclusion

Existing evidence of the level of interest in ceramic tableware amongst the élite in Georgian Ireland demonstrates a shared determination amongst its members to ensure that the most up-to-date and fashionable materials were in use and on display in their households. The careful deliberation exercised in relation to the acquisition of appropriate goods, e.g. as exhibited in the letters of Edward Synge, Bishop of Elphin, and Richard Lovell Edgeworth, emphasizes the growing importance of material culture and consumption in eighteenth-century Ireland. Changes in dining and drinking habits, an expansion in the variety and quality of available tableware, and a corresponding growth in interest in *les arts de la table* – these represent just a few of the factors that influenced evolving trends in material culture in modern Europe. In eighteenth-century Ireland, no less than in England or Colonial America, these trends mirrored those manifested in continental Europe. Georgian Dublin may have been the second city of the British Empire, but in her enthusiasm to master the grammar of the polite table she proved second to none.

Notes

1. The quotation in the title comes from a letter from E. Synge to A. Synge, 8 June 1750, *The Synge Letters: Bishop Edward Synge to his daughter Alicia, Roscommon to Dublin 1746–1752*, ed. Marie-Louise Legg (Four Courts Press: Dublin, 1996): p. 180.
2. *Dublin Daily Advertiser*, 5 February 1737.
3. Founded in 1731, the society aimed to promote development in the areas of science, agriculture, industry and the arts.
4. Over thirteen thousand tons of this special clay was exported to England between 1723–1778 and widely used there in delft manufactories (Francis 1996: 89, 92).
5. Sale 7920, Syd Levethan: the Longridge Collection. 10–11 June 2010, London, King Street.
6. James Delamain (1738–1800), nephew of Henry Delamain, married into a well-established cognac export house in 1759 and was presented with a set of delftware manufactured at his uncle's pottery.
7. Edward Synge (1691–1762), bishop of Elphin from 1740–1762.
8. Blanche or Blandine Jourdan (1705–*c*.1780), governess and companion to Alicia Synge.
9. Chichester Fortescue (1718–1757). an Irish Member of Parliament who represented Trim in the Irish House of Commons (1747–1757).
10. William Bright and Alexander Owens, proprietors of the Rostrevor Pot House, Co. Down; Robert Jocelyn, Lord Newport, later Viscount Jocelyn (1688?–1756). Lord Chancellor in Ireland, 1739–1756; James Caulfield, 1st Earl of Charlemont (1728–199), Irish peer.
11. Richard Lovell Edgeworth (1744–1817), educationist and writer; father to the famous novelist, Maria Edgeworth.

References

Attfield, Judy. 2000. *Wild things: the material culture of everyday life* (Oxford: Berg).
Barnard, Toby. 2004. *Making the Grand Figure: Lives and Possessions in Ireland, 1641–1770* (New Haven: Yale UP).
Barnard, Toby. 2005. *A Guide to Sources for the History of Material Culture in Ireland, 1500–2000* (Dublin: Four Courts Press).
Berg, Maxine. 2010. *Luxury and Pleasure in Eighteenth-Century Britain* (Oxford: Oxford UP).
Breen, Timothy H. 2004. *The Marketplace of Revolution: How Consumer Politics Shaped American Independence* (New York: Oxford UP).
Bush, John. 1769. *Hibernia Curiosa: A Letter from a Gentleman in Dublin to his Friend at Dover in Kent* (Dublin: J. Potts and J. Williams).
Casey, Christine (ed.). 2010. *The Eighteenth-Century Dublin Town House* (Dublin: Four Courts Press).
Clarkson, Leslie A. 1999. 'Hospitality, Housekeeping and High Living in Eighteenth-Century Ireland', in *Luxury & Austerity*, ed. Jacqueline Hill and Colm Lennon (Dublin: U College Dublin P): pp. 84–105.
Clarkson, Leslie A., and E. Margaret Crawford, 1985. *Ways to Wealth: The Cust Family of Eighteenth Century Armagh* (Belfast: Ulster Society for Irish Historical Studies).
Cullen, Louis. M. 1981. *The Emergence of Modern Ireland, 1600–1900* (London: Batsford Academic).
Dawson, Aileen. 2010. *English and Irish Delftware* (London: British Museum Press).
Doherty, Francis. 1986. 'An Intellectual Friendship: Letters of Richard Lovell Edgeworth and the Wedgwoods', *Proceedings of the Royal Irish Academy*. Section C: Archaeology, Celtic Studies, History, Linguistics, Literature, 86C: pp. 231–69.
Francis, Peter. 1994. 'The Belfast Potthouse, Carrickfergus Clay and the Spread of the Delftware Industry', *English Ceramic Circle Transactions*, 15, Pt. 2: pp. 267–82.
Francis, Peter. 1997. 'Recent Discoveries in Irish Ceramics', *Irish Arts Review Yearbook*, 13: pp. 88–101.
Francis, Peter. 2000. *Irish Delftware* (London: Jonathan Horne Publications).
Godden, Geoffrey A. 1979. *Encyclopaedia of British Pottery and Porcelain Marks* (London: Barrie & Jenkins Ltd).

Synge, Edward. 1996. *The Synge Letters: Bishop Edward Synge to His Daughter Alicia, Roscommon to Dublin 1746–1752*, ed. Legg, Marie-Louise (Dublin: Lilliput Press).
Livesy, James. 2013. 'Free Trade and Empire in Anglo-Irish Commercial Propositions of 1785', *Journal of British Studies*, 52: pp. 103–27.
Mac Con Iomaire, Máirtín. 2009. 'The Emergence, Development and Influence of French Haute Cuisine on Public Dining in Dublin Restaurants 1900–2000: An Oral History', PhD thesis (Dublin Institute of Technology: Dublin).
Maza, Sarah. 2005. *The Myth of the French Bourgeoisie: An Essay on the Social Imaginary, 1750–1850* (Cambridge, MA: Harvard UP).
O'Brien, Gillian, and Fiona O'Kane, (eds.) 2008. *Georgian Dublin* (Dublin: Four Courts Press).
O'Connor, Cynthia. 1987. 'Blue and White Services with Irish Armorials', *Irish Arts Review* (1984–1987), 4.1: pp. 58–60.
Rock, Hugh. 2006. *Pub Beer Mugs and Glasses* (Buckinghamshire: Shire Publications Ltd.).
Rynne, Colin. 2006. *Industrial Ireland 1750–1930: An Archaeology* (Cork: Collins Press)
Turpin, John. 1986. 'The School of Ornament of the Dublin Society in the 18th Century', *The Journal of the Royal Society of Antiquaries of Ireland*, 116: pp. 38–50.
Weatherill, Lorna. 1996. *Consumer Behaviour and Material Culture in Britain, 1660–1760* (London: Routledge).
Westropp, M.S. Dudley, and Henry Delamain. 1913. 'Notes on Pottery Manufacture in Ireland', *Proceedings of the Royal Irish Academy*, Section C: Archaeology, Celtic Studies, History, Linguistics, Literature, 32 (1914–1916): pp. 1–27.
Zumthor, Paul. 1994. *Daily Life in Rembrandt's Holland* (Palo Alto, CA: Stanford UP).

The Cow Creamer and the 'Cudster'

Llio Teleri Lloyd-Jones

The animal's appearance is ridiculous in the extreme. She is an absurd cartoon cow in silver, with short spindly legs, a slack drooping udder, and an indescribably inane facial expression … Although bovi-form vessels have a long history, the cow-creamer still comes as a slight surprise.[1]

In its more recent history, the cow creamer has been treated unkindly, dismissed as an eccentricity of the British table. A jug shaped like a cow did not necessarily fit the prevailing twentieth-century fashion for clarity of line and expressions of modernity.[2] In fact, this particular traditional archetype was described in a rather cruel way by P.G. Wodehouse through the voice of Bertie Wooster:

> It was a silver cow. But when I say 'cow', don't go running away with the idea of some decent, self-respecting cudster such as you may observe loading grass into itself in the nearest meadow. This was a sinister, leering, Underworld sort of animal, the kind that would spit out of the side of its mouth for two-pence. It was about four inches high and six long. It's back opened on a hinge. It's tail was arched, so that the tip touched the spine – thus I suppose, affording a handle for the cream-lover to grasp. The sight of it seemed to take me into a different and dreadful world.[3]

Such sentiments were echoed decades later when an article in *The Times* suggested 'author, artist and antiques correspondent' Bevis Hillier might be especially interested in a Sotheby's sale at Gleneagle Hotel because 'he is in the early planning stages for an exhibition on bad taste … in the first day's sale Hillier draws particular attention to an English silver cow creamer "exactly the sort of thing Bertie Wooster's Uncle Tom Travers used to collect".'[4]

The charge levied by Wodehouse and Johns at the creamer is not its frivolity or novelty but the particular representation of the cow. Johns characterizes John Schuppe's silver cow creamer as a pitiful representation of nature's reality. Wodehouse also focuses on the object's unnaturalness, comparing it, unfavourably, to a 'decent, self-respecting cudster'. As these remarks highlight, the cow creamer presents a version of nature and was popularized in the mid-eighteenth century, a period when Britain's dialogue with nature was shifting continuously, from the way we bred animals and farmed the land to the influence of Rococo on fine art and design. While taking pleasure outlining the many swipes at the cow creamer, this paper will consider the history of this particular object and follow it with a focus on one exceptional collection.

The Cow Creamer and the 'Cudster'

The earliest examples of cow creamers come from Holland in the early eighteenth century, with the form reaching Britain around the 1740s. Several of the mid-century examples of silver cow creamers found in Britain are marked by a London-based Dutch silversmith named John Schuppe. They follow the archetype's conventions of a standing cow with its tail looping forwards to create a handle, the back opening for the jug to be filled and the mouth of the cow used as the mouth of the jug. An example in the Victoria & Albert Museum is particularly intricate: made between 1758–1759, with detailing including a lid with a floral pattern and fly finial as well as a collar reading 'H.P. from Laetitia Maydwell a memento of Tyttenhanger'.[5] Those looking closely will spot a fly sitting on the cow's udder that is actually a valve to control the flow of the contents from the mouth.

In terms of the representation there are obvious artistic liberties taken (as Catherine Johns has noted). The relative size of the fly needs to be excessive for anyone to be able to lift the lid. The legs are particularly slender and the hooves flat like discs. The size of the head is disproportionately large, a way to anthropomorphize the animal, giving a sense of character with large open eyes and possibly contributing to Johns' interpretation of the facial expression as 'inane'.[6] The lid of the jug is reminiscent of a saddle that along with the collar are signs of the animal's domestication, while the tail's loop provides the figure with some sense of movement.

While the cow creamer has been manufactured in large quantities over the past centuries, there is little evidence of their use. In reality, the cow creamer is an object that survives, in spite of and not because of, its practicality (the interior shape makes the creamer hard to clean and therefore unhygienic). In practice we are confronted by a play between the natural and the cultural as the cow is re-filled with milk, making the use of the jug a re-enactment of the milking process, albeit turned on its head. Instead of the milk coming from the udders, it pours from the mouth as though regurgitated. The valve system (seen on this particular creamer only, not a usual feature) in the udder points to an internal, biological process, some hidden mechanism and accentuates the machine-like reliability of the animal. It is the very apex of obedience, a performance of man's power over nature.

That the cow creamer came from Holland and found a home in England is not so surprising when you consider the symbolic importance of the cow to both cultures. Paintings of cattle had become a genre in itself in Holland by the eighteenth century with work by artists such as Paulus Potter and Albert Cuyp. Indeed Cuyp 'made a fetish of dairy cows … . [H]e loads his canvas with them. They're enormous, even monumental, with great angular bones and bellies puffed like the sails of Holland's growing colonial fleet.'[7] With their experiments in animal husbandry and crop rotation, the Netherlands' agriculture was a source of pride and David Rimas has posited the country's cattle as an alternative national ideal to royalty or religion.[8]

While Britain learnt much from Holland in terms of agriculture, and indeed imported their cattle, the nation already had a long cultural connection with the cow. British cuisine was often reduced to a tradition of roasting meat, especially beef – Charles Morris's *Jubilee Song* of 1786 even compares the shape of Britain to that of a steak.[9] It was in the eighteenth century that John Bull became a national character, sometimes represented in bovine form in print by caricaturists.[10]

While the cow could be characterized as a benign, national symbol, the eighteenth century saw the dairy become a fashionable accessory for women of high status. Marie Antoinette's predilections for playing the shepherdess and the milkmaid may be well known, but the aristocratic vogue for agricultural pastimes had begun at least a hundred years before in Britain. As Meredith Martin has detailed, Queen Mary II commissioned an ornamental dairy at Hampton Court in the 1690s with Queen Caroline, Princess Amelia, Queen Charlotte, Elizabeth Yorke and Elizabeth Craven following suit throughout the following century. As the word 'ornamental' suggests, these spaces were not for milking cows but were for socializing with other women, sites, as Martin describes, of 'hygiene, temperance and feminine productivity'.

Josiah Wedgwood, that exceptional entrepreneur of Georgian consumerism, produced 'dairyware' especially for these aristocratic dairies. Wedgwood's wares were earthenware in gleaming, white glazes, their forms nodded to the neo-classical style often on show in the buildings' design. In essence, the ornamental dairy was devoted, perhaps paradoxically, to both fertility and purity.

If the dairy was an appropriate setting for aristocratic women in the eighteenth century, the popular character of the dairymaid was more colourful. Taking the milking of the cow as a sexual metaphor, the milkmaid was characterized as 'an ideal of peasant beauty and sexual attractiveness'.[11] Seen as wholesome and healthy, the milkmaid stood in direct contrast to the 'impotent nobility debilitated by urban excess'.[12] Milkmaids appeared in song and theatre, among the rustic entertainments at London pleasure gardens at Vauxhall as well as pastoral paintings by the likes of Thomas Gainsborough. This is not to suggest that to use a cow creamer was to invoke intense sexuality, but that the eighteenth-century cultural context of dairies and milkmaids connected milk with femininity, whether that femininity was virtuous or not.

While both eighteenth-century Britain and Holland had a fondness for the cow as a national symbol, they were also both centres of metropolitan consumption hungry for new wares and luxuries. The function of the cow creamer, to provide milk for taking tea – a practice which gained popularity, and accessibility, as the century progressed – was part of a consumer pastime. A lady's tea-table was a place for polite performance. As Pierre Bourdieu has suggested, the formalities and stylization of the dining table detracts from the material reality of the acts of the eating, and contemplation of what is being eaten.[13] Yet the cow creamer is again an object of balance, one of conformation and resistance to Bourdieu's thinking. It presents a kind of nature, a manicured and miniature version of production that sits upon the table-top.

Earthenware cow creamers became more popular towards the end of the century, with numerous styles coming out of the Staffordshire Potteries as well as South Wales

The Cow Creamer and the 'Cudster'

and Tyneside. Just as the fashion, and access, for tea trickled down the social ladder, so too must the equipment, as the methods of production became cheaper, offering more affordable wares. In the Potteries Museum and Art Gallery, in Stoke-on-Trent, there is a collection of 667 ceramic cow creamers, evidence of the flourishing of styles between approximately 1750 and 1825. Known as the Keiller Collection, the herd was given to the Museum on 1 May 1962 by Gabrielle Keiller.

Keiller, born Gabrielle Ritchie on 10 August 1908, was brought up in Ashwell Rise near Oakham in Rutland. In 1951, after two marriages and a successful professional golfing career, she married Alexander Keiller, the heir to a marmalade firm in Dundee. Alexander was a keen collector with broad tastes from books on witchcraft and demonology to Ancient Egyptian *ushabti*.[14] After the Second World War, Gabrielle sold her part-ownership of the million-acre family ranch in Texas, releasing funds for her collecting. A trip to the Venice Biennale in 1960 introduced Gabrielle to the work of Eduardo Paolozzi, in the British Pavilion, and on the same trip a meeting with Peggy Guggenheim helped to open up the world of modern and contemporary art. That year would mark the start of 25 years of collecting.[15] Gabrielle bought work by Dali, Duchamp, Magritte and many more, and, while her collection focused on Dada and Surrealism, she was also a patron to contemporary artists such as Paolozzi and Richard Long; much of Keiller's impressive collection was given to the Scottish National Gallery of Modern Art in 1995 and was considered 'by far the most important gift made to the Scottish National Gallery of Modern Art since it opened in 1960.'[16]

The Keillers also collected ceramic cow creamers over a period of 35 years.[17] The collection stopped growing in 1961, six years after Alexander's death and one year after Gabrielle's trip to Venice. It was as though her new role as contemporary art patron was incompatible with such expressions of traditional domestic British culture. The collection of creamers commanded an entire room in the Keillers' beloved Telegraph Cottage in Kingston. Arranged across three walls of shelving, the creamers all faced outwards, in regimented rows seemingly ordered by aesthetic typology. The effect is startling; this is most definitely a herd, perhaps even an army. Their individual sense of function becomes less important, instead one is afforded a surreal tour of surface and pattern. Gabrielle Keiller demonstrated her contemporary tastes in her modern art collection, and while the cow creamer had become an almost vernacular archetype it is never too far away the surreal. Squinting at the surfaces one can see twentieth-century surfaces from Picasso to Lucien Day.

Collecting anything in such numbers would suggest a great affection, and it is tempting to make biographical connections between Gabrielle's ranch in Texas and her attraction to these objects, especially given the timing of first creamer purchase a year after her father's death. In fact, the only other comparable collection of cow creamers, numbering 250, is the Rice Collection in Taylor University, Indiana, America. It was amassed by Garnet and Raymond Rice, who made their fortune investing in Dairy Queen, an ice-cream business, in 1945.

The document archive connected to the Keiller collection outlines Gabrielle Keiller's negotiations with the Stoke-on-Trent Museum and Art Gallery in the early 1960s concerning the gift of more than six hundred cow creamers. Throughout the discussions, Keiller was focused on keeping the collection together at all costs, as well as the importance of offering handling access to researchers and getting assurance that two-thirds would be on show at any one time. The collection is referred to by the curator G. J. V. Bemrose as 'amazing' and 'extraordinary' in the various correspondence with Keiller, and yet by 1964, once the Museum had taken hold of the creamers, Keiller's solicitors wrote of her 'extreme dissatisfaction' with their treatment. Keiller was disappointed to hear that her collection had been displayed not in the main gallery but in a 'schoolroom' accessed through a door 'marked "No Admittance" and kept locked'. There were no labels or identification. Keiller had heard a story of one of the Museum's staff referring to 'a collection of animals in the schoolroom'.[18]

Her solicitor wrote to Harry Taylor, the Town Clerk:

> She treasured the Collection in her own keeping and was accordingly rather reluctant to part with it, but on further consideration, she was moved to make a immediate gift in sacrifice of her own personal pleasure of possession for the general benefit of others who might like the opportunity to view the Collection publicly ... . [S]he now feels she has good cause for regret, that she was ever influenced at all to entrust it the care of a collection she had long treasured.

Then, nearly a year later, 'she is almost drawn to the point of demanding the return of the Collection in her own care.'[19] Although there were factors such as a change in curator and the development of the Museum building to consider, Keiller interpreted the treatment of her collection as an institutional slight on the cultural value of the pieces.

The Keiller collection remained within the Museum's holdings, so a resolution must have been found, though it is interesting to note that it is currently displayed within the ceramics galleries, but as a children's activity area. Both in the early 1960s and today, these creamers have been placed outside of the traditional spaces of the museum. Perhaps due to their astounding quantity, or their perceived novelty, the Keiller creamers are consistently presented incidentally, tangentially and for the attention of children, not adults.

So we come full circle to the maligned nature of this object. Apart from a few cruel remarks, the cow creamer has left little trail over the centuries, quietly animating the tea-tables of the wealthy and subsequently becoming part of a wider domestic culture. It may elicit jibes and jokes, it may be novel and humorous, but it also reflects our negotiations with nature, both that which we have mastered and that for which we are nostalgic. It is an object that is so curious it surely deserves a little more thought, after all, there are not many designs that have been in production for over 250 years.

The Cow Creamer and the 'Cudster'

Notes

1. Catherine Johns, *Cattle: History, Myth, Art* (London: British Museum Press, 2011), p. 166.
2. Consider, for example, the cow creamer's antagonism to didactic design moments like Henry Cole's 'Chamber of Horrors' and the foundations of the Victoria & Albert Museum or Gustav E. Pasaurek's 'Cabinet of Horrors' for the Deutscher Werkbund in 1907.
3. P.G. Wodehouse, *The Code of the Woosters* (London: Arrow, 2008), p. 23.
4. PHS, *The Times*, 13 August 1971: p.10 col. A
5. V&A Museum, no. M. 1691–1944.
6. Johns, p. 166.
7. Andrew Rimas and Evan D. G. Fraser, *Beef: The Untold Story of how Milk, Meat and Muscle Shaped the World* (New York: William Morrow & Co, 2008), p. 106. Gillian Riley notes, 'Perhaps the most eloquent comment on the rich dairy product of the Netherlands is to be found in the work of the painter Albert Cupt, whose sleek, well-fed cattle in a golden landscape seem to personify the buttercup-coloured floods of cholesterol which brought wealth to his native town of Dordrecht' ('Cheese in Art', *Milk: Beyond the Dairy – Proceedings of the 1999 Oxford Symposium on Food and Cookery*, ed. Harlan Walker (Totnes, UK: Prospect Books, 2000), p. 289.).
8. Rimas and Fraser, p. 106.
9. Qtd. Walter Arnold, *The Life and Death of the Sublime Society of Beef Steaks* (London: Bradbury, Evans & Co., 1871), pp. 47–50.
10. Ben Rogers, *Beef & Liberty: Roast Beef, John Bull and the English Nation* (Vintage, 2004).
11. Robin Ganev, 'Milkmaids, Ploughmen and Sex in 18th century Britain', *Journal of the History of Sexuality* 16.1 (2007) 42.
12. Ganev, p. 42.
13. Pierre Bourdieu, *Distinction: A Social Critique and Judgment of Taste* (Abingdon, UK: Routledge, 2013), p. 195.
14. Timothy Clifford, 'Gabrielle Keiller: A Biographical Sketch', *Surrealism and After: The Gabrielle Keiller Collection*, ed. Elizabeth Cowling et al. (Edinburgh: National Galleries of Scotland, 1999), p. 12.
15. Clifford, p. 16.
16. Clifford, foreword.
17. It is inconclusive who began the collection, Alexander or Gabrielle. The Potteries Museum considers the collection to be Gabrielle's while Elizabeth Cowley (who worked with Gabrielle on the Scottish bequest) believes Alexander began the collection. What is certain is that Gabrielle continued to purchase pieces for the collection six years after the death of Alexander in 1955.
18. Letter from Edwin Coe to Harry Taylor, 18 June, 1964, Keiller Collection documentation, Stoke-on-Trent City Archives.
19. Letter from Edwin Coe to Harry Taylor, 11 August, 1964, Keiller Collection documentation, Stoke-on-Trent City Archives and later letter from Edwin Coe to Harry Taylor 30 June, 1965, Keiller Collection documentation, Stoke-on-Trent City Archives.

How to Make Solar Cooking Global: a Beginner's Guide

Jeremy MacClancy

Cooking with the sun is the beneficent side of the greenhouse effect: concentrating the sun's rays in a closed environment to cook food. A heaven-sent opportunity to curing so many contemporary problems, its use should be now be near-global. But it isn't, yet. Here I discuss why, and what we all can do to change that present negative into a future positive.

Principles

The rays of the sun strike the earth and convert into infrared radiation. If that occurs in an enclosed space, its temperature rises. If that space is well-insulated, little of the heat is lost. If the walls of the space are opaque, the heat is absorbed. Reflectors placed around or inside the enclosed space can intensify the heat falling on an object in the centre of the space. The result – a solar oven.

Practice

I made several attempts to make solar ovens. All my efforts were carried out during the summer months, on the terrace of our small house – sited in an olive grove in south-eastern Spain.

My first attempt was of the simplest: a solar panel oven. The material to be cooked was put in a large plastic bag, which was then sealed and placed in the centre of a series of panels, which had been cut from cardboard boxes and covered with aluminium foil. The layout of the panels followed directions from an online site dedicated to the home construction of solar cookers. The oven was then placed in line with the sun, which was strong.

This panel oven was almost useless. Why – because even a mild wind moved the panels, and whisked away much of the heat from the surface of the bag. For this kind of oven to work, the panels needed to be of much more durable and heavier materials, securely fastened, and left in an almost windless place.

I attempted to overcome these obstacles by making a solar box oven, again following instructions from an online site. The idea here is to create an insulated space by placing an open cardboard box inside another, larger one, and filling the gap between the two with crumpled newspaper. The top of the gap is covered with card. Aluminium foil is glued onto this horizontal card frame. Foil is also glued onto the inner walls of the internal box; the base is painted black. A large side of a cardboard box is used to make a lid. In its middle, I cut three sides of a rectangle, which were raised up; onto its inner surface I glued more foil; I secured this reflective surface in place (badly) with a piece

How to Make Solar Cooking Global: a Beginner's Guide

Figure 1. A solar panel oven.

of bamboo. The created hole in the centre of the lid was covered by affixing a piece of glass on its lower surface. I protected the result from rain, by covering the exterior of the oven in a sticky-backed plastic, in a fetching red gingham.

How did it work? The rays of the sun either passed directly through the glass or were reflected onto it from the bamboo-secured reflector. Once inside the oven, the rays were intensified by reflection from the foil-covered walls and from the inner surface of the glass. Relatively little heat could escape because of the insulation between the two boxes. Instead, the heat generated was absorbed by the pot. I put a trivet on the base of the oven, so that the heat generated could circulate around the whole of a pot.

It was immediately plain that this oven was much more efficient than the panel one. So long as the wind was not too strong, the reflector stayed in place. With use, however, it became clear that the reflector needed to be made of a heavier, more stable material, with a more secure fastening. While the lid achieved a tight fit, it turned out to be so tight that, over time, it began to fray. My next attempt at one of these ovens will have strengthened lids.

The panel oven took me an hour to make and cost less than two euros. I am a desk-based academic unused to manual labour or constructing objects: the box oven took myself and our two children two afternoons, and cost eleven euros in materials.

What did we cook in it? My wife and I quickly learnt how best to use the oven. The main lesson was that solar box cooking was slow: if we wished to cook something for lunch, it had to be in place, on days when the sun was strong, at least two hours beforehand. Our children and I successfully cooked pizzas, crumbles and cookies. The oven also proved very useful for defrosting and heating baguettes.

Figure 2. A solar box oven.

Promise

The sun's rays beam down on us all. It does not charge. Successful exploitation of the sun's rays can be very, very effective. Coal-fired stoves are about 15% thermally efficient, but solar cookers can reach 65%. One Chinese study suggests four hours of solar cooking meets a rural family's daily cooking and water needs.[1]

Solar cooking lightens the loads of those charged with collecting firewood. Since these tasks are often given to women and children, changing cooking techniques gives women time to do other things, and children more chance to play or learn.

Food in solar ovens doesn't need constant attendance. Cooks, usually women, are freed up for other tasks.

Solar cooking is good for health. The technique eliminates smoke that causes respiratory disorders, reduces burns to children who sometimes fall into the fire, and dramatically decreases the chance of assault and rape while gathering firewood.

Solar cooking is good for the environment. The technique forestalls deforestation; does not produce soot, a major contributor to climate change; and helps combat soil erosion, since dung is not burnt for fuel but used instead as fertilizer.

Solar cooking has a host of other uses. Besides cooking, solar cookers can be used for drying, especially of income-generating fruits; purifying water to combat diarrhoea and other water-borne diseases; ironing; canning; refrigeration, which seems counter-intuitive but uses the energy generated to power cooling units; and 'promotes the development of harmonious society'.[2]

How to Make Solar Cooking Global: a Beginner's Guide

Figure 3. Defrosting bread in a solar box oven.

The perils of preaching: the downsides of solar cooking

Solar cookers are cheap, but still cost. Even a small cost can loom large for the poorest populations. And why should they invest in a novel, strange technology?

Light-fingering. A light box is no burden to a thief. And if Cook is not around, its contents are even lighter. Therefore, Cook needs to hang around.

The earth rotates. Solar cooks, like lovers, know the earth moves. Thus, solar ovens need to be adjusted, every hour or so, to take full advantage of the sun's rays.

Hanging out at the hearth is not a chore. People like to meet over a fire, to tell stories or mull the moments of the day. Often mothers and children especially like to gather there to share relaxed companionability at day's end.

Fires and stoves give light, give off heat. If you've no electricity, fire may be your only source of night-time illumination. Also, even tropical regions can have chilly nights, come the winter. Desert nights can be cold, even in summer. Moreover, if the food-producing area of your home has no fire, insect numbers can spiral very fast.

Solar cooking is slow, very slow. Slow cooking means more planning, which may not fit with people's daily routines. Also, meat must be cut up into small pieces, perhaps smaller than demanded by locals. For example, in Kenya, if you cannot offer guests meaty chunks, you're thought inhospitable.

Box ovens are bulky if you've a family. Also, box ovens cook everything together at the same rate. Some cooks produce two or more dishes, which require different cooking rates. But raising the lid lowers the temperature, lengthening cooking time yet further. Moreover, in some areas of East Africa, families who cannot accommodate the sudden arrival of kin/guests are seen as niggardly.

Figure 4. A successful result.

Only good for some styles of cooking especially baking. No good for frying, which is popular in many parts of the world, partly because it is so quick. Further, some do not appreciate the change in consistency and texture of the food: e.g. a more solid, cake-like cooked staple, rather than the smooth, porridge-like consistency many central Africans are used to. On top of that, some people used to a smoky taste miss its absence.

Who can foresee the state of the sky? In certain tropical areas with almost rainless seasons, it may be possible to predict the day's weather. But elsewhere the threat of clouds makes solar cooking fundamentally unreliable in a way conventional cookers are not.

May disrupt domestic rhythms. In Burkina Faso, for example, many homes have housemaids, who wish to get their daily job over and done with, quickly. For them, solar cooking is too slow, delays their departure. A Central American study suggested husbands opposed their use: what unwanted new freedoms were solar ovens giving their womenfolk? Not surprising, then, that some women choose to cook around a smoky, potentially dangerous fire. The heat and smoke keep men away, and so enable women to create a space for themselves.

Successful introduction of solar cooking is very, very time-consuming. Project after project demonstrates that successful integration of solar cooking into local lifestyles requires a culturally sensitive, lengthy period of training. Projects may fail for many different reasons. Men may not regard time spent by women and children collecting firewood as laborious work, but as what mothers and kids are meant to do. Project leaders have to think ahead to the potential future production of more solar cookers. Thus project leaders have to collaborate with locals even before introducing the cookers.

They have to heed locals' concerns, and to overcome those in a culturally acceptable manner. Locals must feel, in some sense, the project is as much theirs, if not more so, as it is the introducing organization's.

Local values may push solar cooking down the list of priorities. If you're dirt-poor, you care about survival more than about the environment. Getting your family to the end of the day is more important than worrying about the future. One study in the Sudan summed up its findings: locals 'did not care about the effects of cutting trees and burning traditional biomass on the environment'; what did concern them was the price of bought wood; solar cooking only caught their interest when its introducers underlined the extent it could relieve household budgets.[3] In some areas, locals may be more worried about being trendy than treeless. As one commentator on a project put it: 'concern for the environment is a post-industrial concern.... The Basotho are not going to start caring about saving trees until they can stop caring about getting telephone poles erected leading to their houses.'[4] Further, some locals may say they wish to remain as healthy as possible. But usually they discuss this in the language of the very short-term. The cumulative effect of day-to-day phenomena, like smoke, was not openly considered.

Solar cooking's real contribution to forestalling deforestation is very easy to exaggerate. In most areas, firewood does not come from specially cut trees, but from foraged twigs and broken branches.

Where to target solar cooking initiatives? Most country dwellers find most of their fuel wood locally, and without too much difficulty, as they only tend to cook once a day, for the evening meal. Moreover, they may well exploit agricultural detritus, not wood, as their fuel, e.g. corn or millet stalks. In towns, however, many people, now following European eating patterns, light fires three times a day. They tend to use more wood, in large pieces, which they buy. On top of that, they rely more than country dwellers do on charcoal, which usually only contains 11% of the original wood energy. The result is that townspeople use a lot more wood, compared to their country cousins, and of a more difficult type to replace. The important consequence of this is that those who promote solar cooking should switch their efforts from rural sites to urban ones.

Parabolas

Some proponents of solar cooking think parabolic cookers will overcome many of the above disadvantages. The definition of a parabola is that all rays reflected from its surface share a common focal point. If the rays are solar, that point can become very hot, very quickly. On an ordinary sunny day, a kettle with a litre of tap water placed in the focal point will come to the boil in about seven minutes. A comparative project in Somalia found that these cookers were the only ones locals judged acceptable, as their cooking speed was directly similar to that of charcoal.

The elevated temperatures that parabolic cookers can attain mean that a host of cooking styles becomes possible: steaming, blanching, roasting, and frying.

Further, to make them more durable and more reliable, most parabolic cookers are made of metal, the dish covered with reflective tiles. The result is too heavy to lift for most thieves.

The rapid rise in temperature is also being exploited at a large, commercial scale: by food-processing plants (which produce potato chips, jaggery, and marmalade), textile manufacturers, bakeries and waste incinerators. In 1998 the eponymous inventor of the popular Scheffler solar concentrator even started to experiment with solar cremation.

These parabolic variants of solar cookers appear to bypass many of the problems suffered by box and panel ovens. But every technology has its downsides as well as its upsides. First, solar box ovens only need adjusting every hour or so: parabolic concentrators have to be shifted every 30 minutes; if they are not finely adjusted to the position of the sun, their efficiency drops dramatically. Second, the adjustment can be too fine: the food at the focal point cooks very rapidly while the food on the inner edge of the holding-pot cooks much more slowly. In some particularly finely made parabolic cookers, the food at the focal point can burn.

Third, the sun's rays give light as well as heat. Thus a cook who places their face too close to the focal point can temporarily blind themselves: think Galileo. Similarly, a body part (hand, arm, etc.) placed at the point may receive a sudden burn. One solution is to wear sunglasses, and to keep hands away from the focal point. For some, though, the simplest solution is to give up using them.

An imaginative alternative is to split the parabola into two complementary, but separate half-dishes. These 'butterfly parabolic solar cookers' greatly reduce the chance of damage to body or food. An inventor from northern France has recently devised a low-lying, horizontal parabolic concentrator, whose focal point is the underside of the conductive cooking surface.

A further obstacle is that most households wish to cook and then eat at times when the sun is low, at the beginning and end of the day – hence the need to store, and later exploit, the energy generated by the cooker. In 2011 an international development technology organization launched a competition to stimulate advance in storage solutions. The most lauded entries were imaginative, impressive and highly suggestive. Trouble is, most of those entries were reliant on expensive, fragile materials. To overcome that, some suggest quicklime solar storers: calcium monoxide mixed with water liberates energy; when it is sunny, solar energy dehydrates the resultant hydroxide, back to monoxide. But only parabolics with storers have been produced so far, with all the disadvantages listed above. A butterfly concentrator with a quicklime storage unit has yet to be invented.

Globalism for dumbos

Several years ago, I produced an irreverent but scholarly book on the anthropology of food. One of the key points I tried to make there was that the way people prepared, cooked and ate their food was central to what they did and who they thought they were. In other words, a people's cuisine, with all that entails, is a key component of their culture, and thus of their cultural identity. As such, change will usually come only for extremely good reason. Unless there is a strong case for altering their mode of cooking, most traditional peoples on this globe resist the introduction of culinary novelty.

The study of solar cooking only underscores the validity of that statement. A depressingly long list of critical studies shows that, in case after case, the importation of solar ovens does not produce the results development workers had expected. One survey concluded, 'Decades of efforts to implement and improve solar cookers for developing countries have not helped to achieve the breakthrough of this technology.'[5] To take one specific example from south Asia: 'In India, where more than 100,000 box cookers have been disseminated at 50% subsidized rates, the cookers' utilization rates, durability and performance have been unsatisfactory. Also, progress has been relatively slow, i.e. there is still only one cooker in India for each 10,000 people.'[6]

As part of my research into this topic, I contacted a broad number of colleagues who had done fieldwork in areas where solar cooking was viable. All of those who knew of solar cooking projects in their field sites stated that the introduced ovens were no longer being used by the time of their fieldwork. What my anthropologist colleagues tended to see were disused, dilapidated ovens, of no use to anyone.

The information presented by websites of NGOs dedicated to the promotion of this technology provides, unfortunately, little evidence to the contrary. For it has to be recognized that the great majority of these sites are in effect promotional vehicles for the NGOs themselves. All too often, their otherwise laudable projects are not backed up by independent, critical studies of subsequent use of the ovens by the locals. As one environmental anthropologist has confessed, 'They use the solar oven when we're around, but put it away again when we leave.'[7]

So far, it would seem that the area of the globe where solar cooking has been most successfully adopted by locals is Tibet. Why – because there the scarcity of fuel is so great and so clearly acknowledged by villagers, that they have little option but to embrace the new technology. In other words, in most cases, unless a culturally very sensitive, long-term (and thus expensive) programme of solar cooker promotion is carried out in each area where its promoters take it, it is only when people's backs are up against the wall that they will accept using it without too much resistance.

It is possible to argue that other parts of western China also have successful programmes. But it is no coincidence that this adoption of the new technology is occurring in areas where fuel is scarce, people are poor, and the government at times crushingly authoritarian.

Finale: time to help others by helping ourselves?

The initial promise of solar cooking seems so great, and its potential benefits so broad, that it is at times deeply disappointing to have to acknowledge the oft-ignored maxim that, technologies are all profoundly social in origin. We cannot expect to be able to simply transfer a technology, however basic or sound it may appear to us, directly into another cultural setting. Different advantages and disadvantages may occur in each new setting to which these cookers are introduced, and they have all to be taken account of, in each particular case.

There is, however, one last problem I wish to consider, and that is the image of solar cooking. For many people, though seemingly very poor and with few apparent options, still wish to hang on to their sense of personal dignity, no matter how constrained that might appear to us, affluent Westerners.

Let me give some examples of what I mean. In rural Lesotho, many who consider buying a solar oven ask themselves, 'What do white people do?' 'Is this going to make me seem more advanced?' or would people call them country bumpkins for having one around the house? According to the founder of Ladakh Project in India, the locals who tend to adopt solar cookers are the more traditional ones: 'The young and fashionable won't use them; there is no glamour in it.'[8] Cookers are not associated with what is modern and fashionable. In her opinion, what is needed to change attitudes is for an American soap opera, such as *Dallas*, to include the use of one in an episode.

Some promoters are well aware of how they themselves may be viewed. As one put it, 'Of course, it's hard for me to make a persuasive argument for the solar oven when they know perfectly well that I use more fossil-fuel energy in a day than they use in a year. "Do I use a solar oven?", they ask.'[9] One way to surmount this problem is to turn preaching into home practice. In the words of a charitable programme director:

> I can say from personal experience that the fact that I use these technologies myself has gone a long way in terms of technology acceptance in the communities we serve. I suspect that this is because they feel that if someone of greater means chooses to make these technologies instead of being relegated to use them (by lack of other options), that there must be some inherent or perceived benefit from their usage.[10]

In a small effort to follow this best practice, we have lent the solar ovens we have made so far to our rural neighbours in south-eastern Spain, in the hope that they might come to see their value and to make their own. To further the point, I shall put a version of this paper on the web, where it can, of course, be seen by anyone.

Perhaps the best way to sum up our experience and loan of solar ovens is, how can we hope to change the habits of other people, if we are not prepared to change our own?

Notes

1. Solar Cookers International Network, 'China', SCInet Wiki <http://www.solarcooking.wikia.com/wiki/China> [accessed 14 April 14 2013].
2. C. Xiaofu Han Tingcun, 'Development and Application of Solar Cooker in China' (Paper presented at International Solar Food Processing Conference), 2009, p. 5 <http://www.solarfood.org/solarfood/pages/solarfood2009/3_Full_papers/Technologies/9_Tingcun.pdf> [accessed 10 February 2010].
3. M. Rizing and B. Croxford, 'Cooking in a Semi-rural Area in Sudan: A Case Study in al-Sororab' (Paper presented at Solar Cookers and Food Processing International Conference), 2006.
4. W.N. Grundy, 'Solar Cookers and Social Classes in Southern Africa', *Techné: Journal of Technology Sciences* 5 (1995) 4.
5. See P.P. Otte, *Cooking with the Sun: An Analysis of Solar Cooking in Tanzania. Its Adoption and Impact on Development* (Saarbrucken: VDM Verlag Dr. Muller Aktiengesellschaft & Co. KG, 2009) and Ott, 'Solar Cookers in Developing Countries – What is Their Key to Success?' *Energy Policy* 63 (2013) 375–81.
6. H. Bergler et al., *Moving Ahead with Solar Cookers* (Eschborn: Deutsche Gesellschaft für Technische Zusammenarbeit (GTZ) GmbH, 1999) <http://pagesperso-orange.fr/synopsis/gtz.pdf> [accessed 14April 2013].
7. Qtd. B. Diamond, 'Solar, Appropriate Tech, etc.', 2008, p. 23 <http://www.listserv.uga.edu/cgi-bin/wa?A2=ind0802&L=eanth-l&P=R16110&X=7A &X=1BF4100F8BB419678> [accessed 12 March 2008].
8. V. Farwell, 'Solar Box Cookers in Ladakh', SCInet Wiki <http://www.solarcooking.org/ladakh1.htm> [accessed 14 April 2013].
9. Qtd. Diamond.
10. Diamond.

The Rise of the Picnic Hamper: Its Pleasurable and Macabre Uses in Nineteenth-Century Britain

Diana Noyce

The Rat brought the boat alongside the bank, made her fast, helped awkward Mole safely ashore, and swung out the luncheon basket. The Mole begged to be allowed to unpack it all by himself.... [He] took out all the mysterious packets one by one and arranged their contents, gasping 'Oh my! Oh my!' at each fresh revelation.

The Wind in the Willows (1908)

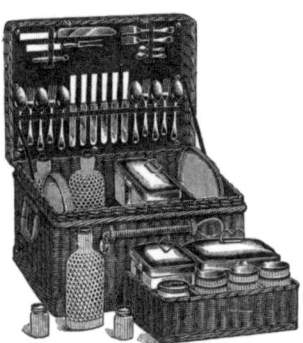

Contemporary literary and visual arts are engaging sources to trace the rise of the picnic hamper, a basket intended to hold and transport food and tableware for a picnic meal that today is standard equipment at many picnics. In Kenneth Graham's enchanting tale *The Wind in the Willows*, for example, Mole's joy in unpacking the basket reflects the British love of picnics.[1] Writer Georgina Battiscombe claims in *English Picnics* that, 'although no climate in the world is less propitious to picnics that the climate of England', picnics became quintessentially an English way of outdoor dining.[2] The pleasurable excursion at which a meal is eaten outdoors (*al fresco* or *en plein air*), ideally taking place in a picturesque landscape, was a new way of sharing food. A picnic became an acceptable fixture of the social calendar for Britain's burgeoning middle class from the second decade of the nineteenth century, together with the use of the picnic hamper.

A picnic, according to the *Macquarie Dictionary*, is 'an outing or excursion, typically one in which those taking part carry food with them and share a meal in the open air'. Although people have always eaten outdoors, it was not for the same reason or in the same way as we know it today. Medieval hunting feasts or Renaissance-style country banquets, for example, required hundreds of servants to carry, prepare and serve elaborate feasts. Field labourers also ate outside, but their meals were usually brought to them, and they ate during a work break, not for pleasure. The idea of tramping out into the country to share a meal while enjoying the scenery was neither possible nor desirable for these early *al fresco* diners.

So how did this new form of sharing food originate? According to Colin Spencer in *British Food*, picnics came into being as meal times shifted, with the midday dinner moving into the evening, and a light luncheon replacing it in the daytime. In Jane Austen's time (1775–1817) breakfast, usually taken around 10 a.m., was followed by dinner at 3.30 p.m. in 1798; at 4 p.m. in 1805, occasionally at 5 p.m.; never before 5 p.m. by 1808, and in fashionable households at 6.30 p.m. As the gap between breakfast and dinner widened and the pangs of hunger were felt between meals, cold meats, pickles, cakes and jellies were laid out on the sideboard, which evolved into luncheon, now a proper meal taken in the middle of the day.[3] The cold collation of portable sideboard dishes could also be packed into a picnic hamper and eaten in the great outdoors.

In tandem with this development, the Romantics, an artistic, literary and intellectual movement that began at the end of the eighteenth century, made nature fashionable. Previously there was a prevailing distaste for nature in her wilder aspects, at least by those calling themselves civilized. Mountains and moors were regarded as places of interest but not of beauty.[4] The Romantics held that society had become fragmented as a result of the French Revolution (1789–1799), industrialism, urbanism, secularization and the Napoleonic wars (1803–1815).[5] Civilization was corruption, and man had to return to nature, implored the Romantic philosopher Jean-Jacques Rousseau (1712–1778).[6] A close connection with nature was mentally and morally healthy, and to eat outdoors, 'liberated the soul', wrote Rousseau.[7]

The works of key figures in literature such as Samuel Taylor Coleridge (1875–1912), Sir Walter Scott (1771–1832) and William Wordsworth (1770–1850), and in the visual arts, the landscape paintings of John Constable (1776–1837) and Joseph Turner (1775–1851) for example, encouraged the enjoyment of picturesque settings and vistas in the countryside. At the close of the Napoleonic wars, William Wordsworth published his epic poem 'The Excursion' (1814).[8] In the poem Wordsworth reflects on the fragmentation of society and the disunity brought about by the French Revolution and industrialism. Instead of articulating solutions that he believed would reunify British society, the poem concludes with a description of a small community taking a pleasure excursion to a remote spot in the country in order to share a rustic meal. The writer Andrew Hubbell interprets this 'picnic' as Wordsworth offering 'a new custom for creating the bonds of identity within a community and between the community and the land.'[9] Indeed, after the French Revolution, royal parks became open to the public for the first time and communal picnics, known as *fêtes champêtres*, became a popular activity amongst the newly enfranchised citizens. The British sometimes referred to a picnic as a *fête*.

Battiscombe states that before the Romantics made nature *au courant,* 'no one connected the idea of pleasure with the notion of a meal eaten anywhere but under a roof.'[10] The term 'picnic', which entered the English language in the second half of the eighteenth century, is derived from the French '*pique-nique*', and originally referred to a meal eaten indoors where each person either paid a share of the cost or contributed to the meal. The short lived Picnic Society, formed in March 1802 (and ending in 1803), patronized by 'persons of fashion' including the Prince of Wales and his mistress, Mrs Fitzherbert, was an event held indoors, but a decade later the word 'picnic' was used only in the sense of a meal eaten outdoors.[11]

Pleasure

The occasion of the outdoor picnic began to appear in the narratives of nineteenth-century English novelists. In Jane Austen's *Emma* (1816), an excursion is proposed to picnic at the picturesque Box Hill which, to this day, is a popular picnic spot. Austen employs the picnic to bring into play conflict in relationships with the possibility of a resolution, as well as the enticing prospect of unchaperoned flirtation.

But plans go awry, and in the event there are two excursions, one to Donwell Abbey to take advantage of the strawberries there, and the Box Hill excursion taking place the following day. There is a debate as to whether the lunch should be taken in or out of doors. One of Austen's characters, Mr Knightly, is reluctant to eat outdoors, preferring instead to have a table spread in the dining room.[12] His disinclination perhaps suggests the transition from indoor dining to outdoor dining was in its infancy. Moreover, to the modern reader, Austen's picnic seems a rather formal occasion – a cold collation of pigeon pies, cold lamb and gathered strawberries, eaten at a table with servants in attendance. Still, what was formal then made a trestle-table in the open countryside seem exhilaratingly abandoned. By the Victorian period (1837–1901), however, outdoor excursions to picnic had become *de rigueur,* and picnickers were happy to sit on a picnic cloth spread on the ground to eat their repast from a hamper.

Whether shared with family members, a group of friends or just an intimate romantic companion, fresh air and natural beauty, adventure, no cooking, no tables and chairs and, despite the constraints of Victorian attire, the freedom to lounge about on a blanket eating cold food with their hands from a wicker basket, was a thrilling reversal of Victorian societal rules and structure.[13] With the sky as their roof and the ground as their table eating a meal in the great outdoors amongst beautiful scenery, confirmed that surely God was the consummate architect as far as the Victorians were concerned.

By mid-century, innumerable societies, including architectural, archaeological, ecclesiastical and temperance, held annual picnics. Sporting picnics also became the acme of fashion, from cricket teas to boating suppers. Picnics had become such a national pastime among the urban middle class that Mrs Beeton, the Victorian arbiter of middle-class tastes and manners, thought it necessary to include, in her *Book of Household Management* (1861), a Bill of Fare as well as a list of 'things not to be forgotten' to be packed in hampers. The collation of cold suggestions suitable for a genteel outdoor meal included joints of roast beef, boiled beef, ribs of lamb, shoulders of lamb, roast fowls, roast ducks, ham, tongue, veal and ham pies, pigeon pies, lobster, collared calf's head, lettuces, baskets of salad and cucumbers.

As well, Beeton's suggestions list stewed fruit well sweetened, and put in glass bottles well corked, plain pastry biscuits to eat with the stewed fruit, fruit turnovers, cheesecake, cold cabinet puddings in moulds, blancmanges in moulds, jam puffs, cold plum pudding (this must be good), fresh fruit, plain biscuits, cheese, butter (this includes butter for tea), bread, bread rolls, plum cakes, pound cakes, sponge cakes, a tin of mixed biscuits and tea. Coffee was thought not suitable for a picnic, being difficult to make.

'Things not to be forgotten' at a picnic included a stick of horseradish, a bottle of mince sauce well corked, a bottle of salad dressing, a bottle of vinegar, mustard, pepper and salt, good oil and pounded sugar. Of course plates, tumblers, wine glasses, knives, forks, spoons and corkscrews were not to be forgotten; as also teacups and saucers, teapots, lump sugar and milk. Beverages should include ale packed in hampers; ginger beer, soda water and lemonade; sherry, claret, champagne, and any other light wine that might be preferred, as well as brandy.[14]

The picnic baskets or hampers ranged from a simple open wicker basket as depicted in Édouard Manet's controversial 1862 painting, *Le déjeuner sur l'herbe*, to one consisting of a single large storage space, usually with a handle and flaps that opened at both ends on the top. More elaborate baskets were made of wood and wicker and boasted lids with intricate metal hinges, hook clasps and handles with clips on the inside to hold plates, utensils, and a large picnic cloth. The latter baskets often bore their owners' initials either inscribed, embossed or embroidered. Picnic hampers were also made of leather. Towards the end of the nineteenth century the motor car began traversing the British countryside, and, in 1901, British luxury-goods retailers like Asprey began stocking hampers filled with tableware for motorists to take on country drives. The travel outfitter G.W. Scott & Sons made picnic hampers complete with copper kettle and burner.

Figure 2. Picnic hamper with owner's initials embroidered on lid, 1920s. (Photo. by the author.)

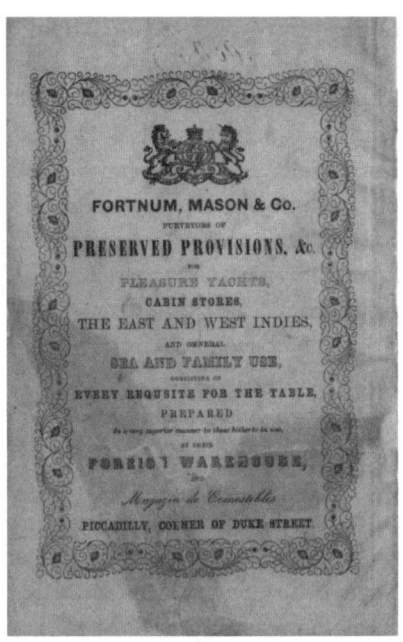

Figure 3. Fortnum, Mason & Co., 1849 catalogue of Preserved Provisions. (Courtesy Fortnum & Mason.)

Commercial picnic hampers were popular amongst the upper echelons of British society. The purveyor Fortnum & Mason were the first to provide ready-made hampers, a service available to this day. The classic wicker basket embossed with the now famous F&M logo was developed in the 1740s to meet the demands of well-heeled travellers journeying by coach to their country estates to see their families and friends, or to 'take the waters' in Bath. The hampers held delicacies such as game pies, fresh bread, West Country butter, scotched eggs, cheese, hothouse fruit and rich fruit cake, with mineral water, small beer and hock to drink.[15] By the time of the Great Exhibition in 1851, ready-to-eat dishes were all the rage. An 1849 Fortnum & Mason catalogue reveals the purveyor provided an enormous range of luxury tinned and prepared foods for travellers, hunting parties and those attending sporting events – ragout of veal, Bombay mangoes, bottled and green truffles, lobster and wild duck which required no cutting, to name a few, as well as wines and spirits.[16]

In the Victorian era, the 'London season' held in the summer months consisted of as many outdoor cultural events as indoor – the Harrow and Eton cricket match, the Henley Regatta, the Cowes Regatta, the Epsom Derby – and Fortnum & Mason supplied picnic hampers for the spectators on these occasions. Derby Day was a particularly important day in the calendar, with carriages queuing from four in the morning to pick up the Fortnum's picnic basket. Charles Dickens wrote in *Harper's New Monthly Magazine* of the Epsom Derby in August 1851: 'Look where I will.... I see Fortnum & Mason. And now, Heavens! all the hampers fly wide open and the green downs burst into a blossom of lobster salad!'[17]

The Rise of the Picnic Hamper

Beginning in September, the 'hunting season' followed the 'London season'. From the hunting feast of Tudor and Stuart times descended the shooting luncheon. It was an opportunity to see and be seen by the élite of the society and perhaps to have a new outfit made for the occasion. In *The Pickwick Papers* (1836–1837), Charles Dickens poked gentle fun at a shooting luncheon when the picnic hamper is unpacked for Mr Pickwick:

> 'Weal pie,' said Mr Weller, soliloquising, as he arranged the eatables on the grass. 'Wery good thing is weal pie, when you know the lady as made it, and is quite sure it an't kittens... Tongue; well that's a wery good thing when it an't a woman's. Bread – knuckle o'ham, reg'lar picter – cold beef in slices, wery good. What's in them stone jars, young touch-and-go?'
> 'Beer in this one,' replied the boy, taking from his shoulder a couple of large stone bottles, fastened together by a leathern strap – 'cold punch in t'other.'[18]

Picnic baskets also became the traveller's companion. Paradoxically, although the Romantic Movement opposed industrialism, and at the same time encouraged people to get out into the country, this movement was not possible until industrialization brought about improved roads and convenient transportation. The railway, an essentially British invention, burst upon the English countryside in the 1840s, providing inexpensive and rapid transportation for the multitudes. The nineteenth-century revolution in transport also produced faster steamships, which dramatically cut travel time and costs. These improvements had a major impact on the development of travel and tourism. Travel for pleasure became a possibility for a far greater number of people.

For rail journeys, reasonably priced picnic hampers made in both wicker and tin could be purchased at railway stations containing a ready-made picnic meal and cutlery (and then returned afterwards). For those travelling further afield, say to the Continent for a month-long grand tour, the picnic basket along with a guide book, an umbrella and a hat box to conceal the chamber pot, made up the accoutrements of the 'pleasure' tourist.[19]

If the Victorians enjoyed the pleasures of picnicking at outdoor events during the 'London season' and at peaceful idyllic settings or while travelling, they were not averse to extending their cultural pursuits not only on foreign shores, but to a war zone.

Macabre: a taste for war

Human beings have always possessed a morbid curiosity. The Romans staged fights between individuals and wild animals to entertain the public at sites like the Coliseum; crowds flocked to public hangings during the medieval period; and the guillotine provided endless entertainment for the proletariat during the French Revolution. The Victorians were no exception.

Through a sense of social engagement and to see their countrymen in action, British tourists ventured to the battle fields of the Crimean peninsula in the Black Sea where the British were engaged in a war along with the French against the Russians. The Crimean War (1854–1856) was the first major war from which photographs and newspaper reportage hit the breakfast tables and parlours of the Victorian middle class and well-to-do. The new 'media coverage' revealed the realities of war which piqued the public's interest and motivated war tourists to see for themselves firsthand the horrors of war, as well as to take the opportunity to extend the 'London Season' on foreign shores.

The first tourist ship to the Crimea, the iron paddle steamer *City of Glasgow*, left London a month before Christmas in 1854 with 100 tourists on board. By spring, tourists (accompanied by their servants) began to arrive in the Crimea by the shipload on private yachts and on steamers. Tourists (both male and female) were able to take advantage of the £5 a head packaged tour on offer in the British press by the shipping firm Inman for a fortnight's travel and accommodation, including visits to Constantinople and the battlefields.[20]

The arrival of tourists started a burst of social and military activity behind the lines. The Crimean war not only became a military campaign but a culinary campaign. The British, that is the upper echelons of British society, were intent on recreating their cultural pursuits on Russian soil. 'Picnics were the order of the day,' wrote Captain Robert Portal to his sister. Lazy picnics were taken on Crimea's craggy coast with its spectacular views of clear blue sea. The women wearing the new crinoline fashion, along with the men, also made inland excursions to picnic amid the bleached bones of the fallen in the valley of the Light Brigade's fateful charge, a battle immortalized by the poet Alfred Tennyson (1809–1892). A favourite picnic spot was the monastery of St George, five miles (8 km) from Balaclava, and tourists didn't mind climbing over rocks and patches of marshland, intersected by narrow paths covered with vines and shrubs to reach it. Coastal trips by yacht within gunshot distance of the Russians, band concerts and cavalry reviews and many 'capital dinners' were put on for the benefit of the tourists, delighted as the men were to have the pleasure of their company.[21]

In the urge to recreate English society in the Crimea, for the British officer class so far from home, spring in the Crimea took on an air of normality with the resumption of the traditional sports of racing, hunting (not the traditional fox, but feral dogs that roamed the Crimea) and cricket matches. 'Can this be a journal of a campaign? I think I must change its name to a new edition of the Racing Calender,' wrote Fanny Duberly in March 1855.[22] Fanny, who had followed her paymaster-husband Captain Henry Duberly to the Crimea, was anticipating the start of the racing season. She thought it 'wonderful, that men who have been starved with cold and hunger, drowned in rain and mud, wounded in action, and torn with sickness', should, in the first warm, balmy days of spring, be eager for 'the sport of kings', 'a national English sport on Russian territory'.[23] Along with the men, the women attended the race meetings complete with parasols, opera glasses and picnic baskets. 'The Russians must certainly think us an odd race of people', observed George Cavendish Taylor, 'to carry all our national institutions about and establish them wherever we go.'[24] Thus, the Crimea became a hermetically sealed part of old England, and by the spring of 1855 it was transformed into one great country club to which the war was increasingly an adjunct.[25]

Picnic hampers purchased at Fortnum & Mason were brought over from London, or provisions for a picnic could be procured from the sutler town of Kadikoi (a sutler was generally a female who was an independent, usually small-time trader whose job it was to sell provisions to military personnel). The German purveyors Oppenheim, 'the Rothschild of the provision market', who had been provisioning armies since the 1700s, had opened up on a half-acre site in the sutlers' town and offered picnic supplies including the best champagne, hock, claret and bottled beer, as well as every kind of cured and potted meat, pickles, preserves and hams, French chocolate, roasted coffee, and tins of Albert biscuits. At Kadikoi, Oppenheim monopolized trade and were so successful that they later were allowed to build a second outlet at the 4th Division camp near the observation point at Cathcart's Hill.[26] However, they soon found some competition. Tourists' numbers had, as the war progressed, increased to such an extent that Fortnum & Mason set up shop too in the Crimea. Now that picnic hampers could be bought on the spot, they no longer needed to be brought over from London.

The appetite for witnessing war first-hand meant the highlight of the Crimean excursions was to see the army in action. A visit to the sites of the battles of Alma, Balaklava and Inkerman, and then thrill to the live action of the soon-to-be-renewed vigour of the bombardment of Sebastopol, was very much part of the tourist itinerary. Impelled by curiosity, the cultural pursuit of visiting battlefields had been established many years before during the Napoleonic wars when the Battle of Waterloo in 1815 was observed from a safe distance by a few male members of the British nobility replete with a Fortnum & Mason picnic hamper.[27] The Crimean theatre of war, however, became a macabre spectator-sport, the common soldiers were the players watched by a tourist audience of ladies and gentlemen from the British middle and upper classes.

Tourists could be seen with telescopes of all sizes roaming about the countryside with picnic baskets in hand jostling for the best views of the 'killing fields'. The tourists settled down in the hope of enjoying a sight that would justify the cost and trouble of their journey. What time was the curtain likely to rise? They looked at their watches. And they looked at their picnic baskets that each little party was going to open between the intervals of battle, and if a stray shot or two from the Russians went in their direction, the visitors accepted the risk as part of the entertainment.[28] And as time wore on, while many were dying every hour in the trenches and British artillerymen were being hurled high into the air by massive explosions, 'their bodies appearing in the distance like birds on the wing', the presence of shiploads of tourists increased.[29]

The third bombardment of Sebastopol, which took place on 8 June, saw a large crowd of spectators gather to catch the view of the massacre of 6000 British and allied troops.[30] Another bombardment took place on 18 June at Cathcart's Hill. Tourists hauling picnic baskets arrived just before dawn and sat all day long in the heat to watch 3500 French soldiers killed and 1500 British cut to shreds in a hail of grapeshot and

Food and Material Culture

Figure 4. A picnic party attended by a servant perched on the hills above the scene of a forthcoming battle during the Crimean War. Artist C. L. Doughty, c. 1971, www.lookandlearn.com.

bullets, and 'the ladies thoroughly enjoyed the fun', wrote Captain Portal.[31]

And it wasn't just the British who enjoyed a good battle while picnicking. Across the Atlantic, some hundreds of American Civil War tourists made a seven-hour carriage ride for a weekend excursion to watch about 50,000 soldiers take part in the First Battle of Bull Run fought on 21 July 1861 in Prince William County, Virginia, near the city of Manassas. Expecting an easy Union victory, the wealthy élite of nearby Washington, including congressmen and their families, had come to picnic and watch the battle. The tourists made pies and packed lunches into picnic baskets. Arriving in the evening, the tourists set up camp and rose at dawn to ready themselves for the impending battle. As the cannons began to roar so did the crowd. Charging to the valley of death as Tennyson had noted in the Crimean war, boys bled and husbands struggled to hold in their insides after grapeshot wounds; while the war tourists picnicked, 4700 lives were lost. The Confederates though, overtook the Union Army, and the roads back to Washington became clogged as panicked civilians attempting to flee in their carriages became entangled with the retreating Union army.[32]

In war and peace alike, picnics were a new way of sharing food that redefined how people engaged with each other and their environment. Thus, picnics and the picnic hamper came to play a significant role in the social life of the British in the nineteenth century, at least for the upper echelons of society. However, picnics are not unique to the British; today people from all cultures and all classes of society enjoy a picnic. Nevertheless, the British model provides compelling insight into how human societies engage through material objects, in this case the picnic hamper and its contents, with the physical world – it demonstrates people routinely use food to express relationships amongst themselves and their environment whether it be in a picturesque setting, while travelling, at a sporting event or perched on a hill above the scene of a bloody battle.

Notes

1. Kenneth Grahame, *The Wind in the Willows*. (London: Vintage, 2012), p. 11.
2. Georgina Battiscombe, *English Picnics* (London: Harvell, 1949), p. 1.
3. Colin Spencer, *British Food: An Extraordinary Thousand Years of History*. (New York: Columbia UP, 2002), p. 256.
4. Battiscombe, p. 63.
5. Andrew Hubbell, 'I picnic lonely as a cloud', *Times Higher Education* (7 March 2003) <http://www.timeshighereducation.co.uk/175225.article> [accessed April, 2013].
6. Maxine Feifer, *Going Places: The Ways of the Tourist from Imperial Rome to the Present Day* (London: Macmillan, 1985), p. 139.
7. Solomon H. Katz, *Encyclopedia of Food and Culture* (New York: Charles Scribner's Sons, 2003), p. 68.
8. William Wordsworth, 'The Excursion', *The Complete Poetical Works* (London: Macmillan and Co., 1888; Bartleby.com, 1999) <www.bartleby.com/145/> [accessed April 2013].
9. Hubbell.
10. Battiscombe, p. 3.
11. Kate Crookenden, Caroline Worlledge and Margaret Wiles, *The National Trust Book of Picnics* (London: National Trust, 1993), pp. 13–14.
12. Jane Austen, *Emma* (London: Penguin Classics, 1996), pp. 330–52.
13. Margaret Visser, *The Rituals of Dinner* (London: Viking, 1992), pp. 150–51.
14. Isabella Beeton, *Mrs Beeton's Book of Household Management,* ed. Nicola Humble (Oxford: Oxford UP, 2000), p. 391.
15. Fortnum & Mason, *The History of the Hamper* <http://www.fortnumandmason.com/c-385-the-history-of-the-hamper-fortnum-and-mason.aspx> [accessed January, 2013].
16. Fortnum & Mason & Co, *Preserved Provisions for Pleasure Yachts, Cabin Stores, The East and West Indies and General Sea and Family Use* (London: Fortnum & Mason, 1849), pp. 1–10. I am grateful to Dr Andrea Tanner, Fortnum & Mason company archivist, for her correspondence and assistance.
17. Charles Dickens, 'Race Horses and Horse Races', *Harper's New Monthly Magazine,* 3:15 (August, 1851) 333.
18. Charles Dickens, *The Pickwick Papers* (London: Penguin Classics, 1999), p. 252.
19. Feifer, p. 172.
20. Piers Compton, *Colonel's Lady and Camp Follower* (London: Robert Hale, 1970), p. 137.
21. Compton, pp. 158–61.
22. Francis Isabella Duberly. *Journal Kept During the Russian War, From the Departure* of the Army from England in April 1854, to the Fall of Sebastopol. (London: Longman, Brown, Green and Longmans, 1856), p. 177.
23. Duberly, pp. 171–73.
24. Helen Rappaport, *No Place for Ladies: the Untold Story of Women in the Crimean War* (London: Aurum, 2007), pp. 197–98.
25. Rappaport, p. 190.
26. Rappaport, pp. 185–86.
27. Annabel Venning, *Following the Drum: The Lives of Army Wives and Daughters, Past and Present* (London: Headline Book Publishing, 2005), p. 186.
28. Compton, pp. 91,166.
29. Rapapport, p. 204.
30. Rappaport, p. 205.
31. Compton, p. 166.
32. Nate DiMeo, 'The First Civil War Tourists', *Slate* (4 August 2011) <http://www.slate.com/articles/podcasts/podcasts/2011/08/the_first_civil_war_tourists.html> [accessed January, 2013].

Vessels and Equipment Used by Street Food-vendors in Istanbul

Banu Özden

Istanbul has been and still is a very vibrant city where life actually takes place on the streets. Such activity is an important factor in the development of street food, and therefore to the development of vessels and equipment used to serve or transport these foods, which ranged from ready-to-eat items to dishes cooked on the spot. As Reşat Ekrem Koçu, author of the famous *Istanbul Ansiklopedisi*, puts it, street sellers are 'tradesmen on foot', and they are crucial to the life of the city: 'Tradesmen on foot are the salt and pepper of great Istanbul, they are Istanbul's trademark' (1960: 44).

In the nineteenth century, street food vendors were all over the city. During meal times, citizens of Istanbul would get a chance to communicate, to interact and share with each other by creating small communities around these sellers. In those times restaurants were not common, but even today street food remains indispensible to the lives of current Istanbul residents. In some cases, street food is even better than the fare of most restaurants as it is fresh, quick and cheap. The foods sold by the street vendors are usually seasonal and obtained locally.

The types of vessels used to transport these foods and drinks varied according to the commodities. There were wooden trays with tray stands, three-wheeled carts, straw baskets, hand scales, mobile grills, brass jugs and other speciality containers specifically designed for certain foods and drinks.

Street food's popularity really increased in the nineteenth century, as residents came to appreciate the easy access to a wide variety of foods. They could shop for different ingredients without straying far from the comfort of their homes or grab a quick, cheap lunch in various parts of the city. But street food has never lost its importance in Istanbul. It is an integral part of the city's colourful street life, displaying Istanbul's diverse cultures and helping people from many backgrounds to carry on their traditions. The vessels and equipment used to transport these foods have had a significant impact on the history of culinary culture of Istanbul. While some of the vessels used to transport these foods have changed over the years, others have stayed the same. These vessels fall into easily identifiable types.

Round wooden trays with tray stands
Round wooden trays have been a significant vessel of Istanbul street food, as they have been widely used to hold and transport the king of street food: *simit*, a kind of bread ring topped with sesame seeds. These round wooden trays vary in size, with a frame that

is about five cm high. Trays were usually carried on the heads of the sellers, balanced on small round cushions, as they walked the streets. In order to rest from time to time, they also carried wooden tray stands. The stands had three legs like a tripod, and were not foldable. The three legs were attached with nails to a wooden ring. Between each leg, there were two pieces of wood, hammered on either side to look like the letter 'X'. The stands could easily be carried over the shoulder of the seller while he carried the tray on his head. These trays lost popularity when the municipalities required *simit* sellers to use four-wheeled carts designated by officials.

Even before the nineteenth century, round wooden trays were the most popular types of vessels used for a variety of products. They were very practical, easy to carry and, when used with the tray stand, they acted as tables to show off the food being sold. Round wooden trays were also used for selling *borek*, a baked savoury pastry made from layers of thin dough like phyllo with various fillings; miniature versions of Turkish delight called *kuş lokumu*; and milk puddings or other puddings in fancy ceramic bowls. The round wooden trays used for puddings were usually painted with floral or leaf patterns.

Wicker baskets

Street food sellers have long used various types of wicker baskets for both previously cooked foods and raw ingredients. A vendor could carry one type of food in one basket or he might carry several differently sized baskets with different kinds of ingredients. The most common of these vendors were greengrocers on foot. These salesmen were the housewives' favourites, as they could shop for their ingredients on their doorstep. These greengrocers walked among the neighbourhoods, announcing their arrival by shouting out the names of the fruits and vegetables they carried. The most common type of basket used for this purpose was *kufe*, also referred to as a pack basket. The largest type of wicker basket, the *kufe* was usually carried like a backpack or sometimes loaded on the back of a donkey.

The *kufe* usually consists of four parts, the base, sides, rim and straps, made from leather in old days and from high-strength nylon material today. *Kufe*-making is considered an art form in some regions of Turkey, but there are fewer and fewer basket makers, and soon the skills may be completely lost as new generations have little interest in learning these art forms. The baskets themselves are most often made from chestnut or willow. The master basket maker uses specific tools to prepare long, flat bands. The basket is made by laying the long sticks in place and then weaving the flat bands together with the sticks. The rim is woven in next, sometimes along with handles. Because the *kufe* is carried like a backpack it has straps, and many vendors add cushions to protect the small of their backs.

These vendors also carried hand scales to weigh out their foodstuffs. Some used a pocket balance with a spring; others carried the traditional scales with two concave dishes, one for the weights and the other for the food being weighed.

In today's Istanbul these types of vendors are still seen on the streets. Nowadays the *kufe* is most commonly used by porters who work in the open bazaar areas where shoppers hire them to help carry their purchases. More amusingly, in the old days porters who owned a *kufe* sometimes provided a taxi service to drunkards. At night, they waited in front of taverns; drunken customers who wanted to go home would hire a porter, get inside his *kufe* and be taken home.

Smaller wicker baskets were used for carrying various types of smaller fruits like lemons or garlic in former times. Today these small baskets are mostly used for selling sandwiches. Sandwich sellers can be seen all hours of the day, especially in busy parts of town. The sandwiches are usually filled with white cheese, parsley, peppers and tomatoes – basically ingredients that won't spoil easily. These baskets are relatively flat with short sides and a wide opening. The vendors either carry them by their handles or place them on tray stands. The sandwiches are fanned out over colourful flower petals and look very appetizing in the baskets.

Wooden Poles

Wooden poles are the simplest vessels used by various vendors, but the most significant of these vendors are the liver sellers. In the beginning of nineteenth century, the liver sellers usually consisted of Albanian immigrants living in Istanbul. In Turkish, 'liver' usually refers to all types of offal, so it might be more accurate to call these kinds of vendors offal sellers. The offal was sold as a complete set, with liver, lungs, heart, kidneys and trachea, hung by the trachea off either sides of the pole. The seller would balance this pole over his shoulders and walk around the neighbourhoods.

The offal seller's worst enemies were flies and stray cats. There was nothing protecting the offal, so undoubtedly they were infested with flies. While these vendors were making a sale, or bargaining the price, accidentally bending to either side would lower the pole close enough to the ground for hungry stray cats to get their paws on the meat.

Three-wheeled open carts

The fruit vendors in today's Istanbul have given up on using the *kufe* and upgraded to three-wheeled open carts to sell their fruits and vegetables on the streets. These carts are made out of pine or hornbeam in sizes that average around 170 cm long and 90 cm wide. The three wheels resemble bicycle wheels, with one in the front and two in the back. The handle to push the cart is at the back. Ideally the vendors lay a blue vinyl cover – their trademark – over the top of the cart and place the fruits and vegetables over the vinyl. This vinyl protects the fruits and vegetables from getting bruised by the frame. The carts usually carry a table scale to weigh the fruits.

These carts are also used by the vendors known as 'cucumber sellers'. These vendors sell apples in the winter and cucumbers in the summer. And, for the very short season when they are available, they add raw melons to their repertoire. When serving apples, they use a vertical spiral slicer, which peels the apples as it slices in a spiral manner, and the spiral apple is presented to the customers in a napkin. When serving cucumbers or melons, they use a vegetable peeler. Peeled fruit is cut partway into four vertical slices that remain attached at the bottom. Sprinkled with some salt, these become a most refreshing snack on a warm summer day.

Similar carts are also used by a new type of vendor selling fruit juices. The fruit juice sellers usually work in winter time; they carry oranges and pomegranates. Using a new version of the vintage heavy-duty iron orange juicer, they provide freshly squeezed fruit juice to their customers who seek natural vitamins to fight off the colds and flu of winter.

Three-wheeled open carts with a grill

Another type of three-wheeled cart, containing a built-in charcoal grill, is a relatively new type of street food vehicle. These carts can usually be seen around stadiums or open air concert venues, and cater to the attendees. The most popular type of food offered is *kofte*, minced meat patties, or *sucuk*, spicy beef sausage, served with grilled tomatoes, peppers, onions and red pepper paste inside a split loaf of traditional white bread. The smells of these carts are really intoxicating when one is hungry.

Kokorec carts

Kokorec is grilled lamb's intestines. They have been one of the most popular types of street food since the 1970s. Cleaned intestines are wrapped around sweetbreads, quite a few times, yielding a large piece of meat that looks like a thinner version of *doner kebab*. To be able to cook and sell *kokorec* properly, a special kind of cart has been built. The cart is made out of stainless steel, and is usually about 1 m high and about 1 m long with a width of 60–70 cm. The top has a long half-circular section with a sliding lid, resembling a bread storage bin. The sliding door is opened to reveal discs that hold the *kokorec* skewers in place. Charcoal heats this section; alongside is a flat iron grill heated with butane gas, located on the bottom of the cart. The small area in front of the grills provides space for a cutting board and knife. Hooks along the cart hold plastic bags full of bread, napkins and wet towels.

Three-wheeled carts with glass case

Carts with glass cases have become the most popular on the streets of contemporary Istanbul. There are a few different types of three-wheeled carts, used for selling different types of street food.

These carts are usually made out of wood. Three-wheeled like the carts described above, these have an upper section with a glass case that holds the food. The glass case has two doors, which are closed while the cart is on the move or to protect the food and keep it clean.

In the carts used for selling rice pilaf with chickpeas, the bottom part of the glass case consists of a sheet of stainless steel sheet above a tub of water heated by butane gas. The hot water keeps the rice pilaf with chickpeas warm.

Another version of this cart is used to sell *pogaca*, a savoury pastry, similar to bread, stuffed with cheese, potato or minced meat fillings. These vendors usually work early in the morning because *pogaca* is a popular breakfast item, especially for those who don't have time to eat at home. In order to keep their *pogaca* warm, these vendors use a similar three-wheeled cart with a heating device underneath the metal sheet. They select these tasty breads with a pair of tongs and serve them wrapped in paper or napkins.

Sandwiches have become another popular breakfast item among contemporary street food. The sandwich sellers use the same glazed carts. Instead of a heating mechanism, there are shelves located inside. The vendors display all their sandwich fillings on plates on the bottom of the glass case, and on the shelves above they store items such as breads, back-up sandwich fillings and sometimes drinks.

Other vendors use these same types of carts to sell different foods, such as various desserts and *cig kofte*, a Turkish version of steak tartare made out of bulgur wheat, minced meat, salt, red pepper flakes, onions, tomato paste and parsley – usually the street food version does not contain meat.

Four-wheeled *simit* carts

Vendors of the most popular street food, *simit*, have been upgraded from round wooden trays to four-wheeled carts, a change mandated by the municipalities of Istanbul from the early 1990s. Unlike the three-wheeled carts described above, these carts are made out of sheet iron. Painted in red, with golden coloured rods and handles all around, they have become fairly standard all over the city. Each cart displays a stamp from its local municipality. Although these carts are mobile, they are usually stationed in fixed locations.

Round tinned copper trays

On a sweet note, the most popular street vendors among children were without a doubt the candy sellers. Although there were street vendors that sold hard candies, the equipment used by the candy paste sellers was more unique. These vendors used a round, tinned copper tray, which was divided into five equal triangles with a tiny round section in the middle. Each of the triangles was used to hold a different flavoured candy paste. The middle round part was used to hold a half lemon. Each candy flavour had its own metal skewer with a wooden handle used to serve this special paste.

In today's Istanbul, these candy paste vendors can only be seen in tourist areas, mostly on weekends, but they sell the pastes in the time-honoured style. Flavours can be combined or sold separately depending on the customer's desire. The candy paste is lifted with the metal skewer and wrapped around the end of a wooden stick that resembles a chopstick. Customers can get as many flavour layers as they want, and with each different flavour and colour the candy looks more and more appealing to the eye. Finally the prepared candy is rubbed with lemon to smooth out the surface and presented to the customer.

Water sacks

Water sellers were very popular in the eighteenth century, though they began to diminish by the end of the nineteenth century, when, during Sultan Abdulhamit's reign, water pipes were built to bring spring water straight from the source to the city centre. However, in the beginning of nineteenth century there were still a few to be found on Istanbul's streets. Vendors carried water in sacks, narrow on one side and wide on the other, made of buffalo skin. The sack was carried on the back of the seller with the help of a leather strap. A hose that resembled an elephant trunk was used to pour the water out of the sack.

Ensemble of *boza* sellers

As mentioned in *Istanbul Eats: Culinary Backstreets*, *boza* is 'a thick, almost pudding-like drink made from fermented millet'. *Boza* sellers were a significant part of cold winter nights in Istanbul; they walked around neighbourhoods, announcing their arrival by 'calling out a long mournful "boooozaaaa"' (Mullins and Schleifer 2011: 44). Vendors carried tin jugs, with lids, that could hold up to twelve kilos of *boza*. In the other hand, they carried smaller pitchers of water to wash the glasses used by the customers. The glasses used for offering *boza* were placed in a tin box, open at the top, attached to a belt at the waist of the seller. This tin box also held a small container of powdered cinnamon. Since they worked at nights, *boza* vendors were required by law to carry small flashlights. It is very rare now to see these vendors in contemporary Istanbul, as *boza* is now bottled and sold in supermarkets.

Sherbet jugs

Sherbet jugs are among the most fancy and decorated vessels used in the nineteenth century. Although they can still be seen at times in historical and tourist areas, they no longer play an important role in the lives of Istanbul residents. Sherbets were popularly sold as a refreshing drink to combat the heat of the summer.

Sherbet jugs were made out of brass that shined like gold and could be spotted from far away. They were shaped like large Chinese vases, narrow at the neck and bottom and quite large and wide in the middle. With attached straps, the jug was carried on the vendor's back like a backpack. The top of the jug was decorated with chains and beads; as the vendor moved, it jingled to announce his arrival. Just like the *boza* seller, sherbet vendors also carried a tin box for holding glasses, again attached at the waist, and a pitcher of water to clean the dirty glasses.

Mobile coffee vendors

Mobile coffee vendors do not exist anymore since coffee is now sold in all restaurants and coffee shops, but in the nineteenth century and earlier coffee makers were a common sight. These mobile vendors carried their own little grill with charcoal, along with a small basket containing coffee pots, cups and coffee. Coffee makers would settle down in front of shops and make coffee for people coming and going from the shops.

Conclusion

Street food vendors still play an important role in the colourful, vibrant city of Istanbul, but in a few years time, strict municipal regulations and health and safety issues may well drive them into extinction. Along with the food itself, the original vessels used to prepare and transport street food will also become obsolete and become mere antiques. However, while it still exists, street food provides a great alternative to eating in restaurants. All over the city, these various vessels really are the 'salt and pepper of great Istanbul'.

References

Ugur Aktas, 2010. *Isanbul'un 100 Esnafi, Istanbul Buyuksehir Belediyesi Kultur* (Istanbul: A.S. Yayinlari).
Ilhan Eksen, 2008. *Istanbul'un Tadı Tuzu* (Istanbul: Everest Yayinlari).
Reşat Ekrem Koçu, 1960. *Istanbul Ansiklopedisi* (Istanbul: Cilt).
Ansel Mullins and Yigal Schleifer, 2011. *Istanbul Eats: Exploring the Culinary Backstreets* (Istanbul: Boyut Yayinlari).
Özge Samanci and Sharon Croxford, 2008. *XIX. Yuzyil Istanbul Mutfagi* (Istanbul: Medya+ik Yayinlari).
Marie Adelaide Walker. 'Pera'da Sokak Saticilari'. *Yemek ve Kultur* (Istanbul: Ciya Yayinlari, 2008).

Ushnān and Perfuming the Banquet

Charles Perry

> In as much as the chief pleasure of this life and the next is the consumption of appetizing food and drink, and since perfuming the body and the clothes is one of the ways to draw near to the ones we love, both men and women, it is incumbent on those who dress themselves, eat and drink to make suitable use of perfumes. Therefore I have compiled this book, which I have named 'The Book of the Link to the Beloved, Concerning the Description of Good Things [to Eat] and Perfume.'[1]

Of the seven great medieval Arabic recipe collections, five include recipes for handwashing preparations to be used before and after the meal, and three also give recipes for perfumes of various kinds. The oldest is *Kitāb al-Ṭabīkh*, representing practice in eighth- and ninth-century Baghdad court circles.[2] From the thirteenth century, *Kitāb al-Wuṣla ilā al-Ḥabīb* and *Kanz al-Fawā'id fī Tanwī' al-Mawā'id* share a considerable repertoire of recipes.[3] A handful of related recipes appear in the roughly contemporaneous *Zahr al-Ḥadīqa* and a very different handful in the North African collection *Fuḍālat al-Khiwān*.[4]

The diner's day

The diner's preparations for a banquet began in the morning, or even the evening before, if he were sucking on a pill to sweeten the breath with aromatics such as mace, clove, cubeb, galingale, cardamom, sandalwood, musk and camphor.[5] *Kitāb al-Ṭabīkh* describes the diner's morning obligations.[6] He would brush his teeth with the *siwāk* (a small stick chewed or pounded at one end to separate it into fibres), rub his teeth with galingale (the aromatic root of *Cyperus longus*) and possibly suck on another breath pill.[7]

After bathing at the *hammām*, he could begin the perfuming. There were dozens of perfumes, the most basic being *'anbarīnā mumassak*, a mixture of ambergris and musk. The same ingredients scented *ghāliya*, the classic men's perfume for the skin and above all the hands, which consisted of ambergris and musk dissolved in *duhn al-bān*, a light oil with a mild, pleasant aroma resembling peanut oil and celery, obtained from the seeds of *Moringa oleifera*. These perfumes, and other aromatic toiletries, were often suffumigated with ambergris, musk, sandalwood or agarwood (*Excoecaria agallocha*, an incense similar to sandalwood but sweeter and more resinous). Altogether a lot of ambergris and musk were involved in going to an important banquet.

Some perfumes were for the hands or face, others for the beard or hair (the last particularly likely to be scented with musk and camphor), still others for the clothing. Clothing could also be suffumigated with incense; *bakhūr yamanī* was for use in winter 'and for furs'.[8] Perfume and incense were not strictly distinguished: breath pills might be burned to incense clothing, and wicks made by kneading ambergris with quince down could be used as incense but they could also be carried in a pocket to perfume the clothes.[9] Perfume might even be worn – in the *Arabian Nights*, a 'smartly dressed' character sports 'a tall green hat, with knots of silk stuffed with ambergris'.[10]

There were also perfumed powders (*dharāʾir*) that could be sprinkled on hair or clothing. They inclined to the same musky, resinous aromas as most perfumes but some included floral notes such as violet, jonquil or orange blossom.[11]

If he feared excessive sweating – perhaps because banquets often had a political dimension as well as being about drawing near to the dear ones – the diner could apply a desiccative powder of zinc oxide. To be on the safe side, it was scented with wormwood and rosewater and suffumigated with ambergris and then agarwood.[12]

At the banquet, the diner might encounter some of the same perfume ingredients in the food. For instance, bread crusts stuffed with pistachios, boiled chicken and spices were fumigated with ambergris, musk flavoured a pilaf made with chicken and pistachios and a stew of lamb and dates.[13] But first the hands must be washed – an important consideration when diners were eating with the hand out of a common dish. In addition to concern for cleanliness, there was the possibility that a particular hand perfume might clash with the flavourings of the food.

For this purpose, there would be soap and a water basin, and the soap would be perfumed, of course. The technique was to mill unscented soap by shaving it very fine and then to knead it with same sorts of aromatic that were likely to flavour the dishes that followed. *K. Wuṣla* mentions rosewater and *maḥlab* (the aromatic seed of a variety of cherry, *Prunus mahaleb*) and adds that cardamom, mace and clove might also be used, but it emphasizes that the crucial ingredient was *maḥlab* – not rose, as we might expect today.[14] Soaps were also given various colours, and professional soap-makers doubtless made more varieties than these recipes describe.

Wherever people eat with the hands, similar codes of etiquette evolve to censure greed, unsanitary behaviour and the inconveniencing of one's fellow diners. In *The Book of Misers*, the ninth-century essayist al-Jāḥiẓ quotes a certain Abu Fātik on etiquette offenders. For instance: 'Everybody knows the Finger-Licker (*laṭṭā*). He licks his fingers and then returns them to the common stew or yoghurt or porridge or the like. The Cutter (*qaṭṭāʿ*) chomps on a morsel and cuts it in half, then dips the half into the condiments.'[15] The diners were provided a dish of spiced salt, and a certain offender dubbed the Sifter (*mugharbil*) 'shakes the salt cellar like a sieve so that all the spices collect in one part and he gets them all.'[16]

It was after the meal that the most distinctive feature of the banquet appeared: washing powders. Common soap consists of an animal fat or vegetable oil saponified by mixing it with lye. The classic Arab washing powder consisted of lye (sodium carbonate, also known as soda ash or washing soda) diluted with a neutral substance such as white clay or rice flour and mixed with aromatics, which could be herbs (marjoram, basil, sweet flag, wormwood), spices (cinnamon, clove, nutmeg, saffron, galingale, cubeb, cardamom, *maḥlab*), incense ingredients (sandalwood, agarwood, frankincense, myrrh), aromatic resins (costus, storax), perfume ingredients (roses, musk, ambergris) or other fragrant substances (almonds, camphor, lemongrass, spikenard).

The lye saponified the grease on the diner's wetted hands, which could then be rinsed in the water basin and dried on a towel. These powders were rather like present-day laundry detergent powder, which often contains sodium carbonate as an anionic surfactant. We also use dry hand-washing products today in industrial contexts where large amounts of grease have to be removed from workers' hands, though it goes without saying that they are not scented like *ushnān*.

It's common knowledge that lye for soap-making is traditionally obtained by dissolving wood ashes in water and then draining the liquid off the lees. The Arabs used the ashes of prickly saltwort (*Kali tragus*), a close relative of that tumbleweed that blows listlessly through the silent ghost town in many a cowboy movie. In Arabic this plant, which flourishes in salty and alkaline soil, was known as *ushnān*, and the same name was also applied to the whole category of hand powders, whether or not they actually contained any lye.

Ushnān posed its own etiquette problems. Abū Fātik named the following types of offender:

> The Kneader (*dallāk*) does not rinse his hand well of *ushnān* but kneads it well on his napkin. … The Greener (*mukhaḍḍir*) kneads his hand in the *ushnān* when it's dirty with grease, so that the *ushnān* turns green and black, then he rubs it on his lips.[17]

Kitāb al-Ṭabīkh gives recipes for two other kinds of post-meal hand washing powders which appeared on the same tray as *ushnān* but differed in that they did not contain lye, so they served primarily to perfume the hands, rather than to clean them. One was *maḥlab*, here meaning ground *maḥlab* kneaded with aromatic oils. This was probably also the *maḥlab* with which one cleansed one's mouth after the meal.[18] Possibly the galingale one rubbed on one's teeth in the morning was a similar paste: galingale kneaded with other aromatics.

The other was *bunk*, made from an ingredient which puzzled the lexicographers. They said vaguely that *bunk* came from Yemen and India (though one recipe calls for Iraqi *bunk*). Some authorities claimed that it was shavings from the root of Egyptian thorn (*Acacia nilotica*), though that does not particularly agree with the repeated observation that it was aromatic. The only thing they agree on is that the best quality was yellow and inferior *bunk* was white.[19] The poet, gourmet and sometime caliph

Ibrāhīm ibn al-Mahdī wrote a verse celebrating *bunk* as redolent of *'abīr* (a perfume consisting of musk, sandalwood and rose water) and silken to the touch.[20]

The conclusion of the meal proceeded as follows, according to *Kitāb al-Ṭabīkh*: after rinsing his hands, the diner would use a special *ushnān* for the mouth, teeth, beard and 'wherever there is grease', which suggests that this *ushnān* actually contained lye, unpleasant to the taste as that sounds.[21] Possibly to get rid of that taste, a fresh batch of *ushnān* and *maḥlab* would be provided to cleanse the mouth, this time possibly an *ushnān* which lacked lye, as the *maḥlab* certainly did. Then more *bunk* and galingale for the mouth (which sounds a bit like perfuming the lily), then rinsing the mouth with water, and finally the diner would wash his face and hands with rosewater and return to his seat.

Kitāb al-Wuṣla ilā al-Ḥabīb ends with a chapter on another class of scents associated with the meal. It begins, 'As we have dealt with hand-washing, and as people perfume themselves with waters afterwards, we should discuss this now.'[22] (It sounds as if these waters were sprinkled on the face and beard.) The chapter is devoted to steam distillation of rose petals, jasmine, jonquil, marjoram, laurel, *nammām* (some member of the mint family, probably oregano), citron peel, orange peel, jujube, basil and cucumber (distilled together), clove, saffron, musk, camphor, agarwood, sandalwood, spikenard and palm spathe.[23]

The ushnān tray

Here are two contrasting examples of *ushnān* from *K. Wuṣla*, a grand one made with ten aromatics which shows the heavy, musky effect that was evidently the aristocratic taste, and a simpler one with a sweet spice aroma. The weights are given in *raṭls* (approximately 400 grams) consisting of 12 *ūqiyas* (33.3 grams). The *dirham* was around 3 grams and the *mithqāl* around 4.25:

> The first, (made from) *ushnān 'aṣāfīrī fārisī*.[24] White cleaned soda ash, 3 *raṭls*. Galingale, 4 *ūqiyas*. Ground sifted white wormwood, a like amount. Yellow sandalwood dissolved in rosewater, 3 *ūqiyas*. Ground white rose petals, a like amount. *Idhkhir* (West Indian lemongrass, *Cymbopogon schoenanthus*), a like amount. Clove, a like amount. Spikenard, 1 ½ *ūqiyas*. Ceylon cinnamon, a like amount. Fine rice flour, 7 *ūqiyas*. Mix everything with the soda ash and knead with rose water. Fumigate with agarwood for a day and a night, then mix every *raṭl* with half a *mithqāl* of camphor. This is *ushnān ḥammūdī*, with which vezirs and caliphs clean their hands.[25]
>
> The sixth kind, from Ibn al-'Abbās: One part *ushnān 'aṣāfīrī*, one quarter part rice flour, one half part each nutmeg, clove and pounded white *maḥlab*. Pound each ingredient separately and bolt through a piece of silk, and add a little saffron.[26]

Kitāb al-Ṭabīkh gives three recipes for ushnān, quite similar in style despite being three hundred years older. The main difference is that white clay can be used in place of rice flour for diluting the washing soda:

Ushnān and Perfuming the Banquet

A lesser *ushnān*. Take washing soda and pound it fine. Pound with it a third as much of white clay and mix with it a sixth as much of ground and sifted lemongrass, a quarter as much of pounded sifted galingale and half a sixth as much of scraped sandalwood. Pour in camphor water and knead well until it no longer appears.[27]

The *maḥlab* mixtures in *Kitāb al-Ṭabīkh* differ from *ushnān* not only in omitting washing soda but in scenting it with aromatic oils, rather than spices.[28] The only *maḥlab* that does use spices is the one described as 'suitable for the common people'. Here is a more typical example (at least for this book which represents court practice):

Recipe of royal *maḥlab* for the élite. Take good *maḥlab* seeds, pick them over one by one and completely peel them [of the enclosing skins], and puff on them so that none of the yellowed and spoiled seeds remain. Grind, sift in a fine sieve and put in a glass bowl. Knead with Persian jasmine oil, [stick this dough onto the interior of the bowl, turn it upside down over the incense] and fumigate with good quality agarwood and camphor 100 times a day for three days. Twice a day stir it up and mix it and stick it [again] to the wall of the bowl. When this is done, put it in a cup and mix it with jasmine oil of Sābūr. Throw on some attar of Persian roses (*duhn ward Fārisī*), balsam oil, citron oil, good [distilled] camphor water and as much crushed camphor as you like, God willing.[29]

The *bunk* mixtures are more similar to *ushnāns* except that they also omit washing soda and always add liquids such as safflower water or apple juice before the process puzzlingly referred to as 'toasting'.[30] Here is one example:

'Toasted' *bunk* for the hands and the bath. Take 30 *dirhams*' weight each of yellow *bunk* and yellow sandalwood, 20 *dirhams* of clove, 15 *dirhams* of rose petals, 5 *dirhams* of saffron and 6 *dirhams* each of thin brown Chinese cinnamon bark (*salīkha*) and spikenard. Pound everything together and grind it and 'toast' it with rosewater. Fumigate it well with raw agarwood, camphor and saffron. Then take 20 *dirhams* each of cardamom, nutmeg and mace and 1 *dirham* camphor. Spread the first mixture in a dish and sieve the spices onto it. Mill it again and suffumigate well [inside] the bowl with agarwood and camphor. It is the very best.[31]

The *ushnāns* in the North African book, divergent from the eastern recipes as they are, may cast light on the curious place of *maḥlab* and *bunk* on the *ushnān* tray. The following recipe uses similar aromatics to the eastern *ushnāns* but omits the washing soda:

Ushnān which cleans the hands, improves the breath, cures the mouth and the gums and removes the odours of fat foods. Take good mealy palm pith, 100 *dirhams*, red rose petals, green apples, dry marjoram, sandalwood, dry citron leaves, fennel leaves, an *ūqiya* of each. Put them on a large stone, crush them and save to wash the hands with after a meal.³²

This could certainly not dissolve grease, but compare the following two recipes, also from *Fuḍālat al-Khiwān*:

A soap which cleans the hands and removes fatty odours. Take 4 *mithqāls* of clove, 1 *ūqiya* of natron and 3 *ūqiyas* of broad bean flour. Pound everything strongly and wash the hands with this. It is good and very beneficial.

Another kind. Grind chickpeas, sift and wash the hands with this after meals. It is suitable for that and is the *ushnān* which the common people use.³³

The first is essentially the *ushnān* of the eastern Arab books, natron being a form of sodium carbonate derived from inorganic sources, diluted with broad bean flour as the eastern recipes use rice flour. It would certainly cut grease. The second recipe contains neither lye nor aromatics, yet the book says that it is suitable for washing the hands. Evidently this recipe, like the *maḥlab* and *bunk* recipes, 'cleaned' the hands by abrasive action alone, but it did not perfume them – it was not suitable for a banquet.

Notes

1. *Kitāb al-Wuṣla ilā al-Ḥabīb*, London, British Library, MS Oriental 6388: p. 18a. Citations of *Wuṣla* will refer primarily to this manuscript of the work because of its accessibility to European scholars.
2. Ibn Sayyār al-Warrāq, *Kitāb al-Ṭabīkh*, eds. Kaj Öhrnberg and Sahban Mroueh (Helsinki: Finnish Oriental Society, 1987); Nawal Nasrallah, *Annals of the Caliphs' Kitchens: Ibn Sayyār al-Warrāq's Tenth-Century Baghdadi Cookbook* (Leiden: Brill, 2007).
3. *Kanz al-Fawā'id fī Tanwī' al-Mawā'id*, eds. Manuela Marin and David Waines (Wiesbaden: Franz Steiner Verlag, 1993).
4. Shihāb al-Dīn Aḥmad b. Mubārak Shāh, *Zahr al-Ḥadīqa fī al-Aṭ'ima al-Anīqa*, MS Orient. A1344, Forschungs- und Landesbibliothek zu Gotha: pp. 38b–39a; this book contains recipes for perfume and breath-sweetening pills but no hand-washing powders. Ibn Razin Tujibi, *Fudalat al-Khiwan fi Tayyibat at-Ṭaam wa al Alwan*, trans. Mohamed Mezzine and Laila Benkirane (Fez, Morocco: Publications Association Fès-Saïs, 1997); this book contains recipes for hand-washing powders but no perfumes.
5. *Wuṣla* p. 94a; *Kanz*, p. 234.
6. Ibn Sayyar, pp. 322–23; Nasrallah, 502–03.
7. *Wuṣla* p. 94a; *Kanz*, p. 234.
8. This recipe happens not to appear in the London *Wuṣla*, but it does in most other MSS, e.g. Arabe 4938, Paris, Bibliothèque Nationale: p. 3.
9. *Wuṣla*, p. 4, p. 20a: *fatā'il nadd*.
10. *The Arabian Nights*, trans. Husain Haddawy (New York: Norton, 1990), p. 206.
11. *Wuṣla*, pp. 21b–24a.
12. *Wuṣla*, p. 24a: *dawā' al-'araq*; *Kanz*, p. 233: *fatā'il lā naẓīr lahu*. The recipe in *Kanz* explicitly says that it prevents armpit odor (*yaqṭa' al-ṣanān*).
13. *Wuṣla*, p. 40b: *ausāṭ miṣriyya*; p. 40a: *ṭabīkh āruzz*; p. 56b: *ma'shūqa*.
14. *Wuṣla*, p. 91a.
15. al-Jāḥiẓ, 'Amr ibn Baḥr, *Kitāb al-Bukhalā'* (Beirut: Dar, 1974): p. 112.
16. al-Jāḥiẓ, p. 111.

17. *Kitāb al-Bukhalā'*, p. 111.
18. Ibn Sayyār, p. 528; Nasrallah, p. 497. This verse describes a young servant passing among the diners and dispensing *maḥlab* from a special bowl with a golden spoon.
19. Another mystery is that all *bunk* recipes describe the mixture as being 'toasted' (*muḥammaṣ*). It's hard to believe that this literally means heated until scorched. For one thing, all *bunk recipes* include ingredients such as rose petals and fragrant herbs which would be destroyed by toasting. For another, in every recipe the ingredients are counter-intuitively moistened just before this 'toasting': One says to 'toast with apple juice,' another to mix 50 *dirhams* (150 grams) of rose water with the *bunk* 'and toast until [or so that] the rose water interpenetrates it.' Evidently 'toasting' is a forgotten term of art, perhaps connected with an earlier sense of the verb *yuḥammaṣ*, 'cause to contract', as when a medical treatment causes a wound to knit. Nawal Nasrallah contends that *bunk* is the earlier form of *bunn*, the Arabic word for coffee bean, and rewrites the *bunk* recipes to go with her vision of people washing themselves with coffee grounds. The moistening issue aside, this identification is implausible for linguistic reasons and the descriptions of *bunk* do not at all accord with coffee beans.
20. Ibn Sayyār, p. 528; Nasrallah, p. 497.
21. Ibn Sayyar, pp. 333–34; Nasrallah, pp. 505–06.
22. *Wuṣla*, p. 91a.
23. Dictionaries commonly translate *ṭal'* as 'spadix or inflorescence of the palm tree', but here the meaning is the spathe, viz. the bracts which surround a spadix (a stem – in the case of the palm, a bundle of stems – covered with tiny flowers): 'ii. spathe. [...] In a first attempt a distilled extract (pentane and ether) of freshly harvested spathes the analysis by gas chromatography revealed a prominence of 1,2-dimethoxyl-4-methyl benzene of up to 75% of total isolated volatiles. [...] It has a pleasant characteristic flavour somewhat like vanilla' *Date Palm Products*, FAO Corporate Document Repository <http://www.fao.org/docrep/t0681e/t0681e11.htm>.
24. Literally, 'Persian sparrow *ushnān*,' reportedly so called because it resembled bird droppings.
25. *Wuṣla*: p. 90a: *ushnān 'aṣāafīrī*. *Kanz*; p. 227: *ushnān al-mulūk wal-umarā' wal-mutamawwilīn*. I do not know the Ḥammūd for which this is named.
26. *Wuṣla*, p. 90b.
27. *Wuṣla*, p. 92b, *ṣifat mā' al-kāfūr*. Ibn Sayyār, p. 327; Nasrallah, p. 495. Camphor water was distilled from a mixture of camphor and rosewater.
28. Ibn Sayyār, pp. 327–28; Nasrallah, pp. 496–97.
29. Ibn Sayyār, p. 328; Nasrallah, p. 497.
30. Ibn Sayyār, p. 528; Nasrallah, p. 497.
31. Ibn Sayyār, pp. 329–30; Nasrallah, p. 499.
32. Tujibi, p. 270. Mezzine and Benkirane translate *ushnān* into French as *soude*.
33. Tujibi, p. 272.

A Federal-era Kitchen:
Hampton's Stew Stove, Iron Oven and Hearth

Patricia Bixler Reber

Figure 1. Hampton Mansion (Patricia Reber, courtesy Hampton National Historic Site, National Park Service).

The state-of-the-art kitchen in Hampton Mansion, completed in 1790 near Baltimore, Maryland, contains an original brick stew stove, a Reip metal wall oven and a hearth. While most people are aware of open-hearth cooking and some basic implements, few know how the other two, much rarer, cooking apparatus worked. Stew stoves (modern term used in US) or stewing stoves (UK), to use two of its many names, were not early 'crock pots' nor were pots always inserted into the stew-holes. There are also misconceptions about metal ovens – not all iron ovens are Rumford Roasters. The mansion was the showpiece of a 24,000-acre estate which was a diverse economic system ranging from a large iron works to a profitable dairy operation. Many of its outbuildings were important in supporting the kitchen to prepare food for the table.

A Federal-era Kitchen

'The best table in America'

When the Revolutionary War ended, construction began on the huge mansion that would take seven years to complete. The Georgian style house contained about 24,000 square feet, more than Mount Vernon and Monticello combined, and may have been the largest private residence in America when it was built.[1] Charles Carnan Ridgely (1760–1829) inherited the new house and most of a vast fortune from his uncle in 1790. Ridgely, who would later become governor of Maryland, entertained lavishly and was 'said to keep the best table in America'. Furthermore, he 'had the fortune that enabled him to live like a prince, and he also had the inclination.' The early labour force that maintained the estate and his lifestyle ranged from slaves, indentured servants and convicts to paid staff.[2]

The Hampton estate was supported by an assortment of revenue producing enterprises: a variety of agricultural endeavours such as corn and wheat, mills, large orchards, herds of livestock and dairy sales; mercantile enterprises, particularly the Northampton Furnace; and investments. The iron works, a mile and a half to the north of the mansion, required a large amount of charcoal, obtained by cutting down a vast number of trees each day. Colliers tightly stacked the wood in mounds under a layer of soil, and did a controlled slow burn for up to two weeks. The resulting charcoal was used in the furnace, but was also burned in the small fireboxes of the kitchen's iron oven and stew stove. Charcoal was preferable to bulky wood because less was needed and it burned hotter with generally less smoke and ash.

Outbuildings related to food production were scattered throughout the property and some still exist, most notably the dairy and the unusually deep icehouse. Other structures were meat houses (wood plank smoke houses), an orangery, fish house and a pump house for water. From 1798 through 1801, almost eleven thousand feet of water pipes were made and installed from the spring to the house and extensive gardens. A gas house to convert coal into gas was constructed in 1857 for lighting and possibly for cooking. The mansion itself was used for food storage: the cellar was divided into areas for cider/apples, lard and wine; another wine room on the third floor held Madeira.[3]

Kitchen

The Hampton kitchen was not a separate outbuilding, but always part of the house in the east wing. This is notable since the 'country seat' was used in the summer (the family spent winters in their Baltimore home) and was one of several Federal-era mansions in the area that did not have a detached kitchen when it was constructed. The kitchen, with its stew stove, wall oven and large hearth, was not static but changed with the times. Cast iron ten-panel heating stoves with an oven were made at the Northampton ironworks and used on the estate. Later, a larger cook stove took over the functions of the hearth and stew stove.

Hampton's first bake oven may have been an early iron oven or the more prevalent brick type. Brick ovens were heated by burning wood for several hours until the bricks

Figure 2. Reip oven and roaster (Patricia Reber, courtesy Hampton National Historic Site, National Park Service).

had absorbed enough heat, then all the coals were removed. Items were placed in the oven, with those needing high heat such as bread put in first, and as the heat diminished to moderate then 'slow' the more delicate foods were added. In 1831, the T. & S. Abbett company installed their 'improved cast iron oven' in the wall, undoubtedly replacing the original brick or metal oven. Twenty-five years later the current metal Reip oven replaced the Abbett model.

Bake oven and Roaster

Reip ovens were produced in Baltimore for at least 40 years. Henry Reip (c. 1781–1859) opened his first double-block tin manufactory in 1810, and became very successful, due in part to the oven he patented in 1825, and by making and selling a variety of iron and tin ware. By the 1840s, his eldest son Alfred (1809–1895), also a tinner, was selling an oven strikingly similar to the patented one and other household items in direct competition with his father. It was an Alfred Reip oven that replaced the earlier metal oven in the Hampton kitchen. The brass plaque on the door had the maker's information:

A Federal-era Kitchen

Premium Patent
Bake Oven & Roaster
By
Alfred H Reip
No. 337 Balto Street Baltimore.

According to Baltimore city directories, he moved five times and was at 337 Baltimore Street from 1854 to 1867, which dates when the oven was installed.

The oval oven was actually two parts. The inner section was the oven with two or three shelves and a double plated bottom. The outer shell had a cut-out in the bottom so the heat from the firebox, which was directly below the oven, went around in the space between the inner and outer sections. The brick mason who installed the iron pieces (oven, firebox and ash-pit doors) made a flue from the inner space and a pipe exiting from inside the oven to the chimney for the heat and smoke to escape. As the charcoal or coal burned in the firebox (the door was only six by seven inches), the ash fell through a grate to the ash-pit below whence it was removed.

While there were some similarities to the better-known round Rumford Roasters designed by Count Rumford (both claimed to be more efficient than brick bake ovens since the small fire-box required less fuel, kept the room cooler and the oven temperature could be maintained throughout the entire baking period), most Rumford Roasters differed by having the firebox heat the air in two pipes which then entered the oven. Either oven could be used to bake or roast (actually bake the meat), but some cooks preferred the bread and pies baked in brick ovens, and the meat roasted in front of a fire. A further impediment to mass acceptance of the metal ovens/roasters was learning the skills necessary to properly prepare food in the sometimes-tricky new apparatus.

Stew stove

The waist-high brick stove at Hampton still retains its two round iron grates and ash-pit doors. While used for centuries in many countries, most eighteenth century homes in America did not have a stew stove, and even fewer exist today. The convenient height allowed for doing a variety of cooking, from frying and making sauces to main dishes, without having to kneel down at the hearth to prepare the food in pans on a trivet over the coals. Other advantages were similar to the small fire-boxes in the iron ovens: the contained fires used less fuel, kept the heat concentrated thus cooking faster, was cleaner, and the room was cooler in the summer. Stewing stoves did have problems; the greatest being the carbon monoxide fumes which caused headaches, illness and even death.

It was fairly easy to use the stewing stove. Grates, located seven inches from the top of each stew hole, held burning charcoal or coal that heated the pots or pans set on trivets on the surface, and the ash fell into the ash-pit. The style of stew stove at

Figure 3. Grate in stew stove. (Patricia Reber, courtesy Hampton National Historic Site, National Park Service).

Hampton did not have a flue system, so the smoke and heat had to exit up the opening; thus the pots could not be inserted into and thus block the stew holes. Hampton's stove was situated under a window by the oven so light from the window helped to view the progress of the item being prepared. Stewing stoves were also located adjacent to the hearth, within a fireplace or under a hood.[4]

Hearth

The fire in hearths found in most homes was used to roast, boil, broil, fry and even bake. Among the many kitchen items in the Governor's 1829 inventory and auction listing were five grid-irons (for broiling over coals), three frying pans and three skillets (frying over coals), eighteen iron pots (boiling over the fire), six bake ovens (baking under and over coals), thirteen muffin bands (baking on griddle), and a Dutch oven and smoke jack (roasting in front of the fire).[5]

The smoke jack, with its chains, spits and dripping pans freed the cook from turning the spit by hand next to the fire. Its fan was attached in the chimney so that when the heat and smoke rose the blades spun causing the gears to rotate, thus moving a chain attached to the wheel at one end of each spit. The meat on the spit rotated constantly in front of the flames for an even roasting. Other types of labour saving jacks included clockwork jacks, bottle jacks, turnspit dog wheels and steam jacks.

A Federal-era Kitchen

Figure 6. Dairy. (Patricia Reber, courtesy Hampton National Historic Site, National Park Service).

Dairy

The stone 'Milk House' was sunk into the ground. It was further cooled by spring water running through a channel around the interior of the building, and extraordinarily the water is still flowing. The cooling effect was also helped by a long roof overlay shielding thin windows at the top of the walls which provided light, while allowing the heat rising from the many pots of body-temperature cow's milk to exit the building. The Hampton dairy sold 4296 pounds of butter for $1764 in 1822, with an additional 860 pounds consumed on the estate. A set of scales, the most expensive item in the dairy, was critical to guarantee the correct weight of the butter sold in the city markets. Under-weight butter bricks or prints would cause all that day's butter to be seized and sold at a reduced price, with the proceeds going to the city.[6]

To produce such large amounts of butter there were 141 milk pots and six barrel churns in the Hampton dairy. By comparison, the wealthy Marylander Charles Carroll, who gained fame as the last surviving signer of the Declaration of Independence, owned only 27 stone milk pots, two barrel churns and two hand churns among the dairy items in his 1832 inventory. Barrel churns were laid horizontally on a base with a handle turning the paddles within the barrel, and were recommended for farmers with many cows. Additional items essential to producing the quantity and quality of butter in the Hampton dairy were six piggins (wooden bucket with one stave longer for a handle), a milk strainer (to remove cow hair and dirt), a milk skimmer (to lift cream which had risen to the top of the milk), nine milk tubs (to collect the skimmed cream before churning), four pewter basins (possibly for washing), two butter prints (stamp to distinguish maker and make uniform size), four butter boxes (ice boxes for transport) and a table.⁷

Icehouse

In addition to keeping the butter cold during transport in the butter boxes, the icehouse ice was also used in the four ice-cream freezers, a wine cooler and one refrigerator. The *circa* 1790 icehouse is 34 feet deep, with a brick dome and stone shaft under a mounded earth top. The hatch on the north side of the mound helped to expel damp air, harmful to the ice, as well as to load the icehouse. On the other side, a staircase led to an entrance about a third of the way down the incredibly deep icehouse. Access to the base would have been by ladder. Several feet above the bottom was a log and wood floor through which the water could drip to the 'sink' area below the ice.

Contemporary authors presented various icehouse configurations and ways to best preserve the ice for longer periods, including two Marylanders, Thomas Moore and John Beale Bordley. The ice was to be cut into smaller pieces and pounded into place; Moore proposed a wood frame next to the wall of smaller icehouses where straw, a nonconductor of heat, would be added for insulation.⁸

Conclusion

The study of *in situ* apparatus reveals a more complex evolution of cooking devices during the Federal or Georgian period than simply the hearth to cook stove transition. Cooks, then as now, were interested in the latest innovations and a few readily removed some (if not all) of the older technology to try the new. In fact, many owners were proud of their up-to-date equipment, such as the Prince Regent (the future King George IV) who guided guests around his modern steam-powered kitchen with a metal wall oven and iron-framed stewing stoves, installed in 1816 at the Royal Pavilion in Brighton.

Hampton National Historic Site, a property of the National Park Service since 1948, preserves 63 of the 24,000 acres of the once-vast estate. Remarkably, many of the original buildings remain, including two double-story stone slave quarters, a mid-eighteenth century farm house, ash house, two racing stables, barns, and greenhouses. Since the Ridgely family had continuously resided in the home from 1790 to 1948, a vast assortment of furnishings and personal processions remain. A massive amount of the family's written records survive, though divided, and are preserved onsite at Hampton NHS, Maryland State Archives, Maryland Historical Society and in other repositories.

A Federal-era Kitchen

Notes

1. Hampton National Historic Site < http://www.nps.gov/hamp/index.htm >. *Hampton National Historic Site Guidebook*, by the staff of Hampton National Historic Site (Towson, MD: Historic Hampton, Inc., 2010). Charles E. Peterson, *Notes on Hampton Mansion*, 2nd ed., rev. ed., Sally Sims Stokes (College Park, Maryland: University of Maryland, 2000).
2. Robert Parkinson, *A Tour in America 1798, 1799, and 1800: Exhibiting Sketches of Society and Manners, and a Particular Account of the American System of Agriculture, with its recent Improvement* (London: Printed for J. Harding, 1805), p. 73. Heinrich Ewald Buchholz, *Governors of Maryland: From the Revolution to the Year 1908* (Baltimore: Williams & Wilkins Company, 1908), p. 85. Items for serving at the table which were not available from any of Ridgely's holdings were purchased overseas or in nearby Baltimore stores and markets. Sugar, molasses, spices, coffee, tea, chocolate, mustard, almonds, oil, rice, cheese, cranberries, crackers, oysters and candles were just some of the items available in the cosmopolitan city. Annapolis, Maryland State Archives (MSA), *Kitchen Cash Book listing Purchases 1825–1826*, G. Howard White Collection MdHR #4681.
3. Charles W. Snell, *Hampton Mansion and Garden, 1783–1909…Historic Structure Report, Historical Data Section* (Denver: Denver Service Center, National Park Service, U.S. Dept. of the Interior, 1980), p. 70.
4. Peter Brears, 'Kitchen Fireplaces and Stoves', *Country House Kitchen, 1650–1900: Skills and Equipment for Food Provisioning*, ed., Pamela A. Sambrook and Peter Brears (Gloucestershire: A. Sutton Pub., in association with the National Trust, 1996), pp. 100–101. Probably the oldest existing stewing stove in England is in the seventeenth century Hampton Court kitchens according to Brears. The locations in the kitchens of the remaining extant stew stoves in the American museums and private homes which I have examined correspond to contemporary images and descriptions, and also with what Brears has found in the UK.
5. MSA, *Baltimore County Maryland Inventories Liber 38 1829*, p. 34. Charles Carnan Ridgely and his wife had eleven children survive to adulthood. When he died in 1829 (his wife had died in 1814), he freed many of his over 300 slaves, bequeathed Hampton to his eldest surviving son John, and divided the various land holdings, townhouses, and finances among his other children or their heirs. The contents of the houses and out buildings were sold in several auctions which were recorded in the *Baltimore County Register of Wills, Accounts of Sales, Liber 14* 1832–1833, p. 9–10 (Kitchen items).
6. *American Farmer*, 24 January 1823, p. 359. *Ordinances of the Corporation of the City of Baltimore* (Baltimore: Warner & Hanna, 1801), p. 86. Butter was sold as one or one half pound prints, and larger sizes from two pound rolls to 28 pound half firkins, 56 pound firkins and 84 pound tubs; some variance in local ordinances. William Marriott, *The Country Gentlemen's Lawyer: And, the Farmer's Complete Law Library* (London: W. Stratford, 1801), p. 17–23.
7. MSA, *Inventories*, 41 1832, p. 75 (Charles Carroll of Carrolton). MSA, *Inventories*, 38 1829, p. 46 (Charles Carnan Ridgely).
8. Historic American Buildings Survey, HABS MD,3-TOW.V,1D-sheet 2. HABS No. MD-226-E. Thomas Moore, *An Essay on the Most Eligible Construction of Ice-Houses. Also, A Description of the Newly Invented Machine called the Refrigerator* (Baltimore: Bonsal & Niles, 1803). John Beale Bordley, *Essays and Notes on Husbandry and Rural Affairs* (Philadelphia: Budd and Bartram, 1799).

Table Manners and what they Looked Like: a Discussion of Visual Evidence for what People Ate and how they Handled it

Gillian Riley

When it comes to the material world, Leonardo said it all in his sketch of a tsunami of worldly goods. Anyone who has moved house will immediately understand his vision of the chaos of possessions as a graphic understatement of a harrowing reality. But if this is so, why did patrons of the Bassano family hang on their walls images of the *trasloco* on the Feast of St Martin (11 September)? Moving house was not just a quaint subject, something the lower classes were obliged to do from time to time, as later comments on these works seem to imply. The Venetian nobility, who cannily put their commercial wealth into property on the mainland, moved every year to their country homes to avoid the torrid heat of summer and oversee the management of their estates. For the most part Palladian villas were working farms, not just rural retreats: the space above the *piano nobile* was used as barns and haylofts, and the elegant loggias and porches concealed mundane farm buildings. Wealthy families undertook the horrors of upheaval, removal and return every year, trundling possessions and livestock with them. Bassano's versions of *The Flight of Abraham* or *The Return of Jacob* were pretexts for familiar representations of this annual event in the Veneto. In these images there is a delight in everyday objects and material possessions, the chaos is well managed, the worldly goods flaunted; they are there to be admired. But what they can tell us about eating and drinking, about table manners? Other works by Bassano include kitchens, food preparation and dining, with the presence of a weary cook, and diligent female helpers, but apart from *Cleopatra's Banquet* there is little information on table manners.

Veronese, their contemporary, produced magnificent banquet scenes, purporting to be *The Marriage at Cana* or *The Feast in the House of Levi*, but in reality images of affluent modern life. Here we can see the flurry and bustle of the banquets described by Scappi in the mid-sixteenth century, get the sense of noise and movement, but depressingly few details. Two glimpses of the use of forks are very helpful, however. One shows a man deep in contemplation, perhaps of an overheard conversation, appearing to be picking his teeth with a fork. Not as uncouth as it might seem, for *stecchi profumati*, perfumed toothpicks, were produced for use during the last course of a banquet, to spear up sticky candied or preserved fruit as well as tidy up the teeth. After the ritual hand-washing in scented water, and drying with fresh napkins, the toothpicks were presented, along with posies of fragrant flowers or artificial ones made of silk. Forks had similar uses. A young woman is shown using a fork, perhaps a sign of refinement or just indicating that this was the final dessert course in the banquet.

A particularly grand feast towards the end of Lent described by Scappi, without meat or dairy products but rich in fish, fruit and vegetables, lists at the end, for the final course, 'Levata la tovaglia, & data l'aqua alle mani si muterà salviette candide, et cocchiari & forcine.' After changing the tablecloth and washing of hands, white napkins are produced, along with spoons and forks. Forks, as well as toothpicks, were used for special occasions. The banquet offered by Cardinal Lorenzo Campegio to the Emperor Charles V in 1536 was even more splendid, with the use of gold forks for the ultimate course from the *credenza*.

This seems to imply that forks were the exception rather than the rule, provided for crowned heads and his Imperial Majesty, luxury items not for everyday use. But the fork as an implement had always been around, or rather pronged, spiked instruments to spear or lift food from the pot, or place before the coals, or steady meat for carving, or pierce for larding. Eating food was done with knife, spoon, and fingers and thumbs. Who could possibly need forks? But evidence from the past seems to show that forks did come in handy for eating, from Roman times onwards, in some shape or form. One of the engravings illustrating Scappi's book shows a set of cutlery: knife, fork and spoon. It would be unwise to draw fixed conclusions from visual and written evidence for the use of forks; a pragmatic overview suggests that they were around, and in use for cooking and eating, but that it took centuries for the use of the fork to evolve from a deviant practice to a convenient socially accepted tool.

St Peter Damian is often quoted on the subject of deviant practices; he fulminated against the effete manners of a Byzantine princess, Maria Argiro, who married Giovanni, the son of Doge Orseolo, introducing the fork and other degenerate habits to the innocent Venetians, and then died of the plague (divine retribution) in 1005. But at this time Peter Damian was only 17 years old and had never been to Venice. Historians have come up with another Byzantine princess in 1071, who fits the bill rather better; she was the wife of Doge Domenico Silvio. Peter Damian's tetchy outburst was part of a politically motivated diatribe against the Eastern Orthodox church, a cheap slur, an urban myth, not an accurate historical fact. Venice was indeed the entry-point for Eastern delicacies and oriental luxuries, for silks and spices and traders and merchants of every race and nationality. Carpaccio pictured them, later Veronese's great set-pieces showed the nobility flaunting these luxuries. This contact with the mysterious and suspect East became for Peter Damian a pretext for discrediting both the Venetian Republic and its citizens, as well as Byzantium, and so eating food with a fork could be presented as a metaphor for deviant Eastern behaviour, degenerate and foppish, a transgression from the healthy Western norm, even if it happened in private among consenting adults. In the dark history of the fork there was thus this intermittent closet use regardless of the general disapproval. The slow evolution from perversion to normality involved many factors, changes in taste, gastronomy and manners.

But if food was not usually eaten with a fork, how did people manage? They ate with a knife, a spoon, and thumb and fingers. This was practical, neat and efficient. A sharp, pointed knife, one's own or part of the table-setting, could be used to cut up food, then spear it and convey it to the mouth, or morsels of food could be picked up by the fingers, perhaps dipped in a sauce, and eaten. The tactile sensations of handling food, tearing soft meat from an obdurate bone, prising flesh from the cartilage of a gently simmered fowl, enhance the pleasures of anticipation, the aromas clinging to the fingers, the taste-buds stimulated, the eye and the brain vibrating in harmony. This is a good way to eat. It did not have to be messy, and if it was, help was at hand; basins of perfumed water and acres of freshly laundered linen were supplied by attentive pages. Some banquet menus specify in detail the sequence of this ritual. The folded napkins enclosing a bread roll can be seen in many images, as can the multiple uses of the lengths of woven and embroidered linen, spread over trestle tables, wound round the lid of a bowl to ensure it gets to the table still hot and untampered with, draped round the forearm and shoulder of the page.

Some images show this hands-on approach to food as an elegant procedure, while the cruder manners of lower orders are sometimes depicted by way of contrast, grasping a chicken leg or even the blade-bone of a small animal in one hand, and gnawing at it. The servants in the hunt picnic depicted in Gaston Fébus' hunting manual are squatting on the grass in the foreground, eating with gusto, while the lord and his companions sit at a trestle table, covered with a fine white cloth, and discuss with refined gestures the characteristics of the fewmets or droppings of their prey. These turds are spread out on the white tablecloth, but are not the dried fruit or comfits we take them for, although the elegant mannerisms are those of the nobility at table.

We get an emerging picture of food brought to table and dealt with using knives and fingers. Illustrations of banquets show a sort of hands-on approach, where touching food and making a whole gamut of ritual gestures around the protocol of offering and receiving tasty morsels is drawn for an audience who understood, in a way we don't, what these gestures meant. Guests are rarely pictured putting food into their mouths, but they can be seen with hands on their trenchers, or the table top, or in a dish, reaching for a morsel, or passing something special to their companion. The sharing of personal space at a banquet extended to eating and drinking from a shared bowl, dish and goblet, and manuals of etiquette demanded strict cleanliness and propriety in all this. Some of the things diners are warned not to do give a horrid insight into what behaviour might have been in reality. Bonvesin de la Riva wrote a handbook of good manners for his fellow citizens in thirteenth-century Milan advising a guest not to blow his nose on his napkin, not to sneeze in a way that sprays snot over the table, to remember to wipe the glass, after eating greasy food, before passing it to one's companion, to keep ones thumb out of a bowl of food when offering it, and never to wipe one's hands on the tablecloth.

Eating with fingers could be messy, however elegantly done. Napkins were used

Table Manners and what they Looked Like

a lot, after the ritual hand-washing at the start of a meal, then at table as the meal progressed, with more bouts of ablutions, involving fresh linen tablecloths as well as fresh napkins, and finally at the end, during the particularly sticky final course of preserved fruit and comfits. One illustration shows a young knight washing his hands before a banquet. Others show table settings with the long linen cloth, with decorative, fringed ends, spread over the length of a trestle table. Matching towels or napkins hang on a rail behind Petronilla's simple domestic arrangements. In a similar scene, a man of some importance eats alone, in an alcove hung with fashionable green tapestry, served by attendants who manipulate with professional skill the extremely long napkins or towels, both practical and flamboyant, that are meant to keep covers firmly in place on food, but were also flourished with dramatic effect as part of the rituals of service.

This profusion of constantly renewed clean linen was necessary for hygienic reasons, washing and wiping hands and lips, and was also a way of flaunting wealth and status. Some of these beautifully made textiles survive, or can be seen in works of art. Layer upon layer of tablecloths were spread one on top of another, sometimes over an oriental carpet, and removed as the banquet progressed. This practice is seen in many sixteenth- and seventeenth-century still lifes in the Low Countries, where the fine damask is carelessly crumpled over a priceless 'turkey' carpet draped over the table, both at risk from the dribbling juices of ripe fruit, oysters and spilt wine. Old fashioned Dutch bars and cafés still have reproduction carpets on the tables, in homage to the Golden Age, which soak up spillage wonderfully.

The use of forks for eating made these frequent changes of linen redundant. Travellers who relied on napkins were dismayed if they were not on offer. Forks had been in use in Italy for some time before they were taken up in other European countries. It has been suggested that the rise of individualism in Renaissance humanist thought prompted this change in eating habits, a wish for one's own personal space, a separate bowl and goblet, perhaps a new fastidiousness in eating, maybe a fork.

Thomas Coryat noted in 1610 how everyone in Italy ate with a fork, claiming that it was more convenient and hygienic, that the transgression was now the messy and unhygienic use of one's fingers. He was mocked by his friends when he got home and took to this way of eating.

Our own insistence on eating with a fork balanced elegantly in the right hand produces some pretty weird gastronomic gymnastics. Fork etiquette has become complicated, using it as a shovel, scoop, or impaler. A spoon would handle peas a lot better. Fingers and teeth are better for lamb cutlets. 'Giglia, un peccato mortale!' said a Roman friend, at my clumsy attempts to eat char-grilled baby lamb cutlets with a knife and fork.

A nineteenth-century painting of the interior of a Roman tavern shows an understandably suspicious young man, glaring at the artist's admiration of his companions, two young women wielding knife and fork in a rustic way, grasping the fork like a pitchfork. A later cartoon shows the same grip on a fork – a welcome corrective to prissy right-handed ways.

Annibale Carraci's *Bean Eater* is difficult to decipher; an uncouth man is eating a dish of black-eyed beans with avidity but somewhat rough manners. He slurps, his hands are not clean, he glowers at us; but his white shirt is crisp and clean, the food is laid on a clean white cloth, he drinks wine from a maiolica jug out of a delicate glass. Art historians surmise that this could be a self-portrait. So we are left puzzled by the ambiguities, whilst enjoying the details; the artist's client must have appreciated the dissonances, and this reminder of the pleasures of rustic food with its seasoning of raw onions, but enjoyed with nice wine and good quality white bread is a reminder of Castelvetro's praise of simple vegetable dishes like this.

The theory that the logistics of eating pasta necessitated the use of forks is not easy to document. We have hardly any visual evidence from the period when forks began to be in general use in Italy. Literary references indicate that forks were around in fourteenth-century Florence, as Sacchetti's tale of Noddo and his friend Giovanni tells us: presented with a shared dish of boiling hot spaghetti Noddo deftly wound the pasta round his fork and shovelled away most of the serving, while poor Giovanni was still waiting for his forkful to cool. Greed, manual skills and an asbestos palate won the day, but the key items were the forks.

We know that pasta, in long strips or short pieces, as filled packets or flat sheets, was being made, commercially and in the home, from medieval times onwards, and enjoyed long before the universal use of forks. The earliest images of pasta making are probably those in the different versions of the *Tacuinum sanitatis*, made in the 1380s in northern Italy, which show women making pasta and spreading strands of it out to dry, but there is no evidence from that period of how this pasta was eaten. The seventeenth-century engraving by Mitelli is enigmatic, made in Bologna, home today of ribbons of fresh egg pasta, for we cannot tell if this is a rustic person behaving in an uncouth way, pulling strands of pasta out of a pot and swivelling them into his open mouth, or the way everybody ate their pasta. The later nineteenth-century Neapolitan coloured engravings, the tourist postcards of the time, are equally misleading; the penniless *lazzaroni* performing barefoot and in rags for the entertainment of wealthy foreigners was both degrading and disturbing, but hardly reliable evidence for how pasta was generally eaten. A fork, though, in the hands of a diva, can work wonders, as Sofia Loren demonstrates.

The spoon was a more versatile implement than it is today, and good for not just liquid food like soups, but sloppy stews, as well as the pulses and mushy porridges of the poor, and many different pasta dishes. Short pasta or dishes like *tortellini in brodo* are easier to eat with a spoon than a fork, and the Chinese way of slurping noodles from a bowl, shovelled along by chopsticks, is a reminder of different ways of eating pasta. It is not clear how some of Scappi's dishes were eaten, where pasta is seemingly used as a garnish for a cooked fowl. Scappi mentions *macheroni romaneschi* and *ravioli sensa*

Table Manners and what they Looked Like

spoglio as well as stuffed ravioli, all of which could have been eaten with a spoon.

A nobleman in an Italian fresco uses a small knife to cut up food, holding it in place with his other hand, a fastidious no-fuss performance. The rituals of serving are observed by the attendant personages with a similar gravitas.

Knives were so much a part of life, a personal possession, article of dress, defensive weapon, tool and status symbol that they came to have symbolic value in later images. In sixteenth- and seventeenth-century Dutch art, knives were almost blunted with symbolism. The knife could imply the making of choices, between good and evil, right and wrong, especially if the handle was decorated with a black and white chequered pattern. The diagonal of a knife's position in an arrangement of worldly goods could imply the angst of these choices, the weight of moral imperatives, predestination versus free choice. What can be deduced about table manners is less clear. We can see from slices cut from a fine fatty ham that the knife would have been sharp, not just decorative, and that the slices were bite-sized portions to eaten with the fingers, without forks.

Forks are not totally absent from the art of the Netherlands, but where they occur they seem to have no symbolic value, or not much. The scantily-clad buxom wench in 'Velvet' Breughel's *The Sense of Taste* is using an elegant little fork to tackle a dish of shucked oysters, whilst grasping greedily in her left hand a goblet of wine in its ornate stand. It is not clear if the use of the fork (after all oysters can be slurped from the shell with ease) is part of the erotic charge of this image, where the trappings of pleasure are condoned rather than condemned. The merry young woman at the centre of a group of inebriated revellers in a painting by Jordaens is triumphantly holding a fork, possibly spearing a helping of a lush tart, which again associates the fork with indulgence and excess.

Usually where forks do appear in still-life or genre scenes they seem to be merely a part of the setting for food and drink, without any double meanings. A detail from a posh meal depicted by Frans Francken shows a spoon being dipped into some sticky preserved fruit, a knife on the table, near to an elegant two-pronged fork, a flat open tart, perhaps a wedding cake with its upright comfits looking like candles, and sprig of fragrant herbs. Another detail shows a group of people attacking an elegant meal, pies, tarts, a fowl, with a knife to dismember it, oysters, mussels, and a spoon for breaking into the pie and extracting the filling, and various skewer-like single-pronged implements of indeterminate use.

The Flegel and Van Walkenborgh scene of a genteel meal in the 1580s shows a flower-strewn table and a gentleman improbably tackling a roast fowl with a spoon. It also shows a young woman at the centre of the composition, with a knife in her right hand, her left either holding a glass, or making a gesture as if to say, 'Shall I carve, darling?' To the left of the knife are two instruments, one of them a two-pronged fork. We can only guess at its use.

Although majestic roasts and fowl were brought whole to the table with much pomp, they were then dealt with by the *trinciante* or carver, who operated before the diners, slicing the beast into bite-sized portions. This became over time a performance art, in which the balletic movements and flamboyant gestures of the carver were designed to impress. Holding a heavy joint in one hand while wielding a selected knife, without spilling a drop of gravy or getting his sleeves soiled, while flashing a sparkling ring on his little finger. Handbooks were published with diagrams of how to cut and slice, the object being to offer morsels easy to convey to the mouth. It is perhaps possible that as the use of forks became more widespread the art of carving declined.

Table manners varied a lot in nineteenth-century Europe. We can compare Van Gogh's *Potato Eaters* with sophisticated Parisian dining. The potatoes are eaten from a common dish with various implements, washed down with strong tea, and there is enjoyment in this satisfying meal. But the table setting of the wealthy upper-middle-class Caillebotte family is grim in its formal perfection. The cut-glass, silver and polished mahogany, the obsequious servant, all reinforce the atmosphere of alienation and gloom. The young man on the right eats in a self-absorbed way, even before his mother has been served. The artist himself is unseen, but his place at the table is just glimpsed, in the foreground. Later in life Caillebotte retired with a generous private income to a house on the banks of the Seine near Argenteuil, where he fished, built himself a racing yacht, and might well have enjoyed relaxed luncheon parties with his friend Renoir and a carefree group of young people, as depicted in *The Boatmen's Luncheon*. Here the end of a meal litters the table on a terrace, as they chat, smoke and the young men show off their biceps. Their manners are free and relaxed, but the conventions have probably been observed, with a standard bourgeois lunch menu, and the usual hierarchy of glass and crockery. The painter's loose technique just about allows recognition of this.

Monet's version of *Déjeuner sur l'herbe*, avoiding the shock of nudity, shows a similar regard for convention, with a tablecloth spread with standard fare from the *traiteur* at the suburban station where the group of pleasure-seekers have just got off the train from Paris – *pâté en croûte*, a cold roast chicken, bread, cheese and wine, and the standard tough but elegant picnic glasses.

By contrast later Post-Impressionist meals by Vuillard show a deliberate flaunting of convention. A group of writers and artists, with their comfortably-off patrons, are at the end of a lunch in Normandy, an unusual choice for a holiday. The tablecloth is checked red and white, the wine has not been decanted, what one can make out of the crockery and glass is local rustic stuff. Even more rustic is the table setting of another meal with sophisticated avant-garde friends, wine from a jug, drunk out of tumblers, and huge slices of melon on coarse blue and white crockery. In another painting, Vuillard's mother, seen in her apartment in Paris, enjoys a more conventional lunch with her baby grandson, standard wine glass and decanter, and an embroidered tablecloth. The presence of a small infant at a family meal is another indication of art illustrating table manners, in this case the civilized French way with children at mealtimes.

A final look at an equivocal vignette of Parisian manners: a pensive young woman in pink, all alone in the sort of café where the artist's wife or mother would never have ventured. Is she a nice girl out of her depth or a nice girl on the make? She sits in resigned acceptance of her destiny: an unlit cigarette (no matches) and the plum in brandy in a glass 'penny lick' but with no spoon. Convention leaves her stranded, and quietly emphasizes her equivocal position.

This and many other works of art can illustrate the relationship between the everyday objects of material culture, and the sometimes complex systems of behaviour that influenced their design and use.

Endless Eating: the Indian *Thali*

Caroline Rowe

In India the varieties of *thali* are as numerous as the gods, if not more so. The Indian *thali*, or plate, is an entire meal in one that serves as a microcosm both of the region in which it is found and of Indian customs and culture as a whole. In this paper, I focus on six broadly defined 'regional' *thalis*, using a typical template of the *thali* to investigate aspects that relate to social, medical and historical factors. I have tried to include a variety of *thalis*, from the extravagant Rajasthani palace *thali* served on silver to the humble Punjabi *dhaba thali*, and each *thali* has become a small study into some aspect of the material culture of the *thali*.

Punjabi *thali*: in the beginning

The typical Punjabi *thali* is a simple roadside *dhaba* because, when all is said and done, the *thali* began life in humble surroundings in the area of what is now the Punjab of Pakistan and India. The word *thali* (Hindi: थाली) finds its origin in the ritual cooking pot used in the Vedic household to boil rice and has changed over time to mean a large flat plate with raised edges on which small bowls, *katoris*, are placed.[1] The Vedic period is generally accepted to have begun around the time of the Rig Veda, the first of the four Vedas, around 1500 BC in the area known as Sapta Sindhu, or the 'seven rivers', which is broadly accepted today as an area covering modern day Afghanistan, Haryana and Rajasthan, but centring in the Punjab of both India and Pakistan which was split at Partition in 1947.

The typical Punjabi *thali* found on the streets of Amritsar or Ludhiana is a fairly simple affair. At the simplest, its components might include a chickpea stew, some pickle, a lemon, a chilli and a large pile of steaming hot *paranthas* laden with ghee and stuffed with potato, *paneer*, or cauliflower. A marginally more complex *thali* might add rice, salad (chopped cucumber, tomato and white radish), a few dry or wet vegetarian curries and a *papad*. A non-vegetarian version might also have a dish such as butter chicken (the origin of the British chicken tikka masala) and some *kheer* (sweet rice pudding) or sweet and sticky *gulab jamuns*.[2] Almost all Punjabi *thalis* feature a *dal* of some sort, perhaps a thick, dark *dal makhani*, or a thinner, more everyday yellow *tadka dal*. A full *thali* featuring ten different items is available in New Delhi (which has a considerable Punjabi population) for 190 Rupees (US$3.35) including a bottle of Pepsi and home delivery. For a simple and more delicious plate in Amritsar, the price could come to less than 50 Rs. These simple *thalis* are none too different from the foods eaten in Vedic India over 3500 years ago.

Endless Eating: the Indian *Thali*

Another example of the simple Punjabi *thali* is that served at the Golden Temple, Sikhism's holiest spot in the city of Amritsar close to the Pakistan border. Everyone is welcome to eat in the temple, so to respect other religions the meal does not include meat. Instead it features a very simple selection of *chapatti* (simple unleavened bread), two *dals*, a basic salad of radish and a sweet rice pudding. The *dals* are cooked in huge cauldrons with donated food stuffs, or those bought with donated funds, and cooked by volunteers. Men and women alike sit around huge *chapatti* rolling platforms in the *langar* kitchen. The volunteer work is called *seva*, and it is expected of every Sikh to carry this community work out in some form or other as much as possible. Any person, Sihk or otherwise, can come into the kitchen and cook for a while. Up to 100 people at a time are seated in rows, or *pangat*, on the floor, regardless of gender, religion or status, and more volunteers move up and down the row ladling out *dal* or with huge baskets of *chapatti*. Service lasts only a matter of minutes and while you are welcome to ask for seconds, you are most certainly not encouraged to linger. Once service is over you are expected to clear your own plates and rinse them before volunteers wash them up. It is frowned upon to waste food, and it is extremely rude not to finish your *thali*. With this sort of superior efficiency, the *langar* at the Golden Temple serves anywhere from 70,000 to 100,000 people per day.

Rajasthani *thali*: material concerns

Great debates rage over the correct material for a *thali*, but broadly speaking economic status and practical concerns prevail. In the south of India a simple banana leaf is used, ceremoniously washed with water before the dishing out commences. In the north a cheap *dhaba* (restaurant) will use a stainless steel *thali*, with indentations in the plate itself, which is inexpensive and easy to stack and clean, while more upmarket places will use *thali* sets with *katori* bowls. Outside temples and at large events disposable Styrofoam *thalis* are used to feed the masses.

Since ancient times, Indian beliefs have maintained that the materials in which we cook and from which we eat affect the nutritional and medicinal values of the food consumed. In the sixteenth century, Abul Fazl recorded that the *hakim* (physician) of Emperor Akbar (1542–1556) advised the *Mir Baqawal* (chief of the kitchen) that rice cooked in copper destroyed gas and cured spleen disease; rice cooked in bronze destroyed all three humours; rice cooked in gold alleviated poisons, warded off indigestion and jaundice, and improved vigour, vitality and arousal; rice cooked in tin cooled the body and so on.[3] These beliefs continue to this day, and copper, considered pure and sacred, is often used for *thalis*, plated with tin to negate the impact of acid to which copper is sensitive. *Peetal* (brass) and *kansa* (bell metal) is also used. *Chandi* (silver) and even *sona* (gold) *thalis* are considered to be the best possible material, being non-reactive and 'pure'. While silver *thalis* are used at some of the country's top restaurants such as Dum Pukht in Delhi and 1135 AD at the Amer Fort, Jaipur, gold is reserved for the homes of royalty and the super-rich.

The *khanna* (food) *thali* used to serve a meal is generally about thirteen to fourteen inches in diameter, with a rim raised about three-quarters of an inch to stop food spilling over and make the *thali* easier to carry. A larger version is called a *thal*; these are fourteen to eighteen inches in diameter. These large *thal* are used to display foods and for major festivals when the centre of the tray is engraved with the name of the celebration. The *thal* is loaded with sweets such as *laddu* (sweet *besan* dumpings) and given out to neighbours, friends and family. A smaller version is called *tashtari*. These are six to eight inches in diameter and are used to serve snacks. Gold and silver *thalis* or *aarti thali* are also used to serve the Gods during a *puja* (religious ceremony).

The somewhat spectacular silver *thali* served at 1135 AD in Amer Fort feels like something of an anomaly when compared to the normally restricted cuisine of what is a largely desert state. A *thali* served at Laxmi Mishthan Bhandar, fondly known as LMB, a famed 286-year-old sweet shop in the centre of Jaipur's walled town, is a pure vegetarian *thali*. There are a number of wet and dry vegetable dishes and *dals*, but there are also appearances from all of Rajasthan's rather limited number of speciality dishes such as *gatte ki sabzi*, a gram flour dumpling dish. The famed dish *dal-bati-churma* is the first example we see of India's rather straightforward technique for naming dishes. Perhaps the polar opposite of the poetic names of dishes in some countries, Indian dishes may be named *chole-bhattura* (chickpea-bread), *dal-bati-churma* (lentils-dough balls-cereal powder) or *idly-sambar* (rice cake-spicy water). *Dal-bati-churma* is the perfect example of making do with what you have. Dry hard balls made from wheat are mixed with a thin *dal* and different sugar-sweetened cereal powders.[4] Another dish appearing in the LMB *thali* is *ker-sangri*, a dish of *ker*, a caper-like fruit of a thorny desert bush, and *sangri*, a bean grown in the desert and dried for future use.[5]

Assamese *thali*: regional variations

The most obvious variety in *thalis* is seen across India's many regions. With 28 states, India is home to 1.24 billion people and, at over 3,000,000 square kilometres, is larger than the whole of Europe less Russia.[6] Unsurprisingly, then, one can sample endless regional *thalis*.

One can broadly – very broadly – separate these *thalis* and their characteristics into north, south, east and west. *Thalis* from south India are based more on rice, often white or red. The meal starts with *payasam* or some other sweet dish and includes plentiful coconut and coconut oil. While 'south Indian' *thalis* served across India are often vegetarian, in Adhra Pradesh *thalis* often contain meat and are very spicy, while in Coorg they may contain pork and even game. In the north the reliance on rice diminishes somewhat, with breads such as *roti* and *puris* served instead. In the Punjab, milk products such as *paneer*, *lassi* and buttermilk make a strong showing, and when rice appears it is often flavoured, appearing as *jeera* (cumin) rice or *pulao*. Sweet dishes are often milk-based, such as *kheer* or *gulab jamun*, and are often eaten at the end of the meal. As with elsewhere across the country, refills of the *thali* are often unlimited.

Endless Eating: the Indian *Thali*

In the west, the Gujarati *thali* is much sweeter than that of any other region; in other western states such as Maharashtra *thalis* are often cooked in peanut oil. Coming to the east, a *thali* culture and distinct personality is found in Bengali *thalis* (often served in the home) and Assamese *thalis*.

The *thali* of Assam is a unique affair, with rice as the primary staple and bread potentially not even making an appearance. The whole north-east of India – Assam, Manipur, Aranachal Pradesh, Tripura, Nagaland, and to a lesser extent Sikkim – enjoys a selection of various rices beyond the usually revered Basmati. A very simple *dhaba* may serve Joha rice, red rice, Bora rice, Manipuri black rice and then Assamese sticky rice for dessert. Rice is not only served as a staple, but is also incorporated into such dishes as chicken rice-flour curry and chicken rice-kernel curry. *Thalis* are generally non-vegetarian and likely to feature fish since Assam's landscape is dominated by the mighty Brahmaputra river and its regularly flooded tributaries. Other proteins are also far less restricted than in states such as Gujarat, with chicken, pork, duck and even pigeon regularly featured.

The Assamese, like the Bengalis, enjoy cooking in mustard oil instead of the peanut oil of Maharashtra, coconut oil of Kerala, or ghee of north India. Cooking methods here too are unique; one common cooking method involves putting a dish's ingredients inside a bamboo tube and burying the whole package in a fire. Reliance on bamboo goes beyond its use as a cooking vessel as seen in common dishes like bamboo shoot curries and meat dishes boiled with bamboo shoots. Other ingredients not much used in the rest of the country include elephant apple, *laishak* (similar to mustard greens), banana flowers, sesame (as a curry base), *akhuni* (an import from Nagaland) and *mejinga* (a close relative of the Sichuan peppercorn).[7]

The Keralite *thali*: medicinal merits

The *thalis* of south India are completely different in their make-up, ingredients, methods of cooking and even their sequence from the *thalis* of north India. Where Punjabis end the meal in a typical western or even eastern fashion, Keralites like to start their meal with a sweet *pasayam*, a vermicelli cooked in a coconut milk sweetened with jaggery and often featuring raisins or nuts or other similar dish as an aperitif or *amuse bouche*. Often vegetarian for festivals and weddings, a Kerala *thali* is served on a banana leaf, not a metal platter. The leaf is first washed with the water provided then the pickles, *papad* and chutney are served first along the upper right hand of the banana leaf followed by the different vegetable dishes along the bottom of the banana leaf, closest to the diner. The rice is then served and followed with various gravies. The rice may be white, but more often than not it is a flavoursome and characteristically local red rice. The sweet dish is served at the top left hand side of the dish, and unlimited refills are taken as desired.

While metal *kakoris* and a metal *thali* are sometimes used in restaurants, the more traditional banana leaf is often used alongside *vatis*, or leaf-cups. Many distinctively south Indian flavours and dishes appear in a Kerala *thali*. A *rasam*, a thin, spicy, sour, pepper-filled tomato and tamarind soup is generally served. Coconut appears in bountiful quantities, as in favourite dishes such as *avival*, a coconut and green chilli-based dish made with drumsticks and other typical local vegetables such as white pumpkin, yellow pumpkin, bitter gourd, yam and raw banana.[8] Dishes are usually soured with either yoghurt or unripe green mangos, unlike further up the coast where *kokum* is used. Non-vegetarian *thalis* often feature the local delicacy pearlspot, the area's most beloved fish.

The Indian *thali* can be viewed as an ancient version of the food pyramid now recommended by health organizations and governments around the world. A scientific system for health and well-being pioneered prior to 1500 BC and recorded in the Vedas, Ayurveda finds its routes in the study of nutrition in *sadhana* (yoga practice).[9] This ancient science has been instrumental in forming the expectations the dishes that appear on a *thali*. According to Ayurveda, each *thali* should have six tastes; bitter, pungent, astringent, sweet, sour and salty, bringing perfect balance to body and mind.[10] Rice and breads, most often whole-wheat, form the base of the meal, similar to the base of the pyramid, providing carbohydrates and fibre in fresh, quickly prepared, and easily digested forms. On that base rest multiple vegetable dishes, providing vitamins, minerals and fibre. In smaller quantities, protein comes in the form of fish or meat in non-vegetarian *thalis*, and in the form of *paneer* or *dal* in vegetarian *thalis*.

Oil is, of course, used in the cooking process, and in many dishes it is poured over the rice as a last minute addition as well. A sweet dish is also featured although the position in the sequence depends very much on regional variations. Milk products such as *raita* or *lassi* are often served, but never pure milk as it increases *kapha* tendencies and is believed to produce mucus in the body. The spices used, such as black pepper, ginger and garlic, have their own medicinal qualities, and the spicy chutney or pickle serves not only to add to the flavour, but also aids in digestion. The keys to the Ayurvedic system are variation, moderation and balance, freshness, seasonality and healthful methods of preparation.

The Maharashtrian *thali*: sequence

The *thali* encompasses a whole meal including dessert. In direct contrast to the Western way of eating in sequential courses, the *thali* provides a circular form of dining that still retains a clear sense of beginning and end.

A study of the Maharashtrian *thali* tells us a lot about order, sequencing and the arrangement of items within the dish. This particular *thali* is set like a clock. Salt features at twelve o'clock. Moving anti-clockwise leads to lemon wedges, chutneys, *koshimbirs* (salad) and *lonache* (pickles). Clockwise from the salt are vegetables such as *paatal bhaji* (vegetable curry) and *paale bhaji* (leafy greens) followed by *suki bhaaji* (dry stir fry), *usal* (bean sprouts) and finally *amti* (*dal*). Cooked white rice along with *varan* (yellow *dal*) topped with a little *toop* (ghee) are on the right hand side of the plate. The rice is never in the centre of the plate, giving the *thalis* in Maharashtra a rather more lop-sided appearance than most. The general arrangement of the dish is meant to be an offering to Ganesha, the most popular Maharashtrian god.

The Guajarati *thali*: touch

Thalis are, of course, always eaten with the hands. While other cultures may find this repulsive – when Oprah Winfrey recently visited India, even she exclaimed, 'You guys still eat with your hands!?' – in India connection to one's food is extremely important. During the preparation of food, it is not touched or tasted by any other person. To touch the food would render it *jhoota*, or spoiled, so the final act of preparation, mixing the food together with rice or bread or condiments on the plate, is left to the one consuming the food. This practice allows for personal tastes to be taken into account and keeps *papads* and breads from becoming soggy. The consumer effectively becomes the chef who dictates the finishing touches.

The hands are not only organs of action, but also our connection to divinity, as is demonstrated in the Vedic chant, 'Karagre vasate Laksmih karamule Sarasvati Karamadhye tu Govindah prabhate karadarsanam', which translates as, 'On the tip of your fingers is Goddess Lakshmi, on the base of your fingers is Goddess Saraswati; in the middle of your fingers is Lord Govinda'. The *shokla* is traditionally said while looking at the hands; reciting it is a reminder that divinity comes to life through human efforts.[11] The hands are said to be conduits of the five elements: through the thumb comes space; through the forefinger, air; through the mid-finger, fire; through the ring finger, water; and through the little finger, earth. This belief stems from the concept of Mudras used during meditation and various forms of classical dance such as Bhartnatyam. The circular motion of the fingers gathering up rice or tearing bread stimulates the appetite, passes divine energy into the food, uses the five elements to request Agni (the Goddess of fire) to bring forth the digestive juices, and completes the enjoyment of all the senses. The right hand is always used, and hands are washed both before and after the meal.

Gujarat seems more affected by religious beliefs than most regions. The area is home to a large community of Jains, followers of a religion with some of the strictest dietary restrictions of any major religion: for the most pious of its 4.3 million followers, meat, alcohol, onions, garlic and even mushrooms and honey are banned. As a result, alcohol is banned and sattvic food elevated even for the non-Jainist Muslim and Hindu communities in Gujarat.

A common theme running through Indian food, though, is that religious restrictions only seem to further inspire culinary creativity, as if such restrictions are merely teasing challenges to chefs, and Gujarat boasts of some of the most delicious *thalis* in India. The *thali* I experienced at famed Gujarati restaurant Golden Star *Thali* in Mumbai is a meal which will always stay with me. With upwards of 25 courses, the meal, or rather experience, is a full-immersion class in Gujarati food. The *thali* defines the concept of endless eating. You may have as many refills of any dish as you want, and are encouraged, or rather forced, to do so. There are four different breads and four to five different sweet dishes. The food overall is sweetened, with many of the savoury dishes reaching a level where they could easily pass for dessert. The Golden Star *thali* involves favourite *farsan*, or snack items, usually something separate from a *thali*, served in the centre of the plate. Among those is the intriguingly textured *dhokla*, made from a paste of rice and chickpeas, fermented for a few hours before, chillis, ginger or baking soda are sometimes added, then steamed for fifteen minutes and cut into pieces before being fried with hot oil and mustard seeds. Asafoetida and green chillis are often also added, and sometimes, unsurprisingly for Gujarat, sugar.[12]

The bright light of the Golden Star universe is undoubtedly the *aam raas*. Available only in season and then only on certain days of the week, the *aam raas* is basically a pulp of the quite magical Alphonso mango. So delicious is the divine nectar that I spotted otherwise upstanding citizens sneaking their unlimited *kakoris* into thermos flasks they had brought specially for the purpose and hidden in their bags under the table.

A *thali* from the Andaman and Nicobar Islands: foodways

While working on this paper I had the opportunity to visit the Andaman and Nicobar Islands. I asked around, in between dives and hammock-time, and was directed by one and all to a restaurant in market #3 on Havelock Island that served 'traditional' Andamanese food. I cycled down to the market and ordered the Andaman *thali*, only to be confronted by a *thali* which included a thin *dal*, fried okra, a tomato-based *paneer* dish, *papads* and a vegetable dry curry with potatoes, carrots and cauliflower! Not a coconut in sight. The only thing that seemed to me not to scream north India was the accompanying fish curry which was resplendent with the spices you might expect on an island that has spent much of its history as a stop along the spice route. The only other dishes, other than easily-spotted tourist favourites, I had seen were fish curry, BBQ fish, and more of the same with the other forms of aquatic life. I was quite confused by the mystery of the Punjabi *thali* on a tropical island until I realized that, after the Indian Mutiny of 1857, the Andamans were used by the British as a prison to hold freedom-fighters from Uttar Pradesh, Bihar Delhi and the Punjab. Aside from the prisoners, there were other Punjabis working for the British administrative service and a sizable naval and trade community. Hence an Indian state which in all likelihood never had its own *thali* adopted one directly from the very state in which it was born.

Navratra *thali*: 'fast food'

On certain, even many days, a pious Indian is required to fast. The concept is very much the same as Christian Lent, but much more restrictive. On days such as *charva chaut*, women are not even allowed to take a sip of water throughout the day. These fast days happen with regularity throughout the year. While it sounds awfully restrictive, Indians, of course, are renowned for their gregarious social nature and their joy of indulgence and pleasure. Therefore what is due to be a day of restriction and self-penance turns into a feast of the highest order. All over the city of Delhi come February, April, July and October, one sees special 'navratra' *thalis* advertised. Navratra is a time when wheat is not allowed, nor lentils, onions, garlic, meat fish, eggs, spice, regular salt or even rice! As such it is a lean time for restaurants, so chefs have been forced to come up with the creative concept of the 'navratri *thali*'. At Indian Accent in New Delhi, a lunchtime *thali*, devoid of any meat ingredient, spices and many other favourites, will still set you back US$19, but that is because the chef, Manish Mehotra, has managed to create a *dal* out of nothing more than *chronji* (*Buchanania lanzan*), creamier and more delicious than the ghee-laden *Dal Bukhara* so beloved by tourists to India. Navratra *thalis* in Delhi have become a culinary form of one-upmanship. Given the most basic ingredients imaginable and the strictest guidelines of fasting for Goddess Durga, restaurants all over the city have come up with one feast each more decadent than the rest.

Conclusion

Thus therein lies the beauty of the *thali*. While remaining sensitive to local ingredients; within the laws of multiple religions of the land; mindful of sequence, materials, and cooking techniques; with the concept of balance of nutrition in mind; and overseen by thousands of years of wisdom and tomes of ancient texts, the *thali* remains a meal which manages to thrill, delight and satiate its consumer. Despite the noble pursuit of heath and moral wealth, the Indian *thali* is, at the end of the day, a delicious eat.

Notes

1. K.T. Achaya, *The Illustrated Foods of India A–Z* (New Delhi: Oxford UP, 2009).
2. Monish Gujral, *Moti Mahal's Tandoor Trail* (New Delhi: Roli Books, 2004).
3. Salma Husain, *The Emperor's Table: The Art of Mughal Cuisine* (India: Roli Books, 2008).
4. Harveen Choudhary, *Taste of Rajasthan* (India: Nita Mehta Publications, 2009).
5. Pushpita Singh, *Rajasthani Kitchen*, fourth ed. (India: Roli Books, 2009).
6. Alan Davidson, *The Oxford Companion to Food*, second ed. (Oxford: Oxford UP, 2006).
7. For more on *Akhuni*, see my 'Fermented Nagaland: An Adventure', *Cured, Fermented and Smoked Foods: Proceedings of the 2010 Oxford Symposium on Food and Cookery*, ed. Helen Saberi (Totnes, UK: Prospect Books, 2011), pp. 263–277.
8. Prima Kurien, *Kerala Kitchen*, third ed. (India: Roli Books, 2007).
9. Radhika Shah-Grouven, '*Thali*: Understanding the System behind Indian Cooking', *THATfirst* <http://www.that-first.com/category/yoga_ayurveda_and_vegetarian_cooking/article/*thali*-understanding-the-system-behind-indian-cooking/>.
10. Acharya Balkrishna, *Ayurved: Its Principles & Philosophies*, second ed. (New Delhi: Divya Yog Mandir Trust, 2007).
11. Rajesh Patel, 'Vedic Wisdom behind Eating with Your Hands', *Hindu Human Rights*, 15 May 2012 <http://www.hinduhumanrights.info/vedic-wisdom-behind-eating-with-your-hands/>.
12. Vijaylakshmi Baig, *Gujarati Kitchen*, fifth ed. (India: Roli Books, 2008).

'Let's all go eat at the Automat': Machines and Miracles in New York City

Laura Shapiro and Rebecca Federman

For nearly half a century, Horn & Hardart's Automat was the most celebrated food-service system in America. It was a machine, yet it was far more than a machine: people who talk about eating at the Automat invariably look back on an interaction that was thrillingly personal. Here's how it worked: first you approached the long rows of glass-front compartments, each holding a portion of food designed for one person, and carefully examined the sandwiches, the pots of beans, the dishes of creamed spinach, the pastries, and the desserts. Next to each compartment was a slot for nickels or quarters. You decided what you wanted to eat, you inserted your coins, you turned a knob and opened the compartment and then you pulled out the very chicken pot pie that you had chosen over all the others. Judging from our research, nobody who had this experience, especially as a child, ever seems to have forgotten the glorious satisfaction of acquiring food in this fashion.

Three years ago we set out to curate an exhibition at the New York Public Library on the history of lunch in New York City, where speed and pragmatism became the defining characteristics of the midday meal starting in the late nineteenth century. (The motto of the feeding-machine that assailed Charlie Chaplin in the 1936 film *Modern Times* – 'Don't stop for lunch! Be ahead of your competitor!' – could have flown on a banner overhead every weekday when the clocks of New York struck noon). Although we knew the Automat deserved centre-stage as the city's best-known lunch spot, we were unsure how to do justice to it. The NYPL is blessed with dozens of cartons of Horn & Hardart manuscripts and photographs, thanks to an Horn & Hardart executive named Robert F. Byrnes, an Automat enthusiast who appears to have saved every document relating to its history that ever crossed his desk. His gift to the Library, the Robert F. Byrnes Collection of Automat Memorabilia, is a treasure-laden archive and one of the best resources for the study of restaurants that exists anywhere. But – it is all pieces of paper. How could we possibly convey what it was like to encounter the machine itself? Then we learned that a visionary collector in upstate New York had acquired many of Horn & Hardart's Automat machines when the restaurant chain went out of business. He was willing to lend us whatever we wanted. These rescue Automats were in poor condition, but an extraordinary team of craftsmen was able to rebuild and repair a full wall of compartments, using only original materials. When 'Lunch Hour NYC' opened in June 2012, a beautifully refurbished Automat stood there aglow, surrounded by documents and artefacts recounting its life and times. Alas, we could not put food in the compartments – they held Horn & Hardart recipes, instead – but for the eight months of the exhibition, the Automat delighted record-breaking crowds just as it had done decades earlier.

The Automat was not unique to New York – it wasn't even native to New York. But like many another newcomer to the city, the Automat became a New Yorker the moment it arrived. For the city-dwellers who stopped in for lunch, or spent a long, slow afternoon with coffee and a piece of pie, the Automat was as fundamental to ordinary life as the sidewalks and the subway. For tourists making a long dreamed-of visit to the Automat, it was an urban icon as recognizable as the Empire State Building. And when those glowing letters spelling 'Automat' appeared on a movie screen, everyone in the audience recognized a scene set in New York. As we worked on the exhibition, and even more so after it opened, we came to believe that it was this deep association with New York – so powerful it would outlive the Automat itself – that explains how an automated food delivery system, impersonal and wholly impassive, was able to seize the hearts and imaginations of millions of people.

Surprising as it may seem to Americans, the Automat was one of the few innovations in hyper-modern culinary efficiency for which the US cannot be blamed. It first emerged in Berlin in 1896, the brainchild of a German engineer named Max Sielaff collaborating with a major German candy company, Gebrüder Stollwerck.[1] Vending machines dispensing Stollwerck chocolates were already in wide use; what Sieloff and Stollwerck decided to do was expand and elaborate on the vending-machine principle to create an entire restaurant. Their 'Automat' – the name they came up with to designate both the machine and the restaurant – was a splendid dining room in the Art Nouveau style, lavishly appointed with mirrors, marble and stained glass. The machines ran along two sides of the room, offering hot and cold food and beverages with seemingly miraculous efficiency, though the actual operation of the machinery appears to have been a bit clunky. Only the cold dishes – sandwiches, salads, desserts – were on display in the windowed compartments, kept at a level just above the door of the compartment. To buy a sandwich, a customer inserted a coin, watched the sandwich move down via dumbwaiter to the level of the glass door, then opened the door and pulled out the plate. When the compartment was empty, the dumbwaiter carried it down to the basement, where all the food was being prepared in a full restaurant kitchen. Workers refilled the compartment and sent it back up. Obtaining a hot dish took several more steps: the soups and stews themselves were not displayed, so the customer chose from a posted menu, dropped the coins into a slot next to a compartment labelled with the name of the dish, pulled a handle, and retrieved a token. Pulling the handle, meanwhile, caused a bell to ring downstairs in the kitchen, which alerted the staff to the order. The food was placed on a tray and sent up to the right compartment, where it sat just above the door until the customer dropped in the token and pulled another handle, at which point the dish descended to door level and could be extracted.[2]

Food and Material Culture

A German postcard advertising the Berlin Automat shows a well-dressed lady and gentleman looking festive and convivial in the midst of the machines. Phrases describing the attractive features of this new concept – 'casual', 'up-to-date', 'quick and good' and 'no tipping' – surrounded the picture.[3] Nowadays the whole idea seems antithetical to our cherished, perhaps romanticized, image of how Europeans traditionally dined – long family meals with wine and conversation – but it was an age celebrating industrialization and all the novelties that came with it. The streamlining of the midday meal, not to mention 'no tipping', had a certain amount of popular appeal; and the company began selling machines to other restaurant operators, both in Europe and the US. But within a decade or two, Europeans had largely lost interest. Not so Americans.

The Automat arrived in the US at the start of the twentieth century, settling so easily into its new habitat that when New Yorkers first glimpsed an Automat on Broadway, they assumed they had invented it. 'For the student of human nature there is much to see in this strange eating place besides the almost human machines which deliver the food,' marvelled a reporter examining the city's first Automat in 1903.[4] He discerned 'half a dozen New-York characteristics' of the new restaurant, including the phenomenal speed at which it was now possible to assemble and devour a full meal. (One minute and 45 seconds was the record set during his visit, impressive even in a city regarded as the quick-lunch capital of the world.) 'What a tribute to American inventive skill!' remarked a customer, and another praised 'the progressiveness of New York'. They were astonished to learn that the Automat was dreamed up in Germany, and that New York couldn't even boast of having the first one in the New World – an Automat had opened a few months earlier in Philadelphia. ('In Philadelphia! Great Scott!')

But despite the reported enthusiasm of the lunchtime crowd, this particular incarnation of the Automat was short-lived. James Harcombe, the restaurateur who imported it from Berlin and set it up at 830 Broadway, closed his Automat for unknown reasons in 1907. It would be the Philadelphia company after all – Horn & Hardart – that would make the Automat the most famous restaurant chain in the country, even as its Philadelphia lineage, not to mention its German inventors, plummeted from public memory.

Joe Horn and Frank Hardart had been running coffee shops and lunchrooms in Philadelphia for a dozen years when Hardart made a trip to Germany in 1900, possibly for the very purpose of getting a look at the Automat. The advantages of what Europeans were calling a 'waiterless' restaurant would have been clear to him right away: machines couldn't demand higher wages, machines couldn't take vacations, machines didn't have to be tipped.[5] He promptly bought a restaurant's worth of Automat machinery and shipped it home, where the Automat made its American debut on Chestnut Street in June 1902, shortly before Harcombe's New York version.

Both these early Automats resembled the Berlin original, with its splendid Art Nouveau flourishes, but the Horn & Hardart company was already taking steps to

Americanize the concept, starting with the elimination of the machine dispensing alcohol. In Berlin it was possible to get beer, wine, spirits and even cocktails at the Automat by inserting a coin and pulling a lever. Harcombe retained the alcohol machine in New York, hoping to lend his Automat 'the features of the European cafe', as he explained to a reporter.[6] But evoking that particular touch of Europe may have been his first mistake. Many Americans tended to associate public drinking not with charming cafes but with the much-reviled 'saloon', frequently depicted as a gathering place for disreputables. Ladies of that era out for a stroll or shopping were unlikely to drop in at a bar of any sort. Horn and Hardart put their faith in coffee.

More fundamental changes were underway in the Automat mechanism itself. John Fritsche, an inventor who worked for Horn & Hardart for many years, patented numerous modifications of the machine and ultimately came up with a system that did away with the dumbwaiter.[7] He housed the glass-fronted compartments in a drum that swivelled when a compartment was empty, to be refilled by workers standing directly behind the machines. Plates of food were kept at the ready, and the compartments could be heated or chilled as necessary. Horn and Hardart also wanted rock-solid protection against theft, and Fritsche did his best to make the system impermeable. The new machine acted as a barrier between employees and the public – they couldn't see each other or make contact in any way – so it became impossible for workers to slip free food to their friends. As for the coins, they tumbled into a locked container behind the machine, accessible only to employees specifically designated to collect them under strict protocols.

Once these refinements were in place, the partners were ready to expand their reach. The Automat was doing well in Philadelphia, but nothing in that quiet, estimable city was going to have the kind of swaggering, high-profile success that would be possible in New York. They chose their new location carefully, avoiding the downtown neighbourhood where Harcombe's experiment had collapsed. Instead they decided to meet the world at an address in one of the busiest neighbourhoods in America – 1557 Broadway, just north of Times Square – and on 2 July 1912, they unveiled a spectacular new Automat. With a facade 30 feet across and two storeys high made entirely of stained glass created by the artist Nicolo Discenso (whose work could also be seen at the city's magisterial Cathedral of St John the Divine), the Automat was the most glamorous place in New York to spend a few nickels on lunch, and it was open to all.

Over the next several decades, Horn & Hardart built dozens of Automats around the city, including a restaurant in the financial district that could handle 10,000 customers a day.[8] New Yorkers were enthralled, and they also recognized a phenomenal bargain. 'There is no trick to selling a poor item cheaply,' Joe Horn used to say. 'The real trick is to sell a good item cheaply.'[9] For the most part Horn & Hardart put out mainstream American cooking, the sort of food New Yorkers could find at hundreds of cafeterias and lunch counters, but it's doubtful that anybody else serving a 15-cent Waldorf salad in 1924 paid such relentless attention to quality. Each five-ounce portion of salad (celery, apples and a mayonnaise-like dressing) sat on 'selected leaves of lettuce', according to the Horn & Hardart rulebook, and had a garnish of walnuts.[10] 'The walnuts will have to be carefully handled or they will become rancid,' the book instructed. 'Keep them sealed up in the 8 ounce milk bottles in which they are sent out, in order to keep the air away from them as much as possible.' All the food served at Horn & Hardart restaurants in New York – soups, stews, breads, pastries, meats, poultry and the renowned baked beans – came from a central commissary where it was prepared fresh for each day's service. Company officials gathered daily at what was known as the Sample Table, where they tasted portions of food from Automats around the city to make sure every outlet was keeping its standards high.[11] They tasted for the saltiness of the butter, the texture of the filling in the lemon pie, the amount of chicken in the soup and always the quality of the coffee. Frank Hardart, who had grown up in New Orleans, understood coffee and knew that it didn't have to be the boiled sludge typically doled out in those days. He and Horn wanted the Automat coffee to be the best in town, and by all accounts it was – a special blend of six different beans plus a little chicory, painstakingly brewed, and dispensed for a nickel from spouts adorned with what the company grandly called 'dolphins'.[12] (They were more like ducks.) By the time of the Automat's 25th anniversary in New York, some 300,000 people a day were eating at Horn & Hardart restaurants and visiting Horn & Hardart retail shops, where they could buy Automat food wrapped to go.[13]

But history has largely forgotten a crucial point about the Automat: even at the height of its success, the machine itself contributed relatively little to the company's day-to-day business. By 1920 Horn & Hardart had stopped running restaurants that only dispensed food by machine, and instead favoured a format that put the Automat machine in one section of the restaurant and a fully-staffed cafeteria in another section.[14] In the cafeteria, customers could choose from a wider variety of menu items than the machines offered, including freshly-sliced portions of ham and beef, grilled sandwiches and other dishes that were best prepared on the spot. Despite the extra service costs, Horn & Hardart could make more money selling the slightly more elaborate food available at the cafeteria, and customers who came regularly for meals seemed to prefer it. Tourists and children would always flock to the machines, but over the years the company built fewer and fewer of them. Either the machines were accompanied by a cafeteria, or the cafeteria stood alone.

Yet the cafeteria played no role in the fame of the Automat. It was the machine that captured the public's imagination: by the 1930s the Automat had become a New York City landmark and a phenomenon of popular culture that criss-crossed the nation in movies, songs and cartoons. *Face the Music,* the 1932 musical by Irving Berlin and Moss Hart, opened with a scene set in the Automat and featured a song – 'Let's Have Another Cup of Coffee'– that became a Horn & Hardart anthem. Numerous Hollywood movies made use of the Automat, especially to evoke the lives of hard-pressed young women trying to survive in New York. (The Automat scene in the 1934 movie *Sadie McKee,* in which a hungry Joan Crawford is ready to pounce on an uneaten piece of pie when its owner casually stubs out a cigarette in it, was still drawing gasps of dismay nearly 70 years later, from people watching the movie clips screened at the exhibition.) Television picked up the same working-girl theme for an episode of the 1960s series *That Girl*, in which Marlo Thomas goes to the Automat to mix ketchup with hot water for a classic starving-artist soup.

Most strikingly, in the realm of popular culture the Automat lost its mechanized character and acquired a mind of its own – sometimes even a heart. In the real-life restaurants, for instance, Horn & Hardart employees working behind the machines were invisible and unreachable. But in the imagined Automat restaurants, customers could always make contact with the people on the other side of the glass compartments. Doris Day, arriving for lunch at the Automat in the 1962 movie *That Touch of Mink*, approaches a seemingly faceless wall of machines and puts in a few coins to buy a small salad. Then, while the compartment door is open, she calls out quietly, 'Connie? Connie! Yoo hoo!' Behind the machine her roommate, Audrey Meadows, is busy filling compartments when she hears her friend's voice. 'Where are you?' she inquires. 'In the cucumbers,' says Day. Once they can see each other through the opening, Meadows slips a chicken potpie to her friend and the two of them chat companionably.

Later in the same film, Meadows, still at work, spies Gig Young through an open compartment and mistakes him for the cad who has been trying to cajole Doris Day into an affair. As he pulls out his lunch, her hand reaches through the compartment and slaps him across the face. This splendid moment – featuring Gig Young's astonished recoil – captured a kind of urban myth that was vital to the imagined version of the Automat. Many, many cartoons over the years showed a hand or an arm or a head comically bursting forth from the Automat, either to strike a customer or more cheerily to offer a treat. In one instance a hand holding a match darts out to flambé somebody's dessert. A famous *New Yorker* cartoon by George Price shows a man shrinking back in terror as dozens of dishes come flying out at him from a single compartment. 'Congratulations, sir,' says an employee. 'You've hit the jackpot.'[15] However efficient it was to get lunch from a machine, people loved the idea that human characteristics – personality, unpredictability, even contrariness – might be delivered along with the macaroni and cheese.

Popular culture never placed these endearingly personalized Automats anywhere but New York. The machine that was practically human became the city's unofficial greeter, waiting under the glowing Automat sign to let people know they had arrived in New York at last. Famously, Horn & Hardart restaurants made no distinctions among customers – a nickel was a nickel no matter whose hand it came from – and the Automat drew a remarkable mix of ages, nationalities, races, occupations and incomes. Early on, that mélange became an icon of the diversity that New Yorkers loved to celebrate about themselves. Of course, the clientele was self-selected; and anybody who shied away from sharing a table with blacks, or people speaking foreign languages, or scruffy students, would have eaten elsewhere. But the Automat's manifest welcome to all, like the Statue of Liberty's, was one of its most powerful features. As a Depression-era ditty summed it up:

> Said the Technocrat
> To the Plutocrat
> To the Autocrat
> And the Democrat –
> 'Let's all go eat in the Automat!'
>
> *New York Evening Sun*, 1933[16]

Horn & Hardart flourished in New York for more than 40 years, but by the 1950s the chain was clearly in decline. A formula that had worked brilliantly for so long – good food, low prices, comfortable surroundings – became difficult to sustain in a post-war era of rising food and labour costs. The coffee crisis of 1950 was a harbinger of bad times to come. The company had long prided itself on selling the best cup of coffee in the city for only five cents, but by mid-century Horn & Hardart was losing three cents on each cup – a shortfall that amounted to some 2,000,000 dollars a year. The coin slots could take only nickels and quarters, so there was no way to raise the price except by doubling it. And there was no way to serve a less expensive brew except by watering down the coffee and diluting the cream with milk, which ruined the drink and annoyed the customers. Finally, on 29 November 1950, the Automat doubled the price of its coffee – and New Yorkers reacted with fury. Coffee sales in the city dropped from 70,000,000 million cups a year to 45,000,000 million.[17] Years later a company executive looked back at the whole debacle – the outmoded machine, the desperate efforts to work around it, the public relations disaster – and concluded, 'For all practical purposes, growth of the original concept virtually ceased at this time'.[18]

The Automat had staked an enormous part of its fortunes and identity on the city of New York, and New York was changing – in exactly the wrong direction. Many of the new office buildings that were going up in midtown had their own cafeterias, so lunch business, which had been central since the beginning, fell off dramatically. Meanwhile more and more city dwellers were moving to the suburbs, so customer counts at breakfast and dinner also plunged. Horn & Hardart tried desperately to cut costs. Freshly prepared food gave way to packaged and frozen products, with a noticeable effect on quality. A food writer from Ohio with fond memories of the Automat tried a sandwich in 1968 and reported with disappointment that the machines were balky and the bread was rock-hard.[19] What's more, the customers who did remain loyal to the Automat were in the wrong demographic – elderly people, low-wage workers, and the poor looking for a warm place to sit. Tourists still revered the Automat, but New Yorkers who afford to spend a bit more for a sandwich at noon were going elsewhere. Thomas R. Hardart, Frank's grandson and a long-time company executive, told a reporter that people talked to him all the time about how devoted they were to the Automat. 'But they don't show it at the cash register,' he said. 'What we're trying to do is attract a wider audience. I don't mean that we want to alienate our so-called blue collar people, clerks and cab drivers, but we do want to appeal to a broader group.'[20]

Horn & Hardart executives studied the field, conducted surveys, met with consultants, and launched experiment after experiment aimed at reinvigorating the original idea of the Automat. They opened an Out-O-Mat – a takeout shop for hot food. They tried a Windowmat – a walk-up machine right on the sidewalk. There was a Mobile-Mat – a truck hauling an Automat machine through the park to reach office workers at noon.[21] They had been running full-service restaurants since 1950; now they opened one with a cocktail lounge, and another with a Wild West theme.[22] They even tried transforming 1557 Broadway – the first Automat restaurant in the city – into 'Showcase World', with a concert stage open at night to youthful performers doing 'country-style folk music and some relatively mild rock music'.[23] Nothing worked; it was a company that had perfected a single concept and was unable to see it through into a new era. In 1973 a couple of Horn & Hardart executives showed up for breakfast at one of the company's full-service restaurants and filed a discouraging report – grimy menus, sticky counters, flies, 'an unkempt griddle man with wild hair and a largely-exposed hairy chest', and terrible service. 'It is probably symptomatic of our whole restaurant problem,' the executives concluded.[24]

Eventually Horn & Hardart management decided that the only way forward was to get aboard the fast-food juggernaut – pizza, hamburgers, gimmicks. A number of concepts or at least names were floated: La Burgerie, Matilda's, Horatio's, The Respite, Cheap Louie's, The Pentagon and the Bamberg Inn ('Home of the Bam!berger').[25] None of these ever materialized; in the end, Horn & Hardart converted many of its properties to Burger Kings. The last Automat restaurant in New York closed in 1991.

Today it seems impossible to reconcile people's warm, vivid memories of the Automat with the restaurant that spent the second half of its lifespan fighting desperately for survival. But at the level of imagination, the Automat turned out to be indestructible. After all, it lived in New York – or more accurately, 'New York', a city that has been created and recreated endlessly in every form of storytelling including memory. Again and again, we heard people in the exhibition describing to companions or even strangers their first visit to the Automat – as a child, as a tourist, as a suburban teenager, as a brand new New Yorker. They were remembering the meal, but most of all they were remembering the city, and how they had pulled it right out of a windowed compartment like a miracle on a plate. 'The Malloys found their way, that afternoon, to the Broadway Automat,' wrote John Cheever in his 1948 story, 'O City of Broken Dreams'. 'They shouted with pleasure at the magical coffee spigots and the glass doors that sprang open. "Tomorrow, I'm going to have the baked beans," Alice cried, "and the chicken pie the day after that and the fish cakes after that."'[26] The Malloys have just arrived from Wentworth, Indiana, with glorious visions of a triumph in the theatre, and in due course they will lose everything except their meagre lives in a deal with a crooked producer. But as Cheever makes clear, that's not going to happen until later in the story. First, they'll go to the Automat.

Notes

1. Angelika Epple, 'The "Automat." A History of Technological Transfer and the Process of Global Standardization in Modern Fast Food around 1900', *Food & History* 7.2 (2009), pp. 97–118.
2. 'Food Automatically Dispensed', *New-York Tribune*, 4 January 1903, part 2, p. 1; 'A Coin-in-the-Slot Café', *Printer's Ink* 42 (14 January 1903), p. 22; Alex Tristin Shuldiner, 'Trapped Behind the Automat: Technological Systems and the American Restaurant, 1902–1991' (unpublished doctoral thesis, Cornell University, 2001), pp. 23–24.
3. Epple, p. 106.
4. *New-York Tribune*.
5. Shuldiner, p. 19.
6. *Printer's Ink*, p. 22.
7. Shuldiner, p. 44.
8. Shuldiner, p. 94.
9. Jack Alexander, 'The Restaurants that Nickels Built', *Saturday Evening Post*, 11 December 1954, p. 100.
10. Washington, DC, Archives Center, National Museum of American History, Horn and Hardart Records, Box 3, Manager's Rule Book, S-44, 29 February 1924.
11. Alexander, 'Restaurants', Part 2, 18 December 1954, p. 55.
12. New York Public Library, Robert F. Byrnes Collection of Automat Memorabilia, Box 10, f. 3, 'Memo from Regina Farmer', n.d.; Byrnes Collection, *Horn & Hardart Herald*, December 1958, p. 7.
13. Archives Center, Box 2, advertisement in *New York Journal American*, 27 June 1937, n.p.
14. Shuldiner, p. 86.
15. *The New Yorker*, 26 September 1936, p. 24.
16. Qtd. in Shuldiner, p. 109.
17. Shuldiner, p. 175–178.
18. Shuldiner, p. 178.
19. Byrnes Collection, Scrapbook 2, Polly Paffilas, *Akron Beacon Jurnal*, 7 November, 1968, n.p.
20. Archives Center, Box 3, Dennis Duggan, 'Slugs at the Automat', *Newsday*, 30 October 1968, n.p.
21. Byrnes Collection, Box 1926–1936, 'Horn & Hardart looks for a new self', *Fast Food Magazine*, November 1966, n.p.
22. Byrnes Collection, *Horn & Hardart Herald*, September 1961, p. 1; Archives Center, Box 3, 'Automat is Moved Outdoors', *National Restaurant*, 19 September 1966, n.p.
23. Archives Center, Box 3, Memo, 13 November 1972.
24. Archives Center, Box 3, Memo, 24 January 1973.
25. Archives Center, Box 3, 'Suggested Names for a Fast Food Module', 5 February 1973.
26. John Cheever, 'O City of Broken Dreams', *New York Stories*, ed. Diana Secker Tesdell (New York: Knopf, 2011), p. 31.

Transformations in Cookery and Clay: the First Thousand Years of Pottery in Prehistoric Oxfordshire

Emilie Sibbesson

Setting the scene

Five to six thousand years ago, Oxfordshire was covered in dense deciduous forest. The River Thames had recently settled into its current course, fed by a post-glacial lattice of smaller streams. Human groups lived alongside the waterways, in small clearings in the forest. They were among the first Britons to use pottery vessels and eat foods from domestic plants and animals. This is the beginning the Neolithic period in British prehistory (see Pollard 2008). Traditionally, the Neolithic is associated with the first appearance of farming, pottery, polished stone axes and sedentism (settled lifestyles). Today, archaeologists recognize that these defining features of the Neolithic period do not always appear together as a 'package' in the prehistoric record. So while the British Neolithic gets underway around 4000 BC, we do not see evidence of fully settled agricultural communities until the middle Bronze Age, 2500 years later (Stevens and Fuller 2012). This means that people were semi-nomadic and relied on both wild and domestic foods for over two millennia. In this paper, I consider the roles of pottery vessels within these complex culinary repertoires.

The mechanisms by which Neolithic-type features were introduced and dispersed across Britain have been debated by archaeologists for several decades. The debate has centred on two main scenarios: the Neolithic 'began' in Britain due to either incoming groups of farmers from the European mainland or through gradual shifts within the indigenous population. However, it is increasingly likely that a combination of these two scenarios resulted in the changes we see in the archaeological record from around 4000 BC. In other words, small groups of people from continental Europe decided to settle in Britain around this time, and they began to interact with indigenous communities. The character of such interactions is still poorly understood. Was it violent? Did members of different communities intermarry? Did they speak similar languages? Some things are left to our imagination, but there is little reason to believe that categories such as 'newcomers' and 'natives' remained significant for long. Whatever the nature of interactions, they soon changed everyone involved. These dynamics can be traced through, for example, the food they ate and the pots they made.

Ceramics of the fourth millennium BC

The earliest known pottery vessels in Britain date from around 4000 BC. The early assemblages contain sherds of finely made bowls of different forms, of which the most widely recognized type is known as 'carinated bowl'. A carination is a sharp shoulder on the profile of the vessel. The skill with which these vessels were made indicates that the potters from mainland Europe were active within an established and actively sustained craft tradition. The vessels are typically thin-walled and made from a gritty ceramic paste. Clays were mixed with sand, crushed flint, shell fragments and/or organic matter to make them more durable or elastic. Ceramic paste recipes varied with local geologies and traditions of practice. All prehistoric pottery in Britain is hand-built – the potter's wheel was brought by the Romans some 4000 thousand years after the beginning of the Neolithic. Traces of the potter's hand are sometimes seen. For example, many vessels were made by the coiling technique and later broke along a coil-joint. Today, 6000 years later, the ways in which the potter pushed and smoothed the clay to join the coils and consolidate the vessel wall are still visible. Many Neolithic pottery vessels also carry scars of the open bonfires in which they were fired.

The first few generations of potters in Britain carefully smoothed or burnished the surfaces of vessels to increase lustre and reduce permeability. Around 3800 BC, potters began to press patterns into the surfaces of pottery vessels. Bird bones, reeds and twisted cords were used to make lines or rows of dots on the ceramic surface. Alongside these sparsely decorated bowls, plain vessels were made, sometimes with handles. A typical ceramic repertoire from the mid-fourth millennium BC in Oxfordshire includes some heavy, straight-sided bowls, a couple of small cups and a few bowls with modest carinations and perhaps some impressed decoration. This kind of pottery is referred to as Early Neolithic bowls, although that label masks plenty of regional and chronological variation.

Sometime after 3500 BC, pottery vessels that are thicker, heavier and more profusely decorated appear on archaeological sites. This style is known in archaeology as Peterborough Ware. However, the distinction between these bowls and the earlier styles may not have been meaningful to the communities who made and used them. The prehistoric record cannot be easily catalogued; like life itself it is messy. The distinction was articulated before the introduction of radiocarbon dating, and we now know that Early Neolithic bowls and Peterborough Ware vessels were made and used alongside each other for a couple of centuries. The latter style was named after the vessels found during an excavation in Peterborough, Cambridgeshire, in the early twentieth century. Since then, this type of pottery has been found on sites in most parts of Britain that date to between 3500 and 2800 BC (Gibson and Kinnes 1997).

In the 1950s, archaeologist Isobel Smith re-examined the sherds from Peterborough itself during her doctoral research. She found them to be 'mud-like' due to inadequate firing (Smith 1956: 81). Indeed, if we take a step back and consider potting traditions throughout the fourth millennium BC, it is clear that the best-made vessels belong in the earlier part of the period. The earlier vessels had thinner walls made with finer ceramic pastes and they were generally fired in higher temperatures. In contrast, vessels from the end of the fourth millennium were 'sometimes incredibly ill-made and ill-fired' (Smith 1956: 106). In other words, potting skills did not steadily improve during the fourth millennium BC. Material culture does not necessarily evolve towards mastery. That is not to say that there are no well-made Peterborough Ware vessels – there are, but the quality of production varies a great deal. A single archaeological site from the later part of the fourth millennium may yield both well made and clunky, under-fired bowls.

These circumstances indicate that pottery was made within increasingly localized craft traditions. Vessel aesthetics were perhaps more highly valued in the earlier part of the fourth millennium, especially in episodes of initial contacts between newcomers and natives. Pottery was a novelty to some, if not all, of the indigenous communities. They descended from hunter-gatherers that had followed wild game into Britain thousands of years earlier as the ice sheets of the last glaciation receded. Prehistoric hunter-gatherer ceramics have been recovered in some parts of the world, including Brazil, Russia, Japan and Scandinavia. Pottery is no longer considered to be an exclusively agriculturalist phenomenon. However, in the British Isles pottery is still strongly associated with the Neolithic, despite evidence for cross-Channel contacts that significantly pre-date the period (e.g. Garrow and Sturt 2011). As the fourth millennium wore on, the distinction between newcomers and natives faded and pottery, along with a few other components of the Neolithic repertoire, became widespread.

Crucially, the spread of pottery across Britain included the know-how of making vessels. In some settings, bowls were made with a specific purpose in mind, and this purpose did not rely on high levels of skill or aesthetic value. However, the ways in which vessels were made, their decorative motifs and ceramic paste ingredients probably still mattered. Notions of group identity, for example, may be strongly expressed through material culture, perhaps especially that made of malleable clay. Yet by the time that the chunkier Peterborough Ware bowls appear in the archaeological record, the collection and preparation of raw materials – clay, grit temper, fuel for the fire – were routine tasks, even though they may have been associated with certain seasons. Each community made and used pottery vessels, and no living memory lingered of a time without ceramics. So what purpose did these pots have?

Molecular traces of food

In 1976, a scientific study of a Roman amphora from Spain was published by Condamin and colleagues. The team 'took into account the porous structure of ceramics and thought that the oil constituents could have migrated through the amphora and be retained there even if in very small quantities. They ought to therefore be traceable either in their original form, or in the form of degradation substances' (Condamin et al. 1976: 195). They were right. Bio-molecules that may have derived from olive oil could be extracted from the powdered amphora sherds. Since then, the techniques involved have been vastly improved and organic residue analysis has been performed on thousands of archaeological pottery sherds from around the world. This development relies on advances in molecular biology, and in archaeology it has motivated a wider shift of attention towards perishable items from the past. The archaeologically more ubiquitous stone tools and ceramics were made and used alongside repertoires of organic materials – leather, wood, basketry and so on – that make up the 'missing majority' of the archaeological record (Hurcombe 2008: 85). Prehistoric organic materials only survive in exceptional environments such as deserts, glaciers and waterlogged deposits. There are obvious implications for food remains, which are traditionally only accessible through animal bone and burnt grain or nutshells on archaeological sites. Consequently, the recently developed bio-molecular techniques hold great potential for the study of ancient food.

Food, drink and other commodities that were contained or cooked in unglazed pottery often absorbed into the walls of the vessel. Alternatively, food residues survive as burnt crusts on the interior surface of vessels. An organic residue is made up of different compound classes, including carbohydrates and proteins, but archaeologists primarily target the lipid (fats, oils, waxes) component. Lipids are insoluble in water and thus survive relatively well when buried in the ground for thousands of years. The most widely used technique (gas chromatography/mass spectrometry or GC/MS) for retrieving the lipids works by separating the extract into its constituent compounds and analysing them according to certain chemical characteristics. However, the data thereby produced is not easily translated into lists of ingredients or menus. The resolution is coarser than that. We can detect constituents of foods such fatty acids, wax esters and sterols, but we cannot generally identify species since many plants and animals share these constituents. A promising line of future research is DNA analysis of food residues (e.g. Foley et al. 2012), but this approach requires exceptional preservational circumstances and state-of-the-art laboratory facilities. For the time being, we interpret GC/MS data by searching for a number of 'biomarkers' and by looking at the distribution and quantity of lipid compounds.

However, not all foods are equally represented in an organic residue. Saturated animal fat is the most chemically stable, whereas fish oils are elusive since they consist of polyunsaturated fatty acids that do not preserve well during cooking and subsequent burial. Many plant foods do not contain appreciable amounts of fats or waxes. As with the plant and animal remains themselves, the picture is therefore skewed in favour of meat consumption. Different food activities also leave different signatures. Cooking with heat is likely to cause lipids to enter the porous ceramic wall. In contrast, dry commodities that are stored in pottery vessels are probably invisible to us. If we are lucky, intact animal fat in the form of triacylglycerols are present, and they enable us to distinguish between dairy fat, tissue fat from ruminants and tissue fat from monogastric animals. That is, the question of whether milk, beef or pork foods were cooked in the vessels can be addressed if the fat residues are well preserved. In short, the prehistoric past survives in fragments and our data will never represent entire food webs or culinary repertoires. Past foodways can only be painstakingly pieced together through a combination of analysis, interpretation, analogy and imagination.

Bowl food

We have seen that the communities living in this region during the fourth millennium BC were not fully settled farmers. Instead, they relied on a wide range of both wild and domestic food species. They were semi-nomadic and lived in a few different locales throughout the year, perhaps on a seasonal basis. Archaeologists have struggled to come to terms with the ambiguous economic status of these groups, due to a disciplinary legacy that imposes a strict conceptual division between hunter-gatherers and farmers. The implication of this legacy for the British Neolithic is that scholars have argued for decades about the calorific input of wild versus domestic foods. Fortunately, the strict division is currently eroding as prehistoric communities that practised some form of 'mixed economy' are coming into sharper focus. The challenge, therefore, is to enhance understanding of the complex foodways practised in the grey area between foraging and farming. To this end, the molecular traces of food offer important clues.

The most comprehensive study of organic residues in British Neolithic pots to date was designed to explore whether dairy fat could be scientifically detected (Copley et al. 2005). It could indeed, and the authors concluded that milk was an important food resource even during the period of incipient cattle husbandry in the early fourth millennium BC. The study obtained samples from pottery sherds recovered at six different Neolithic sites in southern England, including both domestic and 'monumental' sites. At the latter, communities are likely to have gathered for seasonal feasts. Two of the sites are located in Oxfordshire, and another three are found in the wider region of the Thames catchment. Ceramics from a funerary monument in the nearby Cotswold Hills have also been analysed in this way (Copley and Evershed 2007). My own work targets small domestic sites in Oxfordshire and Gloucestershire (Sibbesson in prep.). We can begin to build up a detailed, localized picture of what and how people ate during this period, although our interpretations are subject to the analytical drawbacks mentioned above.

Accordingly, it is becoming clear that a majority of pottery vessels from this period were used to cook. This is a valid conclusion despite the fact that researchers have approached the pottery assemblages somewhat differently. For example, Copley et al. (2005: 524) specifically targeted vessels that were likely to have been cooking pots. In my own work, I selected sherds that represent the entire ceramic repertoire of each community. Either way, absorbed food residues were found in a majority of vessels. What is more, indications of foods being heated over fires were detected in all datasets. This is evident because repeated heating results in chemically altered substances that can be recognized as such. So what was being cooked? Unsurprisingly, most vessels contained a combination of plant and meat food. Traces of dairy fats were present at each site. The laboratory data corresponds well with the larger food remains recovered alongside the pottery. For example, finely chopped and burnt animal bone was found at the domestic sites. The pieces were small enough to fit in a ceramic bowl, and they may have been boiled for broth or in a stew.

If we zoom out and look at this detailed data within the wider inhabited landscape, it seems as though different kinds of places warranted different ways of eating. I believe that large domestic animals such as cattle and pig were only slaughtered at the ceremonial gathering sites at certain times of the year. We often find the remains of large carcasses in the ditches of monuments. In contrast, the smaller domestic sites contain the remains of the joints of meat that were brought back from the feast. Here, nothing was wasted. Even the bone was boiled and the marrow added flavour and nutrients. For the remainder of the year, milk was an important source of protein. We do not generally find the bones of wild animals at these sites, but it is likely that some hunting took place. The scarcity of bone from smaller animals is probably due to a combination of poor preservation in the ground and spatial arrangements of food practices. In other words, for practical or symbolic reasons the remains of hunted animals may not have been disposed of at the inhabited site. We cannot distinguish between wild and domestic food in an organic residue, but information from other sites sheds some light. For example, further downstream along the River Thames, bones of deer, beaver, otter, badger, fox and polecat were found alongside those of domestic animals at the Neolithic settlement site of Runnymede Bridge in Surrey (Serjeantson 2006).

When we consider the data alongside vessel characteristics – including those vessels that did not yield any prehistoric lipids – certain patterns emerge. For example, the cooking pots tended to be of closed forms (i.e. where the mouth of the vessel is not its widest point). In contrast, open vessels may have been preferred for display or consumption of food, which is less likely to leave fat residues. It is also clear that, at any given time, different vessels served different culinary purposes. There is no reason to assume that we are looking at the remains of 'one pot cookery'. On the whole, there is more variation within the datasets than there is consistency. That is, each community would have used their vessels in their own ways. Certain notions about how a pot should look and what was edible were shared throughout the region, but careful analysis reveals subtle differences. For example, at one site the decorated vessels were not used as cooking pots. At another, the cooking pots had smoothed surfaces. This brings us to consider the makers of these vessels.

The cooking potter

We do not have much evidence of clay being worked for any other purpose than to make pots. The rare exceptions include few clay beads were been found at a burial monument in the Cotswold Hills and a handful of instances of clay used in wattle-and-daub walls. For the most part, it seems as though people associated clay with containers, and these containers belonged in a culinary setting. In later periods, clay was used in multiple ways, for example in the making of loom weights. Moreover, ceramic vessels were made for a variety of reasons; funerary urns held cremated human remains, and crucibles for metal smelting were used in bronze production. In contrast, in the fourth millennium BC pottery vessels and food occupied the same social domain. Accordingly, the changes we see in the ceramics throughout the period reflect the requirements placed on vessels by cooking practices. This intimate association between food and pottery raises new questions. However, traditional labour divisions and increasing specialization in archaeology mean that different types of finds are analysed separately. Pottery sherds are counted, weighed, examined and drawn by the ceramic specialist. Macroscopic food remains such as animal bones and plant remains are studied by the zooarchaeologist and the archaeobotanist respectively. The degree of re-integration of these different strands of information depends on the research design, budget and timeframe of the project. I say *re*-integration because past lives involved all of them, together. The categories that we divide them into – ceramic, environmental, inorganic and so on – may not have resonated with the inhabitants of prehistoric Britain.

The ceramic specialist is primarily concerned with the making and breaking of vessels. Analysis of manufacture relies to an extent on geological information, as clay components may tell us where a vessel was made and whether it was traded or exchanged. Aspects of forming, decorating and firing of pottery vessels can tell us a great deal about the cultural contexts in which they were made. At the other end of a pot's life, broken vessels were discarded in ways that shed light on how a site was inhabited. For example, sherds with fire-damaged or worn edges were probably lying around on the ground for some time – perhaps getting trampled on and burnt near a hearth – rather than being purposefully removed from a living area. Until recently, we could only make qualified guesses about the purpose of pots in between manufacture and breakage, although conventional 'use-wear analysis' provides insight if scraping or sooting marks are present on a vessel. For decades, archaeologists have assumed that many pots held food. Today, we can characterize that content in some detail, but this enquiry is pursued by the archaeological scientist with a background in biochemistry, rather than by the ceramic specialist. Consequently, the contents of prehistoric pottery vessels are often discussed in isolation from the making and breaking of vessels, and vice versa.

In my view, the vessels that survive from the fourth millennium BC prompt us to overcome this compartmentalization. They were made by potters who were intimately familiar with cookery practices. In other words, these vessels were not made for trade. They were made by members of the community, as and when more vessels were needed. Increasingly throughout the period, the ceramic repertoire accommodated vessels suitable for food processing. For example, handles were added and walls were made thick enough to withstand repeated heating on the fire. After only a few generations, pottery was made not only by skilled potters. The strong craft tradition of the first settlers fragmented, with varying outcomes. The function of a pot gradually became more important than the way it looked. My argument, then, is neatly summed up by another Symposiast, Mary Wondrausch, in the title of her contribution to the 1988 meeting: 'The cooking potter makes a cooking pot'. This may seem obvious, but archaeologists are trained to deconstruct common-sense conclusions. Rightly so – we often deal with periods so remote that our modern-day concepts may not apply. Yet cooking and eating are experiences that we all share. In the fourth millennium BC such experiences were closely entangled with that new kind of material culture: pottery.

References

J.F. Condamin, M.O. Formenti, M. Michel Metais, and P. Blond. 1976. 'The Application of Gas Chromatography to the Tracing of Oil in Ancient Amphorae', *Archaeometry* 18: 195–201.

M.S. Copley, R. Berstan, A.J. Mukherjee, S.N. Dudd, V. Straker, S. Payne and R.P. Evershed. 2005. 'Dairying in Antiquity III. Evidence from Absorbed Lipid Residues dating to the British Neolithic', *Journal of Archaeological Science* 32: 523–46.

M. S. Copley, and R.P. Evershed. 2007. 'Organic Residue Analysis', in *Building Memories. The Neolithic Cotswold Long Barrow at Ascott-under-Wychwood, Oxfordshire*, eds. D. Benson and A.W.R. Whittle, (Oxford: Oxbow Books), pp. 283–88.

B.P. Foley, M.C. Hansson, D.P. Kourkoumelis and T.A. Theodoulou. 2012. 'Aspects of Ancient Greek Trade Re-evaluated with Amphora DNA Evidence', *Journal of Archaeological Science* 39(2) 389–98.

D. Garrow, and F. Sturt, 2011. 'Grey Waters Bright with Neolithic Argonauts? Maritime Connections and the Mesolithic-Neolithic Transition within the "Western Seaways" of Britain, c. 5000–3500 BC', *Antiquity* 85: 59–72.

A. Gibson, and I. Kinnes, 1997. 'On the Urns of a Dilemma: Radiocarbon and the Peterborough Problem', *Oxford Journal of Archaeology* 16(1): 65–72.

L. Hurcombe, 2008. 'Organics from Inorganics: Using Experimental Archaeology as a Research Tool for Studying Perishable Material Culture', *World Archaeology* 40(1): 83–115.

J. Pollard, ed., *Prehistoric Britain*. (Oxford: Wiley–Blackwell,2008).

D. Serjeantson, 2006. 'Food or Feast at Neolithic Runnymede', *Animals in the Neolithic of Britain and Europe*, eds. D. Serjantson and D. Fiel (Oxford: Oxbow Books), pp. 113–34.

I.F. Smith, 1956. 'The Decorative Art of Neolithic Ceramics in South-eastern England and Its Relations'. PhD thesis, London, Institute of Archaeology, UCL.

S.J. Stevens, and D.Q.Fuller. 2012. 'Did Neolithic Farming Fail? The Case for a Bronze Age Agricultural Revolution in the British Isles', *Antiquity* 86(333): 707–22.

M. Wondrausch, 1989. 'The Cooking Potter Makes a Cooking Pot', in *The Cooking Pot. Proceedings of the Oxford Symposium on Food & Cookery 1988*, ed. T. Jaine, Totnes (UK: Prospect Books), pp. 183–84.

Making Muscular Machines with Nitrogenous Nutrition: Bovril, Plasmon and Cadbury's Cocoa

Lesley Steinitz

This essay examines the visual and material objects used to promote three of Britain's iconic food brands, Bovril beef extract, Plasmon protein powder and Cadbury's Cocoa Essence, during the period from 1890 until the end of the Great War. Specifically, it explores one important theme underpinning the advertising of these foods, their high protein content. The 'nitrogenous nutrition' of the title, which scientists taught was the supreme nutritious substance synonymous with strength and robust good health. The images that advertisers chose, the words that they used and the connections that these made can be used to construct accounts of how individuals viewed food and their bodies in this period. They also provide insights into how individuals used their food and bodies to address key problems in British *fin-de-siècle* society. By focussing on the visual and material objects and their referents and, where possible, reactions to them, this essay explores why eaters trusted and acted on the claims that eating such products would improve strength and healthiness.[1]

Britain's emblematic and burly John Bull ate a lot of meat, and this British meat-eating habit was widely understood as a reason for the country's colonial, industrial and military prowess.[2] During the nineteenth century, one aspect of this story was given scientific legitimacy; meat was rich in the substances containing nitrogen that were essential to life, and which chemists had named 'proteins' in the 1840s.[3] A nation whose population was well fed on meat would therefore be strong and powerful. However, although average meat consumption was higher in Britain than in the rest of Europe, dietary surveys at the turn of the twentieth century showed that working-class diets were woefully inadequate, especially in respect of the quantity of meat and other protein rich food consumed. Almost a third of the population could afford less than 60g of protein per day, half of the amount that most contemporary physiologists agreed was essential for good health.[4] These shocking figures gave extra weight to pre-existing concerns about the fitness of young British working men. Concern had increased as the century progressed, and came to a head during the disastrous British military campaigns of the Boer War from 1899 to 1902, when the poor fitness of army recruits was widely blamed for Britain's military embarrassments. Borrowing concepts of intergenerational change from Darwinian ideas about evolution, these concerns were translated into an increasingly vocal narrative about the degeneration of the English race, displaced from the healthy countryside to live and work in crowded dirty airless cities, with terrible consequences for health, moral values and social behaviour.[5]

Men of science both provided the theory to explain the problem of degeneration, and offered solutions. One of these was to eat protein-rich foods. This new advice was offered by nutritional chemists once proteins had come to represent the supreme nourishing substance from the 1840s. However, protein-rich meat was expensive, and milk often carried disease. Businessmen instead offered consumers access to cheaper proteins, in the form of new processed foods which, they claimed, contained concentrated strength-giving protein. To persuade consumers to eat their products, manufacturers invested in overt advertising, covert advertorials, sensational public displays and celebrity promotions. They used visual and verbal references to material objects and symbols of authority to create positive associations between their products, the credibility of science and the virtues of active masculinity and patriotism. These associations linked the claims of the new science of nutrition to consumers' cultural, economic and social concerns.

Science in late-nineteenth-century Britain was regarded as exciting and useful for economic progress. The booming popular press reported advances in agricultural and nutritional chemistry, displaying a mix of enthusiasm, fear and scepticism over the power of science to solve the world's food supply problems. The press also fed ordinary eaters' interest in matters of direct significance for their bodies, by explaining the new scientific principles of nutrition in newspapers, popular science magazines, women's magazines and household manuals.[6] The number and range of general news articles which mentioned protein indicate that the 'fact' of its necessity for sustaining human life was reasonably well known. Readers could now embody this knowledge practically and personally by eating these foods and feeding them to those in their care, and manufacturers capitalized on this scientific legitimacy to advertise foods containing proteins.

Gaining credibility through science
Cadbury's Cocoa Essence
Cocoa, one of the first processed foods, was no longer an élite drink by the last quarter of the nineteenth century.[7] Prominent among cocoa manufacturers was, of course, Cadbury's, whose Cocoa Essence was a finely-ground pure cocoa without, the company claimed, the additives and fatty cocoa butter found in other brands. This brand became one of Britain's premium products in a society where food adulteration was rife. By the 1890s, however, Cadbury's Cocoa faced tough competition. Its main selling-point was its purity and this was drummed home in their 'scientific' advertising. While many cocoa advertisements depicted people enjoying it, there is no consumption in this expensively produced advertisement. Instead it shows a public analyst in his laboratory, where he tests food and medicines for purity. He is surrounded by the paraphernalia of his profession, a familiar trope in portraits of great men, designed to emphasize their expertise and authority. However, unusually for a portrait, he is shown in profile; we are not the focus of his attention, nor is he ours. Our eye is drawn instead to two

Making Muscular Machines with Nitrogenous Nutrition

Figure 1. The Illustrated Sporting and Dramatic News, *17 August 1891, p. 624. Author's collection.*

of his scientific objects in particular: the test-tube at which he is staring and which demonstrates the cocoa's purity, and the large tin of Cadbury's Cocoa Essence which he holds in his other hand. He invites us to read his notebook which he has helpfully placed facing us: the cocoa is absolutely pure. His analysis cements the scientific authority of the image by quantifying Cadbury's Cocoa's high protein content.

Scientific knowledge about the nature, function and even the proper term for protein was still in flux; however this advertisement suggests that Cadbury's was confident that consumers, from the well-off readers of the *Illustrated Sporting and Dramatic News* to the enforcers of sanitarian legislation who read *Food, Drugs and Drink*, understood that these 'flesh-formers' were central to well-being.[8] Cadbury's cocoa was presented as a superior scientific substance with nourishing properties by linking this everyday product to the authority of scientists and their institutions and practices.

Plasmon

Others, including the manufacturers of Plasmon, a protein powder made from skimmed milk, also used scientific terms and tools to cement their products' nutritional credentials. Skimmed milk had often been sour and nasty until fresh skimmed milk

> **To EAT is not enough!**
> The food we eat must be the right kind of food.
> **PLASMON is the food for old or young,**
> **BECAUSE**
> It contains the Proteid which is lacking in ordinary foods. The concentrated nourishment of 30 pints of fresh milk is contained in an unaltered form in 1lb. of Plasmon.
>
> PLASMON. PLASMON COCOA. PLASMON OATS. PLASMON BISCUITS.
> **BRIMFUL OF NOURISHMENT.**

Figure 2. To EAT is not enough!, The Penny Illustrated Paper and Illustrated Times *(London), 19 January 1907, p. 48 (Image © The British Library Board. All rights reserved).*

became abundant, following the automation of the separation of milk and cream for butter manufacture in the 1870s.[9] Despite the efforts of reformers to persuade people that it was nutritious, it remained culturally acceptable only for the very poorest people. Most of it went to feed pigs or was simply poured away.[10] Entrepreneurial chemists working mostly in Germany and Austria developed new chemical processes to extract the predominant protein in cow's milk, casein, from this waste product. Casein's adhesive properties were used to develop commercial paints, glues and plastics, and from about 1896, edible casein powders could be manufactured using large-scale chemical processes.[11] The cheapest and, according to the *Lancet*, 'best example of a food prepared from milk' was Plasmon, sold as an ingredient for home-made dishes.[12] It was also sold pre-mixed as Plasmon Cocoa, Oats, Biscuits and other staples, which were as expensive as the premium brands. Like Cadbury's, Plasmon's manufacturers used terminology to emphasize that it was a scientific substance. Advertisements quantified a pound of Plasmon as the 'concentrated nourishment of 30 pints of fresh milk' and explained that it consisted of 'Proteid', the most scientific-sounding of the many terms used interchangeably to designate protein.

Plasmon and Cadbury's both used graphs as modern and sophisticated explanatory and legitimizing scientific devices. Invented at the end of the eighteenth century, abstract graphs were widely used in scientific texts to communicate numerical information, but were very unfamiliar in business, advertising and public discourse in 1901.[13] The graphic display in Figure 3 of Plasmon Cocoa's superiority in terms of 'nutriment' or 'flesh-forming substances' (protein) over 'pure' cocoa was very innovative. It underlined Plasmon's scientific status, both explicitly through the information conveyed, and implicitly through the use of this scientific tool. They may have been imitating Cadbury's similar graph in the *Daily Mail* (Figure 4) used to claim that their cocoa powder contained more 'flesh-forming (nitrogenous)' matter even than fresh meat or eggs, both exemplars of good nutrition. Cadbury's treated consumers as at once sophisticated enough to be able to interpret a graph, yet naïve enough to accept as

Figure 3. Plasmon Cocoa, Manchester Courier, *10 May 1901, p. 7 (Image © The British Library Board. All rights reserved.)*

legitimate the comparison between dry cocoa and foods in a natural hydrated state.

Bovril
Bovril was, and still is, a viscous brown beef extract. Diluted in hot water, it resembles beef tea, a traditional invalid remedy. Justus von Liebig, arguably the most influential chemist of the nineteenth century, had stimulated a large market and manufacturing industry for beef extracts from 1865, by legitimizing the traditional remedy with science. Beef extract was manufactured according to Liebig's recipe by steaming boneless ox carcasses, then concentrating the resulting sieved broth. Liebig taught that this extract was especially nutritious because its aromatic mineral salts played an important part in the formation of muscle, even though it contained no protein, so did not fit into the protein/carbohydrate/fat model of nutrition which he also championed. Many people, physicians included, continued to subscribe to Liebig's claims about extract, even though, by the time that Bovril was launched in the 1880s, a new generation of nutritional chemists had denied that meat extracts were nutritious.[14]

This continuing debate was in part stimulated by Bovril's formulation; Bovril contained added pulverized dried meat, nourishing protein, so could claim to be truly nutritious. Competing manufacturers and scientists played out a lively exchange, the 'Battle of the Beef Extracts', in the popular and scientific press during the 1890s.[15] Bovril fought this battle by extending its marketing beyond the symbolic associations with science utilized by Plasmon and Cadbury's to emphasize its strong links with eminent scientists. The most notable of these was Lord Lyon Playfair. Following a distinguished career as scientist and hygienic reformer, Playfair became a Liberal MP in Gladstone's government before being appointed to the House of Lords. He also became Chairman of Bovril. His and other scientists' names appeared in advertisements to legitimize Bovril's

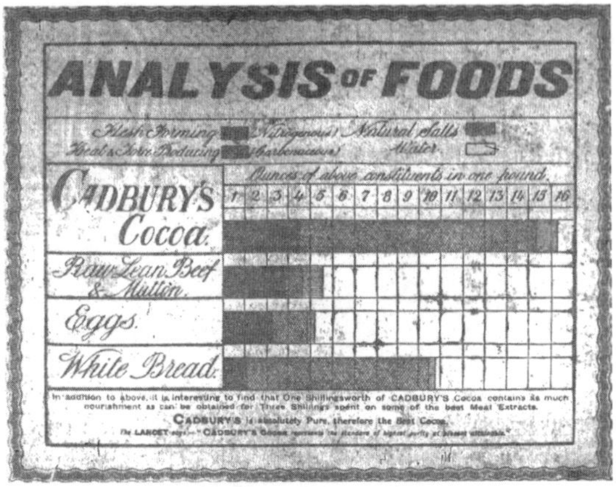

Figure 4. Analysis of foods, Daily Mail *(London), 5 March 1897, p. 8. Author's collection.*

nutritional claims to consumers and to officials provisioning the military, hospitals and workhouses. As well as operating at a political level, the company enrolled many ordinary experts as Bovril advocates. From 1900, they laid on invitation-only tours of Bovril's 'Temple of Sanitation', the company's new headquarters (Figure 5), where the product was hygienically blended and bottled. The building's imposing facade, its grand meeting rooms and its electrically powered factory and laboratories were symbols of modernity and science. Bovril intended the hundreds of invited physicians, nurses, grocers and members of the Sanitary Association to convey this symbolism of Bovril to their institutions and communities.[16] These deep and visible associations with scientists and physicians endowed Bovril with enormous scientific legitimacy consistent with the rise of the sanitation movement.

Figure 5. Bovril offices and factory, Old Street, London (c. 1900). Edinburgh City Archives, records of John Lawson Johnston & Bovril Ltd.

Making Muscular Machines with Nitrogenous Nutrition

Gaining credibility through muscles

While scientists used the terms 'proteid, 'protein' and 'nitrogenous food' interchangeably, they and the popular press often also used metaphors such as 'flesh-formers', 'muscle-formers', 'tissue-formers', 'blood-forming matters' or 'body-building food'. Such expressions underlined the belief that protein literally replaced the muscle and other body parts worn out through work in bodies that, as Rabinbach has shown, were widely represented as machines.[17] Muscularity was therefore a visual symbol of protein consumption. Bovril and Plasmon both used this symbolism in their trademarks, images of muscular active men: Samson slaying a Lion, and a man chiselling out 'PLASMON' (from the Greek 'that which gives form') on a stone pillar. Such portrayals followed the fashionable 'New Sculpture movement', typified by Frederic Leighton's *Athlete Wrestling with a Python*. Like the Bovril and Plasmon trademarks, New Sculpture offered morally uplifting images of idealized male bodies which demonstrated both active physicality and good character as a counterforce to the degeneracy exemplified by both the destitute poor and Oscar Wilde's circle of homosexual artists and writers. These nudes were therefore not shocking or risqué. They represented, Michael Hall argues, icons 'of decency in late Victorian Britain… insistently positioned as a positive ideal.' Many of the clichés used in art magazine reviews of New Sculpture of the late 1800s – 'vigorous, healthy, vital' – were also used by advertisers to describe the effects of eating their protein foods.[18]

Figure 6. From 'Bovril gives strength', The Sketch, 28 February 1894, p. 263. Author's collection.

Figure 7. Plasmon stamp, c. 1900. Author's collection.

Bovril and Plasmon's trademarks also drew on another related but more populist practice that had also risen in response to fears of degeneration and decadence: the Physical Culture movement. Politicians, reformers and celebrities encouraged people to partake in sports, creating a participant and spectator sports culture. One of its biggest stars, Eugen Sandow (Figure 8), claimed he had developed his body on scientific principles and emulated classical revivalist models of body perfection, with sharply defined musculature and greater fleshiness than either the classical or today's svelte ideal body shapes. This Prussian exile's music-hall displays of his extraordinary body, shown off by his statuesque poses and astonishing feats of strength, were wildly popular. He

Figure 8. Eugen Sandow, Strength and how to obtain it *(1901), following p. 127. Author's collection.*

Figure 9. Eustace Miles, 'A Meal at Miles's', The Bystander, 7 August 1907, p. 274. Author's collection.

became a global celebrity, and his body became a visual icon and arguably part of the period's popular material culture.[19] Sandow endorsed both Bovril and Plasmon. Both brands also made extensive use of pictures and testimonials of other muscular men, including intrepid explorers, sports champions and 'ordinary' fit people.[20] Plasmon pictured an anonymous weightlifter in a collectable pop-up trade card, while Bournville F.C.'s team of fit 'ordinary' men enjoyed the manly comradeship of sport, strengthened by Cadbury's Cocoa.[21] The New Sculpture and Physical Culture movements, and these product icons and advertising images more generally, created a spectacle of the male body. All were aiming to become associated with the wider meanings, both physical and moral, of a new masculinity.

Unlike tasty Bovril and Cadbury's Cocoa, Plasmon had none of the usual immediate physiological effects or material properties of food. It had no taste, no smell and no texture; it was not a stimulant, so had no immediate perceptible effect on the body, and it was not substantial or filling, as only a few teaspoonfuls needed to be 'taken' each day. It did not resemble any other types of food available at the start of the twentieth century, and so carried no direct emotional associations with familiar foods that might have made it desirable. Plasmon's asset was in its medical and scientific credibility: when people ate it, they appreciated it for its intellectual, rather than physical or emotional, qualities. Instead of centring its marketing solely around body culture, Plasmon therefore also made overt appeals to the intellect, and became more associated with the ideology promoted by another celebrity of the physical culture movement – the tennis champion Eustace Miles, who was Plasmon's foremost advocate outside the company from soon after the product's introduction in Britain in 1900.[22]

Although Miles's activities, like Sandow's, extended into entrepreneurial businesses around health and fitness products and advice, their ideologies could hardly have been more different. Eustace Miles was a British upper-middle-class intellectual who straddled the worlds of sporting celebrity, intellectual culture, aristocratic society and commercial enterprise. As well as being the World Tennis and Squash Champion, he coached Cambridge classics scholars; was a prolific author of dozens of books and

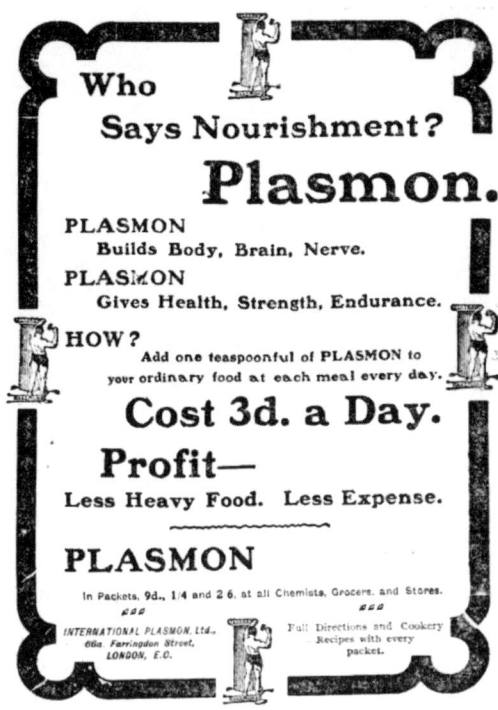

Figure 10. Cost 3d. a Day., Manchester Courier, *21 April 1902, p. 8 (Image © The British Library Board. All rights reserved).*

newspaper articles about history, spirituality, sports, self-help, diet and physical culture; and was a respected health expert and fitness coach.²³ Even his books on sports or memory techniques invariably contained a section about eating.²⁴ Unlike Sandow, Miles wrote endlessly not just about the body, but about loftier matters of morals, the soul and the mind, drawing on the works of an eclectic mix of conventional and quirky scientists and religious figures. The more reserved Miles was only photographed with his clothes firmly on, as in Figure 9 which accompanied an article promoting his new 500-seater vegetarian restaurant. It expresses Miles's (and Plasmon's) serious-minded perspective: eating was a serious matter which should, first and foremost, be part of a moral duty to build up physical and mental health. Even though restaurants were ostensibly about eating and socializing, there was no food on show in this carefully posed tableau. For Miles, eating was not primarily about aesthetics or pleasure. While Sandow ate and drank just about anything, Miles's ideology centred on his teetotal 'lacto-vegetarian' diet, because food influenced, he said, 'not only the body but also the mind and character'.²⁵

Both Miles and Plasmon were representing a particular version of masculinity, characterized by restraint, respect for scientific authority and nature and an emphasis on frugality (Figure 10). Most of Plasmon's advertisements used wordy explanations rather than imagery, and drew on fact and science rather than emotion or humour. Where Plasmon's trademark appeared in Britain, it was usually tiny, and probably served brand

Figure 11. Bovril 'Alas! My poor brother', playing card (back), c. 1900–1920. From design by W. H. Caffyn, c. 1896. Author's collection.

recognition rather than any significant association with the masculinity that the image represented. A typical advert declared that 'To EAT is not enough! The food we eat must be the right kind of food' (Figure 2): having a healthy body was as much about duty as about beauty. While Plasmon associated itself with modern science, it also embodied traditional middle-class masculine values that were slightly out of kilter with the rise in power of the working class, modern consumerism and the body culture which Bovril exploited so effectively at the very end of the nineteenth century.[26]

Gaining credibility through patriotism

Bovril used imagery to create explicit links between this flavoursome food and patriotism across all classes. Meat's cultural legitimacy as one cause for Britain's supremacy meant that beef was a food to which people of all classes aspired. Bovril capitalized on this, using iconography of the ox to link beef extract back to beef. This was not a self-evident approach. The vegan feminist theorist Carol Adams notes that animals have typically become invisible 'absent referents' from representations of meat as food.[27] Today, advertisements for prepared meat products rarely show images of living animals. It is striking that Bovril (and other extract manufacturers) often emphasized and personified the ox to associate the cultural values of Britishness, masculinity, valour and strength to brown gloop. This is most visible in one of Bovril's most popular advertisements, which depicts a tearful ox gazing at a jar of Bovril, saying 'Alas! My poor brother!' (Figure

11). For decades from 1896, the ox was the centrepiece of many Bovril advertising campaigns, representing strength, stoicism, good character and patriotism, as well as the prized British sense of humour.

Bovril built on the product's association with these positive values by linking it to other symbols of national greatness. A politically charged advertisement from 1890 shows schoolboys in front of a chalkboard listing the great powers, 'England, France …'. They have mischievously added 'Bovril' to the list of countries, explicitly elevating Bovril's status to that of a leading nation while implicitly also linking it to the recent sanitarian achievement, universal elementary education.[28] A 1907 postcard shows a Bovril cart in the heart of the City of London raising the status of Bovril with the caption, 'Three well known institutions. Bank of England. Royal Exchange. And Bovril.'[29] A clever folding trade card positioned Bovril as a British icon by showing how another iconic symbol, the Union Jack, was constructed, while ironically claiming that Bovril – which was made from South American and Australian oxen – was 'British'.[30]

Bovril also created military and patriotic associations by presenting the drink as an essential food and comfort for the military, encouraging people to send Bovril to the front to supplement the Bovril supplied by the army. In 1916 an entire front page of the *Daily Express* pictured a huge 'British Bull' telling John Bull that 'If you can't go yourself you might want to send *Me* – I hear they want more BOVRIL at the Front'.[31] The advertisement's catchphrase that Bovril was 'British to the Backbone' was hardly necessary to convey the link between the ox, patriotism, self-sacrifice and Bovril. Bovril represented wartime camaraderie and loyalty, for example in a marketing booklet containing the music for the Allies' National Anthems.[32] Bovril was also shown refreshing the Boer War wounded. Back home, the dozens of young khaki-clad boys who comprised the Bovril War Cables service presented civilians with a striking patriotic image as they cycled energetically, displaying the name 'Bovril', around Greater London while delivering telegrams with breaking Boer War news for display in homes, schools and shops. A 1915 poster showing a drawing of a munitions worker fortified by Bovril was echoed a year later with photographs of the strong torsos of munitions workers testifying to the 'splendid health and energy … [from] the wonderful body-building powers of Bovril'.[33] This complex advert brings together the same themes of physical strength, patriotism and the proven power of Bovril.[34]

The public reaction

We can interpret the messages that advertisers were trying to convey, but the public reaction is less visible. Cocoa was already a commonplace food, and while food adulteration was the subject of much political discussion and consumer concern, Cadbury's Cocoa Essence was not usually a matter of public discussion. Instead, both Bovril and Plasmon were mentioned regularly in popular culture. Bovril's 'Alas! My poor brother' catchphrase was widely appropriated to parody a range of issues within British culture in the press, demonstrating a broadly affectionate public response to Bovril's slogans and images, and consumer adoption of its iconic representation of masculinity, national pride, endeavour, strength and health. Plasmon was frequently mentioned in novels, travel writing, cookery books and women's-page newspaper columns, but it also became a target of satire.[35] For example, the author of a popular volume of 'discursive jottings written from the point of view of a member of the aristocracy, obliged, through stress of circumstances to live among the middle classes', discusses his Plasmon-eating wife's hygienic regime.[36] He moans that 'Once let the subject of Health take firm possession of the mind, and no other occupation is necessary or even possible. It claims all day and night for its own.'[37] For this author, at least, the scientific pursuit of health through eating Plasmon and other faddish foods was a ridiculous and stereotypically middle-class practice.

Turning foods into scientific objects

Advertisements were designed to engage consumers. The symbols that they used can show us what advertisers considered important to the buying public. Advertisers created associations with many different material things: grand buildings, schoolrooms and scientific spaces; the images, names and testimonials of eminent scientists as well as their scientific objects and language; and popular icons of patriotism, from John Bull and his ox to the Union Jack. These were symbols of strength, authority and pride.

The beautifully constructed mythical and 'real' bodies in advertisements portray the fashionable ideal masculinity, a respectable body which showed no signs of degeneration or decadence. While women were largely absent from advertisements that mentioned proteins and strength, they, the housekeepers, may have decided whether to buy these commodities for their men. The appreciation of the ideal male body that was displayed across élite and popular culture suggests that both men and women aspired to this, for themselves or their loved ones. Food manufacturers were busy persuading them that this could be achieved through physical activity and consumption. They used the authoritative symbols of science and patriotism, carefully tailored to specific social groups' agendas about health, morality and embodiment, to link their products to their aspirations and fears. In this age of nutrition science, consumerism and scarcity (for some), eating was not a matter of simply assuaging hunger – it rarely has been. Proper eating and feeding were presented as part of a moral and patriotic duty which required ordinary people to engage with science through consumption, and thereby apply the technologies of modernity to their own bodies. Bovril, Plasmon and Cadbury's Cocoa Essence were not just foods; they were presented as modern articles that could transform bodies into useful and beautiful objects.

Notes

1. Ludmilla Jordanova, *The Look of the Past: Visual and Material Evidence in Historical Practice* (Cambridge: Cambridge UP, 2012).
2. James Crichton-Browne, *Delusions in Diet: Or, Parcimony in Nutrition*, (London: Funk and Wagnalls Company, 1910); Anita Guerrini, 'Health, National Character and the English Diet in 1700', *Studies in History and Philosophy of Science Part C* 43 (2) (June 2012) 349–56.
3. William Brock, *Justus Von Liebig: The Chemical Gatekeeper* (Cambridge: Cambridge UP, 1997).
4. For consumption, see: Derek Oddy, 'Working-Class Diets in Late Nineteenth-Century Britain', *Economic History Review*, 23 2 (1970) 314–23, 319; for requirements, see: Robert Hutchison, *Food and the Principles of Dietetics* (London, 1900), p. 27.
5. Edward J. Chamberlin and Sander L. Gilman, *Degeneration: The Dark Side of Progress* (New York: Columbia UnP, 1985); John Burnett, *Plenty and Want: A Social History of Diet in England from 1815 to the Present Day*, 3rd edn. (London: Routledge, 1989).
6. E.g. Andrew Wilson, *The Modern Home Physician* (London: Caxton, 1905).
7. J. Othick, 'The Cocoa and Chocolate Industry in the Nineteenth Century', in *The Making of the Modern British Diet*, eds. D. J. Oddy and D. S. Miller (London: Croom Helm, 1976), pp. 77–90.
8. Cadbury's advertisement, *Food, Drugs and Drink*, 15 October 1892, p. 12.
9. Peter Atkins, *Liquid Materialities: A History of Milk, Science and the Law* (Farnham: Ashgate, 2010).
10. 'Surplus Milk', *The County Gentleman: A Sporting Gazette and Agricultural Journal* (London 26 June 1886) 812.
11. Robert Scherer, *Casein; Its Preparation and Technical Utilisation*, trans. Charles Salter (London: Scott, Greenwood & Son, 1906).
12. 'The Medical, Surgical, and Hygienic Exhibition', *Lancet*, 31 May 1902: p. 1557. Hutchison says Plasmon is the cheapest.
13. Edward Tufte, *The Visual Display of Quantitative Information* (Cheshire, CT: Graphics, 1983).
14. Brock; Edinburgh City Archive, The Records of John Lawson Johnston & Bovril Ltd collection (BA), SL240/8/6/2, MS Hugh Lawson Johnston, *History of the Early Years of Bovril*, n.d.
15. BA, SL240/7/1/6/1, 'The Battle of the Beef Extracts: What "Bovril" says on the subject.', *The Pelican*, 26 January 1895.
16. BA, SL240/8/6/1, Printer's proof, Pentagon, 'Bovril and its New Home in London', *Grocery*, 2, February 1900; '300 Food Experts see Bovril made. Speech by Sir James Crichton-Browne.', *The Times*, 10 November 1909, p. 4.
17. Anson Rabinbach, *The Human Motor: Energy, Fatigue, and the Origins of Modernity* (Berkeley: U California P, 1992).
18. Michael Hatt, 'Physical Culture: The Male Nude and Sculpture', *After the Pre-Raphaelites: Art and Aestheticism in Victorian England*, ed. Elizabeth Prettejohn (Manchester: Manchester UP, 1999), p. 243.
19. David Waller, *The Perfect Man: The Muscular Life and Times of Eugen Sandow, Victorian Strongman* (Brighton: Victorian Secrets, 2011).
20. Peter Hadley, *The History of Bovril Advertising* (London: Bovril, 1972).
21. Plasmon trade card, c.1900, Author's collection (AC); Cadbury's advertisement, *Illustrated London News*, 29 December 1888, p. 795.
22. Eustace Miles, *Better Food for Boys* (London: George Bell, 1901).
23. Ina Zweiniger-Bargielowska, *Managing the Body: Beauty, Health, and Fitness in Britain 1880–1939* (Oxford: Oxford UP, 2010).
24. Eustace Miles, *How to Remember Without Memory Systems or With Them* (London, 1901).
25. Miles, *Better Food*, p.vii.
26. Hall, D.E., *Muscular Christianity: Embodying the Victorian Age* (Cambridge: Cambridge UP, 1994).
27. Carol Adams, *The Sexual Politics of Meat: A Feminist-Vegetarian Critical Theory* (New York: Continuum, 2000), p. 51.

28. *Illustrated London News*, 9 November 1889, p. 30.
29. 'Three Well Known Institutions', postmark 4 April 1907, AC.
30. 'British to the backbone' trade card (n.d.), AC.
31. *Daily Express*, 29 January 1916, p. 1.
32. Allies' National Anthems (London: Bovril, n.d.), AC.
33. *Graphic*, 28 October 1916, p. 523.
34. For other advertisements see Hadley.
35. C.W. Earle, *A Third Pot-Pourri* (London: Smith, Elder, & Co, 1903).
36. G.W.E. Russell, *A Londoner's Log-Book, 1901–1902* (London: Smith, Elder, & Co, 1902).
37. Russell, pp. 198–99.

Nefs: Ships of the Table and the Origins of Etiquette

David C. Sutton

Introduction: keeping a distance

At the Oxford Symposium of 2012 I presented some thoughts on 'surprise stuffings', that curious medieval idea of filling a pie with live animals – most frequently birds, rabbits or frogs – which then invaded the dining hall when the pie was opened. There was special reference to the English nursery rhyme about 'four-and-twenty blackbirds baked in a pie'.

In trying to find an explanation for these strange banqueting practices, the idea of 'social distance' seemed to be paramount. These were rich people's entertainments, utterly remote and distinct from the ways of peasants, workers or burghers, and adopted by the ruling classes for that very reason. To succeeding generations, however, they appeared ludicrous and outmoded:

> To the modern reader there is a strong element of the ridiculous about these *entremets* exuberances. We are prompted to remember that the French word for stuffing is *farce*. A highly critical assessment of these old-fashioned excesses began during the fastidious reign of King Louis XIV. From around 1660 new attitudes of gastronomic taste-matching, serious appreciation and respect for the flavour of each individual food were becoming the norm in France. The self-indulgence of the *entremets* was seen as archaic, disrespectful and ridiculous. A key destructive text was *Le repas ridicule* (1666) by Boileau (Nicolas Boileau-Despréaux). Within a decade of its publication, the medieval *entremets* had disappeared.[1]

Dispensing with these archaic medieval usages, however, did not mean that the rulers did not want to continue to keep a great social distance between their world and that of the ruled. Indeed, the requirement for distance, on formal occasions and especially at mealtimes, actually grew during the sixteenth and seventeenth centuries.

King Henri III of France was one of the first to insist upon a clear separation between the kingly presence and his immediate entourage. Although his circle of male favourites known as *les mignons* caused much scandal by their elegant and effeminate manners around the King, in fact Henri insisted that there should be strict rules separating them from him and also that they should wear special specified clothes and footwear when entering his presence.

The development which was encouraged by Henri III and strongly reinforced by Louis XIII and Louis XIV was from separation between one social group and another, between the rich as a group and the poor as a group, to a much more hierarchical

Nefs: Ships of the Table and the Origins of Etiquette

pyramid of privilege and relationships, with the king alone at the top. One fascinating manifestation of the new separation was the highly exclusive use of *nefs* (imitation ships with a prescribed place on the banqueting table) in royal banquets.

France in general and Versailles in particular represented the European model for banqueting in this later period. The practices were admired, imitated and treated as the aspirational standard for all the courts of Europe. Several English kings, from as early as King Richard II, proudly displayed their own *nefs*, and a number of popes, including Benedict XIII, adorned their tables at papal banquets with strange and worldly *nefs*. (The *nef* of Benedict XIII extruded fifteen serpents' tongues.)

In two of the less well-known great museums of France, the visitor can trace the evolution of the *nef* from a distinguished piece of tableware to a fabulously special symbol of royalty. At Cluny (Musée National du Moyen Âge), for the thirteenth and fourteenth centuries, one finds simple and elegant *navettes*, table-boats for incense or fine perfumes. At Écouen (Musée National de la Renaissance), for the sixteenth century, they have the extraordinarily elaborate *nef-automate*, mistakenly named after the Holy Roman Emperor Charles V, with its clockwork princes passing deferentially before the emperor, clockwork trumpeters and drummer, and even clockwork mini-bellows to simulate gunfire. This *nef* would propel itself onto the table of the emperor (probably Rudolf II) before beginning its marvellous automated performance. Between the thirteenth and the sixteenth centuries a fine piece of tableware had become a table-extravaganza.

Nefs and the social order

Tableware can symbolize a whole social order. Tureens, *surtouts de table*, pyramids, salt cellars, candlesticks and fruit-bowls, different types of knife and fork, elaborate dishes and artistic handles: these utensils help provide a definition of a historical stratified society.

The *nef*, literally a nave or a ship, became the most exclusive of all the pieces of tableware found on the grandest tables. It would be a wonderful piece of craftsmanship, an intricate representation of a ship which could be small enough to serve as a salt-cellar or large enough to contain a set of towels for the king's toilet.

Bridget Ann Henisch writes with wry humour of *nefs* in her *Fast and Feast*:

> The *nef* was an irresistibly elaborate confection, offering the craftsman unlimited opportunities to show off, with spider's webs of rigging, Lilliputian anchors, diminutive cannon, microscopic bags and bales. Sometimes large enough to hold its owner's napkin and cutlery as well as salt, it had all the charm of a doll's house. Richard II owned one whose forecastle was crowded with eight tiny men holding up the banners of France. Awkward pauses in a feast could be eased when a *nef* was trundled in a stately progress along the table.[2]

The most important characteristic of the *nef* is that its use in secular banquets was reserved for the king or emperor alone. It was consequently even more exclusive within the hierarchy of tableware than the *cadenas*, a similarly grand and ornate vessel which could, however, be used by queens, princes, dukes and other members of royal families, and which often served as a splendid container for forks, knives and spoons.

The great age of the *nef* was that of Louis XIV in France, when every particular of tableware and table manners was refined to the most minute detail. The *nef*, followed by the *cadenas*, came to represent the apogee of the system of etiquette at table which became predominant in the seventeenth century. The Duc de Luynes, writing in 1738 but about the court of Louis XIV, described how all the ladies of the court had to pass by the *nef* on their way to the King's supper, and would offer to the *nef* 'une profonde révérence'.[3]

Other descriptions indicate that before the arrival of the King, the *nef* would be ceremoniously brought into the room and taken to its side-table. All courtiers present would gravely salute the *nef*, the vessel clearly representing the royal presence itself. Before the sovereign's arrival, several armed guards would stand by to protect his *nef*.

The appearance of the table, and the role of the *nefs* and the other exclusive items of tableware, often attracted more attention from the commentators on banquets than the food being consumed. It was essential that the food should meet the criteria for fine dining and good taste, and that the foods selected should be of exclusive high-society quality and type (see Table 1); but the most important attribute of the foods served seemed to be their presentation and appearance within the whole *tableau* of the banquet.

In *L'art de bien traiter*, published in 1674, the author known to us only as L.S.R. makes clear the expectations of his age, and the way in which that age saw its approach to banqueting. What is now looked for in a grand meal, in the view of L.S.R., is not the prodigious abundance of the great tables of the past, nor their use of so many diverse and exotic spices, but 'the exquisite choice of meats, the finesse of the seasonings, the politeness and correctness with which they are served, quantities which are proportionate to the numbers of people present, and finally the general arrangement of matters which make an essential contribution to the appearance of a meal, in which both the mouth and the eyes find their delights'.[4] This is a canonical statement of the rules and the attitudes which governed the banqueting tables of the age of Louis XIV, and it reveals the equal importance given to the exquisiteness of the food and to the manner of its presentation. We note the strong emphasis on politeness, correctness and order. And within the extension of careful arrangement into a prescribed and unchangeable order, we are seeing that the supreme position of the king at table is paralleled by the supreme position of the *nef*.

Meaning and significance

What significance should we attach to these magnificent pieces of tableware? The answer is clearly symbolic and representational, rather than related to any real table function. Whilst objects reserved for royal use would naturally be of splendid and

Nefs: Ships of the Table and the Origins of Etiquette

elaborate appearance, the primary purpose of the *nef* was to emphasize and symbolize hierarchy and the distance between the strata in society. In the context of grand banquets, the distances being emphasized were those between the king and his dukes (even occasionally the king and his brother)[5] and then between the dukes and the gentlemen courtiers, but, clearly and overtly, these gulfs in status were themselves a guarantee of the further gulf between the gentlemen and the common people. At the courts of Louis XIV and Louis XV, the dukes had no access to the *nef*, while the gentlemen courtiers had no access to the *cadenas*. The common people, of course, had no access to anything.

Reading the accounts of social distance at the court of Louis XIV by writers such as the Duc de Saint-Simon and the Marquis de Dangeau, as well as the Duc de Luynes, there can be no doubt that these ostentatious marks of respect and reverence, were taken with the greatest possible seriousness. They may recall the fine ironies of Marcel Proust and the entertaining snobberies of his Mme Verdurin, but there was no irony at all at the court of the Roi Soleil. On the contrary, the elaborate deferences were designed to reinforce a humourless ideology based firmly on the 'monarchie de droit divin' (known in English as 'the divine right of kings').[6]

Furniture as well as tableware played a role in this structure. We read, for example, of one banquet where the King was present and seated on his throne-chair, and it seems that, almost as a natural consequence, all the other diners, without exception, were obliged to sit on rows of benches (in accordance, in fact, with the etymology of the word 'banquet').

Access to items of tableware and furniture was thus highly symbolic of status. Status also required meticulous attention to placement at table, where the hierarchy of seating arrangement was critical. Today, the best-remembered feature of this obsessive interest in placement at table is the idea of being seated above or below the salt.[7]

Other utensils at great tables

Paintings and designs of great tables between about 1550 and 1750 show the prominence accorded to beautifully made and exquisitely decorated tableware. The iconography shows table after table adorned and even dominated by tureens and pyramids, symmetrically spaced and extravagantly designed. The elaborate lids of some of the tureens seem sometimes to resemble Burmese temples or Mongol war-helmets; often the best comparison, however, is with the baroque architectural domes which began to appear on European buildings around 1600. The pyramids and flower-bowls were more exclusively decorative than the tureens (and are therefore ranked higher in the hierarchies of Table 1), and they are similarly distinguished by highly wrought baroque design and embellishment.

At the lower end of the hierarchy of tableware in this same period, we also note the rise of the fork and the decline in status of the knife. The table-fork was gradually introduced into the two leading civilizations of Europe, the Byzantine and the Italian, from the eleventh to the fifteenth centuries. By the fifteenth century, forks were specifically mentioned in Italian cookery books, although they were little known at the time in countries further north, including France and England. In the sixteenth century, the Florentine Queen of France Caterina de' Medici was said to have introduced the use of forks to the French courts of her husband Henri II and her sons Francis II, Charles IX and Henri III, insisting at the same time upon a distinction between serving forks and eating forks.

In his 1605 work *Les hermaphrodites*, looking back to the times of Caterina de' Medici, Thomas Artus, sieur d'Embry, mocked the fork-using pretensions of the court of Henri III. He reports in apparent amazement that the courtiers never touched meat with their fingers, only with forks, no matter how difficult the pieces might be to pick up, and that even the salads were picked up with forks – 'they prefer to have this little forked instrument touch their mouths rather than their fingers'. He smugly enjoys the vegetable course, as the less-skilled fork-users struggle with the artichokes, asparagus, peas and beans and drop food into their plates on the way to their open mouths.

The two-pronged fork, having more of the appearance of a weapon, was the first form to emerge and remained predominant until the mid-seventeenth century. Thereafter the more 'civilized' three-pronged or four-pronged fork became more and more the norm, and by 1750 the two-pronged fork, scourge of the elegant pea-eater, had virtually disappeared.

The rise of the fork was accompanied by the decline of the knife, and especially the sharp knife. One well-known story is that Cardinal Richelieu was so exasperated by a courtier's habit of picking his teeth with the point of his knife that he had all the points of all the man's knives ground down and blunted. The fashion caught on, according to the story, and other courtiers felt that they had no choice but to follow suit and blunt their own knives. Even if the story is (like those concerning Caterina de' Medici) apocryphal, its timing would be historically accurate, because during the years of the Cardinals Richelieu and Mazarin the triumph of the fork over the sharp knife became complete.

The hierarchy of tableware is paralleled by a hierarchy of foodstuffs and is accompanied by a new insistence upon norms of good behaviour and etiquette. It was essential for everyone at court to abide by elaborate codes of social behaviour, which were clearly and repeatedly enumerated, and which came to be widely known as 'etiquette'.

These formative years for etiquette and formalized polite behaviour saw the publication of innumerable instructive works whose title began with the word *Traité*, and especially with *Traité de savoir-vivre*. (The unwary reader should not imagine, however, that the celebrated *Traité de savoir-vivre à l'usage des jeunes générations* by Raoul Vaneigem, published in 1967, is a late version of this sort of manual of behaviour. Vaneigem was a 'situationist' revolutionary in the 1960s, advocating subversion, violent resistance and refusal to work; and his book-title is elegantly ironic.)

Nefs: Ships of the Table and the Origins of Etiquette

Most of the *Traités de savoir-vivre* during the reign of Louis XIV gave minute instructions about what was considered to be acceptable behaviour in high society and what was considered to be 'good taste'. The concept of good taste extended far beyond the oral-sensory, and included good judgement about matters as varied as choice of shoes, when to remove one's hat, how to hold a fork, how to address a lady, and the correct way to fold table-linen.

Good taste was defined in the manuals as distinctively urban. The rural and the regional were disdained, in matters of food, behaviour and ways of speaking. Regional cuisine in particular was marginalized. No matter how delicious or how gastronomic in composition, a dish which could be classified as rural or regional (such as roast duck with turnips or cassoulet with partridge) could not be accepted at court.

Table 1 shows the place of *nefs* within the wider context of etiquette, good taste and social order. It presents five analogous hierarchies of people, tableware and foods as they would be either valued in the banqueting hall, or excluded from the banqueting hall.

AT TABLE	ON TABLE	FISH	FRUIT	VEGETABLES
King	*Nefs*	Turbot	Dates	Asparagus
Royal family	*Cadenas*	Sturgeon	Peaches	Artichokes
Dukes	*Surtouts de table*	Brill	Apricots	Peas
Marquesses	Pyramids	Sole	Cherries	Truffles
Counts	Flower bowls	Red mullet	Pears	*Cèpes*
Viscounts	Tureens (*terrines*)	Bream	Medlars	Cauliflowers
Barons	Food bowls	Sea bass	Raspberries	Sprouts
Knights	Dishes	Cod	Blueberries	Broad beans
Courtiers	Plates	Gurnard	Apples	Mushrooms
Ladies	Salt & pepper	Sardine	Quince	Chestnuts
Middle classes	Forks	Herring	Strawberries	Leeks
Servants	Spoons	Mackerel	Gooseberries	Onions
Common people	Knives	Sprats		Garlic

Table 1. Five examples of table and food hierarchies, 1550–1750

These hierarchies bring in a number of conventions and beliefs which match or parallel the power-structure of the court. With fruit and vegetables, for example, we find an intriguing combination of rarity-value and exoticism with perishability and also height on the plant. So figs arrive at their number-one position by scoring highly on exoticism and perishability and height on the tree, whilst garlic and the other bulbs are ranked at the lowest level both because they grow below soil-level and because of their close association with the common people. With fish, there is a hierarchy of flavour and texture which places turbot at the head, but also a convention that fish which are caught singly are food for the rich whereas fish which swim in shoals are food for the poor. Sweet chestnuts, a staple food of the poor in Mediterranean lands, do indeed grow high in the trees, but they are collected when ripe amongst the leaves on the ground and belong in the lower part of such food hierarchies (several French writers have indignantly attributed the alleged laziness of Corsican peasants to the fact that their favourite staple, the chestnut, simply falls out of the trees for them to eat).

The clear purpose of these hierarchies is to state that, in line with the principles of the divine right of kings, everything has its place in a natural order, everything is in hierarchical obedience, and between the highest-ranked and the lowest-ranked there is a huge social distance. As Norbert Elias stressed in his works on the sociology of courtly behaviour, the distance between the king and his courtiers served as a guarantee of the distance between the courtiers and the common people. As a result of this social stratification, it was inconceivable that the king would eat garlic, and inconceivable that the peasant would eat asparagus or artichokes.

The exclusivity of asparagus was especially evident. Jean-Louis Flandrin, for example, cites two fairly late luxurious menus (of 1751 and 1757) in each of which asparagus is the only food to appear twice.[8] Asparagus and artichokes also formed part of an élite class of delicate, aromatic and urine-scenting foods which were typically eaten accompanied by water rather than by wine. In an urban context, pure water was also an exclusive product.

The food hierarchies began to disappear, or at least to lose their sense of compulsion, during the latter half of the eighteenth century, and by the time of *La cuisinière bourgeoise* (1774) we can find recipes which talk easily of using onions and mushrooms – which in earlier times were amongst the ingredients most rigidly defined as food of the poor. Such was the disdain for mushrooms that we find several earlier sources which describe them as 'les excréments de la terre'.[9] During our suggested period of 1550–1750 the food classifications amounted almost to taboos. The rich abjured hard cheese, salted fish, onions and garlic. Proverbs described leeks as 'the asparagus of the poor'. Poor people themselves would say that they had no stomach for artichokes or peaches, and would affect to fear to eat such elevated foods even if they had the chance.

Etiquette

The place at table of the *nef* and the *cadenas*, the blunting of knives, the rise of the fork and the consolidation of food hierarchies all naturally accompanied the new interest in etiquette.

Etiquette, initiated in the sixteenth century partly to reduce the danger of violence at table, followed principles of restraint and decorum first proposed by Erasmus of Rotterdam. Dozens of manuals instructed that etiquette depended upon model behaviour as well as implements. The underlying bases for etiquette were repression of natural instincts, deference, self-denial, physical constraint, placidity and patience. Key features included:

Nefs: Ships of the Table and the Origins of Etiquette

Upright and uncomfortable seating positions, with elbows never placed on the table.

Eating tiny portions, so as to be able to reply at any time; no storing of food in cheeks.

Prohibition of belching, farting, spitting or laughing; never discussing the food served.

Waiting to be served, never serving oneself, never asking to be served, leaving the best portions for others.

Not licking clean any knife, fork, spoon, plate or dish.

No wine, and often no glasses, on the table; wine-service from a side-table, to be consumed in a single draught and the glass returned.

No re-arrangement of bones or other uneaten pieces on the plate.

No replacement of food in the serving dish.

No use of the fingers.

No staining of clothing, hence copious covering with napkins.

Eating with slowness and deliberation.

Eating without noise: no slapping of stomachs, smacking of lips or clattering of cutlery.

Ladies affecting not to hear any licentious conversation, and being prepared to leave the table rather than be seen to smile or laugh.

In each action (prayers, washing, eating, drinking, arising) awaiting the moves of persons of higher rank.

Anyone who as a child was perplexed as to why they should not put their elbows on the table will recognize the extraordinary durability of these rules of etiquette. They came into being within a clearly defined historical timeframe: in 1520 they did not exist; by 1660 they were standard courtly behaviour.

The origins of etiquette, as a new code of polite behaviour, can be traced to Erasmus, and in particular to his *De civilitate morum puerilium libellus* (A Handbook on Good Manners for Children), which was written in 1530. Erasmus is sometimes portrayed as a dull moralist. In fact, he is a humorous writer (sometimes intentionally, sometimes unintentionally) with a splendid range of original phrases and expressions.

Here are a few examples from the text of Erasmus, which show both his distinctive style and his role in laying down the origins of etiquette:

It's inappropriate to wink at another person. For what is it other than doing yourself out of an eye? We should leave that gesture to tuna fish and one-eyed mythical metal-workers.

It's absurd to lick your lips repeatedly. Pursing one's lips, as if preparing them for a kiss, used to be considered appealing amongst the people of Germany.

It's rude to look around you as you drink, in the manner of a stork turning his neck round towards his back, in case you leave a drip at the bottom, which is impolite.

> To swallow whole pieces of food in one gulp is the practice of storks and clowns. Gnawing on bones is for dogs; using a knife to strip meat away is well-mannered. Greedy gobbling is for ruffians. Some cram so much into their mouths at once that their cheeks swell out on both sides like a pair of bellows.
> It's also rude to shake your head and toss your hair, to cough unnecessarily, to clear your throat noisily, likewise to scratch your head, to pick your ears, to wipe your nose, to stroke your face as if wiping away your shame, to rub the back of your head and to shrug your shoulders, a characteristic we see in some Italians.[10]

These typical phrases formed a basis for parental guidance for more than four centuries, and the rules of etiquette survive in many of the absurdities of white tablecloth and Michelin-approved behaviour. The manuals and treatises on proper conduct avoid any positive reference to enjoyment, pleasure in food or savouring of flavours, and emphasize instead deference, propriety, correctness and restraint.

Conclusion

This review of the wider context shows that *nefs* played a key role in some major changes in the history of feasts and banquets. There is a close inter-relationship between the various rules and hierarchies (animal, vegetable and mineral): structures of society based on huge social distances; the curious hierarchy of tableware with *nefs* at the apex; the concept of food hierarchies, with the clearest of divisions between the food of the rich and the food of the poor; and the new systems of table-behaviour and etiquette which began to emerge during the sixteenth century.

All these inter-related hierarchies reflect the social norms, and hence the banqueting norms, of a highly stratified society between about 1550 and 1750. And these norms of the banqueting tables of high society spread down to influence attitudes in all sectors of society – symbolized perhaps at the lowest levels by the abject status of the sharp knife and the garlic-bulb.

In conclusion, I would like to offer a way of interpreting the significance of the *nef* by reference to another fine piece of tableware which might in many respects be regarded as its opposite: the loving cup.

The loving cup, an ornate drinking vessel for toasts and special occasions, to be shared around the table, has a history dating back to the Anglo-Saxons. Some of the traditions which pertain to loving cups come from a need for self-protection during the banquets of a warlike society. Most obviously, there is a reduced risk of poisoning with a shared drinking vessel, but there is also the tradition of the companion who stood up next to the drinker, which derives from a need for protection from stabbing in the chest whilst in a vulnerable position, drinking with the head thrown back. Loving cups remain a cherished part of the dining rituals of several of the historic livery companies of London, and the loving cup of the Worshipful Company of Distillers is still circulated at their banquets accompanied by daggers.[11]

Nefs: Ships of the Table and the Origins of Etiquette

There is a striking contrast in the traditions associated with these two beautiful pieces of tableware. The traditions associated with the loving cup survive into the twenty-first century, whereas the traditions of the *nef* disappeared with the absolute monarchy which it represented. The loving cup is Anglo-Saxon, participative, inclusive, and shared by everyone around the banqueting table. The *nef* is Norman, feudal, exclusive, at the peak of a hierarchy and strongly associated with an extreme form of monarchy, with the king all alone at its head – alone with his *nef*.

Notes

1. David C. Sutton, '"Four and Twenty Blackbirds Baked in a Pie": A History of Surprise Stuffings', in *Wrapped & Stuffed Foods: Proceedings of the Oxford Symposium on Food and Cookery 2012*, ed. Mark McWilliams (Totnes: Prospect Books, 2013), pp. 285–94, esp. p.286.
2. B. A. Henisch, *Fast and Feast: Food in Medieval Society* (University Park, PA: Pennsylvania State University Press, 1976), p. 164.
3. Sandrine Krikorian, *Les rois à table : iconographie, gastronomie et pratiques des repas officiels de Louis XIII à Louis XVI* (Aix-en-Provence: Presses universitaires de Provence, 2011), p.38, and pp. 30, 65, 77. See also Eric Birlouez, *À la table des seigneurs, des moines et des paysans du Moyen Âge* (Rennes: Éditions Ouest-France, 2011); *Fêtes gourmandes au moyen âge*, textes Jean-Louis Flandrin, Carole Lambert; photographies Claude Huyghens ; réalisation de recettes Yves Pinard (Paris: Imprimerie Nationale Éditions, 1998): esp. p. 46: 'La *nef*, les salières et les tranchoires'; and *La fiesta en la Europa de Carlos V: Real Alcázar Sevilla* (Sevilla : Sociedad Estatal para la Conmemoración de los Centenarios de Felipe II y Carlos V, 2000): esp. pp. 334–36: 'Naveta joyel'. ('*Naveta*' is the Spanish word for '*Nef* '.)
4. Translated from L.S.R: *L'art de bien traiter*, 1674, Préface.
5. The brother of Louis XIV, Philippe d'Orléans (1640–1701), known as 'Monsieur', was the cause of much embarrasment to the king because of his appearance and behaviour. In recent decades he has achieved an established place in the new discipline of gay history. Saint-Simon dwells on his excessive use of perfume, the rouge on his cheeks and his wearing of rings and bracelets. It is said that his preference for wearing women's clothes was encouraged by Cardinal Mazarin from an early age, as an exaggerated ploy to ensure that he was no threat to his brother's power. In spite of the vexations he caused the king, his place at table and at court was always rigidly defined and respected.
6. The divine right of kings is usually described as an extinct historical idea, but this is not quite the case. The lingering influence of this divine right can be seen, for example, in the reluctance of the present Queen of England to contemplate Dutch-style abdication.
7. The expression 'below the salt' reflects both the monetary value of salt and the elaborate vessels in which the salt would typically be served. The salt would usually be situated half-way down the principal table of a banquet, and the social importance of diners could therefore be determined by their place at table as measured against the place of the salt.
8. Jean-Louis Flandrin, *L'ordre des mets* (Paris: Odile Jacob, 2002): first colour plate and p. 123. See also pp. 41–44 and 242–49.
9. 'Les excréments de la terre': used by e.g. Nicolas de Nancel (1581); also Jean Bauhin (died 1613), cited in Madeleine Ferrières, *Nourritures canailles* (Paris : Seuil, 2007), p. 30.
10. Erasmus of Rotterdam: *A Handbook on Good Manners for Children*, trans. Eleanor Merchant. (London: Preface, 2008), pp. 8, 17, 47, 51, 55, 56, 68–69.
11. See The Worshipful Company of Distillers, 'Loving Cup Ceremony', *The Worshipful Company of Distillers* (2013) <www.distillers.org.uk/activities/loving-cup-ceremony>.

Turkish Coffee: *arte* & *factum*, Paraphernalia of a Ritual from Ember to Cup

Aylin Öney Tan and Nihal Bursa

Coffee became an exceptional beverage by being 'intoxicating, heartwarming and utterly pleasurable', as Claudia Roden puts it.[1] Humans have contrived seemingly endless paraphernalia and rituals around it. This study is an attempt to understand a particular type of coffee, Turkish coffee, by examining its physical processes of preparation. It will focus on the interactive relationship between Turkish coffee as a tasteful drink and the rituals of its preparation through the material culture related to processes from roasting raw coffee beans to enjoying the finished cup. While the origins of coffee as a plant and a beverage are mythical, the history of the Turkish method of crafting coffee can be evidenced through its particular methods of preparation. The long pedigree of instruments used during various processes, from roasting to serving, allows us to trace the ways and methods of the craft.

According to popular myth, humans owe much to goats in discovering the coffee plant in Ethiopia.[2] But it was humans, not goats, who found ways to process the fruits of the plant into a drink. Before becoming a hot beverage, coffee was consumed as food. Besides being chewed as a fruit, ripe cherries of the plant were used as ingredients in bread or pounded, mixed with fat and moulded into cylindrical chunks. In reliable accounts of Arab writers, coffee history is traced back to the last quarter of the fourteenth century in Yemen.[3] Records of its use as a brewed beverage until that time are vague, but there are writings claiming that coffee was popular as a drink among Sufi religious sects.[4]

Although not suitable for coffee planting (except in Yemen and Mecca), Ottoman territories started to develop the cultural habitat of a particular type of coffee drinking in the sixteenth century. From that period on, we observe the evolution of this coffee making process through its related instruments and methods. As it became popular, certain customs and manners developed that made coffee a key element in the process of socialization. It was introduced to Europe and the rest of the world through the Ottoman Empire and soon became a widespread phenomenon. This historical aspect requires broad discussion beyond the scope of this present study. However, the social context of the customs and manners developed around preparing and serving Turkish coffee will be discussed in relation to a whole range of equipment used in these processes. This discussion will focus on coffee as a cultural artefact that gives pleasure to the eye and the palate.

Paraphernalia of a Ritual from Ember to Cup

The preparation of Turkish coffee is a particular method common to Ottoman geography. It is one of the earliest known surviving methods of preparing coffee. This particular process can simply be described as simmering powdered coffee in a special pot, in which finely ground, freshly roasted beans are brought to the boil, with or without sugar, twice or thrice before serving the frothy liquid with the grounds. The best Turkish coffee is made from medium-roast high-quality Arabica beans ground to an extremely fine powder. The distinctive experience of drinking Turkish coffee comes from this fine grinding, giving rise to a velvety froth, satisfying mouth-feel and unique fragrance. Later, coffee making and serving became an art in Istanbul palaces and in the Ottoman court, an art with an etiquette and paraphernalia of its own, including a variety of utensils contrived to store, roast, cool, grind, brew and serve coffee. Serving coffee developed into a ceremony involving elaborate tools and vessels. Within the course of this study, storage boxes, braziers, roasters, coolers, mortars, grinders and brewing and serving instruments will be examined in reference to their form and material. This heritage helps show how the material culture of Turkish coffee was enriched by continuous experimentation over time.

An indispensible drink in the everyday life of Ottoman people, coffee created its own culture through related artefacts and manners. It existed as a pleasure in the simple worlds of common people and in the sumptuous lives of the wealthy as well. The need for this pleasure was satisfied sometimes by itinerant coffee vendors in open markets or mosque courtyards and at other times in the sociable environment of a coffee house. Whether used in straightforward and simple service or in ceremonial presentations in splendid palaces and mansions, a rich variety of artefacts display the aesthetic preferences of the era and provide information about the material culture of coffee drinking in Ottoman lands.

The authors both firmly believe that objects tell us not just about manual processes, but also about the minds which create them. Therefore, this study will dwell on the material culture of Turkish coffee as a craft while giving particular emphasis to its design principles. Evaluations will be based on both visual and written documents in history with additional investigation of private and museum collections. Besides works of the skilled craftsmen, new design solutions for coffee preparation and presentation will also be discussed.

Turkish coffee culture offers rich ground to observe how skilled craftsmen developed ways of crafting coffee. The term skill is defined here as trained practice, and it is worth mentioning how Richard Sennett defines its development: 'All skills, even the most abstract, begin as bodily practices and technical understanding develops through powers of imagination. The first argument focuses on knowledge gained in the hand through touch and movement. The argument about imagination begins by exploring language that attempts to direct and guide bodily skill.'[5]

The knowledge through practice, accumulated over time, produces material reality which cannot be divorced from cultural expressions. This material culture speaks through craftsmanship. Craftsmanship is used here as it is defined by Sennett: 'an enduring, basic human impulse, the desire to do a job well for its own sake.'[6] Craftsmanship in this sense could be evidenced by the deep-rooted tradition of Turkish coffee preparation including the artefacts themselves. Within this tradition, a new expertise developed that required a master craftsman: the coffee-maker (*kahvecibaşı*). When coffee became an essential luxury in the Ottoman Empire, *kahvecibaşı* became a key figure among the kitchen staff in the royal palace; he was responsible for accomplishing the whole process of preparation.

Roasting and cooling

One of the most critical stages in determining the taste of coffee is its roasting and this requires careful monitoring. To guarantee consistency, the coordination of hand and mind by traditional craftsman has been replaced by high-tech coffee roasting control systems today. Beans should ideally be medium-roasted, though darker roasts are sometimes preferred for their almost burnt flavour. During the grinding process, a certain amount of heat is produced through friction; thereby, roasting should be adjusted to account for this extra heat.[7]

Traditional methods all depend on the skilled coffee-maker's tacit knowledge acquired over time. The raw green coffee beans were roasted in small quantities over embers in shallow, long-handled wrought iron roasting pans that almost resembled ladles. These were elaborately decorated, and some had stirring spoons attached. Some included innovative details, such as an additional iron plate attached to increase the thickness of its cross section to help maintain consistent heat during roasting. Drums revolving horizontally over embers were generally preferred by the ambulant coffee makers. Proper roasting requires steady heat, usually from embers contained in braziers.

The moment when beans were roasted to the desired degree was crucial. They were immediately transferred into wooden cooling pans to allow the excess oil that developed on the beans' surfaces to be absorbed. These shallow cooling pans could be plain or ornamented with carved or inlaid decoration. Forms sometimes displayed strong connections to nature. Local woods were generally used, non-resinous and impervious woods, like walnut, preferred. Some subtle interactions between wood and coffee probably occur, but the correlation between the required flavour of the coffee and the type of wood remains a matter for speculation.

Grinding and pounding

Pounding and grinding are different ways of processing coffee beans in order to get fine powder. Roasted beans were pounded in huge wooden mortars (*dibek*) with wooden or iron pestles or ground in intricately designed brass hand mills (*kahve değirmeni*). Pounding crushes and smashes the roasted beans, causing the oil in the beans to be slightly extracted; grinding breaks the beans into particles which are comparatively dry. Hence the taste differs. Pounding is the earliest method, but it is difficult to achieve the required uniform fineness for Turkish coffee; however, aficionados of Turkish coffee swear by *dibek kahvesi*, hand-pounded in wooden mortars.[8] When it comes to hand mills, the imagination of the craftsman can easily be traced in surviving examples. Traditional Turkish hand grinders are tall, heavy brass or copper mills convenient to use at home because they enable a fine grind. The tall cylindrical body is mainly composed of two parts: the upper half holds the whole beans, while the lower half collects the coffee grounds. In early examples, the upper part is generally made out of wood or thick leather. Mill stands were usually used in coffee houses and in the great mansions. These have a large wooden base to which a square wooden mill with a drawer is attached.

Storing

The process of grinding or pounding maximizes the exposure to the air. Therefore, coffee becomes extremely vulnerable to the effects of heat, light and moisture. Traditionally, boxes made of copper, brass, wood or gilded copper (*tombak*) with two separate sections, one for coffee and one for sugar, were used to store coffee. In some cases, a detail is attached to the main body or a separate chamber is carved in the wood for holding a spoon. In the Balkans, these boxes become two separate containers, mostly made from copper or brass engraved with decorative designs. Anatolian examples are generally made from wood ranging from naively carved ones to meticulously crafted pieces although they are far from airtight.

Brewing: a Turkish method

Brewing could be defined mainly as heating coffee and water together. The earliest practice was to chew the fruit of coffee plant, which could be considered the most simple and straightforward way of extracting pleasure from coffee. This single stepped method evolved through time and across cultures ending up with a drink. Among the processes, from the plant to the cup, the brewing stage is most important in determining the character of the drink. Needless to say, the distinct character of Turkish coffee owes much to the brewing process. The traditional brewing vessel, the coffee pot, is called *cezve;* it remains a unique way of bringing coffee and water together over heat. That name is rooted in the Arabic word *cadwat*, which means 'red hot cinders' or 'tongs for embers'.[9] The most preferred type in the quest for a perfect cup of coffee is *cezve* made from thick forged copper with a particular form that has been retained throughout the centuries in Islamic and Ottoman lands. The overall form of *cezve* has three features – an enlarged base, a narrowing neck and the spout – that make the brewing process distinct.

Brewing coffee with the proper consistency requires good timing, a keen eye and long practice. A properly manufactured *cezve* is imperative for crafting a cup of good Turkish coffee. Devised for this particular brewing process, it is the product of tacit knowledge gained over time. Being a cleverly designed tool, its functionality is of utmost importance. The tapering form is large at the bottom and becomes narrow

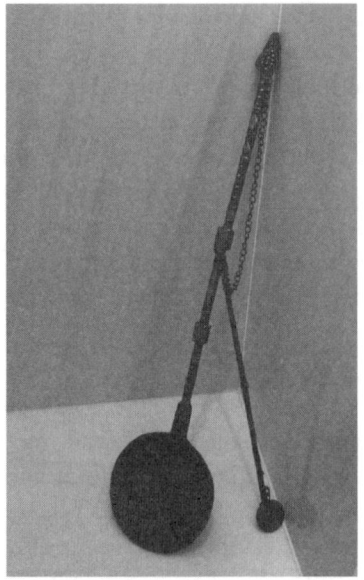

Figure 1. Wrought iron roasting ladle, stirring spoon attached.

Figure 2. Wooden cooling pan.

Figure 3. Grinder, brass and wood.

towards the top. The enlarged bottom plane increases the interface between the heat source and the copper surface of the pot. The thickness of the copper sheet affects the timing and distribution of the heat. Thicker copper's high thermal conductivity uniformly distributes heat across the inner surface of the pot. When the ground coffee and cold water mixture reaches a temperature just below boiling point, the liquid starts to rise. It should never come to a rolling boil, because this is the moment when the froth starts to form. This stage requires close monitoring and delicate timing since a good Turkish coffee has the thickest possible layer of froth on the top. The formation of the desired froth determines the moment of serving. The narrowest part of the *cezve*, the neck, helps to maximize the froth while minimizing the surface area of simmering coffee. In a well-designed *cezve*, the long spout juts directly out from the neck, curving outward to a higher level than the rim. This curved chute helps preserve the thick froth while pouring the coffee. Therefore, the level at which the liquid coffee starts to become foamy should not exceed the neck level, which also leaves enough space for the froth to rise. Comparing recently manufactured *cezves* with historical examples reveals the transformation of the relationship between the pot's pouring part and the main body.

This distinctive design can be easily discerned in other pots for brewing coffee across the eastern Mediterranean: *ibrik* (ewer), *güğüm* (large *ibrik*), *kahvedan* (flagon). The history of coffee in the region often draws on accounts of Western travellers who themselves may have relied on second-hand information, so the names and descriptions of utensils sometimes vary. In the seventeenth century, Dufour describes 'a kind of pot called *ibrik*' used to brew coffee. He wisely speculates that the pot's form contributes to the brewing process, recognizing that the enlarged surface at the bottom maximizes exposure to the heat source, therefore minimizing the boiling period. He appreciates the way the form tapers to a small mouth at the top to help contain the volatile coffee aromas.[10] The coffee pot described by Dufour – a long-spouted copper container with a lid particularly designed to brew coffee – is seemingly a kind of *cezve*. *Ibrik* is an Arabic word meaning *ewer*. Its root in Persian, compounded of two words, *ab* (water) and *rextan* (pouring), tells us much about the consumption of coffee in the mid-fifteenth century in Persia and its spread through the Middle East afterwards.

Aficionados of Turkish coffee prefer their coffee brewed slowly in thick forged copper *cezves* over moderately low heat in the firm belief that thick copper contributes a lot to the taste. A low heat extends the brewing time to keep the finely ground coffee beans in hot water long enough to extract their flavour. This brewing technique brings out acidic notes, contributing a liveliness to the coffee's flavour. The thick copper that helps make this possible was the preferred metal for traditional manufacturers; copper's various properties and capacities also made it cost-effective.[11] Apart from its physical properties which enhance brewing (and cooking as well), there may be chemical interactions with the coffee which affect the basic characteristics of the resulting drink, such as flavour, body and acidity.

Figure 4. Turkish coffee pots (jezveh), copper and brass.

Figure 5. Coffee cup, porcelain, Paris, end of 18th century.

Paraphernalia of a Ritual from Ember to Cup

Traditionally, embers in braziers were the heat source. Sand-filled trays were sometimes placed on the embers to ensure gentle and uniform heat transfer. Braziers were an indispensible part of the technical operation of roasting and brewing, but they also acted as socializing agents, gathering people around their warmth to enjoy a pleasurable cup of coffee. From the simplest in homes or coffee houses to the most ornate, they remain the heart of the space as the irresistible smell of coffee fuels communication.

A cup of pleasure through a ceremonial service

The psychological and emotional effects created by the ritual of Turkish coffee make the resulting experience tasteful both to the palate and to the eye. Serving Turkish coffee has evolved into a ceremony with its own particular set of utensils and vessels depending on where and for whom the coffee is served. The ceremony can be a modest celebration of a cup of coffee accompanied with a glass of water in traditional coffee houses or a perfect setting to display wealth, a confirmation of status among the élites. In that case, a series of exquisite pieces turns the service into an elaborate ceremony whether at a palace or in a mansion.

Given the high expectations for a good cup of coffee, the spatial organization in the house and the relationship between the served and the servant necessitated a hierarchy of utensils. Coffee prepared in the main kitchen of the palace is presented in the spaces for receiving guests, a kind of transition from back stage to the stage itself that required a few intermediary instruments, such as the *sitil* and *sitil* cloth. *Sitil* is a small, hand-held brazier suspended from three chains; it holds the coffee pot during the service. Elaborately made of silver, copper or bronze, *sitil* often has a matching coffee pot. This set is always placed over a circular, intricately embroidered cloth. The ceremony of serving coffee is usually accompanied by Turkish delight or other sweet specialities served on exquisite silver, porcelain or crystal plates. From the mid-nineteenth century on, liqueurs became a Western companion for coffee. In some opulent palaces and mansions, coffee service became so elaborate that the space was even scented by incense burners and rosewater sprinklers before coffee was served after dinner.

Of all the paraphernalia related to ceremonial service, the coffee cup has a unique place. The cup marks both the end for the one preparing coffee through a succession of stages and also the beginning of a pleasurable experience for the drinker. A quick survey of coffee cups displays the relationship between humans and the objects they create which could be defined as 'a love affair and a dependency'.[12]

Coffee was initially served in cups without handles or saucers throughout the Ottoman Empire; towards the end of eighteenth century, cups with handles came onto the scene. Long before the European discovery of porcelain at the beginning of the eighteenth century, coffee drinking was a habit in the Islamic world and in the Empire. At that period, Chinese porcelain was imported to provide tableware for the palace, but it was not used by common people.[13] During the sixteenth and seventeenth centuries,

Ottoman Iznik pottery was preferred by the rich; the modest substitute was pottery from Kütahya. Apart from practical manufacturing reasons, cups without handles seem to fit the practice of coffee drinking developed around the idea of meeting and sharing within the Sufi tradition. The cup without a handle suggests an equal openness to all directions, and therefore facilitates its transfer from hand to hand.

The search for comfort and luxury among the wealthy led to a new category of cups with holders. The cup holders were shaped to embrace the cup containing the coffee to protect hands from the heat. Making the act of drinking more dignified and ceremonial, they stand as vivid examples of how far the act of drinking coffee could be elaborated. Holders made of silver and gold, embellished sometimes with jewels and enamels, were preferred, particularly for the royal family. Copper gilded with gold, porcelain or clay with silver inlays and gold decorations (Tophane style) were also popular in wealthy circles. Some of the cup holders made from these materials were decorated with filigree, which allowed the cup holder's form to be just flexible enough to grasp the inner cup firmly.

From the eighteenth century onwards, ceramic coffee cups were produced in Iznik, Kütahya, Çanakkale and at Eyüp in Istanbul. Besides these types, Tophane-style cups – made out of pipe clay with remarkable floral decorations gilded with gold and silver – were widespread in Istanbul. These cups' earthy feel and thick clay must have created a great contrast with the refined and cold touch of porcelain introduced later to the Ottoman territories. By the beginning of the nineteenth century, prominent manufacturers of porcelain in Europe and Russia began to design porcelain coffee cups for the Ottoman Palace. Some cups were even personalized with the signature and the portrait of the sultan. As Turkish-style coffee drinking became popular among the European élite (especially in France), porcelain manufacturers like Meissen and Sèvres produced cups appropriate in size and form.

The form of the coffee cup and thickness of its porcelain undoubtedly affect the experience, and therefore pleasure, of drinking coffee. Delicate porcelain emphasizes the delicacy of Turkish coffee. The most critical part is the rim of the cup; the favourable froth at the top and the textured feeling of this particular liquid are best appreciated by sipping it across a thin rim. The fine edge allows lips and mouth to meet intimately with the light foamy structure of the froth and the fine powders in the liquid. To prepare the mouth for such an experience, Turkish coffee is served with a small glass of water which should be taken after the sweet companions and prior to coffee. It cleanses the mouth, prepares the appetite, and therefore increases the appreciation of the coffee itself. This ritual makes the gustatory experience unique; after a few sips, it allows the refreshed mouth to experience again the textured feeling created by fine grounds in the liquid.

Some accounts of Western travellers describe additional ingredients used in coffee, such as esmeramber and macun.[14] Opium sometimes accompanied coffee in coffee houses. Cemal Kafadar draws an analogy between the 'linkage of coffee' to various additives and the coffeehouse to 'interlinked activities'.[15] For example, a guild in

Cairo produced pills made from a honey and opium mixture.[16] The use of additional ingredients can be seen in some coffee cups dating back to those times. Some cups included a perforated metal cage or capsule inside the bottom surface; this small chamber helps the surprise ingredient to mix gradually with the coffee. Here the cup, seemingly passive, actively changed the coffee's flavour.

A cup of stories

For many, fortune-telling has become an indispensible complement to the pleasurable experience of drinking Turkish coffee. A cultural habit developed around coffee drinking, groups of drinkers use the coffee grounds as a trigger for soul-feeding stories. Shapes in the grounds suggest meaning, even names, and inspire a kind of psychic reading of the present and the future. Whether consoling or entertaining, the stories definitely leave one longing for the next cup. The desire to read coffee grounds may even play a role in the design of coffee cups!

Tradition vs. innovation

Until recently, the method for Turkish coffee preparation seemed to be so tied to tradition that it could never be adapted to modern technology. Turkish coffee preparation, with its careful and patient waiting over the coffee pot, simply could not be reproduced in electrical appliances. However, a design team came up with the idea of simulating the traditional process of Turkish coffee making. Observing human behaviour and studying the traditional method of making Turkish coffee, the team ended up developing a machine protected by eight patents.

Telve, the new Turkish coffee machine, is designed to simulate the process of manual preparation of coffee. To simulate spoon swirling by hand, the machine ejects water through nozzles, thereby creating a vortex that mixes the water, coffee and sugar; putting the pot on the fire is mimicked by moving a hot plate underneath the pot, gently raising the mixture into a simmer; watching the rise of the froth is done by constantly monitoring the level of coffee and water mixture by sending thousands of signals per minute to the surface; and finally the process is terminated by automatically removing the hot plate to stop heat contact. This final product is a tribute to innovation with deep roots in tradition.

Conclusion

Studying the traditional material culture used to make a cup of Turkish coffee seems to necessarily evoke all psychological and emotional factors involved in its tradition, even in this new high-tech design for brewing a valued old style of coffee. Remembering Sennett's description of craft – something that evokes 'the desire to do a job well for its own sake' – the craft of making Turkish coffee must be kept alive today to preserve these cups of pleasure. It is the understanding of the craft, rather than the physical or manual labour, that must be retained.

Notes

1. Claudia Roden, *Coffee: A Connoisseur's Companion* (London: Pavilion Books, 1994), p. 9.
2. In this ubiquitous story, one day an Ethiopian goathard notices his flock moving with unusual energy at the end of the day and staying awake through the night. The next day, he observes them in the pasture eating berries of a shrub. The story goes that he verifies his observations by tasting the berries himself.
3. Ralph Hattox, *Kahve ve Kahvehaneler; Bir Toplumsal İçeceğin Yakındoğu'daki Kökenleri*, trans. Nurettin Elhuseyni (Istanbul: Tarih Vakfı Yurt Yayınları, 1998), p. 14.
4. Hattox, pp.14–17; Hattox refers to Abd al-Qadir al-Jaziri as the most important sixteenth-century coffee writer on the spread of coffee in Yemen. He also discusses the way coffee is consumed by chewing or by drinking while dwelling on the verbs in Arabic.
5. Richard Sennett, *The Craftsman* (New Haven, CT: Yale UP, 2008), p. 10.
6. Sennett, p. 9.
7. The specifications about roasting are defined by The Association of Turkish Coffee Culture and Research and enlisted in its official website <http://www.turkkahvesidernegi.org/images/pdf/Standartlarimiz.pdf#page3>.
8. The size of 70–75% of the particles must be 75–125 microns according to the standards of Turkish coffee <http://www.turkkahvesidernegi.org/images/pdf/Standartlarimiz.pdf#page3>..
9. Sevan Nişanyan, *NişanyanSözlük* <http://www.nisanyansozluk.com>.
10. Hattox, p. 76.
11. Copper is a malleable material that becomes ductile during hot forging. Hot forging eventually makes copper extremely dense with a refined grain structure, making it strong and highly resistant to cracks and flaws. In this ages old artisanal work, a steel hammer is used to produce articulate forms in small and thin sections. Copper also has a biostatic and corrosion-resistant nature which does not allow organisms grow on its surface._
12. Neil MacGregor, *A History of the World in 100 Objects* (New York: Penguin Books, 2011), p. 13.
13. Suraiya Faroqhi and Christoph K. Neumann point out the rarity of porcelain pieces in the 1770 inventory of household utensils and vessels of a wealthy family in the Ottoman Empire; see *Soframız Nur, Hanemiz Mamur*, trans. Zeynep Yelce (Kitap Yayınevi, 2006), p. 298.
14. Hattox, p. 73.
15. Cemal Kafadar, 'A History of Coffee' <http://www.docstoc.com/docs/53906610/A-History-og-Coffee>: p. 56.
16. Hattox, p. 97.

The Material Culture of the Classical Greek Banquet

Stephanos Tanis

This essay looks at the material culture of the Greek banquet during the classical and late classical periods. In particular, it examines the equipment used in the dining chambers and kitchens of the social élites. From the broad body of sympotic material evidence – archaeological and literary records from the archaic, classical and Hellenistic periods – this study focuses on material from Delos, a PanHellenic sacred island associated with Apollo's cult and a vigorous, busy market, and from Vergina and Derveni, both sites on the periphery of Pella, the capital of Alexander the Great and his successors. The drinking equipment examined in this paper comes from five intact classical burials, two from Vergina that were probably royal and another three from Derveni that were surely high-aristocratic. The *hydriae* kitchen equipment examined here comes from the building remains of villas and marketplaces. Valuable collections of kitchen utensils come from classical and late classical Delos, an island also famous for its cooks and culinary culture.[1] References to Macedonian kitchen equipment are restricted because of the limited research on the subject.[2] Painted and plain pottery items mainly from Delos, the Vergina and Derveni material, a few masterly mosaics from Macedonia, as well as literary sources and a painted frieze, provide the frame for the following discussion on the equipment, activities and atmosphere inside both the dining chambers and the kitchens during symposia.

Figure 1. The sympotic frieze of the Aghios Athanasios Macedonian Tomb after Tsibidou-Auloniti 2005, plates 30-1. (© ΥΠΠΟ/ΙΣΤ΄)

We commence with the painted frieze of the monumental barrel-vaulted tomb at Aghios Athanasios, Thessaloniki, which dates to the last quarter of the fourth century BC.[3] The tomb's almost four-metre-long frieze uniquely encapsulates, in typical classical formulaic fashion, the world of the Greek aristocratic symposion: in the centre of the composition six reclining symposiasts enjoy themselves, entertained by two female musicians – a harpist and a flutist – and served by a young boy, while welcoming two groups of special guests coming from either side of the venue to join the party.[4] Imaginary or real, the aristocratic male gathering depicts the most important phase of the Greek banquet, the *sumposion*, drinking together, or simply *potos*, drinking, while nibbling savoury and sweet snacks, *tragemata*, served in little plates of metal or clay.

Here it seems dinner itself, the *deipnon*, has already been served.[5] Omitted from the scene for thematic reasons is all kitchen equipment; cooking activity is subtly suggested only by the presence of a dresser (*kulikeion*) loaded with plates and vessels for wine and water to be served by the *oinochoos*.[6]

We can imagine the kitchen of any such wealthy domicile – Athenian, Pellaean, Rhodian, Halikarnassean, Syracusan or Alexandrian – a short distance away, indoors, shady and cool for better preservation of cooked or raw foodstuffs, water and other liquids, spirits or not. Wine was kept in clay containers in cooler storage spaces, namely the *pithon* or *oinon* (the ancient equivalent of the wine cellar / *cava*), with the appropriate temperature and air circulation.[7] The most common pottery types for the long storage of liquids, as well as crops, were the *amphoreus* / L. *amphora*, the *pithamphoreus* and the *pithos*, with the latter being in everyday use, particularly for olive oil and grains, by Greeks until the present day – and in almost unchanged shape (although most often unvarnished but still satisfactorily impervious). The technology, dimensions and shape of such containers depended on the nature of the material being stored as well as other factors such as local traditions, individual workshop practices and aesthetics, market needs and convenience in transportation.[8] Other containers include the *stamnos* and the large *kados* with a lid (also for honey, syrups and ready-made sauces), as well as other types of containers for liquids that were made of stone or organic materials such as wood and animal skin (*askos*), practices almost extinct today.[9] Ice, a great luxury for very few in the pre-refrigerator era, was stored in the coolest part of the house or in a special place underground.

As in everyday life, part or most of the cooking for special events took place outdoors, as it still does in many rural parts of Greece, around the Mediterranean and beyond, for reasons of convenience, necessity and safety, since it involved open wood or charcoal fires. Both written sources and archaeology attest to the existence of a plethora of items used in ancient Greek cooking methods.

Grilling was undertaken with the help of long wooden or metal spits or skewers, *obeloi* (identical to the traditional Greek wooden or metal *soublakia*, cf. the broader blade of spits for the oriental kebab) on metal fire dogs, *krateutes*, or on an iron or clay pan of fire, *eschara* (see Figure 2d) used since prehistoric times for thin cuts of meats, fish, vegetables, roots and a certain type of bread (*escharites*)[10]

Boiling (which along with grilling is synonymous with cooking in several cultures, old and modern, including Greek) was done in clay, metal or even leather cooking pots such as the *chytra* in variable sizes and shapes (e.g. *chytris* and *chytridion*); the metal or clay *lebes* (modern Gr. *lebeti*) for great quantities of food; the wide-mouthed *kakkabe* and its variants *kakkabos* and *kakkabion*, all used for stewing, and the name of which is recognizable in a broad variety of traditional Greek fish soups (*kakkabia*); and the (very common as finds) *lopas* and *lopadion* (see Figure 2a), a shallow pot type excellent for fine braised dishes, which could have been also prepared in the quite similar *patane* (since the fourth century BC), which was originally of metal before appearing also in clay.[11]

The Material Culture of the Classical Greek Banquet

Figure 2. Cooking equipment from Delos. From top to bottom: a) lopas *items, b)* patanai, *c) a frying pan, d) grilling equipment, after Chatzidakis 2000b, plate 318. (© ΥΠΠΟ/ΚΑ'/Delos Museum)*

Frying took place in metal or clay pans such as the *teganon* or *saganon* (Byz. Gr. also *steganon*) (see Figure 2c), a term that today survives in the name of a Greek special fried cheese, shrimp or mussel dish (*saganaki*), in shallow variants of the *lopas* and the *patane* type (also *patellion*/ It. *padella*), as well as in the *seison* or *phrugetron* type of pan, a rare item used, as it seems, for the light frying, browning or roasting of spices and herbs, including fresh pulses such as broad beans and chick peas.[12]

Roasting, as today, occurred in metal or clay tray-like utensils with or without a lid, such as the *pnigeus*, also appearing as a kind of oven (*LSJ* s.v.: πνιγεύς), apparently for the *pnikton* category of dishes (*LSJ* s.v.: πνικτόν) which were prepared also in the *lopas* type, and the *gastroptes* which was also used as lid for the *lopas* type, among other still unidentified objects for roasting purposes.[13]

Baking sweet or savoury breads, pastries and cakes was usually done in ovenware similar or identical to that for open roasting, and was placed in clay ovens refrred to by the words *kribanoi* or *klibanoi*. Ancient Greek ovens were either portable or built in a fixed place. Their varied sizes and shapes sometimes had side openings wide enough to allow the insertion of whole stuffed animals such as lambs and goats (quite a fashionable practice since classical times). Nevertheless, the most common type of oven throughout Greek antiquity and Roman times resembled the Asian tandoor oven with the characteristic opening on the top.[14]

The list of items at the disposal of an ancient cook in a 'well-equipped' kitchen does not end here. Chatzidakis has identified 126 terms for cooking utensils in Aristophanes' comedies alone.[15] Yet not all well-equipped kitchens could have displayed even half of the items mentioned by Aristophanes, nor would all cooks, and especially their lords and

Figure 3. The Derveni krater *from Tomb B, after Themelis-Touratsoglou 1997, fig. 14. (© ΥΠΠΟ/ΙΣΤ΄)*

Figure 4. Silver kantharos *from Derveni Tomb B, after Themelis-Touratsoglou 1997, Plate 9 B5. (© ΥΠΠΟ/ΙΣΤ΄)*

ladies, have found them all necessary. Despite our continuing confusion as to whether each reported term signifies an individual item – names are also subject to individual preferences whether to rules of fashion or to dialect – or an entire category of objects, many of the items in Aristophanes' list are detectable in the archaeological record. Among cooking pots and pans, tripod-like bases or flat-topped cooking platforms, equipment for grilling and ovenware, the list also includes items for weighing, measuring, grating, grinding, cutting and forking, stirring and sampling, spooning and ladling, decanting and sieving all sorts of liquids (water, wine, including other spiritous or alcohol-free refreshments, as well as syrups, oils and sauces) and solids (grain, cured or fresh meats, including fish, dried or fresh vegetables, herbs and spices, fish roe, cheese and pickles such as olives, capers and hyacinth bulbs among many others).[16]

Several of these utensils have maintained their shapes, styles and purposes to the present day, in Europe and beyond. Strikingly unchanged, for example, are ladles for stirring or serving, pins and flesh-hooks (the *kreagra*), as well as the funnel for decanting liquids (*chone*).[17] Knives, too, have only slightly changed in shape; for example, knives for slicing fish steaks (e.g. tuna, greater amberjack, grouper) are identical to those with the broad blades preferred by many fishmongers today. There are also few differences in shape with regard to the various kinds of wooden, metal or stone pestles, *hypera*, and mortars most commonly termed as *holmoi* and *thueiai*; the ancient term *igdion* most probably denotes both the pestle and the mortar just as modern Greek does with the generic word *goudi*.[18]

The frequency in which both items come to light (with mortars being more frequent finds than pestles, which could have been made of organic materials like wood, just as today) in excavated buildings in Delos, Macedonia and elsewhere in the Greek world indicates their importance in the ancient kitchen for rich and poor alike. Indeed, many lower-class households would not have been able to afford more than a mortar (or a little mill) and a cooking pot; grilling, the most basic cooking method, demands little equipment, much of which could have been manufactured at home along with other basic tools and utensils such as wooden flesh-hooks and ladles, as well as straws and fans to keep the fire going. Mortars were far more necessary than today for the daily grinding of cereals for breads and porridges; pulping ingredients for sauces, pastes and spreads; and grinding and crushing herbs and spices. The terms *thueia*, which is always bowl-shaped, and the conical or bell-like *holmos* mentioned above may well denote the purpose for which each object was made. In Greece today we come across both shapes: the bronze bell-like mortars are always used for crushing spices (usually pepper), whereas bowl-shaped ones (wooden or stone) serve better for paste and sauce making.

In all cultures, practical experience and technological advances are the most important factors that dictate the survival of or change to a tool's shape. Frying pans, knives and flesh-hooks, for example, have only slightly changed over time; when changes appear they most often accompany alterations in cooking methods. This principle seems to hold for all cooking pots – even including pressure cookers with their characteristic pressure-relief valve – whether clay, metal or stone.[19] Whether prehistoric Japanese, Middle Eastern, Egyptian, classical Greek and Roman, Byzantine or central European, pots have remained virtually identical: half spherical or oval and bowl-like in form and shape, with or without lids, and with or without handles that are either vertical or horizontal, whether lug or loop in shape.

When ready for serving, food was transferred to vessels or fine pottery platters and then to individual dishes, again made of metal or clay. Wealthy houses could display and enjoy silverware, or even gold, and the finest of pottery along with items in bronze, whereas the poor had only simple clay or wooden dishes – and even clay or wooden objects were not always affordable for all. Our inventory of silver tableware for eating from classical Greece is limited, so far, to little plates and salt-cellars. The items we possess are few, and the finest examples come from Derveni and Vergina (Tomb III).[20] Free from decoration, the Derveni silver tableware items still impress today, as they surely did in the past, not so much for their simple and smooth lines as for their actual value and high symbolic significance both in real life and as a funerary offering to the deceased.

Unlike silver tableware, pottery items are found in far greater quantities, particularly from settlements. There are several types, with each of them serving specific, and sometimes multiple, purposes: shallow dishes for appetizers; plates for meats, fish, vegetables or fruits; deep bowls for soups, porridge and stews; and saucers for numerous kinds of dips and sauces, warm or cold. Shapes and styles vary: with or without handles (vertical, horizontal, twisted and curved), suspension holes, stems or lids. Fish plates (*pinakia*) with the characteristic navel or dip in the centre, which perhaps functioned as liquid collector/drainer, are well recorded, but it remains unclear if the so-called 'fish plates' were dishes for fish or were named after the fish painted on them.[21] In general, the main differences in the decoration of pots used for eating, such as dishes, bowls and platters, and of drinking equipment such as cups and jars, seem mainly, if not only, to relate to their function: plate painting was more often (but not always) about food, whereas the themes of wine and drinking are pursued on cups and the like.

On decoration, written sources are generally poor except when they indicate the existence, use and purpose of tableware types that either are now lost forever or have escaped archaeological digging. Classical comedies are particularly useful here, whether old (Aristophanes) or new (for example Menander and Alexis). Of all the Hellenistic works, Athenaeus' *Deipnosophists*, a fictional symposium with semi-fictional characters, stands out as the most valuable source on equipment for eating and drinking as well as on food and sympotic culture in general. The great value of Athenaeus' work is due not only to the detailed information it provides but also to its many quotations from works that remain unknown to us or lost. However, since its quotations of both contemporary and earlier works are often unattributed, attempts to date equipment, foods, cooking methods and table habits are confusing at best.

Classical and Hellenistic sources list items for the serving and handling of food, such as several types of silver platters and plates of various sizes and shapes (for flesh,

The Material Culture of the Classical Greek Banquet

eggs, cheeses, vegetables and fruits); knives for carving and as cutlery; saucers for warm sauces and cold dips; salt-cellars and little bowls for spices and herbs, as well as spoons for sauces and soups, pins to serve as forks (in general, however, ancient Greeks and Romans ate with their fingers), and finally basins and bowls for hand-washing and necessary libations. A great deal of classical Greek equipment is probably lost forever, but its existence is either attested in literature and/or suggested by its Roman equivalent. For example, for silver platters we must turn to material from Roman times. Fine complete sets of silver tableware have been discovered in Pompeii and as far north as Hoxne and Mildenhall in England and Chaourse in north-east France.[22] Many pieces from these hoards can be dated even some hundred years earlier than the date when they were concealed by their last owners; this fact allows us to reconsider, cautiously, the variety of classical Greek tableware in silver in particular and metal in general.

In contrast, our record of Greek equipment for drinking is far larger. The recovered pottery material is virtually boundless, and its study and classification is a painful but highly profitable process that has been under way for almost a century. Our record in metal is comparatively smaller in quantity, but the most magnificent and most complete sets of classical equipment for drinking in silver and bronze discovered at classical Vergina and Derveni satisfy all expectations about the opulence that might have existed in the residences of the upper echelons of the Greek society, in this case Macedonian, during the age of Philip II, Alexander the Great and his successors. The sympotic equipment from Vergina Tomb II, or the tomb of Philip II, includes twenty items in silver, two in bronze and six in clay; Tomb III held 22 items, including a masterly *kados* and a *hydria*, both in silver.[23] The Derveni material is as impressive.[24]

Luxury was the style of the royal Macedonian court, and the symposion became a vital element of status for the state and the king himself; local aristocracies followed suit. The Vergina and Derveni sets would have been used during the symposion phase of the banquet. In Greek gatherings the drinking session was far more important than the meal, and in general Greeks, unlike Romans, preferred to keep the drinking session separate from that of eating. (The infamous Roman 'vomunt ut edant, edant ut vomunt' was not a Greek practice and went far beyond even the stigmatized Greek Sybarite dining culture and lifestyle.) Dinner itself, the main event today, was consumed in a relative hurry with a moderate amount of wine.

The principal phase of the gathering, the *sumposion*, began at the signal of pipes or trumpets, depending on the occasion. All tableware was removed, floors were cleaned, and hands were washed with perfumed water brought in bowls (*phialai*) or basins (*lekanai*).[25] After the necessary libations, toasts of unmixed wine took place. Wine was poured into individual cups of many shapes and sizes – including *kylikes*, *kotylai*, *skyphoi*, animal-shaped *rhyta* and Dionysus' favourite, *kantharoi* – from wine jugs, *oinochoai*.[26] Water was kept in various kinds of jars (*hydria*, *plemochoe*, *kalpis* and *stamnos* to mention only the most important types); wine in *amphoreis* and *kadoi*.[27]

Wine was preferred diluted, and experts (*oinochooi*, today's butlers or sommeliers) were needed for its accurate mixing with water, sweetening with honey and flavouring with herbs and spices. The chosen wine cocktail was prepared in a large mixing bowl, usually a *krater* or *dinos*, taken out with a ladle (*arytaina*), sieved from impurities and then served into drinking cups. Cooling was achieved by the insertion of a bulb-like pot (*psykter*/ cooler) filled with ice or cold water in the mixing bowl.[28]

Nearly all types of drinking cups, jugs and jars are found in pottery and metal; often items in metal functioned as prototypes for pottery items. Metal items, especially gold and silver, were for the rich while the lower classes could afford only pottery (often imitating luxurious metal vessels), the finest of which nevertheless remained beyond their means.

Whereas cups in gold, silver and bronze impress with their high value, projecting wealth and social status, drinking items made from pottery attract the eye with their variety of shapes, colours and, especially, decoration. Painters' repertoires spanned from plain or combined colours and geometric patterns to themes inspired from everyday life and nature, inland and aquatic.[29] Didactic and entertaining scenes included the daily activities of the gods and humans, heroic deeds from myths and legends, the constant battle between good and evil and the on-going struggle between civilization and barbarism join depictions of idyllic settings, love stories, sensuous male and female bodies and erotic or sympotic inscriptions; these decorations might provide subjects for discussion in everyday life as well as during banquets, adding to the entertainment of the gathering. Pottery decorations were not only visual: a number of the so-called 'eye-cups' had feet decorated in relief with or even replaced by forms of male genitals, much to the surprise of the drinker about to raise the cup.[30]

Mosaics, many with Dionysiac themes, added further to the atmosphere and theatricality in the Greek dining chamber (*andron*).[31] Dionysos, god of wine, ecstasy and theatre was the dominant figure in all sympotic equipment, decoration and activities. The presence of Dionysos and his entourage (*thiasos*) is also striking in the brilliant sympotic record of the Derveni and Vergina tombs as we see in the lavishly decorated Derveni *krater* (see Figure 3) and in a variety of drinking cups such as *kylikes*, *skyphoi* and *kantharoi* (see Figure 4). No less elegant are buckets (*kadoi*) and *hydriai*, fine ladles with a swan-headed handle ending, a feature throughout classical antiquity, and sieves for sieving and serving wine beverages.[32] The Vergina and Derveni sympotic sets in metal accord with what our sources attest about the opulence of royal and aristocratic Macedonian symposia and with what we see in the sympotic frieze of the Aghios Athanasios Macedonian tomb.

To sum up, we only know about the equipment used for cooking, eating and drinking in classical Greece from literary sources and the archaeological record. Cooking equipment has not changed much since antiquity in terms of shape, style and purpose. By contrast, equipment for storing and drinking wine has changed significantly. From clay containers we have moved, fortunately, to wooden barrels. Also, no wine expert today would recommend the practice of mixing and ladling fine wines; glass has rid wine from the characteristic taste of metal and oxidization that this mixing may have helped cover. But something is lost in this transition: Greek wine drinking cups appeared in more versatile shapes, and the clay ones were far more colourful, informative, didactic and even sexy than ours. Finally, the brilliance of sympotic silverware from the rich funerary contexts at Vergina and Derveni, tells us much about the taste, finances and sophistication of the society that produced and used them, both in real life and as funerary offerings to distinguished individuals. The wedding feast of the Macedonian aristocrat Karanos that Athenaeus describes in full detail (*Deipn.* 128a–130e) and the magnificent sympotic frieze of the Aghios Athanasios Macedonian tomb allow us great insight into the pleasures that the classical aristocracy was keen to enjoy in both life and afterlife.

Acknowledgements

I should like to thank the ΙΣΤ' (for Figures 1, 3 and 4) and ΚΑ' (for Figure 2) Ephorates of Prehistoric and Classical Antiquities and (respectively) the Ephors V. Misailidou-Despotidou and Dr P. Chatzidakis for the permission to use all the images presented here. I am also grateful to Dr Panagiotis Chatzidakis, Ephor of the ΚΑ' Ephorate of Prehistoric and Classical Antiquities, and Stergios Lioulias, archaeologist (ΙΖ' Ephorate), for their bibliographical recommendations and useful suggestions as well as Dr Anna Davies (Liverpool University) for proof-reading the text.

Notes

1. P.I. Chatzidakis, 'Opsopoiika skeue apo te Delo: kai hutras phemi euruthmon phainesthai eukrinos keimenas (Xenophontos Oikonomikos)', Ε' Επιστημονική για την Ελληνιστική Κεραμική. Χρονολογικά Προβλήματα, Κλειστά Σύνολα – Εργαστήρια (Αθήνα: ΤΑΠ, 2000), pp. 123–24. (Subsequent citations refer to this source as Chatzidakis 2000a.)
2. The material from the palace at Vergina still awaits full publication, and the few related reports from the vast palatial and market complexes at Pella – which undoubtedly have much to reveal in future – are insufficient to support any extensive discussion at this point. I examine Olynthos in Chalkidike in another study.
3. M. Tsibidou-Auloniti, *Makedonikoi Taphoi ston Phoinika kai ston Agio Athanasio Thessalonikes* (Αθήνα: ΤΑΠ, 2005), p. 108.
4. For an extended discussion on the Aghios Athanasios frieze, see Tsibidou-Auloniti, pp. 114–49. For earlier depictions of banquets, painted or in relief, in funerary monuments and temples from Lydia, Ionia and the Aegean, see E. P. Baughan, 'Sculpted Symposiasts of Ionia', *American Journal of Archaeology* 115.1 (2011), pp. 19–53; on Lycia, see J.-M. Dentzer, *Le motif du banquet couche dans le Proche-Orient et le monde grec du VIIe au Ive siecle avant J.-C.* (Rome: BEFAR, 1982); on Etruria, see L.B. Van der Meer, 'Kylikeia in Etruscan Tomb Painting', *Ancient Greek and Related Pottery*, ed. H.A. Brijder (Amsterdam: 1984), pp. 298–304 and K.M.D. Dunbabin, *The Roman Banquet: Images of Conviviality* (Cambridge: Cambridge UP, 2003), pp. 25–32.
5. Tsibidou-Auloniti, pp. 134–42. Athenaeus *Deipnosophists*. XIV. 48–50.
6. Tsibidou-Auloniti, pp. 134–35 and 123 with indicative bibliography.
7. On Macedonia, see P. Adam-Veleni, 'Dionusos kai paragoge oinou ste boreia Ellada (Makedonia kai Thrake) kata tous istorikous chronous', Το Δώρο του Διονύσου (Θεσσαλονίκη: Αρχαιολογικό Μουσείο Θεσσαλονίκης, 2011), p. 90 and I. Akamatis, 'Ek tou Keramikou tes Pellas: To kleisto sunolo tou stromatos katastrophes kai e chnonologese tou. Oi Choroi A kai 1', ΣΤ' Επιστημονική για την Ελληνιστική Κεραμική.

Χρονολογικά Προβλήματα, Κλειστά Σύνολα – Εργαστήρια (Αθήνα: ΤΑΠ, 2011), pp. 383; on Delos, see Chatzidakis 2000a, p. 116.
8. J. Boardman, *The History of Greek Vases* (London: Thames and Hudson, 2001), pp. 153–68, 282–89.
9. Chatzidakis 2000a, p. 122, fig. 3.1.
10. For spits and firedogs as offerings in late archaic and early classical burials, indicatively Sindos, *Katalogos tes Ektheses* (Αθήνα: ΤΑΠ, 1985), p. 85, figs. 125–26; on the fish, see Chatzidakis 2000a, p. 128, especially for *eschara ichthyoptris*, quoting *Polyd*. vi. 88; on *escharites*, see Athenaeus *Deipnosophists*. III. 109c–d.
11. On the *chytris* and *chytridion*, see Chatzidakis 2000a, p. 126 and 'Ta mageirika skeue stous archaious Ellenes komodiographous kai ste Delo', *ΣΤ' Επιστημονική για την Ελληνιστική Κεραμική* (Αθήνα: *Ταμείο Αρχαιολογικών Πόρων και Απαλλοτριώσεων*, 2000), pp. 647–49, Plate 7 (subsequent citations refer to this source as Chatzidakis 2000b); on the *chytra*'s importance in cooking and symbolical significance, see Chatzidakis 2000b, pp. 647–48; on the *lebes*, see Chatzidakis 2000b, p. 653, Plate 319a; on *lebes gamikos*, see Boardman, pp. 232, 263; on *kakkabia*, see Chatzidakis 2000a, p. 126 and Chatzidakis 2000b, p. 652; on *lopas* and *lopadion*, see Chatzidakis 2000b, pp. 649–50, listing fourteen epithets of the *lopas* item; on the *patane*, see Chatzidakis 2000b, p. 651.
12. On the *teganon* or *saganon*, see Chatzidakis 2000b, pp. 650–51, Plate 318a, left; on the *seison* or *phrugetron*, see Chatzidakis 2000a, pp. 128–29 and Chatzidakis 2000b, p. 652.
13. Aristophanes, *Wasps*. 511; Chatzidakis 2000b, p. 654.
14. Chatzidakis 2000b, p. 654.
15. Chatzidakis 2000b, pp. 642–43.
16. For ancient Greek culinary culture, see A. Dalby, *Siren Feasts: A History of Food and Gastronomy in Greece* (London: Routledge, 1996); on Archestratos of Gela, see S. Douglas Olson and A. Sens, *Archestratus of Gela: Greek Culture and Cuisine in the Fourth Century BCE* (New York: Oxford UP, 2000).
17. Chatzidakis 2000a, p. 120.
18. For mortars from Pella's *agora*, see A. Bouboulis and A. Laftsidis, 'Agora Pellas: Notios Dromos. E Periptosse ton Lakon', *Egnatia* 15 (Θεσσαλονίκη: University Studio Press, 2011), p. 177 and 182; on Delos, see Chatzidakis 2000a, p. 124.
19. On pressure cookers from Delos, see Chatzidakis 2000a, p. 127 (also on the use of dough or plaster for pot sealing).
20. On Vergina Tomb III, see M. Andronikos, *Vergina: The Royal Tombs* (Athens: Ekdotike Athenon, 2004), p. 209; on Derveni Grave II, see P. G. Themelis and G. P. Touratsoglou, *Oi Taphoi tou Derveniou* (Αθήνα: ΤΑΠ, 1997), pp. 67–68, Plates 66–67, 69–70.
21. Boardman 2001, p. 256, fig. 282.
22. P. Roberts, *Life and Death in Pompeii and Herculaneum* (London: British Museum Press, 2013): pp. 235–37, figs. 272, 274–79.
23. For Tomb II, see Andronikos, pp. 145–46, figs. 104–24; for Tomb III, see pp. 209–14, figs. 162–63, 170–83.
24. Themelis-Touratsoglou; B. Barr-Sharrar, *The Derveni Krater: Masterpiece of Classical Greek Metalwork* (Princeton: The American School of Classical Studies at Athens, 2008). For more sympotic sets in silverware and metal from Macedonia, see *Ancient Macedonia* (Athens: Greek Ministry of Culture, National Hellenic Committee - ICOM, 1988), pp. 293–98, figs. 244–49 (Sevasti), pp. 374–76, figs. 339–42 (Stauroupolis); *Au royaume d'Alexandre le Grand, la Macedoine antique,* Catalogue de l' exposition 'Au royaume d'Alexandre le Grand, la Macedoine antique', Paris, musee du Louvre 2011–2012 (Paris : Samogy Editions d'art, 2011), pp. 400–06, figs. 252–59 (Nikisiani, Paliouria, Mauropigi, Makrygialos, Alykes Kitrous, Edessa).
25. Boardman, pp. 256, 266.
26. On *kantharoi*, see Boardman, pp. 246–50; on *oinochoai*, see pp. 37, 250–51, fig. 40.
27. Boardman, pp. 76–77, fig. 108 of a Caeretan hydria.
28. Boardman, p. 250, figs. 274–76.
29. Boardman, pp. 168–243.

30. R. Osborne, *Archaic and Classical Art* (Oxford: Oxford UP, 1998), p. 133, fig. 68.
31. Ch. Makaronas and E. Giouri, *Oi Oikies Arpages tes Elenes kai Dionusou tes Pellas* (Αθήνα: Αρχαιολογική Εταιρεία, 1989); *Ancient Macedonia*: p. 307, fig. 260; M. Lilimpaki-Akamati and I. M. Akamatis, *Pella and its Environs* (Αθήνα: ΤΑΠ, 2004), p. 25, fig. 15.
32. On the Derveni *krater*, see Barr-Sharrar and Themelis-Touratsoglou, p. 31 and figs. 1, 30–31 and pp. 70–71, figs 13–17, 73–75; on drinking cups, see Andronikos, pp. 150–53, figs. 113–14 (Tomb II) and pp. 212–13, figs. 179–80; on *kadoi*, see Andronikos, pp. 146 and 209, figs. 104–05, 176–77; on *hydriai*, see Andronikos, p. 202, fig. 214; on ladles, see Themelis-Touratsoglou, p. 70, fig. 11; on sieves, see Andronikos, pp. 149 and 209, figs. 108, 178.

A 'Knack' for Cooking: what are the Required Tools?

Amy B. Trubek

Culinary historians tend to associate cooking practice primarily with a place (French cuisine) or with an identity (be it 'women's work' or 'professional chef'). In an earlier project looking at the development of the culinary profession, my primary concerns involved such a connection. I wanted to know why French *haute cuisine* was the culinary code that needed to be mastered by aspiring chefs, inside and outside of France. In my attempt to understand these cooks and their cooking, I looked at cookbooks, professional journals, culinary memoirs, restaurant criticism, travel guides and other primary sources to make sense of the power of France to their professional identity.[1]

Cooking reflects the predilections of the group and the vicissitudes of a place, but cooking is also an individual skill. And although we all may intuitively understand that the ability to cook is not innate, much like a myriad of other human practices (playing music, hunting animals, building houses), surprisingly little sustained scholarship has looked closely at cooking skill: the acts, knacks and tips that make a person a cook. This might be due to that perennial problem which arises when looking at anything related to food: constant and everywhere, how can any practice related to food be analytically contained? But starting with the premise that cooking is first and foremost a skill opens up our culinary horizons. In order to cook, we must first learn; ability is always linked to both experience and access to knowledge.

A shifted focus on cooking practice as part of a web of social relations, including those who teach and those who learn how to cook, is inspired by the work of anthropologist Tim Ingold, who has long argued for an integration of knowledge and practice, one that brings together 'the whole person, indissolubly body and mind, in a richly structured environment'.[2] The cook is always cooking somewhere for someone. The skilled practice of cooking never occurs in isolation. And neither does the transmission of knowledge: 'skills are not transmitted from generation to generation but are re-grown in each, incorporated into the *modus operandi* of the developing human organism through training and experience in the performance of particular tasks'.[3] We cannot assume that everyone in France learns to cook a *crêpe* or a *pot au feu* purely through osmosis; each cook has to learn how to heat the *crêpe* pan correctly, to swirl the batter at the right speed, to cover the lid to the Dutch oven tightly. So, can we learn to cook without learning about the tools of the trade? How can we understand or evaluate such transfer of knowledge and acquisition of skill? In particular, can starting with a cook and his or her know-how change the way we understand cooking tools, to see them as 'the practice of a skill rather than the operation of a technology'.[4] And what are the necessary tools

A 'Knack' for Cooking: what are the Required Tools?

for contemporary home cooks? Finally, how timeless are objects for cooking in the objective of everyday cooking? This paper will explore these questions. And what do such processes mean when we attempt to make sense of cooking tools and technologies, of cooks and cuisines?

I began a new research project on domestic cooking skills and knowledge several years ago, with a focus on the contemporary United States. As always, I was interested in examining cooking as an everyday practice in light of larger social systems and cultural values. The research included: ethnographic interviews and videotapes of people from rural and urban areas in the north-east cooking in their homes; archival research on iconic cookbooks of the twentieth century; participant observation in an artisan bakery and a commissary/catering kitchen; analysis of contemporary survey data, labour statistics and mass media; and more.[5] For the ethnographic portion of the project, we focused on the New England region, working with people from rural, suburban and urban locales in Vermont as well as urban Boston. Researchers visited each participant's home on two separate days. In the initial visit, researchers administered a semi-structured interview, presented a questionnaire and conducted the first video-recording of the preparation of a typical dinner-time meal. During the second visit, the researcher collected the questionnaire and videotaped a second meal preparation (that did not have to be the same meal as the first visit). The videos recorded participants preparing a dinner-time meal, starting with raw ingredients and ending with the finished product. Videotaping was also a way for the researchers to follow up on questions from the interview or ask additional questions that did not fit within the timeframe of the interview.

As the interviews and videotapes accumulated, and we began to look closely at people's practices and listen carefully to what people said, we were surprised by what we were documenting. Contrary to our original assumptions that we would find an overall decline in cooking knowledge and cooking skill, we discovered that our informants had a good basic level of cooking skill and knowledge; they simply did not use that skill and knowledge all the time. So this practice is now episodic rather than intrinsic to daily life. At the same time, we realized that cooking practice has expanded. Instead of a categorical imperative of human (particularly women's) existence, cooking is a practice that can be categorized in multiple ways, for example, as daily drudge, as creative possibility and as complex livelihood.

Hence our realization that domestic cooking can be analysed using Ingold's formulation: a skill that remains central to an integrated engagement of the mind and body with a 'structured environment'. However, documenting this engagement requires a wider aperture, for the landscape of cooking is varied, and people's relationship to that landscape is rich and diverse. Mapping this landscape can tell us much about the relationship of place and identity to cooking skill and knowledge. We need, though, to start with actions, and from such acts build frames of meaning. The decision to combine interviews with videotapes greatly expanded the ability to analyse action.

Capturing people's actions permanently has allowed for repeated viewing and analysis of what people do; listening to what they say at times informs and at times contradicts these actions. We have analysed and reanalysed the words and images numerous times, identifying a number of emergent themes now central to the larger inquiry into modern domestic cooking.

Here, the focus is on how the videotapes of cooks in their kitchens yielded a rich trove of evidence as to people's engagement with tools. Their hesitance, their dependence, and their passion for the various cooking tools are captured for study. The larger stories these encounters tell – of identity, of social relations, of culinary organization – reveal both the relevance and irrelevance of tools in everyday cooking practice. Here, four vignettes are closely examined: a young girl and her citrus press, an elderly man and his spray bottles, a young man and his measuring cup and a woman and her salad bowl. Investigating these vignettes, these moments when cooking knowledge is mediated by a cooking tool, brings us back to central culinary questions: How do we know what we know about cooking? What do our relationships with our tools say about who we are as cooks?

Four cooks and four tools

Vignette one

A young girl, the oldest of four children, is in the kitchen with her parents as they make an evening meal. She really wants to help, perhaps because cooking this particular meal will be videotaped, but perhaps, also, because she wants to learn. Of all the children, she is most engaged in the process. The parents are talking about their everyday cooking practices at the same time they are moving around the kitchen, preparing dinner. Isabel keeps interrupting, 'Daddy, Daddy, can I help?' After several minutes, the father acquiesces. He gets her to stand on a chair and instructs, 'you can juice the lemon'. He sets on the counter the following items: a lemon, a juicer made of metal, a cutting board. In the pantheon of possible tools to extract juice from a citrus fruit, this tool is fairly simple. The bottom half is a simple metal bowl; on the top half the centre is a rounded, moulded piece of metal with numerous surrounding ridges connected to a flat pierced area. The top half is connected to the bottom with a hinge. Isabel then picks up the whole lemon, lifts to the top part of the juicer, puts the lemon in the bottom bowl, and presses down on the lemon with the top half. Nothing. The lemon stays exactly the same, and there is definitely no juice. Quickly realizing there is something wrong with her method, she calls out to her father: 'Daddy, can you cut this open?' Isabel then carefully places the lemon on the cutting board, and noticing that the sell-by sticker remains on it, she peels it off. Her father comes over, and here is their subsequent interchange:

> When you're juicing something (*yeah*), cut it in half (*yeah*). You take it and smash it as hard as you can. *(Isabel takes a half a lemon and slams it onto the ridged metal)*

A 'Knack' for Cooking: what are the Required Tools?

No, no, put it on there, sorry. And then you turn it back and forth while you are pushing down. You can do it. (*And then she does. The juice is extracted from the lemon*)

Anthropologists often compare learning to cook with learning a language. There are implicit and explicit rules. There is grammar, syntax and even punctuation to cooking. Some knowledge seems intuitive, received by cultural osmosis (the words – hello or bonjour – and the ingredients – peanut butter or horsemeat) but other knowledge seems more conscious (the colon and semi-colon; the chicken cut up in pieces and cooked slowly in liquid in a clay pot over an open flame, or roasted whole in an electric oven). And the required knowledge is not universal; rather it is very specific to time and place. The ingredients vary. The tools and techniques shift. The tastes change. The expectations of the cook are not consistent. But somehow, somewhere, someone has to bring all the components together into an edible dish. And just as new members of a generation must learn the language of their family or culture, new members of a generation must learn how to cook. When Isabel tries to get the juice out of the lemon without cutting the lemon in half, what is the significance of the tool to the lesson she learns?

Such everyday lived experience of cooking has also been studied by anthropologist David Sutton. In his videographies of cooks in Kalymnos, there is a relationship of 'language to all kinds of practices, the use of tools in the kitchen, kitchen organization, bodily movements and postures as cooks interact with non-cooks or fellow cooks, an entire kitchen choreography.'[6] When Isabel sees the drama unfolding, she wants to participate, to not be a bystander. Taking on the lemon is a first step. So how do cooking tools function in the process of learning the language of cooking and creating Sutton's 'kitchen choreography'? At the same time, what is the meaning of such complex cooking tasks? Perhaps, as Ingold argues, 'the tasks you do depend on who you are, and in a sense the performance of certain tasks *makes* you the person who you are'.[7] Isabel is a student learning how to cook but also asserting herself in her family environment.

Vignette two

After retirement, Joel, an older man in his seventies, becomes the main cook. His wife used to make all the daily meal decisions, but now he has taken charge. He is an intuitive cook, resisting learning from others:

First of all, I very seldom use a cookbook.... Measurements we usually try to avoid, in other words how much of this and how much of that. I think a lot of it is instinct. You never want to over salt for example, but many recipes say a pinch, well, what is a pinch? A pinch to you might be different than a pinch for me.

When he cooks, Joel uses many tools, often in unpredictable ways. When he makes a chicken soup, he introduces me to his 'tools of the trade'. He opens up a drawer next to the stove, full of dried spices from a well-known mail-order spice company. He says, 'this is my box of paints'. He picks up different spice bottles and then decides what to put into his soup pot. He points to his blender. After he has boiled all his soup ingredients for some time (including a whole chicken), he will 'blenderize' them all, before sieving the concoction to get his final dish.

Later on, he introduces me to his 'secret weapons', standard-issue spray bottles used for household cleaning tasks. He uses them to mix marinades, which he then sprays on many different types of meat and fish. When Joel discusses his technique for making striped bass ('I just made this up in my head'), he starts with a fillet that is placed on a sheet of tin foil. Next he chops several sprigs of dill and spreads them on top of the fillet. He adds butter and extra virgin olive oil, salt, pepper and a little Tabasco. Joel's voice rises a bit, and he says, 'Now I will show you my great secret ... I invented ... years ago.' He reaches up into a cabinet over the stove and pulls down a spray bottle. This particular bottle contains four wines: sherry, madeira, marsala and port. He then spritzes the entire fillet with his wine mixture. He explains why: 'again, it is like mixing paint. If you have all blue, or yellow, or green or black, it's not very good. But if you can find a way to mix those colours, then you have something good.' He then folds the foil over the fish, makes a tight packet, and puts his creation in the oven to bake.

When Joel declaims about his 'mystery marinades and his secret weapons' (the spray bottles), what do we learn about him as a cook, but also about cooking more generally? He uses a musical analogy:

> You might compare it, I suppose, to learning to play the piano. When your mama or dada says, now I am sending you to get piano lessons, in the beginning you might say this is awful and then after a year or two you give it up. But then the person who enjoys the piano keeps doing it all their life and they come home at night and the first thing they want to do is sit down and play something and so what might have been a chore or demanded by your parents when you are little can change entirely.

Joel categorizes his cooking tasks as individualized interpretations of dishes using any variety of tools to assist in his improvisations. Basic skills are transformed into creative acts. Tools assist in the creative process: 'I use the analogy of a painter. ... A painter is a creative artist and the painter does not paint by numbers in the little box. ... A painter paints and mixes his different colours and sometimes he has to throw it away, sometimes it's okay.' He cheerfully admits that such improvisatory cooking is not for everyone (as is the case with playing piano), but for Joel, cooking is jazz.

Vignette three
Karen, in her late twenties, is a single professional living in urban Boston. As she admits herself, she is a planner in all aspects of her life, and certainly in her approach to preparing a meal. She likes to host dinner parties on the weekend, and clearly enjoys the entire process, from creating the menu, to shopping and cooking, to hosting the event:

A 'Knack' for Cooking: what are the Required Tools?

if I'm having a dinner party on Saturday, I plan my Saturday so that I can clean the house, clean the kitchen, get all my stuff ready, go food shopping, make sure that I have everything.... I kind of have a timeline.

One cooking session we observe is for a dinner party; she wants to share her love of hospitality. Karen proudly displays the printed menu for the evening's dinner, and then goes on to display her 'tricks of the trade'. One is a baked brie appetizer:

The secret to this is you don't buy the baked brie they sell to warm up, you just buy a wedge, slice some apples and put that in halfway through, heat it for twenty minutes, put in the apples and pour on maple syrup.

She serves this to her guests and then continues to prepare the main dish. Another secret is spending money on ingredients: 'this is a forty-dollar bottle of olive oil, which makes a huge difference.' Karen's kitchen is small, so many of her 'tricks' involve negotiating her space. This extends to her use of kitchen tools; she built a special shelf for all her utensils since there is so little room for storage. She puts her empty salad bowl in the refrigerator to save the space; after she has made the salad she can just put the full bowl back in the fridge. When Karen makes the salad, she has a cutting board next to the sink for the lettuce while the bowl and the compost bucket are placed right in the sink. She then can cut the lettuce, putting the leaves in the bowl and the stems in the compost bucket in several fluid movements. When she wants to add canned sweet corn, she opens the corn with a hand-held can opener and reaches over the salad bowl (now filled with lettuce, fennel and sliced cherry tomatoes) in order to find a small open space where she can drain the liquid out of the can. Salad done, Karen puts the bowl back in the fridge.

Which came first, Karen's desire for organization or her ability to organize? Claude Levi-Strauss's dictum – food is good to think – seems appropriate here.[8] Karen's approach shows that cooking is also good to think: she, like all cooks, does not randomly act, but develops a system to navigate between her tools and her environment. She demonstrates that cooking is also good to categorize. Or as Roland Barthes, a scholar eloquent on both structure and meaning, puts it, '[the] essential object is the taxonomy or distributive model which every human creation, ... inevitably establishes, since there can be no culture without classification'.[9] And there are many ways to categorize and classify. Karen's cooking is planned cooking, and her tools facilitate that classification.

Vignette four
David lives with several other young male bike enthusiasts in the largest urban area of Vermont. His relationship to his cooking space and his cooking tools could be best described as casual, but perhaps there is an underlying method to his seeming madness. David's kitchen is fairly large, with the major appliances against the wall and a large centre island with an electric cookstove in the middle. He is making a meal (and

making up the meal), as he moves through the kitchen. In one case, he has decided to make sautéed vegetables with rice. He decides to put the water on to boil for the rice. A stainless steel pot gets put on the stove, and then David walks over to the sink. The faucet gets turned on, and then he looks for a measuring cup. He puts the measuring cup under the faucet, fills it up close to the brim, and then walks over to the stove with it; all these actions occur as the water continues to pour out of the faucet. Later, he decides to measure the rice to put in the pot of water. This action seemingly requires more precision. He pours the rice into the same cup that previously was used to measure the water, and then bends over to read the measurement line. He adapts to his tool. All tools, large and small, become part of his fluid cooking shuffle. David's refrigerator functions as the storage centre of his culinary environment. He opens it up and forages for ingredients multiple times every time he prepares a meal, leaving it wide open as he hunts through the packed contents. During one such foray, after a minute or so of rummaging, he finds a bag of frozen vegetables, which he places on the edge of the centre island. As he moves on to another cooking task, the bag falls on the floor; at some point he picks the bag up off the floor. David also adapts his habits to the available tools. During another meal preparation, he is handling an acorn squash. He finds a large sharp knife to cut it open, but how will he scoop out the seeds? He looks around and makes his choice: the end of a fork will do.

David's cooking knowledge seems to integrate organically with his cooking environment, in a sort of ecological relationship. He constantly responds to the tools, large and small, in his surroundings, and adapts his practice accordingly. The task at hand, getting the seeds out of the butternut squash, needs a tool. The closest one available, the fork, will be sufficient. And later on, when the onions in the pot need to be stirred, the fork works again as a tool for David.

Conclusion

The four cooks profiled have a lot in common (live in the same geographic region, cook the same style food, cook solely in the domestic sphere), but should their cooking practices solely be generalized by such commonalities? Ingold's assertion, that any person's skill comes from 'training and experience in the performance of particular tasks', helps explain the importance of tools, because in the case of all the cooks profiled above, the tool plays a pivotal role in how the cook operates in a structured kitchen environment. So tool use and skill are interdependent. But how can such an array of categories – the variable engagements with the tools – be accounted for? The action with the tool and the meaning of the use and the result – which comes first?

We could spend some time considering the differences in the tools used: a metal manual lemon juicer, a plastic salad bowl, a spray bottle, an electric blender, a glass measuring cup, a freezer. So many materials used to make the tools: plastic, metal, glass. Some of the tools are used manually, two require electricity. The bowl is an ancient cooking tool, the measuring cup has been in constant use for over a century, and the blender is a relatively new addition to the kitchen pantheon. We could also consider what these tools have in common. The juicer, spray bottle, blender and measuring cup all assist in the cooking process. But can we make sense of the meaning of these tools without seeing how they are used in a particular structured environment? The spray bottle makes Joel a jazz artist. The juicer helps Isabel realize what she still has to learn. The bowl holds and reserves space, helping Karen implement her plans. The measuring cup and the fork facilitate David's on the spot problem solving. The tools reveal varying types of skilled practice. But all these actions can be connected to a category of action, bringing structure to each individual's cooking environment. In these vignettes, the individual's skill does not exist outside of how the individual categorizes his or her know-how: a student, an artist, a planner, an adapter.

With the axioms of earlier culinary scholarship removed (for example cooking and nationalism, or cooking and gender, or cooking and technology), tools can take on new meaning. For example, how do physical and social environments structure, enable or constrain our cooking? Which comes first, the tool or the way someone classifies the tool? What are the implications for looking at cooking across time and space?

Notes

1. Amy Trubek, *Haute Cuisine: How the French Invented the Culinary Profession* (Philadelphia: U Pennsylvania P, 2000).
2. Tim Ingold, *Perception of the Environment: Essays on Livelihood, Dwelling, and Skill* (New York: Routledge, 2000), p. xvii.
3. Ingold, p. 4.
4. Ingold, p. 291.
5. Along with three graduate students from the University of Vermont, I interacted with people from rural and urban areas of New England. I also have done supplementary historical research, examining primary sources as diverse as historical labour statistics and fan letters to Julia Child.
6. David Sutton, *Introduction to the Course of True Knowledge: Cooking, Skill and the Senses on a Greek Island* (Berkeley: U California P, forthcoming).
7. Ingold, p. 291.
8. Claude Levi-Strauss, *The Raw and the Cooked: Mythologiques* (Chicago: U Chicago P, 1983).
9. Roland Barthes, "Science versus Literature," *The [London] Times Literary Supplement* (28 September 1967), pp. 897–98.

The Qederah: the Everyday Cooking Pot of Talmudic Times

Susan Weingarten

The rabbis of late antique Palestine laid down in some detail the basics a husband must provide for his wife.[1] The third-century collection of religious laws known as the Mishnah includes both a list of basic foods and a list of basic personal equipment: bed, bedcover or mat and clothes. The Tosefta, another collection of laws probably also from late antiquity, adds a list of basic kitchen equipment which he must supply: pots, a lamp and a wick. The different pots are specified by name: *kos*, a cup; *havit*, a large jar, for water and/or wine; *qederah*, a cooking pot; *pakh*, a small jar usually containing oil.

The *qederah* (pl. *qederot*) was thus the most ordinary and everyday of pots. It is mentioned several hundred times throughout the Talmudic literature, both in the Mishnah and Tosefta, as well as the later Talmuds, written in Palestine and Babylonia between the fifth and seventh centuries, and other exegetic works called *midrashim*. I have collected these references and in this paper I intend to analyse them to see what we can learn about this pot: what it was made of and what it looked like; how it was used; what was cooked in it and how it was cooked. We shall see that this most everyday object figures in proverbs and metaphors, and like English 'dishes' and 'casseroles', is used metonymically for the food that was cooked in it.

According to the Talmudic literature, the *qederah*, the pot, was made by a *qadar*, a potter, who fired his wares in a kiln and sold them to the householder. This was a local industry, and the pots were made of local clay.[2] The Galilean centre for the pottery industry was a village called Kfar Hananiah, which according to the *midrash* supplied *qederot* for Judaea as well.[3] There were also more expensive versions made of copper, which would not be subject to breakages or splitting on the fire: a *midrash* dealing with alcoholism describes a man who sells off his household goods to buy wine, claiming a ceramic *qederah* is as good as a copper one.[4] The *qederah* was globular in shape, with a round bottom: the word *shulayim* which normally means 'sides' of a pot is used also for the bottom of the *qederah* where left-over lentils collect, so there was clearly no distinction between sides and base.[5] It was topped by a raised neck, which was smaller than the body: a *midrash* tells us of a dog which put its head into a *qederah* of meat, was unable to get it out again and ran away with its head still inside.[6] There were one or two handles to hold or hang it by.[7] The Tosefta mentions the habit of stacking *qederot* on top of each other, presumably in a hollow in the earth floor and/or propped in a corner: 'A pile of *qederot* is stacked inside the house, rising from the floor to the ceiling, always with the bottom of the pot above resting on the mouth of the pot below.'[8]

The *Qederah*: the Everyday Cooking Pot of Talmudic Times

Figure 1: Qederah: Yavneh-Yam, Israel: mosaic villa, fifth-sixth century layer, unpublished: inventory no. YY07–0119 (Copyright permission: Professor Moshe Fischer, Tel Aviv University).

The commonest cooking pot found in excavations in ancient Palestine from the Iron Age to the eighth century CE fits this specification, and has thus been identified with the *qederah*. Its round body varies in size over time, but there is always a raised neck smaller than the body and one or two handles drawn from shoulders to neck or rim.[9]

With use, the lower parts of the *qederah* would blacken. Many *qederot* found archaeologically are found with blackened bottoms. It has been suggested that this is the origin of the name: from *q-d-r*, black.[10] Other suggestions connect it with the Greek cooking pot, the *chutra* or *kuthra*, which was used especially for cooking legumes.[11] It is interesting to note that early reports of the excavations in the Athenian agora record very few of these pots, but Susan Rostoff has discovered that earlier researchers looked for more exotic pots, and simply failed to record the very frequent local *chutrai*.[12] The everyday occurrence of the blackening of the pot (cf. the English saying 'the pot calling the kettle black') became metaphorical for anger: a pair of rabbis each had eight pairs of students dressed in gold embroidered clothes (i.e. they were very high-status rabbis) but when they disagreed with each other their faces went as black as the bottom of a *qederah* (i.e. they behaved like the common people), we are told.[13] They must have been boiling inside, too. The blackening process is also said to typify the sufferings of the wicked in the fires of Gehenna, when their faces will become as black as the bottom of the *qederah*.[14]

An order of cooking in a *qederah* is specified in the Tosefta: lighting the fire, putting on wood, putting on the *qederah*, adding water, meat, and then flavouring.[15] Other sources, however, say that the food to be cooked was placed in the *qederah* before the wood was placed on the fire to heat it.[16] There were clearly a number of ways of cooking in the *qederah*. The heat source was not necessarily a wood fire: charcoal could also be used, in a simple hole in the ground or on a stove, *qalatut* or a *kirah*, a kind of brazier which sometimes had space for two *qederot*, but at its most basic consisted of just three pins over the fire.[17] It was forbidden to rake the coals under these installations on the Sabbath.[18] The food could also be cooked by putting the *qederah* in an oven.[19] Cooking food from scratch was forbidden on the Sabbath – a woman who filled her *qederah* with lentils and lupines and put it in the oven before the Sabbath began was not allowed to eat from it even after the Sabbath had ended, because the cooking had all taken place on the Sabbath.[20] It was however, permissible to simply keep food warm in the *qederah* on the Sabbath by covering it in hot ashes and leaving it overnight. However, since this might cook the food further, the food had to be just about edible, even if not thoroughly cooked, before the *qederah* was placed in the ashes. 'Edibility' was defined as being acceptable to Ben Drosai, a legendary bandit, who was notorious for gobbling his food only a third cooked. In his case it was oxmeat, not lentils, which went into the pot![21]

Clearly the process of cooking in the *qederah* had to be carefully supervised or food would burn. There is a lot of evidence about this in the Talmudic sources, including discussions of cooking for Jews by non-Jews. If a traveller gives a non-Jewish inn-keeper food to cook, and watches her setting the *qederah* on the fire, the rabbis tell us he need not stay to supervise her, as she is unlikely to add forbidden food in his absence.[22] Similarly, if a Jew and a non-Jew are partners in a *qederah*, the Jew need not worry if the non-Jew takes the *qederah* off the heat to stir or shake it, and then puts it back: once again, the non-Jew is considered unlikely to add anything forbidden.[23] Little pieces of cloth were used to hold the *qederah* when taking it off the heat to shake or stir it, and a ladle *zoma lastron* (Greek *zomarustron*) for stirring.[24] The process of shaking or stirring the lumps of food in a liquid in the *qederah* gave rise to a simile: the book of Exodus writes of the defeat of the Egyptians at the Red Sea, when God overturned both horse and rider in the water. The rabbis of the Talmud ask why the horse should be mentioned before the rider, and explain that because just as stirring or shaking the *qederah* means the food that was at the bottom rises to the top and vice versa, so it was at the Red Sea.[25] God here is metaphorized as a cook.

However, it was usually women who stirred their *qederot*, pots of boiling food. And just as European male anxieties gave rise to the image of the witch stirring her cauldron,

The *Qederah*: the Everyday Cooking Pot of Talmudic Times

similar fears arise in the Talmudic literature. Women are depicted as using various magical practices to control the lengthy cooking process, some of which were identified as witchcraft and forbidden by the rabbis: 'If she puts sticks through the handles of the *qederah* so it should not boil over, this is witchcraft. But it is permitted to add sticks of mulberries or broken glass to the *qederah* to make it cook quicker. But the rabbis forbade broken glass as being too dangerous.'[26]

The Roman author Pliny also says sticks (from figs, rather than mulberries) added to the pot will make ox-meat cook quicker, and save fuel.[27] It is also considered witchcraft for a woman to urinate in front of her *qederah* to make it cook faster.[28] The daughters of Rav Nahman were reported have stirred their *qederah* with their bare hands. At first it was thought that this was because they were so virtuous, but later they were accused of witchcraft.[29] The eighty witches of Ashkelon who were notoriously sentenced to death for sorcery in Hasmonean times appear in the Talmudic account of this event together with their *qederot*.[30]

These witches' *qederot* have lids, and it is clear that these were used at times: a *tsamid petil*, a very closely fitting lid is noted as not allowing smells (or uncleanness) to come out.[31] The lid was relatively small in comparison to the *qederah*, as we see from the following comparison:

> Egypt is 400 parasangs square. Egypt is one sixtieth of Ethiopia, Ethiopia is one sixtieth of the world, the world is one sixtieth of the garden, the garden is one sixtieth of Eden, Eden is one sixtieth of *gehenna*, so all the world is like the lid of a *qederah* to *gehenna*.

Here, as with the metaphors of the blackened bottoms, once again we see the concept of hell as a *qederah* full of boiling stuff. Not all *qederot* had lids, however: only a few of those excavated archaeologically have a grooved rim to rest one on.[32] If there was no lid, women would tie on a cover to their *qederah* with knots which were 'meant to be untied'.[33] From another source, we know that such covers were made of paper or skins.[34] A woman who goes out and leaves a *qederah* of food when her neighbour is present can be sure she will uncover it, says the Mishnah, for no woman can resist the temptation of seeing what her neighbour is cooking.[35]

When there was no cover for the *qederah*, steam rose from the boiling food. This was called *hevel qederah*, and these vapours rising from the *qederah* were compared to the soul or breath leaving the body on the day of death, explaining why the book of Ecclesiastes writes, 'the spirit returns to God who gave it', and then follows this with *hevel havalim*, vapour of vapours, all is vapours (12, 7–8, translated by the AV as 'vanity of vanities, all is vanity').

The *qederah* is often mentioned together with another pot, the *ilpas*, or *lepes*, a name which comes from the Greek *lopas*. Everything which can be cooked in the *qederah*, we are told, can be cooked in the *ilpas*, but not vice versa. The *ilpas* was generally smaller and shallower than the *qederah*, with straight sides and a close-fitting lid with a vent hole, used for draining vegetables. It was lighter than the *qederah* and seems to have been used for more delicate cooking: the lightest of eggs beaten up in an *ilpas*. It is notable that the Greek author Galen also cooks his eggs gently in the same pan, *lopas*.[36] The Jerusalem Talmud asks what can be cooked in the *ilpas* but not in the *qederah*, and answers *hal man nunia*. Nunia refers to fish in Aramaic, but scholars disagree on the meaning of *hal man*. One suggests it means greasy, suggesting frying in the *ilpas*, and another salt, since *hal* is salt in Greek. If so, this might mean that fish were salted in this wide, shallow pot, perhaps because they would not fit in the narrower neck of the *qederah*. The evidence that vegetables, olives and locusts were salted in the *qederah* is much clearer.[37]

What was cooked in the *qederah*? *Ma'aseh qederah*, something made in a *qederah*, was, as we saw above, typically a boiling liquid, with or without lumps in it. It was made from very basic ingredients. If someone swore he would not eat *ma'aseh qederah*, he would only be forbidden to eat boiling food, *retahta*, but if he swore not to eat anything which goes into a *qederah*, he would be forbidden anything in a *qederah*. So what is *retahta*? asks the Jerusaelm Talmud, and answers: *hilqa, tragis, tisan, solet, orez, zarid, arsan*.[38] *Hilqa* is Latin *alica*, and refers to emmer meal; *tragis* is from Greek *tragos*, wheat that had been wetted to remove the husks.[39] *Tisan* is Greek *ptisane*, Latin *tisane*, and refers to a barley gruel.[40] *Solet* is fine flour, *orez* is rice, *zarid* is a porridge of broken groats and *arsan* may be a mixture of flour and water.[41] Thus *ma'aseh qederah* was a sort of porridge or gruel made out of different sorts of grains. It was considered the most basic food of the poorest people: when listing what food to give to mourners – loaves of bread, meat, fish, lentils – it is added at the bottom of the list, as only being given in places where this was the custom.[42] Similarly, it was customary to leave over some food for the poor, widows and orphans, called *peah*, from food made in the *ilpas*, but not from *ma'aseh qederah*.[43] However, not everyone agreed, and the story is told of Rabbi Joshua who once stayed with a widow who gave him some cooked groats (*grisin*), but he did not leave any over for her in the *qederah*. The same happened the next day, but on the third day she added a lot of salt to the food and he did not eat any:

> Why didn't you eat? she asked. I have already eaten, he replied. So why did you eat the bread? she asked. Perhaps you intended to leave me *peah*? If so, why did you not leave any for me the other days?
> Rabbi Joshua admitted that this widow was one of the few people who had ever got the better of him.[44]

Flour cooked in the *qederah* with oil and honey made a more desirable dish, called *havitz qederah*. Most of the other foods we have seen appear to have been eaten both in Palestine and Babylonia, but this appears to have been purely a Babylonian dish, and it is interesting to note that a sweet pudding called *khabis* appears in the tenth century in the cookbooks of the caliphs of Baghdad.[45]

The *Qederah*: the Everyday Cooking Pot of Talmudic Times

Pulses were also cooked in the *qederah*, and the Mishnah distinguishes between pulses congealed into a lump and those separate from each other.[46] We noted above that both lentils and lupines are mentioned, the latter having to be soaked many times to get rid of their alkaline poisons before cooking. In fact there are three different words used for lentils: *adashim*, *assissiot* and *telophhim*, although we do not know the differences between them. Beans were also cooked in the *qederah*.[47]

Other food cooked in the *qederah* included noodles, *itriot*. It was permissible to cook them on a festival, as they would be used on the festival, but not to make them to dry for use after the festival.[48] Vegetables were also cooked in the *qederah*, especially leeks, but the only fruit mentioned are quinces, which are noted as being the only fruit that is inedible unless cooked.[49] We might note here that quinces are often found in Arab recipes from the tenth century, where they are commonly cooked with honey.[50]

The blandness of the groats, pulses and noodles meant that the food in the *qederah* needed flavouring: all food cooked in the *qederah* needs salt, says the Babylonian Talmud, but not all needs spices.[51] We have already seen a widow adding a lot of salt, and other anonymous *tavlinim*, spices and/or flavourings are mentioned, including a bunch of herbs, which may no longer have any flavour when moved to another *qederah*.[52] The only herbs mentioned by name are dill, *shevet*, cress, *shahlayim* and safflower, *moriqa*.[53] Other flavourings added to food in the *qederah* were leeks, onion, cumin and pepper.[54] Flavourings could not be added to the *qederah* on the Sabbath, in case the heat cooked them, but they could be added after the food had been poured out into a bowl or plate.[55]

As we saw with the *havitz qederah*, sweet flavourings were also added to the *qederah*, including dates and dried figs.[56] It is in fact possible that the honey in the *havitz* was also date honey, rather than bees' honey.

With all these flavourings, it is clear that a *qederah* made of coarse pottery would absorb cooking tastes. Thus, since it was forbidden to cook meat and milk together, it was also forbidden to cook meat in a *qederah* that had had milk cooked in it previously.[57] Similarly, it was forbidden to cook Passover food in a *qederah* that had had leaven (forbidden on Passover) cooked in it, unless the *qederah* was boiled three times first.[58] The same applied if the *qederah* had had the priests' portion cooked in it, which was forbidden to ordinary people.[59] However, if the taste of the forbidden food was bad, it was permissible to eat it![60] By extension of this concern with the taste left by food in the *qederah*, a man is warned not to cook in a *qederah* his neighbour has cooked in: i.e. not to marry a divorced woman while her first husband is still alive. For if a divorced man marries a divorced woman, warn the rabbis, there will be four opinions in bed.[61]

Meat is also mentioned on a number of occasions as being cooked in the *qederah*. It is unclear whether this was because it was indeed commonly eaten, or whether, because it was not commonly eaten, the rabbis wanted to be sure that people did not transgress the rules when cooking it.[62] Thus, although baking on a festival for the day after was not allowed, people were allowed to fill a *qederah* with meat and cook it even if they only intended to eat one small piece out of it on the festival itself.⁶³ The Babylonian Talmud distinguishes between cooking times for different types of meat: young kids will cook quickly, whereas an old goat will take a long time.⁶⁴ Other meat noted came from rams.⁶⁵

Some of the references to cooking meat in the *qederah* certainly refer to theoretical situations related to sacrifices in the Temple which had been discontinued for many hundreds of years.⁶⁶ Others are found in the Babylonian Talmud, and it is generally considered likely that there was more meat available in ancient Babylonia than in late antique Palestine.⁶⁷ The archaeologist Jodi Magness has noted that, after the eighth-century Arab conquest of Palestine, there is a change in the shape of the *qederah* found in archaeological excavations. She proposes that the change in shape of the *qederah* was due to new ways of using this pot, with an increase in boiling large lumps of meat in a stew, which meant the neck would get in the way, unlike with pulses and groats. The Arabs would have brought these with them from Babylonia to Palestine.⁶⁸ Magness uses a rather wide time bracket for her Babylonian meat stews, calling into play evidence of stewing meat from ancient Sumer, as well as Baghdad of the caliphs, and suggests that there may have been local continuity. She also points out that there is very little evidence of stewed meat dishes in the Roman Apicius. However, we have seen that some Talmudic sources do report cooking meat in a stew in ancient Palestine, as well as Babylonia, and we would conclude that there is not enough evidence here to confirm or deny her interesting theory.

We have seen that food in the *qederah* was typically cooked by boiling in a liquid, *retahtah*, but the *qederah* could also be used for a kind of roasting: the Jerusalem Talmud says the Passover lamb must be properly roasted directly on the fire, and opposes this to roasting in a *qederah*, as well as on a spit or grate.⁶⁹ This method may have produced the food called *tzli qedar*, literally pot roast, although this is only mentioned once in the Babylonian Talmud and may not have been eaten in Palestine.⁷⁰

Apart from the everyday foods cooked in the *qederah*, there is also a group of Babylonian sources which talk about *tziqei qederah*, clearly a very desirable luxury food (eaten by kings' daughters, among others) which included plenty of wine. The word *tziqei*, which only occurs in this context, may come from a root meaning something poured into a mould. One source speaks of making this dish from horns, hooves and skin. Previous commentators have found this problematic for a luxury food, but it is just possible that *tziqei qederah* was the equivalent of calves' foot jelly, a traditional and much-loved Jewish dish in later times, sometimes made with wine in non-Jewish contexts in the Middle Ages.⁷¹

But I end on a less cheerful note. The *qederah* was the pot in which people cooked everyday food, but they did not always have food to put into it. Ordinary people in late antique Palestine and Babylonia lived on a knife-edge. Food was not always plentiful and often it would only take a few bad harvests for famine to threaten the poorest. And, as always, war could lead to destruction of crops and stores, and to inhuman responses

The Qederah: the Everyday Cooking Pot of Talmudic Times

to the consequent shortage of basic food. The Talmudic sources bear witness to this with several harrowing famine readings, which even if they are written years later than the events they describe or contain clearly legendary elements, certainly reflect the ever-present fear of famine.

The first tells of the shame of poverty in a normative society. The wife of R Shimon b Halafta was so ashamed not to have food for Passover that she put her empty *qederah* on the fire and boiled water in it so the neighbours would not know she did not have food to put in it.[72] On seeing this, her husband is said to have prayed until a precious stone was sent him from heaven and he went to buy meat and wine and vegetables for the festival. His wife was suspicious of this unusual plenty, and he owned up to what he had done. Isn't it enough I am ashamed in front of the neighbours here, she said, should I also be ashamed when I get to heaven? He went and prayed again and everything was taken back. This was a greater miracle than the first, the *midrash* tells us, but does not tell us where they got the food to survive on afterwards.

The defeat of the second century CE revolt against the Romans in Palestine led to mass killings and to captivity and deprivation for the survivors. *Midrash Lamentations Zutra* was written in the wake of the revolt, and recounts terrible stories. Two of these centre round the *qederah*. A woman who had only one spoonful of flour left cooked it in her *qederah* and spilled one drop. Her four sons killed each other in their fight to get the spilled drop.[73] Another story from the same collection tells of two brothers who had gone to the war. When they came back, their mother had nothing to give them to eat and served them up their baby brother cooked in the *qederah*. When they found out what they had eaten, they both jumped off the roof.[74] In these stories, the sufferings of the Jews of Palestine after the failure of the revolt are carried by the *qederah*, empty or horribly full.

Notes

1. Mishnah Ketubot v, 8. This is preceded by a list of the works a woman must perform for her husband. For an explanation of the Talmudic literature, see my paper 'Nuts for the Children' in *Nurture: Proceedings of the Oxford Symposium on Food and Cookery 2003*, ed. R. Hosking (Bristol: Footwork, 2004), p.264.
2. D. Adan Bayewitz, *Common Pottery in Roman Galilee: A Study of Local Trade* (Ramat Gan: Bar-Ilan UP, 1993).
3. Midrash Lamentations Zutra i, 5.
4. Leviticus Rabbah xii, 1.
5. BTBeitzah 16a and see J. Brandt, *Ceramic Vessels in Talmudic Literature* [Hebrew] (Jerusalem: 1953), p.473.
6. Midrash Deuteronomy Rabbah parshat Eqev, ed. Lieberman p.78.
7. Hanging: M.Oholot v, 7; U. Zevulun, Y. Olenick, *Function and design in the Talmudic* period (Tel Aviv, 1979); F. Vitto, 'Potters and pottery manufacture in Roman Palestine' *University of London Institute of Archaeology Bulletin* 23 (1986) 47–64.
8. Tos Oholot 10.12, tr. Zevulun and Olenik, n.7 above. Vicky Hayward tells me that al-Andalus cookery used pots or jugs stacked on top of each other and sealed with flour and water paste for cooking. This

is similar to Tos Shabbat iii, 23, where a seal of dough is used for keeping food warm in stacked *qederot*, but not for cooking.
9. Vitto, p.49; J. Magness, 'Conspicuous consumption: dining on meat in the ancient world'. I am grateful to Jodi Magness for letting me see an early draft of her unpublished paper.
10. Zevulun and Olenik, n.7 above.
11. Brandt, n.5 above.
12. S. Rotroff, *Hellenistic Pottery: The Fine Wares. The Athenian Agora 33* (Princeton, 2006): 165–166 [*non vidi*], qtd. in W. Flint Dibble, 'The Archaeology of Food in Athens: The Development of an Athenian Urban Lifestyle', MA thesis, U of Cincinnati, 2010.
13. JT Hagigah ii, 2.
14. BT Rosh haShanah 17a.
15. Tos Shabbat xi 5; BT Beitzah 34a.
16. BT Pesahim 27a.
17. M Kelim viii, 9; M Kelim vii 1; BT Shabbat 102b.
18. JT Shabbat ii 5.
19. MKelim viii 4.
20. JT Terumot ii, 1; JT Shabbat iii,1.
21. JTShabbat i 10.
22. TosDemai iv, 32.
23. JT Avodah Zarah ii 10; 42a and cf. BT Hullin 6b.
24. BT Shabbat 29a; Tos Shabbat xiv, 1.
25. Italian Jews still have food commemorating the defeat of the Egyptians at the Red Sea, but not cooked in a *qederah*: *ruota di Faraone*, which is a round dish of baked noodles with a sauce containing diced goose breast, raisins and pine nuts. The noodles are said to represent the waves of the sea, and the diced goose and raisins the heads of the Egyptians! Q.v. A. Toaff, *Mangiare alla Giudia* (Bologna: Il Mulino, 2000), p.133.
26. Tos Shabbat vi, 14.
27. Pliny, Nat. Hist. 23, 127.
28. BT Shabbat 67b.
29. BT Gittin 45a.
30. JT Hagigah ii, 2 77d–78a and cf JT Sanhedrin vi, 6.
31. Tos Kelim Bava Qama vi 10.
32. Zevulun and Olenik, n.7.
33. JT Shabbat xv 2; BT Shabbat 112b.
34. M Kelim x,4.
35. M Tohorot vii,9.
36. Galen vi 769. See on this my paper 'Eggs in the Talmud' in *Eggs in Cookery: Proceedings of the Oxford Symposium on Food and Cookery 2006*, ed. Richard Hosking (Totnes, UK: Prospect Books, 2007), pp. 270–81.
37. Vegetables: M.Tohorot ii, 1; olives: BT Taanit 24b and parallels; locusts: Midrash Exodus Rabbah xiii, 7.
38. JT Nedarim vi 2 39b.
39. For problems of identification of *tragos*, see C. Perry, '*Trakhanas* Revisited' *PPC* 55 (1997): pp. 34–39. I am grateful to Charles Perry for bringing this to my notice.
40. Dalby, n .43, p.46.
41. Jastrow, *sv* 'a-r-s.
42. Semahot xiv, 13.
43. Derkh Eretz iv, 13.
44. Lamentations Rabbah i, 1 9 19.
45. N. Nasrallah, *Annals of the Caliph's Kitchens* (Leiden: Brill, 2010), pp. 388–401. These versions of *khabis*

The *Qederah*: the Everyday Cooking Pot of Talmudic Times

are all made with expensive ingredients in a *tanjir* (copper cauldron with rounded bottom); C. Perry et al., *Medieval Arab Cookery* (Totnes, UK: Prospect Books, 2001): sv *khabis* in the index. Perry quotes a source that identifies *khabis* as rich Persian food, p.151.

46. M Tevul Yom ii 5.
47. BT Hullin 45b.
48. JT Beitzah i 7 60d.
49. BT Nedarim 54a; Nasrallah, n. 4; JT Maaserot i 2.
50. Nasrallah, n.48; p. 486 (with honey); p. 480 medicinally with honey, vinegar and spices; p. 276 in chicken stew.
51. BT Beitzah 14a.
52. M Orlah ii 15; BT Shabbat 90a etc.; JT Terumot xi 1.
53. Tos Tohorot ii 2; BT Beitzah 14a.
54. JT Orlah ii 5. Pepper: BT Hullin 97b.
55. BT Pesahim 40b, cf. JT Maaserot i 4.
56. Tos Uqtzin iii 14.
57. Tos Terumot viii 16.
58. JT Pesahim iii 1.
59. JT Terumot xi 4.
60. BT Pesahim and parallels.
61. BT Pesahim 112a.
62. e.g. M Shabbat xv, 2; Tos Eruvin viii, 4; JT Shabbat xv, 2 and parallels ; BT Hullin 84a etc.
63. Tos Beitzah ii 5 and parallels.
64. BT Shabbat 18b.
65. BT Hullin 98b.
66. BT Bekhorot 33a; BT Temurah 24a etc.
67. A. Oppenheimer, 'Purity of Lineage in Talmudic Babylonia', *Manières de penser dans l'Antiquité méditerranéenne et orientale, Mélanges offerts à Francis Schmidt*, eds C. Batsch and M. Vârtejanu-Joubert (Leiden: Brill, 2009), pp. 145–56.
68. Magness, n. 9.
69. JT Pesahim vii 1–2.
70. BT Megillah 7b.
71. This is a complex subject that I discussed in detail in my presentation at the Symposium, but there is no room to expand on it here. Sources for *tziqei qederah*: Avot de Rabbi Natan A, 6; BT Ketubot 65a; BT Pesahim 56a; BT Yoma 75a etc; made of bones etc.: BT Hullin 77b; wine: Ménagier de Paris. 15 Entremès, fritures et dorures : pour faire quatre plats de gelée de char.
72. Midrash Tehillim xcii,8.
73. Midrash Lamentations Zutra i 10 33.
74. Midrash Lamentations Zutra i 11, 34.

Travelling Tools and Mobile Kitchens: the Role of Extra-domiciliary Kitchens in Great Household Victualling Strategies, c. 1400–1600

Ryan Whibbs

Figure 1. Anon., The Field of the Cloth of Gold *c. 1545 (Royal Collection Trust / © Her Majesty Queen Elizabeth II, 2013. Used by permission.)*

The 'interview' at the Field of the Cloth of Gold was a famous Tudor diplomatic spectacle designed to foster peace between England and France. Occurring over a number of weeks in June, 1520, Henry VIII of England hosted Francis I of France to an outdoor meeting at a large field near Balinghem, Pas-de-Calais, France. Determined to impress Francis with his ability to muster resources in the English-held region, Henry spared no expense equipping the field with a banqueting house for serving sweets and drink, a jousting arena and an array of domestic quarters established under elaborately-adorned tents. The interview was a great success with both monarchs returning to attend another at the same site in 1532.[1]

While the interviews of 1520 and 1532 remain celebrated events in the political histories of France and England, we know surprisingly little about food provision at the field. Who cooked the magnificent feasts that Henry, Francis and their retinues enjoyed? Where were the kitchens located? Who provided the *batterie de cuisine* and other materials necessary for cooking?

Travelling Tools and Mobile Kitchens

This paper will survey practicalities of fifteenth- and sixteenth-century European great household food provision during periods of travel. Evidence indicates that there was a widespread practice among the élite of sending advance parties of kitchen servants to locations where masters intended to rest or lodge in order to transport kitchen materials, to maintain regular mealtimes and to serve appropriate food to masters and servants upon their arrival. Although the topic currently draws little scholarly attention, some well-known sources including Chiquart's *Du fait de cuysine* (1420) and Bartolomeo Scappi's *Opera* (1570) as well as a number of lesser-known household ordinance and account books mention advance kitchen parties and describe their practical arrangements. By requiring servants to devise methods of providing the household with suitable food during travel, masters initiated development of highly complex mobile victualling strategies that are not currently associated with the range of tasks required of early modern great household kitchen workers.

Temporary feasting kitchens

Large feasts are one of the most noted features of medieval dining. Many great halls and castle kitchens continue to stand across Europe and testify to the grandeur of late medieval royal and noble dining habits. While these rooms convey a sense of the vast scale of cooking and serving space necessary to feed great households, textual evidence indicates that, by the late medieval period, some great lords hosted feasts of such magnitude that cooking areas needed to be moved out-of-house and established under temporary structures.

Master Chiquart, celebrated master cook to Duke Amadeus VIII of Savoy, outlined the special preparations necessary for extra-domiciliary feasting kitchens in his 1420 cookery manuscript, *Du fait de cuysine*.[2] While Chiquart's work is famous for its recipes, large portions were also taken up with advice on hosting feasts attended by 'kings, queens, dukes, duchesses, counts, countesses, princes, princesses, marquises, marchionesses, barons, baronesses, lords of lower estate and nobles also a great number.'[3] In cases when so many notables assembled, along with their retinues, the volume of required food seems to have been more than even a large kitchen could process. In total, Chiquart recommended to have on hand at least 100 cattle, 120 pigs, 130 mutton, 200 kids, 200 lambs, 100 calves, 100 piglets, 2000 head of poultry, and 6000 eggs, noting that the feast would occur over a number of days.[4]

Buried in Chiquart's text are a number of peculiar notes surrounding the organization of the kitchen. He noted:

> The master of the household, the master cook and other cooks should assemble and come together three or four months before the feast to organize, visit and find good and sufficient space to do the cooking and this space should be so large and fine that workbenches can be setup in such fashion that, between the serving sideboards and other tables, cooks can easily pass and receive dishes…. There

should be made a large and fair building [*si faire se peut, un beau et grand hôtel*] close to the kitchen having space for two large ovens for making meat and fish pies, tarts, flans, *talmouses*, *ratons* and all other things which are necessary.[5]

His advice that cooking space must be 'visited' and 'found' is peculiar given that the Château de Ripaille, Amadeus's VIII's primary residence, already had monumental stone kitchens and bakeries.[6] Even more peculiar was the suggestion that staff 'make' (*faire*) a 'building' (*hôtel*) whose proximity should be close to the kitchen. It seems likely that the kitchen Chiquart described was actually an extra-domiciliary kitchen, established temporarily outside Ripaille, and used to cope with so many guests.

Further evidence of the kitchen's extra-domiciliary nature can be found in the composition of Chiquart's recommended *batterie de cuisine*:

And for this there should be provided great cauldrons for cooking large meats and other medium ones in great abundance for making potages and other things necessary for cookery and great pans for cooking fish and other necessary things and large common pots in great abundance for making soups and other things, twelve fair large mortars, … and there should be twenty large frying pans, twelve large casks, fifty casks, sixty bowls with handles, one hundred wooden buckets, twelve grills, six large graters, one hundred wooden spoons, twenty-five slotted spoons both large and small, six hooks, twenty iron shovels, twenty 'chapel' and goat rotisseries … you should have one hundred twenty iron spits which are strong and are thirteen feet in length and there should be other spits, thirty-six which are of the aforesaid length but not so thick, in order to roast poultry, piglets and river fowl … and also, forty-eight small spits to use for gilding food and to act as skewers.[7]

Though vast in scale, most of the various cauldrons, pots and pans were among the normal articles of a *batterie* that one would expect to find in a fifteenth-century great lord's kitchen. More exceptional were the twenty rotisseries.[8] Though Ripaille's kitchens were large, they almost certainly did not have sufficient space nor ventilation to operate twenty rotisseries indoors. Instead, the large numbers of rotisseries seem to have allowed Amadeus's cooks to prepare the thousands of fauna required at feasts away from Ripaille's kitchen and without reliance on its permanent stone hearths.

When we consider Chiquart's intended readership, the notion that these were special preparations becomes clearer. He prepared the work at the request of the duke mentioning that Amadeus sought instructions for his household cooks to guide them through preparations required at times of feasts and festivals; this was not a guide for everyday cookery and it was tailored specifically to Amadeus' household.[9] The original manuscript, held at the Médiathèque du Valais, Switzerland, was dictated by Chiquart to a local notary, Jehan de Dudens, who transcribed it by hand on unembellished paper quires.¹⁰ Addressed to the duke, one gets the sense that Chiquart was not aware that he was creating a work that would be read far outside the duke's household. Within this context, it would have been clear to Chiquart and the duke's servants that the instructions surrounding 'finding' and 'visiting' space for kitchens referred to spaces other than the kitchens of Ripaille. Similarly, it would have been clear that the instructions to make a 'large and fair building' for pastry work referred to a place other than the permanent stone bakery that was located within Ripaille's foundations. Less clear is the kitchen's location relative to Ripaille: was this kitchen close to the castle and used to augment the castle's own kitchen, or was the entire feast held away from Ripaille?

While Chiquart did not provide answers to those questions, specifically, some answers can be gleaned from a similar feast held exactly a century after Chiquart completed his manuscript: Henry VIII's feasts held in honour of Francis I at the Field of the Cloth of Gold in 1520. Receipts from the event, transcribed in the *Letters and Papers, Foreign and Domestic, Henry VIII, Volume 3: 1519–1523*, indicate that the highest élites were, indeed, willing to uproot their *batteries de cuisine* and cooks in order to host extra-domiciliary feasts when the number of guests or political situation required it.¹¹ Like the staggering quantities of food served at Duke Amadeus VIII's feasts, Henry also ensured that his guests at the three-week feast were supplied with seemingly unending quantities of food: 350 oxen, 2000 sheep, 1200 capons, 800 veal, 19 sturgeon, 1 dolphin and 2400 quail among tens of thousands of other aquatic and terrestrial fauna.¹²

Visual and textual records reveal that the kitchens used at the field were derived from a combination of rented buildings and purpose-built areas.¹³ The Royal Collection's oil painting, *The Field of the Cloth of Gold* (c. 1545), offers some insight as to the arrangement of the kitchen tents and oven that served the field.¹⁴ On the right-hand side of the painting, two tents housed cooking spaces; one houses a roasting area with rotisseries while the other houses cauldrons. An enormous brick baking oven is seen being tended by bakers, their peels lying atop. Separating the cooking and serving areas were a number of long work benches; some used by cooks and bakers for preparing food, while one holds stacks of serving platters and seems to be tended by cooks and servers. While the painting offers some idea of kitchen arrangements in the field, other aspects are not pictured.

In the months leading up to Henry's arrival, his agents in Calais, Sir Edward Belknap and Sir Nicholas Vaux, rented several other properties to augment the field kitchen.¹⁵ Margett Goldsmith and Mychell Byndea rented their houses to the royal household for six weeks to provide space for butcheries.¹⁶ Two other houses were rented to provide space for a spicery and a scalding house.¹⁷ The great brick baking oven shown in the oil painting was augmented by the baking services of Cornelius Baker and Mary Thomas whose Calais bakery was rented for the entirety of the interview.¹⁸ Through tents and hired businesses Henry was able to provide enough cookery space for his highly skilled kitchen servants to create feasts of historic proportions.

Food and Material Culture

Figure 2. Anon., The Field of the Cloth of Gold (detail) c. 1545 (Royal Collection Trust / © Her Majesty Queen Elizabeth II, 2013. Used by permission.)

Supplying a *batterie de cuisine* at the field presented additional challenges. Henry's cooks could bring some tools with them from his palaces, though the demands of serving so many people required rental of extra equipment. The 'cooks of London' allowed the royal household to rent a huge assortment of spits, pots and frying pans at a total cost of £17.7s.8d.[19] Despite this, other tools had to be bought outright. William Company sold the royal household three flesh axes, six dressing knives, three mincing knives and ten lashing knives for £1.3s.4d.[20] Nicholas Pynson supplied a number of skimmers and ladles.[21] Philip Fewacre provided new hippocras bowls, coal shovels, bread graters and oven peels; possibly the peels pictured being used in the oil painting.[22] Once obtained, the 'kitchen stuffe' was first transported by sea to Calais at a cost of 19s.7d., then inland from Calais by wagon.[23] Not surprisingly, the latter portion of the trip was delayed after the wagon carrying the *batterie* 'broke' requiring wagon repair at a further cost of 2s.[24]

Waiting to use the *batterie* when it arrived were at least 84 cooks and kitchen workers that the royal household had transported from London.[25] The *brigade de cuisine* that they were organized into at the field closely paralleled their normal division of labour when in-house.[26] Various receipts mentioned provisions bought for the bakery, privy kitchen, hall kitchen, scalding house, boiling house, pantry and buttery.[27] Some cooks were mentioned by name such as Robert Constantine, cook in the hall kitchen, and John Alumbye, groom of the boiling house, though most are unknown.[28] To provide housing and sleeping space, the royal household rented local houses for the cooks as well as a separate house for kitchen supervisors.[29] In addition to these cooks, a number of speciality craftsmen were also hired. Thomas Tayllor provided 'cream for the King's cakes' and John Ricrofte was hired to make 4000 wafers.[30]

Travelling Tools and Mobile Kitchens

Extra-domiciliary feasts were the exception rather than the rule. While most feasts happened indoors, some of the largest and most impressive could sometimes involve erection of temporary kitchens and even short- or long-distance travel. One might wonder if such an idea was well advised; with so many nobles in attendance and with cooks working under irregular circumstances, disorganization in the kitchen could prove highly embarrassing. However, evidence indicates that, in addition to feasts of exceptional magnitude, cooks of late-medieval royal and noble households often had a good deal of experience in devising systems in order to provision their master's household while in transit.

Great household kitchens in transit

Whereas extra-domiciliary feasting kitchens were designed for extraordinary meals and required long periods of time to prepare, daily cookery arrangements used by travelling nobles took more mobile forms. On longer journeys whose routes included a number of towns or cities, provisioning servants likely relied, in part, on local cookshops, bakers and so on.[31] Other times well-placed individuals could rely on friends who lived along the planned route for billeting and food.[32] However, when travelling élites could not rely on friends or a town with enough cookshops, cooks were often brought along for the journey.

Chiquart mentioned the habit in passing, noting that one had to incorporate extra space and tools in feasting kitchens to accommodate cooks that would arrive in guests' entourages.[33] Although Chiquart stopped short of explaining the duties of travelling cooks, a vivid description of their work comes to us from Bartolomeo Scappi's 1570 *Opera*. Scappi, personal cook (*coquus secretus*) of Popes Pius IV and V, produced the *Opera* as a culinary *tour de force* that also included long passages of kitchen management advice. Accompanying the text, Scappi commissioned a series of copperplate engravings to illustrate to readers many of the tools and arrangements discussed in the book. One of the engravings, Field Kitchen (*Cucina per Campagna*), illustrated the arrangements necessary for cooking for a great lord while in transit.

Although Scappi's work is famous, this particular image has received little attention. Earlier in the text, Scappi noted that the field kitchen was to be used 'for a trip any great prince might wish to take'.[34] The engraver depicted a kitchen that was equipped with tools designed to complement speed and mobility. Two different types of andirons – fixed and hinged – were designed to allow cooks to boil food in cauldrons and roast meat on spits at once. Importantly, the andiron's design allowed wood to be set directly on the ground, simplifying preparation of the fire pit. Shelter was provided by a simple canopy without any of the *hôtels* or brick ovens associated with Amadeus's and Henry's more substantial feasting kitchens. The lack of work tables and ovens seems to indicate that menu options were modified to allow for simple, faster cookery methods: boiling, roasting and possibly frying. Breads and other food items could be purchased *en route*. Wicker saddle-baskets hold tools in the foreground while longer, three-sided cases hold

Figure 3. Field kitchen (Cucina per Campagna)*, Bartolomeo Scappi,* Opera, *1570 (Courtesy of the Thomas Fisher Rare Book Library, University of Toronto)*

a collection of other equipment. The three-sided shapes of both sets of cases seem to indicate that they were designed to be hung along the side of a horse's saddle or along a wagon for transport. None of the cases was fully unpacked; the cook simply removed tools required for that meal. As much as the engraving explains about transitory field cookery, it raises a very practical question: if this kitchen was used for quick meals on the road, what did Scappi's master – the Pope – do while waiting for cooks to light fires and boil large cauldrons of soup? It seems too banal a problem to delay popes' business, and indeed, it surely was.

In a few rarely cited passages of his *Opera*, Scappi explained the mechanics of the field kitchen, noting that its function would be useful to great households in general:

> Should it become necessary for him who is deemed of use and service to a lord to go travelling, he should be able with authority and propriety to select skilled and reliable men and, while still appropriate for the office [kitchen], the lightest and most functional equipment, not overlooking mounts for his assistants, scullions and pastry workers who have to go on ahead with the first kitchen; and mounts likewise for those who have to remain behind with the second one, and he has to

arrange that the scullions who will follow on foot will not lack shoes and other things normally given to them, nor the porters who accompany such kitchens, loading and unloading the packs, not forgetting wind-proof torches and their wind vane when the kitchen sets out on a journey.[35]

Scappi's detail in explaining the two-kitchen provisioning system was unique among sixteenth-century cookery manuals. The 'kitchens' in these cases were not rooms but rather workers accompanied by their tools. The use of two fully-equipped groups of kitchen workers allowed one group always to 'go on ahead' of the main body of the household in order to establish a new field kitchen in time for the lord's arrival. The second kitchen may have departed ahead of the household's completion of the meal in order to establish the next field kitchen. Need for more than one travelling kitchen seems to have been mandated by the time it took to transport and use the *batterie* in the field; one kitchen always had to be present serving their master while the other continued on to attend to preparations required for the next meal. Scappi was in a unique position to be aware of these travelling systems, not only because the papal household was constantly travelling throughout the Papal States, but also because he was in touch with the cooks of many royal, curial and noble households referencing their kitchen management practices throughout his introductory epistle.[36]

When great lords owned a number of residences, outdoor field kitchens sometimes played a lesser role in provisioning, though a two-kitchen travelling system was still crucial. Henry Percy, Fifth Earl of Northumberland (1477–1527), required his kitchen servants to enter into a very specific division of labour at each 'removal', or journey, between residences. One of the great northern land magnates, Percy was integrated into the networks of influence at Henry VIII's court. Percy accompanied Henry to the Field of the Cloth of Gold and was even listed as a judge at the jousting tournaments held there in 1520, so his household servants had a good deal of experience in travelling with their master between his seats in Northumberland, Yorkshire, London and occasionally on his trips to France.[37] The 1512 *Northumberland Household Ordinance Book* notes that Percy divided the year between his properties and, like many Tudor noblemen, required his servants to pack and transport the bulk of his household chattels at every removal.[38] Of the 166 servants listed in his household ordinance book, about forty worked in household food service departments including kitchens, buttery, pantry and cellars.[39]

In the days before removals, Percy's servants were required to put forward five workers that would go 'afore unto the place wheir his Lordeschip remevith unto,' including a groom and usher of the bedchamber, an usher of the hall and a clerk and groom of the kitchen.[1] This small band of servants was used 'for making redy for my Lorde' and would be joined by the rest of the household upon Percy's arrival.[41] Although Scappi's *Opera* mentioned horses and wicker and wooden cases as transport devices for the *batterie*, Percy's household used three wagons to carry all kitchen tools. Of the three, one was used for the 'keching stuff as spittes, pottes, pannes, traffettes, raks and pastrystuf'; another was used for cloths, serving vessels and beds for the kitchen staff; and a third transported 'the stuff belonginge the bakhous with the bedde for the bakers, [and] the bed for the brewers.'[42] It is difficult for us to image the scale of work necessary to facilitate such removals, though the fact that Percy's household had preordained labour arrangements in place to deal with these journeys speaks to a regular need to organize such systems.

A similar system of travelling kitchen departments served the household of Thomas Cranmer, Archbishop of Canterbury. The first reformed archbishop to hold the See of Canterbury, Cranmer occupied the post through the turbulent period between 1533 and 1553. Cranmer's *Ordinance Book* of *c.* 1540 included a single short ordinance pertaining to governance of the household while on journeys:

> Yt is ordeyned that every personne of howshold as such seasons as my Lord rideth, ryde not owt of my Lords company, except such as shallbe appoynted wth the Sumpter horse officers purvior, and other wch shallbe assigned by the hedd officers for preparing of vitalls and other stuffe.[43]

Though far less descriptive than the 1512 *Northumberland Household Ordinance Book*, a similar pattern emerges of household victuallers separating from the household 'for preparing of vitalls and other stuffe.' Like other sources, conveyance was accomplished by means of a sumpter horse.[44] Cranmer's main residences were located at Canterbury, Croydon and Lambeth with a number of other properties throughout Kent. With such a network of residences, it is likely his household provisioners could rely on residence kitchens as opposed to the field kitchens Scappi recommended.

Overall, travelling kitchens present us with a diverse group of management systems not typically associated with great household victualling departments. When a lord announced their desire to go on a journey, they put into motion a series of preordained management systems designed to transport two essential elements of a professionally-staffed kitchen: a *batterie de cuisine* and workers. The spaces in which these two elements came together varied between field kitchens or, in the cases of Percy and Cranmer, various castle and palace kitchens. Although Cranmer's *Ordinances* only mentioned separation of victualling servants from the household, the *Opera* and the *Northumberland Ordinance* specified the use of advance kitchen departments. This need for advance arrival, I suggest, was the result of masters' unwillingness to wait for pots to boil after a long day of travel. The solution, in these cases, was to have workers and tools in place before masters' arrivals.

Advanced kitchen parties reveal a side of early modern great household kitchen operations that is rarely recognized in scholarship on the topic. While grand residences usually served as settings for magnificent feasts, aristocratic cooks had to be proficient at moving between residences and cooking outside such well-equipped environments. Although surviving castle and palace kitchens speak to the monumental scale of

Travelling Tools and Mobile Kitchens

demands placed on early modern great household cooks, they do not reveal the complexity of kitchen operations when the household was travelling. By examining the lengths that servants went to in order to provide food to élites during periods of travel, we can begin to understand a new dimension of early-modern great household culinary materiality. The many kitchen tools and materials that we typically think of as stationary and associate with the interiors of early modern great household kitchens were, in fact, sometimes transported across the countryside by specially-organized household culinary workers in order to see to masters' alimentary needs wherever they might be.

Notes

1. Richard Turpyn, '1532', *The Chronicle of Calais*, ed. John Gough (London: Camden Society, 1846), pp. 116–29.
2. Maître Chiquart, *Du fait de cuisine*, eds. Florence Bouas and Frédéric Vivas (Arles: Actes Sud, 2008), p. 158.
3. Chiquart, p. 57.
4. Chiquart, p. 57.
5. Chiquart, p. 58, 61.
6. Max Pierre Marie Bruchet, *Le Château de Ripaille (1907)* (repub. Thonon-les-Bains: Laffitte, 1980), pp. 260, 485, 552.
7. Chiquart, pp. 58–59.
8. Chiquart, p. 59. I speculate that 'Chapel' rotisseries may have been similar in design to the hinged andirons seen in the engraving of the 'field kitchen' found in Scappi; when spread out in tandem over a fire pit with spits across both sides, the rotisserie's form resembled the pitched roof of a chapel or narrow hall. No additional information about their form comes to us from Chiquart.
9. Chiquart, p. 56.
10. Chiquart, pp. 55, 158. Original manuscript currently held as MS Sion Médiathèque du Valais S 103.
11. Anon., 'Expenses at Guisnes for the Interview', *Letters and Papers, Foreign and Domestic, Henry VIII, Volume 3: 1519–1523*, ed. J.S. Brewer (London: Longmans *et al.*, 1867), pp. 334–36.
12. Anon., 'Expenses at Guisnes', pp. 334, 337.
13. Anon., 'Expenses at Guisnes', pp. 334–36.
14. Anon., *The Field of the Cloth of Gold*, c. 1545, Royal Collection, Inventory Number: 405794, OM 25.
15. Turpyn, *Chronicle*, p. 293.
16. Anon., 'Expenses at Guisnes', p. 335.
17. Anon., 'Expenses at Guisnes', p. 334.
18. Anon., 'Expenses at Guisnes', p. 332.
19. Anon., 'Expenses at Guisnes', p. 336.
20. Anon., 'Expenses at Guisnes', p. 335.
21. Anon., 'Expenses at Guisnes', p. 335.
22. Anon., 'Expenses at Guisnes', p. 335.
23. Anon., 'Expenses at Guisnes', p. 335.
24. Anon., 'Expenses at Guisnes', pp. 334–35.
25. Anon., 'Expenses at Guisnes', p. 337.
26. The most comprehensive survey published to date on the division of labour in late-medieval English great households can be found in Peter Brears, *Cooking and Dining in Medieval England* (Totnes, U.K.: Prospect Books, 2008).
27. Respectively, the king's kitchen, the kitchen that served nobles and lesser attendees, a kitchen used for blanching and plucking large volumes of poultry in preparation for further cooking, a kitchen used for

cooking braised meats and broths, a department specializing in the serving of bread and a department responsible for portioning and serving drink.

28. Anon., 'Expenses at Guisnes', pp. 334–35.
29. Anon., 'Expenses at Guisnes', p. 335.
30. Anon., 'Expenses at Guisnes', p. 335.
31. Françoise Desportes, 'Les métiers de l'alimentation', *Histoire de l'alimentation*, eds. Massimo Montanari and Jean-Louis Flandrin (Paris: Fayard, 1996), pp. 433–34.
32. For example, Henry VIII rested at the archbishop's palace in Canterbury before leaving for the Field of the Cloth of Gold, see Turpyn, '26–31 May 1520', *Chronicle*, 28; also, records of Catherine de Medici and Charles IX's various tours of France during 1554–1556 detail their reliance on both friends' chateaux and the royal household's own travelling provisioners when staying in poor (*pauvre*) locales; see Abel Jouan, *Recueil et discours du voyage du roy Charles IX, 1554–1556*, ed. Jean Bonfons (Paris: Jean Bonfons Libraire, 1566).
33. 'And because at this feast there are some lords or ladies as was said above who have their own master cooks whom they command to prepare and make ready certain things, for such there should be given and made available to the said master cook quickly, amply, in great abundance and promptly everything for which he asks and which he needs for the said lord or lady or both so that he can serve them to his taste' (Chiquart, p. 61).
34. Bartolomeo Scappi, *Opera* [1570], ed. and trans. Terence Scully (Toronto: U Toronto P, 2008), p. 641.
35. Scappi, pp. 131–32.
36. Scappi, p. 131.
37. Percy was listed in the general list of nobles accompanying Henry VIII, see Turpyn, 'The apoyntment for the kynge to atend upon hym over the sea to Caleys in the xij. yere of his reigne, 1520', *Chronicle*, 20; and among the 'Juges deputed for the felde for the kinges parte', *Chronicle*, 89. Also, in terms of the question of whether Percy's household servants accompanied him to France, Turpyn noted that when nobles accompanied Henry to Calais in 1520, earls were allowed to bring 'xxx servants, whereof vi gentlemen and x horses'. It likely that some of Percy's retinue was comprised of his personal domestic servants including cooks, see Turpyn, *Chronicle*, 27. For descriptions of his English residences, see Anon., *Regulations and Establishment of the Household of Henry Algernon Percy, 1512*, ed. T.P. (London: 1770), pp. 451–64.
38. *Percy Household Ordinances 1512*, pp. 386–92.
39. *Percy Household Ordinances 1512*, pp. 253–55.
40. *Percy Household Ordinances 1512*, p. 153.
41. *Percy Household Ordinances 1512*, p. 250.
42. *Percy Household Ordinances*, p. 388.
43. Lambeth Palace MS 884, fol. 9v–10r, 'Ryding in the Company of the Lord', *Household Ordinances of Thomas Cranmer, Archbishop of Canterbury*.
44. A medium-sized horse used in transport.

Renewing the Second Skin: Kee Wah Bakery's Mooncake Packaging Makeover in the 1990s

Jennifer Wong

Much food-related research has focused on the cultural identity of food and its ability to respond to the surrounding environment. Taking a closer look at the contemporary market for edibles, however, it is often the food packaging that acts as the key agent in stating its contents' identity rather than the food item itself. Not only does the packaging provide the first impression for consumers, but it also carries practical information such as the ingredients, origin and nutrition value. Yet as much as food packaging is a determining factor in our purchasing choice, we seem to forget its power once the food is unwrapped. The packaging that once ignited consumers' desire quickly loses its purpose and enters the next phase of its social biography as either a highly cherished decorative object or simply unwanted trash. However, as this paper will show, packaging can also be a site for unpacking interactions between the local and the global, as well as between tradition and modernity. The design history of the Hong Kong-based Kee Wah Bakery's mooncake packaging, which protects one of the most representative foods in Chinese festivals, also demonstrates the different relationships packaging can share with its edible contents.

As one of the few remaining local businesses with 75 years of history, Kee Wah Bakery has witnessed many social and political changes in Hong Kong. Though rooted in Chinese culture, the city was a British colony for over 150 years before returning to Communist rule in 1997. Due to instability in China since the nineteenth century, including the Taiping rebellion, the Chinese Civil War, the Sino-Japanese War and the Cultural Revolution, steady waves of migrants had made Hong Kong their new home from the 1840s to early 1980s. In addition, as a key entrepôt and financial centre in East Asia, visitors from across the world frequented the city and many chose to settle down permanently. Therefore, Hong Kong's identity is far from homogenous: citizens need to negotiate innovatively to retain even part of their respective cultural traditions.

By focusing on Hong Kong, then, we are not ignoring but inciting global discussions because 'locality itself is a historical product and … the histories through which localities emerge are eventually subject to the dynamics of the global.'[1] Although expatriates and other ethnic groups have had their contributions to the development of the Hong Kong identity, for the purposes of this paper, I will mainly focus on Hong Kong's Chinese citizens, who make up 95% of its total population. Not only are the various Chinese identities, traditions and customs coexisting, but they are also negotiating with global forces. Inevitably, Hong Kong has developed a 'Chineseness' that is different from that of Mainland China or elsewhere because of its special course in history. The resulting local identity is 'both Chinese and Western, *as well as* ... non-Chinese and non-Western.'[2] The manifestation of this unique local identity has attracted the attention of specialists from different disciplines, including art history, design studies, anthropology and sociology.[3]

Like people, food carries specific characteristics that mark its cultural, national or ethnic origin.[4] Aside from being an expression of 'self', food can also serve as an ambassador of place. Tourists who are seeking 'authentic' experiences may visit local food outlets and take edible souvenirs home with them. In Hong Kong's local history, food has been one of the key agents that blur ethnic boundaries 'in the form of the Chinese adoption of non-Chinese foodstuffs, the syncretization of Chinese and European traditions, and the consumption of these foods.'[5] The culinary diversity in Hong Kong is most evident in Lan Kwai Fong and Soho, where over fourteen distinct cuisines can be found within 500 metres in the city's most popular entertainment districts. Cooking techniques and flavours of distinctive origins are combined together to create local signature dishes, such as the Hong Kong-style baked pork chop rice: a slice of juicy pork chop is placed on top of a skillet of plain fried rice, covered in a tomato- or ketchup-based sauce, and baked to perfection. Other food items that are deeply associated with local customs, such as mooncake, often serve as a reminder of ethnic traditions. The origins of mooncake can be traced back to the twelfth century, and the pastry has become an indispensable part of celebrating the Mid-Autumn Festival, which takes place annually on the fifteenth day of the eighth month in the Chinese calendar, when the lunar phase reaches the full moon.[6] Arguably, the very act of ingesting mooncake has also become a tradition. Since the social significance that is imbued in food is often shared by its packaging, mooncake packaging also plays an important role in retaining such social meanings. As the inseparable second skin of the pastry, it has to relay the traditional message that its food content carries.

The packaging also serves, of course, as a sign of the producer. Local family businesses in Hong Kong have often been forced to devise strategies to survive in this ever-changing international city. On a global scale, family businesses are disappearing and giving way to public corporations. Maintaining a family business is extremely difficult, as succession is not as easily planned as in public corporations. The rate of survival decreases over generations, with only 30% managing to pass the family business to the second generation, 12% to the third and around 3% to the fourth and beyond.[7] Kee Wah began as a neighbourhood grocer in 1938, and has grown into a company with around eight branches specializing in Chinese traditional bridal cakes, mooncakes and other baked goods. Since its foundation, the bakery has faced stiff competition from other traditional bakeries, as well as from the Western-style bakeries that emerged in the 1960s.[8] In the case of mooncake, many factors make it a challenging product to promote in a competitive market. To begin with, mooncake is a seasonal item, meaning there is a limited sales window each year. In addition, most traditional mooncakes look

Kee Wah Bakery's Mooncake Packaging Makeover in the 1990s

Figure 1. Reproduction of Kee Wah Bakery's Chang'e mooncake packaging before 1995. Courtesy of Kee Wah Bakery Limited.

very similar – they typically have a rich filling contained within a relatively thin crust.[9] The impression on top of each mooncake marks the bakery's name, but is not apparent enough to distinguish one bakery's product from another. Hence, packaging design has become an increasingly important medium for expressing each bakery's identity.

In Kee Wah's early days, packaging served a functional rather than aesthetic role. Like a protective skin, the wrapping paper and container box ensured the safety of the pastries and facilitated the transportation process, and were secondary to the pastries. The modern notion of brand distinction only appeared when the company commissioned a square tin box packaging for mooncakes in the 1950s and 1960s: the boxes bore two common symbols that signify the Mid-Autumn Festival: the full moon and moon goddess Chang'e.[10] Dressed in a traditional dress, the goddess is set against a typical landscape backdrop and holds a fan with the inscription, 'celebrate the Mid-Autumn [Festival]'.[11] She is painted in a manner similar to that of the Chinese calendar posters which gained popularity during the 1920s.[12] The Chang'e tin box not only protected its contents, but its newly acquired decorative quality also made it identifiable as 'Kee Wah mooncakes', marking the arrival of the important festival with style.

However, just as any skin will age, the Chang'e design that was once in vogue became outdated by the 1990s. Even though the bright colour scheme and beautiful goddess were once considered 'modern', the overall design was considered overly Chinese and traditional for a society that had preferred internationalism since the late seventies.[13] Also, the design would not have stood out in the market as most mooncake boxes of other traditional bakeries were executed in a similar style and included identical symbols.[14] The lack of a distinctive design identity caused consumers to lump Kee Wah into the general category of Chinese-style bakeries, especially when juxtaposed against

Western-style bakeries and international companies that had high brand recognition because of their popularity. Its anachronism was especially pronounced when compared to the more streamlined packaging of Western-style bakeries. For example, the mooncake packaging of Western-style bakery Taipan Bread & Cakes abandoned the standard square-shaped tin box that holds four mooncakes for an oval one. Even though Taipan's packaging also has a Chinese celestial being on the box, it is much smaller than the moon goddess on Kee Wah's packaging. The overall execution of Taipan's mooncake packaging design is cleaner, having only one figure contained in the centre of the box against a plain red background with minimal floral decoration.

The dominance of Western-style bakeries in the 1990s caused others 'producing traditional Chinese pastries [to be] seen as a sunset industry'.[15] To avoid elimination from the market, Kee Wah urgently needed a brand reformation to fight for recognition and expand its market audience. Internally, marketing and art departments were set up to develop a cohesive brand identity. External help was sought from designers to find the appropriate market positioning and design profile for the company. Graphic designer Suen Siu Wah was hired in the mid-1990s to lead the project.[16] Significantly, the Kee Wah project was one of the first attempts to utilize design to repackage the heritage and identity of a local company that produces traditional Chinese-style goods in the nineties. The objective is easier said than done: an international and Western design language had increasingly dominated the Hong Kong design scene since the mid-twentieth century.[17] Douglas Young, the interior designer of Kee Wah's retail shops during the renewal, testified to the originality of the project.[18] At that time, rebranding an old company 'often meant throwing everything old away and starting all over again. So we ... were one of the first to use their company's ... archive and ... their unique heritage to design.'[19] The end result is a careful balance of being 'modern' and 'classic' in order to highlight the bakery's heritage while showcasing its ability to adapt to the ever-changing city.

The mooncake was the first product line to be released after the makeover. The new packaging had to distinguish itself from those of fellow traditional bakeries, yet not entirely lose its 'Chineseness' and be mistaken as a product from a Western-style bakery. Suen performed a lot of research for the project, as he had never handled any cases that required a strong Chinese visual language. While Hong Kong designers may identify their personal cultural roots as Chinese, they are not necessarily familiar with Chinese visual history. This is similar to Hong Kong's local identity, which is 'neither wholly-Chinese, but clearly also not non-Chinese'.[20] Determined to find a fresh and recognizable look for Kee Wah's mooncake line, Suen flipped through ancient print manuals and referred to multiple Chinese decorative pattern books. He made a bold decision by replacing Chang'e and the full moon with the portrait of the legendary first emperor in Chinese history, Huang Di, in muted gold against a black background. The emperor holds a plaque incised with the words '*zi zyun*' [supreme], which is also the title of the new line of mooncakes. The restrained colour palette strongly contrasts with

Kee Wah Bakery's Mooncake Packaging Makeover in the 1990s

Figure 2. Suen Siu Wah, Kee Wah Supreme Mooncake gift box, designed 1995.

the common choices of bright red, blue and yellow in traditional mooncake packaging. Black is definitely a daring choice for traditional festive products because of its negative association with death and illegal activities.[21]

By naming the new line 'Supreme Mooncakes' and associating it with the founder of Chinese civilization, Suen implies that Kee Wah mooncakes are of superior quality, endorsed by royalty and perhaps true descendants of the original line of mooncakes. The repeated cloud motif in the background references the clouds in traditional Chinese imagery, further signifying the Chineseness of the design. The cascade of Kee Wah logos and the maroon 'Kee Wah Supreme Mooncake' label serve as a constant reminder of the brand name. Even though most consumers may not be able to recognize the figure as Huang Di, his headdress strongly suggests his identity as an emperor. The emperor's head and the cloud motif serve as classical signifiers of Chinese culture while the understated colour scheme and careful proportion of the overall design signal that this design is not passé but up-to-date.

In addition to experimenting with new colour schemes and introducing a new figure to the Mid-Autumn Festival iconography, Suen also challenged the existing form of the packaging. He felt that the standard square tin box packaging was not actually the most practical design for carrying mooncakes. Not a lot of shopping bags have square bottoms, so the mooncake box cannot lie flat and has to be inserted vertically on its rectangular side. Usually, for other products like a pack of biscuits or sweets, it does not matter much at which angle one places the packaging within a bag. But since 'mooncakes are quite heavy, the box would – bum [sound effect] – pop open'.[22] Therefore, he took inspiration from the everyday stacked lunch boxes and elongated the normal mooncake box to develop the '*Gam Deng* Mooncake Gift Box'. The resulting

Figure 3. Suen Siu Wah, Kee Wah Golden Summit Mooncake gift box, designed 1995.

vertical box not only has a handle convenient for carrying, but also saves space when placed in a shopping bag. The term '*gam deng*' literally means 'golden summit', and the box shares that same name with the peak of Mount Emei, which is one of the Four Sacred Mountains of Buddhism. This is a fitting title to the gift box as the golden cover is emphasized when paired with a maroon body. Once again, Suen is elevating the status of a product by referencing significant Chinese cultural terms and landmarks in the naming process.

For anyone foreign to Chinese culture, the design language of the Supreme Mooncake series immediately conforms to the stereotypical imagery of ancient China. However, on many levels the Huangdi packaging is an innovative design. By recruiting Huangdi to the mooncake box, the company successfully created a new visual vocabulary for the Mid-Autumn Festival and thereby challenged a seemingly unchanging tradition.[23] Interestingly enough, it is the historical background of the company that legitimized this move. In addition, the packaging broke visual taboos by using the colour black, which had picked up its Western association with funeral attire and thus represented inauspiciousness. Most importantly, the Huangdi design transcended packaging's status as merely the second skin of the edible product by leveraging the emperor's historical authority to endorse Kee Wah's mooncakes. By doing so, the packaging is nowhere near being secondary to the product – it has reversed its role and become indispensible in defining its edible content.

The popular theme of nostalgia in Hong Kong design circles during the nineties perhaps further encouraged the acceptance of Kee Wah's redesign efforts. If the transfer of sovereignty from British colonial rule to China in 1997 created another discontinuity for Hong Kong, then 'nostalgic reconstruction of history at once seems to extinguish history's temporal distance, while providing for a pleasant experience through the repression of its negative aspects.'[24] After being separated from mainland China politically for more than a century, the majority of Hong Kong's people lacked a shared memory with fellow countrymen and had taken on a Chinese identity that was quite different from that in China. Hong Kong had been absorbing so many foreign influences that it has become a city with little physical traces of Chinese origin. Naturally, anxiety increased in the eighties when the city began to face its imminent return to Chinese sovereignty.

If no certainty can be found in the future, then perhaps looking backwards is the best way to reconnect with the motherland. As Fred Davis argues, perhaps the purpose of nostalgia is 'to assuage apprehension of the future by retrieving the worth of the past'.[25] It might have been difficult for Hong Kong to identify with a China that had been through the Cultural Revolution and the Tiananmen Square Protests of 1989, so the alternative was to seek points in Chinese history when the city was also part of the greater China. This mentality is reflected in the works of local designer Alan Chan and fashion brand Shanghai Tang, who both appropriated historical imagery and material culture from pre-war port cities Shanghai and Canton as the major inspiration for their products.[26] Another form of nostalgia tends to reminisce about existing local cultures that are under threat of disappearing before the possible engulfment by the seemingly monolithic Mainland Chinese culture, as seen in Douglas Young's brand G.O.D.

However, the nostalgia present in Kee Wah's makeover is of a different scale and nature from those of Alan Chan, Shanghai Tang and G.O.D. The Supreme Mooncake series does not draw upon a particular moment in Chinese history, but rather evokes a romanticized vision of classical China. Kee Wah's makeover, which happened two years before the handover, was not born out of social context and can be seen as participating in Hong Kong's collective search for identity and creation of a postcolonial memory. Although its design elements are not as often critically recognized, the bakery's packaging design has permeated Hong Kong society and culture in a way that individual brands and designers have not. On a wider level, the history that Kee Wah was borrowing came from the root of Chinese civilization and could be related to by all Chinese descendants, whether from Hong Kong, mainland China or elsewhere. By using imagery of the first emperor of China from whom all Chinese descended, Kee Wah appeals to the underlying sense of what it means to be Chinese. On a pragmatic level, the company is using classical Chinese signifiers to bolster its corporate image and heritage. But the makeover is ultimately an active maintenance of tradition through encouraging the consumption of mooncake and, more importantly, the marking of a traditional festival.

This case study of Kee Wah's mooncake packaging demonstrates three distinctive relationships food packaging can share with its contents. It can be merely functional and secondary in importance, evolve to become the 'second skin' of the product and, finally, act as to enhance and endorse its contents. Ultimately, in Kee Wah's case, the packaging allows the edible product to refresh its appearance without compromising the pastry's inherent traditional values. The Huangdi packaging also serves a unifying purpose, linking different Chinese communities to their common root in history. Most pertinently, this case study highlights the reliance edible products now have on their second skins to maintain their survival in the market. The implications of this case study are relevant to food studies of different geographies, as what Kee Wah experienced is one of the many local responses to the global narrative of modernity. Therefore, it is time for researchers to cast the spotlight on the superficial yet inseparable mediating agent of packaging.

Notes

1. This paper is based on my past research: Jennifer Wong, 'Kee Wah Bakery Redesigned: Tradition, Appropriation and Innovation in Hong Kong, 1994–2011' (unpublished master's dissertation, Royal College of Art/Victoria and Albert Museum, 2012). Arjun Apparudai, *Modernity at Large: Cultural Dimensions of Globalization* (Minneapolis, MN: U Minnesota P, 1996), p. 17.
2. Siumi Maria Tam, 'Eating Metropolitaneity: Hong Kong Identity in *yumcha*', *The Australian Journal of Anthropology*, 8 (1997), pp. 303–04.
3. For more information on Hong Kong art history, see David Clarke, *Hong Kong Art: Culture and Decolonization* (London: Reaktion, 2001); for a summary of the local design identity, see Wendy Wong, 'Design Identity of Hong Kong: Colonization, De-colonization, and Re-colonization', *The 6th International Conference of the European Academy of Design Conference Proceedings* (Bremen: University of the Arts, 2005), pp. 1–13; to further understand Hong Kong's reaction to the 1997 handover, see Ackbar Abbas, *Hong Kong: Culture and the Politics of Disappearance* (London: U Minnesota P, 1997).
4. For example, Emiko Ohnuki-Tierney's work focuses on the social meaning of rice in Japan and explores how the construction of 'self' identities can be done through setting up dichotomies with 'others', such as Japanese short-grain rice versus Chinese long-grain rice; see 'Food as a Metaphor of Self: An Exercise in Historical Anthropology', *Rice as Self: Japanese Identities through Time* (Princeton: Princeton UP, 1993), pp. 3–11.
5. Sea-ling Cheng, 'Eating Hong Kong's Way Out', *Asian Food: The Global and the Local*, eds. Katarzyna Cwiertka and Boudewijn Walraven (Honolulu: U Hawaii P, 2001),p. 18.
6. We do not know when exactly the festival became a tradition, but it is suggested that the festival slowly evolved from the ancient rite of worshipping the moon during autumn by Chinese emperors. See Yan Liao, *Food and Festivals of China* (Philadelphia: Mason Crest, 2004), p. 69.
7. Family Business Institute, 'Succession Planning' <http://www.familybusinessinstitute.com/index.php/Succession-Planning/> [accessed 1 November 2011].
8. Western-style bakeries sell *sai beng*, literally meaning 'Western cakes', including a wide range of products such as croissants, baguettes, custard tarts, napoleons, etc. Despite having various Western origins, these baked goods have been integrated into Hong Kong citizen's everyday life.
9. There are a lot of regional varieties among mooncakes, but this paper will focus on the Cantonese-style mooncakes that are known to be *pei bok haam leng*, meaning having thin crust with excellent fillings.
10. The legend of Chang'e, the moon goddess in Chinese mythology, is strongly associated with the festival. There are many variations to her legend, but the common thread is that Chang'e ingested her husband's medicine of immortality and floated to the moon.
11. All Chinese terms within this paper are in Cantonese romanization.

12. For further reading on the history of calendar poster art, see Ellen Johnston Laing, *Selling Happiness: Calendar Posters and Visual Culture in Early Twentieth Century Shanghai* (Honolulu: U Hawaii P, 2004). For more on the transferral of the Shanghai modern style to Hong Kong, see Matthew Turner, *Made in Hong Kong: A History of Export Design in Hong Kong 1900–1960* (Hong Kong: Urban Council, 1988).
13. Hong Kong desired diverse dining experiences in this period, such as visiting hotel grillrooms and Western restaurants, and eating other Asian cuisines. Cheng, p. 25.
14. For example, even though Wing Wah's mooncake box does not include the moon goddess, it also has the full moon and a sky-blue background. The name of the bakery is also marked in red.
15. Pink Cheung, 'Brand Standing', *Silk Road*, July 2009, p. 36, Kee Wah Bakery Ltd., Archive.
16. Suen graduated from what was then the Swire School of Design at Hong Kong Polytechnic University in 1982 and was the creative director of The Peninsula Hotel Group in the late eighties. His simple and minimalistic design style could be described as international, because his previous works did not necessarily carry any geographical markers and could easily be identified as designs seen in other international cities.
17. Commenting on Hong Kong's design expectations, Turner argued that foreign manufacturers suppressed local creativity after the 1950s by instilling 'the West's prevailing belief that the 'Modern' style of design was one universal visual language ... which, like the English language, should be learned by everyone else as a key to industrial and commercial progress' (Turner, pp. 14–15).
18. Young later founded a renowned local lifestyle company G.O.D. To learn more about his work, see Wessie Ling, 'From "Made in Hong Kong" to "Designed in Hong Kong": Searching for an Identity in Fashion', *Visual Anthropology*, 24 (2011), pp. 106–23.
19. Douglas Young, Personal Interview, 5 December 2011.
20. Hazel Clark, 'Back to the Future, or Forward? Hong Kong Design, Image, and Branding', *Design Issues*, 25 (2009), pp. 12–13.
21. Black was not an inauspicious colour in Chinese history, but perhaps due to the influence of Western culture, it has come to be associated with death and illegal matters. For example, black attire is worn to funerals nowadays, and 'Black society' means criminal societies in Cantonese.
22. Suen Siu Wah, Personal Interview, 13 December 2011.
23. Eric Hobsbawm's writing argues that traditions are not unchanging, and can be invented and constituted through repetitive enforcement; see 'Introduction: Inventing Traditions', *The Invention of Tradition*, eds. Eric Hobsbawn and Terence Ranger (Cambridge: Cambridge UP, 1983), pp. 1–14.
24. Daniel J. Huppatz, 'Designer Nostalgia in Hong Kong', *Design Issues*, 25 (2009), p. 14.
25. Fred Davis, *Yearning for Yesterday: A Sociology of Nostalgia*, (New York: The Free Press, 1979), p. 71, qtd. Huppatz, p. 15.
26. For further reading on the use of nostalgia in Hong Kong design, see Clark and Huppatz.

The Waurás in Brazil Have a Pan that Speaks to the Fire

Marcia Zoladz

Objects and implements from cultures different from our own tend to fascinate us, not only because of the substance they are made from, be it clay or silver, but also because of the way they trigger our imaginations. But our imaginations are limited by our cultural context, by the way we, as part of Western culture, see the world. That limitation is what makes it so appealing to include, as part of the Symposium's exploration of material culture, a pan from the Waurás, a group with a quite different way of seeing the world. The Waurás, or Waujas, are an indigenous population in Central Brazil, in an area that today is the Xingu Indian Park, a large reservation for indigenous people. Their culture is very rich: they produce beautiful ceramics, weave fibres into masks for festive occasions and have productive lives on the banks of the Batovi River, where they have lived for more than one thousand years.

The Waurás make beautiful – actually quite amazing – pans and pots, in sizes varying from as small as four or five centimetres to very large ones with a diameter of more than a metre. Some are shaped like animals such as bats, frogs, armadillos and turtles. Interestingly, only those with decorations on their bottoms, where the flame of the fire touches them, can be used for cooking, and only they can be called pans. The other vessels are simply pots.

Besides characterizing a pan as such, the decorations are part of a complex system in which the material and spiritual world coexist for the Waurá. Aside from its use as a cooking object and a container, the pan's purpose is to speak with the supernatural world while in direct contact with the flames. While it looks like the paintings have meaning in themselves, their true meanings are only revealed as part of a much more complex communication system in the Waurá's worldview.

Why a pot is not like a pan

The first contact I had with Waurá culture was at home. My mother, Professor Rosza Wigdorowicz vel Zoladz, a sociologist of art, worked in the Museu Nacional, the National Museum, of the Federal University of Rio de Janeiro, the largest ethnological and anthropological research centre and repository of the Amerindian cultures of Brazil. There is an equally important research and preservation institution in the city, the Museu do Índio (Museum of the Native People) where Ione Couto, one of my mother's former students, helped me access information about the Waurás, including how a pot differs from a pan and its relation with the fire while cooking meals. I wanted to know how a pan differs from other vessels, and why it speaks with supernatural beings. It turns out that, in in Waurá culture, the pan has a voice.

The Waurás in Brazil Have a Pan that Speaks to the Fire

The Brazilian context

Visitors to Brazil confront a complex local culture. Since Europeans started arriving in the late sixteenth century, each new group has steadily appropriated and integrated local habits into an evolving vernacular. At first, this early social and cultural organization was influenced by the Amerindians, the Portuguese and peoples from various regions of Africa, soon joined as well by young unmarried Englishmen, converted Jews and French pirates.

Later, as the Portuguese monarchy moved from Lisbon to Rio de Janeiro in 1808, the country received Swiss small landholders, Italian winemakers from the Veneto region; Syrian-Lebanese immigrants and Sephardic Jews, also called Turks because of their passports issued by the Ottoman Empire, arrived by the end of the nineteenth century. Around the Second World War, Eastern European Jews and Russians arrived, and the large number of Japanese who moved to São Paulo made it the second-largest Japanese city after Tokyo. There are also Chinese in north Brazil and Koreans and Bolivians in the south-east, and many other nationalities make valuable contributions.

The freedom of appropriating and including new cultural traits with such apparent ease, as if they had always been part of everyday life, is what makes Brazilian culture so lively. The cultural diversity adds layers of charm, or better, a higher degree of interest, to the amazingly beautiful and rich natural resources of the region with its large number of plants and animal species.

From the beginning of the colonization, this layering, this lack of a constraining social order, has attracted Europeans and North Americans to Brazil. This perpetual embracing of practices and beliefs from multiple sources that has contributed to the Brazilian ethos has not always been plain sailing however: there were violent clashes, murders and land boundary fights between the Amerindians and the newly arrived, and later arrivals have encountered conflict at times too. The blending of cultures can also make the practices and beliefs of individual groups, especially early ones, difficult to see. Even when part of the society think they are invisible, and another part does not seem interested in how they fare, the Amerindians still have an important role in defining the country's identity.

And then the Indians disappeared

Because of the long history of cultural exchange, it is very hard to write about Amerindian culture separately from Brazilian life. First, the Indians, as they are called in Brazil, are part of the country's contemporary culture with a recurrent role in urban and rural life. Second, they have a crucial voice in national conversations despite many efforts to deny their rights, restrict their lands and limit their political participation, efforts that began the moment the Portuguese arrived.

For 500 years, Amerindians have been objects of curiosity for Europeans. At different times, they have been seen as 'good savages' who should live without any interaction with local society, as examples to be copied because of their balanced way of living close to nature, or, especially during colonial times, as dangerous heathen that should be enslaved and Christianized.

Throughout this long history, however, Amerindian lives have remained intertwined with the lives of Brazilians. This importance begins almost from the cradle, when little children hear stories about their mythology, usually involving animals that change into humans and back. Later, in school, children have obligatory visits to museums to see large anthropology and ethnography collections. Older children in Brazilian literature classes read *The Guarani*, a novel by José de Alencar; it tells the seventeenth-century story of Peri, a brave warrior from the Guarani tribe, who rescues his love Ceci, a daughter of a colonial farmer.

By high school, students' education shifts from reading this romantic novel to a more scientific explanation introduced through the work of Claude Lévi-Strauss. Students usually read one or two chapters of *Tristes Tropiques* (1955), where the anthropologist recounts his experiences with Amerindians while teaching at the University of São Paulo in the 1930s. In this book he describes his travels to the Kadiweu, Nambiquaras and Bororos in central Brazil and Tupi-caraíba in the Amazon. It was the seminal work that would define his structural theory.

Many students also read parts of Lévy-Strauss's *Les structures elementaires de la parenté* (1948) and discuss the differences between family organizations and the symbolic role of parents in European and Amerindian cultures.

While Amerindians have a growing voice in Brazil – and may, perhaps, have found a receptive audience in the country's youth – one rarely hears about the way they see and understand the world outside the community of anthropologists and photographers that work with them.

But it was not always so. During the nineteenth century, perhaps because of the relatively untouched nature of the Atlantic and Amazon forest, where a multitude of birds, animals from tiny frogs to large jaguars, different trees, orchids and bromeliads in endless varieties that even today overwhelm its visitors, scholars studied the Amerindians in hopes of discovering the past. It was almost as if, by observing the Brazilian Amerindians, they thought they might be able to imagine how small groups of people lived and understood the world in prehistoric times.

Even intellectuals like Elizabeth Cabot Agassiz focused on this comparative question when she visited Brazil with her husband Louis Agassiz, in 1865. She was a pedagogue, a founder and the first president of Radcliffe College, and her husband, a professor at Harvard, was perhaps the world's best known palaeontologist and ichthyologist. And yet, they were fascinated by the possibility of studying plants of certain species, like fern trees, that had been around since prehistoric times.

She wrote a diary, *Journey in Brazil,* recording their observations about the country. Her level-headed descriptions commented on the local élites' support for slavery and captured simple details like how the emperor Pedro II, a scientist and well-read man, made a point in greeting them personally and even organized a series of lectures for members of the scientific expedition. But the journal's focus was on the couple's search for clues that would link local flora and fauna with prehistoric times, and they seemed to view the Amerindians in a similar way, as groups of people living at an earlier stage of human development, as links to Stone Age or Iron Age ancestors.

A people in the present or the past?

When the first Europeans arrived in Brazil, Amerindians were seen as political equals, or almost so. Texts refer to the king of the Tupinambás in the same way as others note European barons or princes, for example. But, as the colonial enterprise became more established, the way the new arrivals thought of the Amerindians changed.

Unlike Asia and Africa, where Europeans could trade with – or attack – large coastal cities, Brazil's social order seemed truly a new world. Most Europeans learned about this new world through books, and travellers' tales responded to and fed curiosity about what seemed like life in a raw natural state. For example, a German adventurer named Hans Staden wrote about his travels in Brazil; his lurid tales of surviving the cannibals' cauldrons – twice – became a sixteenth-century bestseller. Such stories reached Europeans at the same time as philosophical discussions were asking whether the natives of the newly discovered lands had souls.

By the end of the eighteenth century, new scientific methods of exploring geography, botany and zoology led to expeditions, sometimes including important visitors from the academic world: in the early nineteenth century Alexander von Humboldt travelled the Orinoco River, now in Venezuela, and northern Brazil, and Johan Baptist Von Spix, a biologist, and Karl Friedrich Von Martius, a botanist, travelled in the Amazon River basin and the Atlantic Forest. Unlike earlier explorers, these scientists did not seek gold or silver but knowledge. In addition to methodically describing the region's flora and fauna, these expeditions documented the existence of several ethnic groups as well.

In their work, these scientists attributed a childlike understanding of the world to the 'savages', and the 'Indian question' changed as a result. Portuguese legislators stopped thinking of Amerindians as owning the land on which they lived; instead, they began to identify these original residents as crown tenants. This was – and ironically still is – part of an unequal dispute between the Amerindian population and representatives of the government. Conflicts still occur over land. Brazilian agribusiness wants to use the reservation areas to produce soy and rice today, in the same way others wanted to plant sugar cane in the seventeenth century. Those that oppose Brazil's Amerindian rights to reservations often claim that the natives do not do anything productive with their lands. After 400 years as two sides of complementary cultures in one country, neither has clearly established their rights. There are many reservation areas throughout the country, but as large agricultural areas grow around them the consequence is a constant conflict of interests and sometimes armed confrontations. The pan that cooks the meals for the tribe cannot be isolated from the social interaction of the Waurás with the Brazilian society.

Figures 1 and 2. Published with permission of the Museu do Índio/FUNAI – Fundação Nacional do Índio, Rio de Janeiro, 2013.

The Waurás in Brazil Have a Pan that Speaks to the Fire

Figure 3. Published with permission of the Museu do Índio/FUNAI – Fundação Nacional do Índio, Rio de Janeiro, 2013.

And the jaguar arrived
The Amerindian world has a complex cosmography. Their world, in the case of the Waurás, is divided between material and invisible spirits, known as *apapaatai*. They influence everyday life, playing roles in determining people's moods and health. The Waurás believe that, at the beginning of the world, all beings were originally human, and despite their metamorphosis into animals they retain within their bodies some percentage of their original humanity. The shamans – who also can change their shapes – can see this humanity in the animals. This partial humanity leads to a series of alimentary prohibitions: after all, to eat your own kind would be to practise cannibalism.

The shaman therefore has a huge importance in the life of the group. As he is the only one allowed to see this otherworldly population, his ability to understand the spirits brings health and balance to life. Since the supernatural space is so attractive, anyone not trained as a shaman would have a difficulty returning to the material world. The shaman's training allows him to translate this world's desires to the other world, helping him to cure the sick and to keep bad spirits at bay.

How not to be a cannibal
Because Amerindians believe everything was originally human and still has some humanity, eating is difficult. The shaman must establish what is and is not edible.

Since the supernatural world cannot be seen, material existence is only partial. Many potential foods are simply prohibited: mammals, snakes, turtles, crocodiles and most birds cannot be eaten, and other species can only be consumed on particular occasions, like after giving birth. Before preparing the things that can be used as food, cooks must rely on the shaman to ask for rightful authorization to clear all the spirits. The pan's drawings are a kind of sign language to make sure that no wandering spirit drops in and gets hurt by mistake. This practice allows the Waurás to avoid cannibalism.

Waurá families cultivate corn, manioc, beans, peanuts, squashes, bananas, watermelons and two indigenous fruits, *pequi* (*Caryocar brasiliense*) and *mangabas* (*Hancornia speciosa*). *Pequi* is more than part of their diet; it is also used in ceremonies to honour the dead. The oil extracted from its stones is used as a fixative of the *urucu* (*Bixa orellana*), the red colour used to paint their bodies.

How the Waurás arrived at the Batovi River

The clay used for the pan that speaks to the fire is related to the Waurás origin myth. The Waurás live along the Batovi River, and they believe they were brought there by a gigantic snake, carrying the whole group mounted on its back. The snake ensured they would have the clay they would need for pots and pans. In one version of the story, the snake defecated on the clay; in another, it chose to settle the Waurás by a large clay deposit and remains asleep nearby, meaning that the women who collect the clay to make pots and pans must be very silent to keep the snake from waking up and eating them.

The Waurás are well-known ceramicists who sell their wares to other groups inside the Xingu Indian Park and in shops in cities around the country. They have a very guarded life and are well organized and politically active. For instance, at the moment they are negotiating to retrieve the property of a huge area outside the Xingu Park reservation which is a sacred place for them. And it is also where their largest clay deposits lay. Unfortunately, the Government did not take that fact into account when they set the limits of the Xingu Indian Park. Many ceramics manufacturers are now established in this area.

Time for a change

The Waurás lived relatively unnoticed by Europeans until 1884, when the German ethnologist Karl Von Den Steinen visited them. They were only contacted again in 1946/1947, when the Brazilian Government surveyed the interior to learn how many tribes were still alive and living in isolation. The census was the first step to protecting these cultures by studying them and integrating them under state authority. In addition, the government was concerned about health issues like vaccination. One sign that health policies are working is that the birth rate among Amerindians is growing again.

What the jaguar has to tell us

In the Xingu Indian Park, fifteen ethnic groups live, interact and use the same services, including medical facilities. Even with so many different language groups, it is inevitable that they sometimes intermarry and often absorb Brazilian regional habits, especially since many tribesmen go to school in the villages and to college, usually in Brasília, under the protection of the FUNAI, *Fundação Nacional do Índio* (Indian National Foundation), the government organization that represents them.

As these new relationships develop the Waurás' pans play less important roles. They are still used, but large aluminium pans, the ones used to cook lunch at schools, are replacing them. This transformation has been occurring for some time, as seen in the research of Aristóteles Barcelos Neto, currently at the University of East Anglia; he subtly shows these changes in his movie *Apapaatai*. It is very difficult to keep contemporary groups isolated, without bridges of cultural and material exchange.

Feeling comfortable
The Museu do Índio has a collection of small flat clay sculptures with the shape of armadillos, frogs, bats, capybaras and turtles. They are sculpted, or rather scraped, to form these new shapes out of the ceramic fragments of broken pans. This collection was transferred to the museum without much explanation; what is known is that after its service cycle the pan is broken, and then the fragments are sculpted and, eventually, thrown away. It is almost as if – and this is entirely speculation on my part – the pan has to be returned to its human or supernatural shape.

Another explanation could be that the fragments are reshaped simply because they are there. In a society that has no accumulative model, they are not kept. Modern societies have a tendency to attribute a symbolic value to anyone or anything that fits into a vision of a world at peace with nature. Such assumptions limit an understanding of who the Amerindians are, making their lives in many ways harder. As a result, many are often surprised that they should claim their rights in the same terms as farmers and other groups.

According to Claude Lévi-Strauss in *Mythologies*, the invention and use of ceramics represents a step away from a natural state, because it involves knowing how to use the fire to vary temperatures carefully. In this view, the small animals sculptured from the pan fragments are not a reversal to their original animal or natural shapes but rather suggest that, as objects cooked by the fire, they assert the strength of culture over an animal state that eats food raw. Throwing the sculpted fragments into the flowing waters of a river is like spreading the voice of a culture.

What about the fire?
The Waurá legend of how the fire was conquered is one of intelligence, cunning and fear, and can be read in detail in a book by Harald Shultz, who collected such stories with an informant and a translator in the early 1960s. At first the fox owned the fire, but the Sun and the Moon, brother and sister, decided to steal it. To catch the fire, the Sun hid inside a fish and the Moon sat inside a large clam in a lake where the fox used to

Figures 4, 5, 6, 7. Fish, capybara, jaguar, and bat, published with permission of the Museu do Índio/FUNAI – Fundação Nacional do Índio, Rio de Janeiro, 2013..

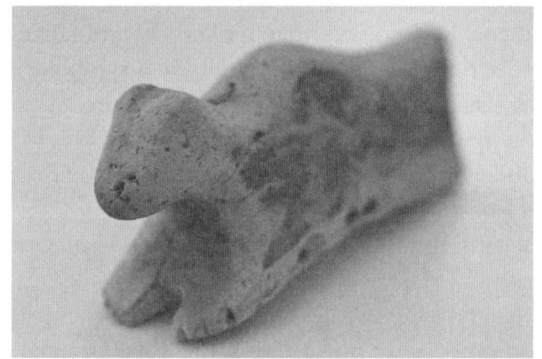

fish. As the fox captures them and heats them over the fire, they reveal themselves, steal the fire and run away. Thus the Sun became the real fire because it does not extinguish itself, and the Moon became a false fire.

Fires are quite common in the forests and prairies of Central Brazil. The tribes around the Xingu Indian Park are constantly training to combat them, and some, like the Waurás, have to patrol their limits and maintain observation posts. Fires can start in two ways. The first is criminal: farmers burn vegetation bordering on the reservation to gain more arable land by destroying the original trees and bush. During the dry season fires often burn out of control and enter the territory of the many national parks in the Amazon Basin and Central Brazil. The second is unavoidable as lightning strikes set off fires. And this is the kind that needs a fox to explain its power.

As potters, the Waurás have extensive knowledge of how to control the fire's temperature and how to vary the clay to keep it from breaking as it heats. But mastering kitchen fires is different, and that task has to be conquered daily. This is another reason why the pans go through so many rituals before a meal can be cooked. In the Amerindian world, there is constant conflict in the relation of nature, culture and the supernatural, although the message is that culture – that made by humans – must predominate.

A difficult life for a pan

The main question today is not so much whether we can live with the Amerindian cosmography that integrates different types of existences – animals, humans and supernatural, living together in a almost collective understanding of the world – but whether Western society has not already, metaphorically at least, adopted such a cosmology. With human relations based more and more in virtual reality – frequently taking place through some device, a computer or a mobile phone – material culture now has quite explicit virtual existence, shadow representations of actual objects in virtual realms. Perhaps the rapid growth of the virtual world is bringing everyday life closer to a kind of supernatural experience. It may be that the devices that give us access to this virtual world, the material culture of phones, tablets, and computers, are acquiring a shamanic place in western society.

References

Elizabeth Cabot Agassiz and Louis Agassiz, *A Journey in Brazil* (Boston: Ticknor and Fields, 1868).

João Bandeira de Mello, 'Em audiência, índios que invadiram museu rejeitam proposta da *FUNAI*', *Jornal O Globro* (The Globe) 25 March 2013 <http://g1.globo.com/rio-de-janeiro/noticia/2013/03/emaudiencia-indios-que-invadiram-museu-recusam-proposta-da-funai.html>.

Aristóteles Barcelos Neto, *Apapaatai* (São Paulo: LISA – Laboratório de Imagem e Som em Antropologia at the University of São Paulo: 2007),

——, 'Mil anos de história Aruak no Alto Xingu'. *Blog Povos indígenas no Brasil.* <http://pib.socioambiental.org/pt/povo/wauja/1115>.

Claude Lévy-Strauss, *The Jealous Potter* (Chicago: U Chicago P, 1988).

——, *The Raw and the Cooked: Mythologies*, vol. 1 (Chicago: U Chicago P, 1983).

——, *Tristes Tropiques* (New York: Penguin, 1992).

Vera Penteado Coelho, 'A festa do pequi e do zunidor'. *Schweizerische-Amerikanisten Gesellschaft* 55–56 (1991–1992): pp. 37–56 <http://www.ssa-sag.ch/bssa/pdf/bssa55-56_07.pdf>.

Ribeiro, Darcy, *O povo brasileiro* (Brazil: SuperFilms, 2000) <http://www.youtube.com/watch?v=2gqz4BHYcck> and <http://www.youtube.com/watch?v=x6YeSItLLro>.

Harald Shultz and Vilma Chiara, 'Mais lendas Waurá'. *Revista do Museu Paulista* 60 (1971), pp. 105–35 <http://www.persee.fr/web/revues/home/prescript/article/jsa_0037-9174_1971_num_60_1_2071>.

Eduardo Viveiros de Castro, 'Exchanging Perspectives: The Transformation of Objects into Subjects in Amerindian Ontologies'. *Common Knowledge* 10:3 (Fall 2004) pp. 463–84.

Von Spix, Johan Baptist and Karl Friedrich Von Martius, *Reise in Brasilien*, (Munich: 1823).

Our Kitchen in 1940s Baghdad

Sami Zubaida

The house of my childhood in Baghdad had two courtyards, *haush*, Middle Eastern style. The larger one was the centre of the main living area, with rooms and terraces ranged around it on two levels. The smaller *haush* was the kitchen area, *beit al-matbakh*, with a room on one side containing a range of kerosene-fuelled rings at ground level, and in one corner a wood-burning boiler for the attached Turkish-style *hammam*. Beside the boiler was a *kanoun*, a square frame of stone and plaster over which pots could be placed over wood and coal burning in the middle, mostly for slow cooking when the fuel was reduced to embers and ash. This is where the Saturday *tebit* of stuffed chicken and rice was cooked overnight.

In one corner of the kitchen courtyard was a *tanour*, better known globally as *tandur*, a clay pot built into a metal oil drum (more commonly built into the wall) with an opening at the bottom where a wood fire burned to heat up the clay walls. Flat rounds of dough were stuck on the walls to make *khubuz*, flat bread; *jeradiq*, thin, crisp flat bread; and *makhbouz* or *keleicha*, sweetened and buttered dough pastries, stuffed with cheese, dates or almond and sugar. *Sambousak* was the name of the crescent-shaped pastries stuffed with cheese or almond/sugar (distinct from the *sambousak bil-tawa*, larger folds of dough stuffed with heavily spiced and onioned mashed chick-peas, then fried in hot oil, more akin to the Indian *samousa*). Bu`bu` (plural, bu`abe`) was the round bready pastry stuffed with date paste.

Elsewhere in that courtyard, more kerosene rings, chopping boards, knives and pestle and mortars, *hawan*, of various sizes were to be found. There was no oven: domestic ovens are recent innovations in many parts of the world. Banquet dishes, of meat or fish, on large trays, were sent to neighbourhood bakers' ovens, also a common practice elsewhere. On special occasions a lamb would be slaughtered over the drain in the courtyard and butchered there by a hired specialist.

Between the two courtyards stood a store-room where hessian sacks of rice, sugar and flour were stored, as well as drums of oil and various packets of other provisions. We children played in that room and were once delighted to find a large cache of chocolate bars (was it forgotten by the adults?). That was during the rationing period following the Second World War and so especially welcome. Also in that room was the ice box, and later the electric Frigidaire. The ice box was a wooden cupboard with various compartments, lined with zinc, in which a block of ice, delivered periodically from the factory, would be placed, wrapped in hessian, and food and drink distributed around it in the compartments. The arrival of the electric fridge was a delight, especially in the Baghdad summer months, with unlimited supply of cold water and sherbets, as well as the coveted ice creams, previously only available from specialist shops or itinerant pedlars shouting 'Eskimo!' the trade name of the popular ice.

These were the spatial parameters of my childhood food world. It was presided over by my mother and her mother, the latter a diminutive and quiet woman who seldom left the house. In her last years in the London home of her son she was bewildered, her horizons having always been domestic and local: her grandchildren took it in turn to granny-sit. She was a good domestic cook, as was my mother. They were aided by one or two resident maids (who lodged in corner spaces around the kitchen, where mattresses were spread at night), as well as the younger women of the household, in preparation of chopping, mincing and pounding (endless, loud pounding) and in cleaning and tidying up.

Shopping and provisioning were male tasks. At one point it was an elderly maternal uncle staying in our house (thrown out, we were told, by his vicious wife) who undertook the early morning trip to the markets for meat and fresh products. My father would shop for the 'dry goods' from the main bazaar, the *Shorja* (an Arabization of the Turkish *Çarşı*), on his way back from work. Meat was bought from a *kasher* butcher in the largely Jewish Hannouni market, who had a longstanding relationship with the family. The butcher would get to know your requirements and deal as honestly as possible to keep your custom. Even then, the cooks were not always satisfied with the quality or the cuts. Meat was not sold as specific cuts of leg or shoulder, for instance, but as lean or fat, with or without bone. Fruit and vegetables also came from that market.

Fish, an occasional treat, was always bought live from a fisherman on the nearby corniche of the Tigris. *Shabbout*, a kind of barbell, was the fish of choice (now largely fished out, after being monopolized by Saddam Hussein and his entourage), or slices of a very large fish called *bizz*. A large *shabbout* was a banquet dish, cooked in domestic imitation of the iconic *mazgouf*, barbecued, typically by river bank eateries or fishermen, much prized in Iraq and considered a national dish.

The fish would be opened flat, like a kipper, by cutting it along the backbone and gutting it at the belly. It would then be skewered on twigs, the twigs stuck into the sandy ground, so that the fish stood vertically to face the fire ignited by its side; thus grilled on the open side, it was then laid flat with the skin side on the hot embers of the fire. It was served seasoned with strong spices, sometimes curry powder or chilli, with tomatoes and onions in the middle, enriched with the inevitable `anba*, mango pickle.

The domestic version followed this closely, except that the cooking was done in a neighbouring baker's oven. This would also be the centrepiece of dinner parties to which we were invited in non-Jewish homes, the thoughtful hosts mindful of Jewish abstention from non-kosher meats. The *bizz* pieces would be cooked as a *salona*, braised with onions, tomatoes and spices, with slightly sweet and sour flavouring. Fish was always special, not an everyday food.

Milk would be delivered from dairy farms on the outskirts of Baghdad. The quality and purity of the milk was a matter of constant concern, for good reasons. At one time

Our Kitchen in 1940s Baghdad

we acquired a share in a cow, and the milkman would bring us our portion of the milk in an urn carried on a donkey. Did he, at one point, actually bring the cow itself and milk it on our doorstep, or is that a trick of memory? In any case I detested milk, which I was pressured to drink, largely because it had to be boiled, and the smell and taste of that boiled milk was repugnant to me. While adults drank their breakfast tea plain, with sugar, or with a drop of milk, English style, we children were required to drink boiled milk with a hint of strong tea. Condensed milk, in tins, was a boon.

Yoghurt was mostly made at home, sometimes drained in linen bags. Occasionally we bought rich, thick, buffalo milk yoghurt, as well as *gaimer*, thick clotted cream (the word being the Iraqi corruption of the Turkish *kaymak*, known elsewhere in the Arab world as *qishta*) from the Bedouin women who kept water buffalos in the shantytown of rural migrants from the Marshes in the south. The *gaimer*, combined with *dibis*, date syrup, on fresh, hot *khubuz*, flat bread, washed down with strong tea (no milk), made a dreamy breakfast, the stuff of nostalgia. I, alongside some other Iraqis in London, try occasionally to reproduce this taste with English clotted cream and imported date syrup, on flat bread: good, but not quite the same.

After dinner of an evening, my grandmother and mother would discuss forthcoming menus and specify their shopping requirements, noted by my father and whoever was detailed to do the markets.

On schooldays we kids arrived at lunch time, hungry, and would walk directly to the kitchen house to see what was cooking. Almost every day, the pervasive aroma was that of chopped onions frying in pungent sesame oil. This was the final step in cooking rice. The rice would be picked over for small stones and other impurities in large trays with a servant sifting and throwing the grains from one side to the other. It was then washed and soaked, drained and thrown into a pot of boiling water, drained when nearly ready and put back in the pan. Finally, the fried onions would be poured over the rice, then covered and allowed to steam. With an aromatic, native variety of rice called `anbar, amber, it made for a fragrant, nutty taste.

This rice was a feature of almost every lunch and sometimes dinner. With it would be served a stew, typically of lamb or chicken with various vegetables and condiments, and sometimes with dumplings of rice and meat called *kibbah*. The simplest would be lamb, in pieces on the bone, with beans, green or white/dried, *fasoulia*. Our favourite was the lunch made every Friday, a *bamia*/okra stew with lamb and *kibbah*. This was called *hamidh*, sour, which was half the story, as this was sweet and sour, many families appreciating ultra-sweet tastes, achieved with sugar or date syrup. The sour would be lemon, vinegar, and/or dried limes, *noumi basra*, whole or ground. The dumplings/*kibbah* were made by pounding rice and a little meat or chicken in a mortar, then shaping portions into little balls stuffed with a mixture of ground meat, onion and herbs, which were cooked in the sauce. This sauce was the meat juice with tomato paste, sweet and sour agents, mint or penny royal and garlic. The meat for this dish would be typically fatty, usually ribs. The very characteristic aromas of *bamia*, mint and garlic, would assail the Jewish neighbourhoods of Baghdad every Friday at midday.

An occasional alternative to the *bamia* in the *hamidh* would be chopped beetroot. But there was always *bamia*, all the year round: fresh *bamia* in season would be threaded on strings, like necklaces, and dried for use out of season. This is done all over the Middle East and parts of Africa.

Another rice *kibbah*, usually of larger size and flatter shape, was put into 'sweet' stews, *helou*, as against *hamidh*, sour. This did not contain sugar or a sweetener, and was only 'sweet' in that it was not 'sour'. Typically this would be a stew of squash and/or aubergine with meat. The blandness of the stew contrasted with the sourness and spiciness of the *kibbah*, its meaty stuffing flavoured with ground dried lime and black pepper.

For Jewish households several days of the week were marked by dishes. Thursday evening was always *kitchri*, a spicy pulau of rice and lentils, of Indian origin. Following the Friday lunch preparations described above, Friday evening and Saturday saw Sabbath dishes, dominated by chicken. The Friday evening *qaddous* ceremony (the blessing of the vine and the bread) culminated in a dinner in which the primary dish was a chicken pulau (*plaw b-jeej*). The chicken, in pieces, was first boiled: chickens were tough, especially when freshly killed, which was the custom. Even when modern industrial chickens arrived people could not believe that you could roast or fry chicken without first boiling it. Rice would be boiled in the chicken stock, with tomato paste (red rice) and light seasoning. The chicken pieces were then fried in oil to give them colour and crisp the skin. Peeled almonds and raisins were fried in the same pan then everything was placed over the rice and served. Each member of the family had his or her favoured piece of the chicken: mine was the drumstick. Girls were given the wings so that they would fly to their matrimonial homes!

Saturday meals revolved around chicken, but in a different form, called *tebit*, indicating 'overnight' cooking. The chicken was stuffed with rice, chopped meat and/or giblets, seasoned with salt and black pepper. To 'extend' the chicken in some households, including ours, the bird was skinned, retaining the skin, before being cut in half horizontally into breast and back, then the skin sewed with needle and thread over each half to create two pouches, which were stuffed. The pieces were boiled in a stock mixed with tomato paste and aromatic spices: pepper, cloves, cardamom and perhaps cinnamon. When the chicken was nearly cooked a quantity of rice was added to the stock under the meat. This was done on a Friday afternoon. A wood fire was lit in the *kanoon* and reduced to embers. The large pot containing the chicken/rice was then placed over the embers, covered with old blankets and cushions and allowed to cook overnight. The embers were calculated to die slowly by morning or midday on Saturday, while the covers retained the heat. By the time it was ready to serve there was no fire so that cooks committed no ritual sin by handling fire on a Saturday. The *tebit* was served with portions of chicken meat and the two forms of rice: the dry, peppered stuffing rice and a pudding cake of the surrounding rice, slightly crusted at the bottom, aromatic and rich with the chicken juices. This Saturday dish was emblematic of the Jewish household, and much admired by our Muslim and Christian neighbours, who would occasionally be sent samples.

Tebit eggs (*beidh al-tebit*), were placed on the rim of the same pan, under the covers, to cook slowly in the steam, giving the resulting hard-boiled egg a mahogany colour and a smoky flavour. These were enjoyed at breakfast, when the men returned from the synagogue and before we kids departed for the morning matinee at the cinema, an indication of the mixture of religious observance and errant secularism that prevailed amongst most Jews in those days. The eggs would be eaten with bread and salad, sometimes with aubergine slices that had been fried the day before, and the quintessential Baghdadi relish of `anba, mango pickle from India. This pickle was so popular amongst us kids that we even ate it in sandwiches, to the concern of adults worried about our digestive systems.